Micro-Economics

WILLIAM G. SHEPHERD · ANN PUTALLAZ · W.H. LOCKE ANDERSON

◄ University of Michigan ►

PRENTICE-HALL, INC., Englewood Cliffs, N.J. 07632

Library of Congress Cataloging in Publication Data

SHEPHERD, WILLIAM G.
   Microeconomics.

   Includes index.
   1. Microeconomics. I. Putallaz, Ann F. II. Anderson,
W. H. Locke. III. Title.
HB172.S527 1983   338.5   82-12217
ISBN 0-13-581033-7

PHOTO CREDITS

The Bettman Archive/page 231
Culver Pictures, Inc./page 9
The Granger Collection/page 10 (Marshall)
New York Public Library/357 (Walras)
United Press International Photo/
pages 10 (Keynes), 42, 43, 357

Development editor: Gerald Lombardi
Production editor: Sonia Meyer
Interior design and layout: A Good Thing, Inc., and Christine Gehring-Wolf
Cover design: Christine Gehring-Wolf
Cover photo: PASTNER/FPG
Assistant Art Director: Linda Conway
Manufacturing buyer: Ed O'Dougherty

© **1983 by Prentice-Hall, Inc., Englewood Cliffs, N.J. 07632**

Printed in the United States of America
10 9 8 7 6 5 4 3 2 1

ISBN 0-13-581033-7

Prentice-Hall International, Inc., *London*
Prentice-Hall of Australia Pty. Limited, *Sydney*
Editora Prentice-Hall do Brasil, Ltda., *Rio de Janeiro*
Prentice-Hall Canada Inc., *Toronto*
Prentice-Hall of India Private Limited, *New Delhi*
Prentice-Hall of Japan, Inc., *Tokyo*
Prentice-Hall of Southeast Asia Pte. Ltd., *Singapore*
Whitehall Books Limited, *Wellington, New Zealand*

Contents

PREFACE, xv

◄ **1** ►

The Economic Approach, 1

Economic Systems, 1
Scarcity and Choice, 2   Economic Goals, 3   Positive
and Normative Economics, 4

Economic Analysis, 7
Early Economic Thought, 7   Classical Economics, 8   Neoclassical
Economics, 8   The Literature, 12   Schools and Groups, 13
The Economic Approach: Matters of Logic and Degree, 13

Summary, 14
Key Concepts, 15
Questions for Review, 15

◂ 2 ▸

Basic Economic Principles, 17

The Economy as a System, 18
Households: The Decision Units for Selling Inputs and Buying
Goods, 19   Enterprises and Inputs, 20   Maximizing Behavior, 21
Market Exchange, 22   The Circular Flow, 23

Microeconomic Principles, 24
Opportunity Cost, 25   Marginal Conditions, 25
Diminishing Marginal Effect, 26   Efficiency and Scarcity:
The Production Possibility Boundary, 27
Equilibrium, 31   Public Choice, 32

Macroeconomic Principles, 33
The Circular Flow, 33   Income and Output, 34
Demand and Income, 34   Changes in Output, 35
Potential Output, 35   Stabilization Policy, 36

Summary, 37
Key Concepts, 37
Questions for Review, 37

◂ 3 ▸

Methods
and Measurements, 39

Diagrams and Their Use, 40
Linear Equations and Their Graph, 41   Economic Models, 44
Time Series, 48   Distributions, 49

The Interpretation of Numbers, 50
Problems of Bias and Deception, 50   Stocks and Flows, 51

Summary, 53
Key Concepts, 54
Questions for Review, 54

◂ **4** ▸

Demand and Supply, 55

Demand, 58

Influences on Demand, 58   The Demand Curve, 59   Quality Demanded
and Demand, 61   Price Elasticity of Demand, 63   Elasticity and Total
Revenue, 66   Determinants of the Price Elasticity of Demand, 67
Income Elasticity of Demand, 67   Cross-Elasticity of Demand, 70

Supply, 71

Influences on Supply, 71   The Supply Curve and Its Upward
Slope, 72   Quantity Supplied Versus Supply, 73   Elasticity
of Supply, 75   Determinants of Elasticity of Supply, 77

Interaction of Supply and Demand, 78
Summary, 81
Key Concepts, 83
Questions for Review, 83

◂ **5** ▸

Demand and Supply
in Action, 85

Effects of Elasticities on Market Outcomes, 86

Elastic Demand and Supply, 86   Inelastic Demand and/or
Supply, 87   The Price of Oil, 90

Interferences with the Market Process, 91

The Burden of a Sales Tax, 91   Price Controls, 94
Controls on Quantity, 97

Measuring Supply and Demand, 98
Summary, 101
Key Concepts, 102
Questions for Review, 102

◂ **6** ▸

Individual Demand, 103

The Analysis of Utility and Demand, 104

Rational Choices by Consumers, 105   Diminishing Marginal
Utility, 107   Individual Demand Curves: Preferences and Income, 110
Scarce Goods and Free Goods, 111   Marginal Utilities and Prices
in Equilibrium, 113   Shifts Versus Movements Along Demand Curves, 116
Consumer Surplus, 117   Market Demand Is the Sum of Individual
Demands, 118   Derived Demand, 120

The Validity of Demand Analysis, 120
Summary, 121
Key Concepts, 122
Questions for Review, 122

◂ **7** ▸

The Enterprise, 123

Patterns of Actual Enterprises, 124

Private Enterprises, 124   Other Types of Firms: Public Enterprises,
Nonprofit Firms, and Cooperatives, 135

The Enterprise, 135

Choices and Outcomes, 136   Inputs, Outputs, and
Production, 137   Simple Accounting, 138   Success Indicators:
Profitability and Stock Prices, 141

A Case Study: Starting a New Enterprise, 142

Choosing What to Produce, 142   Starting, 143   Lessons, 144

Summary, 145
Key Concepts, 145
Questions for Review, 146

◄ **8** ►

Supply: The Nature of Costs, 147

Basic Concepts: Technology, Opportunity Cost, and Economic Profit, 148

Technology, 148   Opportunity Cost, 149   Economic Profit, 151

Productivity and Costs in the Short Run, 153

Short Run and Long Run, 153   Productivity in the Short Run, 153   The Law of Diminishing Marginal Returns, 157   Costs in the Short Run, 158

Productivity and Costs in the Long Run, 163

Derivation of the Long-Run Average Total Cost Curve, 164   Economies of Scale: The Shape of the Long-Run ATC Curve, 167   The Marginal Conditions Necessary for Least-Cost Production, 171

Summary, 173
Key Concepts, 174
Questions for Review, 175

◄ **9** ►

Pricing and Output Under Perfect Competition, 177

The Rules for Maximizing Profits, 178

Should the Firm Produce at All? 178   How Much Should the Firm Produce? 178

Setting Output Under Perfect Competition, 180

The Nature of Pure Competition, 180   Competition: A Process and a Zone of Choice, 180   Rivalry and Pure Competition May Give Similar Results, 181   Firm and Market Demand in Perfect Competition, 181   Marginal Cost, 182   The Firm's Short-Run Supply Curve in Perfect Competition, 183   A More Complete Analysis, 184   The Short-Run Market Supply Curve Is a Summation, 188   Shifts in the Firm and Industry Supply Curves, 189   Short-Run and Long-Run Equilibrium in Perfect Competition, 190

Long-Run Supply, 193
The Firm's Long-Run Supply Curve, 193   The Long-Run
Market Supply Curve, 194

Efficient Allocation Under Competition, 194
Summary, 196
Key Concepts, 197
Questions for Review, 197

‹ **10** ›

Monopoly, 199

Varieties of Monopoly and Competition, 200
Monopoly and Its Effects, 200
The Characteristics of Monopoly, 200   How Monopoly Power Is Created
and Maintained, 203   The Effects of Monopoly Power, 204
Price Discrimination, 213

Cases of Monopoly, 216
Standard Oil, 217   Electric Companies, 217

Summary, 218
Key Concepts, 218
Questions for Review, 219

‹ **11** ›

Degrees of Competition, 221

The Dominant Firm, 222
Definition of Dominance, 222   Instances and Effects of
Dominance, 223   Possible Causes of Dominance, 224

Oligopoly, 229
Concentration and Leading Firms, 229   Conflicting Incentives Can Make
Oligopoly Unstable, 232   Types of Collusion, 234   The Central Tendency
Under Oligopoly, 235   Rigid Prices: Kinked Demand
Curves, 236   Economies of Scale: A Cause of Oligopoly? 239

Monopolistic Competition, 240
Patterns and Trends in Real Markets, 241
Aggregate Concentration, 241   Concentration in Individual
Markets, 242   Conglomerate Firms, 244

Summary, 246
Key Concepts, 247
Questions for Review, 247

‹ 12 ›

Policies Toward Monopoly Power: Antitrust, 249

Origins and Standards of U.S. Antitrust Policies, 250
Three Waves, 250   Standards of Efficient Policies, 252

U.S. Antitrust: Forms and Coverage, 253
The Agencies and Laws, 253   History, 254   Antitrust
Criteria, 256   Precedents, 257   Mergers, 258   Economic Effects, 258

Specific Parts of Antitrust, 259
Antitrust Actions Toward Existing Concentration, 259   Antitrust Policies
Toward Mergers, 264   Policies Toward Price Fixing
and Other Actions, 267

Summary, 269
Key Concepts, 270
Questions for Review, 270

‹ 13 ›

Policies Toward Monopoly Power: Regulation and Public Enterprise, 271

Regulation of Utilities, 272
Patterns of Regulation, 272   Decisions on Price Levels and
Structures, 275   Four Economic Issues of Regulation, 277

Public Enterprise, 283
Coverage and Purposes, 283   Subsidies and Efficiency, 286

Summary, 287
Key Concepts, 287
Questions for Review, 287

‹ **14** ›

Input Markets, 289

The Demand for Inputs, 290
The Level of Input Use, 290   Marginal Revenue Product, 290   The Profit-Maximizing Level of Input Use, 292   Deriving the Firm's Demand Schedule for an Input, 293   Elasticity of Demand for an Input, 294   Shifts in the Marginal Revenue Product Schedule, 295   Comparison of Input Use of a Perfect Competitor and a Firm with Monopoly Power, 295

Supply and Equilibrium in Input Markets, 297
The Supply of Inputs, 297   Economic Rent, 299   Taxing Economic Rents, 301   Who Provides the Value of Production? 302

Summary, 303
Key Concepts, 304
Questions for Review, 304

‹ **15** ›

The Economics of Labor and Unions, 305

Labor Supply, Demand, and Market Outcomes, 306
The Marginal Utility of Work, 306   The Choice of a Job, 307   Individual Labor Supply Schedules, 308   Price and Income Effects, 308

The Market Supply Curve of Labor, 309   The Demand for Labor, 311
Equilibrium Between Supply and Demand, 313

Differences in Labor Skills, 315

Variations in Pay Rates, 315   Investment in Human Capital: The Cost of
Training, 316   Scarcity of Talent, 319

Departures from Competitive Market Outcomes, 320

Monopsony and Competitive Supply, 325   Bilateral Monopoly, 325
The Effects of Labor Groups on Workers' Incomes, 326

Summary, 328
Key Concepts, 329
Questions for Review, 329

◄ 16 ►

Capital, Investment, and Technological Change, 331

Capital and Investment Decisions, 332

What Is Capital? 332   Actual Capital and Investment, 332   The Decision
to Invest, 333   Market Demand and Supply for Capital, 337

The Return to Capital, 338

Risk and Return, 338   Interest, 341   Profit, 342

The Value of Assets, 343

Fluctuations in Asset Values, 343   Expectations Govern Asset Values, 346
Bonds and Stocks, 347   The Choice Process Equalizes
Returns, 348   Three Levels of Knowledge, 348   Stock Markets as a
Control System, 348

Capital and Technological Change, 349

Trends of Capital and Productivity, 349   Forms and Components of
Technological Change, 351   Decisions to Innovate, 352   The Patent
System, 353

Summary, 353
Key Concepts, 354
Questions for Review, 354

‹ 17 ›

General Equilibrium, 355

The General Process Toward Equilibrium, 356

Conditions and Processes of General Equilibrium, 358
The Conditions, 358   Ripple Effects, 361

Limits on Competitive Efficiency, 364
External Costs and Benefits, 364 · Distribution May Be Unfair, 367
Cultural Values Are Not Necessarily Provided, 368
Monopoly, 368   Natural Resources, 369

Summary, 370
Key Concepts, 370
Questions for Review, 370

‹ 18 ›

Public Finance, 373

Economic Concepts of Optimal Public Policies, 374
Social Goods, 374   External Effects, 377   Public Expenditure:
Cost-Benefit Analysis, 378   Cost-Benefit Analysis for Specific
Projects, 380   Alternatives to Public Spending and Taxes, 383
Categories of Spending and Taxes, 385

Taxes: Impacts on Distribution and Incentives, 386
Incidence: Analyzing Who Bears the Burden of Taxes, 386   Incentives:
How Taxes May Affect Choices, 387   Distribution: The Effects of Taxes
and Spending, 389

Major Patterns of Public Finance, 392
Trend and Share, 392   Composition: Local, State, and Federal
Shares, 393   Purchases and Transfer Payments, 394   The Variety
of Spending Programs, 395   Taxes, 396

Summary, 398
Key Concepts, 398
Questions for Review, 399

◄ **19** ►

Inequality, Poverty, and Discrimination, 401

Income Differences and Their Causes, 402
The Degree of Inequality, 402   Technical Causes of Apparent
Inequality, 404   The Economic Forces Shaping the Income
Distribution, 405

Discrimination, 406
Employment Discrimination, 406   Discrimination in Housing, 408

Public Policy and Income Distribution, 409
Tax Policies, 410   Public Expenditures, 413   Equal Opportunity
Programs, 413   Minimum Wage Laws, 416

Summary, 417
Key Concepts, 418
Questions for Review, 418

◄ **20** ►

Education, Social Regulation, and the Military, 419

The Economics of Education, 420
Private Benefits of Education, 420   Public Benefits
of Education, 421   Actual Expenditures on Education, 422   Public
Schools and the Issue of Choice, 423   Financing Public Colleges:
Efficient? Fair? 425

Social Regulation: Protecting the Environment, Workers, and Consumers, 428

Environmental Issues and Programs, 428   Cost-Benefit Issues, 430
The Use of Rules to Limit Pollution, 432   The Use of
Incentives, 433   Programs Protecting Worker and Consumer Safety, 435

Military Spending, 437

Avoiding Waste in Producing Military Goods, 438   Efficient Military
Levels and the Arms Race, 440   The Economic Basis for a Volunteer
Army, 442

Summary, 445
Key Concepts, 446
Questions for Review, 446

◂ **21** ▸

Natural Resources: Concepts and Policies, 447

Basic Concepts, 448

Conservation: Reaching the Optimum Rate of Use, 448   Five
Determinants of the Optimum Rate, 452   Private Markets Can Optimize
the Use of Resources, Except . . ., 455

Agricultural Economics, 457

Basic Conditions, 457   Farm Policies, 459

The Economics of Energy, 462

Basic Trends, 462

Future World Resources, 465
Summary, 466
Key Concepts, 467
Questions for Review, 467

GLOSSARY, 469
INDEX, 478

Preface

Teachers know, and their students soon learn, that economics is an evolving field. Yet the basic concepts are relatively stable. In this book we present those concepts, as they are shared and used by economists. We try to convey both the simple beauty of economic logic and the complex variety of its practical uses in the world.

Economics is exciting and important, but parts of it can also be puzzling and genuinely difficult to master. Some students approach economics as a duty: a hard subject that's sure to be dull and not very rewarding. Yet economists know it instead as a fascinating field, which can clarify an astonishing range of topics with a few tools.

To help students advance from reluctance to enjoyment, we present logic, facts, policies, and other materials both in good balance and in an effective sequence. We stress *logic* because economics is above all a connected set of logical concepts and hypotheses. But logic alone is not enough. We must also emphasize the *matters of degree*, which good economists learn to judge carefully. Logic and degree—hypotheses and facts—are a two-sided theme for students to watch as they learn both to grasp the tools and to evaluate real conditions.

Beyond that, we have another paired goal for students: first, to learn economics as it is, but also to acquire a healthy skepticism about economists' work and advice. Because economics is a human creation, it involves human errors and contradictions. By learning this, students come to understand that economic knowledge always has gaps and soft spots as it evolves, and that it cannot accomplish all—or even half—of the tasks we ask of it.

This sort of sympathetic realism need not undercut students' motives to learn the analysis. Instead, by gently dispelling students' hopes of finding something that is infallible, it encourages them to take a sensible view of the whole world. This demystifying process can in turn make it easier to learn.

Students often resist this balanced treatment, asking instead just to be told what material they "have to learn." We think that all students can learn both the basic ideas and the economist's skeptical, independent-minded approach. That is the spirit which we have tried to convey.

The text We have labored long to make this book short. Despite its substantial size, the volume is a compact presentation of principles and examples. Every line reflects difficult choices we have had to make about depth and detail. Our choices have been guided by three main goals. The first is to be *clear*, using plain English concisely. The second is to be *complete* on technical analysis, making sure that the prose is thorough, step by step. The third is to give sufficient *variety* of "real" illustrations and cases, showing readers the important practical uses of the concepts.

The format The order of topics has been carefully chosen to provide a progression from basic concepts to more advanced issues. The chapters proceed generally from fundamental analysis to more complex, applied, and policy-oriented issues. The whole sequence of topics allows for flexibility in emphasizing some topics or omitting others, even among sections within chapters.

Distinctive features Apart from its whole approach, we have built into the book a number of special features, large and small, including the following: chapters 1 to 3 provide a thorough foundation of concepts and methods, rather than just an introduction. Special features beyond the standard topics include:

Chapter 1 Economic goals. The economic literature and the development of economics. The economist's approach.

Chapter 2 Microeconomic principles (opportunity cost, marginal conditions, diminishing marginal effect, scarcity, equilibrium, public choice). Macroeconomic principles.

Chapter 3 The linkage of diagrams, hypotheses, and models. Organizing and presenting data. Stocks and flows.

The next chapters present allocation analysis thoroughly and with unusual concern for general equilibrium.

Chapter 4 A focus on supply and demand concepts. Thorough treatment of elasticity.

Chapter 5 Supply and demand concepts and cases are knitted together; agriculture, oil prices, tax incidence, market controls. Measures of elasticities.

Chapter 6 Focuses on individual demand. Consumer surplus. An assessment of utility analysis.

Chapter 7 Uniquely thorough coverage of the enterprise. Actual patterns of firms. A tour of *Wall Street Journal* data. Nonprivate firms. Accounting, motives, and success indicators. A case study of starting up a firm.

Chapter 8 Intensive coverage of cost analysis. Link between productivity and cost. Economies of scale.

Chapter 9 The nature of competition, marginal cost, and efficiency conditions.

Chapters 10–13 cover monopoly power and its policy remedies with an industrial-organization focus.

Chapter 10 Varieties of markets, from pure monopoly to pure competition. Concise causes and effects of monopoly. Case studies of monopolies. Price discrimination fully explained.

Chapter 11 The dominant-firm case. Numerous practical instances, including newspaper markets. The Schumpeterean process. The contrast between tight and loose oligopoly. New data on the rise in competition since 1960.

Chapter 12 Antitrust agencies, trends, and criteria. A detailed presentation of cases and their economic effects.

Chapter 13 The economic content of regulation. Commissions and their setting. Key economic issues: marginal cost pricing, inefficiency, and deregulation. Public enterprise: its coverage and economic criteria.

Next come inputs and general equilibrium in Chapters 14–17. Both labor and capital are given detailed attention.

Chapter 14 Thorough analysis of input choices. Economic rent. Inputs' roles in creating value.

Chapter 15 The utility basis of work choices. Human capital and returns to education. Effects of labor unions.

Chapter 16 Uniquely thorough, integrated coverage of capital (physical and portfolio) and technological change. Investment choices, cost of capital, return to capital; risk and asset values. Expectations and stock prices. Stock markets as the control system of capitalism. Trends and elements of technological change.

Chapter 17 Complete coverage of equilibrium and allocation. Ripple effects and input-output tables. Limits on the invisible hand.

We round out microeconomics by analyzing major public policy choices in Chapters 18–21.

Chapter 18 A thorough analysis of social goods, external effects, and cost-benefit analysis. Taxes and incentive effects. Trends of taxes and spending.

Chapter 19 Trends and causes of inequality. Analysis of discrimination. Actual incidence of taxes and spending.

Chapter 20 Analysis of resource conservation: criteria and free-market efficiency. Common-property resources. Agriculture, the energy sector, and future world resource scarcities.

Throughout, there are "boxes" presenting unusual topics, special cases, or extended discussions. Also, each concept is printed in boldface type when it is first presented, and definitions of the concepts are gathered in a glossary at the back of the book.

Teaching aids Each chapter begins and ends with a brief summary of its main points. End materials also include a list of key concepts in the chapter, plus questions for review.

To complement this textbook, there is a set of additional materials: The *Study Guide* (which, along with the test bank, was written by Ann Putallaz with the assistance of Therese Mendola) is designed to help students identify and resolve areas of confusion, and to develop their ability to apply theoretical concepts in solving problems. For each chapter, true-false and multiple choice questions and applied problems are presented. The questions focus on concepts with which students frequently have difficulty. Detailed explanations of answers to the questions are provided to ensure that students do not answer a question correctly without understanding why it is correct, and that they are not unduly frustrated by having answered a question incorrectly and not knowing why. The problems help students learn to apply theoretical concepts correctly. Students who work with the study guide will be able to identify sources of confusion, and can build confidence in their ability to apply the material through problem solving. Throughout, an attempt is made to keep students' attention focused on core material, and to encourage them to feel at ease with the subject matter.

The *Test Bank* (available only to instructors) contains multiple choice questions for each chapter. The questions vary considerably in difficulty. Within each chapter, questions are generally arranged sequentially according to the location of the relevant material in the text. Frequently, more than one question is available for a given topic to allow instructors flexibility in designing tests. The test bank is stored in a computer file so that the publisher can provide instructors with individually tailored semester exams. The procedure for ordering these exams is described in the introduction to the *Test Item File*.

The *Instructor's Manual* (prepared by the authors and available only to instructors) is written with the needs of the instructor in mind. It emphasizes the goals of the text, chapter by chapter, and calls the instructor's attention to crucial concepts and diagrams and to areas that students may find particularly difficult. It also gives answers to selected review questions that appear at the end of the text chapters.

A *Transparency Package* containing the most important analytical diagrams is also available from Prentice-Hall.

Acknowledgments

We are deeply indebted to many people for supporting us in shaping this book. For special help from our colleagues at the University of Michigan we want to thank Alan Deardorff, Richard Porter, and Gavin Wright. Our teaching fellows have also given good advice from their classroom experience with the book.

Many scholars at other campuses have provided extensive reviews of early drafts. They include Rich Anderson, Texas A & M University; Marion S. Beaumont, California State University, Long Beach; Peter Bloch, Grinnell College; Daniel S. Christiansen, Albion College; Robert W. Clower, University of California, Los Angeles; J. Ronnie Davis, Western Washington University; James M. Ferguson, Federal Trade Commission; Alfred J. Field, University of North Carolina, Chapel Hill; Max E. Fletcher, University of Idaho; Ralph Gray, DePauw University; John R. Hanson II, Texas A & M University; Barry Hirsch, University of North Carolina, Greensboro; Tom Kniesner, University of North Carolina, Chapel Hill; Kenneth A. Lewis, University of Delaware; Michael Magura, University of Toledo; Robert Moore, Occidental College; Kent W. Olsen, Oklahoma State University; Larry Radecki, Federal Reserve Bank of New York; Michael Salemi, University of North Carolina, Chapel Hill; Allen Sanderson, Princeton University; Len Schifrin, College of William and Mary; James Starkey, University of Rhode Island; John A. Tomashe, California State University, Los Angeles; Holly H. Ulbrich, Clemson University; Tom Ulen, University of Illinois, Urbana; and Jeffrey Wolcowitz, Harvard University.

We have benefitted from research assistance by Barton Lipman, Abdolhamid Mohtadi, George Shepherd, Theodora Shepherd, and Gilbert Skillman.

The publisher has also provided excellent technical support. The editorial gifts and personal commitment of Gerald Lombardi have improved the book on every page. David Hildebrand has steered the book with unfailing talent and devotion. The technical skills, hard work, and sharp eye of Sonia Meyer were invaluable aids to the production of the book.

Among the superb typists who have graced the book are Suzanne Gurney, Judith Jackson, Isabella Leach, Theodora Shepherd, and Joan Susskind.

Finally, our children have sacrificed to make this book possible, by doing without our attention from time to time. We thank them, too, with hopes that they will some day learn from reading it for themselves.

◄ 1 ►

The Economic Approach

As you read and study this chapter, you will learn:

- the basic economic issues of scarcity and choice
- the main types of economic goals and economic systems
- the development of economics as a field
- how the economic approach focuses on matters of logic and degree

Economics is the science of production, exchange, and consumption in economic systems. It shows how scarce resources can be used to increase human wealth and welfare.

Its central focus is on *scarcity and choice*. Scarcity is the fundamental economic condition of human life. The resources available to produce goods are limited, so that the goods themselves are scarce. Economic scarcity requires people to make economic choices, and economics is about comparing alternatives and choosing among them.

The need for choices is evident at all levels of life, from personal affairs to matters of worldwide urgency. On a personal level, one might like to have excellent food and clothes, spacious living quarters furnished in style, frequent travel, and so on. Yet because their incomes will provide only modest amounts of these goods, most people must always choose among them. For example, the price of a new coat may equal 50 gallons of gasoline, a weekend trip home, 10 restaurant meals, or a 2 degrees' warmer

1

room temperature all winter. Each purchase may foreclose buying the others. Such decisions are made routinely by everyone because scarcity requires an endless series of choices.

Companies are also forced by scarcity to make careful choices among alternatives as they convert inputs into outputs. Both a local baker and the huge General Motors Corporation, for example, must decide each day and week how many workers and other inputs to employ, and then use them efficiently in producing bread or automobiles.

At the national level, there are also important economic choices to be made. For example, an increase in the nation's military forces and weaponry might make the country more secure from attack. But the added military spending might have to be obtained by cutting back on programs to inoculate children against disease and to provide medical care to the aged. Better roads may entail worse libraries; more funds for health care may mean less for education. Even more broadly, actions to reduce price inflation may cause national output to fall and unemployment to rise.

To all such small and large choices, economists apply **economic analysis,** a system of concepts and logical hypotheses that has been developed over more than two centuries in debates among generations of economists. The debates continue, and economics itself is still changing.

This chapter is your introduction to the field of economics. First you will be introduced to the most basic economic questions. We show how different types of economies handle these questions in quite different ways. Then you will learn the goals by which economic systems can be judged, and why these goals are often hard to achieve.

Then we present the main lines of the United States economy, in which you are naturally involved. The chapter ends by showing the distinctive approach that economists apply to problems. Our hope is that this approach will soon become yours.

Economic systems

Scarcity and choice

Choice and cost are at the heart of economics. Choosing between alternatives, each with its own costs, is the central task of economics. There are three brief questions that summarize the most basic economic problems:

1. **How much of each good and service should an economy produce?**
2. **How should these goods be produced?**
3. **To whom should these goods be distributed?**

These questions involve choice because of a fundamental aspect of human life: *the interaction between scarce resources and the sum of individual wants.* Resources are limited in quantity—when used to produce one good, they cannot be used to produce another.

Given the problem of scarcity, the three questions of *how much* of each good to produce, *how* to produce it, and *to whom* to distribute it become critical. If people wish to have more of one good, they must usually give up something else. As economists often phrase it, a "trade-off" is involved. *Choosing efficient methods of production is important, because resources are limited: If inputs are used inefficiently, then the total production of goods will be lower.* Finally, since the economy may not be able to produce abundant goods for all, distribution—dividing the goods among the populace, rich and poor, young and old, and among regions—becomes urgent. Often, the more goods

Table 1 **The main economic goals**

The Economic Goals	Symptoms of Poor Performance
1. *Efficiency, High Productivity, and Technological Progress*	Low income per person
An efficient allocation of resources	Simple waste, poor management, misallocation among markets
Growth of capacity and output	Low growth rates
New products and techniques	Stagnant products and technology
2. *Fairness in Distribution and Work*	An extreme inequality of wealth and income, not related to productivity or effort
Alternative criteria include: Equality of result and opportunity Rewards for effort and/or talent Meeting people's needs	Unequal opportunity
The sharing of responsibility and of unpleasant work	Unequal access to control and to the best jobs
3. *Stability: Full Employment and Stable Prices*	Sharp recessions, with mass unemployment
Steady jobs for all, suited to workers' skills and preferences	Chronic long-term unemployment
Stable or declining prices	Price inflation
4. *Wider Values*	
Freedom of choice for people as consumers, workers, managers, and investors	Narrow, restricted choices
Security from extreme hardship	Many people in hardship

that one person gets, the fewer goods that will be available for others.

But recognizing that the choices must be made is only the first step. The second involves making these choices by deciding which trade-offs are best. To deal with these choices, every nation has evolved its own peculiar economic system, whether by historical chance or by design.

Each economy is a system in which the production and distribution of goods are organized around people's wants. No **economic system** is tight and rigid, like a factory assembly line, nor as loose as, say, the world's weather "system." It is more like a large city, in which many people live, work, and play. All of them go their own ways, and yet their actions mesh with and respond to one another.

Economic goals

There are many criteria for appraising the performance of economic systems. Table 1 summarizes the main *economic goals* that economists agree on. Certain goals that are relatively easy to measure, such as output, incomes, or unemployment rates, can be reduced to a few simple numerical scales. Though the measures are not perfectly precise, they are widely used to compare different economies and to study long-term economic trends.

Even if every detail on the list of economic goals and indexes were accepted by all economists, judging an economy's performance would still be difficult for several reasons. First, the goals range from those that are fairly easy to measure, such as total output or employment rates, to those that are extremely hard to quantify or measure, like freedom. Second, people may differ about which goals are most important. For example, you may think that freedom of choice is paramount, but the person sitting next to you may give the most value to efficiency, while a third person may rank fairness or security first.

There is still another difficulty in applying the goals and indexes. It is a fundamental problem, which arises from the difference between positive and normative economics.

Positive and normative economics

Economic analysis operates on two levels: positive and normative. ***Positive statements*** are about facts, *what is* or has happened, or how certain conditions are related to each other. "Six percent of the work force was unemployed last year" is a positive statement, which could ultimately be affirmed or rejected by scientific measurement.

Normative statements are about value judgments, about *what ought to be*. A normative statement usually expresses ethical standards and values. People naturally accept those normative statements that fit their own values and reject those that do not. Thus, "Six percent unemployment is too high" is normative, comparing the fact of 6 percent unemployment with a standard of what is unreasonable.

It is hard to find a widely acceptable *normative* standard of reasonable performance. Judging economic performance takes several steps, each one difficult and debatable. First, you must measure what is happening and why (positive knowledge). Then you develop your normative standards of good performance, such as high incomes and low unemployment. This step includes assigning values to the relative importance of the goals. Finally, you compare the actual performance with the standards.

The possibilities for normative disagreements are great. One economist may rate high incomes as most important, while another may emphasize avoiding unemployment. With the goals being given different values, judgments about how well an economy is doing may differ sharply. Nonetheless, economists often must make such judgments as best they can. Indeed, judgments of both positive and normative elements are a delicate but routine task for economists from the moment they begin introductory economics.

Thus far we have presented economic systems in general terms. You also need to grasp some details of the U.S. economy in order to understand the economic issues discussed in this book. At this point, the U.S. economy will be summarized to give you a factual background. Later you will be able to fill in the outline with much richer detail and insights.

The main features of the modern U.S. economy are quite similar to those of other industrialized economies, such as Japan, Canada, and Western Europe. As Figure 1 suggests, these economies are composed of four major sectors. First, there are the basic *utility* industries (power, transport, communications, city services) that underlie and support all other economic activities. Next are the *primary* industries, such as agriculture, fuels, and mining. Most of their goods flow into the *industrial* sector, whose activities range from the processing of raw materials to the manufacture of goods. Finally, there is the *service* sector, which includes sales, repair, government, education, and health. As Figure 1 indicates, these four sectors of the economy are interrelated. All sectors also draw on financial and labor markets. Moreover, a set of *governments*—federal, state, and local—absorbs large amounts of output and influences activities in many markets.

Table 2 shows these sectors' relative importance. Initially, agriculture was

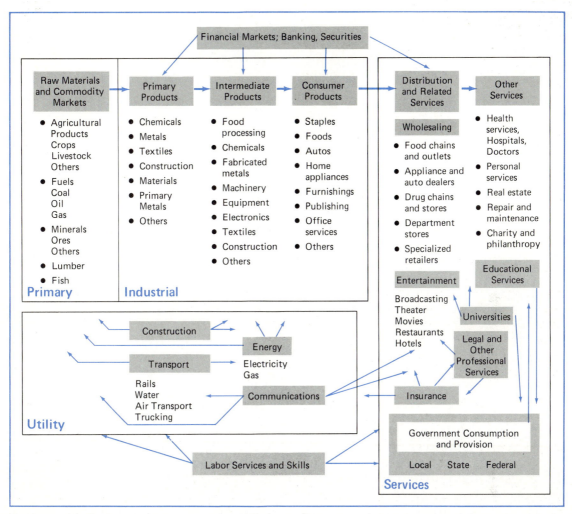

Figure 1   The main sectors in an industrialized economy

The three main parts are utilities, industrial, and services. Each part has many industries and thousands of individual markets within it. Although this diagram only sketches the complex flows and arrangements among them, it does suggest the main kinds of sectors where microeconomic activity occurs in the economy.

dominant; most people worked on farms. Manufacturing and utilities became more important as industry grew from 1870 to 1920. Today, the service sectors (including government services) have come to dominate the mature U.S. economy. Especially since 1930, governments have absorbed a growing share of national production.

The U.S. economy has an enormous capacity to produce goods and services. Part of this capacity comes from the coun-

try's rich *natural resources*. Another part comes from the *skills* that Americans bring to their work. The remaining capacity comes from human-made *capital*, embodied in factories, offices, roads, rails and harbors, cities, farms, houses and apartments, electric and telephone systems, and all the rest.

The growth of production occurs partly because these factors increase, raising the capacity of the economy. Techno-

Table 2 *The main sectors of the U.S. economy, 1840–1950*

Share of Total Value of Output (percent)

	1840	1900	1960	1980
Primary				
Agriculture, forestry, and fisheries	48	23	4	3
Mining and construction	7	10	7	6
Manufacturing	12	24	30	26
(Foods, clothing, wood products, chemicals, oil, metals, machinery, transportation, equipment, and others)				
Utilities	6	11	8	8
(Transportation, communications, electric, gas, urban services)				
Services	23	25	38	41
(Wholesale and retail, financial, real estate, and others)				
Governments	3	6	12	15
Total	100	100	100	100

Sources: *Statistical Abstract of the United States* and *Historical Statistics of the United States.*
Note: Details do not add to 100 because of rounding.

logical progress also makes the factors more productive. New methods of production are embodied in new investments, using the latest techniques. The populace also grows more skilled, more able to operate complex processes.

Population and production correlate closely with the distribution of income. High incomes are focused in industrial areas and in states with large farms. As the map shows, these high-income areas are mainly in the Northeast and parts of the Great Plains and West Coast states. Low incomes are concentrated in small farms and rural areas, particularly in the South and Southeast.

This diversity of agriculture and industry is matched by a great *diversity in the size of enterprises*, ranging from tiny one-person shops to the American Telephone and Telegraph Company (AT&T: the Bell System), which employs one million people. You may picture the U.S. economy as made up of corporate giants like AT&T and General Motors. Yet, most economic acitivity occurs in small and medium-sized firms with 1,000 or fewer employees.

During economic *recessions*, which seem to occur every four or five years, several million people are thrown out of work, some of them for long intervals. Among some groups of workers, such as young black men, unemployment stays above 30 percent for long periods. Unemployment rates this high are not simply an "interesting" economic phenomenon: They are also a severe social problem.

The production of goods and services creates income and wealth. **In the United States, as in most developed countries, the *distribution of this wealth* is distinctly unequal.**

One feature of this inequality is that while the United States has one of the highest per capita incomes in the world, *poverty* is still widespread. In 1980, about 25 million people, or approximately 12 percent of the U.S. population, had incomes below the officially designated "poverty level" of about $8,000 per year, unable

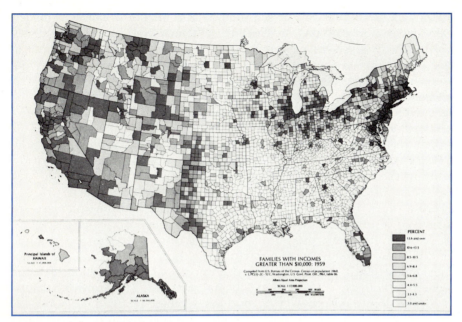

Figure 2   Geographic distribution of family income
The darker shadings indicate counties with higher incomes.
Source: U.S. Bureau of the Census

to afford more than the barest necessities of life.*

In short, the U.S. economy mobilizes a vast array of capital, raw materials, and labor to produce a staggering $3,300 billion worth of goods and services per year. Yet, impressive as the performance of the U.S. economy is, its functioning is far from perfect. Its economic record, like that of all the countries of the world, is both good and bad. It resembles a glass that is partly full of water—or partly empty, depending on your viewpoint. While most people in the United States are rich by world standards, severe economic problems remain.

One of the important skills you will develop by studying economics is the ability to look clearly at the U.S. and other economies and to assess their strengths and weaknesses. This process of analyzing problems and searching for solutions is the key to understanding how economic thought has developed. As you will see in the next section, much of the history of economic thought has been shaped by economic problems themselves. New questions have forced economists to search for new answers and techniques.

Economic analysis

Early economic thought

In ancient Sumeria, Babylonia, China, Egypt, Greece, and Rome, people tried to understand and improve the economic process. Plato and Aristotle analyzed trade, production, and values at some length. All of the modern concerns—production, jobs, prices, monopoly power over

*The poverty benchmark varies among regions and towns to reflect differing costs (in rents, heating, etc.). The benchmark values have risen over time as general price levels have increased.

markets, public works, money, interest rates—were vigorously debated more than 2,000 years ago. Much of the analysis was primitive and vague, but the concern about economic issues was there, along with some important insights.

Economic thought, which had become increasingly sophisticated under the Roman Empire, was then forgotten or neglected during the "Dark Ages" from A.D. 400 to 900. It was only in the 1200s, with St. Thomas Aquinas's discourses on the "just price" and interest rates, that economic analysis was revived. From 1400 to 1700, expanding trade, the discovery of new worlds, and the rise of early industry caused economic development to move ahead faster than economic thought.

From 1600 to 1750, the dominant economic doctrine was mercantilism. Mercantilists believed that economic wealth was embodied mainly in precious metals, whose possession by the state helped to enlarge military capacity and national power. To amass this wealth, states relied on taxes and trade restrictions. The French Physiocrats (1760–1780) argued against the mercantile view. They stressed that wealth is economic capacity rather than gold, productive resources rather than money.

Classical economics

Classical economics differed from most of the earlier economic schools in its insistence that national wealth is the capacity to produce goods or material products. Yet, unlike the French Physiocrats, the classical economists viewed capacity as resources, labor, and capital, a far broader definition than that of the Physiocrats.

Adam Smith's *Wealth of Nations*, published in 1776, synthesized for the first time the ideas of Smith's immediate predecessors into one grand system of analysis. Smith (1723–1790) stressed that people were guided by the "invisible hand" of

self-interest in their economic choices. These free choices would lead to the development of exactly the appropriate mix of skills and capital necessary to increase national output or "opulence."

Smith's optimism was attacked by later economists. Thomas Malthus (1766–1834) argued in 1798 in his *Essay on the Principle of Population* that unchecked population growth would strain the world's food supply and pull the population back toward poverty. David Ricardo (1772–1823) analyzed how economic growth could overcome the scarcity of resources, but he also foresaw barriers to economic growth. Together, Malthus and Ricardo earned economics the reputation of being "the dismal science." Yet, Smith's optimistic outlook seemed justified to many, as British industry boomed and spectacularly increased its output.

Some exponents carried the doctrines of free choice to extremes. Defenders of unbridled capitalism argued that even the ugliest industrial exploitation was inevitable and acceptable to achieve the efficiency of free markets. These writers were called the "Manchester School" after their location in that leading British industrial city. It was the excesses of early capitalism with its riches for the few and grinding labor and poverty for the many that stirred the French Socialists, along with Karl Marx in *Capital*, to stress the cruel and self-destructive nature of capitalism.

Neoclassical economics

By the late 19th century, Europe had become so wealthy that many Europeans could afford to purchase goods far beyond the subsistence level. This greater latitude for consumer choice was one reason that several brilliant economists began working independently in the 1860s and 1870s on the theory of consumer choice: Stanley Jevons (1835–1882) and Alfred Marshall

Five Leading Economists

Each of these five famous economists represents a different stage and emphasis in the development of economics.

Adam Smith (1723–1790) was professor of moral philosophy at the University of Glasgow. He resigned to travel and write *The Wealth of Nations* (1776) and then remained an influential economist while an official in the British customs service. A wry-humored Scot and a close colleague of the controversial philosopher David Hume, Smith was both learned and worldly wise. Though a leading advocate of free choice in private markets, he recognized that private enterprises are often inefficient and prone to fix prices with their supposed competitors.

David Ricardo (1772–1823) was a successful London stockbroker and a member of Parliament, as well as the leading classical economist of his time. Gifted in abstract thinking, he submitted the leading economic problems of the times to penetrating analysis. He attacked restrictions on agricultural prices and other market barriers. He originated the concept of economic rent as received by owners of land and other resources, developed the theory of relative prices (giving labor a main role), and created the basic analysis of international trade. A cheerful, kindly gentleman, he was widely loved and respected.

Karl Marx (1818–1883) was first a German revolutionary (co-author of the *Communist Manifesto*, 1848), and then a powerful social historian and economic analyst in his three-volume *Capital*. In attacking capitalism, he attributed value mainly to labor rather than capital (thus taking Ricardo's view to

the extreme), and forecast more suffering for workers until a revolution replaced capitalism with socialism. Eccentric, irascible, and usually poor, he toiled in London on his immense and often barely intelligible volumes. At his death in 1883, only one had been published. The whole set has had enormous

influence, and Marxian economics is officially accepted by the Soviet bloc nations and China.

Alfred Marshall (1842–1924) was an early pioneer of neoclassical economics. As the Cambridge University professor of political economy, Marshall was highly influential in the fledgling field of economics and as a commentator on public affairs. Though skilled in mathematics, he always subordinated mathematical technique to the content of economic ideas. His *Principles of Economics* (1890) is still a powerful and lively summary of neoclassical economics.

John Maynard Keynes (1883–1946) was brilliant in economics, successful in commodity and stock speculation, a leading intellectual in public debates, and a lover of high culture. He was a member of the Bloomsbury Group that included Virginia Woolf and Lytton Strachey, and started on a diplomatic career. After spectacularly (and correctly) denouncing the peace treaty after World War I, he became a leading expert on British monetary affairs. The calamitous Great Depression of the 1930s stimulated his *General Theory*, which explained why an economic collapse might not be self-correcting. This made him instantly the leading exponent of

modern macroeconomics. Witty, generous, and tireless, just before his death he helped devise the world monetary system that made possible the long prosperity of 1945–1970.

(1842–1924) in England, Carl Menger (1840–1921) in Austria, and Leon Walras (1834–1910) in Switzerland were the leading neoclassical pioneers. **The framework of neoclassical economics erected at that time still dominates Western economic thought.**

Leon Walras showed in 1874 how an economy's many markets fit together to form a complete economic structure. He stressed that each market both influenced and was influenced by every other market,

as part of an internally consistent whole. A century later, Walras is still viewed as one of the greatest mathematical economists.

By 1890, Alfred Marshall had combined in his *Principles of Economics* much of the best of the older classical analysis and the newer neoclassical analysis. Marshall's text analyzed cost, productivity, demand, and output choices in an economy composed of competitive markets. These topics are in the branch of economics called *microeconomics*, which focuses on one economic actor (such as a consumer or producer) or one market at a time. In England and Austria, theories of capital and business cycles were being developed during 1870–1920, stressing the self-correcting tendency of competitive markets. This belief in the innate stability of national economies was shaken in the United States by the financial crash of 1929 and the Great Depression of the 1930s.

In 1936, John Maynard Keynes (pronounced "canes") published the *General Theory of Employment, Interest and Money,* in which he held that depressions may not be self-correcting. Instead, deliberate government policy might be needed to move the economy of a mature Western nation back to full employment. Keynes' work led to the modern field of *macroeconomics,* which analyzes the economy as an aggregate. Keynesian economists who stressed the need for government spending to cure depressions had developed macroeconomics to full flower by the 1960s.

The Great Depression of the 1930s severely embarrassed economists, for their traditional theories could not explain or cure the devastating economic stagnation. Keynes' systematic analysis of the causes and cures of depression, plus the economic recovery late in the decade, restored much of their self-confidence. World War II reversed conditions by causing an all-out boom in production. Economists were drawn into managing much of the price controls, planning, and financing of that war.

They then helped guide Europe's postwar recovery and America's long boom during 1945–1965. The steady economic growth of the 1960–1966 period in the United States was a triumph for Keynesian economics. Leading macroeconomists were at the president's elbow, "fine-tuning" the economy to achieve full employment with little inflation.

But that brief golden era was the peak of the Keynesian success. President John-

son escalated the Vietnam War; its great expenditures overstrained the economy's capacity and started rapid inflation. The steep rise in oil prices after 1973 spurred the inflationary rise, and a high and persistent rate of unemployment accompanied it. Keynesian analysis had few clear answers to the problem of simultaneous unemployment and inflation.

New situations call for new theories and tools, and the search for new answers began. Monetarism, "supply side" economics, "Reaganomics," and other approaches have been advanced since the mid-1970s. Macroeconomics remains unsettled, and the problems remain unsolved.

Microeconomics has also encountered urgent new problems. For example, the sharp rise in energy prices since 1973 has forced major new choices about the use of coal, oil, nuclear power, and solar energy. Race and sex discrimination in employment are stubborn problems that have an important economic component. Does the minimum wage law hurt or help minority workers? Should government's roles in fields such as education, railroads, and communication be reduced? If so, in what form and to what degree? Should governments set safety standards in factories? If so, which methods of protection are most economical? Should antitrust policies reduce corporate power? These and the many other microeconomic issues are controversial, often stirring the sharpest political debate. Yet, microeconomists insist that rational answers to them begin with a careful weighing of the economic costs and benefits.

Economists have always worked on both theory and practical problems, often or even usually immersed in intense controversies. Before 1930, they were a small band of generalists, mostly teachers on college campuses, who did some research and occasionally debated public policies. They were often brilliant, but were few in number. Now the field consists of a sizable army, some 50,000 specialists, most of them with advanced degrees. A few economists are still generalists. But most—whether they teach, do full-time research, advise political leaders, work in government or for private industry—concentrate in a specialized field and focus on narrow technical problems.

The literature

Like other scientists, economists analyze issues, conduct research, and publish their findings. *Their writings form the literature of economics:* articles, books, and reports in which concepts and facts are debated. New ideas are advanced to replace old ones, old ones are defended, and the sifting process retains—it is hoped—the best ones. Often older ideas are "rediscovered" and replace some of the newer ideas! Economists write with a purpose: to change ideas and to make their own reputations. The literature embodies those debates as the field evolves.

The core of the literature consists of the professional journals and specialized books, written by professional economists.* The literature consists of layers, as illustrated in Figure 3. New professional articles and books form the core of the literature. Written by economists to persuade and inform their fellow economists, these core publications provide a growing stream of new ideas and facts. Textbooks (like the one you are reading) are rarely at this creative core of the literature, although they do reflect professional standards of objectivity.

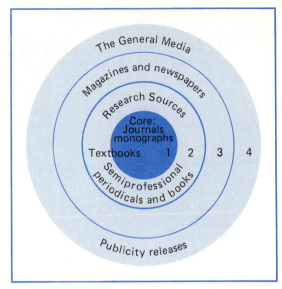

Figure 3   Layers in economic literature

Texts try to present the main concepts that have come to be accepted among economists, not to change economic thinking or engage in debate. Magazine articles and many government reports are far from the core: They are often merely second-hand—and one-sided—accounts of what economists are saying.

The field of economics is always evolving; it never reaches a final set of tools or answers. By 1860, classical economics seemed to be complete and refined; then came the neoclassical revolution. By 1965, Keynesian economics seemed to have the answers, but new problems requiring new answers arose in the next ten years. Throughout economics, the debates go on.

Reading in the literature can give you a sense of its changes and the ability to judge each piece for its value in the ongoing debates. Each piece of professional work at the core helps to make the changes. Some books—like Smith's *Wealth of Nations*, Marx's *Capital*, and Keynes' *General Theory*—have a massive effect. The thousands of others move ideas

---

*The leading U.S. journals are the *American Economic Review*, the *Quarterly Journal of Economics*, and the *Journal of Political Economy*; there are perhaps six other important ones. There is also a host of prestigious specialized journals, such as the *Review of Economics and Statistics*, the *Journal of Economic Theory*, and the *Journal of Economic History*.

by inches: some forward, some perhaps backward! You can enjoy economics for such elements of change and human drama, while mastering the basic tools.

Schools and groups

Every field has its "schools" and groups. They have differences of opinions that may go to the very roots of methods and values. The groupings often involve subtle shades of opinion along a spectrum, rather than diametric clashes. Still, it is often helpful to recognize these points of view.

One is composed of "liberal" economists, trained in both neoclassical and Keynesian analysis from the 1930s to the 1970s. They expect the market system to perform reasonably well. When it fails, they often propose corrective government action: to prevent or ease recessions, reduce pollution, regulate industry, promote competition, and the like.

To the right are conservative economists—often called classical liberals, or "free-market" economists, or the "Chicago School." They rely on people's private choices as the rational basis for the economic system. Therefore, they trust the free-market system to deliver efficiency and technological progress. They deeply distrust government actions, which interfere with the incentives applied in a market system.

On the left, "radical economists" including Marxists and other critics see fatal flaws in free-market capitalism. In their view, the capitalist system is dominated by financial power; it exploits workers and is subject to frequent depressions and mass unemployment. Despite a patchwork of cures designed by "liberal" economists, the radicals believe that the system is basically unsound and unfair to most of the people. The system needs to be changed outright, they say, not just improved or allowed to run free.

The economic approach: Matters of logic and degree

Economists have a distinctive approach to problems. It is best to present that **economic approach** now, so that you can develop it in your own thinking from the start. It has several main parts.

Logic and matters of degree *Economic concepts are matters of logic*, which can be refined and analyzed to a high degree of precision. Used clearly, these concepts can cut razor-sharp through complicated human affairs, exposing the essentials. *But economic conditions are also matters of degree.* The logic needs to be applied with a sound sense of reality, weighing the size of conditions and the force of many crosscurrents. Thus, logic and matters of degree are both involved. Simple formulas cannot solve difficult problems. If they could, problems would no longer be tough, and economics could be done by clerks applying rules of logic. Economics is partly a science, with clear logical lines, but it is also an art, requiring good judgment and good sense.

Systems and deeper causes Above all, economists see the economy as a system with interacting parts. These parts—consumer, factory, or market—can be studied separately, but their actions also affect one another. To be able to see the whole system and its parts—and to trace changes as they ripple through the system—is the mark of economic skill and wisdom. Thinking about systems is second nature to economists, for economics itself is a system of related concepts.

So each issue is tackled with an eye to its extra economic elements. Economists always cast their net wider than most immediate issues, searching for hidden, unexpected costs that others have neglected. They probe for real causes, ignoring the superficial events that crowd the daily news.

What is *really* causing high unemployment, or inefficient factories, or poverty, they ask? What have others forgotten to analyze? Again and again, economists show how a narrow problem has larger roots and effects.

Comparing effort with reward (costs with benefits) Economists are always comparing alternatives. Usually they compare an effort with a reward—a cost with the benefit it gives, a sacrifice with its resulting return—and they ask, "Is the reward worth the effort?" Thus, if a firm adds $6 million to its costs by building a new factory, will the resulting increase in its sales revenue more than equal the added costs? If unemployment rises from 6 to 8 million, will inflation drop by 4 percent or 2 percent or not at all? If $10 million is spent to control pollution, will the added value of the cleaner air justify the cost? In each case, is the value of the change *worth* its costs? In numberless practical cases, economists ignore Shakespeare's advice that "Comparisons are odious." Comparisons are, in fact, the very stuff of economics.

Tracing alternatives—their costs and benefits—is the economist's standard work. Often, though not always, it is easy to figure out the facts, to see what *is;* but the economist must also study what *might be.* That helps to understand present conditions more clearly.

Marginal changes **The economist expects things to change by degrees, not by opposites. A little more here, or a little less there, will cause a degree of change in other things. These small or "marginal" changes can often be compared accurately: *Such marginal analysis is crucial throughout much of economics.* If one talks only of either-or's, of jumps from one condition to another, one is probably not talking good economics.**

Clinical analysis Most economists care deeply about poverty and injustice, progress and freedom. Their aim is to help people by improving the economy's performance. But the analysis must first be objective, to show correctly the exact processes at work. Only if the processes are seen clearly can the causes and results be judged accurately. Then, and only then, does the careful economist apply that knowledge to show which remedies might cause the economy to do better.

Common sense All valid economic concepts can be tested in the end by common sense. Indeed, you will sharpen and extend your own good sense as you become an economist. You will need to master concepts clearly and use them with technical skill, as you would any new language. But that technical precision needs to be allied with good sense and balance.

An independent mind Above all, economics requires independence of mind. Chapter by chapter, you will learn increasingly to *think for yourself.* Economic analysis can give sharply diverging answers, even though the core concepts are pretty much agreed upon. You will need to be skeptical of every answer and claim, skeptical even of the concepts themselves. Once they are tested and familiar, the economic tools and habits of mind will become part of your thinking.

Summary

The aim in this chapter has been to show the essentials of economics as a field of study. The leading points of the chapter are summarized below.

1. Scarcity is a fundamental condition of life and of economics. Since there

are not enough resources to produce outputs sufficient to satisfy all wants, hard choices must be made.

2. Economic systems must cope with the choices set by the three most basic economic questions: *how much* of each good to produce, *how* to produce the goods, and *to whom* the goods should be distributed.

3. In judging economic performance, and in any other economic analysis, one needs to separate *positive* statements concerning what exists, from *normative* statements concerning what ought to be. Positive matters are strictly factual, though often hard to grasp; normative issues involve ethical values.

4. Economic issues have been debated intensely for many centuries, but modern economics is generally agreed to have begun with the publication of Adam Smith's *Wealth of Nations* in 1776. The classical economists (including Smith) viewed wealth as productive capacity. They stressed the contributions of free choice and specialization to the growth of national wealth. The advent of neoclassical theory after 1870 and Keynesian economics in the 1930s provided many of the main tools of modern economic analysis.

5. There are three main schools of economic thinkers:
   a. "Liberal" economists, who believe that although the market usually gives good results, governments can often correct market failures by specific actions, rules, and reforms.
   b. Conservative or "classical liberal" economists, who trust the market system thoroughly and distrust all government actions.

   c. "Radical" economists, including Marxists, who see basic flaws in free-market capitalism and urge that the system be radically reformed or replaced.

6. It is important to learn the economic approach in applying economic concepts to the conditions of the world. The main elements of the economic approach are:
   a. To deal both with matters of logic and matters of degree.
   b. To see the economy as a system.
   c. To compare alternative costs and benefits.
   d. To compare small or "marginal" changes, not extreme jumps from one condition to another.
   e. To apply an objective analysis.
   f. To keep an independent mind.

Key concepts

Economic analysis

Economic system

Market economy

Centrally planned economy

Economic goals

Positive and normative statements

Economic approach

Questions for review

1. "The problem of scarcity, which haunts so much of the world's population, can hardly be said to exist in the United States. With its vast array of re-

sources, the U.S. economy can produce almost unlimited amounts." Discuss.

2. Using Table 1 as a starting point, rank in order of importance the five goals that you think are the most significant in judging an economy's performance.

3. Explain whether the following statements are positive or normative:

a. "The unemployment rate was 6.8 percent in 1982."

b. "American capitalism is an efficient system of production."

c. "The availability of consumer goods is an important criterion of economic performance."

2

Basic Economic Principles

As you read and study this chapter, you will learn:

▶ the circular nature of flows in the economic system

▶ microeconomic concepts including opportunity cost, marginal choices, equilibrium, and specialization by comparative advantage

▶ macroeconomic concepts including inputs and outputs, aggregate demand and income, and policies to stabilize economic activity

Even the most complicated card games are played by applying a few simple principles. Take bridge, for example. The play of the hand by the declarer, or person who has the bid, presents an endless variety of problems. There are more different arrangements of the cards than you probably care to think about. Yet a winning strategy is always pieced together by combining a few elementary stratagems: the finesse, ruff, drop, squeeze, strip, holdup, and throw-in. What distinguishes the master from the ordinary player is the imagination, concentration, and sense of timing with which he or she applies these principles. The principles themselves can be learned from a book. Skill in applying them comes from experience in playing the game. If you have ever played bridge seriously, you know how exciting it is when you first realize that you can rise to the challenge of a new problem, piecing together a strategy of your own.

Economics, too, has a relatively small number of principles. Just as in bridge, the master is distinguished by the imagination, concentration, and sense of timing with which he or she applies these few principles. Gaining this skill is simply a matter of practice. And again, success is exciting.

In Chapter 1 we introduced the economy as a system. Our first task in this chapter is to present that system's main parts: *households*, which consume, and *enterprises* (also called firms), which produce. For simplicity at the start, we will focus on these two fundamental parts. Two other sectors are important but will be saved for later chapters. One is *government*, which influences the economy through its spending and taxing, and through regulations that influence the behavior of households and firms. The other is *foreign trade*, which includes what an economy buys from and sells to other countries.

First we will discuss the economy's basic circular flow, to show how the parts are related. Then we will define the choices and motives of households and enterprises. Next we will introduce the concept of the **market,** the arena where households and firms meet. Finally, we will unite these economic units—households, firms, and markets—in a more complete version of the **circular flow of goods and money.**

The economy as a system

Every economy is a system in which the production of many goods is organized to fit people's many wants. The system has an underlying circular pattern, which connects its many markets and economic actors. As illustrated in Figure 1, the two main kinds of economic units in a system like the U.S. economy, *households* and *enterprises*, are linked by a circular pattern of economic activity.

The choices and actions of these two main units are the driving force of economic activity. In their households, people make two sets of decisions: (1) *selling the inputs they own*, primarily their labor, but also land and capital, and (2) *buying goods with their incomes*. Meanwhile, enterprises *engage in production*, using the labor and other inputs bought from households. The goods produced by the firms are sold ultimately to the households. In Figure 1, the inputs and goods flow clockwise, as shown by blue arrows. The money paid for these items flows counterclockwise.

The interactions of households and firms bring together the two sides of economics: demand and supply. The action occurs in two sets of markets: that for inputs and that for outputs. In the input markets, households offer their labor, land, and capital. Firms buy those inputs at prices set in the markets. Notice that

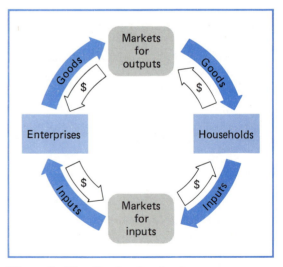

Figure 1   The simple circular flow of goods and money

Inputs flow from households to input markets, are exchanged there, and flow on to enterprises. Production occurs in the enterprises, the resulting goods flow to output markets, where they are sold, and then flow to households to be consumed. The physical items flow clockwise, while money flows in the counterclockwise direction.

households are the suppliers and firms are the consumers in input markets.

The two roles are reversed in output markets. There the households are the consumers while the firms are the suppliers. The households' demand (how much they want to buy at alternative prices) interacts with the firms' supply (how much they will offer at alternative prices). The result is a definite price and quantity in each market.

The whole circular system, therefore, yields specific levels of production and consumption in each period. It answers the three basic questions—**what** goods to produce, **how** to produce them, and to **whom** to distribute them. Demand and supply interact throughout. For example, if in 1983 there are 3.1 billion bushels of wheat, 1.2 million new houses, and 6 million new bicycles sold in the United States, those amounts reflect demand and supply working throughout the system.

Households: The decision units for selling inputs and buying goods

A **household** is any unit in which people live and make decisions about work, consumption, and the disposal of personal property. In America, the conventional household has been the nuclear family. But many households consist of only one person or temporary pairings of some kind. College students sharing an apartment, for example, would be considered a household. Most households have one or more members who work, but some are composed of retired or unemployed couples or of singles who consume but get no income from work. Despite this variety, all households must make the same basic decisions.

In making *consumption decisions,* households budget their spending and assign it among goods to buy. Their incomes come mainly from work, though some households receive income from property or live on pensions or welfare. Households must keep their purchases within their in-

comes, often making hard choices within small budgets. Households can go into debt, of course, but the debts must be repaid eventually. Income can often be raised by working longer hours, perhaps by having more household members work, or by taking on extra part-time jobs. But those ways of enlarging income have their limits, since they cut into family life and leisure time, which are themselves goods.

The ultimate determinants of how much people are willing to work in exchange for income, and what they will buy with the income, are *human wants.* Everyone wants or needs food, clothing, and shelter. These needs are basic, universal, and easy to understand. Nonetheless, much of the world's population has to struggle to gain even a minimum of these rudiments.

In general, *economists take personal preferences as a given.* Preferences, in fact, make up a person's identity and are accumulated over a lifetime of experience. They need not be rigid, requiring fixed amounts of each good for each person. On the contrary, preferences involve *degrees of choice* among goods, as prices vary. In applying their preferences, people continually adjust their choices as conditions change.

Preferences also govern people's choices about the other half of household choice: *choosing work and managing personal property.* The work choice is often complex. Which kind of work to do, for which employer, at what rate of pay, and under what hours and other conditions—these must all be decided, often day after day and month after month. Choices about training for work must also be made, in deciding about college or other specialized programs. Often these choices involve several household members at the same time, in a complicated balancing of interests.

Managing the household's property also expresses preferences. Assets can be held in a variety of forms, with varying risks and possible profits. Stocks, bonds, and other paper assets; farms, houses, and other real estate; jewelry and other valuables—all these offer numberless choices to households with money to invest. The choices can be an important expression of preferences.

Finally, households themselves *also engage in productive activity:* washing clothes, preparing meals, health care, cleaning, do-it-yourself projects, child care, and other work. Households are minifactories that have consumption and production activities. Unlike firms, however, their production is not for sale on markets.

Enterprises and inputs

Enterprises (or firms) are the basic units of production, converting inputs into outputs. *Like households, enterprises face constraints. They must repeatedly make choices, keeping their expenditures within their money income.* They obtain that income by selling their outputs at specific prices to their customers. They spend to acquire the inputs necessary to produce the finished products. The difference between a firm's income and its production costs is *profit.* **Maximizing profit is the primary aim of private enterprises.** To maximize profit, firms must choose the right level of output to produce, buy the right mix of inputs, and keep production as efficient as possible.

Along with the private firms that dominate most market economies, there are also public firms, cooperatives, and nonprofit enterprises. Examples include most hospitals, city bus systems, and your own college. They do not seek profits, at least not as a formal objective. But they all have to balance income and expenditures.

Recall that *households are the basis of consumer demand:* Incomes, market prices, and preferences shape the demand for goods by households. Similarly, *enterprises are the basis for supply:* The potential income from sales, prices, and the productivity of inputs shapes the supply of goods. *Inputs* are resources, which are purchased by enterprises, processed, and turned into outputs. They are not only an important part of the flow of goods and services—they also are the basis of the economy's ability to produce.

Categories of inputs For centuries, economists have spoken of *labor, land, and capital* as the three fundamental categories of inputs. These are the *factors of production,* the endowment of resources that makes production possible and also determines how large it can be.

The inputs are brought together in production, as workers use equipment in workplaces to process materials into goods. The combinations of inputs vary greatly from industry to industry. In some industries, a few workers may manage enormous machines, cooking up large volumes of complex chemicals. In other industries, masses of workers apply simple hand tools to wood, metal, or cloth. In still other industries, workers may use pens, typewriters, computers, or other apparatus—along with their mental capacities—to do office work. In all cases, though, output is achieved by some combination of the three major classes of input.

Labor is the physical and mental effort of people applied during periods of work: hours, weeks, years. The economy's stock of skills ranges from simple labor to highly trained technical and professional capacity. Since training itself is expensive and time consuming, the stock of human talent is a form of human capital that is an important part of the economy's productive capacity. Yet even highly trained specialists do not work in a vacuum. They need the appropriate capital equipment with which to work.

Capital is the set of productive resources—buildings, machinery, roads,

and other tangible means of production—
*that has been created by production and
investment in the past.* Capital is distinctive because (1) it is made by human production rather than by "nature"; and (2) it
is used to produce other goods or services.
Capital embraces a great variety of equipment: Buildings, roads, harbors, sewers,
dams, electric wires, and other engineering
works are all examples of capital. A violin
and a broom are also pieces of capital; so
are a sledgehammer, a jumbo jet, a typewriter, a courthouse, and a mine.

A primitive society may have vast natural resources but little capital other than
knives, hammers, and hoes. An industrial
economy invariably has a large stock of
capital, much of it highly complex and
specialized. The classic image of capital is
the "dark satanic mill" of a century or two
ago, a vast factory or arsenal with huge
furnaces where people toiled among heavy
machinery. Compared to that, much capital today is both quiet and complex.

All economies use capital in production. If the capital is owned privately, the
economic system is called **capitalism.** The
U.S. economy is mainly a capitalist system
because most of its enterprises are privately owned. A successful firm enlarges
its sales, holds its costs down, and reaps a
financial surplus of sales revenue over
costs. *This surplus or profit goes to the
firm's owners.* The workers are paid for
their labor, while the owners of capital get
the extra value that arises when the business prospers. Of course, the owners also
bear the risk of possible losses.

*Land is the broad term for both (1)
geographic area and (2) natural resources.*
Since most production activity occupies
space, land is inevitably a factor of production. Farming uses large amounts of land;
office work requires very little. The price
paid for the use of land varies, in some
cases to great extremes, according to the
land's location and quality. Thus a rich

acre in Iowa or a plot in lower Manhattan
Island draws a much higher purchase
price or level of rent than does scrubland
in Utah or swampland in Alabama. In
cities, the location of each parcel of land is
crucial in determining its value, while for
farming the quality of land is usually critical.

There are many types of natural resources. They occur in land, streams,
oceans, and air. The main categories of
natural resources are:

Nonrenewable: fuels (coal, oil, gas),
topsoil, ores, chemical deposits, natural beauty sites.

Replaceable at great cost: wilderness,
certain rivers and lakes, clean shore-
lines.

Renewable: other rivers and lakes, forests, fish, grass cover.

Virtually inexhaustible: fresh air, solar
heat.

Now that you are more thoroughly acquainted with the household and business
sectors, one fact should be obvious: Both
sectors of the economy are continually
confronted with choices. Households and
firms must accept some alternative plans
of action and reject others, always mindful
of the constraints under which they operate. To choose the "right" course of action,
they must have some goal—some principle—by which they can organize their production and consumption decisions. What
principle motivates them? The economist's
answer is *self-interest,* or in more technical
terms, *maximizing:* each unit doing the
best that it can for itself.

Maximizing behavior

*Economists consider the primary motive
of households and firms to be self-interest.*
The technical term for it is **maximizing.**
Households select the group of purchases
that will *maximize their satisfaction within*

the limits of their incomes. On the supply side, firms choose the combination of inputs and level of output that will *maximize their profits.* Self-interest is the proper basis for microeconomic analysis because almost all people and firms are guided by it almost all the time. Your family, the corner grocer, General Motors Corporation—these and the millions of other units all pursue their own self-interest.

Maximizing organizes people's actions, just as a string passed through a row of beads converts them into a necklace. Each purchase by a family is part of its whole effort to do its best, given the constraints of its income. Each such purchase involves a choice among alternatives in which more of one thing means less of another. More bread means less potatoes, and for most parents, putting a child through college means less dining out and fewer vacation trips. This balancing among choices to achieve the most satisfaction is how consumers maximize.

For firms, too, maximizing gives coherence or pattern to a string of specific actions. The owners of a local restaurant, for example, adjust their buying among meat, flour, plates, cooks' and waiters' time, and set the prices of the meals, all as steps along the road to making money. Maximizing their profits is what spurs and unifies all of those actions. It is the same, too, with the other 15 million private firms in the United States, plus millions more in other countries.

The "As If" proposition   This pursuit of self-interest need not be complete, conscious, or infallibly correct in every detail. Real choices often involve trial and error, but they are still organized by the principle of maximum advantage. For example, consider a choice that seems to violate the principle: you buy a car that does not work. The result is a loss of satisfaction, not a gain. Yet you were trying to maxi-

mize: The "lemon" is merely a factual error, not a lapse of motive. Such errors are part of the inevitable variations and adjustments that occur even for the most finicky maximizers. For economic analysis, what matters is that maximizing is the consistent underlying motive.

All maximizing theory assumes is that people's choices are *mainly* guided by self-interest most of the time. They will therefore act *as if* they were maximizing their advantage and follow the patterns predicted by maximizing behavior. This *as if* proposition is simple and fundamental, and it gives the logic of maximizing a firm practical basis.

Market exchange

A market is a grouping of the buyers and sellers of a good, in which they make exchanges. Their choices and exchanges determine the good's price and quantity. An economy is a mosaic of many such markets. Each market is an arena in which the supply of a good and the demand for it meet. Their interaction determines the value of the good, as shown by its price.

Market exchange   In any exchange, two parties agree to a mutual trade. In a market exchange, one person trades a physical item (a *good,* such as a shirt, or a *service,* such as a taxi ride or a piano lesson), while in exchange the other person trades money to purchase the item. The amount of money exchanged per unit is its *price.*

The exchange is voluntary. Each of the parties regards it as better than no exchange at all. That crucial fact deserves a careful explanation: Both sides in an exchange might hope for better terms than they actually get. The seller would prefer to obtain the highest price possible, while the buyer would like to pay as low a price as possible. Yet some price in the middle may be both higher than the seller's alternative opportunities and lower than what the buyer would have to pay in the next-best choice. Therefore, the sale at that price gives some advantage to each side.

Value and price As these exchanges occur, the value of the good, reflected in its price, is determined by supply and demand in the market. ***The market value is the market price.*** The price will move up or down as changes occur on the demand or supply side. For example, a house near your campus may be priced now at $60,000. If more people suddenly wanted to buy housing near campus, the value or price of that house would probably increase. In a properly functioning market, the price adjusts until the buyers (on the demand side) and the sellers (on the supply side) want to exchange the same amounts. *"The market clears" as demand and supply are brought into line: There is no physical shortage or surplus of the good. The price, then, reflects the workings of both supply and demand.*

Economics focuses much of its analysis on markets. That is natural because much of economics since Smith's and Ricardo's time has been the theory of value, of what determines prices, and markets are where economic value is mainly determined.

You have looked at households, enterprises, and the process of exchange in markets, all in some detail. It is now time to fit these pieces together, treating the economic system as a whole.

The circular flow

Figure 2 shows the economy's underlying circular pattern in more detail than Figure 1. Guided by the primary motive of self-interest, the 70 million households and 15 million enterprises go about their daily business of purchasing, consuming, and producing. What happens in one part of the system, in one household or one enter-

prise, can affect conditions throughout the system.

As you can see from the diagram, this interaction of households and firms occurs in three broad types of markets. First are the *markets for inputs*, where households supply labor, resources, and the services of their financial capital, accumulated from past savings. Firms are the buyers. They pay wages, rents, and capital incomes, such as interest and dividends. Second are the *markets for consumer goods.* Third are the *financial markets* in which households supply new financial capital from their current saving out of income. In exchange, firms promise to pay interest and dividends in the future. These promises may be in the form of stocks, bonds, or savings accounts. The firms use this new capital to finance their purchases of machinery, buildings, and other inputs used in their processes of production.

The whole process seems simple, and is, just as the circulatory system of the human body is basically simple. Inputs of labor, land, and capital services flow through the factor markets from households to firms. In firms, they are combined with raw materials and semifinished goods to produce outputs. Some of these outputs flow to other firms and some to households. The flows of money payments run in the opposite direction. *The circular flow is thus really two separate but equal flows— the "real" flow of goods and services through countless markets, matched by a "money" flow of dollars moving in the opposite direction.*

Simple as it is, the process unites an overwhelmingly complex array of units and markets. All manner of consumer choices, from bland to bizarre, are serviced by millions of firms. Some markets are tiny local ones; others, dominated by big business, are national in scope. Yet the circular flow operates in and connects them all.

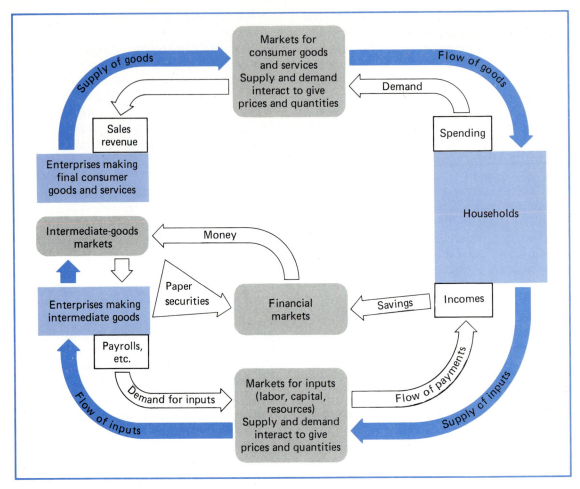

Figure 2 The detailed circular system

Households and enterprises make the main economic choices, and deal with one another in markets. Firms sell their products on output markets. Some of their output goes to other firms, and some goes to households. Households get their income from selling labor, land, and capital services to firms in factor markets. Part of this income goes back to enterprises to pay for consumption goods, and part goes through the financial markets, as households exchange their current saving for promises of future income. The circular flow of goods, services, and money permeates the entire economy, as millions of households and firms deal in millions of markets.

Microeconomic principles

Having studied the main parts of an economic system—the households, enterprises, and markets—you understand that these parts fit together to form a system. Economists who deal with the individual sectors or markets of this economic system work in the branch of economics known as *microeconomics*. **Microeconomics** concen-

trates on the smaller details of the economy, on parts of the whole. Studies concentrating on household or firm behavior, or on supply and demand conditions in individual markets, all deal with microeconomic issues. They often analyze only a tiny part of the economy at a time.

In fact, the three basic questions—*what* and *how much* of the various goods to produce, *how* to produce them, and to *whom* to distribute the goods—are all microeconomic issues, since each question focuses attention on one part of the circular flow. How much to produce focuses on household wants, how to produce focuses on firm behavior, and for whom to produce focuses on distribution of income among the households in the economy.

The principles of microeconomics are few, but they are powerful and of general validity: opportunity cost, marginal conditions, diminishing marginal effect, scarcity and efficiency, comparative advantage, equilibrium, and public choice. The more familiar you become with these principles, the better you will be at microeconomic analysis.

Opportunity cost

Opportunity cost is a fundamental concept of microeconomics. *It is the value of the best alternative.* This basis for measuring true cost pervades all economic choices. Every choice involves taking one action rather than others. For each choice, *the person compares the benefits and costs of each alternative, trying to get the maximum net benefit (the benefit minus the cost).*

The *benefit* side is usually clear and easy to appraise. The satisfaction and advantages from acquiring a car, meal, concert, or even a year of college are usually matters of direct personal experience. But the *cost* side is often much more subtle and difficult to measure. The true economic cost—the opportunity cost—*may* be simply the price you pay for the good. But instead, the opportunity cost may differ sharply from the simple dollar figure because other real costs are incurred.

These other real costs are often hidden, or indirect, or **implicit costs,** to use the technical term. *An implicit cost is a sacrifice that does not involve the paying of money.* An example: Arthur goes to a

movie the night before an examination for which he has not prepared. The movie's price is $3.50, which is the direct cost. But by not spending that time studying, Arthur gets a C rather than an A on the examination. That lower grade is the implicit cost of the movie. The total opportunity cost of the evening at the movie is $3.50 plus the difference between an A and a C.

Four examples of opportunity costs are given in the box on the next page. In all cases, opportunity cost depends on the true value of the best alternative. That value often requires a careful appraisal for hidden elements. For example, the true cost of college noted in the box does include the job earnings sacrificed by not spending the year at a paying job. But there are further elements. Only the earnings *after taxes* are true costs, since the taxes would not have been kept by the worker. And the cost of living while a student is *not* part of the true cost of college because it would have been spent in either case.

Marginal conditions

Most economic choices involve **marginal** changes. To be most precise, marginal means adding just one more unit. *A decision "at the margin" compares the benefits and costs of small changes.* For a consumer, the choice involves buying one more unit of a good, such as a hamburger or a gallon of gas. Producers' marginal choices involve using one more unit of an input or producing one more unit of output.

Marginal choices have been the central focus of neoclassical microeconomics since its inception over a century ago. The approach is valid because *most maximizing behavior by consumers and producers does indeed involve marginal choices.* Most decisions involve small adjustments rather than radical changes. Alfred Marshall

Calculations of Opportunity Cost

Commonsense Instances

1. With just 2 days before exams, you could either study economics exclusively, thereby raising your course grade from a B to an A, or only chemistry, raising that grade from a C to an A. The *opportunity cost* of an A in chemistry is therefore getting a B in economics rather than an A.
2. Your parents bought a house for $20,000 some years back. They could sell it for $45,000 now. The accounting cost of their staying in the house now is $20,000. The *opportunity cost* is $45,000.
3. College costs for you this year are $3,000 tuition and $3,000 living costs (food, lodgings, clothing, etc.). That totals $6,000. But you could have earned $8,000 after taxes on a full-time job if you weren't in col-

lege. The *opportunity cost* is $3,000 tuition *plus* the $8,000 not earned at a paying job: This equals $11,000 (the $3,000 for living costs would have been spent in either case). The opportunity cost differs from accounting costs both in amount and in the kinds of items included.

An Example of a Commercial Decision

4. A firm has $1 million of retained earnings left over from the previous year. The firm can invest the funds in either Plan A or Plan B. Plan A will pay 15 percent rate of return, while Plan B offers 18 percent. The accounting cost of the firm's use of the funds is zero. The *opportunity cost* of the funds for any use other than Plan B is 18 percent.

stressed this by adopting the Latin phrase *Natura non facit saltum*—nature does not make jumps—as the motto on the title page of his *Principles of Economics*. Marginal analysis is firmly rooted in reality.

Moreover, the effects of marginal changes can be precisely defined and measured. Therefore, marginal analysis has developed many exact conclusions, which can be verified by practical tests.

Six main marginal concepts are at the heart of modern economics. They are listed in Table 1. Though few in number, they are among the most frequently used economic tools. Marginal decisions are the cutting edges of economic activity. They determine value and cost in markets. They

are the standard for judging the efficiency of the economy.

Diminishing marginal effect

Marginal concepts guide economic choices made by consumers, enterprises, workers, investors, and the rest, in all parts of the economy. They give definite outcomes because of an important marginal principle: **diminishing marginal effect.** *The effect of any good or input tapers off as more of it is used.* This holds true for both demand and supply situations. It is also a common phenomenon that can be verified by personal experience.

Table 1   The main marginal concepts

1. *Marginal utility:* The change in satisfaction gained from consuming one more unit of a good.
2. *Marginal product:* The change in output arising from the addition of one more unit of an input, assuming that other inputs are held constant.
3. *Marginal cost:* The change in cost resulting from the production of one more unit of output.
4. *Marginal revenue:* The change in revenue resulting from the sale of one more unit of output.
5. *Marginal benefit:* the economic gains (in utility, satisfaction, or other values) obtained from having one more unit of a public or private good.
6. *Marginal propensity to spend:* The proportion of a change in income that will be spent.

First, consider *demand*. As you consume more of any good, the pleasure from each added bit diminishes. The day's first glass of orange juice may seem wonderful; the fifth glass is less refreshing; the fifteenth would make you sick. You prove diminishing marginal effect every time you pour a certain amount of juice to drink, but not an ounce more. Why did you not have a fifth or twelfth glass? Diminishing marginal effect is the answer. This eventual decline in marginal pleasure or satisfaction (called "marginal utility") from consuming additional units of a good is called the *law of diminishing marginal utility.*

Next, consider *supply*. As more of an input is added to production with another input held constant, its contribution to output—called its "marginal product"—declines. For example, the first waiter hired for a small restaurant accomplishes a lot; the fifth waiter will add less because four waiters are already at work, while the sixth or seventh waiter might just get in the way of the others, perhaps subtracting from production rather than adding to it. This effect is called the *law of diminishing returns*. It applies throughout factories and shops, and helps to determine how much of each input to use.

Diminishing marginal effect sets the range within which each type of action (consuming a good, using an input to produce an output, or investing in capital) makes sense. It sets limits and discourages going "too far." Everyone consumes scores of food items, not just a lot of one or two. Firms use many inputs together, not just one. Because of diminishing marginal effect, economic choices reach balances among many elements, rather than being lopsided or extreme.

Efficiency and scarcity: The production-possibility boundary

You have read about how people decide between alternative courses of action (opportunity cost), how marginal conditions are crucial, and how choices are limited by diminishing marginal effect. This continual choosing or deciding among alternatives is necessary because of a fundamental human condition: *scarcity*. No person—no country, for that matter—can have as much of everything as he or she wants. Given scarcity, it is important not only to produce the most "desirable" goods, to make the right output decisions, but also to produce these goods *efficiently*. Efficient production conserves society's scarce resources.

Efficiency is important because human wants outrun what can be produced from the available resources. If the resources can be used efficiently, then the maximum value of production can be obtained. Efficiency has meaning and importance because of scarcity.

Efficiency is achieved when a given level of output is produced using the least amount of inputs. Any switch of inputs to other uses will reduce the total value of output. Efficient production is also referred to as the *least-cost* method of production.

Firms seek to minimize their costs by adjusting their production so as to use relatively cheap inputs. If an input grows scarcer, its value (as shown by its price) will rise. Firms will respond by using less of this input, substituting others for it at the margin. As all firms respond in this way to relative scarcity, the whole economy will adjust so as to minimize costs.

The concepts of efficiency and scarcity are clearly shown by the simple diagram in Figure 3, called a **production-possibility boundary.** The figure illustrates not only efficiency and scarcity, but also choice, opportunity cost, and diminishing marginal effect. The principles shown by this diagram, which represents an economy that *produces two goods,* can be applied equally well to an economy producing the usual vast array of goods. (The vast array of goods, however, cannot be easily portrayed in a two-dimensional diagram.)

The economy represented by Figure 3 allocates its resources between two categories of goods: food and shelter. The curve itself depicts the supply side of the economy. *It represents the maximum combinations of food and shelter that can be produced, given the country's resources and technology.* Each point on the curve is therefore a combination of the two goods that can be attained when all resources are being used, and used efficiently. Each point is an alternative to other points that could be reached by using the same available resources. Thus, point F is for 480,-000,000 units of food and 20,000,000 units of housing, while point C is for 150,000,000 food units and 110,000,000 housing units. All other possible combinations are also shown on the curve.

The enclosed shaded area represents the economy's capacity to produce. That capacity may be large or small, so that the economy may be wealthy or poor. Curve 1 in Figure 3 represents high capacity, compared to the limited potential output shown by Curve 2.

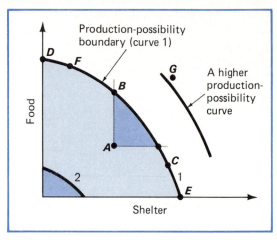

Figure 3   A production-possibility curve for food and shelter

Combinations of output that fall in the shaded zone can be produced. Amounts outside the zone are beyond the economy's capacity. The boundary of the zone is the production-possibility curve (curve 1). Point A is an inefficient point, for more of both goods could be produced by moving to the northeast. Curve 2 is a production-possibility curve for a smaller economy with fewer resources, which can produce much less.

The rounded shape of both curves reflects diminishing marginal returns. Thus, to get more food beyond point B (up to point D), farmers have to resort to increasingly barren land. Also, they have to hire construction workers (skilled only at building houses) as farm workers. The conversion grows harder and harder to do successfully. At point D, the last carpenter—who is least competent at farming—has finally been put to work in the field.

The physical amounts of food and shelter shown are:

	Food	Shelter
A. (inefficient)	200,000,000	60,000,000
B.	400,000,000	60,000,000
C.	150,000,000	110,000,000
D.	500,000,000	0
E.	0	125,000,000
F.	480,000,000	20,000,000
G. (impossible)	450,000,000	110,000,000

The boundary itself separates the attainable from the unattainable quantities of goods. All points on or *inside* the production-possibility boundary are possible. All points *outside* the boundary, like Point G, are unattainable. They are beyond the economy's capacity. To operate *inside* the production-possibility curve, at a point like A, is inefficient. If the economy is at Point A, it means that some resources are unemployed and/or that resources are being used inefficiently. More of both goods could be produced by moving closer to the boundary, as the economy achieves a more complete and efficient use of its resources.

The curve has a negative slope, downward from right to left, reflecting *scarcity*. To get more housing, the populace must give up some food, since resources must be taken from one good in order to provide more of the other. Scarcity does not apply inside the boundary, for from any inner point more of both goods can be obtained.

Once production has moved out to a point on the boundary, then scarcity requires that hard choices be made. *Each marginal increase in the amount of one good involves a marginal sacrifice or decrease in the amount of the other good.* Therefore, the production of each good has an **opportunity cost,** which is shown precisely by the slope of the curve. The population can have more food only if it is willing to give up some shelter, and vice versa. If the economy must give up three units of housing to obtain an additional unit of food, then three units of housing is the opportunity cost of that additional unit of food. Inside the curve, of course, the opportunity cost of an additional unit of food would be zero, since more of both goods could be had without sacrifice.

Diminishing marginal effect or returns is reflected in the rounded or concave shape of the production-possibility boundary. It shows that shifts of resources to either good will encounter diminishing marginal returns. To get larger and larger amounts of shelter, for example, one has to draw away resources that are best suited to growing crops and put them to work on increasingly crowded building sites. This is illustrated in

Figure 4. Therefore, there is diminishing marginal productivity—as units of input produce successively smaller additions to output—in producing shelter. Thus, the rise in housing production tapers off, as it takes more and more inputs (and sharper decreases in the amount of food) to produce another unit of housing.

For example, at Point A in Figure 4, if the economy gives up 50 million units of food, it can add 25 million units of housing. But at Point B, a 50-million-unit reduction in food will add only 5 million units of housing. Thus, the opportunity cost of each good rises as more and more of it is produced. The same effect also works in the other direction. As the economy produces increasing amounts of food, the additional units of food are gained only by larger and larger sacrifices of housing.

The only escape from the scarcity along the curve is to shift the whole boundary outward by expanding the economy's capacity to produce. The expansion can come from several main sources, illustrated in Figure 5. *Population may grow*, enlarging the labor force, as in Panel I. Rapid population growth could move the boundary out swiftly, but of course the additional people would also add to consumption, so that the production *per person* might not rise.

Technology might improve, as in Panel II, giving higher production from unchanged inputs. Many economists credit such technological innovation with a large share of actual economic growth in the last century. Technology need not enlarge the capacity for both goods equally. For example, rapid improvements in farming technology (in equipment, fertilizer, and hybrid seeds) could shift out the boundary as shown by the dashed line in Panel II. Indeed, such a contrast between progress in farming and in housing construction probably has occurred in recent decades.

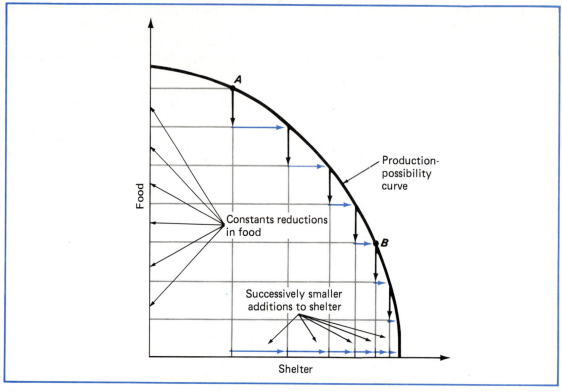

Figure 4 Diminishing marginal effect
Along the production-possibility curve there is diminishing marginal effect in both directions. One direction is shown by the stair-step arrows. They indicate the amount of additional shelter that can be produced with the resources released by giving up constant marginal amounts of food. In each step, the same amount of housing is sacrificed, but the transferred inputs give smaller and smaller additions to shelter.

Growth in the capital stock will also shift out the boundary. But such growth requires investment, which diverts production from present consumption. Panels III and IV illustrate this choice. The two goods are now assumed to be consumption goods and investment goods. Higher amounts of investment goods in one period cause the boundary to move out farther in the next period. In Panel III, year 1 involves a level of investment represented by point A. The curve for year 2 is therefore well outside the initial curve. But in Panel IV, a lower amount of investment occurs, represented by point B, so that the boundary moves out very little by year 2.

The amount of resources devoted to investment is of great importance. Japan is often said to be like Panel III because its investment levels are above 20 percent of total production and its growth rates average about 10 percent annually. In the U.S. economy, investment has been about 10 percent of total output, and the growth rate has been only 5 percent per year. Continued over many years, these trends may bring dramatic changes in economic affluence and power.

Finally, we return to the simple food-shelter choices in Figure 3 to note that *not all points on the curve are equally desirable.* At Point D the population might eat well but have no protection from the weather or other dangers. At Point E, in contrast, the population might live in stately mansions but would soon starve to death. A degree of balance is obviously needed, somewhere in the middle of the range. But whether the choice will lean toward food (as at Point F) or shelter (as at Point C) would depend upon consumer preferences, on the demand side, rather than on supply conditions.

Equilibrium

An equilibrium is a condition reached when all influences balance each other out, so that there is no pressure for further change. An economic equilibrium may exist for an individual consumer or firm, for a market, or for the entire eco-

nomic system. Much of economics is about defining such equilibrium situations and the forces that may disturb them.

An equilibrium is usually not a state of rest, with action coming to a halt (such as three balls in a round bowl). Rather, it combines various forces in a way that keeps the resulting outcome (such as price or quantity) the same. The concept is common in fields outside economics (such as chemistry), as well as in ordinary life. For example, a moving bicyclist is in equilibrium; so are a sleeping person and an airplane flying at its cruising speed. There is motion, perhaps with sharply counter-

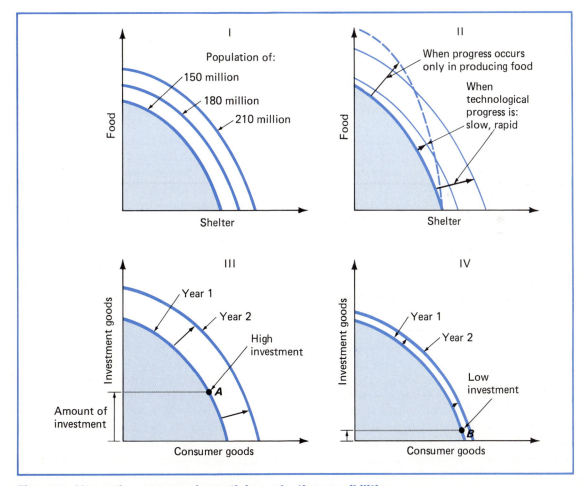

Figure 5 Alternative sources of growth in production possibilities

posed influences (as in the terrific forces within the airplane's jet engines), but *the result is an unchanging level of activity*.

In economic equilibrium, people are satisfied to maintain their level of activity, so that the economic outcomes—in prices, quantities, or any other item—are constant. The outcomes may be fast or slow, high or low, normal or bizarre, but they remain constant.

Such pure situations are unusual, though they precisely convey the concept. Actual economic processes involve continual changes, which require adjustments. Therefore, a total, exact equilibrium with perfectly constant values is rare. *Yet most people behave as if they were aware of what their equilibrium choices would be and are moving toward them.* Most markets are in the range of their equilibrium outcomes most of the time.

The economic system as a whole also continually moves toward an equilibrium. In this case, the balance must be between total demand for all goods and services and total or aggregate supply. If people want to purchase more goods than are available, firms will see their inventories going down and orders up, and realize that output should increase. If the units in the economy do not want to purchase all of the goods and services available, then firms will see their inventories piling up and orders falling, and they will decrease output. It is only when total demand and supply balance that the economy is in equilibrium.

In equilibrium, not only are total supply and demand balanced, but each and every market must also be in equilibrium, for any disturbance in one part of the economy will affect the whole system. For example, a bumper crop of wheat will have effects on other food markets, which will spread to restaurants, grocery stores, and so on. As these ripples spread out, they dwindle—diminishing marginal effect

again!—and the whole system moves toward a new equilibrium.

Remember that in any economy there are always disturbances and uncertainties at work, so that a precise equilibrium is never reached. Yet changes that move the economy away from equilibrium are automatically met by forces that move the economy back toward equilibrium. This automatic pull toward equilibrium is important, since it gives the market system a self-correcting stability.

Public choice

The final microeconomic principle applies to choices by governments. Such choices are important because the private market system frequently creates *external effects* (often called spillovers or third-party effects) that cause real harm to others, such as when a factory pours out smoke or toxic chemicals as part of its own profit-maximizing choices. If the firm causing the pollution ignores this harm, government action may be justified to correct it.

External *benefits* may also occur, such as from a lighthouse that guides ships, or roads that are open to all, or a police department that protects the citizens. The extreme case of external benefit is called a *public good*. No private firm can profitably provide it because its benefits are widely shared among those who do not pay for it. Such public goods are another economic responsibility of governments.

As governments make the economic choices that treat external effects and provide public goods, those choices can be judged against economic standards of efficiency. The standards are based on *cost-benefit analysis*, which defines the correct level of public regulation and public goods in each case. In precise terms: *An efficient public action proceeds until its marginal benefits just equal its marginal costs.* The correct amount of regulation or spending is chosen in light of the alternative uses of resources. For example, a city's road repair program costs $14 million per year. If it is efficient, the fourteenth million dollars provide at least $1 million in benefits from smoother traffic flows. For another example, the decision whether to build a new public school should weigh the cost of the school against the benefits it will provide.

Macroeconomic principles

Macroeconomics has the same workaday subject matter as microeconomics: firms and households, inputs and outputs, demands and supplies, prices and incomes. But instead of looking at economic life up close, unit by unit or market by market, **macroeconomics** looks from afar at the broad outlines of the economy. Microeconomics is more interested in the detail of economic life. But if you have ever studied or visited a great Gothic cathedral, you know that to appreciate the genius of its creators, you cannot just concentrate on the altarpiece, the stained glass, and the sculptures. You must also concentrate on the beauty of its overall conception.

Strictly speaking, macroeconomics has few principles of its own. Its main results come from applying the same principles and methods of analysis used in microeconomics, such as comparative advantage or equilibrium, to the collective behavior of the large interdependent groups that make up an entire economy.

The contrast between the two major branches of economic science can best be brought out by comparing the kinds of questions each branch focuses on. Here are some examples:

Micro: Why have food prices been rising faster than clothing prices?

Macro: Why did prices in general rise more rapidly in the 1970s than they did in the 1960s?

Micro: Why are the wages of blacks so much lower than those of whites?

Macro: Why did the general level of wages (in real purchasing power) fall throughout most of the 1970s?

Micro: Why is the unemployment rate in Michigan so far above the national average?

Macro: Why did the national unemployment rate rise so sharply from 1973 to 1975?

In each of these pairs of questions, the first question applies to a part of the economy, the second to the economy as a whole.

Since macroeconomics deals with the economy as a system, its central concept is *interdependence*. The economy is not simply the individual unit writ large. It is a system of people and groups that interact. Without appreciating these interactions, you cannot understand the ebb and flow of the business cycle or the long-term trends in production and prices. The logical starting point for macroeconomic analysis, then, is with the most graphic description of this interdependence: the circular flow.

The circular flow

Think back to the circular flow whose pattern you saw in Figure 2. It charts the flow of economic activity—goods, services, and money. Households supply inputs—their land, labor, and capital. In return, they get wages for their work and property income from their land and capital. Firms use this labor and property to produce goods and services. Some of these products are destined for other firms. They may use them as intermediate goods, as steel is used as an input in the production of cars. Or they may accumulate these goods as capital— machinery, inventories, and buildings that are necessary to their processes of production. Other goods are destined for consumer markets where they will be bought by households.

As this dual circular flow of goods and money payments occurs, some parts of it must always balance, while other parts balance only if the economy is in equilibrium. *These identities and equalities make up the main substance of macroeconomics as a body of theory.* As you review these principles in the sections that follow, try to keep firmly in mind the central concept of **interdependence,** which means that a change in any one part of the circular flow must cause changes elsewhere.

Income and output

To see more clearly what occurs in the dual circular flow of goods and money, consider a simple purchase like a $20 shirt. First, think of the chain of goods and services that went into the production of that simple commodity: fibers, plastic for buttons, labor, machinery, electricity, fuel, rent, profit, and so on. The actual list of inputs for even this simple item would be quite long.

Now think of the money side of the flow, the $20 that you paid for the shirt. Starting with the retailer, it makes its way back down the chain of suppliers. For example, the retailer may pay $5 of this $20 to employees as wages, $10 to the shirt manufacturer, $3 to other suppliers such as the utility companies or landlord, and have $2 left in profit. Now the shirt manufacturer may pay $3 to its employees, $5 to its suppliers, and keep $2 in profit. As you trace this $20 back through the circular flow, the wage and profit figures keep mounting. In fact, if you traced the payments back through all the producers involved in the production of the shirt, the accumulated wages, rent, interest, and profits would mount until they equaled $20, or the entire value of the shirt.

This illustrates one of the most important facts of macroeconomics—*all expen-*

ditures on goods generate an equal amount of income in the form of wages and property income. The total value of all goods, then, must equal the total income received from their production.

This equality is an *identity*. It must hold true, regardless of what is happening in the economy. Whether the economy is doing well or poorly, whether it is in equilibrium or not, the value of output will equal the income generated by its production.

Demand and income

From studying the circular flow, you already know where manufactured goods go: to households and firms. But what happens to the income generated by production? It also goes to households and firms. Since wages are paid to employees, they become part of *household income.* So do rent and interest. Profits may be paid to the owners of businesses, so that they become part of household income, or they may be retained by the firm as business saving. Thus, all wages and part of profits become household income. Some of this income is spent by households; some is saved.

Firms invest in plant, equipment, and inventory, and they must somehow raise the money to pay for these goods. Part of these purchases are financed by business saving, but a large part is financed by business borrowing. It should be obvious that the business sector can borrow only what the household sector is willing to save. And somehow, funds must be channeled from the savers to the borrowers. This transfer of funds is the job of the *financial markets.* In exchange for lending their money, savers get title to *future* income from stocks, bonds, savings accounts, and similar assets.

Since saving and investment decisions are made separately, there is no obvious reason why the amounts that households collectively wish to save must equal the amounts that firms collectively wish to borrow. Because savers and investors are different people, facing different problems, looking at an uncertain future from different perspectives, the amounts people try to save and invest can differ from one another. *When saving and investment plans do not match, desired or planned demand will not equal production.* Suppose that firms want to invest *more* than savers want to save. If planned investment is greater than saving, then planned demand (planned investment plus consumption) will be *greater* than income (saving plus consumption). Remember that income must equal actual output. Thus, if planned demand is greater than income, it must also be greater than actual output.

By the same token, if firms want to invest *less* than savers want to save, then planned demand (planned investment plus consumption) will be *smaller* than income (saving plus investment). Since income must always equal output, then demand must be less than output. Thus, only if the plans of savers and borrowers harmonize will demand and production be equal.

But what happens if demand and output do not match?

Changes in output

Start with the case in which planned investment is less than saving, so that planned demand (investment plus consumption) is smaller than income from production (saving plus consumption). Firms will be unable to sell their output, and producers will accumulate unwanted inventories of finished goods. They will want to cut back on their output, of course, and perhaps on prices too. But think of what happens when production falls to meet demand. Since income and production must be equal, income will fall along with production. With less income, households will consume less, and firms will

find it a poor time to invest in expanding their capacity. Demand will fall still lower. What will happen is that the downward movement of production to meet demand will trigger further drops in demand, and therefore production, that are referred to as the downswing of the business cycle. (The popular term is *business cycle*, even though the swings do not occur with clockwork regularity.)

This whole process also works in reverse, of course. If planned investment is greater than saving, planned demand will be greater than output. Firms will find inventories being drawn down and customers being turned away. Excess demand will make them want to increase both output and prices. As production increases, income will rise and households will want to consume more. Firms will find that it is a good time to invest in more capacity. Thus, as output increases to meet demand, the upward movement of production to meet demand will trigger further increases in demand, and therefore production, that are the upswings of the business cycle.

But is this equilibrium level of output and income a "good" one? Does it represent a healthy economy, or one in which production is so low that unemployment is a worry, or so high that shortages make constant price increases a worry? To judge how well the economy is doing, you need to compare the equilibrium level of output with *potential output.*

Potential output

In the microeconomic section of this chapter, you encountered the *production-possibility boundary,* the outer limit to the combination of goods that an economy can produce with its resources. Macroeconomics has its own nearly identical concept: **potential output, *the maximum value of all goods and services that the economy can produce without generating shortages and widespread inflation.*** In other words, it is the amount of output that the economy can produce without straining its capacity.

When the upswing of the business cycle carries economic activity past potential output, shortages develop, causing wages and prices to rise. As the downswing of the business cycle moves the economy away from potential output, the strain on the economy is alleviated, and wage and price inflation subsides. The cost, however, is unemployment and excess productive capacity. The ups and downs of the cycle sometimes carry the economy hard up against the production-possibility boundary, where there is genuine scarcity, and sometimes to the interior of the curve, where there is waste and unemployment.

A nation in good macroeconomic health is always close to its potential, so that it wastes very little, but is never beyond its potential long enough to generate a chronic pattern of rising prices.

Stabilization policy

The ups and downs of the business cycle, with their alternating episodes of inflation and unemployment, are among the most distressing aspects of economic life. While all economists agree that these episodes should be avoided, there is no single remedy that every economic physician would prescribe. Indeed, how best to stabilize the economy at a level of income close to potential output is one of the major controversies of modern economics.

One group of economists feels that it is the government's responsibility to curb the upswings and downswings of the business cycle. These "liberal" economists believe that the government ought to pursue an active macroeconomic policy. It should stimulate the economy in bad times by spending more and promoting easier credit, and should curb the economy in prosperous times by reducing government spending and tightening credit. These economists feel that such a government *stabilization policy* will improve the functioning of the private economy.

On the other side are the more "conservative" economists, who regard the government itself as a major source of economic instability. These economists believe that the government should simply balance its budget at modest levels, rather than trying to stimulate or contract the economy by changing the size of the budget. Similarly, they would urge the government not to influence the level of income by manipulating interest rates. They would like the government simply to ensure that the supply of money and credit expands at some steady rate consistent with overall price stability.

To these economists, nearly all governmental attempts to stabilize the economy are poorly timed, and the lags in the economy's reaction to change are too uncertain. The result is that policies aimed at reversing the downturn will take effect too late and simply overaccelerate the inevitable upturn.

The participants in this debate generally agree on goals: to avoid unemployment and inflation. But the two groups are far apart on how to reach these goals. Like all major scientific controversies, it is a heated dispute, and one, moreover, in which everyone in the economy—yourself included—has a stake, since we are all affected one way or another by the cycle of prosperity and depression.

Macroeconomics, therefore, focuses on issues that are of great importance to all of you. The debates are often sharp and lively. Even in the heat of argument, however, no competent economist should exchange logical analysis for impassioned rhetoric (although logical analysis can certainly be lively!). Like microeconomics, macroeconomic analysis must be constructed carefully, concept by concept. Its major subjects are: *interdependence; the necessary equality of income and output; how the relation between savings and investment affects output; the desirability of coming close to potential output, and finally, the controversies centering on how the right level of economic activity can be achieved.*

Summary

This chapter takes a detailed look at three aspects of economics: the U.S. economic system as illustrated by the circular flow, and the two major branches of economics, microeconomics and macroeconomics.

1. The two basic units of the economy are households and firms.
2. Firms and households meet and interact in markets: groupings of buyers and sellers of a good. In a properly functioning market, the price adjusts until the buyers and sellers want to exchange the same amount of the good.
3. The underlying circular pattern of the economic system can be clearly seen by examining the circular flow diagram. This shows the dual flows of goods and money that circulate among the units of the economy.
4. When economists deal with the individual sectors or markets that make up the circular flow, they are working in the branch of economics called *microeconomics.*
5. The *production-possibility boundary* is a diagram that shows the maximum combination of goods that can be produced, given the economy's resources and the known technology.
6. *Macroeconomics* is the branch of economics that considers the economic system as a whole, rather than the individual units or markets of the economy. Interdependence, meaning that a

change in any one part of the circular flow must cause changes elsewhere, is the key to macroeconomic analysis.

Key concepts

Enterprise
Inputs; factors of production
    labor
    capital
    land
Opportunity cost
Marginal analysis
Diminishing marginal effect
Efficiency
Production-possibility boundary
Household
Maximizing
Market
Circular flow diagram
Macroeconomics
Microeconomics
Specialization by comparative
    advantage
Equilibrium
Potential output
Stabilization policy

Questions for review

1. You decide to spend more of your money on clothes and less on food. Chrysler introduces a new line of compact "K" cars, and cuts back on production of larger cars. Can you see any common motive that might explain both actions? Discuss.
2. Economists talk about "constraints" that limit the choices of consumers and firms. List the constraints that you face as you make your own consumption decisions.

3. Why is the circular flow sometimes referred to as a *dual* flow?

4. Pick any three decisions that you had to make today. What was the opportunity cost to you of these decisions?

5. Explain how diminishing marginal effect limits your own consumption of some particular good.

6. Consider the following situation: The UAW calls a strike against GM. Explain the chain of reactions that will take place throughout the economy, showing the interdependence of the units of the economy.

3

Methods and Measurements

As you read and study this chapter, you will learn:

▶ what economic models are

▶ how graphs can show economic patterns

▶ how to guard against deceptive graphs

▶ the main accounting concepts of flows and stocks

▶ how economists treat specific issues

Occasionally, if you are a regular reader of the Sunday paper, you will run across an article about someone who has made a 6-foot model of the Eiffel Tower out of toothpicks. The builder is usually in prison, with a lot of time to serve. Another favorite hobby for those with time to kill is collecting the "world's biggest" ball of twine—although you usually can't work on this in prison. Still other people seem to enjoy calculating π to an immense number of decimal places. This preoccupation with activities that have no purpose beyond themselves is a uniquely human trait. Many animals are playful, but only men and women seem able to waste their time in deadly earnest.

The academic equivalent of the 6-foot Eiffel Tower is found in the higher reaches of pure mathematics. To work comfortably at this intellectual altitude, a person must be in love with logic for its own sake.

Economics differs from pure mathematics. Though economic concepts have a certain logic of their own, they ultimately matter only if they can clarify the complexities of the real world. You probably had practical objectives in mind when you decided to study economics. Practicality, in fact, is the hallmark of economists, as well as of economics. Nearly all of the great economists have had their feet planted firmly in the world of affairs—whether business, politics, or social revolution. Economists are also incurably empirical—they like to learn from facts. They have always tried to fit and apply their concepts to the facts of economic life.

Empiricism requires measurement. Yet, precise measurements are often difficult to make, even in the dollars-and-cents world of economic life. Every crucial condition—such as unemployment, price trends, costs, total production of goods, profits, pollution, or the benefits of public programs—can usually be measured in several ways, each of which often gives different results. Moreover, cause and effect are often muddled, even after decades of research. Do two variables fluctuate together because one causes the other to change? If so, which is the cause and which is the effect? Or, do both change in response to a third variable?

To complicate things further, major economic issues are sensitive matters that involve large stakes. They attract partisans of vested interests, who often make their points with biased data and deceptive charts. You have already been bombarded for years with debatable "facts" about the economy from television, magazines, newspapers, and other sources. The economist's task is to sift the reliable facts from this outpouring of data, and to discard the trivial and the distorted. Printed numbers, like printed words, are fallible. Often, the more exact a published "fact" seems to be, the more distorted it really is.

This chapter will show you how basic economic ideas can be applied in practical forms. If you are already comfortable with graphs and linear equations, you can pass quickly over some parts of this chapter. But if graphs and equations seem daunting, then this chapter can help to overcome your aversion. Read it slowly and carefully. You will discover that diagrams and measurements can make economics much easier to understand. Take your time with the material. When you finish, you will be acquainted with every mathematical concept you will need in order to understand the whole text.

The first section deals with graphs and their uses. First, we present simple linear or straight-line equations and their graphs. Then, we use this information to show how a simple economic model can be constructed. Next, we discuss other types of graphs often used in economic analysis—time series and distributions. The second section shows how to interpret numbers and graphs to avoid problems of bias and deception. Finally, we present the distinction between stocks and flows.

Diagrams and their uses

To relate economic theories to the data and facts of the real world, economists often rely on diagrams. If diagrams intimidate you, try to think of them simply as cartoons, useful for illustrating ideas and facts in a simple way. They are used widely in economics to convey the sense of words and numbers. Although good economic analysis can be expressed clearly in plain words, diagrams (also called graphs, figures, or charts) can often portray facts and relationships with greater clarity.

Suppose, for example, that you are told that people's total savings (1) increase as their after-tax income increases, (2) decrease as income decreases, (3) are zero at some level of income, and (4) can even become negative. It would take you some time to sort out and assimilate all that information. Even those of you with only a slight acquaintance with graphs would probably find this information much easier to digest if it were accompanied by a diagram. A graph makes the information about the income-saving relation both easier to understand and easier to remember.

Don't fall into the trap of skipping over diagrams and hoping that they don't matter. Study them carefully and become skilled at drawing them. Practice drawing different versions of them over and over. Use diagrams to clarify your own thoughts when you are studying or taking exams. You will soon see how much they add to your understanding rather than to your confusion.

There are three main types of diagrams that can be used to convey many different kinds of economic concepts: (1) graphs that present a simple *economic model* showing the relationship between two variables or concepts—between price and quantity, for example, or consumption and income; (2) graphs called *time series* that show how an economic variable (such as prices, unemployment, or national output) has changed over time; (3) finally, graphs called **distributions** that show how an economic variable such as income or wealth is spread throughout the population. Does a small percent of the population have most of this country's wealth, or is it fairly evenly distributed among the population? A distribution can give the answer.

First, let us discuss the type of diagram that shows the relationship between two variables. The emphasis will be on those relationships that can be shown as a straight-line or *linear relation*. First, you will see how to interpret and graph a linear relation. Then, using this knowledge, you will learn how to construct a simple

economic model. Those of you who have not worked much with linear equations and graphs will probably be surprised at how clear and simple it is to use them. After dealing with the equations and graphs of simple economic models, we will then take up the two other major types of graphs used in economics: time series and distributions.

Linear equations and their graphs

Many economic theories merely relate two quantities. Often, the relationship can easily be pictured or approximated by a straight-line graph. In Figure 1, for example, the straight line summarizes the possible relationship between people's consumption and their after-tax or disposable income. By studying the graph, one can see how consumption changes when disposable income changes. As shown, when disposable income changes by $100, consumption changes by $80. This graph of the income-consumption relation can be described or represented by a **linear equation.** A linear equation has the general form of: $y = a + bx$, where a and b are constant numbers (or coefficients). The **independent variable**—the cause—is represented by x. This is the variable that is thought to cause changes in the **dependent variable,** represented by y. In the consumption-income relation, changes in income are believed—on the basis of logic and the observation of real behavior—to cause changes in consumption. In the linear equation representing this relation, x would represent income, while y would represent consumption.

When the straight line representing the equation is graphed, the convention is to put the independent variable or x on the horizontal axis, while the dependent variable or y appears on the vertical axis. (In economics, there is one major exception to this: the graphing of demand and supply curves showing the price and the quantity

Economics Requires Measurement as Well as Theory

Every year since 1969 a Nobel Prize in Economic Science has been awarded to one or two economists, who are shown below. Many of these preeminent economists have focused on the measurement of economic conditions, developing the tools of *econometrics*. All of the Nobel winners have dealt extensively with economic facts.

Winners of the Nobel Prize for Economics

1969
Ragnar Frisch
Norway (L)
Jan Tinbergen
Netherlands (R)

For pioneering work on mathematical economics and econometrics, developing models that could test economic concepts with real-world facts.

1970
Paul A. Samuelson
United States

For varied contributions which have raised the level of scientific analysis in economic theory. He also writes widely on applied economic issues.

1971
Simon S. Kuznets
United States

For pioneering work in developing the measurement of economic activity and analyzing the causes of economic growth.

1972
Kenneth J. Arrow
United States (L)
John R. Hicks
Britain (R)

For advancing the theory of general equilibrium and demonstrating special problems that can arise in complex economic systems.

1973
Wassily Leontief
United States

For the development of the input-output technique to portray and analyze interdependencies within the economy.

1974
Friedrich A. von Hayek
Britain (L)
Gunnar Myrdal
Sweden (R)

For their contrasting approaches to economic problems. Myrdal developed criteria for stabilizing and promoting growth, while Hayek urged against government intervention.

1975
Leonid V. Kantrovich
Soviet Union (L)
Tjalling C. Koopmans
United States (R)

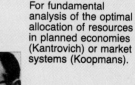

For fundamental analysis of the optimal allocation of resources in planned economies (Kantrovich) or market systems (Koopmans).

1976
Milton Friedman
United States

For research stressing monetary conditions as the crucial economic factor in business cycles, and for his influence upon monetary policies.

1977
James E. Meade
Britain (L)
Bertil Ohlin
Sweden (R)

For path-breaking contributions to the theory of international trade and international movements of capital.

1978
Herbert A. Simon
United States

For exploration of the goals, structures, and decision-making processes within large organizations.

1979
Arthur W. Lewis
Britain (L)
Theodore W. Schultz
United States (R)

For research on world poverty, economic development, and the economic yields to human capital.

1980
Lawrence R. Klein
United States

For developing econometric models to analyze and predict fluctuations in economic activity.

1981
James Tobin
United States

For research on the relations between financial and real markets, as they affect aggregate economic activity.

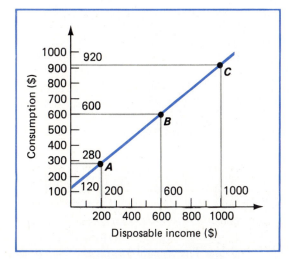

The formula is:

$$C = 120 + 0.8\ YD$$
where C = consumption
and YD = disposable (or after-tax) income.

Point	Value of Disposable Income	Value of Consumption
A	200	280
B	600	600
C	1000	920

Figure 1 A diagram of the consumption–disposable income relation

of a good that is purchased or sold. Alfred Marshall put price, the independent or *x* variable, on the vertical axis, and this has become the unshakable tradition. In all other diagrams, economists put the independent variable on the horizontal axis where it belongs.)

The equation of a straight line must contain enough information to draw the line correctly. This information is conveyed by the constants a and b. To see why, look again at the equation

$$y = a + bx.$$

If $x = 0$, then $y = a + b$ (0), or simply $y = a$. If you look at Figure 1, you can see that when $x = 0$, the line cuts the y axis at a value of 120. This point is called the **intercept.** So for this line, the value of a (or the intercept) is 120.

Now for the slope of the line, look again at the general form of the linear equation. If x increases by 1, by how much will y increase? Try some numbers. Since a is constant, you can see that if x increases by 1, y will increase by an amount equal to the value of b, which is the coefficient of x. The value of the coefficient b is 0.8. So b represents the $\dfrac{\text{change in } y}{\text{change in } x}$ or $\dfrac{\Delta y}{\Delta x}$. (Read it as: delta y divided by delta x.) By definition, $\dfrac{\Delta y}{\Delta x}$ is the slant or **slope** of the straight line. So, knowing the value of a gives us the height of the line for $x = 0$. Knowing the value of b gives us the slope or tilt of the line.

That is all the information you need to draw any straight line. For our income-consumption diagram, the linear equation describing the graph is:

$$y = 120 + 0.8\, x.$$

Because b, the slope of the line, is constant, the relationship has a straight-line or linear form. If b were variable, the line would have a genuinely curved shape. The shape of the line—straight or curved—depends, of course, on what the data tell us about the actual relation between the variables.

The values for a and b may be large or small, positive or negative. A positive value for b means that x and y move in the

same direction: More x causes y to rise. This results in a line with an upward or *positive* slope. The graph of the income-consumption relation shown in Figure 1 is a good example of such a *direct* relation.

A negative value for b means that x and y move in opposite directions. As x increases, y will decrease. This results in a line with a downward or *negative* slope. An example is a demand curve, relating prices to quantities bought. As a good's price increases, consumers usually want to purchase less of it. The result will be a line with a *negative* slope, similar to Panel II of Figure 2.

In fact, Figure 2 contains four different variations of linear equations. For each equation, a few x and y values are given. Make sure that you understand how to calculate the y values, given the x values. Make sure also that you could have sketched in each line, given the actual values of a and b for each equation.

Of course, the relations between variables may be curved, not straight. Many are. Figure 3 gives two examples. Those two curves will often be found later in this book. Panel I shows a typical total revenue curve, while Panel II's curve is an average cost curve.

By this time, you should be starting to feel comfortable with the meaning of linear equations and with the graphs that portray them. Now it is time to move on to the next step, which is to use this skill to construct a simple economic model.

Economic models

Economic analysis is mainly a set of theories about cause and effect: "Condition A makes result B occur." These ideas are often given exact form as *economic models. An economic model is simply a precise formal statement of one or more economic relationships.* The idea begins as words, of course, but it is often put in equation form. The model can be as small and as simple

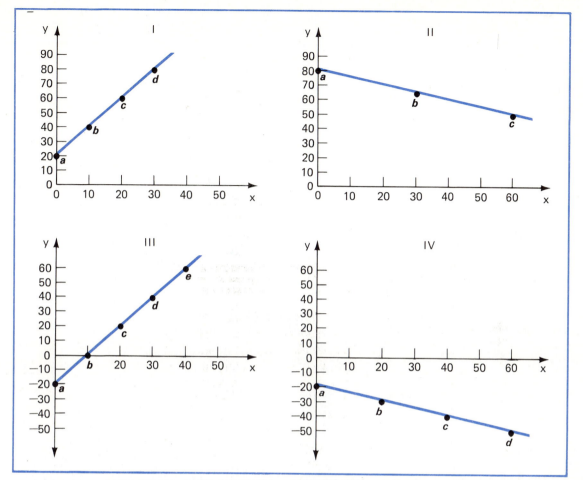

Figure 2   Four different linear relationships

I. This relationship is a line with the formula:

$$y = a + bx$$
$$= 20 + 2x.$$

Point	Value of y	Value of x
a	20	0
b	40	10
c	60	20
d	80	30

The line has a *positive* intercept and a *positive* slope.

II. For this line, the formula is:

$$y = a - bx$$
$$= 80 - .5x.$$

Point	Value of y	Value of x
a	80	0
b	65	30
c	50	60

The line has a *positive* intercept and a *negative* slope.

III. This line's formula is:

$$y = -a + bx$$
$$= -20 + 2x.$$

Point	Value of y	Value of x
a	−20	0
b	0	10
c	20	20
d	40	30

The line has a *negative* intercept and a *positive* slope.

IV. Here the formula for the line is:

$$y = -a - bx$$
$$= -20 - .5x.$$

Point	Value of y	Value of x
a	−20	0
b	−30	20
c	−40	40
d	−50	60

The line has a *negative* intercept and a *negative* slope.

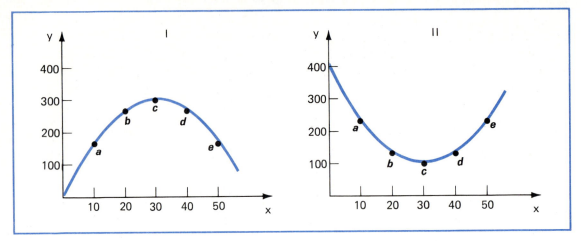

Figure 3   Two illustrative curves

In Panel I, the relationship is:

$$y = a + bx - cx^2$$
$$y = 0 + 20x - .33x^2.$$

The five points shown are:

Points	Value of x	Value of y
a	10	167
b	20	267
c	30	300
d	40	267
e	50	167

as a single short equation relating two variables. For example, a demand curve is a model relating the price of a good to the quantity of it that people buy. Models can also be big and complex, with many long formulas containing dozens of variables. Macroeconomic models are often that large. Yet even the biggest economic model is a simplified version of the real world—a set of ideas about how economic conditions relate to one another.

Suppose that you decide—as seems logical—that a change in disposable income will cause a change in consumption. Disposable income (which we will label *YD*) is then considered the *independent variable,* which causes or explains the change in consumption. Consumption (or *C*) is the *dependent variable,* since it depends on or is determined by income. Trying to think logically about this income-consumption

In Panel II, the formula is similar, but the signs of coefficients *b* and *c* have been reversed:

$$y = a - bx + cx^2$$
$$y = 400 - 20x + .33x^2.$$

The five points shown are:

Points	Value of x	Value of y
a	10	233
b	20	133
c	30	100
d	40	133
e	50	233

relation, you could well reach two other tentative views. First, you could decide that the income-consumption relation can best be expressed as a simple *linear* relation shown by a straight line. You could then present the idea—or theory or model—as a linear equation of the $y = a + bx$ type. Second, you could conclude that the logical relation between income and consumption is a *direct* one, with consumption increasing as income increases and falling as income falls. That is surely logical. This means that the straight line that shows the relation between income and consumption will have an upward slope.

Now, starting with the general form of a linear equation:

$$y = a + bx$$

you can substitute actual variables and assumptions into this general form and arrive at a linear equation specifically designed for your model. Consumption (or C) replaces y as the dependent variable. Disposable income or YD replaces the more general x as our independent variable. The slope of the line (or b) should have a positive sign because of the direct relation between consumption and income. Finally, you would expect a, the intercept, to have a positive sign because consumption can never be negative. So, your linear model can now be expressed as:

$$C = a + b\,YD.$$

Notice how the logic of the model—the cause-effect relation—is highlighted by having the cause (or independent variable) always on the right-hand side of the equation and the effect (or dependent variable) on the left. The graph of this line would take the general form shown in Figure 1. The independent variable is on the horizontal axis, and the dependent variable is on the vertical axis.

At this point, you should pause and ask if the model fulfills the first important criterion by which the soundness of any model should be judged: Is the model ($C = a + b\,YD$) logically valid? It seems to be, since the assumptions of the model make sense: From what we know, people do buy more when their income rises. Moreover, the logic of the model does not appear to have inner conflicts.

You can now proceed to the second step: How well does the model fit the facts of the real world? Now you move from theorizing to data collecting and processing: from points of *logic* to matters of *degree*.

When you plot actual observations of consumption-income combinations on your graph, the result may be a "scatter" of points, as in Figure 4. They appear to reflect a pattern. A line may now be fitted to the dots, to suggest what the relation be-

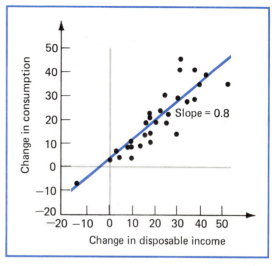

Figure 4 Annual changes in consumption and disposable income 1950–1979 (in billions of 1972 dollars)

This figure relates changes in total national consumption to changes in total disposable income. Each dot represents one year's data. The dots correspond to actual data for the U.S. economy during the 1950–1979 period. A straight line with a slope of 0.8 approximates the data fairly well. By fitting curves or straight lines to historical data, economists are able to measure how some economic variables change in response to other variables.

tween consumption and income is. This is a tiny example of what *econometrics* does: testing and fitting relationships with real-world facts. You can draw free-hand a line that fits the data points, or you can use computers to fit the line precisely, by statistical methods. In either case, following good statistical techniques, you first collect all the data necessary to derive or "fit" the linear relationship. This task of data collection is often much more difficult than it sounds, for you need to collect data not just on quantity and income, but also on all the other "noise" variables, such as population, that you would want to hold constant.

At this stage, you might decide that although the model made logical sense, it is simply not borne out by the facts. In that case, you would want to reconsider either the model or the soundness of your data and statistical techniques. Perhaps income was too weak an influence on consumption to have any clear influence on quantity. Perhaps the data were inaccurate. Or perhaps the relation between income and consumption could be better expressed by a curve instead of a straight line. In any case, the model must be modified or the data refined.

If the model does appear to fit and to explain the facts of the real world, it has passed the second important criterion by which its soundness can be judged: *It is testable and consistent with the facts.*

Once you have fitted your model with actual data, you have actual values for both *a* and *b*. For example, the model may now have these values:

$$C = 120 + .8 \ YD.$$

Not only do you have a precise definition of the relation between consumption and income, but you can also use the model to predict future changes in consumption as income changes, other things being equal. For example, given the above equation, a $1,000 change in families' disposable income will, on average, lead to an $800 change in their consumption

$$(b \text{ or } .8 = \Delta \ C/\Delta \ YD).$$

There is, however, one more criterion of a sound model to consider: *completeness.* Real markets have many crosscurrents: Five, ten, or even more influences may be at work on one variable. Total consumption clearly depends on the size of the population and on incentives to save, as well as on income levels. Your model need not include every such possible influence. A simple model like $C = 120 + .8 \ YD$ is complete enough, if your major interest is finding out how responsive consumption is to changes in income. But if your aim is to predict consumption precisely, a simple two-variable model will not do. You will need a much larger and more complex model, perhaps with ten or fifteen independent variables, allowing for every likely influence on consumption.

An important factor in constructing useful models is to develop a sense for the main economic forces. Always guard against theories that are either too simple or needlessly overcomplicated, given the purpose for which they are being constructed. Beginning students in economics sometimes scoff at models for not accurately picturing all of the world's complexities. Yet, like Newton's three laws of motion, such simple models may be both valid and powerful. They do not explain all details, but they contain the essence or core, the starting point for more detailed study.

So far, the discussion has concentrated on graphs portraying the relation between two variables. It is time to examine the two other types of graphs mentioned earlier: time series and distributions.

Time series

A *time series* shows how an economic variable has moved or behaved over time. A suitably long time series can be remarkably helpful in clarifying the basic pattern of growth or decline. Short time series, however, are often suspect, since they show only the latest shifts, which are difficult to interpret out of their historical context.

Usually, the vertical axis of a time series is an ordinary number scale, as in Figure 5, graph A. Equal increases are represented as equal distances. But if the growth process is believed to be a steady percentage rise that cumulates or steadily increases over time, such as the growth in national output, you might use a ratio scale on the vertical axis, as in Figure 5, graph B. (It is also called a logarithmic scale.) With a logarithmic scale, equal ratios are represented as equal distances. With such a scale, a constant percentage

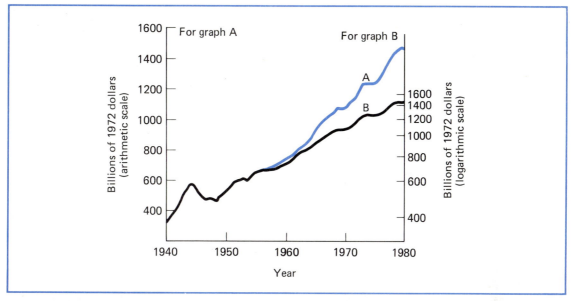

Figure 5   Two ways to show a time series

Graph A and Graph B give the same information. They show the path of U.S. GNP (in constant dollars) for four decades. A is to be read relative to the left-hand scale, which is an arithmetic or absolute scale. Equal dollar amounts appear as equal distances. B is to be read relative to the right-hand scale, which is a logarithmic or ratio scale. Equal percentage amounts appear as equal distances. The graphs have been placed so that they virtually coincide in the early decades. But as GNP gets larger in later decades, equal percentage increases show up as ever-increasing dollar increases. B conveys the correct impression of a fairly steady rate of growth over time. A conveys the incorrect impression of an ever-accelerating rate of growth.

rise results in a straight line rather than an accelerating up-slope. The ratio scale is thus a good way to keep a growth process in perspective. Any change in the proportional rate of growth shows up immediately as a change in the line's slope.

The decision to use a number or a logarithmic scale depends on whether the nature of the change itself is cumulative (that is to say, continually increasing). Since unemployment rates rise and fall with no necessary trend, a number scale would be the best choice for them. But for growth that increases national output cumulatively over time, a logarithmic scale would best convey the information. When interpreting a time series graph, try to imagine how the alternative version would look. This will help you to avoid deceptive graphs.

Distributions

Distributions of numbers are often important in economic analysis. They can be presented in a bell-shaped curve, called a **normal curve.** Such a distribution shows values clustering symetrically around the average value and then trailing off at the upper and lower ends of the distribution. "Grading on a curve" means following such a bell-shaped distribution, as Figure 6, panel I shows. There is a small percentage of the extremely high and low grades of A+ and E. Most grades cluster around the average grade of C.

Most distributions of economic variables such as income and wealth do not follow this bell-shaped distribution. They usually lean toward or are skewed toward high or low values. The more skewed they are, the more unequally the variables they

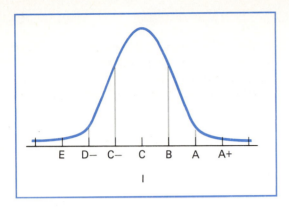

I

Figure 6   I   A normal distribution of grades

Here, letter grades of A+ through E have been assigned to reflect a *normal curve*. Grades cluster around the average value or grade of C. Very few students receive grades of A+ or E, which lie at the upper and lower extremes of the grade range. In this particular class, the distribution is:

Grade	% of Students
A+	2.5
A through B+	13.5
B through C−	68.0
D+ through D−	13.5
E	2.5

present are distributed (although any distribution, even if it is symmetrical, involves *some* inequality).

For example, consider the distribution of income and wealth illustrated in Figure 6-II. The distribution is skewed toward the rich. In 1980, the richest 20 percent of the population held 76 percent of the wealth in the United States, while the poorest 20 percent had virtually no wealth. The richest 20 percent of the population received 42 percent of the income, while the poorest 20 percent received only 5 percent. You can see how the distribution shows the inequality of wealth and income in the United States more quickly and clearly than would be possible in words.

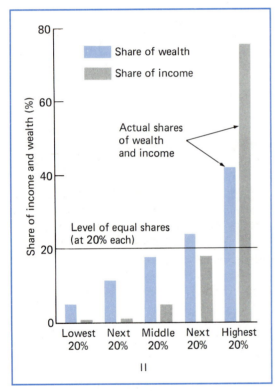

II

Figure 6 II The distributions of income and wealth in the United States

The population has been ranked according to income and wealth and then divided into five groups. The poorest households are to the left, while the richest households are at the right end of the scale. The distribution shows that the poorest one-fifth of households received 5 percent of all income, while the richest one-fifth of households received 42 percent of all income.

The wealth distribution was even more unequal. The poorest one-fifth of the population had virtually no wealth, while the richest one-fifth of households held 76 percent.

Source: *Statistical Abstract of the United States.*

The interpretation of numbers

Problems of bias and deception

By now you realize that economists form their concepts in words and test them with numbers. Economists measure many things, such as prices, trends in output, and relationships between variables such as income and consumption.

Yet numbers by themselves do not convey meaning. They are interpreted and presented by people, often in ways that can twist or bias their message. Graphs are especially liable to deception. One must treat every graph with caution. Even an honest graph can deceive, and many graphs are *designed* to deceive.

Graphs can be biased on two levels. *First,* they may contain data that are poor or off the point. An economist usually has several kinds of measures of an economic concept to choose among. Each may give a different impression.

The *second* level of possible bias is the form of the graph itself. Several common deceptions involve shortening the vertical axis, stretching or shrinking the axes, putting a low ceiling on the graph, extrapolating carelessly into the future, and using deceptive forms of bar charts. Though these tricks are well known, they still recur daily in newspapers and magazines. Often the deception is not intentional: The artist merely tried to fit the graph into a limited space or sought to dramatize the point. Indeed, every layout stresses *something*. Remember: There is no perfectly neutral basis for a graph.

Stocks and flows

To interpret numbers carefully, you often have to know if the data refer to a flow or a stock. **Flows** refer to processes or values occurring *during a period of time*. For the flow to be understandable, its precise time interval must be stated. For example, knowing that a person earns $5,000, or that a store sold 10,000 pairs of shoes, is not enough. Is the person earning $5,000 a month or $5,000 a year? Did the store sell 10,000 pairs of shoes in a week, a month, or a year? Knowledge of the time element is essential if the volume of a flow is to make sense.

Stocks, in contrast, are concerned with the value *at a point in time*. Thus, a reservoir is a stock of water, while a river leading out of it is a flow of water. A factory is part of the stock of a nation's capacity to produce. Inside that factory, the production activity is a flow.

Table 1 shows the main stocks and flows both of the three domestic sectors of the economy—households, firms, and governments—and of the economy as a whole. *Note that stocks and flows can be measured in either physical or monetary terms. When you are studying an economic concept, always try to be clear on whether you are studying a flow, a stock, or a relationship between the two.*

Households The members of each household engage in such flow activities as work and consumption. Their actions are measured in *physical terms* such as hours worked per week and numbers of loaves of bread eaten per month. There are corresponding *money* flows, of dollars of income from the work, of dollars spent for consumption goods, and of dollars saved when spending is less than income.

Households have physical stocks of possessions, primarily their houses, land, automobiles, appliances, furniture, and so on. Their monetary stock data have two sides: One side is the ownership value of those physical assets, plus whatever money assets the household has (cash, bonds, stock certificates, savings deposits, etc.). The other side is liabilities, such as debts, loans (house mortgages), and bills owed. The household's net worth is its assets minus its liabilities. Net worth can be negative or positive.

Firms The flows within firms are the volumes of inputs coming in (labor hours, raw materials, and services), the levels of production activity, and the amounts of outputs going out (such as thousands of bushels of wheat, or thousands of tons of copper). These flows are measured in money values, by multiplying their physical volumes times the price of these items. For example, if Ford sold 1,925,000 cars in 1981 at an average price of $7,500, then the sales revenue was $14,437,500,000 per

Table 1 Flows and stocks for the three domestic sectors and for the entire economy

	Flows		Stocks		
	Physical	Monetary	Physical	Monetary	
				Assets	Liabilities
Households	Time and effort in work	*Income*	Land, houses, cars, appliances, etc.	Ownership of: *Tangible assets:* land, house, etc.	*Loans* mortgages *Bills owed*
	Time and amounts of consumption activity	*Spending*		*Monetary assets* cash, bonds, stocks, etc.	
Firms	Production Inputs used	*Saving* *Sales revenue* *Current costs* *Profit − taxes* *Profit after taxes* a. Dividends b. Reinvested in the firm	Land, buildings, equipment, inventories, etc.	*Total Assets* *Fixed assets* land, plant, machinery, etc. *Inventories* *Monetary assets*	*Total Liabilities* *Debts* Long-term bonds Short-term loans *Equity* of stockholders
Governments (national, state, local)	Employees Amounts of activities and services performed	*Investment* *Tax revenues* Income tax Sales tax Property tax Profits tax *Expenditures* Purchases of real goods and services Transfer payrnents Additions to assets	Land, buildings, equipment, inventories, weapons, roads, and harbors	*Total Assets* *Long-term physical assets* (land, buildings, etc.) *Inventories* (stockpiles of metals, grains, etc.)	*Total Liabilities* *Debt* U.S. government bonds (the national debt) state bonds local bonds *Money* (paper and metal)
Entire Economy (local or national)	Production (items and totals) Employment levels Unemployment levels	*Gross National Product* (GNP) *Sources,* by sectors *Uses* Consumption Government use of goods and services Investment (= to saving)	Land, buildings, equipment, roads, natural resources, inventories, etc.	*Total Assets* *Fixed assets* (land, buildings, etc.) *Inventories* (gold, other metals, other goods) National currencies *Total Assets*	*Total Liabilities* *Ownership claims* *Money supply*

year. If costs included 110,000 worker-years at an average cost per worker of $22,000, then labor costs were $2,420,000,000 per year. Its profit was another flow: total revenues minus total costs.

Firms' physical stocks include the obvious land, buildings, and machinery, plus the inventories of inputs ready for use and of outputs that have not yet been shipped out. These physical items all have their monetary values, such as the Bell System's $100 billion of assets in its present telephone system. Firms also have money assets, such as cash and securities. And firms have debts, in the form of their loans and bonds. The common stocks owned by shareholders are also liabilities.

Governments Still other versions of these flow and stock categories exist for governments. Their flow activities include the employees they hire, the levels of their operations, and the services they provide. The monetary flows have two sides, just as for households and firms. Tax revenues provide an inflow of funds from a variety of taxes on income, sales, property values, profits, and other things. Governments spend to pay for employees, services, and other purposes. As for stocks, governments use large volumes of physical assets, such as land, buildings, stockpiles, and equipment (a police station, a submarine, a road). Governments also issue bonds and money as liabilities.

The entire economy All of these magnitudes add up to form flow and stock values for the whole economy. The physical flows include production, consumption, growth rates, employment levels, and others. These flows are valued in money terms to give the various measures of gross national product, national income, consumption, investment, saving, and many other components.

The economy's physical stocks include the familiar land, buildings, equipment, roads, natural resources, inventories, and other types. They are all valued as assets in money terms, and there are various ownership claims on them.

From the vast economy-wide totals down to minute levels for individual units, the values of flows and stocks all fit into the same basic logic.

Summary

This chapter has focused on the economist's basic tools of measurement and modeling. The major points of the chapter are as follows:

1. Diagrams summarize ideas and facts. They often convey information more clearly than words.
2. Linear equations and their graphs are often used in economics to summarize the relationship between two variables. A linear equation has the general form: $y = a + bx$, where a and b are constant numbers. The constant a represents the *intercept* of the line, the point at which it touches the vertical axis. The constant b represents the degree of slant or *slope* of the line. The letter x refers to the independent variable, the variable that is thought to cause the change in the dependent or y variable.
3. Once the model is constructed, its usefulness should be judged by three important criteria:
   a. It should be *logically valid*. The assumptions should make sense.
   b. It should *fit the facts* of the real world. In other words, it should be testable and consistent with the facts.
   c. It should be sufficiently *complete*, but not needlessly overcompli-

cated, given the purpose for which the model was constructed.

4. A *time series* is a graph that shows how an economic variable has behaved over time. A time series may be presented on a number scale or a logarithmic scale.

5. *Distributions* are graphs that show how such economic variables as income or wealth are spread among the population. The usual distribution shows the majority of cases clustering around an average value, with fewer cases in the upper and lower ranges.

6. To interpret information correctly, it is important to distinguish between stocks and flows. *Flows* refer to processes or values occurring over a period of time. A *stock* is a value at a point in time.

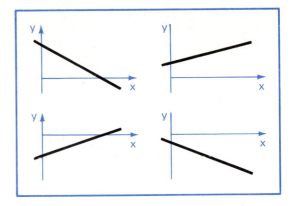

Key concepts

Linear equation:
    dependent variable
    independent variable
    intercept
    slope
Economic model
Time series
Distribution
Normal curve
Flow
Stock

Questions for review

1. Suppose that a linear equation has the form of: $y = -10 + .5 \ x$. Using the equation, calculate some values for x and the corresponding values for y. Sketch the equation.

2. For each of the following graphs, write the general form of the linear equation that would represent the specific relationship.

3. Two variables that obviously increase and decrease together may not belong in the same model. Explain why.

4. Using the general rules that serve as a guide to whether a time series should be presented on an arithmetic or a ratio (logarithmic) scale, explain which scale you would choose for the following:
  a. Unemployment rate.
  b. Price levels.
  c. Income.

5. Suppose that you have constructed a time series showing how income levels in the United States have changed over the past few decades. Would there be any point in constructing a graph of the distribution as well? Would it give you any additional information?

6. Given the following list of economic variables, determine whether each is a *stock* or a *flow:*
  a. Salary.
  b. Sales.
  c. Wealth.
  d. Volume of trading on the New York Stock Exchange.

4

Demand and Supply

As you read and study this chapter, you will learn:

- the simple analysis of demand
- three main elasticities of demand: price elasticity, income elasticity, and cross elasticity

- the simple analysis of supply
- the elasticity of supply
- how supply and demand interact to determine price and quantity in the market

The main task of microeconomics is to explain the relative values of economic goods. Those values are mostly determined by forces operating in markets throughout the economy. *The resulting market values are prices, and prices are at the core of microeconomics.*

Table 1 presents a wide variety of such prices. They are real—formed and changed incessantly in real markets. Their *relative* levels are crucial. To see the importance of relative prices, imagine that you own a one-ounce gold coin. It is a small object, barely able to cover your fingertip. Yet that little piece of metal has recently been worth $452. And, as Table 1 shows, with that one gold coin you could buy 481 pounds of beef, 4,475 pounds of potatoes, 32,873 pounds of old newspapers, or 11 airplane trips between New York and Detroit. How can such a small bit of gold buy so many other goods? There are other puzzling comparisons. For example, why is the value of 583 dozen eggs only equal to 307 pounds of coffee, 13 barrels of oil, or 20 hours of an electri-

Table 1 *Prices of Selected Commodities and Retail Items on a Recent Day*

Commodity (unit of measurement)*	Price per Unit	Amount of the Commodity Equivalent to 1 ounce of Gold Priced at $452 per ounce
Foods		
Beef, 700–900 pound carcass (per pound)	94¢	481 pounds
Butter, grade AA (per pound)	$1.52½	296 pounds
Chicken broilers, dressed (per pound)	45¹⁄₆¢	1,001 pounds
Coffee, Brazilian (per pound)	$1.47	307 pounds
Eggs, large white (dozen)	77½¢	583 dozen
Orange juice, frozen concentrate (per pound)	$1.16	390 pounds
Pork bellies (per pound)	57¢	793 pounds
Potatoes, round white (per pound)	10.1¢	4,475 pounds
Sugar, cane, raw (per pound)	16.46¢	2,746 pounds
Grains and Feeds		
Corn, No. 2 yellow (per bushel)	$2.59½	174 bushels
Oats, No. 2 millings (per bushel)	$2.33	194 bushels
Rice, No. 2 milled (per pound)	22¢	2,055 pounds
Sunflower seed, No. 1 (per pound)	11.3¢	4,000 pounds
Wheat, No. 2 soft red (per bushel)	$4.15¾	109 bushels
Fibers and Textiles		
Cotton, 1¹⁄₁₆-inch strand (per pound)	57.5¢	786 pounds
Print cloth, cotton, 48-inch (per yard)	78¢	579 pounds
Wool, fine staple (per pound)	$2.85	159 pounds
Metals		
Aluminum, ingot (per pound)	76¢	595 pounds
Copper, refined (per pound)	80¢	565 pounds
Lead (per pound)	35¢	1,291 pounds
Nickel, plating grade (per pound)	$3.50	129 pounds
Steel scrap, 1 heavy melt (per ton)	$80.00	11,300 pounds
Tin (per pound)	8.24¢	5,485 pounds
Precious Metals		
Gold (per troy ounce)	$452.00	1 ounce
Silver (per troy ounce)	$8.59	52.6 ounces
Petroleum		
Crude, Saudi Arabia light (per barrel)	$34.00	13.29 barrels
Gasoline, regular, wholesale (per gallon)	$1.00½	450 gallons
Gasoline, unleaded, wholesale (per gallon)	$1.02½	441 gallons
Miscellaneous Commodities		
Cowhides, light native (per pound)	57¢	793 pounds
Newspapers, old, No. 1 (per ton)	$27.50	32,873 pounds
Rubber, smoked sheets (per pound)	45³⁄₈¢	995 pounds
Retail Items		
Apartment rent, 1 bedroom, unfurnished (per month)	$195.00	2.32 months
Ball-point pen	29¢	1,559 pens
Discount air fare, Detroit to New York, one-way	$39.00	11.90 trips
Motion picture ticket	$3.50	129 tickets
Unskilled labor, minimum wage (per hour)	$3.60	126 hours
Skilled labor, electrician (per hour)	$22.50	20.1 hours

Sources: *Wall Street Journal,* Department of Commerce, *Business Week* magazine.
*Most commodity prices are for delivery in New York. Some retail prices are estimates.

cian's labor? What causes nickel to be ten times as valuable as lead, and wool five times as valuable as cotton?

Note, too, that the gold has great power over human labor. That one-ounce coin will buy 126 hours of unskilled labor, which is more than three weeks of full-time work. One pound of gold will buy you nearly an entire year of full-time work by an unskilled laborer.

Table 1 is long, but it is only a small selection from thousands of commodities and retail items. Every day the market system adjusts all of these prices by numberless interactions of supply and demand. *The prices express the relative values of the goods.* Altogether they are at the heart of microeconomic activity.

Microeconomics seeks to explain those relative values, by using a relatively few powerful tools. Moreover, microeconomics shows how market prices can reconcile major social conflicts by solving two fundamental problems. First, markets *coordinate the actions of producers and consumers,* even though the two groups may never meet or communicate directly. Wheat farmers need to sell their grain. Bakers need flour to bake bread. Families need bread. The markets for wheat, flour, and bread enable them to serve one another's needs, while pursuing their own separate interests. Second, markets *resolve conflict.* Wheat farmers want high prices. Families want cheap bread. The markets that link them together resolve this antagonism in an impersonal way, without bitter face-to-face strife.

Microeconomics relies heavily on *comparative static analysis,* which works as follows: First, an equilibrium situation is defined (for example, certain supply and demand conditions for oil yield a price of $34 per barrel and a quantity of 20 million barrels per period). Then the value of one variable is changed, and the resulting effect on the outcome is traced through (a 10

percent rise in world incomes causes oil's price to rise to $36 and the flow to 22 million barrels). The method compares the first static outcome with the second; hence the name "comparative statics."

The method requires holding many complex factors constant, so that attention can be focused on single changes. Moreover, it works especially well with small *marginal* changes. Since comparative statics has such a narrow focus, it can disentangle the many forces at work in complex economic processes.

The first step in microeconomics is to explain the outcomes of individual markets. The market is the arena where demand and supply meet. ***The term market has a precise economic meaning: a grouping of buyers and sellers who exchange a specific good at a price.*** Many people participate, and there is competition among both buyers and sellers. A market also has rapid adjustments in prices and quantities.

Each market is described by two main dimensions: the nature of the good and the geographic area. Each market is defined so that it contains only goods among which consumers can freely substitute. For example, two brands of English muffins would be in the same market, but sledgehammers and saws are in different markets. Atari and Odyssey electronic games are not identical goods, but they would both be included in the market for such games. The second dimension of a market, *geographic area,* is also important in defining markets. Since bread is usually baked and sold locally, the Chicago bread market and the Detroit bread market are separate markets. On the other hand, since microwave ovens are transported nationwide, the market for a particular brand would be the entire United States.

Once a specific market is defined by both its product and its geographic area, then one can examine the workings of demand and supply in that particular market setting. That is precisely what you will be doing in this chapter. The demand and supply sides of the market are presented separately. Then we show how demand and supply forces interact to determine market price and quantity.

Demand

Influences on demand

The analysis of **demand** focuses on the consumers' (or buyers') side of the market. It seeks to explain what demand is and how it affects market price and quantity. As you know from experience, many factors determine how much of a commodity consumers are willing to buy at various prices.

The *price* of the good is an obvious and important influence on purchases. Simple intuition tells you that at higher prices people will purchase less of a good than they will at lower prices, if all other things remain unchanged.

Income (or buying power) is another important influence on the quantity of a good that people will want to buy. As your income rises, you can afford to buy more, and your purchases of many goods will increase. Yet there are also goods that you would buy less of as your income rises. For example, if your own income were suddenly increased, you might buy less hamburger and more steak, or less margarine and more butter.

Preferences determine the relative importance of other variables in determining how much of each product will be bought at each price. Preferences are not always easy to explain, but economists regard them as a crucial influence on demand. The companies selling consumer goods also recognize the importance of preferences; they spend over $40 billion a year in the United States on advertising in attempts to direct consumer preferences toward their own products.

The amount of a good that consumers wish to purchase is influenced not only by the item's own price, but also by the *price of other goods*. These other related goods can be *substitutes* or *complements*. A substitute is a good that can be used in place of another commodity. For example, margarine and butter are widely recognized as substitutes for each other. If the price of butter increases, consumers may substitue margarine. Thus, the amount of margarine purchased will change because of the price change of butter. In contrast, goods that are complements are used together rather than instead of each other—for example, cars and gasoline. As the price of gasoline increases and people buy less of it, you would also expect fewer cars to be sold as consumers switch to buses, form car pools, or move closer to their jobs.

Population will also affect the amount of a good purchased. More consumers mean that more of a good will be purchased, other things being equal.

Patterns of consumption will also be affected by *income distribution*. In a country with a very even distribution of income, there will be less demand for certain luxury goods than there would be in an economy with the same total income divided very unequally among the very rich and the very poor.

Finally, *expectations about future prices* can affect purchases. If consumers expect the price of a good to rise sharply in the near future, they may buy more of the good now to avoid paying higher prices later. If consumers expect a price to fall, they are likely to postpone purchases.

All of these conditions can influence the quantity of each good that consumers will purchase. The economist's task is to disentangle all of these different factors. How does microeconomics isolate the effect of just one of these factors on the quantity of a good that consumers will want to purchase?

The procedure is fairly simple. First, hold all the influences constant at a given level and measure the quantity that consumers will want to buy. Then allow one influence to vary, while still holding the other influences constant. For example, hold income, population, and all of the other influences on demand constant, and only vary the price. Since price is the only influence on demand that is allowed to vary, any changes in quantity must be caused by the changes in price. Thus, you can define and isolate the specific relation between price and quantity. Note that the other factors that affect demand are not ignored; their influence is simply held steady.

You can hold all factors constant and then vary any one influence. If you vary income, you are isolating the income-quantity relation. If you vary population, you are identifying the population-quantity relation. If you allow price to vary to bring out the price-quantity relation, then you can derive an important tool of economic analysis, the *demand curve*.

The demand curve

The demand curve for any good relates the quantities of the good that consumers wish to buy to the *price* of the good. The underlying logic in deriving a demand schedule can be summarized as shown below. All influences except price are held constant. Then quantity varies only as price varies, so that the demand curve reveals the relationship between price and quantity.

Table 2 Conditions for a Simple Demand Curve

Price	Quantity (gallons per week)
$3.50	6,200
3.00	8,000
2.50	10,000
2.00	12,300
1.50	15,000
1.00	18,000
.50	21,500

A demand curve can represent the price-quantity relation either for an individual consumer or for an entire market. This chapter concentrates on *market* or total demand curves, which come from adding all of the individual demand curves for a particular good.

The market demand curve can best be shown by an example. A demand schedule for gasoline is presented in Table 2, showing how many gallons of gasoline consumers would be willing to buy at various prices. For example, at a price of $1.00 per gallon, consumers would be willing to buy 18,000 gallons of gas per week. From your experience as a consumer, what is likely to happen if the market price of gasoline increases? At a higher price, people will probably want to buy less gasoline. This *inverse relation between price and quantity* makes intuitive sense: **At higher prices, people will want to buy less of a good; at lower prices, they would be willing to buy more.** The figures in Table 2 illustrate precisely that.

Influences on Demand

The quantity of a specific good that consumers will buy	depends on	The price of that good	Consumers' income levels The number of consumers Income distribution	Consumers' preferences The price of related goods Expectations about future prices

The Demand Curve Relates These Two Variables

These Influences are Held Constant

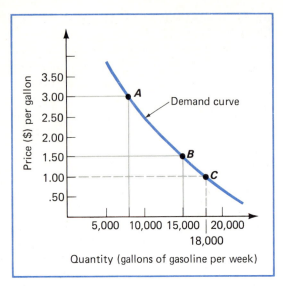

The inverse relation between price and quantity becomes even clearer if the figures in Table 2 are graphed, as in Figure 1. The demand curve showing the relation between price and quantity has a negative or downward slope, because as price rises, consumers want to buy less of the good.

Although the downward slope of the demand curve probably seems obvious, you should be able to explain the inverse relation between price and quantity in more precise terms than intuition. There are two major reasons for the downward slope:

1. **Substitution effect.** As the price of good increases, the substitutes for it (with their now relatively lower prices) look more attractive. Consumers are therefore likely to buy more of the substitutes and less of the good whose price has gone up.

2. **Income effect.** As the price of a good increases, the consumers' purchasing power decreases. Consumers can afford to buy less of all goods, including the one whose price has risen. If the price of razor blades or a bag of pretzels increases, the income effect will be insignificant. But for goods like housing or heating oil that account for a large percentage of people's budgets, the income effect may be substantial. For example, suppose that dormitory rental rates and apartment rents increase considerably. Since housing costs account for so much of your student budget, you will probably have to consume less housing space by rooming with more people than you had originally expected to room with. Instead of two roommates in your apartment, you may have four. Furthermore, to pay the rent you will probably also have to reduce your consumption of *other* things, such as new clothes and entertainment.

For these two reasons, then, your intuition that there is an inverse relation between price and quantity is sound.

Several other points about the demand curve should also be kept firmly in mind. First, the time period for demand must be exactly specified. To know that consumers want to buy 15,000 gallons of gasoline at $1.50 is not very helpful, unless one knows whether that is 15,000 gallons a day, week, month, or year. Without that information, you cannot define demand in any meaningful way. Second, the various quantities expressed in Table 2 and Figure 1 are alternative *desired* quantities, at alternative prices. They represent the amounts that consumers would like to buy at the various prices, and not the amounts they actually succeed in purchasing. For example, at $2.00 a gallon, consumers might want to buy 12,300 gallons of gas *if they could.* But suppose that 12,300 gallons of gas are not available. Actual purchases would then fall short of 12,300 gallons, but that does not alter the demand curve. The curve expresses consumer preferences, not necessarily actual market outcomes. In short, the demand curve is the relationship between price and desired purchases, which may not actually occur.

Finally, you can think of a demand curve in two different ways. Consider the demand curve in Figure 1. (1) The curve shows the maximum quantity of the good people want to buy at a given price—15,000 gallons of gas at $1.50 per gallon. (2) The curve also shows the highest price that consumers will pay to get a given quantity of the good—$1.50 per gallon for 15,000 gallons. People would rather be under the curve, paying less for each given quantity, but the curve itself shows the *maximum* that they are willing to pay.

Because it is diagrammed as simply a line, the demand curve may seem trivial. But, in fact, it summarizes very important information. It shows how much money people are willing to sacrifice to get a good. Of course, you could try to discover preferences by asking all consumers detailed questions, but that would be extremely difficult and give doubtful results. Meanwhile, every day in thousands of markets, consumers put their preferences on the line by making practical choices and payments. These actual and expressed preferences are embodied in the demand curve, making demand an important and powerful concept. To use demand curves correctly, though, the distinction between *demand* and *quantity demanded* must be drawn carefully and precisely.

Quantity demanded and demand
Quantity demanded *refers to a specific price-quantity combination: a particular point on a demand schedule.* In Table 2, 15,000 gallons would be the quantity demanded at $1.50. This would correspond

to Point *B* on the demand curve in Figure 1.

Demand refers to the entire price-quantity relationship: to the whole demand curve in Figure 1, or the entire column of figures in Table 2.

The difference between quantity demanded and demand is crucial in analyzing changes in a particular market. Since quantity demanded refers to a particular point on a demand curve, *a change in quantity demanded refers to a movement along the demand curve from one price-quantity combination to another.* In Figure 1, the movement from Point *B* (15,000 gallons at $1.50) to Point *A* (8,000 gallons at $3.00) would be a change in quantity demanded. Along a given demand curve, the only change that can cause a change in quantity demanded or a movement along the demand curve is a change in price.

Since demand refers to the entire price-quantity relation, the phrase *"a change in demand" refers to a shift in the entire demand curve.* Such a shift in demand can be caused by a change in any influence on quantity *except price.* Take Figure 2 as an example. Curve I is the original demand curve. Now suppose that population increases, all other things remaining unchanged. Because there are now more consumers, a larger quantity of the good would be demanded at every price. The entire demand curve shifts upward and to the right, illustrated by the shift from Demand Curve I to Demand Curve II. Now at a price of P_a, consumers wish to purchase the higher quantity of Q_b.

If population decreases, or if a change in preferences makes consumers like the good less, then consumers would demand less of the good at every price. This decrease in demand would be represented by a leftward shift of the demand curve. But remember that a change in price cannot by itself cause a change in demand. The result of a price change is a *movement along the*

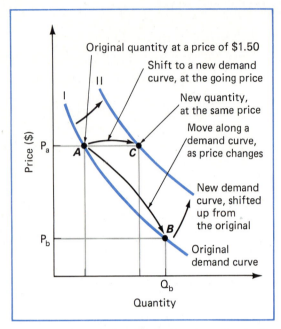

Original quantity at a price of $1.50

Shift to a new demand curve, at the going price

New quantity, at the same price

Move along a demand curve, as price changes

New demand curve, shifted up from the original

Original demand curve

Figure 2   The distinction between a change in demand and a change in quantity demanded

If price falls from P_a to P_b, consumers would move along the demand curve from Point *A* to Point *B*. If any other influence on quantity changes, the demand curve will shift, and a different quantity of the good will be demanded at any given price.

demand curve, not a shift in the entire schedule. Keeping changes in quantity demanded (movements along a demand curve) separate from changes in demand (shifts in demand curves) is crucial when you use demand to analyze changes in markets.

By now, you should have a fairly good idea of how to work with demand curves. You know what causes shifts of these curves and what causes movements along demand curves, and you know why demand curves have a downward or negative slope. But while the general downward-sloping form of demand curves has been discussed, one issue that has not yet been dealt with is the exact *shape* of demand curves, which depends upon how responsive quantity is to price changes.

Consider the two demand curves in Figure 3. Curve I is relatively steep, while Curve II is relatively flat. If the price increases from $1.50 to $2.00, both curves show a decrease in quantity demanded. In the case of the steeper demand curve, Curve I, the drop in quantity from the 50-cent increase in price is 1,500 gallons per week, from 15,000 to 13,500 gallons. For the flatter Demand Curve II, the 50-cent rise in price causes a larger drop in quantity of 5,000 gallons per week, from 15,000 to 10,000 gallons. In other words, quantity

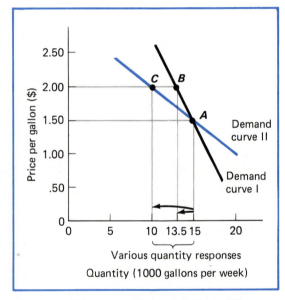

Figure 3   The responsiveness of quantity demanded to changes in price

Both Demand Curve I and Demand Curve II show quantity demanded falling when price increases, and rising when price decreases. Yet the degree of responsiveness of quantity demanded to a given price change is different for each curve. For example, suppose that the price increases from $1.50 to $2.00. Along the steeper demand curve, Demand Curve I, the quantity demanded falls from 15,000 to 13,500 gallons, a decrease of 1,500 gallons. Along the flatter demand curve, Demand Curve II, the quantity demanded falls from 15,000 to 10,000 gallons, a decrease of 5,000 gallons. *For the given price change from $1.50 to $2.00, the quantity demanded represented by Demand Curve II is more responsive to price changes than the quantity demanded represented by Demand Curve I.*

demanded is less responsive to price changes along the *AB* segment of Demand Curve I than along the *AC* portion of Demand Curve II.

How responsive quantity is to price changes is of great importance to any producer or supplier of a good. The reason lies in the influence this responsiveness has on total expenditure or revenue. Total revenue can be expressed as:

Total Revenue = Price per unit × Number of units sold

or

Total Revenue = Price × Quantity.

Suppose that a producer decides to raise prices to increase the total revenue taken in from the sale of a good. The plan may not work. You already know that as price increases, quantity demanded decreases. But while the increased price would, in itself, cause the firm's total revenue to increase, the resulting decrease in quantity would exert an opposite or downward pull on the total revenue gained from consumers' spending. Total revenue may therefore increase or decrease as a result of the price increase. Figure 4 illustrates what may happen to total revenue as price increases. If the price is increased from $2 to $5, the quantity demanded drops from 500 units to 300 units. Total revenue *increases* as a result of this price increase, from $2 × 500 = $1,000 to $5 × 500 = $1,500. But if price is increased further, from $5 to $7, total revenue *decreases* from $5 × $300 = $1,500, to $7 × 100 = $700.

Whether total revenue will increase or decrease when price changes depends on which change is larger—the change in price or the change in quantity. To measure the relative sizes of price and quantity changes, economists use the concept of price elasticity of demand.

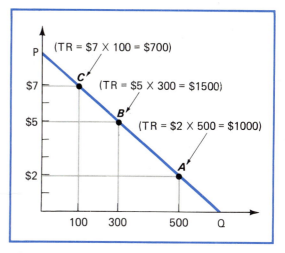

Figure 4   Total revenue at different points on the demand curve

Total revenue may either rise or fall as price increases.

Price elasticity of demand

Price elasticity of demand *measures the relative responsiveness of quantity demanded to a change in price.* The formula for elasticity is:

Price elasticity
$$= \frac{\text{percentage change in quantity}}{\text{percentage change in price}} \text{ or } \frac{\%\Delta Q}{\%\Delta P}.$$

Any elasticity is simply a ratio between a cause and an effect, always in percentage terms. The cause goes in the bottom half or denominator of the ratio, while the effect is in the top half or numerator. For price elasticity, assume that the price change is the cause, and the change in quantity is the effect.

When you calculate elasticities, it is important to work with percentages to avoid the problem of scale. After all, it would hardly be fair to declare that the quantity demanded of gasoline is more responsive to changes in price than automobiles, because a $1.00 change in the price of each good called forth a bigger change in gasoline sales than it did in car sales. By using percentages, the $1.00 price change is put in perspective.

Note that since price and quantity are inversely related, always moving in opposite directions, price elasticity will always be a negative number. The custom is to *ignore the negative sign and discuss only the absolute level* of the price elasticity.

An example can clarify both what elasticity means and how to measure it. Suppose that the price of gasoline rises from $1.50 to $2.00 a gallon in your town, while all other influences on the quantity of gasoline demanded remain unchanged. This causes the local motorists to cut their use from 15,000 to 13,500 gallons per week. The change is shown in Figure 3 along Demand Curve I, represented by a movement from Point *A* to Point *B*. Price elasticity can then be calculated as:

$$\text{Elasticity} = \frac{\text{effect}}{\text{cause}} = \frac{\% \text{ change in } Q}{\% \text{ change in } P}$$

$$= \frac{-1{,}500/15{,}000}{+\$.50/\$1.50} = \frac{-10\%}{+33.3\%} = .30.$$

This method gives the elasticity over the range between Points *A* and *B*, using *A* as the reference or starting point. Unfortunately, this raises a technical problem, for if Point *B*'s values were used instead as the reference in calculating the percentages, the elasticity figure would differ:

$$\text{Elasticity} = \frac{-1{,}500/13{,}500}{+.50/\$2.00} = \frac{11.1\%}{25\%} = .444.$$

The difference in the estimates would be even larger if price doubled to $3.00. The rise would be *100 percent*, but an exact reversal to $1.50 would be only a cut of *50 percent* of $3.00.

To avoid this problem, the midpoint of the range is commonly used as the base. In the present case:

$$\text{Elasticity} = \frac{-1{,}500/14{,}250}{+.50/\$1.75} = \frac{10.53}{28.57} = .367.$$

This gives the average elasticity for that segment of the curve. Another approach would be to measure tiny changes (e.g., a price rise from $1.50 to $1.52), but that would be difficult.

Price elasticity of demand may vary between zero and infinity. With a zero value, demand is *perfectly inelastic*, as shown in Panel I of Figure 5. In this case, quantity demanded does not respond at all to price changes. At the other extreme, where elasticity is infinite, demand is said to be *perfectly elastic*, as shown in Panel II of Figure 5. In this case, people will demand an indefinitely large quantity of the good at the present price, but a zero quantity if the price rises even slightly. Between these extreme cases lie most actual demand situations: Quantity usually responds in some finite degree to price changes, such as with the demand schedule in Panel III.

Make sure that you do not confuse the *slope* of a demand curve with elasticity. The slope of a demand curve between two points would be $(P_2 - P_1)/(Q_2 - Q_1)$. Its elasticity for this same segment would be $\frac{Q_2 - Q_1}{(Q_2 + Q_1)/2} / \frac{P_2 - P_1}{(P_2 + P_1)/2}$, using the midpoint method. A straight-line demand curve, as illustrated in Panel III of Figure 5, will have a constant slope, but *there will be differing elasticities at each point*. This is shown in Figure 6. Generally, at the upper end of a straight-line demand curve, the elasticities are greater than at the lower end.

Aside from the zero and infinite elasticities represented in Panels I and II of Figure 5, there are few exceptions to this rule of differing elasticities along a demand curve. One such exception is the rectangular hyperbola illustrated in Panel IV of Figure 5. At each point, price times quantity yields a total expenditure that is the same as at every other point. This means that price changes must always be

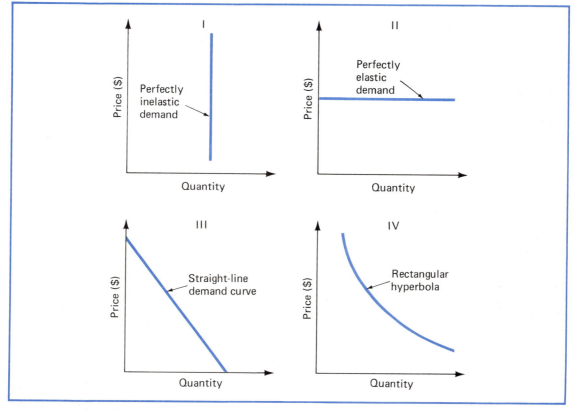

Figure 5   Four examples of demand curves: Perfectly inelastic, perfectly elastic, a straight line, and a rectangular hyperbola

The vertical demand curve (I) is perfectly inelastic. No price change is large enough to change the quantity demanded. The horizontal demand curve (II) is perfectly elastic. At that price, people are willing to consume any amount from zero to infinity. Even a slight price increase will cut their purchases to zero. The straight-line demand curve shown here (III) touches both axes. Elasticity varies along it. The hyperbolic demand curve (IV) has a constant elasticity of 1 throughout.

met by equal and offsetting quantity changes. Therefore, the curve has a constant elasticity at every point.

Once you have learned to calculate an elasticity, you still have to interpret its value. What should you make of an elasticity of 0.088, or 0.3, or 3.0, or 9.67? What do these elasticities tell you?

Elasticities are divided into three simple categories, according to which change dominates: the percentage change in quantity or the percentage change in price. If elasticity is greater than 1 (remember, by convention, the minus sign is ignored),

then the percentage change in quantity (the numerator) must be greater than the percentage change in price (the denominator). For example, a 10 percent rise in the price of hang gliders causes a 20 percent fall in the number bought: elasticity is 2.0. This case is called *elastic demand*, in which quantity demanded is considered *relatively responsive* to changes in price. If elasticity is less than 1, then the percentage change in quantity (the numerator) must be less than the percentage change in price (the denominator). This is a case of *inelastic demand*, in which quantity de-

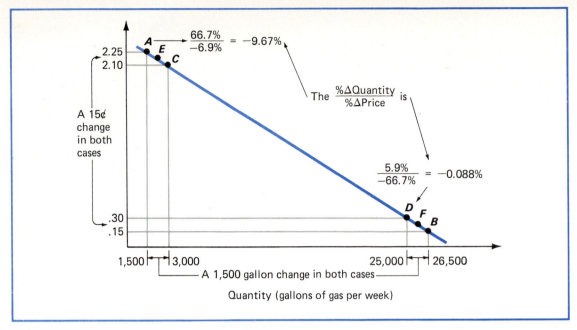

Figure 6 Elasticity varies along a straight-line demand curve
Segments *A–C* and *B–D* have the same slope, but the elasticities—which involve different percentage changes—are sharply different. They are calculated here using the midpoint formula (the two midpoints are *E* and *F*).

manded is considered relatively unresponsive to changes in price. Finally, cases in which elasticity just equals 1, meaning the percentage change in quantity equals the percentage change in price, are considered to be borderline cases, referred to as *unitary elasticity*.

Elasticity and total revenue

Once you know the price elasticity of demand, you can predict how total revenue will change when price changes. Remember that total revenue equals price times quantity. When price changes, all other influences remaining constant, quantity will move in the opposite direction. Total revenue, pulled in two different directions, will

move toward the dominant change. This is because price elasticity tells which change is larger, the change in quantity or the change in price. Knowing that, you can predict in which direction total revenue will move.

If demand is *elastic*, then the quantity change dominates, and so total revenue will move in the same direction as quantity. If demand is inelastic, then the price change dominates the change in quantity, and total revenue will move in the same direction as price. If the elasticity is unitary or 1, then the percentage changes in price and quantity are equal, and there is no change in total revenue. The relation between elasticity and total revenue can be summarized as:

Elasticity (%ΔQ/%ΔP)	Direction of Change in P	Direction of Change in Q	Direction of Change in TR
Elastic demand (Elasticity > 1; %ΔQ > %ΔP)	increase	decrease	decrease
	decrease	increase	increase
Inelastic demand (Elasticity < 1; %ΔQ < %ΔP)	increase	decrease	increase
	decrease	increase	decrease
Unitary demand (Elasticity = 1; %ΔQ = %ΔP)	increase	decrease	no change
	decrease	increase	no change

Determinants of the price elasticity of demand

You have seen how to measure and interpret elasticity, but an important question still remains: What influences the price elasticity of demand? Why, in other words, is the demand for some goods very elastic or responsive to price, while the demand for other goods is very inelastic, changing only slightly when price changes? The following four influences are usually regarded as being the most important in determining each good's elasticity of demand:

1. *Necessity: Certain elementary things are necessary for life, such as food, water, and shelter.* The more you need such goods, the harder it is to cut back on purchases when the price increases. This would make demand for the good relatively inelastic. Other examples of necessities are certain medicines, textbooks, a bed, and heating fuel. Of course, the degree of necessity for some items can vary from one person to the next. Coffee may be an absolute necessity to you, but an optional good to someone else.

2. *The number of available substitutes.* If a good has many close substitutes, it is easy to cut back on purchases in response to a price change. This would make the demand for the good relatively elastic. This is why demand for a specific type or brand of a good is likely to be more elastic than demand for the general category of that good. For example, demand for a new Ford or Dodge will be more elastic than demand for new cars in general.

3. *Time.* As prices change, consumers plan to adjust the quantity they purchase, but this takes time. Plans must be changed; other purchases must be altered. The longer the interval, the greater the changes can be. Therefore, demand over longer time periods tends to be more elastic. For example, suppose that the price of gasoline rises from $1.50 to $3.50 a gallon. Consumers may immediately try to decrease their consumption of gas, but their opportunities for immediate changes are limited. After a period long enough for people to begin to rely on public transport, form car pools, move closer to work, buy bikes, or trade in gas-guzzling cars for more fuel-efficient models, you would expect to see a larger adjustment in quantity: that is, a more elastic demand.

4. *The percentage of income spent on a good.* If you spend a large amount of your income on a particular good, then you are forced to adjust when the price increases. This would tend to make the demand for that good relatively more elastic. For example, dormitory fees or apartment rentals probably account for much of your student budget. If those fees or rentals increase, you may be forced to buy less living space by sharing your apartment with more students. On the other hand, if the price of cole slaw increases, you hardly have to make major adjustments in your purchases. The price increase is simply not significant.

Income elasticity of demand

The income elasticity of demand *measures the responsiveness of quantity demanded to changes in income.* The formula for income elasticity is:

Income elasticity

$$= \frac{\text{percentage change in quantity demanded}}{\text{percentage change in income}}$$

$$= \frac{\%\Delta Q}{\%\Delta \text{Income}}.$$

In this case, all influences on demand other than income are held constant. As income varies, the relation between quantity demanded and income can be determined.

To calculate income elasticity, consider a town in which family income averages $15,000 per year. Average family purchases each year are 40 pounds of

Estimate an Elasticity Cautiously

It is often possible to estimate elasticities from actual price and quantity changes. But when other factors are changing too, the estimates are hazardous.

For example, a recent *New York Times* news story included adjacent charts of gasoline prices and quantities. They showed that while gasoline prices rose in the United States from 70 cents to about $1.30 per gallon during 1979–1981, the quantity of gasoline sold fell from about 9.4 to about 8.0 billion gallons per month. Not only do the directions of the two changes fit basic logic, but they also permit one to calculate a specific value for elasticity as follows:

The price rise was 60 cents per gallon. That is a 60 percent rise, calculated using the midpoint of the 70-cents-to-$1.30 range, which is $1.00. Meanwhile, the flow of gallons declined by 1.4 billion per month, which is 16 percent of 8.7 billion gallons (the midpoint of the 9.4-to-8.0-billion range). The elasticity of demand appears to be

(% change in gallons) ÷

$$\text{(\% change in price)} = (-16\%) \div (+60\%)$$
$$= -0.27 = 0.27.$$

(The minus sign is ignored, of course.) Evidently the simple logic of elasticity can be applied to real data.

But there are two main cautions. First, other factors have certainly also changed during this period, so that the

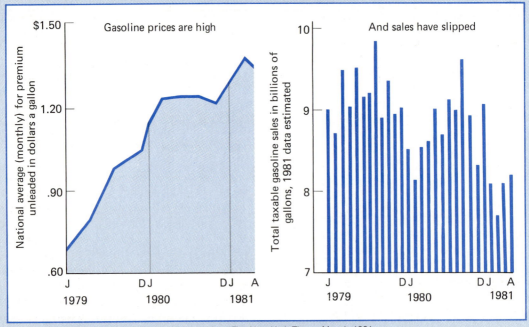

Source: (both charts): Lundberg Survey, Adapted from The New York Times, May 1, 1981.
© 1981 by The New York Times Company. Reprinted by permission.

pure logic of the elasticity—to hold everything constant except price—has been violated to some degree. For example, consumers' incomes changed, and the prices of automobiles rose. Therefore, the "elasticity" number reflects more than just the change in gasoline's price. Perhaps if the other changes were small or mutually offsetting, then the calculated elasticity might not be far from the true value. Moreover, only the general magnitude of the elasticity matters (such as "about .3" or "probably between .20 and .35"). Even when the data seem to be precise, there can be errors, distortions, or unexpected factors. Therefore, the careful analyst usually speaks of approximate, not highly exact, values.

Incidentally, note that the *Times* artist cut the vertical axes dramatically on both diagrams, to make the changes more sharply visible. That is risky practice.

---

margarine, 5 pounds of butter, and 64 loaves of bread. Suppose that family income rises by an average of $1,500 to $16,500. As a result of this change in income, the average family now consumes 36 pounds of margarine per year, 7 pounds of butter, and 65 loaves of bread. The income elasticities of demand for these goods would be (using the midpoint method):

Income elasticity of margarine

$$= \frac{\dfrac{36-40}{38}}{\dfrac{\$16,500-\$15,000}{\$15,750}} = \frac{-10.52\%}{+9.52\%} = -1.11$$

Income elasticity of butter $= \dfrac{\dfrac{7-5}{6}}{\dfrac{\$16,500-\$15,000}{\$15,750}}$

$$= \frac{+33.33\%}{+9.52\%} = 3.50$$

Income elasticity of bread $= \dfrac{\dfrac{65-64}{64.5}}{\dfrac{\$16,500-\$15,000}{\$15,750}}$

$$= \frac{+1.55\%}{+9.52\%} = +.16.$$

Do *not* ignore the sign of income elasticities. Unlike price elasticity where the sign is always negative, income elasticity may have either a positive or a negative sign. That sign provides an important clue to the nature of the good.

If the quantity of a good purchased moves in the same direction as income—increasing as income increases and decreasing as income decreases—then income elasticity will be positive. Goods with a positive income elasticity are called *normal goods*. Consumers buy more of these goods when they can afford to. In the earlier example, both butter and bread were normal goods.

If the quantity purchased of a good moves in the opposite direction from changes in income—decreasing as income increases and increasing as income decreases—then income elasticity will be negative. Goods with a negative income elasticity are called *inferior goods*. Consumers buy less of these goods as their income increases because they are substituting more desirable (but more expensive) alternatives. In the preceding example, margarine was an inferior good. As income rose, consumers switched from margarine to butter.

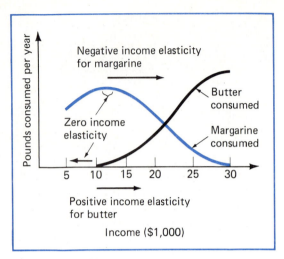

Figure 7 Income-quantity patterns for margarine and butter

At between $5,000 and $10,000 income per year, consumers purchase more margarine as their income increases. It is a normal good. For this same income range, butter shows a zero income elasticity: Increases in income do not cause any increases in the quantity of butter demanded. At incomes over $10,000 per year, consumers will switch from margarine to butter. Now margarine becomes an inferior good, as increases in income cause the quantity demanded to fall. Butter becomes a normal good, with increases in income causing the quantity demanded to rise.

Income elasticity can vary with income levels. A good may be a normal good for most consumers up to a certain level of income, but become inferior at higher income levels. Figure 7 shows this for both butter and margarine. Margarine is a normal good until income rises above the $10,000 mark. Then it becomes an inferior good. Butter has a zero income elasticity up to $10,000. Consumers can't afford to buy any butter at all. At income levels above $10,000, butter becomes a normal good.

Poor families may consider potatoes and cheap cuts of meat to be normal goods. For a while, they are delighted to buy more of these goods as their income rises. But at still higher levels of income, they begin to consume less of these goods, switching perhaps to French bread and

fancy steaks. Potatoes and cheap meat, once normal goods for these families, have become inferior goods at the new and higher income level.

Within the broad categories of normal and inferior goods, economists use the exact values of income elasticity to determine just how responsive quantity is to income. If the value of income elasticity is greater than 1, then the good is said to be a normal good with an *income-elastic demand*. If the value is less than 1 (but not negative), then the good is said to be a normal good with an *income-inelastic demand*. A value of 1 indicates a good with unitary income elasticity. A value of zero shows that quantity demanded does not respond at all to changes in income. And a negative value indicates an inferior good. In the earlier examples of income elasticities, butter, with an income elasticity of +3.50, was a normal good with an income-elastic demand. Bread, with an income elasticity of +.16, was a normal good with an income-inelastic demand. Margarine, with an elasticity of −1.11, was an inferior good.

Cross-elasticity of demand
Cross-elasticity of demand *measures how responsive one good's quantity demanded is to changes in the price of another good.* A pair of goods may be related because they are *substitutes* for each other (margarine and butter), or because they are used together as *complements* (gasoline and cars). The formula for cross-elasticity is:

Cross-elasticity of demand for Good A

$$= \frac{\% \text{ of change in quantity of Good } A}{\% \text{ of change in price of Good } B}$$

$$= \frac{\%\Delta Q_A}{\%\Delta P_B}.$$

First, consider two goods that are *substitutes*, such as Chevrolets and Fords. If the price of Chevrolets rises, while all else (including Ford prices) stays the same, some people who would have bought Chevrolets will now buy Fords. Thus, an increase in the price of Chevrolets would cause an increase in the quantity of Ford cars purchased. With the price of Chevrolets and the quantity purchased of Fords changing in the same direction (both increasing), the cross-elasticity will be *positive*. A *positive cross-elasticity indicates that two goods are substitutes*. The higher the value of the cross-elasticity, the closer the degree of substitution. For example, the cross-elasticity between Chevrolets and Fords is certain to be higher than the cross-elasticity between Chevrolets and bicycles.

Now consider two goods that are *complements*, such as automobiles and gasoline. If the price of gasoline increases, people will purchase both less gas and fewer of the goods used with gas, such as autos and tires. Because the increase in the price of gas causes a decrease in the quantity of cars purchased, the cross-elasticity will be negative. For example, the values might be:

$$\text{Cross-elasticity} = \frac{\%\Delta Q \text{ of cars}}{\%\Delta P \text{ of gasoline}}$$

$$= \frac{-40\%}{+100\%} = -.4.$$

The negative cross-elasticity shows that the goods are complements. A negative value larger than -0.1 or -0.2 would show that they are close complements.

Close complements are not numerous. If you can think of even a few examples, you are doing well. In contrast, close substitutes are common. You should be able to think of a substitute for nearly any good or service.

Up to this point, the chapter has concentrated on the demand side of the market, analyzing how consumers' choices are expressed in demand. To complete the analysis of market quantities and prices, the next section deals with producers' choices on the *supply* side of markets.

Supply

The analysis of supply focuses on the producers' (or sellers') side of the market. Issues dealing with supply concentrate on what determines the amount of a good that producers are willing to offer. Since willingness to supply is based on several considerations, the logical starting place for an analysis of supply is with an examination of the factors that influence it.

Influences on supply

Price is one of the major influences on the quantity of a good that a producer is willing to offer. At higher prices, a producer will usually supply higher quantities of a good because, other things being equal, the higher price makes it more profitable to do so. The incentive to produce is directly related to the level of the price.

The *costs* of producing the good also influence the amount that producers will offer. Costs, in turn, are determined by two major factors:

1. *The prices of inputs.* Given the state of technology, the prices of inputs determine the cost of production. If input prices rise (e.g., when wages rise), then cost will rise and producers may have to receive a higher price to cover their costs. A fall of input prices will reduce costs and permit supply at a lower price.

2. *Technology.* Technology refers to the known ways in which inputs can be combined to produce a given output. If technology improves, so that the output can be produced using fewer inputs, then costs will be lower. That en-

ables the producers to supply each amount of the good at a lower price.

Thus, either a decrease in input prices or an improvement in technology will cause production costs to fall. The producer would then be willing to offer any given quantity of the good at lower prices.

The *goals of a firm* also influence the amount of a good that producers are willing to offer. A firm aiming to maximize its profits may offer less of a good at a given price than a firm that is trying to increase its share of market sales.

The *number of firms* offering the good will also influence the total amount of the good that producers are willing to supply, just as population affects the demand for a good. This is because the total market supply comes from summing the supply of all firms. The more firms there are, the greater will be the total quantity offered.

Changes in *the prices of related goods* also influence the amount of a good that producers will offer for sale. On the supply side, two goods are related if they use a common input. For example, a farmer may produce a variety of crops, including soybeans. If the market price of soybeans increased, all other conditions remaining the same, the farmer would find it profitable to reallocate some land from other crops to soybean production because changes in relative prices affect relative profitability. When the price of soybeans increases relative to the price of the other crops, it becomes more profitable to produce soybeans. The farmer cuts back on other crops to produce more soybeans.

Finally, *expectations about future prices* can affect producers' decisions as well as consumers' decisions. For example, if the price of a product decreases, and producers expect the price decline to be temporary, they may make only slight alterations in output. But if they see this decrease as the beginning of a long-term downward trend in prices, producers will begin a much more substantial cutback. Even if there, is no current change in prices, producers may increase or decrease output on the basis of long-term predictions of the direction in which the industry is moving.

All of these influences help to determine the quantity that producers will offer. To isolate and study the influence of one specific factor on quantity offered for sale, apply the same procedure as for demand. Hold all influences constant, and then allow only one influence to change. If price is the variable that is held constant, this procedure isolates the price–quantity supplied relation, which is the market supply curve.

The supply curve and its upward slope

Table 3 and Figure 8 illustrate the supply curve. Note that as price increases, quantity supplied also increases; and as price decreases, quantity supplied decreases. Because both quantity supplied and price move in the same direction, the supply schedule has an upward slope.

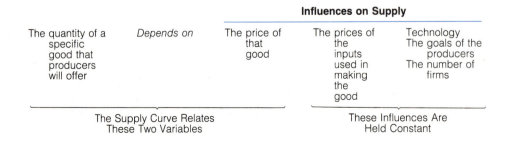

Influences on Supply

The quantity of a specific good that producers will offer	*Depends on*	The price of that good	The prices of the inputs used in making the good	Technology The goals of the producers The number of firms

The Supply Curve Relates These Two Variables

These Influences Are Held Constant

Table 3 *A market supply schedule for gasoline*

Price	Quantity Supplied (gallons per week)
$3.50	17,400
3.00	15,800
2.50	14,100
2.00	12,300
1.50	10,300
1.00	7,800
.50	5,000

Some of the points that were important in understanding demand are also important for supply. First, the quantity figures must be linked to some specific period of time, such as quantity per week, month, or year. Without this information, the quantity figures would be impossible to interpret. Second, the quantities represented by the supply curve represent the *desired* quantities of sales. They are the amounts producers are willing to offer or sell at

each price, not the amounts they actually succeed in selling.

An additional point pertaining specifically to supply should be made. The supply curve—the precise relation between quantity offered and specific prices—exists only for certain types of industries; those in which the producers see themselves as *controlled* by a market price, rather than as *controlling* price in the market. Nonetheless, the general principles of supply—what will increase or decrease each producer's desire to offer various quantities at a certain price—are still useful in discussing supply conditions in all industries.

Quantity supplied versus supply

Quantity supplied and *supply* are terms that must be used as precisely as quantity demanded and demand.

Quantity supplied *refers to a specific combination of price and quantity, which is just one point on the supply curve.* A change in quantity supplied is represented by a movement *along the supply curve from one price-quantity combination to another,* such as from *A* to *B* on Supply Curve I in Figure 9. A change in quantity along a supply curve can be caused only by a change in price.

Supply *refers to the entire relationship between prices and quantities supplied; that is, to the entire supply curve. A change in supply is caused by a change in any of the influences on supply, except price.* A change in the cost of an input or in the number of firms, for example, would cause a different quantity to be supplied at any given price. The only way to show this is to shift the entire curve. If the producers will offer more of a good at any given price, then the supply curve will shift to the right. This is shown in Figure 9 by the shift from Supply Curve I to Supply Curve II.

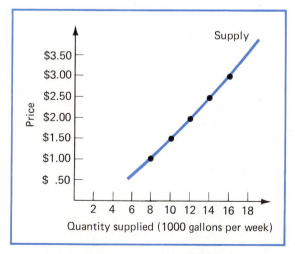

Figure 8 A market supply schedule for gasoline

The supply schedule traces out the quantities that producers are willing to supply at various prices. The upward slope of the supply curve illustrates the fact that higher prices will cause larger amounts of the good to be supplied.

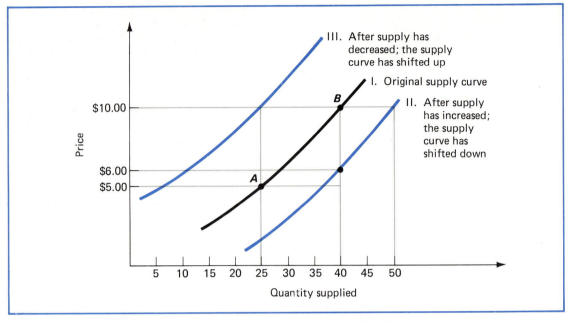

Figure 9   A movement along the Supply Curve differs from a shift of the curve

A change in quantity supplied is caused by a change in price. It is represented by a movement along the supply curve, such as the move from Point *A* to Point *B* on Supply Curve I. A change in supply, caused by a change in any influence on supply except price, means that a different quantity will be supplied at a given price. An increase in supply, with more being offered at a given price, is represented by a rightward shift in the supply curve, such as the shift from Supply Curve I to Supply Curve II. A decrease in supply, with less being offered at a given price, is represented by a leftward shift in the supply curve, such as the shift from Supply Curve I to Supply Curve III.

This shift can be interpreted in two different ways. The increase in supply can be viewed as a larger quantity being supplied at every price. Or, instead, the increase in supply can mean that each quantity is being offered at a lower price. In Figure 9, with supply increasing from Supply Curve I to Supply Curve II, 50 units are now available at a price of $10 instead of 40 units. Or, in the other view: 40 units are now available at a lower price, at $6 rather than $10.

If producers' willingness to supply a good decreases, then the supply curve will shift to the left. Less will be offered at every price; or each quantity will be offered at a higher price. When the curve moves down, or to the right, one says that "supply has increased." If instead the curve shifts up, or to the left, then "supply

has decreased." It may seem odd that an *upward* shift in the curve means that supply has *decreased*, but that is correct. To avoid confusion, think in terms of leftward and rightward shifts of the supply curve, rather than upward and downward shifts.

Finally, the supply curve itself can be interpreted in two different ways. Consider Supply Curve I in Figure 9. It shows the highest quantity that will be supplied at each price (40 units at $10), or the lowest price that suppliers will accept for each level of output ($10 for 40 units). Viewed either way, greater levels of output will be offered only at higher levels of price. This is because extra production requires extra effort and cost. How sharp an increase in price is necessary to bring forth a given increase in supply can be measured by the *elasticity of supply*.

Elasticity of supply

The elasticity of supply *measures how responsive the quantity of supply is to changes in price.* The change in price is the cause; the change in quantity the effect. The formula for supply elasticity is:

Elasticity of supply

$$= \frac{\text{percentage change in quantity supplied}}{\text{percentage change in price}}$$

$$= \frac{\% \Delta Q \text{ supplied}}{\% \Delta P \text{ supplied}}.$$

This elasticity is similar to price elasticity of demand, but there is a difference. Since the supply curve is upward sloping—showing a direct relation between price and quantity—the elasticity of supply will have a positive sign. Both halves of the fraction move the same way. If price increases, quantity supplied will increase. If price decreases, quantity supplied will decrease.

If the elasticity of supply is greater than 1, economists say that the good has an *elastic supply*, with quantity supplied being relatively responsive to changes in price. If the elasticity is less than 1, the good is said to have an *inelastic supply*, with quantity supplied being relatively unresponsive to changes in price. A supply elasticity *equal* to 1 is the borderline case in which the percentage change in price and in quantity supplied are equal.

Elasticity is not identical to slope As with demand, the supply curve's slope is not the same as elasticity. The slope is simply $(P_1 - P_2)/(Q_1 - Q_2)$, while the elasticity, using the midpoint method, would be

$$\frac{Q_1 - Q_2}{(Q_1 - Q_2)/2} \Big/ \frac{P_1 - P_2}{(P_1 - P_2)/2}.$$ The slope of a straight-line supply curve will be constant, while the elasticity of supply will usually vary from point to point along the curve. That is illustrated in Figure 11 by a straight-line (constant slope) supply curve, whose elasticity values range from 6.0 to 2.0 and 1.6.

But in three special cases, supply curves have a constant elasticity throughout. Two of these cases are shown in Figure 10. At one extreme, shown in Panel I, supply is *perfectly elastic*, represented by a horizontal curve, with elasticity equal to infinity throughout. The other extreme, shown in Panel II, is the case of *perfectly*

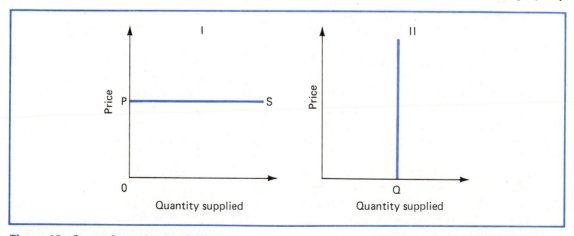

Figure 10 Case of supply elasticities

For an infinitely elastic supply (Panel I), any amount will be supplied at the going price, but nothing will be supplied at a lower price. For a perfectly inelastic supply curve (Panel II), price has no influence on quantity supplied. The supply is fixed at a given level.

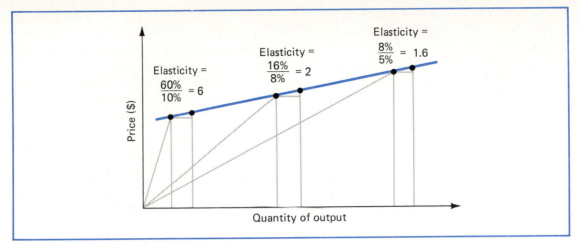

Figure 11   Elasticity varies along a straight supply curve (if it is not a ray or line through the origin)

The variation of elasticity is shown by calculating elasticity at three points. Moving to the right, the elasticity starts high and then declines. Eventually it would go below 1.0. Why does the decline occur? Because the *percentage* rises in price decline more slowly than do the *percentage* rises in quantity.

inelastic supply, in which the supply curve is vertical and has an elasticity of zero throughout. In this case, price has no influence on the quantity supplied. The quantity is fixed, no matter how high or low the price may go. Most actual supply elasticities lie between these two extremes.

The third exception to differing elasticities at each point on the supply curve is the case of a supply curve that lies along a ray from the origin. *For such supply curves, elasticity is constant and equal to 1 at each point.* This is illustrated by Schedules *A* through *C* in Figure 12. Though their *slopes* differ, these schedules all have a constant elasticity equal to 1 throughout their lengths.

Students often find this rule implausible at first, because *A* looks less elastic than *C.* Yet the slopes are constant, and so are the elasticities, along the rays. This constancy contrasts with demand curves, where a straight-line curve has differing elasticities at every point (except for the vertical and horizontal extreme cases).

This unitary value of supply elasticity along rays from the origin is extremely helpful in estimating quickly how elastic a supply curve is. It provides the general rule: Wherever a supply curve is steeper

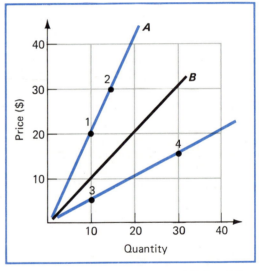

Figure 12   There is constant elasticity of 1 along supply curves that are rays from the origin

This can be verified by calculating the elasticities at points 1 and 2, and at points 3 and 4. The percentage changes in quantity and price will always be identical to each other, so the elasticities will all be equal to 1.

than a ray from the origin passing through it, the curve is *inelastic.* Wherever the curve is flatter than a ray from the origin, it is *elastic.*

Thus, a quick test for supply elasticity is to draw a ray from the origin through

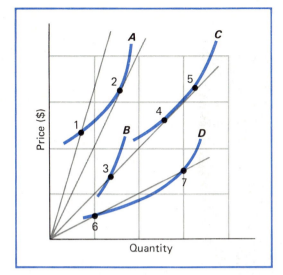

Figure 13 Testing elasticities of supply by using rays from the origin

Consider Curve *A*. The section of the supply curve containing Point 1 is flatter than the ray from the origin drawn through that point. Point 1 must be located on an elastic portion of Supply Curve *A*. Supply Curve *A* is tangent to the ray at Point 2, so its elasticity equals 1 at that point. Along Curve *B*, elasticity is less than 1.0 at point 3. Along Curve *C*, elasticity equals 1.0 in the segment between Points 4 and 5. Along Curve *D*, elasticity is above 1.0 at Point 6 but below 1.0 at Point 7.

whatever part or point of the curve you are interested in. Then just note which is steeper, the ray or the curve. The method also works for *curved* supply schedules, as is shown in Figure 13. If you learn to draw rays lightly on any supply curve diagram, you can quickly show the relative elasticity or inelasticity of any part of any supply curve.

Determinants of elasticity of supply

Four major factors influence elasticity of supply.

1. *Time.* Just as with demand, the elasticity of supply varies directly with the length of the time period: A longer period gives a higher elasticity. The longer time period allows producers to make a fuller adjustment in quantity in response to price changes.

2. *Size of the industry.* Industries that purchase only a small percentage of the total output of their input suppliers can usually buy more inputs quickly with only small increases in price. A large increase in their input use requires only a small increase in total production by suppliers of the input. A local restaurant, for example, can easily expand by hiring a few more waiters and increasing its food purchases, without putting any strain on the entire local labor market or food suppliers. At the opposite extreme is an industry whose demand for inputs accounts for a large percentage of total demand for the input. Growth in the industry, and therefore in its demand for inputs, may severely strain the capacity of the input suppliers. The input suppliers' cost will rise, leading to an increase in the price of inputs.

3. *Special inputs in limited supply.* A specific input that an industry needs may be limited in supply for other reasons. Resource-based industries—such as farm products, lumber, metals, chemicals, or oil—often face this situation. Their supply curves slope up because their key inputs are physically limited. To get more of these inputs, the firms may have to offer steeply higher prices to bid the inputs away from other uses. Or they may have to alter the production process in costly ways to stretch the key inputs further. As a result, the supply curve will be relatively inelastic, showing that more output will be available only at sharply increased prices.

4. *Capital intensity. Heavy industries* use large amounts of capital, such as specialized machinery or equipment, in their production process—for example, blast furnaces in steel plants and oil-refining equipment. Because ordering, receiving, and putting new equipment into operation takes a long time, short-run supply will be relatively inelastic. An increase in price will cause only limited increases in quan-

Supply Elasticity Increases with Time

1. *Coal.* The price of coal rises by 100% because demand increases. Responding to the rise in price, coal companies move their coal stockpiles to market within a week. If this allowed a 10 percent rise in quantity, elasticity for that one-week period would be 10% ÷ 100% = 0.10. In a month, many high-cost coal mines are reopened. Quantity may rise by 30 percent, suggesting an elasticity of 0.30. In a year, 20 entirely new coal mines may have been opened and be starting production. Output is up by 125 percent, suggesting an elasticity of 125% ÷ 100% = 1.25.

2. *Houses.* The price of housing rises by 50 percent because demand shifts upward. Within a week, a few lofts have been spruced up for renting, raising the quantity of new housing per year by 3 percent. Supply elasticity for a one-week period appears to be 3% ÷ 50% = 0.046. In six months, construction has been speeded up to get half-finished houses ready, and the quantity of housing per year is up by 20 percent. Supply elasticity for the period is 0.40. Within a year, the existing stock of housing has risen sharply by 100%, so that the elasticity of supply is 2.0.

tity supplied in all but the longest time periods. In *light* industry, such as small appliances, or local trades, the use of capital is less specialized and extensive, so that capacity is more flexible and can be much more easily adjusted. An increase in price, therefore, can call forth larger increases in quantity supplied. Supply will therefore be relatively elastic.

These four factors—time, size, special inputs, and capital intensity—all work to determine how responsive the quantity supplied will be to changes in price. If supply is relatively elastic, then increases in demand can be accommodated by suppliers with only moderate increases in price. If supply is relatively inelastic, then increases in demand are harder for producers to accommodate. The increase in demand will be met by only

moderate increases in quantity and relatively large increases in price.

Interaction of supply and demand

You have now examined both demand (the buyers' side of the market) and supply (the sellers' side of the market). By fitting together demand and supply analysis, you arrive at one of the most important parts of economic analysis: the determination of market price and quantity.

Consider the gasoline market illustrated by the demand and supply information given in Figure 14. Imagine that you have been asked what the equilibrium price and quantity are. You may not even know what "equilibrium prices and quantity" mean, but your attention would probably be drawn to the price and quantity

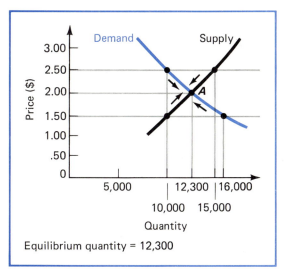

Equilibrium quantity = 12,300

Figure 14   Equilibrium is reached where supply and demand intersect

At a price of $1.50, consumers want to buy far more gallons than suppliers offer. At $2.50, the reverse occurs: Consumers want less than the suppliers offer. Only at Point *A*, at the intersection of the two curves, are the quantities and prices of the two sides—consumers and suppliers—just equal. Note that at any price above equilibrium, there is excess supply. At any price below the equilibrium price, there is excess demand.

Demand		Supply	
Price ($ per gallon)	Quantity (gallons per week)	Price ($ per gallon)	Quantity (gallons per week)
3.50	6,200	3.50	17,400
3.00	8,000	3.00	15,800
2.50	10,000	2.50	14,100
2.00	12,300	2.00	12,300
1.50	15,000	1.50	10,300
1.00	18,000	1.00	7,800
.50	21,500	.50	5,000

combination of $2.00 and 12,300 gallons that exists at the intersection of the supply and demand schedules. That intersection is the only point where quantity supplied equals quantity demanded.

To see why, consider any price above $2.00, such as $2.50. At that price, suppliers will bring 14,100 gallons of gasoline to the market, while consumers wish to buy only 10,000 gallons of it. There is an *excess supply* of 4,100 gallons. What hap-

pens? To sell the excess supply, suppliers will have to lower the price of a gallon of gas. As the price of gasoline falls, suppliers offer smaller amounts of gasoline, and the quantity supplied drops. This can be represented by movement down and to the left *along the supply schedule.*

Meanwhile, as the price falls, the consumers want to purchase more gasoline. This increase in quantity demanded occurs as a rightward movement down along the demand curve. The excess supply of gas begins to dwindle. The pressure to reduce the price will continue until the amount of gas that suppliers wish to offer is just matched by the amount of gas that consumers wish to buy. This equality of quantity supplied and quantity demanded will occur only at the point where the two curves intersect, at a price of $2.00 and quantity of 12,300 gallons of gasoline. At that point, the excess supply has been eliminated and there is no further downward pressure on price.

Now suppose that price had originally been below $2.00, such as at $1.50. At that price, consumers wish to purchase 15,000 gallons of gas, while suppliers are willing to offer only 10,300 gallons. There is an excess demand of 4,700 gallons, which shows up as lines of cars at gas stations. Seeing the long lines of unsatisfied customers, the station operators will quickly realize that there is a greater demand for gasoline than they can meet. In a free market, they will respond to this shortage by increasing price to try and raise their profits. As the price of a gallon of gasoline increases, suppliers will be led to offer more gasoline, moving to the right along their supply curve. Consumers will then respond to the higher price by reducing the amount of gas they are willing to purchase, moving to the left along their demand curve.

The price will continue to rise, along with the increase in quantity supplied and the decrease in quantity demanded, until the point is reached at which suppliers are willing to offer exactly the amount that consumers are willing to buy. Once again, the price and quantity gravitate to the combination represented by the intersection of supply and demand—a price of $2.00 and a quantity of 12,300 gallons. The price and quantity will now remain stable until some further change in supply or demand conditions occurs.

The intersection of the supply and demand curve represents market equilibrium. *Equilibrium is a balancing of forces. At the point where the supply and demand curves intersect, supply and demand forces are perfectly balanced, so that the quantity supplied equals the quantity demanded.* If the market is operating at some point other than the equilibrium, the excess supply or excess demand sets in motion the market forces that will cause price and quantity to move back toward equilibrium. Once that equilibrium is reached, the price and quantity will tend to persist until there is a change in some underlying supply or demand condition. This would be represented by a *shift* in the supply or demand curve. The market price and quantity would then move toward the new equilibrium.

Such a shift can easily be illustrated, as in Figure 15. Suppose that demand for gasoline has decreased because the price of automobiles (a complementary good) has risen sharply. (Note: The curve need *not* shift parallel to its original position.) At the old equilibrium price of $2.00, consumers wish to buy only 8,000 gallons, though suppliers are still ordering 12,300 gallons for sale. Excess supply is 4,300 gallons. To dispose of it, the suppliers cut the price and reduce their orders. Moving to the left down the supply curve, they finally reach Point *B,* the new equilibrium. Price is $1.40 and quantity is 10,000 gallons. (Incidentally, the elasticity of supply over

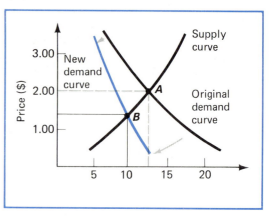

Figure 15   A shift in demand causes a new equilibrium

The original equilibrium is at Point *A.* Then demand shifts down. At a price of $2.00, there is a physical surplus of 4,300 gallons, because buyers want only 8,000 gallons, but suppliers are offering 12,300 gallons as before. The new equilibrium is reached at Point *B,* where both price ($1.40) and quantity (10,000 gallons) are lower.

this part of the supply curve is [−20.6%] ÷ [−35.3%] = 0.58.)

A shift in supply causes a similar adjustment with a movement along the demand curve to the equilibrium. The new equilibrium will always be the new intersection of the demand and supply curves.

These steps lead to an outcome that fits economic logic. As Figure 15 shows, the fall in demand has caused both price and output to decrease. Consumers' desire for gasoline is now less than before, so that the fall in price and quantity bought is precisely what you would expect. Moreover, the change has come about spontaneously, by market actions that cause the new equilibrium to be reached.

One last point: There is nothing morally "good" about equilibrium. Price and quantity are not necessarily fair or just or equitable in any normative sense. Market equilibrium is simply the price and quantity combination at which the market clears, with the quantity supplied equal to the quantity demanded.

Summary

This chapter examines the demand and supply sides of the market separately and then brings them together to show how the market equilibrium is determined. The main points in the chapter are:

1. Supply and demand forces interact in markets. Each market is defined by both the nature of the product and the geographic area in which the product is sold.

2. The factors that influence demand include: (a) price; (b) income; (c) preferences; (d) price of other goods, such as substitutes and complements; (e) population; (f) income distribution; and (g) expectations about future prices.

3. If all influences on demand are held constant, and only price is allowed to vary, then the relation between price and quantity demanded can be isolated and studied. This relation is shown by the *demand curve.*

4. *Quantity demanded* refers to a particular point on the demand curve that represents a specific price-quantity combination. A *change in quantity demanded,* caused by a change in price, refers to a movement along the demand curve from one price-quantity combination to another. *Demand* refers to the entire price-quantity relationship; the entire demand curve. A *change in demand* refers to a shift in the entire curve, caused by a change in any influence on demand except price.

5. *Price elasticity of demand* $\left(\dfrac{\%\Delta Q}{\%\Delta P}\right)$ measures the relative responsiveness of quantity demanded to changes in price. Because of the inverse relation between changes in price and quantity, price elasticity will always be negative.

6. There is an important relation between price elasticity and total revenue $(TR = P \times Q)$. If demand is elastic, total revenue will move in the direction of quantity changes. If demand is inelastic, total revenue will move in the direction of price changes. If price elasticity is equal to 1, a change in price and quantity causes no change in total revenue.

7. The main influences on price elasticity are: necessity, the number of available substitutes, time, and the percentage of income spent on the particular good.

8. *Income elasticity* $\left(\dfrac{\%\Delta Q}{\%\Delta \text{Income}}\right)$ measures the responsiveness of quantity demanded to changes in income. A *positive* income elasticity indicates that the good is a *normal* good, with quantity demanded increasing as income increases. A *negative* income elasticity indicates that the good is an *inferior* good, with quantity demanded decreasing as income increases. If the value of income elasticity is greater than 1, the good is said to be a normal good with an *income-elastic demand:* Quantity demanded is relatively responsive to changes in income. If the elasticity value is between 1 and zero, the good is said to be a normal good with an income-inelastic demand: Quantity demanded is relatively unresponsive to changes in income. A value less than zero indicates an inferior good.

9. *Cross-elasticity* of demand $\left(\dfrac{\%\Delta Q \text{ of Good 1}}{\%\Delta P \text{ of Good 2}}\right)$ measures how the

quantity demanded of one good responds to price changes of another good. A *positive* cross-elasticity indicates that the goods are *substitutes*. A *negative* cross-elasticity indicates that the goods are *complements*. Complementary goods are used together, as, for example, cars and gasoline.

10. Influences on supply include: (a) price; (b) costs, which depend on costs of inputs and technology; (c) goals of firms; (d) number of firms; (e) changes in the price of goods related on the production side; and (f) producers' expectations about future prices.

11. If all influences on supply are held constant and only price is allowed to vary, the quantity supplied–price relation can be isolated and examined. This relation is illustrated by the *supply curve*. The curve has a positive slope, showing that more of the good will be supplied at higher prices.

12. *Quantity supplied* refers to a particular point on the supply curve that represents a specific combination of price and quantity. A *change in quantity supplied* refers to a movement along the supply curve from one price-quantity combination to another, caused by a change in price. *Supply* refers to the entire supply curve relationship. A *change in supply* refers to a *shift* in the supply curve, caused by a change in any influence on demand except price.

13. Elasticity of supply $\left(\dfrac{\%\Delta Q \text{ supplied}}{\%\Delta P}\right)$ measures the relative responsiveness of quantity supplied to changes in price. Because price and quantity supplied are directly related, supply elasticity will be positive. If elasticity is greater than 1, supply is said to be elastic, with quantity supplied being relatively responsive to changes in price. In most cases, supply elasticity will differ from one point on the supply curve to another.

14. The important influences on supply elasticity are: time, size of the industry, flexibility of supply of inputs, and capital intensity. A summary of the main types and ranges of both demand and supply elasticity is provided in Table 4.

Table 4   The main types and ranges of elasticities

	Phrase	Value of the Elasticity Ratio
Demand		
1. *Elasticity of Demand*	Elastic	Greater than 1
	Unitary elastic	Equal to 1
	Inelastic	Less than 1
2. *Income Elasticity*	Normal Good	Greater than zero (positive)
	Inferior Good	Less than zero (negative)
	Income elastic	Greater than 1
	Income inelastic	Less than 1
3. *Cross-elasticity of Demand*	Substitutes	Greater than zero (positive)
	Unrelated	Zero
	Complements	Less than zero (negative)
Supply		
1. *Elasticity of Supply*	Elastic	Greater than 1
	Unit elastic	Equal to 1
	Inelastic	Less than 1

15. The market price and quantity are determined by the interaction of demand and supply. The price-quantity combination at the intersection of the supply and demand schedules is the *equilibrium* price and quantity. This point of market equilibrium is the only one at which the quantity supplied and the quantity demanded are equal.

Key concepts

Market
Substitution effect
Income effect
Demand
Quantity demanded
Price elasticity of demand
    elastic demand
    inelastic demand
    unitary demand
Income elasticity of demand
    normal good
    inferior good
Cross elasticity of demand
    substitutes
    complements
Quantity supplied
Supply
Elasticity of supply
Market equilibrium

Questions for review

1. Consider the following list of goods and services. Would you place them in a local or national market? Explain your reasoning.

    bread   milk
    automobiles   bicycles
    fresh tomatoes   doctors' services
    small appliances   cameras

2. Suppose that you are trying to determine what influences the quantity of jogging shoes purchased in the United States. List the factors that you feel would be important influences on the demand for jogging shoes. Since you are working with a very specific good, you should be able to add specific influences to the list of general influences given in this chapter.

3. List three goods for which you feel your demand is elastic, and three for which your demand is relatively inelastic. By comparing your lists, can you determine the factors that influenced your elasticity of demand for these goods?

4. Suppose that the trustees of your college decide that the college needs more revenue. They therefore vote for a 15 percent hike in tuition. Will the tuition hike necessarily accomplish their objective? Explain.

5. List three goods that you would classify as inferior goods and three goods that you consider to be normal goods. If you were earning $50,000 a year instead of living on a student income, would you still consider all of these last three goods to be normal goods? Explain.

6. Thinking of your own purchasing patterns, name some goods that you consider substitutes, and some goods you consider complements.

7. Suppose that you were grading exams and came across the following statement: "Quantity supplied refers to the amount that producers sell to consumers at various prices." Could you give full credit for the explanation? Why or why not?

8. Would you expect supply to be relatively elastic or inelastic in the following cases?

a. steel industry
b. lemonade stand
c. wheat farming
d. canned fruit
e. local doctors' services
f. local real estate services

9. Each of the following examples represents a change that will affect the wheat market. Using supply and demand diagrams, explain how each change is likely to affect the supply and demand side of the wheat market. Make sure that you indicate how equilibrium price and quantity are likely to be affected, and explain carefully whether the change will be either a change in quantity supplied or demanded, or a change in supply or demand.

a. There is an exceptionally large harvest of wheat.
b. Consumers hear that some wheat supplies have been contaminated with a toxic substance.
c. The cost of fertilizer used by wheat farmers increases.
d. Consumers develop an increased desire for products made with wheat.
e. Excess supplies of wheat are building up.
f. An increased desire for rural living causes more people to become wheat producers.
g. The population of the United States increases.
h. Substantial improvements in the technology of wheat farming occur.
i. U.S. income per capita increases steadily.
j. The price of soybeans increases while the price of wheat remains constant. (Farmland can be used for either wheat or soybeans.)

◀ 5 ▶

Demand and Supply in Action

As you read and study this chapter, you will learn:

- ▶ the simple analysis of demand and supply in equilibrium
- ▶ how lessons of demand and supply work in practice
- ▶ how to analyze the effects of distorting

the market solution, in four practical cases

- ▶ the simple problems of measuring demand and supply in real markets

You have probably discussed subjects about which people hold strong views, such as U.S. foreign policy, the welfare system, or minimum wage legislation. What starts as a friendly conversation can become an angry debate if people begin to exchange value judgments and opinions rather than facts.

To call the minimum wage law a harmful interference with free markets is a provocative statement of opinion that invites a heated response. To say that the minimum wage can contribute to inflation is a little more specific and invites a more reasoned response. To say that the minimum wage can raise prices and reduce the number of jobs, and then to explain why that might be so, is even more positive and less normative. By using economic analysis to reach specific answers, one has the best chance of encouraging an equally reasoned and rational response. One is discussing specific theories and facts rather than airing broad conclusions.

People often know more theory or facts about economic top-

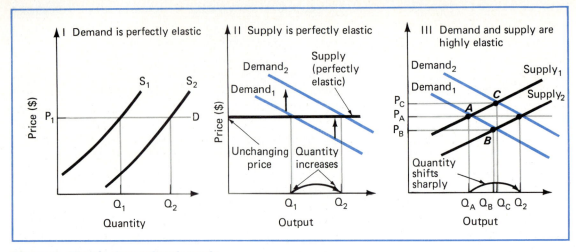

Figure 1   Elastic demand and supply

In Panel I, perfectly elastic demand is represented by a horizontal line. An indefinitely large amount will be demanded at the present market price, while nothing will be demanded at a higher price. A change in supply, such as the shift from S_1 to S_2, will cause a change in quantity (from Q_1 to Q_2) but no changes in price. In Panel II, perfectly elastic supply is represented by a horizontal line. An indefinitely large amount will be supplied at the present market price. A change in demand, such as the shift from D_1 to D_2, will cause a change in quantity (from Q_1 to Q_2) but no change in price. P_A and Q_A represent the equilibrium price and quantity when market conditions are represented by D_1 and S_1. Think of possible changes in the market. Demand might stay at D_1, while supply increased to S_2. Market equilibrium would move from A to B. Price would move from P_A to P_B, while quantity would move from Q_A to Q_B. Or supply might stay at S_1, while demand increased from D_1 to D_2. Market equilibrium would move from A to C. Price would move from P_A to P_C, while quantity would move from Q_A to Q_C. In both cases, note the relatively large changes in quantity.

ics than they realize. But it takes practice to learn how to apply theory to such issues and to use the most relevant information. This chapter is devoted to just that kind of practice. It applies the supply and demand theory introduced in Chapter 4 to various issues, such as the impact on market price and quantity of supply and demand changes, the effects of minimum wage legislation, and the relative burdens of sales taxes. When you have finished the chapter, you should have a better feeling both for the tools of supply and demand analysis and for how to apply theory to a specific problem.

Effects of elasticities on market outcomes

Supply and demand analysis helps determine the impact of market changes on both price and quantity. These market changes show up as shifts in supply and demand schedules. The size of the resulting price and quantity changes depends not only on the magnitude of the shifts, but also on the elasticity or shape of the supply and demand schedules. The analysis of many important issues, such as the impact of the minimum wage on workers' income or the share of a sales tax borne by consumers, depends crucially on elasticity.

You know from Chapter 4 that both supply and demand elasticities can vary from zero to infinity. The market adjustment process is the same, regardless of the elasticities, but the sharpness of the market changes will depend closely on those elasticities. The classic way to grasp the role of elasticities is to consider first the four extreme cases of elasticity, as follows.

Elastic demand and supply
If the demand curve is elastic, quantity changes relatively more than price, in per-

centage terms. Panel I of Figure 1 illustrates perfectly elastic demand. Any amount of the good up to infinity will be bought at P_1 but nothing will be bought at a higher price. Here, market price is determined by demand, and quantity is determined by the location of the supply schedule.

As you will see in Chapter 9, certain firms face a perfectly elastic demand schedule. They can sell as much as they wish at the going market price. While demand is seldom perfectly elastic, the more elastic the demand for the good, the bigger the change in quantity and the smaller the change in price that will result from a given change in supply.

For *perfectly elastic supply*, as shown in Panel II of Figure 1, *the price is determined by supply, and the quantity is determined by demand.* Changes in demand will cause quantity changes but not price changes. The more elastic supply is, then, the larger the changes in quantity and the smaller the changes in price that will result from a given change in demand. Easy adjustments in output resulting in very elastic supply are typical of many narrowly defined, small-volume products, such as candies, small metal products, dresses, and printing. For such goods, output can be increased quickly, simply, and inexpensively in response to changes in demand.

If supply and demand are *both* highly elastic, as shown in Panel III of Figure 1, shifts in supply and demand will cause relatively large fluctuations in quantity and relatively small changes in price. The large changes in quantity occur because consumers can easily adjust their rate of consumption to price changes, and suppliers also have no difficulty adjusting the quantity they supply to changes in demand. Industries with relatively elastic demand and supply include small appliance manufacturers, restaurants, grocery stores, and other retail trades.

Inelastic demand and/or supply

If demand is inelastic, price changes relatively more than quantity, in percentage terms. In a *perfectly inelastic demand schedule,* as in Panel I of Figure 2, consumers will buy the same amount of the good regardless of price. Market price is determined entirely by supply conditions, but quantity is determined by demand. While perfectly inelastic demand is rare, the more inelastic the demand, the larger the change in price that will result from a given change in supply. Extremely inelastic demand would be found for goods such as medicines or textbooks for which there are no practical substitutes.

A *perfectly inelastic supply schedule* is shown in Panel II of Figure 2. Since quantity is fixed, a change in demand can only affect price, not quantity. *Price is determined by demand, while quantity is determined by supply conditions.*

Goods with an inelastic supply, whose quantities are fixed, include land in specific locations, Old Master paintings, antique furniture, and vintage wine. A Rembrandt that sold for $200,000 in 1950 cost $7 million in 1982 because demand moved up a nearly vertical supply curve. Yet, even when supply *seems* to be completely inelastic, the increases in price caused by increases in demand may induce some increase in supply. Swamps, for example, can be drained to create more arable land. The more inelastic the supply, however, the greater the change in price and the smaller the change in quantity that will result from a change in demand.

When demand and supply are *both* highly inelastic, as in Panel III of Figure 2, shifts in supply and demand will cause relatively large changes in price and small changes in quantity. For example, both supply and demand are highly inelastic in the market for U.S. agricultural products. The demand for many foods is fairly inelastic. Even if the price of bread, milk, or

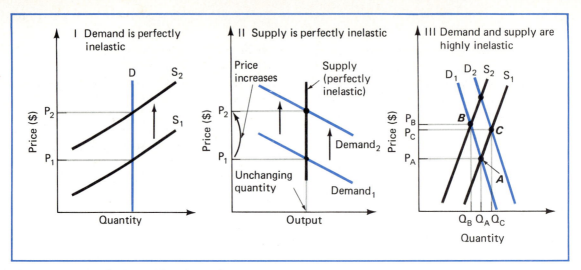

Figure 2 Inelastic demand and supply

In Panel I, perfectly inelastic demand is represented by a vertical line. The same quantity will be purchased regardless of price. In such cases, a change in supply, such as the shift from S_1 to S_2, will cause a change in price (from P_1 to P_2), but no change in quantity demanded. In Panel II, perfectly inelastic supply is represented by a vertical line. The same quantity will be supplied regardless of price. In such cases, a change in demand, such as the shift from D_1 to D_2, will cause a change in price (from P_1 to P_2), but no change in quantity supplied. In Panel III P_A and Q_A represent the equilibrium price and quantity when market conditions are represented by D_1 and S_1. Think of possible changes in the market. Demand might stay at D_1, while supply decreased from S_1 to S_2. Market equilibrium would move from Point A to Point B. Or, supply might stay at S_1 while demand increased from D_1 to D_2. Market equilibrium would move from Point A to Point C. In both cases, note the relatively large change in price and relatively small change in quantity that occur when supply or demand shifts.

potatoes is cut in half, there is a limit to how much of these foods people want to eat. Therefore, changes in price will call forth relatively small changes in the quantity demanded.

The supply of agricultural products is also inelastic because significant adjustments in crops and livestock must wait for a new planting or breeding season. Even longrun adjustments are limited because farmland cannot easily be expanded.

The combination of inelastic supply and demand can cause a paradox: Good harvests can result in low farm incomes, poor harvests in high ones. You might find this baffling without a knowledge of elasticity. But if you understand that elasticity measures the responsiveness of quantity to price changes, the paradox is easily resolved. (Try out the paradox on a friend who has never studied economics. You will see how much you have already learned.)

Suppose that S_1 and D_1 in Figure 3 represent normal or average supply and

demand conditions in the market for wheat. (Ignore government price supports and assume that market forces operate freely.) Now suppose that there is an especially plentiful harvest. The supply schedule for wheat would shift to the right, as shown by the shift from S_1 to S_2 in Figure 3. To get people to buy the increased amount of wheat, the market price of wheat will fall. The effect of this quantity increase and price decrease on total revenue depends, as you know, on the elasticity of demand. If demand is relatively inelastic or less than 1, as it is for agricultural products, the percentage change in price will be greater than the percentage change in quantity: Farm incomes will fall. When crops are poor, as represented by S_3, market price will increase in response to this decrease in quantity, as shown by P_3 and Q_3. Since the percentage change in price dominates, total revenue will increase. You can see the influence of the size of the total wheat supply on farmers' income by comparing the rectangles representing total revenue for both a good harvest (P_2 B Q_2 0) and a poor one (P_3 F Q_3 0). The rectangle representing total revenue for the relatively poor harvest (P_3FQ_30) is clearly larger.

The fall in income when crops are good and the rise in income when crops are poor are intensified by the inelasticity of supply. Even with the inelastic demand, shifts in supply would have a milder impact on both price and quantity if supply were more elastic. This is illustrated in Panel II of Figure 3. A set of elastic supply curves (S_E and S_E') and a set of inelastic supply curves (S_I and S_I') are drawn for equivalent changes in quantity. Note that the same horizontal shift in supply from A to B results in a much smaller change in price and quantity when supply is elastic than when it is inelastic. For the more

elastic supply, the price change will equal $P_A - P_E$ and the quantity change will equal $Q_A - Q_E$. For the inelastic supply, the price change is $P_A - P_I$ and the quantity change is $Q_A - Q_I$.

These examples, based on differing elasticities, show how important elasticities are in determining the outcome of actual cases. By using the concept of elasticity carefully and frequently, you can develop good judgment about the likely outcomes of market changes in many familiar markets.

The rest of this chapter gives examples of other situations in which supply and demand analysis is important. In some cases, the elasticities and other market conditions are so well known that the analysis can give precise answers. In others we have to estimate market conditions or trends, because the data are less complete. The results can only be approximate, such

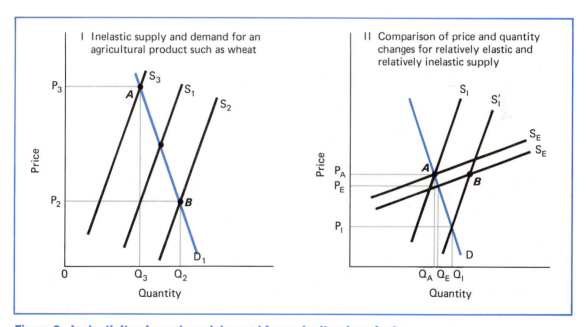

Figure 3   Inelasticity of supply and demand for agricultural products

S_E represents a relatively elastic supply schedule, while S_I represents a relatively inelastic supply schedule. When both are shifted by the same horizontal distance representing a change in quantity from A to B, note the different impacts on equilibrium price and quantity. The shift of the elastic schedule causes a relatively small change in price (P_A to P_E) and quantity (Q_A to Q_E). The shift of the inelastic schedule causes a much larger change in price (P_A to P_I) and quantity (Q_A to Q_I).

as: "If supply is elastic and stable, then oil prices will rise slowly." Yet, even such inexact predictions are often valuable.

The examples that follow suggest the great variety of problems that simple economic analysis can clarify. Some of your own personal choices in markets may be sharpened by using supply and demand analysis. On a larger scale, the same type of analysis can also clarify even the most urgent national and global issues. The first example (in the second main section) shows how a market works when it is left to function on its own. The second set of examples (in the third main section) illustrates how outside interferences in the market process can affect the market outcomes involving price and quantity.

The price of oil

Since 1972, the price of oil has risen sharply, to $32 per barrel in 1980 from less than $3 per barrel in 1972. OPEC, the oil producers' organization, may have influenced that rise, but since 1980, OPEC has had little effect.*

Let us assume that oil supply will be essentially competitive in the future, so that oil prices will now depend solely on shifts in the supply of and demand for oil. Present demand and supply are illustrated by curves D_1 and S_1 in Figure 4. No one can predict with certainty how these might shift. But economic analysis can contrast alternative sets of circumstances, to illustrate the range of likely outcomes for a given year, such as 1990.

First consider a "low price" case. Suppose that conservation efforts by oil consumers are thorough and effective, and that other energy sources such as solar heat and fusion power are developed.

---

*In Chapter 21 we consider whether the 1970s oil price rise occurred for basic reasons, rather than because of OPEC's influence.

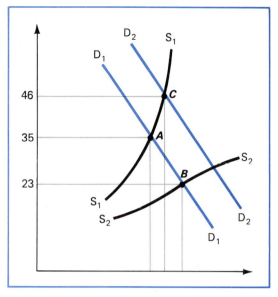

Figure 4   Shifts and elasticities govern the future price of oil

Point *A* is the present market equilibrium for oil. Point *B* is the year 2006 market equilibrium, which would result from a combination of shifts in supply and demand conditions favorable for the United States. Supply increases and becomes more elastic, while demand grows slowly compared with recent decades. Point *C* is the year 2000 market equilibrium, which results from an unfavorable set of supply and demand changes. Supply stays inelastic and grows little, while demand continues increasing at its present rate. Point *C*'s price is twice as high as the price at Point *B*.

These events would slow down the rate of growth in the demand for oil. Suppose, for simplicity, that demand in the year 2000 is identical to D_1 in Figure 4, the present curve. On the supply side, suppose that the search for more oil and gas is highly successful. This increase in supply can be represented by a rightward shift in the supply curve from S_1 to the blue line S_2.

The market equilibrium would move from Point *A* in 1980 to Point *B* in the year 2000, where the new demand and supply curves D_2 and S_2 intersect. The new equilibrium at Point *B* shows more oil available at a lower equilibrium price than at the original equilibrium. Yet this optimistic forecast holds only if there are favorable conditions on both the supply and demand sides of the market.

Now consider a "high price" result. Suppose that further conservation efforts are ineffective. Moreover, the development of other fuel sources is slow. Given these circumstances, the demand for oil may rise 5 percent per year. In Figure 4, Demand Curve D_2 illustrates the demand for oil in the year 2000. Meanwhile, on the supply side, suppose that the discoveries of new oil fields are sparse. Supply in the year 2000 would not be much greater than in 1980—about the same as at present, represented by Supply Curve S_1. The market equilibrium would move from Point A to Point C in the year 2000, where D_2 and S_1 intersect. The year 2000 market equilibrium for oil shows less oil supplied than at present for a much higher price per barrel.

Interferences with the market process

So far, we have dealt with cases in which the market was allowed to function freely. The following examples deal with interference with the market process and show how the free market result can be modified or displaced.

There are three main kinds of interferences with the market process: taxes, price controls, and quantity controls. Because they alter the results given by voluntary exchange, these actions may cause important distortions.

The burden of a sales tax

Sales taxes (often called excise taxes) are imposed in most states of the United States. While they raise revenue, they also influence the market process. Who really pays this tax? You pay at the cash register, but the producer of the good might also

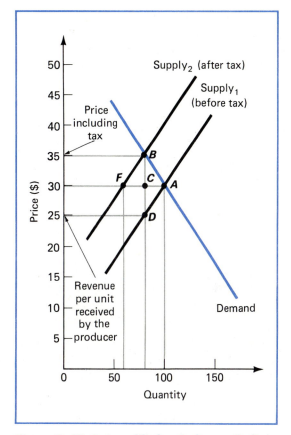

Figure 5 Market equilibrium before and after the imposition of a sales tax.

bear some or all of its burden. With supply and demand analysis, it is easy to see how sales taxes affect both consumers and producers. Elasticity allows you to show who will bear the biggest portion of the tax.

Consider Figure 5. The free market equilibrium price and quantity are $30 and 100 units. This before-tax equilibrium is represented by Point A. Now suppose that a tax of $10 per unit is imposed on this good. What happens? Since the producer will need to receive the same price for any given quantity supplied, with or without the tax, *the supply curve simply shifts up at every point by $10*. In short, the tax is simply added to the costs of production.

One hundred units will now be supplied to consumers at a price of $40: $30 for the producer (the same revenue for each unit as before the tax) and $10 for the government. This $10 increase in the supply price for each unit is represented by the leftward shift of the supply curve from Supply$_1$ to Supply$_2$.

Now what happens? At the old price of $30, quantity demanded at Point A is greater than the amount that producers are willing to supply (Point F). This shortage of the good at a price of $30 causes the price to be bid up. The price rises until the quantity supplied is once again equal to the quantity demanded. This new equilibrium will occur at Point B, reflecting a higher price ($35) and a lower quantity (80 units) than before the tax. Although the tax was $10, the price per unit rose only $5 (from $30 to $35). That means that consumers are not bearing the full burden of the tax. Some of that burden must also fall on the producers.

To see precisely what the consumers' and producers' shares of the tax are, look again at the new equilibrium at Point B in Figure 5. The vertical distance between the old and new supply curve at the new equilibrium quantity of 80 units, measured by B–D on the diagram, represents the $10 tax. The consumers' portion of the tax is simply the difference between the old and new market price, represented by B–C on the diagram. In this example, B–C must be equal to $35 – $30 = $5. Now if the entire tax is $10, represented by B–D, and the consumers' portion is $5, represented by B–C, then the producers' share of the tax must be the remaining segment of C–D. This would be equal to the $10 tax minus the $5 consumers' share, or $5. The C–D segment is simply the difference between the pretax producer revenue of $30 and the posttax producer revenue of $25. The decrease in revenue per unit represents the producer's share of the tax.

But on whom will the tax burden fall most heavily? The answer depends on the elasticity of demand and supply.

Figure 6 depicts various cases of demand elasticity. Panel I illustrates perfectly inelastic demand. Here, the price increase, representing the consumers' burden of the tax, is equal to the entire vertical distance between the supply curves—in other words to the full amount of the tax. Panel II represents perfectly elastic demand. Here, the upward shift of the supply curve resulting from the imposition of a tax causes no change in price at all. Consumers bear none of the burden of the tax.

Most cases of demand elasticity lie between these two extremes. If you keep in mind that consumers pay all of the tax if demand is perfectly inelastic and none of the tax if demand is perfectly elastic, then it should be easy to see how the consumers' burden of the tax varies with demand elasticity. The more inelastic the demand, the greater the tax burden borne by the consumer, other things being equal. This should make intuitive sense to you, since inelastic demand implies that consumers would rather pay higher prices than reduce their consumption of the good by very much. On the other hand, the more elastic the demand for a good, the smaller the burden of the sales tax that consumers will bear, other things equal. In this case, consumers will more readily give up a good rather than pay higher prices.

The importance of demand elasticity in determining how much of the tax a consumer will pay is illustrated in Panel III of Figure 6. With a sales tax, the supply curve shifts from S_1 to S_2. For relatively elastic demand, shown by D_1, equilibrium price increases from P_e to P_1. But with the more inelastic demand represented by D_2, the price increase or consumers' portion of the tax is much greater: The price increases from P_e to P_2. The consumer obviously

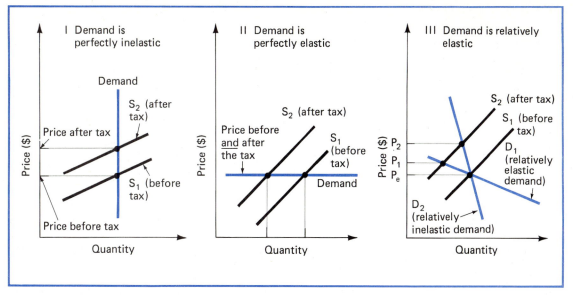

Figure 6   How demand elasticity affects the relative portions of a sales tax borne by the consumer and producer

If demand is perfectly inelastic, as it is in Panel I, a tax will raise the price of the good by the full amount of the tax and have no impact on quantity supplied. The consumer bears the full burden of the tax.

If demand is perfectly elastic, as it is in Panel II, the tax will have no impact on price. The full burden of the tax is borne by the producer.

If the demand is relatively elastic, as with D_1 in Panel III, the tax will cause a smaller increase in price to the buyer than it will if demand is relatively inelastic, as represented by D_2. In general, the more elastic the demand, the smaller the consumer's portion of the tax.

bears more of the tax the more inelastic consumer demand is.

However, the relative burdens of the sales tax are not determined solely by demand elasticity. Supply elasticity is also important. Figure 7 illustrates the various cases of supply elasticity. Panel I illustrates the case of perfectly inelastic supply. Here, the tax will not affect the supply curve, since the same quantity will be offered regardless of price. Since there is no change in price to the buyer, the producers bear the full burden of the tax. Panel II illustrates perfectly elastic supply. Here, the price increase equals the full amount of the tax. The producers receive the same revenue per unit after the imposition of the tax as they did before the tax, and thus bear none of its burden. Yet, the output falls to Q_1.

Most cases of supply elasticity lie between the extremes of perfectly elastic and inelastic supply. The more inelastic the supply is, other things being equal, the

smaller the price increase will be. Therefore, the greater will be the reduction in the producers' revenue per unit, which represents the producers' share of the tax. The more elastic the supply, the greater will be the increase in price, and the smaller will be the producers' tax burden, represented by the decrease in producers' revenue per unit.

The effect of supply elasticity on the producers' share of the tax can be seen in Panel III of Figure 7. S_a is a relatively elastic supply curve, while S_b is a relatively inelastic supply curve. When the tax is imposed, both supply curves shift up by an amount equal to the tax. Look at the new equilibrium when supply is inelastic, with supply shifting from S_{b1} to S_{b2}. The producers' share of the tax is the difference between the before-tax revenue per unit of P_E and the after-tax revenue per unit of r_b. This reduction in producers' revenue per unit is shown by the segment a–b. When supply is more elastic, shifting from S_{a1} to

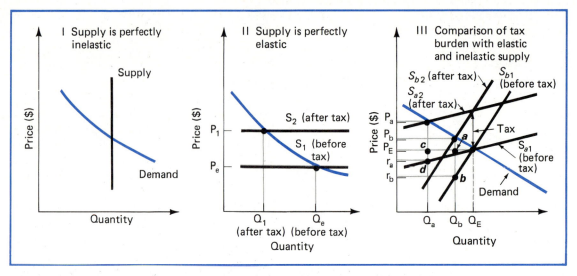

Figure 7   The influence of supply and demand elasticity on the effects of the sales tax

If supply is perfectly inelastic, as in Panel I, a tax will have no effect on supply since the same quantity of the good will be offered regardless of price. Here, because there is no change in price, the producers bear the full burden of the tax. If supply is perfectly elastic, as in Panel II, the price will increase by the full amount of the tax. The producers bear none of the tax burden. In Panel III, S_a represents a relatively elastic supply curve, while S_b represents relatively inelastic supply. With a tax, both supply curves shift up by the same amount, equal to the tax. For inelastic supply, (S_{b1} and S_{b2}), the equilibrium price rises from P_E to P_b. For elastic supply (S_{a1} and S_{a2}), equilibrium price rises by a larger amount, from P_E to P_a. The smaller increase in price when supply is relatively inelastic indicates that the producers are bearing a larger burden of the tax than with elastic demand, where the price rise and therefore the consumer share of the tax is larger.

S_{a2}, the producers' share of the tax—the difference between the before-tax revenue of P_E and the after-tax revenue per unit of r_a—is clearly smaller. It is shown by the segment c–d.

Combining both supply and demand elasticities, you should now be able to determine when the consumers would bear the biggest burden of the tax and, conversely, when the producers would bear the largest share. The consumers' portion of the tax will be larger, other things being equal, if supply is inelastic and demand is elastic. The producers' share of the tax will be larger when supply is inelastic and demand is elastic.

The general lesson is that taxes fall hardest on those who have the least flexibility (elasticity) in avoiding them. Governments have long followed this rule in deciding which goods to tax: *Tax goods whose elasticities are low.* If the demand

for a good is inelastic, then even with the higher prices resulting from the tax, consumers will find it difficult to reduce their consumption of the good by very much. Since the government will only receive tax revenue from units of the good that are sold, it assures itself of the highest tax receipts if there is only a small drop in quantity sold as a result of the tax—that is, if demand is inelastic. Good examples of heavily taxed commodities with an inelastic demand are such habit-forming items as liquor and tobacco, and such necessities as gasoline today and salt in the Middle Ages.

Price controls

In all of the examples so far, a change in supply or demand resulted in market conditions automatically bringing price and quantity back to a new equilibrium or market-clearing level. Remember, though, that there is nothing inherently fair or just, in a normative sense, about such equilibrium prices or quantities. They are simply the price-quantity combinations at which the market clears. Quantity supplied equals quantity demanded, so that there is neither an excess supply nor a shortage of the good.

There are cases in which the public believes that market forces will lead to a price that is unfairly high for consumers or unfairly low for producers. In these cases, the government may limit how high or low the market price may go. Now the market may be prevented from clearing because, by law, the price may be forced away from the equilibrium level. The following sections discuss the impact on a market of *price controls.*

Price ceiling   A *price ceiling* is a legal limit on how much a supplier may charge for a particular good or service. Price ceilings "protect" consumers by holding prices down. Often, price ceilings are applied to essential goods in short supply, such as food or housing. The rationale is that such goods should be available on an equal basis to all, not just to those who can afford to pay the high prices brought about by the short supply.

Such price ceilings have been attempted since time immemorial. There are many recent examples. General price controls were applied in the United States during World War II, the Korean War, and, to a smaller degree, in 1971–1974. Several cities, including New York, have long had rent controls, and many other cities have added them since 1965. Nearly every state has had a "usury" law limiting the rate of interest on loans. Natural gas prices have been controlled since about 1960, and oil prices were controlled during 1974–1981.

Panel I of Figure 8 shows what a price ceiling would do in a typical market. Without government interference, market forces would result in the equilibrium price P_E and the equilibrium quantity Q_E. What happens if the government imposes a price ceiling? If the price ceiling is above

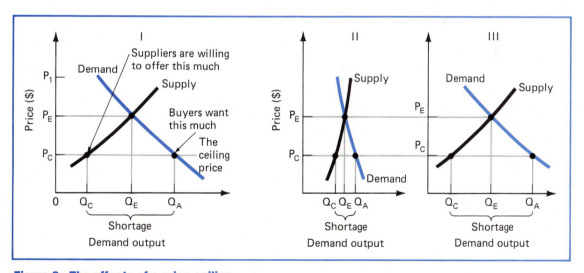

Figure 8   The effects of a price ceiling

In Panel I, representing a typical market, a price ceiling imposed *below* the equilibrium price prevents the market from clearing. At the ceiling price, consumers want more of the good than suppliers are willing to offer. A shortage of the good develops. Panel II shows the effects of a price ceiling when demand and supply are relatively inelastic. Panel III illustrates the effects of a price ceiling when demand and supply are relatively elastic.

the equilibrium price, such as at P_1, nothing happens. The price would not rise above P_1 anyway. The market can still clear at P_E and Q_E. To affect market, the price ceiling must be *below* the equilibrium price, such as at P_C. Now the price is prevented by law from rising to equilibrium, and the market cannot clear. At a price of P_C, consumers wish to purchase Q_A, while producers are willing to supply only Q_C. A physical shortage of the good develops, equal to the difference between Q_A and Q_C.

The effects of a price ceiling, then, are a lower price and a lower quantity supplied. Without the price ceiling, Q_E would have been supplied, rather than Q_C. Thus, while some consumers do benefit from the lower price, less of the good is available. The problem, then, is who is to get the good? Since price is no longer allowed to ration it, some other allocation system must be found.

One form of rationing is lining up or *queuing*. The people who can spend the most time waiting in line will then get the good. Or the government may impose its preferences by instituting *rationing*. Or, *sellers' preferences* may prevail. During gasoline shortages, for example, gas station operators often supply the scarce fuel only to their regular customers. Finally, bribes often guide the exchange of goods. Black markets—the illegal exchange of goods at prices above the price ceiling—often spring up.

How sharply a price ceiling cuts back on the quantity supplied will vary with the elasticities of supply and demand. Try drawing a price ceiling for a good with a relatively high inelastic supply and demand, and for a good with a relatively high elastic supply and demand. This is done in Panels II and III of Figure 8. You can see that if both supply and demand are highly inelastic, as in Panel II, then the lower-than-equilibrium price will not cause much of a reduction in quantity supplied, or much of an increase in quantity demanded. In that case, the shortage resulting from the price ceiling will be small and, perhaps, easily managed. But if both supply and demand are highly elastic, as in Panel III, a price ceiling will cause a severe shortage, and allocating the quantity will be a serious problem.

Once again, you are in trade-off territory. The benefits of the lower price, especially to the most needy groups of people, must be weighed against the costs from having a lower quantity supplied.

Price floor A *price floor* is a legal limit on the minimum price that a supplier may charge for a particular good or service. Price floors benefit the suppliers of a good or service. Agricultural price supports are one form of price floor that has been common since the 1930s. You saw earlier in the chapter that inelasticity of demand for agricultural products, coupled with the variability of the size of harvests, causes farm incomes to fluctuate. Agricultural price supports have sought to stabilize farm prices, given the unpredictable nature of harvests.

Figure 9 shows what a price floor would do in a typical market. Without government interference, market forces would result in an equilibrium price of P_E and an equilibrium quantity of Q_E. What happens if the government imposes a price floor of P_1 *below* the equilibrium price of P_E? Nothing. The price would not fall below P_1 anyway. To affect the market, a price floor must be *above* the equilibrium price, such as P_F in Figure 9. Now the price cannot fall to the equilibrium level, and the market cannot clear. At a price of P_F, the buyers wish to purchase Q_A, and the suppliers wish to offer Q_F. Thus, a *surplus* or excess supply of the good occurs, equal to the difference between Q_A and Q_F.

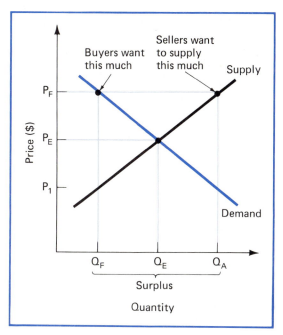

Figure 9   The effects of a price floor

For agricultural price supports, the surplus is crops that must be stored. From the 1930s to the present, farm price supports have caused large surpluses to build up in hundreds of storage sites around the country, at a cost of many billions of dollars.

Controls on quantity

So far, you have seen that price controls always affect the quantities supplied and demanded. Sometimes, however, a government tries to control quantity directly. As you might expect, this affects prices.

The most obvious and common form of **quantity control** is a flat prohibition of a good, such as marijuana. Suppose that if there were no restrictions on growing, selling, and using marijuana, the supply and demand curves would be represented by S_1 and D_1 in Figure 10. The market equilib-

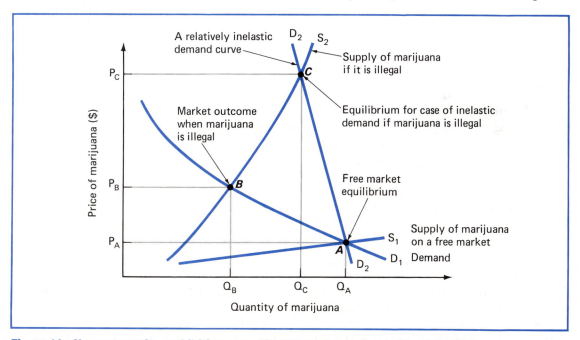

Figure 10   How a quantity prohibition may affect the price and quantity of marijuana

The prohibition is formally meant to yield a supply of zero. But S_2 results, causing both a significant reduction in quantity and a significant increase in price. The more inelastic the demand, the smaller the decrease in quantity and the larger the increase in price. You can see this by comparing the changes resulting in the case of relatively elastic demand D_1 (Q_A to Q_B and P_A to P_B) with the changes resulting in the case of relatively inelastic demand D_2 (Q_A to Q_C and P_A to P_C).

rium for this good would result in P_A and Q_A. A totally effective prohibition on the use of marijuana would mean that supply would be zero at every point—simply a vertical line coinciding with the Y axis.

In practice, even though it is illegal, quantities of marijuana are bought and sold covertly. But the supply situation is completely different from that shown by Curve S_1, since supply is now much more costly. Efficient local farming of marijuana is largely prevented, so that supplies are imported, which greatly adds to the expense. Suppliers must also expect an occasional confiscation, fines, and jail terms as part of the cost of doing business. Supply Curve S_2 might now apply, illustrating that quantities will be available only at higher prices.

If demand remains at D_1, the new equilibrium of P_B and Q_B shows just what you would expect—a higher price and a lower quantity. If the demand for marijuana is highly inelastic, as shown by D_2, the prohibition on marijuana results in a staggering increase in price. At the equilibrium represented by C, much more money is being spent on marijuana than at the original equilibrium of Point A, and most of this revenue is going to criminals.

Yet, because the purchase of marijuana is now a criminal offense, many purchasers drop out of the market. They are not willing to risk a fine or imprisonment to obtain the drug. The ultimate impact on equilibrium price and quantity of these duals shifts—the decrease in both demand and supply—depends upon the relative size of the supply and demand changes. The quantity exchanged will clearly decrease, as an effect of both the decrease in supply and the decrease in demand. But the impact on price is not so easy to determine. The decrease in supply would cause the price to rise, while the decrease in demand would cause the price to fall. The ac-

tual impact on price cannot be determined unless the relative sizes of both the supply and demand shifts and the elasticities are known. The experience in the United States seems to indicate that the price for marijuana is higher than it would be if it could be openly exchanged under competitive conditions.

Measuring supply and demand

You have now seen how useful supply and demand can be in explaining the market outcomes in a wide variety of situations. Even without knowing much actual data, you can use supply and demand analysis to show which way price and quantity will move.

But to make precise estimates of the new equilibrium prices and quantities is much more difficult. That is because demand and supply are not easy to measure. Consider why.

In any given period, one price-quantity combination prevails in a market. That actual price and quantity shows one common point on both the demand and supply curves for that market. That is all that can be measured directly. The price-quantity combinations that are known from past periods may have come from supply and demand curves that had different positions. In fact, demand and supply schedules often do shift from one period to the next.

If the demand curve remained stationary while only the supply curve shifted, a demand curve would be traced out. If the supply curve stayed stationary and only the demand curve moved, then a supply curve would be traced out. These two cases are shown in Panels I and II of Figure 11.

Yet, both curves are often shifting at the same time. The series of points showing price-quantity combinations in successive periods is then simply a scattering of

Example of a Price Floor:
How the Minimum Wage Creates Unemployment

Suppose the equilibrium wage is $3 an hour, but the government sets the minimum wage at $3.65 an hour. What happens? As the figure shows, the quantity of labor demanded decreases (from B to A), while the quantity supplied increases (from B to C). In other words, more people want to work even though there are fewer jobs for them. The resulting unemployment and the size of workers' incomes depend on the elasticity of the demand for labor. When it is inelastic, unemployment will be less and income will rise. When it is elastic, there will be more unemployment, and income will fall.

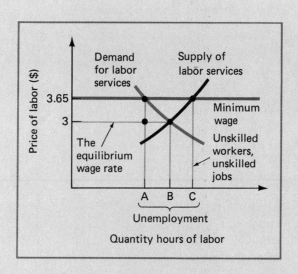

dots that proves nothing, as is illustrated in Panel III of Figure 11. The time series of price-quantity values will never allow us to trace out both the supply and demand curves, and only rarely will it allow us to trace out one curve with great confidence.

Nevertheless, economists have developed econometric methods to identify the true supply and demand curves from real-world data. Agricultural products have been most intensively analyzed, but other goods have also been studied. These measured demand and supply elasticities are estimates, not definitive values. Yet, they often show the elasticities with some accuracy.

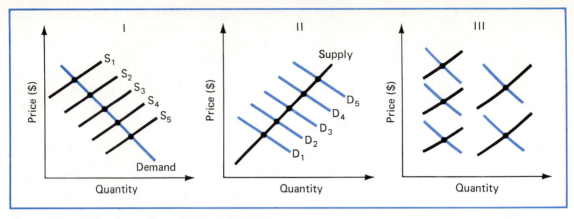

Figure 11   Shifts of supply and demand curves
In Panel I, the demand curve remains stationary while the supply curve shifts, tracing out the demand curve. In Panel II, the supply curve remains stationary while the demand curve shifts, tracing out the supply curve. In Panel III, both the supply and the demand curves are shifting. The resulting scatter of points tells nothing about either supply or demand.

Table 1   Measures of price elasticities of demand for selected goods and services in recent years

Good or Service	Short-Run Price Elasticity	Long-Run Price Elasticity
Gasoline (transportation only)*	−.20	−1.50
Automobiles and parts	−.72	−1.10
Furniture and household equipment	−.27	−.90
Food and beverages	−.23	−.58
Clothing and shoes	−.20	−.33
Gasoline and oil	−.07	−1.03
Housing	−.006	−.37
Transportation	−.09	−.55
Tobacco products	−.46	−1.89
Shoes	−.73	−1.21
Jewelry and watches	−.41	−.67
Toilet articles and preparations	−.20	−3.04
Automobile repair	−.40	−.38
Radio and TV repair	−.47	−3.84
Movies	−.87	−3.67
Theater and opera	−.18	−.31

	Price Elasticity
Bread†	−.15
Beef†	−.64
Lamb and mutton†	−2.65
Eggs†	−.32
Hospital and physician service‡	−.10
Electricity (long-run commercial and residential)*	−.88

Sources:
*J. M. Griffin, *Energy Conservation in the OECD, 1980–2000* (Cambridge, Mass.: Ballinger, 1979).
†P. S. George and G. A. King, *Demand for Food Commodities in the United States with Projections for 1980* (Berkeley: University of California, 1971).
‡Joseph P. Newhouse and Charles E. Phelps, "New Estimates of Price and Income Elasticities of Medical Care Services," in Richard N. Rosett, ed., *The Role of Health Insurance in the Health Services Sector* (New York: National Bureau of Economic Research, 1976).
All others: H. S. Houthakker and Lester D. Taylor, *Consumer Demand in the United States: Analyses and Projections* 2nd ed. (Cambridge, Mass.: Harvard University Press, 1970).

Table 2 *Estimated elasticities of supply for selected agricultural products*

Commodity	Short-Run Price Elasticity	Long-Run Price Elasticity
Green lima beans	0.10	1.70
Cabbage	0.36	1.20
Carrots	0.14	1.00
Cucumbers	0.29	2.20
Lettuce	0.03	0.16
Onions	0.34	1.00
Green peas	0.31	4.40
Green peppers	0.07	0.26
Tomatoes	0.16	0.90
Watermelons	0.23	0.48
Beets	0.13	1.00
Cantaloupes	0.02	0.04
Cauliflower	0.14	1.10
Celery	0.14	0.95
Eggplant	0.16	0.34
Kale (Va. only)	0.20	0.23
Spinach	0.20	4.70
Shallots (La. only)	0.12	0.31

Source: M. Nerlove and W. Addison, "Statistical Estimation of Long-Run Elasticities of Supply and Demand," *Journal of Farm Economics*, November 1958.

A selection of measured elasticities is shown in Tables 1 and 2, for both demand and supply. Note the wide range of the values, from low to high elasticities. Compare these estimates with the values that you would expect for each type of good. Note that *long-run* demand elasticities are all higher than the corresponding short-run elasticities, for reasons explained in Chapter 4. Note, too, that such basic items as food and clothing have, as expected, lower elasticities than luxuries such as toilet articles or movies.

In sum, the logic of supply and demand analysis can show the direction in which the economic outcome will go. But it often cannot predict exactly *how far* the changes will go or *where* the new equilibrium will be. Economists can usually make valid (though imprecise) predictions, even if they can rarely settle an issue completely.

Summary

This chapter shows how supply and demand analysis can be used to examine various market situations. The major points of the chapter are:

1. All markets are influenced by changes in supply and demand conditions. When supply and demand shift, the resulting changes in market prices and quantities will depend crucially on the elasticities of supply and demand.

2. In some cases, market changes are triggered by events within the market itself.

3. In some cases, market changes are triggered by government intervention in the market process.

4. The burden of a *sales tax* is usually borne by both the consumer and the producer. Their relative shares are determined by the supply and demand elasticities.

5. A *price ceiling* is a legal limit on the maximum price that a supplier may charge for a good or service. Such ceilings are intended to protect consumers by holding prices down. If the market price is held below the equilibrium level, a shortage of the good will occur, since quantity supplied will be less than quantity demanded.

6. A *price floor* is a legal limit on the minimum price that a supplier may charge for a good or service. Such price floors are meant to benefit the supplier. If the market price is held above the equilibrium price, an excess supply of the good will result, since the quantity demanded will be less than the quantity supplied.

7. Controls on quantity are often a flat prohibition, such as on marijuana. The effect of such a quantity control will usually be higher prices and lower quantities exchanged. If demand for

the good is highly inelastic, the increase in price will be enormous, and the decrease in quantity will be small.

8. If the demand curve is stationary while the supply curve shifts, a demand curve will be traced out. If the supply curve is stationary while the demand curve shifts, a supply curve will be traced out. If both curves are shifting at the same time, the series of points representing price and quantity combinations from one period to the next is simply a scattering that shows nothing.

Key concepts

Sales taxes
Price controls
    price ceiling
    price floor
Quantity control

Questions for review

1. a. Start with a basic supply and demand graph. On your diagram, show the effects of the enactment of a per unit sales tax. Indicate both the consumers' and producers' share of the tax.
   b. List some goods for which you would expect either the consumers' or producers' share of the tax to be relatively large. Explain.

2. Using supply and demand analysis, explain why agricultural price supports are often accompanied by quantity restrictions, such as a limit on the number of acres planted.

3. Suppose that observations of actual price-quantity combinations in a particular market show the following scatter of points:

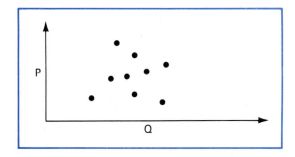

Would it be reasonable to conclude that this is one good for which quantity demanded is not influenced by price?

· 6 ·

Individual Demand

As you read and study this chapter, you will learn:

▸ the basis of rational consumer choices

▸ the law of diminishing marginal utility

▸ the consumer's equilibrium conditions

▸ the determinants of demand

▸ how to derive market demand from individual demand

▸ the underlying meaning and limits of demand analysis

The Scene: Supper time in the Broomfield family dining room.

Richard: Dad, can we get a better car? Our car is too old.

Mr. Broomfield: Maybe we could, but it would be expensive. Then we'd have to eat out less, buy fewer new clothes and records, and take shorter vacation trips.

Mrs. Broomfield: Maybe we could sell Dad's motorboat—

Mr. Broomfield: Wait a minute, wait a *minute*.

Karen: Why, Mom? We need all of these things.

Mrs. Broomfield: We can't afford them all on our income. Having more of some means that we'll have to get by with less of others.

Karen: Oh, you mean that we must adjust the quantities as we optimize our spending to reach equal marginal conditions among all goods?

Mr. Broomfield: That's economic jargon. We're talking about real life.

Karen: But the two are the same!

Indeed, like millions of other families, the Broomfields are applying their preferences, considering prices, and continually adjusting toward their best combination of purchases. Will they sell Dad's motorboat to buy the new car Richard wants? Read on to learn the economic basis for their—and everyone's—decisions.

To show you that, we will take you behind the simple line of the market demand curve. You will learn how demand arises both from people's individual preferences and from the money they have to spend. You have already seen how consumer preferences are summed up in the market demand curve. Now we narrow the focus of our economic microscope to the individual consumer or family as it decides how to divide its income among all the goods that are available in the economy. The demand curves presented in this chapter do not show the total amount of the good purchased in the whole market at various prices. Rather, each one shows the quantity of a good that an *individual* will buy at various prices over a certain time.

Since the market demand curve is derived by adding up individual demand curves, the two types of demand schedules have much in common. Above all, the market demand curve slopes downward, as you know from Chapter 4. **That occurs because *individual people's demand curves*—from which market demand is derived—slope down.** You will soon see why that is true, as you learn how consumers endlessly adjust their choices as prices vary.

The starting point is a pair of basic facts about people's preferences. First, people are *alike*. They all need food, shelter, clothing, and a few other items. But people are also *different*. They insist on liking different things. Jones loves grand opera; Thomas hates it. Cruz loves pickles and drag racing; Newman hates them. Steingut loves her 20th-floor high-rise apartment in Chicago; Wyatt yearns for a ranch under Wyoming's big sky. You yourself are a bundle of specific likes and dislikes: Hawaiian shirts? Elvis Presley records? Pinstripe suits? Classical ballet? Diet foods? Cigarettes? Many of these differences are felt intensely.

Somehow an efficient economy needs to accommodate these differences, offering Jones his opera, Cruz her pickles and drag racing, and Steingut her apartment. For that to happen, these preferences must be expressed. In a market economy, the preferences are embodied in *individual demand*. This chapter shows the causes and nature of that demand.

First, we present the basic concepts. Declining marginal utility is the key concept in rational consumer choices (as we previewed in Chapter 2). Next, we show how the rational consumer reaches equilibrium in choosing among many goods. Then we explain several technical features of demand and derive the market demand curve. Demand analysis is not perfect or all-powerful, but the second section discusses its great underlying strengths.

The analysis of utility and demand

It is best to begin by learning the consumption patterns in the economy as a whole, as summarized in Table 1. There are about 75 million U.S. households (families, singles, and others), with a yearly average of $15,000 in consumption purchases. Altogether, the largest share of personal spending (21.3 percent in 1979) goes for food, beverages, and tobacco. Clothing, transportation, and housing-related expenditures are also important.

These averages mask sharp variations among individual consumers. Some families have modest housing but eat expensive

Table 1 *Where the money goes: A typical U.S. family*

	The Share of Personal Spending			Amount for a Typical Family
	1950 (%)	1965 (%)	1979 (%)	1979
Food, beverages, and tobacco	30.3	24.9	21.3	4,159
Clothing, accessories, and jewelry	12.3	9.4	7.8	1,523
Personal care	1.3	1.8	1.3	254
Housing	11.3	15.2	16.0	3,124
Household operations	15.2	14.2	14.5	2,831
Medical care	4.7	7.0	9.7	1,894
Personal business	3.4	4.6	5.4	1,054
Transportation	13.2	13.5	14.1	2,753
Recreation	5.8	6.0	6.7	1,308
Other	2.4	3.4	3.2	625

Source: *U.S. Statistical Abstracts*, 1978, p. 431; 1980, p. 442.

food. Some families travel a lot, others not at all. And within each category (such as food), many families vary even more sharply in their specific choices (e.g., among turnips, cheeseburgers, lobster, and ribs). The averages only hint at the full variety of consumer spending.

You can also see from Table 1 that spending patterns shift over time. Between 1950 and 1979, for example, the share spent on both food and clothing dropped by nearly one-third. Meanwhile, the shares spent for housing rose by nearly half, and medical care's share more than doubled. These large changes reflected many causes, including changes in consumers' tastes and relative prices. Income elasticities also were important as average incomes rose. Families apparently moved from relatively inferior goods (food, clothing) to such high-income-elasticity goods as housing and medical care.

The table's neat columns of percentages and numbers are a shorthand way of summarizing the choices of the U.S. population. Those choices reflect people's real preferences and budgets as they take hold

in real markets. The crucial task is to analyze how these consumer choices are made.

Rational choices by consumers

Some consumers are single people who live alone and make their choices strictly by themselves. But most live in families or other groups, sharing in the household choosing and spending. The same logic, however, applies to all of them. By "the consumer," economists mean any decision unit, with one or several participants. (The Broomfield family at the start of this chapter is one such unit, hammering out its preferences and choices.)

Rational choices by a consumer will lead to the highest possible level of satisfaction, given the amount of income that the consumer has to spend. The economist's technical term for consumer satisfaction is **utility.**

Economists assume that more utility is better than less. Each good can give some utility, but there are many goods to choose among. The consumer must select

Utility and Marginal Analysis

The concept of utility originated with an eccentric English philosopher, Jeremy Bentham (1748–1832), and his group of fellow "utilitarians" in the 1780s. Their goal was to improve the welfare of individual people, defined as their utility or satisfaction.

Utility acquired precise meaning only in the 1870s, with the neoclassical marginal utility analysis of William Stanley Jevons (1835–1882) and others. By stressing utility, Jevons put demand on par with supply as the two determinants of value. In his *Theory of Political Economy*, his first diagram of declining marginal utility—reproduced here—is much like those that economists still often use.

Jevons' pioneering effort, together with work by Carl Menger, Leon Walras and Alfred Marshall formed much of the neoclassical revolution that established marginal analysis as the core of economics. Marshall's main contributions included not only the concept of elasticity, but also the advanced analysis of consumer surplus and economic rent. His massive *Principles of Political Economy* both assembled and refined the body of new neoclassical thought for many decades of later economists.

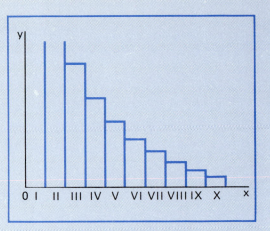

Jevons' marginal utility diagram

The *x* on the horizontal axis is food. The *y* axis shows the degree of utility. The first two units of food give utility that is not specifically measured because "those portions of food would be indispensable to life, and their utility, therefore, is infinitely great." Diminishing marginal utility is readily apparent.

WILLIAM STANLEY JEVONS

the array of goods that will result in the greatest amount of utility possible, within the limits of his or her budget. *The goal of the consumer, in short, is to maximize utility subject to a budget constraint.*

Because utility is only a state of mind, each person has to make his or her choices independently. The utility-maximizing choices can't be arranged from outside by someone else. Indeed, your preferences are not just an economic datum. They express much of your whole personality. Such intensely personal inner conditions are ultimately the wants that the economy ought to service. Therefore, when economists focus their analysis of demand on *utility*, they are trying to expose how some of life's most important decisions are made.

Note also that utility cannot be measured accurately, as by some electronic meter. Pleasure is measured in feelings and attitudes, not according to rigid formulas. No consumer will actually use this chapter's precise concepts and diagrams to make consumption choices. For the same reason, no bluejay needs to study aeronautical engineering to fly. Bluejays can fly without advanced training, and consumers can make reasonably wise decisions without reading this chapter.

Yet the analysis of demand is nonetheless valid. **The mass of consumers usually reach choices that are much the same as if they were applying the precise analysis of utility that follows.** This *as if* hypothesis is crucial and powerful. It enables us to see order in the vast flow of human decisions, many of them made seemingly in haste and without planning. Even the person deciding impulsively to buy a shirt, a book, or a used car is probably behaving *as if* the choices were rational. In this light, the economist's task is to derive a clear logical analysis of the spending decisions that a consumer makes intuitively.

Diminishing marginal utility

In Chapters 4 and 5 we showed that market demand curves slope down: Price and quantity are inversely related. The explanation for that fundamental condition centered on income and substitution effects. Now our focus shifts from markets to the individual consumer. **Individual demand curves also slope down because of the *law of diminishing marginal utility.***

Total utility Consider any economic good —hamburgers, for example. A standard hamburger can provide utility. Economists

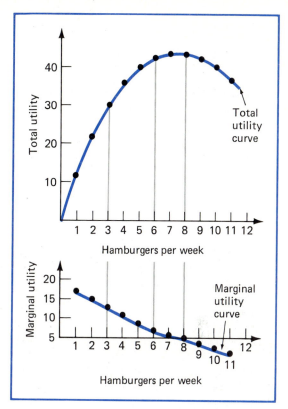

Figure 1 Marginal utility is related to total utility

Total utility rises as consumption of a good increases, but the rise tapers off. The rate of rise is shown by the slope of the total utility curve, which is the change in total utility for each added unit of the good consumed. Note that this is precisely the definition of *marginal utility*. Thus, while total utility rises, marginal utility—the slope of the total utility curve—declines. At eight hamburgers per week, marginal utility has sunk to zero: No more hamburgers are wanted at all. Beyond that level, each hamburger reduces total utility. All of this illustrates the law of diminishing marginal utility.

speak of utility as a degree of pleasure that arises from consuming specific goods. They do not expect to measure it directly, in units of satisfaction, or "utils." But economists suppose that utility is experienced as a magnitude that can be illustrated, as in Figure 1. Accept this convention for now; the meaning of utility will be discussed again later in the chapter. Returning to the hamburgers: As you eat one and then another, the **total utility** you derive from hamburgers may rise, as is illustrated by the curve at the top of Figure 1 and the

Table 2 *Total and marginal utility: An illustration*

Number of Hamburgers per Week	Total Utility	Marginal Utility
0	0	—
1	12	12
2	22	10
3	30	8
4	36	6
5	40	4
6	42	2
7	43	1
8	43	0
9	42	−1
10	40	−2
11	37	−3

numbers in Table 2. There we measure the total utility from hamburgers eaten per week.

Total satisfaction rises as you go through the first six hamburgers per week, but the rise tapers off. The first hamburger provides 12 "utils," while the second contributes only 10 units to total utility. Since both amounts are positive, total utility still rises. But by the sixth hamburger, the marginal utility is only 2, and when you reach the seventh hamburger of the week, you feel that the next one won't make you happier at all. And from the eighth hamburger on, you endure decreasing total utility. Each added hamburger makes you feel worse than before and more worried about gaining weight.

This rise and then decline of total utility is virtually a universal pattern. It holds for every ordinary economic good and for every ordinary consumer. It is true even though each person's unique preferences give a unique, specific total utility curve. It also remains true even though utility cannot be precisely measured. The total utility curve merely shows formally how a person feels about the various amounts of the good.

Marginal utility But it is on *marginal utility* that economists focus to show the pattern even more clearly. *Marginal utility is the change in total utility from adding one more unit of the good.* It is shown in the bottom part of Figure 1, lined up precisely below the total curve. The horizontal axis—the amount of the good—is the same for both diagrams. The marginal utility of that third hamburger is therefore 8, and that value is shown in the marginal utility curve straight below.

The marginal utility curve shows with special clarity how consumption levels affect satisfaction. Notice that marginal utility declines throughout. The decline reflects the basic fact that the first unit is the best; marginal utility declines as consumption increases. By definition, marginal utility is still positive as long as total utility rises. That occurs in Figure 1 up to the seventh hamburger. But when total utility peaks, marginal utility is zero and heading into the negative range below the horizontal axis. Marginal utility is declining throughout the diagram, but it actually becomes negative as the quantity increases from eight to nine per week.

Negative marginal utility means *displeasure; it is called disutility.* Therefore, you find the ninth hamburger (and all additional ones) *bad,* not good. The marginal utility curve shows this crossover point— between added pleasure and added displeasure—even more clearly than the total utility curve above it.

The logic of the analysis can be confirmed by comparing this diagram with your own feelings about a number of goods that you regularly consume—eggs, blankets, and shampoo, for example. You find them useful goods, but their marginal utility declines as you use more of them. And at some level, such as 8 eggs per day, 5 blankets on your bed, and 12 bottles of shampoo per month, you wouldn't really want any more of them, even if they were

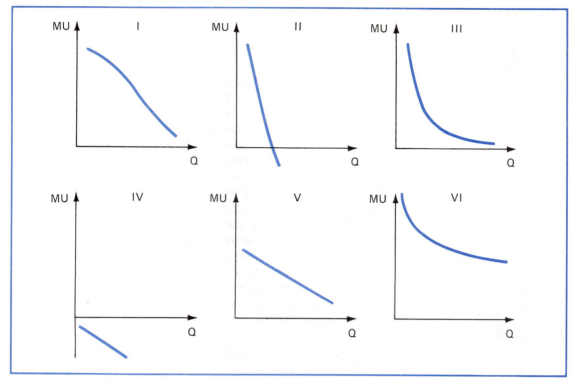

Figure 2 A few of the many forms that marginal utility curves can take

given to you free. The lesson: The marginal utility of each good does decline, and you judge rather clearly where the marginal utility curve cuts zero. With careful thought, you can locate the crossover point for every good you use.

You can also make these rough judgments from what you and your friends *do*. If you or a friend drank a third glass of orange juice with breakfast, it probably had positive marginal utility. If you see people taking seconds of salad or apple pie, their marginal utility was positive. But when you decline a fourth hamburger—or any other offer—your marginal utility is zero or negative.

Variety Because people's preferences vary, their marginal utility curves differ. For example, some people love liver; others won't touch it. Having a .45-caliber pistol at hand makes some people happy; others would hate it. No two people will emerge

from a supermarket with exactly identical carts full of groceries, and often their choices are radically different. The variety of human preferences is an important fact of economic life.

Utility analysis makes this variety clear. As Figure 2 illustrates, marginal utility curves may be high or low. They may slope down sharply or be nearly flat. They may have all kinds of bends and twists, *as long as they do slope down*. Even for the greatest delights, repetition dulls the pleasure.

The curves may be entirely in the negative range, as is Curve IV in Figure 2. Each person has many dislikes, and such "bads" are shown by negative marginal utility. The person considers them a form of garbage, even though other people may love them.

It is helpful to practice drawing marginal utility curves for 10 or 20 different goods, getting a feel for different preferences and cases. Include some goods that you really don't like at all, as well as some of your favorites.

At any rate, marginal utility is the bedrock of consumer choice. Economists show marginal utility by curves that (1) slope down, (2) can take many shapes, and (3) can lie entirely in the negative range.

Individual demand curves: Preferences and income

The marginal utility curves illustrate states of mind, which are based on inner preferences. They are independent of income and the prices of the goods. They are also private and hard to express precisely. But they govern what people actually do in the marketplace, and that is what matters for the economic process. *These consumer actions are embodied in individual demand curves.* Each curve relates price and quantity for one good and one person. It shows how much a person will buy at each alternative price.

Since the individual demand curves are what make up market demand curves, many of the influences on market demand that we presented in Chapter 4 will also influence individual demand: the price of the good, the price of other goods, expectations about future prices, income, and preferences. (Income distribution and total population are the two influences on market demand that are not relevant for an individual demand curve. After all, the amount of a good you choose to consume does not depend on how many other consumers there are or what their incomes are.)

A person's demand curve is derived by allowing only price to vary while keeping the other influences fixed. At each price the consumer will choose to buy a specific amount of the good. Varying the price generates a series of such points. Together, those points make up the demand curve.

The demand curve will slope downward. This reflects the law of diminishing marginal utility: Marginal utility declines as additional units of a good are consumed. If additional units of a good add less and less to your satisfaction, you will only purchase these units if the smaller increases in satisfaction are matched by lower prices. The price reflects what you sacrifice of other goods by not using the money to buy them. If the tenth unit gives you less satisfaction than the first unit of a good, you will not be willing to pay as much for the tenth unit as you were for the first.

Those choices rest closely upon personal preferences, for it is preferences that move people to act. Therefore, the demand curves have the same general shapes and slopes as the marginal utility curves. If marginal utility is high at first but then slopes sharply down, the demand curve will also. If your marginal utility for a good drops off rapidly, it will take fairly large price decreases to persuade you to consume more. If your marginal utility for a good drops off slowly, then it will take smaller decreases in price to persuade you to purchase more of the good. Both the demand curve and the marginal utility curve will cut the horizontal axis at the same quantity. And for a "bad," with a marginal utility curve that is negative throughout, a person's demand curve will also lie entirely below the horizontal axis.

Preferences are crucial. *But equally important is the consumer's income*, which controls how much he or she can afford to spend. The consumer's income affects the vertical height of the demand curve. Wants must be backed up by money to be expressed in market choices. Suppose that both Smith and Jones have similar conditions of utility as shown in marginal utility curves, but Smith is very rich while Jones has only $5,000 income per year. Smith's

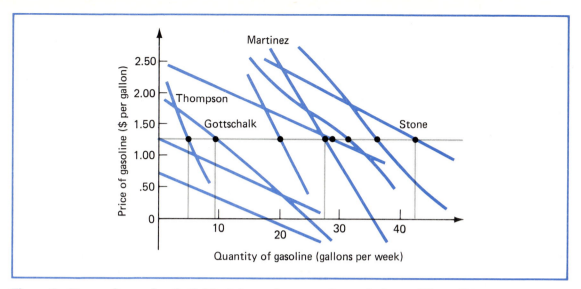

Figure 3   At any given price, individual demand curves show what quantities will be taken
At $1.25 per gallon, the gallons consumed by these ten people are as shown. Some people consume none at all; others take as much as 42 gallons per week.

demand curves for most goods will lie far above those of Jones. Indeed, even if Jones's longing for the goods were far more intense than Smith's, Jones simply could not afford to buy very much of them.

Thus, both preferences and purchasing power determine individual demand curves. These demand curves can be drawn and compared in the same diagram, as in Figure 3. Marginal utility curves, in contrast, cannot be directly compared among people. The fact of comparability among demand is important. By contrast, your preferences for goods are private matters, hard to express in words or numbers. Also, you can't really compare your utility levels numerically with those of other people. Yet what you will *pay*, in money, converts those noncomparable attitudes into money values that are precisely comparable and measurable. They are definite and have a common basis.

The individual demand curves will vary from person to person. Some demand curves will be high; others will be low or in the negative range, as Figure 3 illustrates. Some will slope steeply, others gently; some will be straight lines, others

curved or wavy. Yet all of them will slope down, reflecting the "law" of diminishing marginal utility.

For each price, each buyer will take a specific amount. For example, in Figure 3, when gasoline is $1.25 per gallon, the amounts purchased by Thompson, Gottschalk, Martinez, Stone, and six others are as shown. Different prices will result in different quantities being purchased by each person. One person will buy no gasoline at all at the going price.

Scarce goods and free goods
Scarce goods   Economic goods are scarce goods. They have prices attached to them, set by the interaction of demand and supply. They are scarce because costs have to be incurred to supply them. If the price is not paid, the supply is not provided: Stores will not provide goods to you (such as clothes, gasoline, or groceries) unless you pay the prices.

On a deeper level, suppliers cannot continue producing costly goods unless consumers pay them enough to cover their costs. Consumers are willing to pay a price for the good because it is in the range of

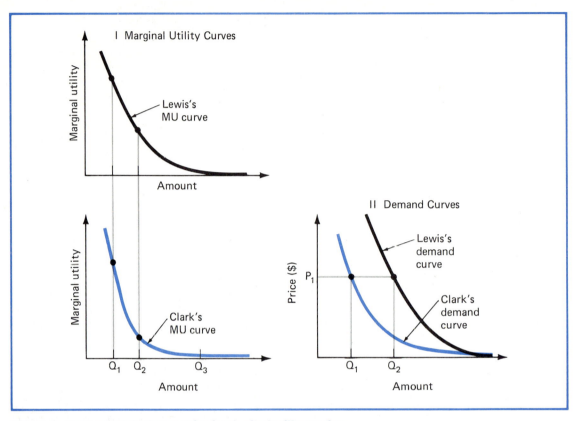

Figure 4   Two people's demand for fresh air: An illustration

Clark's and Lewis's marginal utility curves for fresh air are as shown. Both people would be willing to pay for fresh air when it is scarce, as shown in Panel II. But Lewis's demand curve lies above Clark's, because Lewis either has higher marginal utility, or is richer, or both. Therefore, at a price such as P_1, Lewis will buy more fresh air, for example, by taking more trips to the country, or by living in a more expensive but better ventilated part of town.

scarcity in their marginal utility and demand curves. Since marginal utility is positive, consumers will want more units of the good intensely enough to pay money to get them.

Free goods   But many valuable goods are so abundantly available that two conditions hold: (1) the cost of supply is zero, and (2) consumers use them at rates that bring them into the range of zero marginal utility. Such free goods include natural resources like air and sunlight. All people value and consume them in large amounts, but they are free. If they were scarce, then

people would have high marginal utility for them and be willing to pay for them.

As illustrated in Figure 4, a limited quantity of fresh air at Q_1 would leave the two people with high marginal utilities. Lewis's and Clark's marginal utility would be less if the quantity of fresh air increased to Q_2, but it would still be positive. By the quantity level Q_3, their marginal utilities are virtually zero.

Their demand curves reflect both their preferences and their purchasing power. Lewis, being richer than Clark and also possibly liking fresh air more intensely, has a higher demand curve than Clark. If fresh air were priced at P_1, they would buy amounts Q_b and Q_c. Varying prices would cause varying purchases, as shown by the demand curves. Since the price is zero, they both use about Q_{bc}.

Moreover, many "free goods" do involve costs, even though they are provided at a zero price. Two important categories are: (1) many goods provided by governments, and (2) prepaid goods. Governments provide many "public" goods and services at a zero price, even though the goods are costly. Examples are roads, parks, schools, police and courts, and the national defense. Some of these are consumed as a matter of choice, especially roads and parks. *Because they are provided free, people use them to the point where their marginal utility is zero.* That may be well above the levels of consumption that would be chosen if a price were imposed.

Prepaid goods are also consumed up to the quantity where marginal utility is zero. The consumption of food is often a good illustration of such prepaid goods. In college dining halls and at the family table, the consumer usually does not pay a specific price for each item chosen. The dining hall bill is paid in advance, and family members are certainly not asked to pay for each thing they eat. Commonly the food is abundant, and often there are seconds available on many items.

Therefore, the consumers' choice is often as shown in Figure 5. The average cost of providing the food may be $1.50 per meal. Yet at the point of choice, the price of the food is zero. Therefore, the person eats the amount A, where the demand curve is at zero (the effective price of the meal). That quantity is more than the amount B, which would be the amount chosen if each item were paid for separately. Since the food appears to be free, the person consumes it to the point where its marginal utility is zero. The result is of-

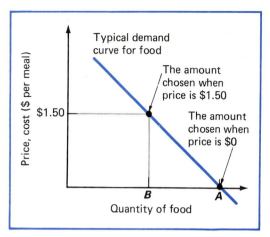

Figure 5 The amount of eating at a dorm may not reflect price

The consumers' demand has a degree of price elasticity. If charged a higher price, the person would eat less. Since the meals are not priced individually and people can take extra amounts at no additional charge, eating will proceed out to Point A. If the $1.50 average price were charged and no extras were permitted, only the amount B would be eaten. The difference between A and B is: (1) overeating, (2) healthy nourishment, (3) economically inefficient, or (4) all three?

ten more total utility, more eating, and more weight!

Would another pricing scheme (such as item-by-item meal tickets for students) be more efficient? That depends on the elasticity of demand for food. If the elasticity is low, then the amount of "extra" eating at A is not much above B. But if elasticity is high, then students may eat much more because the food is "free." (Ultimately the food is not free, for it must be paid for by the family or in the student's total yearly food bill. It just seems "free" at the point of consumption. That is the special feature of the pricing.)

Marginal utilities and prices in equilibrium
Economists also use marginal utility to define the conditions that the consumer reaches in equilibrium. We now show those equilibrium conditions.

Reaching the equilibrium Each consumer allocates his or her spending among hundreds of items. This allocation is done intuitively, in line with personal preferences. For example, you may suddenly feel that you have come to like movies more than eating out. Accordingly, you will rearrange your spending toward movies until it fits your new preferences. Your whole purpose is to allocate your spending so that the resulting set of goods will *maximize your utility*. When this best allocation is reached, you will feel that no further changes in spending will increase your satisfaction. This process is done routinely every day by millions of people. They simply do what seems best to them, without preparing any precise formulas or technical details.

But economists can define that process precisely, using the concept of marginal utility. *The best allocation of income on goods will be reached, they say, when the consumer reaches amounts of goods that give this set of equalities:*

$$\frac{\text{Marginal utility of Good 1}}{\text{Price of Good 1}} = \frac{\text{Marginal utility of Good 2}}{\text{Price of Good 2}} =$$

$$\frac{\text{Marginal utility of Good 3}}{\text{Price of Good 3}} = \ldots \frac{\text{Martinal utility of Good } n}{\text{Price of Good } n}.$$

Utility is maximized, whether the consumer does it by intuition or by deliberate estimates of actual utilities. These equalities are the conditions reached by a consumer when utility is at its maximum.

To understand this set of marginal conditions, concentrate first on the meaning of an individual ratio. Marginal utility is the increase in satisfaction that you receive in each period from consuming the final unit of the good. If marginal utility for the last ball-point pen you bought is 10, for example, then that last pen contributed 10 units to your satisfaction. If you paid $1 for the pen, then marginal utility/price = 10/$1 = 10. The final dollar that you

spent on the fifth pen gave you 10 units of satisfaction or utility. **The marginal utility/price ratio** simply shows the amount of utility received from the last dollar spent on the good.

To examine the meaning of an equality among marginal utility/price ratios, economists usually begin with examples involving two goods. Suppose that your present pattern of consumption is seven pens and five magazines per month. The marginal utility of pens = 10, and the marginal utility of magazines = 50, while the price of pens = $1 and the price of magazines is also $1. The marginal utility/price for pens = 10/$1 = 10, while the marginal utility/price for magazines = 50/$1 = 50. The last dollar that you spent on pens gave you 10 units of satisfaction, while the last dollar you spent on magazines gave you 50 units of satisfaction.

These calculations look impossibly precise, but they show the same result that you would reach intuitively. The ratios are not equal: *You are buying too many pens and too few magazines.* The last dollar that you spent on magazines gave you five times more satisfaction than the last dollar that you spent on pens.

To increase your total satisfaction without spending any more money, simply switch $1 or more from pens to magazines. When you spend $1 less on pens, you give up approximately 10 units of satisfaction, but that $1 now spent on a magazine will gain approximately 40 units of satisfaction (now 50, because of diminishing marginal utility). The net gain in satisfaction or utility would be 30. As you continue shifting dollars and consuming more magazines, the marginal utility of magazines will decrease. You purchase fewer pens (moving back up the marginal utility curve), and so the marginal utility from pens at your spending level will rise. As the switching continues, the marginal utility/price ratio for magazines falls while the

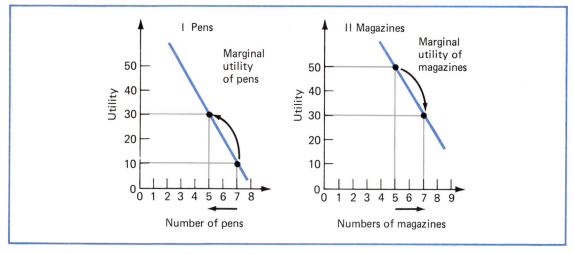

Figure 6   Reaching an equilibrium between two goods

Initially you consume 7 pens and 5 magazines per month. But the MU/price ratios are unequal: 10/$1 = 10 for pens and 50/$1 = 50 for magazines. You cut back on pens, switching the money to buy more magazines. At 5 pens and 7 magazines, the ratios are both 30/$1 = 30, and you are in equilibrium. The adjustment has increased your total utility by 40.

Table 3   Illustrative marginal utility values for pens and magazines

Pens		Magazines	
Number	Marginal Utility	Number	Marginal Utility
1	70	1	90
2	60	2	80
3	50	3	70
4	40	4	60
5	30	5	50
6	20	6	40
7	10	7	30
8	0	8	20

$$\frac{\text{MU pens}}{\text{Price pens}} = \frac{30}{\$1} = 30$$

$$= \frac{\text{MU magazines}}{\text{Price magazines}} = \frac{30}{\$1} = 30.$$

By shifting from the first situation, you have lost 30 units of satisfaction from pens (10 plus 20) but gained 70 units from magazines (40 plus 30). Total utility has risen by 40, while total spending on pens plus magazines is unchanged at $12 per month.

The general rule is: Unless the ratios of marginal utilities/price for all goods are equal, you can always reallocate your dollars and increase your total utility, while keeping expenditures constant. Once the marginal utility/price ratios are equal for all goods consumed, then the last dollar spent on each good gives the same amount of satisfaction or utility. *At that point, no further reallocation will increase your satisfaction.* You are receiving the highest total utility that you can receive, given your preferences and the constraints of your budget. Since there is no reward or incen-

marginal utility/price ratio for pens rises. At some point, the ratios will come to be equal.

The process is illustrated in Figure 6, whose curves are derived from Table 3. The marginal utility curve for pens is shown in Panel I, for magazines in Panel II. While moving back up the MU curve for pens, you free dollars that can be transferred to magazines, which provide higher marginal utility. At 5 pens and 7 magazines, you reach equilibrium, with

tive for additional change, an equilibrium has been reached.

The equilibrium reflects a reconciliation between (1) your *preferences* and (2) the *external limits* set by your income and by the prices of goods. You don't just "buy what you want." Instead, you consider the cost of each good to you (its price), and compare that against the marginal benefits to you (its marginal utility). Here again is the familiar economic comparison of *costs* with *benefits*. Consumers do it repeatedly to reach their individual best allocations.

Restoring an equilibrium   Suppose that you have indeed achieved an equilibrium in your consumer spending. The marginal utility/price ratios for all goods that you consume are equal. You feel satisfied with the allocation of your money. Now consider two main changes—in prices and in preferences—that may disturb the equilibrium.

THE PRICE OF ONE GOOD INCREASES   For that one good, the marginal utility/price ratio will now be lower than for other goods. To restore equality, you will have to buy less of this good and more of other goods. This decrease in the purchase of the good whose price has increased ties in with the *substitution effect*, which we noted (in Chapter 4) as one reason for the downward slope of the market demand curve. The substitution effect states that as the price of a good increases, alternative or substitute goods always become relatively more attractive. That also fits market realities: As the price of an individual good increases, most consumers will purchase more substitute goods.

By focusing on the marginal utility/ price ratios, economics shows why other goods become more attractive as the price of a particular good increases. The result-

ing adjustments may be negligible for an inexpensive item. But if a large item such as housing or food has a big price change, the resulting shifts in purchases of all goods may be substantial.

YOUR PREFERENCES MAY CHANGE   Suppose that your interest in magazines suddenly drops off. Since you get less utility from them, their marginal utility curve from Figure 6 shifts downward, as shown in Figure 7 and Table 4. The MU/price ratio for the seventh magazine is now 10/$1 = 10, definitely unequal to the pens' ratio of 30. You now adjust by cutting back on magazines, moving back up that MU curve. Using the money from magazines, you move down the MU curve for pens. Equilibrium is reached quickly at six each of pens and magazines, where the ratio is 20/$1 = 20 for both. The result also fits common sense: When you lose interest in something, you will buy relatively less of it.

Shifts versus movements along demand curves
As with market demand curves so it is with individuals' demand curves: It is important to distinguish between shifts of demand curves and movements along them. The whole issue of shifts versus move-

Table 4   *Adjusting to a drop in utility from magazines*

Pens		Magazines	
Number	Marginal Utility	Number	Marginal Utility
1	70	1	70
2	60	2	60
3	50	3	50
4	40	4	40
5	30	5	30
6	20	6	20
7	10	7	10
8	0	8	0

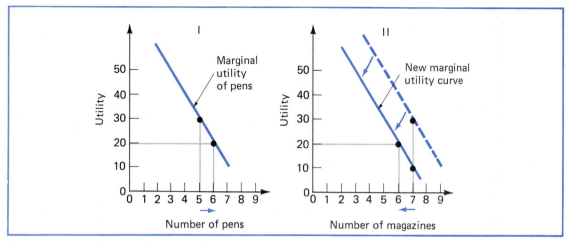

Figure 7   Adjusting to a drop in utility from magazines
The new marginal utility curve for magazines is below the old one. If you still consume 5 pens and 7 magazines, the MU/price ratio for magazines is now only 10/$1 = 10, well below the 30/$1 = 30 ratio for pens. So you switch from magazines to pens as shown, to reach a new equilibrium at 6 pens and 6 magazines and MU/price ratios of 20.

ments along curves was dealt with in Chapter 4. To summarize that discussion: **Quantity demanded refers to a particular point on a demand curve, while demand refers to the entire demand curve. "A change in quantity demanded" refers to a movement along the demand curve from one price-quantity combination to another.** *Such a movement can only be caused by a change in price.*

Individual demand has great power to explain human choice. Think of all consumers as making these balancing choices and adjustments among everything that they buy. *People are all marginalists in their consumption choices, making and adjusting such selections day in and day out.* **In fact, almost every decision you make involves such a balancing among its** *benefits* **(marginal utility) and its** *costs* **(the price you have to pay)** *at the margin.*

Few people think about such choices in the precise economic terms of equating the ratios between marginal utilities and price. Yet, they usually behave *as if* they were doing roughly that: adjusting the levels of activity so as to bring marginal benefits (utilities) and costs into line.

Consumer surplus

The demand curve shows an important condition of consumer demand: *Consumers receive more value from purchasing a good than the money value they pay to the supplier. This extra value is termed consumer surplus.* It is shown quite simply with a standard demand curve, as in Panel I of Figure 8.

First note that you pay $20 to buy 20 units at $1 each. That $20 is shown by the area of the unshaded rectangle Prices times Quantity ($1 times Q_1). The $20 is your sacrifice to get all 20 units. You chose to take 20 units because the 20th unit is just barely worth its $1 price to you.

But you receive the other 19 units, all of which you were willing to pay more than $1 for. Your demand curve shows that you would have paid $5 for the 5th

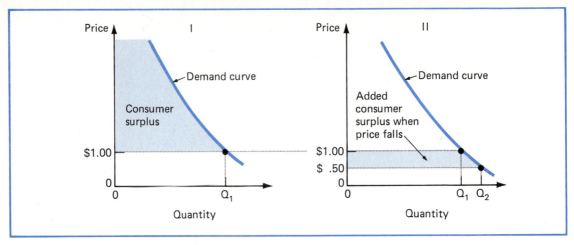

Figure 8 Consumer surplus

When price is $1.00 and the consumer buys Q^1 units, then ($1.00) Q^1 is paid for the good. The consumer also receives the benefit shown by the shaded area under the demand curve in Panel I. This is the consumer surplus. If the price falls to 50 cents, as in Panel II, an added amount of consumer surplus is realized, as shown by the shaded area between $1.00 and 50 cents.

unit and $2 for the 14th unit, if it were necessary. Since the price is $1, you only have to pay $1 each for all 20 units. Therefore, you receive a surplus value above $1 on 19 units. That value is shown by the area under the demand curve and over the $1 price line.

This consumer surplus is a universal phenomenon, occurring whenever a consumer buys more than one unit of a good. By establishing one price for the good, the market assures that consumers can gain extra value above what they must pay for the good. The lower the price, the larger the consumer surplus is. If the price should fall to 50 cents, for example, as in Panel II of Figure 8, then all of the shaded area is added to the consumer surplus. If the price dropped to zero, making the good a "free good," then all of the area under the demand curve would be realized as consumer surplus. (There are many such cases. Public goods such as roads, public schools, fire protection, and many parks are provided at no price to the individual user.)

The amount of consumer surplus for each good depends on the elasticity of the consumer's demand curve, as shown in Figure 9. A high elasticity of demand means that consumer surplus is small (Panel I), while a low elasticity goes with a large consumer surplus (Panel II). That is entirely logical. Inelasticity exists for goods that are urgently wanted, such as a life-giving drug or other such "necessities" as water, food, and housing. *When urgent wants can be met at a low price, you receive a large consumer surplus.* Highly elastic goods, by contrast, are those you want only mildly. You would give them up entirely if the price rises a little.

Consumer surplus is an important economic phenomenon. Though the consumer decides by focusing on the marginal units, the result is extra value on all the nonmarginal units of the good. Economists use the concept of consumer surplus frequently in evaluating the efficiency of the economy.

Market demand is the sum of individual demands

Deriving market demand from individual demand is a short and easy step. Simply add up the individual curves horizontally to get the market demand curve. The market, after all, is simply the sum of the actions of all the people acting in it.

The process of summation is illustrated in Figure 10, using the ten individ-

118

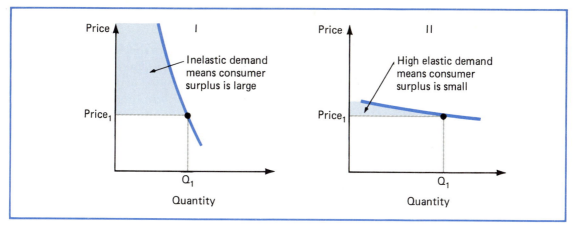

Figure 9   The amount of consumer surplus depends on elasticity of demand

ual demand curves shown in Figure 3. For the moment, assume that the market contains only these 10 consumers (many markets have millions of consumers, while others have as few as 50 or less). At a given price, each consumer in the market will take a definite quantity, which may be zero or larger. For example, at a $1.50 price, the ten consumers whose demand curves are shown in Panel I of Figure 10 will together buy exactly 150 gallons per day (with one of them buying none). If the price were $3.00, these ten consumers would purchase only 52 gallons per day (with six of them buying none). At a price of $3.50, only one consumer would purchase any gasoline at all, approximately 13 gallons per day.

As the quantity demanded by each consumer at each price is added to the others, the market demand curve is given precisely. The curve shows the alternatives that consumers would take at different prices. At any given time the market out-

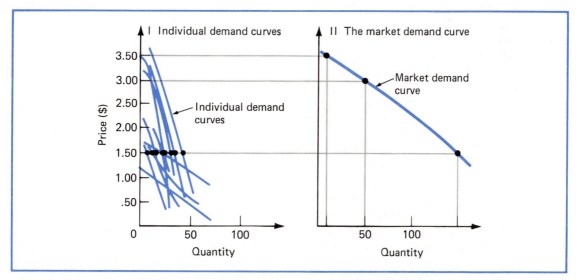

Figure 10   The market demand curve is the horizontal sum of the individual demand curves

At $1.50 per gallon, each person takes the amounts as shown in Panel I. They, plus the other consumers in the market, take 150 gallons per day altogether, as shown in Panel II. The amounts at other prices are traced out by the same horizontal addition.

come is just one point on the demand curve, which shows the actual quantity that was bought at the given price. The complete demand curve merely shows what might have happened at alternative prices.

Consumer surplus also exists on a summed basis under the market demand curve. The analysis is the same as for individual demand. At the going price, consumers pay an amount shown by price times quantity. They also receive consumers' surplus, as shown by the area under the demand curve but above the price. If price falls, the area of consumer surplus increases, parallel to the lesson of Figure 8, Panel II. The size of the consumer surplus depends inversely on the elasticities of the market demand curve, similarly to the patterns in Figure 9. If demand is inelastic, the consumer surplus is large; highly elastic demand provides only a small consumer surplus.

Derived demand

So far we have been discussing only the demand of households for goods that go directly for household use. This is often called "final" demand, for it comes at the end of the chain of production. But that chain—which goes from raw materials, to processed materials and parts, to semifinished goods, and to final goods—can have many stages. At each stage, demand and supply interact to set prices and quantities.

The demand at each early stage is called "derived demand," for it is derived backward from the final demand of households. For example, households buy bread. To bake the bread, bakers have to buy flour. Their derived demand for those goods is met by flour companies. The flour companies, in turn, buy grain; their derived demand goes back to the farmers who grow the grain. The farmers, in turn,

have a derived demand for tractors, seeds, gasoline, fertilizers, and so on.

Derived demand arises in companies, not households, but the analysis for it is much the same as for households' final demand. Each firm has its own individual demand curve, and the market demand curve is the sum of these individual curves. Like personal demand curves, these derived demand curves can shift if other variables change. There can also be substitutes and complements in derived demand, just as in final demand.

The validity of demand analysis

The analysis of individual demand is crucial to microeconomics. Here, as in other parts of economics, we focus on marginal choices, which weigh the costs and benefits of additional units. Yet, doubts about the microeconomic theory of demand have been vigorously debated ever since marginal utility analysis emerged in the 1870s. Since some of them may have occurred to you, we pose them here. The answers will show that the analysis of demand has cogency and power in explaining the mass of consumer behavior.

Question: Aren't these measurements and ratios really *too precise to believe?* No consumer could possibly hope to make choices with such perfect exactitude.

Answer: People *tend* toward rational choices, *as if* their decisions were guided toward equal marginal utility/ price ratios. They may indeed never reach the desired equality conditions, for life is full of changes and approximations. But even if consumers are always out of equilibrium, making a series of rough-and-ready choices, the ratios are still valid for explaining the main directions of their choices.

Question: Aren't the marginalist concepts *irrelevant to real choices?* Nobody actually uses these concepts when making real choices about what to buy. Even the most zealous marginalist-trained economist doesn't calculate marginal utility/price ratios when buying a loaf of bread, or a stereo, or any other good. Instead, people make rough choices one by one, using hunches, impulses, or feelings.

Answer: No, the concepts are still valid. As long as people are trying to obtain the greatest satisfaction they can, within the constraints on their purchasing power, their marginal decisions will be much the same as if they had gone through the analysis and made precise measurements. There will often be mistakes and imprecision, but the whole outcome will be in line with the analysis.

Question: *The consumer is treated as selfish,* interested only in maximizing his or her own satisfaction or pleasure. Doesn't this ignore the altruistic or charitable actions of many consumers?

Answer: The analysis does focus on people's buying choices, which are mostly based on self-interest. Charity and help to others do not fit neatly into the economic calculations. Such unselfish action can be included, though, by recognizing that they give pleasure or satisfaction to the giver as well as to the receiver. In other words, $10 given to a charity may yield the giver the same amount of pleasure or utility as $10 spent on a bottle of wine. Indeed, the analysis would say that the marginal utilities of the two $10 payments *will* be equal.

Question: The pleasures from consuming *economic goods are only one source of happiness.* There are at least two other major sources. First, the best things in

life may be free, or at least many of them are. Love, health, a beautiful day, good friends—these and many other important things in life can't be bought with money. Indeed, paying cash for them would often spoil them. Second, a person's job is often a prime source of meaning and satisfaction. After all, it occupies most of one's waking hours and thoughts. Success at work often dwarfs the satisfaction from anything that is bought. For these two reasons, aren't consumption choices only a sideshow to the real sources of happiness?

Answer: This can be true, especially for people who are young, well off, and in fine jobs. Even so, the consumption choices are important. Moreover, for the rest of the population—the majority who are not so well favored—the spending choices are more important. For older people with mediocre jobs, for example, what money they have must be spent carefully to avoid serious troubles: debts, family quarrels, skimping on necessities, loss of status, and so on. For most people, consumption choices are urgent, and making rational choices can improve their whole sense of well-being. As for job choices, marginal utility is, in fact, the basis for explaining them, as we will show in the chapter on labor economics.

Summary

1. A consumer's goal is to *maximize utility*, that is, to select the array of goods that will result in the greatest amount of utility or satisfaction, within the constraints of the consumer's budget.

2. As more of a good is consumed, total utility or satisfaction rises, at least up

to a point. Yet each additional unit of the good contributes less and less to total utility. This addition to total utility from consuming an additional unit of the good is called *marginal utility*.

3. The downward slope of the individual demand curve expresses the *law of diminishing marginal utility:* Marginal utility declines as additional units of the good are consumed.

4. The shape and height of the marginal utility curve, expressing *willingness* to buy a particular good, will influence the shape and height of a consumer's demand curve for that good. The height of a consumer's demand curve for a particular good will also be influenced by income—the consumer's ability to purchase the good.

5. When a good's price is zero, it is a free good. Such a good will be consumed until its marginal utility is zero.

6. When a consumer has reached an equilibrium or balance in consumption, the marginal utility/price ratios for all goods consumed will be equal.

7. Distinguishing between changes in quantity demanded (movements along the demand curve) and changes in demand (shifts of the demand curve) is just as important in dealing with individual demand curves as in dealing with market demand curves.

8. Consumer surplus is the difference between the total value of the good to the consumer and the money value that has to be paid for it. It is the area under the demand curve but above the price of the good.

9. To derive the market demand curve for a good, simply add up the individual demand curves horizontally.

10. Although utility cannot really be measured or calculated in practice, consumers behave in about the same patterns and intuitively make the same choices *as if* they were actually measuring utilities and equating marginal utility/price ratios.

Key concepts

Rational choices to maximize utility
Utility
Law of diminishing marginal utility
Total utility
Marginal utility
Marginal utility/price ratios

Questions for review

1. Think about the range of goods available for you to consume.
   a. Can you think of any goods whose total utility for you must be negative for every unit? What is the clue that these goods have a negative total utility for you?
   b. Consider some of the goods that you actually consume each week. Can you make any intuitive guesses about which goods have:
      i. sharply declining marginal utility curves
      ii. fairly flat marginal utility curves.

2. Suppose that, for two goods you consume:

$$\frac{MU \text{ pickles}}{P \text{ pickles}} = \frac{MU \text{ ice cream}}{P \text{ ice cream}}.$$

   a. What would this equality mean? Explain carefully.
   b. Suppose that the price of pickles now increases.
      i. What happens to the equality?
      ii. What kind of adjustment would you make in your purchases? Explain.

7

The Enterprise

As you read and study this chapter, you will learn:

- the broad patterns of private business enterprises in the U.S. economy
- other types of enterprises, and the main kinds of industries
- the basic nature and choices of enterprises

- the main indicators of success for the firm
- typical conditions in the creation and growth of a new enterprise

Now we take you across the great divide in microeconomics, moving from the demand side and its households over to the supply side and its enterprises. You already know that the supply curve slopes upward, has elasticities, and helps to determine the market equilibrium. We will now present the foundations of the supply curve, showing how the costs of firms in each competitive market add up to form the supply curve.

In analyzing firms, economists concentrate on certain basic, clinical concepts. Yet actual businesses involve astonishing color and variety, with much human drama and strife. Moreover, the supply side is pervaded by deep social issues. Each company is a workplace, an expression of the people who work there year after year. The pale word "firm" covers all manner of tiny, giant, robust, and decrepit enterprises in a variety of industries.

The economic analysis of supply is about the reality of business activity, not some remote abstraction. Enterprises provide jobs and careers, establish prices and outputs, develop technology, make family fortunes, and set much of the social and cultural tone of society. Most of your relatives probably work for business firms, and perhaps you will too in due course. You already know many enterprises and industries, some of them intimately, because you deal with them every day.

This chapter presents some of that reality, setting the stage for the concepts of production and cost that follow in the next two chapters. First we give the main lines of the business population in the range of real industries. We also cover conglomerate firms, stock ownerships, and *non*private forms of enterprises.

In the second section of this chapter, we survey the main practical kinds of inputs, outputs, and production conditions that firms have. We then show how firms organize differently to produce single products and a wide diversity of products. We also present the main success indicators of firms (profits and stock prices).

Finally, we draw the parts together in a case study, tracing a small firm through its first few years. Throughout we aim to prepare you to understand cost and supply both in the abstract and as they can be seen directly in real enterprises.

Patterns of actual enterprises

Some patterns of actual enterprises are familiar to many readers. Other features are less well known. We present private firms first, for they are the most common form in the United States and other Western economies. Next come other types of firms, such as public enterprises and coopera-

tives. Then we note the variety of industries within which firms operate.

Private enterprises

A *private enterprise* is a firm owned by individuals or by other firms and operated with the primary aim of making profits for its owners. There are almost 14 million such private firms in the U.S. economy, ranging from tiny corner shops to the largest corporations. **They all seek to *maximize profits,*** even though their specific settings and choices vary enormously.

The private business population in the United States includes a range of firms from small to large. Small businesses are the most numerous by far: 13.4 million out of the total 13.7 million firms sell less than $500,000 worth of goods each per year. However, since those small firms together account for only 17.1 percent of total sales, many observers regard the large firm—especially the large corporation—as dominant in the U.S. economy. Yet, small and medium-sized firms are very important and worth considering in some detail.

Small business   The smallest businesses include about 11 million units that take in less than $100,000 in revenue each year. These are the familiar neighborhood stores and tiny workplaces that are run by one or two people, with a small, local clientele. Some of these shops have existed for decades, but most of them close after a short time.

Most owners worked at a production job before starting their own business with a small amount of capital, and often a dedicated spouse. Usually the space and equipment are rented rather than bought. Joining the legions of small business is remarkably easy in this free economy.

What's hard is making a profit. We will trace a case study of a successful small business in the third section of this chapter, showing the severe stresses such a business entails. Unless the firm has a large special advantage, it must contend not only with the internal problems of getting started but also with competition from other firms. Production must be organized, and customers must be attracted who will pay enough in revenues to cover the costs of the business. It may be necessary to offer special low prices at first to draw in new customers. The firm must establish an identity, as well as produce efficiently so that its costs per unit are below the prevailing market price. And it takes time to set up production, train people, get secure supplies of inputs, and develop demand for the firm's product by advertising and other methods.

Accordingly, most new businesses disappear within two years. Some owners go bankrupt, but most simply close down, pay their debts, and return to other jobs, wiser, sadder, and poorer. Successful firms, however, may sell out at a handsome gain or merely continue as a rewarding way of life for their owner-managers.

Most small firms are family held and do not become corporations. But many small firms do incorporate, and nearly all medium-sized and large firms are corporations. We now must consider corporations and their role.

Corporations *Corporations are firms that issue voting stock, which investors can buy and sell.* These owners (the stockholders) are not responsible for all of the corporation's debts or actions. The most they can lose financially is the value of their shares, if the price of those shares should fall to zero in the stock market.

The corporation is the dominant form of U.S. business, and has been for many decades. That is true also of West European industrial economies and of Japan.

But the domination of large corporate business has distinct limits.

That can be seen by considering medium-sized firms. There are about 35,000 U.S. firms with yearly sales revenues between $10 million and $1 billion. They can be regarded as medium-sized, compared to the approximately 425 large firms that have sales above $1 billion.

These medium-sized firms are usually substantial, well-established companies, producing a variety of products and selling on a regional or national scale. They have continuity and identity in the market. Their management is usually specialized to handle complex tasks with professional skill. Of course, many of these firms encounter special problems, and some of them eventually fail. But as a group, these firms' quality, size, and continuity distinguish them from the mass of small businesses.

These 35,000 medium-sized firms form the bulk of the U.S. economy. Their combined sales and assets are over half of the economy-wide totals. In all sectors except farming and services (two sectors where the small family firm is dominant), these medium-sized firms are a major factor.

Large corporations The largest corporations include about 300 manufacturing firms with sales above $1 billion, plus about another 125 in such other sectors as banking, retailing, transportation, and utilities. These firms operate on a national or global scale, often in many different industries. They have at least 15,000 workers each, with the largest seven of them employing over 300,000 workers apiece. The 500 largest firms (of all kinds) in 1981 had about $2 trillion in sales, which was about 40 percent of all sales in the economy.

Portions of the manufacturing, utility, and financial sectors lend themselves to large-scale technology, which, in turn, re-

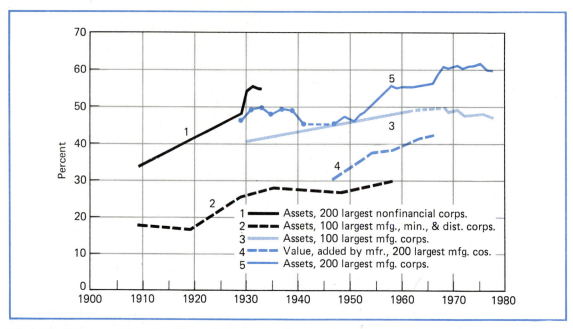

Figure 1 Scope and trends of large U.S. corporations

No single measure of size—assets, sales, employees, etc.—is the sole index of the share of large firms in the economy. Here several alternative measures convey a consistent impression: a strong rise to 1960, tapering off to a possible decline after 1970.

Sources: Adapted from John M. Blair, *Economic Concentration* (New York: Harcourt, Brace, Jovanovich, 1972), Chap. 4; and David W. Penn, "Aggregate Concentration: A Statistical Note," *Antitrust Bulletin* 21 (Spring 1976):91–98.

quires large firms. That is why large corporations are prominent in these sectors.

The role of large corporations in the manufacturing sector is suggested by Figure 1. From 1910 to 1960, the largest 100 or 200 firms significantly increased their shares of total assets and value-added. But their shares appear first to have stabilized in the 1960s and then to have slightly declined in the late 1970s. Therefore, the twentieth-century dominance of the economy by big business now appears to have tapered off and is, perhaps starting to be reversed.

The largest firms The very largest corporations warrant a closer inspection, for they are influential in their markets and in many regions where they operate. These corporate giants are shown in Table 1. They include many familiar names be-

cause their products are widely advertised and sold. They also figure prominently in U.S. economic conditions, such as employment, profits, and growth.

Diversification Most of the large firms focus on just one or a few product lines, such as Exxon in oil, IBM in computers, and AT&T in telecommunications. Other firms, however, are highly diversified, with operations in many kinds of products. Such firms—ITT and United Technologies, for example—are often called "conglomerate" enterprises.

The diversification among the largest manufacturing firms is enormous. In 1965 one third of the firms operated in 5 or fewer of the 440 industries defined by the U.S. Census Bureau. Among the rest, diversification was extensive. Some 284 were in 6 to 25 industries apiece. Thirty-three firms operated in 25 to 50 industries. At the extreme, five firms operated in more than 50 industries each. Some of these firms had more than 100 separate companies—each with its own president and other officers—within their conglomerate structure.

In short, large firms are often highly diversified and have to make complicated choices involving large numbers of inputs and outputs. These choices can be analyzed (as the next chapter will show) with much the same basic tools that apply to simple decisions by single-product firms.

Ownership and control In the millions of small businesses, ownership and control are combined in one person, who makes the decisions and also benefits from whatever financial success the firm achieves. If profits are high, the owner-manager may be able to sell the business at a large capital gain. If there are losses, the owner-manager may lose all of the capital as the firm becomes worthless. Even if the small firm is a corporation, the manager often owns most of the stock, so that ownership and control are still closely combined.

But as size increases, *ownership tends to become divorced from control.* The stocks are bought and sold among many investors, while the managers become a more specialized group who draw salaries and may own little of their company's stock.

This divorce of ownership from control evolved after 1890 as large corporations grew and stockholding became diffused. In a landmark book published in 1932,* Berle and Means argued that this divorce—a "managerial revolution"—had changed the nature of large corporations. The managers were now free from close control and able to run the firms largely as

---

*A. A. Berle and Gardiner C. Means, *The Modern Corporation and Private Property* (New York: Macmillan, 1932; rev. ed., Harcourt, Brace & World, 1968).

they wished. Since 1932, the trend has continued, so that in virtually all of the largest 1,000 corporations there is no major controlling block of shares.

The board of directors still supervises the executives and has to approve all major decisions. But both the board and the executives are largely independent of stockholder control and can select their own members and set their own guidelines. Indeed, on most boards of directors, the executives themselves hold key positions and dominate the discussions. Single owners or large financial institutions (banks, insurance firms) may hold 2, 5, or even 10 percent of the stock in some of these companies. But control is still largely held by the managers.

This divorce between owning and controlling need not be economically harmful. Instead, it encourages executive continuity and professionalism by replacing the old-style industrial buccaneer with the cool modern manager. This may cause two differences in the manager-controlled corporation. First, actions are usually more predictable and objective, rather than reflecting the personality and whims of a single powerful owner. Second, the managers may focus less on maximizing profits for the owners and more on growth, managerial perquisites, and other results that enhance their own importance.

This second effect, which would dilute the central role of profit maximizing, has been studied closely by economists. So far, they have found only slight hints that it occurs normally. A few manager-controlled firms occasionally depart visibly from profit maximizing. But on the whole, the managerial revolution has scarcely affected the primacy of profit as the central goal of private firms, both large and small.

Stock ownership In recent years, between 20 and 30 million people in the United States have owned stock. Most of these

Table 1 *A selection of the largest firms in various sectors (as ranked by sales)*

Industrial

Name of Company	Main Products	Main Dimensions in 1980			Average Rate of Profit as a % of Equity, 1976–1980
		Sales ($mil.)	Assets ($mil.)	Profit ($mil.)	
General Motors	Cars, trucks, buses	57,728	34,581	(−763)	15.3
Ford Motor	Cars, trucks	37,085	24,347	(−1,543)	12.2
International Business Machines (IBM)	Computers, office equipment	26,213	26,703	3,562	21.0
General Electric	Electrical equipment	24,959	18,511	1,514	18.5
International Telephone and Telegraph (ITT)	Telephone equipment	18,529	⁻5,417	894	10.9
E. I. du Pont de Nemours	Chemicals	13,652	9,560	716	14.2
U.S. Steel	Steel and products	12,492	11,747	504	5.0
United Technologies	Aircraft engines, elevators	12,324	7,326	393	13.3
Western Electric	Telephone equipment	12,032	8,047	693	13.7
Proctor & Gamble	Toiletries, household products	10,772	6,553	642	17.6
Dow Chemical	Chemicals	10,626	11,538	805	18.9
Union Carbide	Chemicals	9,994	9,659	890	13.8
Eastman Kodak	Cameras, film, copiers	9,734	8,754	1,153	17.5
Boeing	Aircraft	9,426	5,931	600	19.9
Dart & Kraft	Food products	9,411	4,650	383	14.2
Chrysler Corporation	Cars	9,225	6,617	(−1,710)	4.1
Caterpillar Tractor	Earthmoving equipment	8,597	6,098	564	18.2
Westinghouse Electric	Electrical equipment	8,514	6,812	402	9.4
R. J. Reynolds Industries	Tobacco products	8,449	7,355	670	17.8

Oil Firms

	Sales ($mil.)	Assets ($mil.)	Profits ($mil.)	
Exxon	103,142	56,576	5,650	16.3
Mobil	59,510	32,705	3,272	16.2
Texaco	51,195	26,430	2,642	13.2
Standard Oil of California	40,479	22,162	2,401	16.0
Gulf	26,483	18,638	1,407	12.4
Standard Oil of Indiana	26,133	20,167	1,915	16.6

Utilities

	Main Products	Operating Revenues ($mil.)	Assets ($mil.)	Profits ($mil.)	
American Telephone & Telegraph (AT&T)	Telephone service	50,791	125,450	6,079	11.7
General Telephone & Electronics	Telephone service	9,978	19,720	477	13.3
Southern Company	Electricity	3,763	11,466	344	9.9
Pacific Gas & Electric	Electricity, gas	5,258	11,295	524	10.5
American Electric Power	Electricity	3,756	10,952	348	10.9
Consolidated Edison	Electricity, gas	3,947	7,459	334	10.1

Retail

	Main Products	Sales ($mil.)	Assets ($mil.)	Profits ($mil.)	
Sears, Roebuck	Household merchandise	25,194	28,053	606	11.3
Safeway Stores	Groceries	15,102	3,338	119	13.1
K-Mart	Household merchandise	14,204	6,102.5	260	16.4
J. C. Penney	Household merchandise	11,353	5,863	233	11.1
Kroger	Groceries	10,316	1,997	94	13.3
F. W. Woolworth	Household merchandise	7,218	3,171	160	10.9
Great Atlantic & Pacific Tea Co.	Groceries	6,684	1,230	—	1.4

Banks (ranked by loans)

	Loans ($mil.)	Assets ($mil.)	Profits ($mil.)	
Citicorp	69,915	114,920	499	14.1
Bank of America Corporation	62,482	111,617	643	15.8
Chase Manhattan Corporation	46,506	76,189	354	10.6
Manufacturers Hanover Corporation	30,348	55,522	228	13.1
J. P. Morgan & Company	25,972	51,990	341	14.5

Insurance (ranked by assets)

	Assets ($mil.)	Premium & Annuity Income ($mil.)	Investment Income ($mil.)	Profits ($mil.)
Prudential	59,778	8,668	3,562	444
Federal National Mortgage Association (FNMA)	58,470	5,203	(N.A.)*	14
Metropolitan	48,309	6,010	3,449	479
Aetna Life	22,270	5,412	1,392	185

Source: Fortune Magazine, *Directory of the 500 Largest Industrial Corporations* and *Directory of the Largest Non-industrial Companies,* annual.
*N.A.: Not applicable to FNMA.

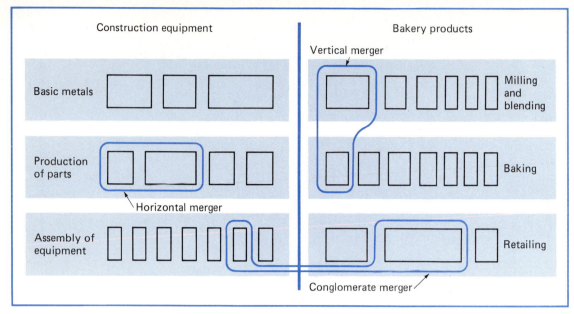

Figure 2   The three kinds of mergers

owners are small investors, with only a few shares. At the other extreme are the wealthiest plutocrats, some with hundreds of millions of dollars' worth of stock. There are also many large "institutional investors," such as insurance firms, pension funds, and banks' trust departments. About three fourths of the trading on the stock exchanges, in fact, is done by these institutions.

The skills of investors vary. The typical small investor is an amateur who learns about stocks mainly from the local newspaper or a local stockbroker. Such an investor usually buys a few shares to hold on to, hoping that their price will rise as the years pass. Only if the price does rise will this person be able to make a (small) gain.

The big-block traders, on the other hand, bring professional skill and detailed knowledge to their operations. They follow conditions minute by minute and their information is thorough. They deal in the most complex, esoteric stock devices. They trade quickly and repeatedly, often acting days or months before crucial information becomes available to small investors (by

then, it is too late to be profitable). These professionals can routinely make money on a falling or fluctuating market by using opportunities that the small investor is scarcely aware of.

Mergers *A merger joins two or more separate firms into a combined firm.* **Each former firm is now part of a larger enterprise, but without the creation of new production capacity.**

Mergers are numerous and commonplace in the U.S. economy. There is an active market for corporate control: the buying and selling of whole companies. In recent years, there has been an average of about 1,000 mergers a year. Most mergers are small, but some are enormous. The assets acquired totaled about $12 billion a year in the 1970s, but the merger boom of 1980–1982 raised that level to over $18 billion a year.

There are three main kinds of mergers. *Horizontal mergers* occur between firms in the same market, as Figure 2 shows. *Vertical mergers* join firms at different but related steps in the production chain. *Conglomerate mergers* include all the rest, in

A Tour Through *The Wall Street Journal*

The daily facts of the business world are collected compactly each working day in the *Wall Street Journal*. We now take you on a brief tour through the paper, to show where large amounts of information about supply can be found. Try to have a copy of the *Journal* at hand when you read this box.

Individual Companies and Industries
The first 20 pages or so have news stories about companies and industries. Some stories report small events. Others dig deep into the basic problems of companies. Any important event or condition is covered.

Stock and Bond Prices
The last six pages are packed with the stock and bond prices of the previous day. About 5,000 of the country's largest firms are covered in precise detail, as shown in Table A. One finds the price of the stock, its rate of dividends, the number of shares traded, and the range of the stock's price both during the previous day and for the year to date. Similar data are given in the bond tables.

Commodities Prices
Just before the bond tables come tables (B and C) with the prices of about 30 major commodities during the previous day. The products range from pork bellies and coffee to heating oil, plywood, and zinc. Precious metals prices (gold, silver, and platinum) are shown; there are not only current "spot" prices, but also "futures" prices for metal to be delivered 1, 2, 3, 12, and more months in the future.

Interest Rates
There is a small table (shown here as Table D) with the current interest rates for various kinds of loans or bonds. Notice that the rates differ, often for reasons that even the experts cannot explain. Yet, the rates all move broadly together as credit conditions change. In the bond price tables, one can also learn the interest rates paid by specific bonds.

Foreign Currencies
Also nearby is a table (Table E) with the prices of the world's major currencies. These exchange rates are expressed in dollars. For example, a $1.83 price for the British pound sterling means that each pound can be bought for $1.83. There are also futures prices for currencies, showing the present prices for currencies to be delivered in one, two, three, and more months.

Others
One also finds occasional compilations of other economic facts. Regular sections have articles about current conditions in bond markets, stock markets, commodity markets, and foreign currency markets. U.S. automobile sales are reported model by model once a week. Data on world oil production and stocks, foreign stock markets, and national levels of income, money supply, and production are also regularly listed. The first three pages of the second section of the paper give stories about foreign companies and markets.

These and still other data add up to a treasure trove of detailed, precise information. Each day the price activity of

Table A

52 Weeks High	Low	Stock	Div.	Yld %	P-E Ratio	Sales 100s	High	low	Close	Net Chg.
5	2⅜	APlan		..	3	11	2⅝	2½	2½	....
17	8⅝	APrecs	s.32	3.2	6	20	11	10	10	−1¼
3⅝	2⅝	Ampec n		..	..	26	2¾	2⅝	2¾	....
10⅜	4⅝	ASciE	.35t	7.8	26	60	4⅞	d 4½	4½	−¼
17	10⅞	AmSeat	.20	1.5	4	2	13½	13½	13½	....
23⅞	9¾	AndJcb		..	34	8	11	10¾	10¾	−¼
14¾	7	Andrea	.60	5.5	14	20	11	10⅝	10⅞	−⅛
35⅛	12½	AngloE	.27	2.1	4	80	13¼	12¾	12⅞	−⅜
25	12	AplDta		..	12	22	21	20⅝	20⅞	+⅜
20½	7⅞	ArgoPtr		..	22	177	8½	8⅛	8⅛	¼
5⅛	2¾	Armtrn		..	3	18	4⅜	4¼	4⅜	....
8⅞	5⅜	ArrowA	.20	3.2	89	6	6¼	6¼	6¼	....
16⅞	8	Asamr	g .40	..	7	101	9⅜	9⅛	9⅛	−⅛
18⅛	10⅜	Astrex		..	10	6	12⅜	12⅛	12⅛	−⅜
8⅞	7½	AstrDr n		..	4	2	7⅞	7¾	7¾	....
4¾	1⅞	AtlsCM	.08e	4.0	22	101	2⅛	2	2	....
8⅞	3⅛	Atlas wt		..	..	25	7	6⅝	6⅝	−⅛
20⅛	11¾	AtlasV	s .20	1.5	5	51	13⅜	13	13⅜	+⅛
9¼	3¾	Audiotr	.16	2.9	12	49	5½	5⅜	5½	+⅛
38⅞	26¾	AutoSw	.80	2.7	13	3	30	29⅞	30	+⅜
11⅞	8⅝	AVEMC	.54	5.0	7	35	10¾	10⅝	10¾	+¼
		– B–B–B –								
16½	15½	BDM	n .15e	.9	12	2	16¼	16⅛	16¼	+⅛
2⅝	1⅛	BRT		..	..	10	1½	1½	1½	....
7⅜	5⅜	Baker	.16	2.2	11	2	7⅛	7⅛	7⅛	−¼
8	5½	BaldwS	.32a	5.7	..	12	5⅝	5½	5⅝	....
28⅝	21⅛	BanFd	4.70e	21.	..	1	22⅝	22⅝	22⅝	+¼
11½	3⅜	Banstr g		..	..	58	6⅛	5⅞	6	....
3⅝	2⅜	Barco	.12	4.4	14	2	2¾	2⅝	2¾	+⅛
9	3½	BarnEn		..	..	12	3⅞	3¾	3¾	....
10¼	3¾	BaryRG		..	12	49	4¼	4	4	....
22⅞	7⅞	Baruch	.43t	5.2	7	8	8¼	8	8¼	+⅛
15⅛	7¾	Beard	n .08	1.0	10	21	8⅜	8	8	−⅛
9⅛	6¼	Behiv n		..	5	85	6½	6¼	6¼	−⅛
4	1¾	Beltran	.10	4.7	..	114	2⅛	1⅞	2⅛	+⅛
24⅛	14	BnfStA	s .40	2.1	8	113	19⅜	19	19⅜	+⅜
24	14½	BnfStB	s .40	2.1	8	21	19⅜	19	19⅜	+⅜
34¼	19⅞	BrgBr	s .48	1.9	12	65	26¼	25½	25⅞	+⅝
		– D–D–D –								
4¾	2½	DWG	.34t	14.	3	44	2⅝	2½	2½	....
14½	7½	DaleE	n.08e	.9	8	40	9⅝	9¼	9⅜	−⅛
5⅝	2⅝	Damon		..	9	34	5	4⅝	5	+½
18⅛	7⅜	Damson	.34t	4.1	12	242	8⅝	8⅛	8⅜	+½
8⅝	2½	Damsn wt		..	..	3	2⅞	2⅞	2⅞	+⅛
20¼	1¼	DataAc	.15e	5.0	3	94	3½	3	3	....
44½	17⅛	Datapd	.30	1.6	14	127	18¾	17¾	18¼	+½
8	5½	Datrm n		..	14	8	5⅝	5½	5½	....
4	1⅞	DeRose		..	13	7	2¼	2¼	2¼	....
2¾	1	Decorat		..	..	3	1⅛	1⅛	1⅛	−⅛
22⅜	13¾	DelLab	.60	4.1	6	3	14½	14¼	14½	+⅜
6⅝	2½	DesgnJ	.38t	9.8	4	42	3⅞	3¾	3⅞	....
35⅞	20⅜	Digicon		..	12	111	24¾	23⅞	24⅝	+½
24⅞	12⅝	Dillard	.40	1.8	5	12	23	22⅝	22⅝	−⅜
21¼	7⅞	DomeP s		..	..	2227	8¾	8½	8⅝	+⅛
31½	16¼	Domtr	g 2	..	..	17	16¾	16⅝	16⅝	−⅛
26⅜	14⅝	DorGas	.16	.9	12	176	17⅞	17⅜	17⅜	−½
10¾	7¼	Dghty	.30b	3.8	7	21	8	7⅞	7⅞	....
8⅜	2¾	Downey	.28	7.0	..	15	4	4	4	....
23⅞	8½	Dreco g		..	..	39	8¾	8⅝	8¾	....
25¼	13½	Driller n		..	7	32	14¼	13¾	13¾	....
11⅞	7¾	DrivHr		..	..	1	8¼	8¼	8¼	+¼
27⅜	18¼	Ducom	n.70b	3.5	10	18	20	19¾	20	+¼
28⅝	15⅜	Dunes n		..	11	38	17	16⅜	17	+⅝
16	11¾	Duplx	.68	5.1	5	3	13¼	13¼	13¼	+⅛
15⅝	9¾	DurTst	.40a	4.0	9	1	10	10	10	....
11¾	5⅝	Dynlctn	.10e	1.2	6	71	8⅜	8¼	8⅜	....
19⅛	11¼	Dyneer	s.70	5.2	6	1	13⅜	13⅜	13⅜	+⅛
		– E–E–E –								
8⅜	4¾	EAC	.36	6.0	5	58	6¼	6	6	....
19	6⅛	EECO	.28	4.1	15	59	6¾	6¼	6¾	....
20¾	10⅜	EDO	.40b	2.8	11	35	14⅜	14⅛	14⅜	+⅛
5⅞	2	ElAudD		..	..	3	2⅛	2⅛	2⅛	....
46	21	ElcAm	1.40	6.4	7	2	22	22	22	−¼
8¾	3¼	ElecSd		..	23	6	3½	3⅜	3½	+⅛
13⅛	4⅞	Elsinor		..	10	175	6¾	6½	6⅝	+⅛
9¼	2⅞	EmpCar	.50	10.	..	55	5¼	5	5	−¼
14¾	6¼	EnMgt n		..	10	74	8⅛	7⅝	7¾	−⅛
12⅛	3⅝	EngMin	.71t	17.	23	151	4⅛	3⅞	4⅛	+⅛
19⅜	9	EngyRs	.24	2.5	10	27	9¾	9¼	9½	+½
21½	8⅝	EnrSv n		..	5	77	10¼	9⅝	9⅝	−⅜

EXPLANATORY NOTES

(For New York and American Exchange listed issues)

Sales figures are unofficial.

The 52-Week High and Low columns show the highest and the lowest price of the stock in consolidated trading during the preceding 52 weeks plus the current week, but not the current trading day.

u–Indicates a new 52-week high. d–Indicates a new 52-week low.

s–Split or stock dividend of 25 per cent or more in the past 52 weeks. The high-low range is adjusted from the old stock. Dividend begins with the date of split or stock dividend.

n–New issue in the past 52 weeks. The high-low range begins with the start of trading in the new issue and does not cover the entire 52-week period.

g–Dividend or earnings in Canadian money. Stock trades in U.S. dollars. No yield or PE shown unless stated in U.S. money.

Unless otherwise noted, rates of dividends in the foregoing table are annual disbursements based on the last quarterly or semi-annual declaration. Special or extra dividends or payments not designated as regular are identified in the following footnotes.

a–Also extra or extras. b–Annual rate plus stock dividend. c–Liquidating dividend. e–Declared or paid in preceding 12 months. i–Declared or paid after stock dividend or split up. j–Paid this year, dividend omitted, deferred or no action taken at last dividend meeting. k–Declared or paid this year, an accumulative issue with dividends in arrears. r–Declared or paid in preceding 12 months plus stock dividend. t–Paid in stock in preceding 12 months, estimated cash value on ex-dividend or ex-distribution date.

x–Ex-dividend or ex-rights. y–Ex-dividend and sales in full. z–Sales in full.

wd–When distributed. wi–When issued. ww–With warrants. xw–Without warrants.

vi–In bankruptcy or receivership or being reorganized under the Bankruptcy Act, or securities assumed by such companies.

thousands of firms and markets is made fully visible.

The *Journal* is not the only source of business information. Such business magazines as *Business Week, Forbes, Barron's,* and *Fortune* also offer useful information. And detailed financial reports by Moody's and Standard & Poor can be found in most college libraries. But the *Journal* is a remarkable compilation of price and financial information, which gives the reader direct contact with company actions and outcomes.

Table C

Cash Prices

Thursday, February 25, 1981
(Quotations as of 4 p.m. Eastern time)

FOODS

	Thurs.	Wed.	Yr. Ago
Flour, hard winter KC cwt	$10.25	$10.35	$10.85
Coffee, Brazilian, NY lb	n1.50	1.50	1.23
Cocoa, Accra NY lb	z	z	z
Potatoes, rnd wht, 50 lb, NY del y z		z	6.75
Sugar, cane, raw NY lb del	.1731	.1691	.2511
Sugar, cane, ref NY lb fob	.2860	.2910	.3610
Sugar, beet, ref Chgo-W lb fob	.2840	.2840	.3390
Orange Juice, frz con, NY lb ...	b1.225	1.25	1.32
Butter, AA, Chgo., lb.	1.47	1.47	1.47
Eggs,Lge white, Chgo doz.	.72½-.73	.71½-.72	.66¾
Broilers, Dressed "A" NY lb ...	x.5060	.5026	.5105
Beef, 700-900 lbs, Midw lb fob 1.04		1.04	.95-.96
Pork Loins, 14 down Mdw lb fob	.96	.98	.91
Hams, 14-17 lbs, Midw lb fob ...84		.81¾	.65½-.66
Pork Bellies, 12-14lbMdw lb fob	.66	.66	.45½
Hogs, Sioux City avg cwt	e48.20	48.80	41.05
Hogs, Omaha avg cwt	e48.10	48.60	41.20
Steers, Omaha choice avg cwt	64.75	64.75	61.75
Steers, Sioux City ch avg cwt	65.75	65.75	61.38
Feeder Cattle, Okl Cty, av cwt	e65.62	65.37	73.00
Pepper, black NY lb	a.78	.78	.79

GRAINS AND FEEDS

Alfalfa Pellets, dehy, Neb., ton 81.00		81.00	106.-107.
Barley, top-quality Mpls., bu 2.90-3.15		2.90-3.15	3.65-4.0
Bran, (wheat middlings)KC ton	n72.50	74.50	85.50
Brewer's Grains, Mlwke, ton ...	81.00	82.00	93.00
Corn, No. 2 yellow Chgo., bu bi	2.60¼	2.602	3.47½
Corn Gluten Feed, Chgo., ton	113.67	113.67	114.00
Cottonseed Meal, Memphis, ton	n140.00	143.75	196.20
Flaxseed, Mpls., bu	n7.65	7.65	8.15
Hominy Feed, Ill., ton	67.00	67.00	99.00
Linseed Meal, Mpls., ton	n150.00	151.00	145.00
Meat-Bonemeal 50%-pro, Ill.,ton ... 205.00		205.00	230.-235.
Oats, No. 2 milling, Mpls., bu	2.12-2.20	2.10-2.20	2.22-2.25
Rice, No. 2 milled fob Ark. cwt	18.0-19.0	18.0-19.0	25.0-27.0
Rye, No. 2 Mpls., bu	3.95	4.00	3.85
Sorghum, (Milo), No. 2 Gulf cwt	5.07	5.18	6.50
Soybean Meal, Decatur, Ill. ton	187.00	187.00	204.00
Soybeans No1 yellow Chgo bu bi	6.06¾	6.04¼	7.25¼
Sunflower Seed, No. 1 Mpls. cwt	n12.00	12.00	11.35
Wheat, Spring 14%-pro Mpls, bu	4.17	4.13	4.69
Wheat, amber durum, Mpls, bu	4.25-4.90	4.25-4.90	6.15-7.75
Wheat No2 soft red Chgo bu bi	3.44¼	3.43¾	4.16¼
Wheat, No. 2 hard KC, bu	4.14¾	4.19¼	4.46¾

FATS AND OILS

Coconut Oil, crd, N. Orleans lb	z	z	.25¼
Corn Oil, crd wet mill, Chgo. lb	.25¼	c25¼-¾	.23½
Corn Oil, crd dry mill, Chgo. lb	n.26	.26	.24
Cottonseed Oil, crd Miss Vly lb	.19	.19	.24½
Grease, choice white, Chgo lb	.16¼-½	.16¼	.17¾
Lard, Chgo lb	a.22½	.22½	.19½
Linseed Oil, raw Mpls lb	.29	.29	.32
Palm Oil, Neutral, N.Y. lb ...	z	z	.28¼
Peanut Oil, crd, Southeast lb	n.30	.30	.38
Soybean Oil, crd Decatur, lb	.1778	.1791	.2244
Tallow, bleachable, Chgo lb	.16¾-.17	.16¾-.17	.17¾
Tallow, edible, Chgo lb	.19¼	.19¼	.19½

FIBERS AND TEXTILES

Burlap, 10 oz. 40-in. NY yd	n.2295	.2285	.2590
Cotton 1 1-16 in str lw-md Mphs lb	.5977	.5932	.8612
Print Cloth, cotton, 48-in NY yd	s.70	.70	.73
Print Cloth, pol/cot 48-in NY yd	t.48	.48	.57
Satin Acetate, NY yd	.62	.62	.60

a-Asked. b-Bid. c-Corrected. d-Dealer market. e-Estimated. g-f.o.b. harbor barge. Source: Oil Buyers' Guide. i-To arrive by rail within 30 days. k-Dealer selling price in lots of 40,000 pounds or more, f.o.b. buyer's works. n-Nominal. p-Producer price. r-Day's trading range. s-Thread count 78x76. t-Thread count 78x54. x-Less than truckloads. y-Long Island origin; varies seasonally. z-Not quoted.

					Lifetime		Open
Open	High	Low	Settle	Change	High	Low	Interest

—GRAINS AND OILSEEDS—

CORN (CBT)—5,000 bu.; cents per bu.

	Open	High	Low	Settle	Change	High	Low	Interest
Mar	259½	259¾	256½	256¾	− 3½	406½	253	28,358
May	272	272¼	270	270¼	− 2¼	410¾	262½	39,409
July	281	282¼	280	280¾	− 1	399	267¾	30,289
Sept	285¼	286¾	284¼	286	.....	388½	268¾	34,370
Dec	292	293¾	290½	292¾	.....	345½	271	24,261
Mar83	305¾	307¾	305¼	307	.....	320¾	294	4,138

Est vol 62,532; vol Wed 42,686; open int 133,329, −1,667.

OATS (CBT)—5,000 bu.; cents per bu.

	Open	High	Low	Settle	Change	High	Low	Interest
Mar	206½	208	205½	205½	− .55	239	183½	2,490
May	197	199	196½	197	+ ¾	231½	177½	2,432
July	186½	188	185½	186½	+ ¾	207	168½	2,087
Sept	181½	182½	180½	181	− ½	204¾	167	678
Dec	186	187	184¾	186½	+ ¾	199½	182	187

Est vol 1,918; vol Wed 1,528; open int 7,874, 19

CATTLE—LIVE (CME)—40,000 lbs.; cents per lb.

	Open	High	Low	Settle	Change	High	Low	Interest
Apr	65.20	65.30	64.75	65.00	− .55	72.40	53.50	25,156
June	64.15	64.20	63.65	63.80	− .85	72.30	54.75	16,218
Aug	61.80	61.80	61.40	61.65	− .47	66.85	54.30	6,650
Oct	60.00	60.00	59.40	59.60	− .42	65.90	53.70	3,151
Dec	60.02	60.02	59.60	59.92	− .35	64.65	54.90	1,032
Feb83	60.05	60.05	59.80	59.80	− .25	60.90	58.45	38
Apr	60.25	60.50	60.25	60.50	no comp	60.50	60.25	9

Est vol 14,554; vol Wed 16,602; open int 51,174, +521.

GOLD (CMX)—100 troy oz.; $ per troy oz.

	Open	High	Low	Settle	Change	High	Low	Interest
Mar	367.00	367.00	367.00	365.70	− 2.30	410.00	360.50	390
Apr	371.00	373.10	368.20	369.80	− 2.60	898.00	362.70	44,556
June	380.00	381.00	376.50	377.90	− 2.60	925.00	371.00	25,165
Aug	387.80	389.50	384.30	386.20	− 2.60	887.00	379.00	14,549
Oct	395.00	397.00	395.00	394.70	− 2.50	842.00	387.00	16,468
Dec	405.30	406.00	401.50	403.50	− 2.40	666.50	396.00	11,057
Feb83	410.50	410.50	410.50	412.50	− 2.30	642.00	405.00	17,644
Apr	421.60	422.80	421.60	421.60	− 2.20	604.00	415.00	9,310
June	....	....	....	430.90	− 2.10	596.00	425.00	1,649
Aug	....	....	....	440.20	− 2.00	515.50	451.50	619
Oct	....	....	....	449.70	− 1.90	500.00	449.50	466
Dec	....	....	....	459.30	− 1.80	495.00	381.60	38

Est vol 35,000; vol Wed 33,670; open int 141,911, −1,747.

HEATING OIL NO. 2 (NYM)—42,000 gal.; $ per gal.

	Open	High	Low	Settle	Change	High	Low	Interest
Mar	.8650	.8885	.8650	.8850	+ .0276	1.1385	.8135	4,000
Apr	.7890	.8015	.7875	.8000	+ .0180	1.1276	.7760	6,204
May	.7780	.7810	.7735	.7793	+ .0089	1.1300	.7675	3,030
June	.7845	.7860	.7795	.7835	+ .0057	1.0800	.7730	1,964
July	.7900	.7940	.7870	.7915	+ .0064	1.0800	.7825	1,572
Aug	.8025	.8050	.8020	.8045	+ .0060	1.0850	.7975	368
Sept	....	....	....	.8230	+ .0070	1.0850	.8100	81
Oct	.8280	.8415	.8280	.8350	+ .0100	1.0950	.8250	367
Nov	.8560	.8560	.8560	.8500	.....	.8560	.8560	0
Dec	.8625	.8680	.8625	.8680	+ .0080	.9475	.8525	143

Est vol 7,000; vol Wed 6,275; open int 17,779, +176

SILVER (CMX)—5,000 troy oz.; cents per troy oz.

	Open	High	Low	Settle	Change	High	Low	Interest
Mar	799.0	801.5	786.0	788.5	− 9.3	2830.0	779.0	5,307
Apr	810.0	810.0	802.0	799.0	− 11.0	835.0	787.0	21
May	820.0	822.5	806.0	809.0	− 10.0	2895.0	799.0	14,136

CBT—Chicago Board of Trade; CME—Chicago Mercantile Exchange; CMX—Commodity Exchange, New York; CSCE—Coffee, Sugar & Cocoa Exchange, New York; CTN—New York Cotton Exchange; IMM—International Monetary Market at CME, Chicago; KC—Kansas City Board of Trade; MPLS—Minneapolis Grain Exchange; NOCE—New Orleans Commodity Exchange; NYFE—New York Futures Exchange, unit of New York Stock Exchange. NYM—New York Mercantile Exchange; WPG—Winnipeg Commodity Exchange.

Table D

Foreign Exchange

Thursday, February 25, 1982

The New York foreign exchange selling rates below apply to trading among banks in amounts of $1 million and more, as quoted at 3 p.m. Eastern time by Bankers Trust Co. Retail transactions provide fewer units of foreign currency per dollar.

Country	U.S. $ equiv. Thurs.	U.S. $ equiv. Wed.	Currency per U.S. $ Thurs.	Currency per U.S. $ Wed.
Argentina (Peso)				
Financial	.000100	.000100	10025.00	10025.00
Australia (Dollar) ...	1.0770	1.0786	.9285	.9271
Austria (Schilling) ..	.0601	.0602	16.64	16.62
Belgium (Franc)				
Commercial rate ..	.023047	.02308	43.389	43.32
Financial rate	.021282	.02147	46.989	46.57
Brazil (Cruzeiro)	.00733	.00733	136.41	136.41
Britain (Pound)	1.8365	1.8335	.5445	.5454
30-Day Forward ...	1.8374	1.8345	.5442	.5451
90-Day Forward ...	1.8415	1.8387	.5430	.5439
180-Day Forward ...	1.8470	1.8439	.5414	.5423
Canada (Dollar)	.8191	.8199	1.2208	1.2196
30-Day Forward ...	.8187	.8198	1.2214	1.2198
90-Day Forward ...	.8181	.8198	1.2223	1.2198
180-Day Forward ...	.8171	.8190	1.2238	1.2210
China (Yuan)	.5497	.5498	1.8190	1.8190
Colombia (Peso)	.0166	.0166	60.07	60.07
Denmark (Krone) ...	.1259	.1259	7.94	7.9418
Ecuador (Sucre)	.0404	.0404	24.75	24.75
Finland (Markka) ...	.0210	.0210	4.5238	4.5243
France (Franc)	.1654	.1658	6.0460	6.0325
30-Day Forward ...	.1654	.1658	6.0470	6.0325
90-Day Forward ...	.1651	.1655	6.0550	6.0405
180-Day Forward ...	.1644	.1646	6.0840	6.0755
Greece (Drachma) ..	.0164	.0163	61.15	61.39
Hong Kong (Dollar)	.1699	.1696	5.8875	5.8975
India (Rupee)	.1082	.1083	9.24	9.23
Indonesia (Rupiah)	.00154	.00154	648.00	648.00
Ireland (Pound)	1.4925	1.4985	.6700	.6673
Israel (Shekel)	.0569	.0569	17.59	17.59
Italy (Lira)	.000787	.000788	1271.00	1269.00
Japan (Yen)	.004244	.004272	235.65	234.10
30-Day Forward ...	.004275	.004306	233.90	232.25
90-Day Forward ...	.004336	.004364	230.65	229.15
180-Day Forward ...	.004419	.004452	226.30	224.60
Lebanon (Pound) ...	.2041	.2041	4.9000	4.900
Malaysia (Ringgit) ..	.4336	.4344	2.3065	2.3020
Mexico (Peso)	.0267	.0256	37.50	39.00
Netherlands (Guilder)	.3840	.3846	2.6040	2.600
New Zealand (Dollar)	.7880	.7880	1.2690	1.2690
Norway (Krone)	.1668	.1666	5.9950	6.00
Pakistan (Rupee) ...	.0976	.0976	10.245	10.245
Peru (Sol)	.00185	.00185	540.97	540.97
Philippines (Peso) ..	.1207	.1207	8.285	8.285
Portugal (Escudo) ..	.01445	.0147	69.19	68.19
Saudi Arabia (Riyal)	.2925	.2925	3.4185	3.4185
Singapore (Dollar) ..	.4751	.4753	2.1050	2.1040
South Africa (Rand)	1.0285	1.0285	.9723	.9723
South Korea (Won)	.0014	.0014	708.00	708.00
Spain (Peseta)	.00973	.0097	102.78	102.75
Sweden (Krona)	.1732	.1731	5.7722	5.7779
Switzerland (Franc)	.5318	.5329	1.8805	1.8765
30-Day Forward ...	.5353	.5363	1.8680	1.8645
90-Day Forward ...	.5416	.5418	1.8465	1.8455
180-Day Forward ...	.5497	.5500	1.8190	1.8180
Taiwan (Dollar)	.0270	.0270	37.00	37.00
Thailand (Baht)	.0435	.0435	23.00	23.00
Uruguay (New Peso)				
Financial	.0847	.0847	11.80	11.80
Venezuela (Bolivar)	.2329	.2329	4.2937	4.2937
West German (Mark)	.4218	.4224	2.3710	2.3675
30-Day Forward ...	.4235	.4241	2.3612	2.3577
90-Day Forward ...	.4271	.4275	2.3413	2.3394
180-Day Forward ...	.4320	.4325	2.3148	2.3120
SDR	1.12952	1.13300	.885334	.882613

Special Drawing Rights are based on exchange rates for the U.S., West German, British, French and Japanese currencies. Source: International Monetary Fund.

Table E

Money Rates

Thursday, February 25, 1982

The key U.S. and foreign annual interest rates below are a guide to general levels but don't always represent actual transactions.

PRIME RATE: 16½%. The base rate on corporate loans at large U.S. money center commercial banks.

FEDERAL FUNDS: 13¾% high, 13% low, 13¾% near closing bid, 14% offered. Reserves traded among commercial banks for overnight use in amounts of $1 million or more. Source: Mabon, Nugent & Co., N.Y.

DISCOUNT RATE: 12%. The charge on loans to member commercial banks by the New York Federal Reserve Bank.

CALL MONEY: 14% to 15%. The charge on loans to brokers on stock exchange collateral.

COMMERCIAL PAPER: placed directly by General Motors Acceptance Corp.: 13⅜%, 30 to 270 days.

COMMERCIAL PAPER: high-grade unsecured notes sold through dealers by major corporations in multiples of $1,000: 13¾ to 90 days.

CERTIFICATES OF DEPOSIT: 13¼%, one month; 13½%, two months; 13.90%, three months; 14 1/0%, six months; 14¼%, one year. Typical rates paid by major banks on new issues of negotiable C.D.'s, usually on amounts of $1 million and more. The minimum unit is $100,000.

BANKERS ACCEPTANCES: 13.40%, 30 days; 13.40%, 60 days; 13.40%, 90 days; 13.35%, 120 days; 13.20%, 150 days; 13.15%, 180 days. Negotiable, bank-backed business credit instruments typically financing an import order.

EURODOLLARS: 14⅜% to 14¼%, one month; 14⅝% to 14½%, two months; 14⅞% to 14¾%, three months; 14 15/16% to 14 13/16%, four months; 15 1/16% to 14 15/16%, five months and six months. The rates paid on U.S. dollar deposits in banks in London, usually on amounts of $100,000 or more. The higher rate for each maturity is LIBOR, the London Interbank Offered Rate.

FOREIGN PRIME RATES: Canada 16½%; Germany 13%; Japan 6.90%; Switzerland 8%; Britain 13.50%. These rate indications aren't directly comparable; lending practices vary widely by location. Source: Morgan Guaranty Trust Co.

TREASURY BILLS: Results of the Monday, February 22, 1981, auction of short-term U.S. government bills, sold at a discount from face value in units of $10,000 to $1 million: 12.430%, 13 weeks; 12.695%, 26 weeks.

SAVINGS RATES: on instruments offered to individuals; minimum amounts vary. Money market fund-a 13.99%; six month money market certificate, 13.958%; 30-month savings institution small-saver certificate (accounts 2½ to less than 4 years) b-14.80%; one-year "all savers" tax exempt certificates, 10.79%; savings institution passbook deposit-c 5.5%; U.S. savings bond, 9%.

a-Annualized average rate of return after expenses for past 30 days on Merrill Lynch Ready Assets Trust, the largest of such funds; this isn't a forecast of future returns. b-Commercial bank rate. Savings and loan associations and savings banks are permitted to pay .25% more than commercial banks. c-Commercial banks are limited to paying .25% less than savings and loan associations and savings banks.

which the partners are neither horizontal nor vertical. (Chapters 11 and 12 present these mergers' effects on competition.)

Since 1960, most mergers have been conglomerate in nature. This is mainly because antitrust policies have prevented most horizontal and some vertical mergers. Conglomerate mergers appear to be affecting the shape of American business by creating firms that are more diverse than before. Probably most of the products that you buy are made by companies that are really just branches of other larger firms.

Most economists regard conglomeration as interesting but of only secondary importance in analyzing firms' main decisions and outcomes. The economic logic of the firm's investment, production, and pricing are largely the same whether the firm is independent or owned by a larger enterprise.

Other types of firms: Public enterprises, nonprofit firms, and cooperatives

Much of this chapter's content applies not only to the private profit-making firms, but also to public, nonprofit, and cooperative firms.

All firms need to make efficient choices about inputs, outputs, and investments. But these other types of firms differ from private enterprises in that profit is not the single motive for their policies and actions. They usually have social goals as well. Some of these firms seek to supply goods to needy people at low prices. Others provide important services that no private firm could supply at a profit. Still other firms provide "utility" services (such as municipal electric systems and the U.S. Postal Service) for which private operators, having a monopoly position, might charge too high a price.

Taken together, these nonprivate firms are a diverse and important group of enterprises, covering nearly one fourth of all U.S. economic activity. Economists, however, have given them little study, focusing instead on private enterprise.

Public enterprises are found in all sizes at national, regional, state, and local levels. Their conditions are treated in Chapter 13.

Not-for-profit enterprises also include a great variety of firms. They are "owned" by charitable groups and often have some special social purpose. Examples include most hospitals, private schools, and colleges, the Red Cross system, city orchestras and cultural centers, and many daycare centers. Many of these units sell their services, but most rely heavily on contributions. Some struggle along always short of funds; others enjoy ample financing and rapid growth.

Cooperatives are enterprises owned by their customers or suppliers. Millions of farmers sell their crops, livestock, and milk through farm cooperatives, and they buy much of their supplies from them too. In the retail sector, cooperative food stores proliferated in the 1970s. In all cases, the cooperative enterprise tries to cover its costs with sales revenue, and it channels its "profits" back to its owners (customers or suppliers).

There are other types of enterprises, even more uncommon, such as worker-owned firms. But virtually all business in the United States is conducted by private firms, public firms, nonprofit enterprises, and cooperatives.

The enterprise

The essence of the enterprise (or firm) is clear and simple: "Enterprise" is just a term for any unit where people produce a good or service. The enterprise may consist of one local plant (factory or office) or more, on up to many hundreds of plants. The corner drugstore is an enterprise, and so are General Motors Corporation, the

Chicago White Sox, the hospital where you were born, and your own college.

Choices and outcomes

Whatever its size or form, the enterprise has the basic task of combining inputs in a production process to create output. These choices *compare benefits with costs,* as do other economic choices. *Inputs* are costs, while *outputs* provide benefits in the form of the sales revenue. The manager carries each choice to the point where its marginal benefits just equal its costs. And in total, the manager tries to maximize the excess of benefits (revenues) over costs.

The basic process is shown in Figure 3. The firm makes choices: what good or service to produce, what kinds and amounts of inputs to use, what quantities of output to make, and what price to set for its output. Not only are these choices numerous, but often the range of choice is also very wide. Once the firm decides and proceeds, the resulting outcomes are quite definite.

But behind each definite outcome lies *a range of alternative values that could have been selected.* It is the economist's task to explain how the firm chooses among all of these alternatives.

The firm plays two main roles in its task of turning inputs into outputs. **First, it is an *owner and manager of real capital,* which is used in production.** In this role, the firm raises funds and then invests them in building up its physical plant and equipment. This activity is reflected in the firm's yearly balance sheet, which shows the *stock* of value contained in the capital.

Second, *the firm is a producer, using labor and capital to process materials into outputs.* The *flow* of costs of inputs and the revenues from outputs is presented in the firm's yearly income statement.

The cost paid out for each input is simply its price times the quantity used in a given period. ***Total cost*** paid out to inputs by the firm is then simply the sum of all these separate input costs: the labor, raw materials, capital, and so on. On the revenue side, ***total revenue*** is equal to the price of

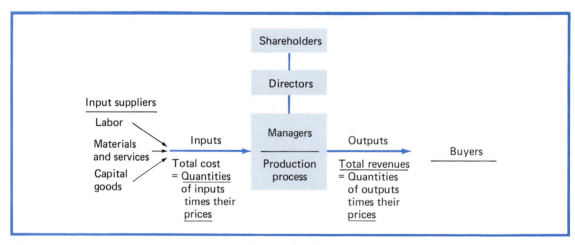

Figure 3 The basic economic elements of an enterprise
The firm uses inputs to produce outputs via some process of production. Each input has a price and is used in a definite quantity during the period. The price times the quantity is the cost of that input. The input costs together make up total cost. Similarly, each output has a price and is sold in a definite quantity during the period. Each output's sales revenue is its price times its quantity. Together, the outputs' revenues make up total revenue.

each unit of output times the quantity of output sold. Total revenue is often called sales revenue or gross receipts.

Net income or profit is simply the revenue left over after all required costs are accounted for:

Net income = Total revenue − Total cost

$$\text{Net income} = \left(\begin{array}{c}\text{The sum of all the}\\ \text{output values}\end{array}\right)$$
$$- \left(\begin{array}{c}\text{The sum of all}\\ \text{the input costs}\end{array}\right)$$

If the firm is privately owned, its managers' main aim is to maximize the firm's profits. They try to use the "right" mix of inputs in an efficient production process to produce the most profitable amount of output. The firm's manager may have a degree of choice in choosing the price-quantity combination. Or, instead, the output prices may be set by market competition, so that the manager is only free to choose the right amount of output, given the price. Although the managers try to keep revenue up and costs down, profits are not assured. Successful performance depends crucially on skillful estimation of consumer preferences and cost conditions. Wrong choices about what to produce and how to produce it will be penalized by losses. Input and output choices, then, are motivated by the search for profits.

Production is therefore merely an outcome of the pursuit of profits. If the markets are working well, the pursuit of profits will lead private firms to provide the array of products that consumers want, at minimum costs.

Inputs, outputs, and production

Inputs As their name indicates, inputs include all items put into the production process. The three traditional main classes of inputs are labor, capital, and land (which includes all natural resources).

Labor is the application of human effort, both in physical force and mental skills. The effort is provided by workers, selling their services by the hour, day, week, or month. Labor comes in many types, ranging from simple actions like digging or fastening, on up to complex professional skills. Managers are also a form of labor input. These various kinds of labor are priced at varying values. Chapter 15 analyzes labor and wages in detail.

Capital is the stock of productive assets created by past investments. It includes buildings, equipment, roads, and any other improvement to natural conditions such as dredging a harbor or clearing stones from a field. Capital increases productivity by enlarging what labor can do. Thus, a hammer and a 20-ton drop forge both increase the ability of workers to bend metal. Computers increase calculating abilities, and jet airplanes increase the speed of travel. Capital is discussed more fully in Chapter 16.

Land is a broad term for all natural resources and raw materials. It includes oil, minerals, forests, farmland, and even fishing shoals. Resources range from nonrenewable ones (ores, coal) to virtually inexhaustible ones (air, solar energy).

Besides these three classes of inputs, there are goods that firms sell to other firms. Thus, a steel plate is an output of a steel company but an input to a machinery firm. Such **intermediate goods** fall into three classes of their own. One is finished goods sold to firms for use in *their* products—for example, tires and batteries sold to automobile companies. Second is semi-finished goods, such as iron slabs, industrial chemicals, paper, rubber, or flour, which will undergo further processing. Third is services, as distinct from physical products. Examples are electricity, insurance, advertising, and the transport of goods.

Such varied inputs provide large degrees of choice to firms. They must decide not only which inputs to use but also how much of each one to buy. The decisions depend on two fundamental sets of conditions—*technology* and *the prices of the inputs*. Technology, the "state of the art," governs how inputs can best be combined. For example, aluminum, steel, and plastic can be used in various parts of automobiles. Each has certain technical advantages of strength, lightness, and flexibility.

But technology alone does not decide the choices among these three. The other basic determinant is the *prices of the inputs*. Thus, if aluminum's price rises sharply compared to plastic's price, then plastic may extensively replace aluminum to minimize the total cost of an output.

Outputs The two main categories of outputs are goods and services. *Goods* are physical things, such as a gallon of gas, a ton of bricks, or a box of corn flakes, and can be stored. *Services* are less tangible and often have no lasting physical form— TV repair, insurance, legal advice, and a blood test, for example. Often goods and services are mingled: A new car may have a guarantee of certain repair services.

Outputs are usually defined by their *location* or *timing* and by their physical features. As for location, a ton of coal delivered to your door differs, economically, from a ton located at the mouth of the mine. Strawberries available at the grocery store differ from those still unpicked at the farm. As for timing, a plumber's repair call made on Sunday night differs from one made on Monday morning. In all these cases, both (1) the cost and (2) the nature of the good itself can be different, despite the seeming uniformity.

Production is any process that converts inputs into outputs, as shown in Figure 3. Production occurs in all manner of plants, under a great variety of conditions. There are dark clanging mills, spotless electronic assembly lines, deep mines, bustling stores, and countless other productive scenes.

The diversity of production techniques is quite clearly reflected in the size of firms. In some industries, such as steel, automobiles, and the production of electricity, production techniques require large size for efficiency. For example, the smallest auto manufacturer, AMC, hires 27,000 workers and owns $1.1 billion worth of capital. In the retailing industry, in contrast, corner grocery stores coexist with nationwide sellers such as A & P.

Simple accounting

Each year the diversity of firms' activities is distilled into standard accounting measures. As we have already noted, there are two parts to such measures: the income statement and the balance sheet. These give the precise accounting data about what the firm has done. The **income statement** sums up the results of the firm's production choices, while the **balance sheet** covers the firm's management of its physical and financial assets. You can gain practice in interpreting such accounts by looking up real companies' accounts in *Moody's Industrial Manuals*, comparing their entries with those discussed here.

Note that we are discussing *accounting* costs and profits. The more rigorous *economic* concepts of costs and profits will be treated in Chapters 8 and 9. The two versions are related, but the economic analysis is deeper and therefore different in certain parts, especially in the definitions of costs and profits.

Income statements The top line in an income statement represents the firm's sales revenue, as shown in the sample statement in Table 2. The next lines cover the various

Table 2 Yearly accounts for a typical firm (millions of dollars)

Income Statement

	1982	1981		1982	1981
Sales Revenue	219	191	Earnings before Tax	41	27
Cost and Expenses	178	164	Taxes on Earnings	19	13
Labor and materials	85	80	Net Income after Taxes	22	14
Materials	53	48	Dividends	8	6
Services	19	16	Retained Earnings	14	8
Depreciation	8	7			
Interest expense	13	13			

Balance Sheet

Assets	1982	1981	Claims on Assets	1982	1981
Current Assets	51	47	Current Liabilities	27	25
Financial	43	40	Accounts and rates payable	20	19
Inventories	8	7	Other	7	6
Gross Plant and Equipment	290	268	Long-term Liabilities: Debt	130	128
Less depreciation	62	54	Stockholders' Equity	122	108
Net Plant and Equipment	228	214	Common stock (22 million shares at $1 par)	22	22
			Retained earnings	100	86
Total Assets	279	261	Total Claims on Assets	279	261

costs, which the firm must pay from its revenues. Most accounts lump the operating or production costs together; they include wages and salaries, materials and services. The wages and salaries paid to labor are usually the largest single cost, averaging about 50 percent of all costs. Materials are usually next in size. After operating costs come two *costs of capital.* The first is *depreciation,* representing the yearly wearing out and obsolescence of machinery and buildings. This decline in the value of the capital is made good by setting aside funds for the replacement of the capital. The second cost of capital is *interest* on the company's debt (its bonds and borrowings).

The difference between revenues and costs is earnings (or accounting profit) before tax. From those earnings, the federal tax on profits usually takes about 45 percent. The **after-tax profit** is the company's yearly financial payoff for its ownership and production actions. The profit can be large, small, or negative. Since profit usually differs from year to year, it is necessary to take the *average* profit over a period of time to determine the firm's true profitability.

The firm usually pays out some of the accounting profits to shareholders as **dividends.** The paying out of dividends is optional; the firm can omit them, change them, keep them steady, do whatever it thinks best from year to year. The remainder of the profits, about two thirds on average, is then kept by the firm as **retained earnings.** These funds can be used for expansion or other actions that will increase the value of the firm.

Balance sheets The firm has productive assets, which appear on the left-hand side of its balance sheet. The firm has issued paper securities in the form of stocks and bonds to the people who gave it the money to buy these assets. These paper assets are liabilities to the firm, since they represent claims against its wealth. They appear on the right-hand side of the firm's balance sheet. The stocks are the owner's claim on the firm's assets. By accounting methods, the total values in the asset and claims sides of the balance sheet are always equal.

Assets include two categories: current assets and long-term assets. They are listed in decreasing order of "liquidity," which is the length of time ordinarily needed to convert them into cash. *Current assets* are mainly cash, accounts receivable, and inventories. Only cash represents actual money. Receivables are the amounts owed to the firm. Inventories are the raw materials, work in process, and finished goods available for sale. The receivables and inventories will presumably be converted into cash eventually.

Fixed assets are the real plant and equipment that the firm has built up over the years. They include machinery, buildings, land, and any other valuable and lasting capital that is used in production. They are listed first at their *gross original value,* which is the sum of all the prices paid for the items when they were acquired. There is also the sum of *depreciation* accrued in order to offset the deterioration of the capital. The difference is the net accounting value of the firm's fixed capital, called *net plant and equipment.*

The *claims against these assets* are of two types. First, *liabilities* are amounts of money owed by the firm to its bondholders and to others who have lent money to the firm in loans of varying lengths. Liabilities remain constant except as they are directly paid off or added to by more borrowing. Liabilities impose the cost of interest payments, which must be made if the firm is to remain in business. Failure to meet those payments results in insolvency, which, if continued, may lead to bankruptcy.

Second is *equity* (or net worth) of the firm: assets minus liabilities equals stock-holders' or investors' equity. If the asset values were to decline, that would cause equity to decline, for liabilities remain constant unless changed directly. Therefore, the risk that asset values will decline is borne by the shareholders. If asset values rise, on the other hand, the benefits go to the shareholders.

The accounting value of stockholders' equity arises from two main sources. One is the original money acquired by selling stocks when the firm was created. *Retained earnings* make up the rest of equity. They are simply the sum of all income retained earnings over the years of the firm's existence.

Accounting values for equity represent the owners' stake in the business, but only in accounting terms. *The actual market value of the firm as judged by investors is determined by the daily buying and selling of the firm's stock in the stock market.* The stock's price may fluctuate widely. Often the firm's market value moves broadly in line with the book value of its assets and stockholder equity, but there is no direct tie. Indeed, the challenge for management is to deploy the firm's assets so that their value in use—in generating excess profits—will be much greater than their cost. The extra value can be created by good management, luck, monopoly power, innovation, or simply by inflation.

The accounting values for equity do not show these opportunities. Rather, they merely record the sum of past amounts. Typically the retained earnings will be the largest part of total equity. For example, Procter and Gamble's equity was recently $4.2 billion, of which $3.6 billion was retained earnings from earlier decades.

The firm's aim is to have large and growing profits as a return on stockholders' equity, so that it can both pay dividends to the stockholders and build up the business through investment. The stockholders can benefit either way. The dividends give them an immediate reward. The plowing back of retained earnings will increase the firm's capacity and prospects for future profits. That will, in turn, increase the value of the business and cause the firm's stock to be bid up in the stock market. Therefore, retained earnings can give the owners a capital gain in their stock prices, as opposed to the immediate gain they receive from the direct payment of dividends.

Success indicators: Profitability and stock prices

Profitability is the main index of a private firm's economic performance. The company will naturally publicize its other socially attractive activities, such as the number of jobs it creates, its production of high-quality outputs, its exports, innovations, and so on. But these are all secondary to the firm's main goal: to earn a large and increasing flow of profits for its investors.

Profitability is a matter of degree, not of absolute amounts. The simple total of dollar profits is not enough to show how profitable a firm is. A local lumber company with $1 million in profits in a year may have a higher degree of profitability than the largest oil firm, Exxon, with its yearly total profits of over $3 billion. The reason is that *profit as a percentage of capital* or **rate of return on equity** is the correct measure of profitability, for that shows how well the firm is managing its owner's capital.

Note that profits as a percentage of capital is *not* the same as profits as a percentage of sales or costs. A bookstore's profits on the textbooks it sells, for example, may be only 3 percent of its sales of those books—"a few pennies on the dollar." Suppose, however, that the bookstore has yearly sales that are ten times as large as its capital (its capital is mainly just the building, shelves, and inventory). Then its

3 percent profit margin on *sales* would be a 30 percent return on its *capital*. That would be a high rate of return on the investment, not a low one. So, once again, *always appraise profits as a return on capital.*

The simple formula for profitability is:

$$\text{The rate of return} = \frac{\text{Net income after taxes}}{\text{Capital}}$$

$$= \frac{\text{Total revenue} - \text{Total cost and Taxes}}{\text{Invested capital}}$$

For total invested capital, the usual accounting figure is stockholders' equity. You can easily calculate it for the sample firm's 1982 results in Table 2:

$$\text{The rate of return} = \frac{\$22 \text{ million}}{\$122 \text{ million}}$$

$$= \frac{\$219 \text{ million} - \$178 \text{ million} - \$19 \text{ million}}{\$122 \text{ million}}$$

$$= 18.0 \text{ percent.}$$

This figure is for one year. To judge the firm carefully, you must consider the average profit over some three to five years, so as to even out any odd yearly fluctuations.

Each owner and manager seeks profit rates much higher than the 8 to 10 percent that is the average rate of return. Their nightmare is to run losses. Only by managing production well and keeping costs low and revenues high can the firm's officials produce good profits for the owners.

Stock prices are the other main success indicator for the private firm. Each share of stock offers its owners a chance to get future dividends and capital gains (that is, a rise in the price of the share itself). The firm's managers want to satisfy the investor-owners by making the company prosper, so that (1) dividends will grow and/or (2) the stock price will rise and provide capital gains. The share's price depends on demand and supply in the stock market. And both supply and demand, in turn, depend on what investors think of the company's performance.

Since most large-scale investors are pretty well informed, they act quickly. Therefore, stock prices usually move swiftly and sensitively. If prospects for the company turn better, then more investors will want to buy shares in the company immediatcly to be able to share in future benefits. Since fewer investors will want to sell, the increase in investor demand will cause the stock price to rise without delay. Conversely, a downturn in a company's future prospects will cause investors to sell the stock now, before the price goes down. Yet that will quickly cause the stock's price to fall, for sellers will have increased while buyers will have decreased. The only way to sell the stock is to accept a lower price for it. In either case, investors hoping to act before a price change will, by their very actions, bring about that change immediately.

Accordingly, the market value of a stock largely depends both on the firm's *future* prospects and on its current performance in maximizing profits. There are some other influences also, such as the general level of interest rates and broad shifts in average prices for the entire stock market. *Yet current stock prices are usually a sensitive, quickly adjusting index of investors' judgments about each firm's whole performance, both present and expected.* Stock prices reflect expected future gains. We will show in Chapter 16 how this discounting feature of the stock market tends to apply steady pressure on firms to maintain their efficiency.

Profits are also a signal for investment. When an industry has high profitability, it is a signal that that industry needs more investment. A high rate of profit shows that the value of the firms' output is well above its cost. Therefore, extra output would be worthwhile because

people will pay more than the present level of what it costs to make it. To increase output, one must expand capacity. To expand capacity, one must invest more. High profits are like a green traffic light, signaling more capital to come ahead.

In contrast, financial losses are like a traffic light flashing red, showing a need to reduce investment and to contract capacity. Consumers in the market will not pay enough in sales revenues to cover the cost of the output. Therefore, the output's value is less than its cost. Lower levels of output should be produced, and capacity should shrink. That requires cutting back on investment or even admitting that some of the existing capital has lost its value (in accounting terms, one "writes off" the now-valueless assets). The process of shrinking the amount of capital is logical, since private investors will naturally shun a company that is losing money.

A case study: Starting a new enterprise

To draw together the concepts in this chapter, we will now trace the typical steps involved in starting a new enterprise. We will cast you as the firm's founder.

Choosing what to produce

First the creator of a new firm must perceive an unmet need. The need might be for a new local newspaper, a special hand tool, an electric car, or a housecleaning service. It is wise to avoid crowded markets, where supply is already ample and no firm can currently make high profits. One looks for "new" markets, where the sellers are few and there are good chances for unusually high profit rates. One needs a clear concept of the new good to be offered, a good sense of market realities, skill in organizing, and considerable stamina. You will be competing both against the established firms and with other ambitious people who decide to enter the market after you.

You will need to plan ahead about the product, its inputs, the method of producing it, where to make it, and the customers for it. The plans for costs, prices, and financing must cover at least the first several years of operations, not just the first few months. Estimating conservatively, the investment must offer at least a 15 percent return on capital, plus a premium (5 or 10 percent more) for the extra risk in the business. Otherwise, no banker or investor group will provide finance—a clear sign that the venture will probably fail.

You narrow the choices down to three possibilities: A restaurant featuring wholesome food, set in an uncrowded location, seems to offer a 40 percent return on capital. A fast-food franchise is available, which might yield a 25 percent return. Or you could organize a "House Care" firm, which performs painting, fixing, cleaning, and so on. It would pay a 30 percent return on investment, but at a higher risk. Assessed objectively, the fast-food franchise is too easy to imitate, and house care would be too hard to supervise (absenteeism, arguments over quality of work, etc.). The restaurant venture offers more security and growth, and so you choose it.

Starting

The first requirement is to obtain capital; the second, to organize production. Recall that these are the two basic functions of a firm: to manage assets and to produce. Your request for financing is turned down by numerous bankers and investors, who consider your undertaking too risky. Finally you raise $500,000 from various investors, including relatives. You incorporate the company and issue shares in the business to the investors. The shares are equity capital; the firm will pay dividends on them when it seems best to do so.

You lease the location, rent the restaurant equipment, and remodel the interior. You hire the staff, design the menu, order supplies, and begin advertising. (The determinants of these input decisions—about equipment, workers, food, and other supplies—will be explained in the next chapter.) Your grand opening occurs one year after your original decision to start a new firm.

The pace of activity is slow at first, because consumers take time to adjust to new products at new prices. The restaurant operates below half of its capacity even at peak mealtimes. Because sales revenues are lower than costs, the firm is losing money. Though initial losses were expected, they are now large enough to strain the firm's finances. You increase advertising, improve the services, and offer price discounts. The rate of operations rises, and soon the restaurant is regularly filled. After one year, the venture is still running losses, as Table 3 shows. There are two major problems: (1) daytime costs are high but traffic is low, and (2) overhead costs are high compared to your small space. There is a need to develop daytime sales and to add space. Your choices are now very risky.

At precisely this moment, a local investor offers $1 million if you will issue shares giving him 75 percent of the firm's stock and thus control of the enterprise. The additional funds would cover the expansion, but it would end your control. Instead, you persuade the original backers to provide the expansion funds. The budget is tight but the restaurant is getting established. It earns $150,000 profit during 1982, which after taxes (including an offset of $50,000 for the first-year loss) is a 10 percent return on the $1 million investment.

Table 3 *Yearly results for the new restaurant enterprise*

	1981	1982	1983	1984	1985	1986	1987	1988	1989
Workers	15	28	28	28	28	80	80	80	80
Sales volume ($1000)	300	800	900	850	1050	2500	2800	3200	3200
Costs ($1000)	350	650	630	630	700	1900	2100	2100	2100
Accounting profit ($1000)	−50	150	270	220	350	600	700	1100	1100
New investment ($1000)	500	500	0	0	0	2000	0	0	0
Assets ($1000)	500	1000	1000	1000	1000	3000	3000	3000	3000
Profit (before tax) as a % of investment	−10%	15%	27%	22%	35%	20%	23%	37%	37%
Profit (after tax) as a % of investment	−5%	10%	14%	11%	18%	10%	12%	19%	19%

The restaurant is also profitable during 1983, but in 1984 trouble arises. The staff goes on strike for two weeks, and profits decrease. Officials of a restaurant chain offer to buy the firm for $1,050,000 (that is, at a net 5 percent profit to the investors). You persuade the firm's board to reject the offer. In 1985, the finances recover, and you start two more restaurants in other towns at an additional investment of $2 million. They are completed in 1986, and during 1987–1989, the whole firm (with its three plants) is profitable.

The business is now established, despite the crises of the first years. You worked hard and took great risks, for a modest salary. Congratulations! You have succeeded by choosing an excellent location and an attractive style, by applying business sense and skills, and by enjoying the support of your investors. But in 1989, new competition enters, as similar restaurants are opened nearby. You now assess the prospects. Sales are likely to stabilize at about $3.2 million per year. The yearly after-tax profits are $550,000, which gives a 19 percent return on investment. That flow will probably continue into the future.

The firm is now extremely valuable. The $550,000 yearly profit stream is worth perhaps $5 million in the financial market, because buyers would probably pay a capital value of about ten times the level of new income. Indeed, a national restaurant chain does offer to buy the firm for $6 million. The shareholders would all gain, since they had only put in a total of $3 million. By selling your one third of the firm's shares, you would gain $2 million in capital value. The years of hard work would have made you a millionaire. But by selling, you would become just a branch manager, and you might then be fired or demoted, rather than kept on or eventually promoted to an executive position in the national chain. Of course, you could now found another firm, drawing on your experience and financial connections.

This choice is a fork in the road. It arises for many successful small businesses. Which direction would you take?

Lessons

The case study has illustrated six lessons:

1. A firm's output must have a value to buyers that exceeds the costs of producing it, by an amount large enough to pay for the owners' risks and the managers' efforts. When the production costs continue to exceed the revenue, the firm will, and should, stop producing. Once again, the economic

comparison is between benefit and cost.

2. The new firm usually has a difficult start-up period. Only when it is established may profits be expected to flow in.

3. Competing in the market is risky, especially for new firms. The prospect of extra profits can induce people to take those risks. If the risks are greater than the returns, then the investments should *not* be made.

4. The pursuit of commercial success is responsible for much of the unremitting activity of capitalism. Production, jobs, and innovation are side effects of the drive for profits.

5. Failure is easy, especially when planning, financing, and day-to-day operations are not done with utmost care. To start an "independent" business in the "free enterprise" system is usually to undergo strong financial and market pressures. The range of choice is often small, especially at first.

6. The financial market continually assesses a firm's performance and prospects. Success often brings efforts to take over the firm, with or without the consent of its managers. The market for corporate control, for buying and selling whole companies, operates parallel to all of the markets for goods and services.

We will return to this case study occasionally in the next several chapters.

Summary

1. Small and medium-sized enterprises perform most U.S. economic activity. Large firms are important but are concentrated in a few sectors.

2. The firm is the basic unit of production and supply. Each firm has two main functions: It owns and manages assets, and it produces outputs from inputs. Inputs involve various kinds of costs. The outputs are sold at market prices, bringing in sales revenue. Profit (if any) is the excess of revenues over costs.

3. The rate of profit on invested capital shows how profitable the firm is.

4. Sales revenues and all costs are shown in the firm's income statement. Costs include both depreciation of the firm's capital and interest payments. Profits may be paid out to shareholders in dividends or reinvested in the firm.

5. The balance sheet shows the firm's assets and claims on those assets; their totals always equal each other. Assets are current and fixed. Claims on assets include debt and stockholders' equity.

Key concepts

Private Enterprise
Inputs
Outputs
Total cost
Total revenue
Net income (profit)
Production processes
Income statement
Balance sheet
Dividends
Retained earnings
Assets
Claims against assets
Liabilities

Equity

Profitability: rate of return on equity

Questions for review

1. Why do so many new businesses fail?
2. Why has ownership increasingly become divorced from the control of U.S. corporations? What are some possible effects of this situation?
3. Explain why a firm's accounting values for equity can be different from its actual market value.
4. Firm A earned $3 million in profit last year; firm B earned $1.5 million in profit. Is firm A therefore more profitable than firm B?

8

Supply:
The Nature of Costs

As you read and study this chapter, you will learn:

▶ basic concepts of technology, opportunity cost and profit

▶ the analysis of productivity and costs in the short run, including the law of diminishing returns

▶ the analysis of long-run productivity and costs

In 1980, there was a spectacular contrast between AT&T, the telephone company, and Chrysler Corporation, the automobile producer. AT&T earned $6,079,000,000 in profits after taxes, while Chrysler lost $1,709,700,000. AT&T was resoundingly prosperous; Chrysler was on the verge of corporate death.

To recover, Chrysler mounted a promotional blitz to increase demand for its cars. But its most direct and desperate actions were internal, as it wielded the knife to cut its costs. Plants were closed, staff was pruned, and production workers were laid off. The surgery was painful but necessary.

Indeed, keeping costs down is every competitive firm's main economic task. Managers will drive their engineering staff to the breaking point to save half a cent on the cost of a mass-produced item, since half a cent may be the difference between a profit and a loss. No firm that wants to succeed in any industry can afford for long to ignore opportunities to reduce its costs. Chrysler's agonies are merely an extreme case of this universal problem.

147

This chapter is devoted to the study of costs from the economist's point of view. Its main function is to provide the underpinnings of the theory of supply. Its three main sections are devoted to basic concepts, cost variations in the short run, and the determination of cost in the long run.

Basic concepts: Technology, opportunity cost, and economic profit

Technology

Technology is the starting point, the bedrock of cost. It is the *state of the art*, the knowledge about the best techniques of production. In each industry, the current technology defines the firm's alternative choices in using inputs to produce outputs. By choosing the best combinations of inputs, the firm can minimize its costs. Technology exists in every age, but it also evolves. For example, the technology for modern computers and jet aircraft did not exist in 1930, but it did in 1960. Indeed, modern industry differs radically from 19th-century industry, because technology has advanced so far in so many industries.

Technology usually offers a wide variety of choices. Whether you bake bread, smelt iron, or weave cloth, there are many methods of production to choose among. To take a simple case, suppose that a firm wants to machine 5,000 metal parts. It may be able to do this with 10 people and 5 large machines, or 15 people and 12 small machines, or 40 people and 40 hand tools. Which method should it choose?

One important step toward maximizing profits is to make sure that a given level of output is being produced at the lowest possible cost—that is, with the best possible mix of inputs. A firm can hardly be maximizing its profit by producing 2,000 units at $5 per unit if those 2,000 units could be produced at $3 per unit.

Thus, any profit-maximizing firm must choose the technology that is the *least-cost* or *economically efficient* method of production for its level of output.

How does a firm find this least-cost or most efficient technology? It must consider both the physical technology of combining inputs (reflecting engineering relations and physical processes) and the relative prices of inputs (which reflect their relative scarcities). At each point in time, with existing technology and input prices, there is a method of production that minimizes costs for a given level of output.

Reasons for variety While the criterion for choosing the most economically efficient technology is straightforward, the process of choice is not. Even firms that produce the same output may choose different technologies or mixes of inputs. For example, a firm's location may influence its costs and therefore input choices. One firm may be located in an area of cheap labor, so it chooses a labor-intensive method of production.* Another firm may be near a low-cost ore deposit, so it chooses a technology that makes much use of ore. A third may have poor access to transportation, so it uses inputs that are close to the plant.

Technological choices also differ because human judgments about the least-cost method of production may differ. After all, technology involves complex choices with uncertain outcomes. One manager may expect labor costs to rise rapidly compared to the price of machinery, so he may choose a technology involving relatively more capital and less labor. By contrast, because another manager

*When a technology uses an input in unusually high proportions, it is expressed as "intensive." Thus, a labor-intensive method uses a high proportion of labor compared to other inputs—for example, the hand picking of farm crops. A capital-intensive method would use large machines operated by only a few people.

may expect capital costs to rise more rapidly, she might choose a technology involving relatively more labor and less capital. To complicate matters further, the known technology or state of the art is constantly changing. The best choice this year may be outdated next year or the year after.

If all of these complications were discussed now, you would be swamped with detailed ifs, buts, and howevers. Instead, it makes sense to begin the analysis simply, concentrating on the most basic principles of cost and supply. Technology is assumed to be fixed, so that definite choices can be made. This is called *static* analysis, and it allows a clearer look at input choices, productivity, and costs at a given time. The best technology is also assumed to be well known, and not uncertain. With these conditions, economic tools can be applied more clearly to show how a firm chooses its inputs. Of course, once you have grasped the basic principles, you can apply them to increasingly complicated situations. For example, a later chapter deals with dynamic issues, involving changes in technology and innovation.

Opportunity cost

You already know that one goal of a firm is to produce its level of output at the lowest cost possible. But what do economists mean by *cost?* Your immediate response might be the dollars that the firm pays out or owes to others. That is certainly important, but it is only part of cost. To see why, start with a very general definition of cost as *the value of inputs used in the process of production.* If you think back to Chapter 2, you will remember that value comes from scarcity. An input has value, then, because it is scarce—if you use the input to produce one good, it is not available to produce something else. An economist, therefore, measures cost by using the concept of *foregone alternatives.* The cost of taking one action is measured in terms of what was given up—in terms of the most highly valued alternative that is sacrificed. And the cost of producing one good measured in terms of foregone alternatives is what could have been produced instead. **When cost is calculated by using this idea of foregone alternatives, it is called *economic cost* or *opportunity cost.***

The concept of economic cost applies to far more than just production. Every action that you take involves an opportunity cost. For example, what is the opportunity cost to you of attending an economics class? Well, first consider all of the alternatives. What could you have done instead? You might have slept an extra hour, studied for another course, listened to a record, jogged, or worked at a part-time job. From your list, pick the most valuable alternative to attending the economics class. That is the opportunity cost of going to class. For you, the opportunity cost might be that foregone hour of sleep. For a classmate, it might be an extra hour studying history. What are you doing Saturday evening? Going to a party or a movie? Sleeping? Studying? Whatever you decide, try to calculate the opportunity cost involved.

Opportunity cost is forward looking, based on a range of choices. The firm compares the alternatives before choosing one of them. The cost of the best alternative is the value that the next best alternative would give. Once the choice is made, the economic content is over, the cost is fixed, and events can then run their course. At the end of the year, actual costs are recorded and rendered in the accounts. In the restaurant example in the last chapter, the decision to expand during 1982 involves complex comparisons of values for the $500,000 of added investment. By 1982, that investment was made: It had become a fixed cost, *not* an opportunity cost.

The accounting costs are backward looking and rigidly specific. They are merely the surface numerical outcome of the economic choices that were made earlier. One must keep opportunity cost and accounting cost in separate mental boxes. The meaning of opportunity cost is like a secret password of microeconomics. Economists know it precisely; most other people don't. Rational firms use its content, but they often don't state or apply the concept explicitly.

The economic cost or opportunity cost of production must include a value for all scarce inputs used. That would include all inputs that have an alternative use. Many inputs are bought or hired by a firm. If the market is working properly, the price paid for the input will reflect its value. Part of the cost of the firm can be calculated by simply adding up the dollars paid out by the firm. These are the **direct costs,** or **explicit costs,** or **accounting costs** of the firm. Direct costs include the purchase of raw materials, equipment, wages paid to hired employees, rent, interest, and utilities.

But think of all the scarce inputs that a firm uses, for which there are no market transactions. For example, suppose that you own your own store and put a lot of your own time and money into the business. Certainly your time and money are scarce inputs, since they have many alternative uses. If a value for them is not included in your firm's costs, then the true cost of production is not being given. But how do you estimate a value for your time and money? And what about the cost to your firm of other inputs for which there is no market transaction, such as the use of machinery, depreciation, or the use of a patent, formula, or brand name that you could have sold instead of using yourself?

Remember that value comes from foregone alternatives. Why not use this concept to estimate a value for the scarce inputs for which there is no market transaction? Simply *impute or estimate* a value for these inputs equal to the return they would get in their best or highest-paying alternative use. This measure can be called **imputed cost** or **implicit cost.** For example, you might believe that the highest-paying alternative to running your own store would be to manage a branch of a chain store for $49,000 a year. The $49,000 figure, then, is your best estimate of the value of your time. Regardless of what salary you actually assign to yourself, the salary figure entered into the costs of operating your store should be $49,000.

The same procedure can be used for all other scarce inputs that are not bought or hired. Suppose that the best alternative investment of your money would have yielded a return of 15 percent. The cost of investing $20,000 in your business, then, is $20,000 × 15 percent or $3,000 in foregone interest.

Since economic cost includes both accounting costs and an estimate of the value of all inputs that are not included in accounting costs, it comes much closer to giving the true value of the resources used in the process of production.

Sunk costs Economists also stress **sunk costs** as a prime instance where opportunity costs differ from accounting costs. Any fixed cost that has already been incurred is a sunk cost. It is irretrievably gone, even if it is now seen as a mistake.

By definition, *once a cost is fixed, it should be forgotten,* and not be allowed to influence what is done next. The invariable economic maxim is: *Bygones are bygones.* Always ignore sunk costs. In plain English: Don't throw good money after bad. Look ahead in your economic decisions, not backward. The box headed "Calculations of Opportunity Cost" illustrates several cases of sunk costs.

Calculations of Opportunity Cost

A. Examples of Commercial Decisions

A1. Apex Products, Inc., bought a grinding mill in 1950 for $10 million, and it has depreciated the full value of the mill since then. Yet the mill is in good shape and could be sold for $15 million at current prices. Apex's use of the mill has an accounting cost of zero. The *opportunity cost* to Apex of using the mill, rather than selling it, is $15 million.

A2. A firm keeps a cash balance of $2 million to meet unexpected difficulties that may arise. It could get a 10 percent return on bonds. The *opportunity cost* of the emergency fund is $200,000 per year ($2 million times 10 percent). The accounting cost of keeping the funds is zero.

A3. A chemical factory releases toxic wastes into a nearby river. This method of waste disposal does not cost the firm itself anything. The cost of the chemicals that the firm produces—its output, in other words—is $8 per pound. But cities downstream must pay $2 million to purify the water. This works out to $2 per pound of the chemical sold. So the *total opportunity* cost of the chemical is $10 per pound, not just the $8 private cost to the firm.

B. Examples of Sunk Costs

B1. *A Bad Course.* You work hard at a calculus course for four weeks. But you can't get the knack of all those derivatives, and meanwhile your career interests change toward graphic arts. Should you struggle on in calculus to justify the work you have already put into it? No, the time and effort are a *sunk cost*.

B2. *Football Tickets.* Iowaska University builds a giant football stadium seating 100,000 fans, but then its football program flops and only 20,000 people come to each game. Should it charge them $15 for each ticket, enough to cover all costs, including the investment cost of the stadium, or $3 to cover just the operating costs? The correct answer is $3, for most of the investment cost for the now-too-large stadium is *sunk cost*.

B3. *Value of a Car.* Mervin Piccolo buys a new sedan for $9,800, but his wife declares it unsafe and tells him to sell it. He tries to sell it for $9,750, but $7,300 is the highest offer he gets. The $2,500 drop in value (from $9,800 to $7,300) occurred when he drove from the dealer's lot onto the street, changing the new car into a used car. The $2,500 is a *sunk cost*.

Economic profit

Economists define profit just as anyone else would: Profit = Revenue minus Cost. Given this definition, most people think of profits as the money left over after all the bills are paid. They are really thinking of revenue minus only direct costs. When costs are defined as economic costs, then profit has a different meaning. Since the cost figure is calculated on the basis of foregone alternatives, the profit figure also depends on the value of alternatives. ***Economic profit*** doesn't just indicate how much money is left over after all the bills are paid. It tells you how a firm is doing, compared to the best alternative use of its resources. Consider the three possible profit situations:

Economic profits equal to zero If economic profit equals zero, revenue must equal direct plus imputed costs. The firm must be covering its dollar costs and making a return equal to the return it could earn in the highest-paying alternative use of its resources. Knowing this, the firm has no incentive to transfer its resources to another line of production, since it is already making as much as it could in its highest-paying alternative. If a firm's economic profits equal zero, it is making a *normal return,* a return just high enough to keep it in its present line of production. A normal return does not imply that a firm will not try to do better. It simply implies that the firm recognizes that, given its resources and present market conditions, it cannot do better by transferring resources.

Economic profits equal to zero may strike you as undesirable. You are used to thinking of profits as the revenue remaining after the bills are paid. But economic profits are calculated net of *both* the amount needed to pay the bills (direct costs) *and* the amount that could be earned on the firm's own resources (imputed costs). In other words, the accountant's concept of profits includes several imputed costs, whereas the economist's definition of profits includes both the direct costs recognized by accountants and all the imputed costs. To the economist, profit is a return over and above all the costs that must be covered to keep the firm operating indefinitely.

Economic profits less than zero If economic profits are less than zero, revenue is less than the sum of direct and imputed costs. The firm *may* be able to pay its bills, if revenue is at least as great as direct costs. But the firm's return is obviously lower than it would be if it were making its best alternative use of resources. In this case, the firm is not making enough to keep it in its present line of production; it could do better by transferring its resources.

Economic profits greater than zero If economic profits are greater than zero, revenue must be greater than the sum of direct and imputed costs. The firm, then, must be earning a higher return than it could in the highest-paying alternative use of its resources. By transferring its resources to another use, the firm could only do worse. It will therefore stay in its present line of production.

You can see that economic profit is a much deeper concept than simply the dollars left over at the end of the period. Such an economic calculation of profits helps the firm to decide if its resources are being put to the best or most profitable use. In other words, economic profit is the criterion the firm should use in deciding whether to continue in its present business or to transfer its resources to another use.

To illustrate, Jerry and Mary Molnar quit their office jobs as accountants, each at $14,000 per year, for the excitement and independence of running their own sporting goods store, the Fast Track. They both work ten-hour days, seven days a week. After three years, the shop has a steady clientele, $300,000 in sales revenue, and $280,000 in operating costs (including nominal salaries of $7,000 each drawn by Mary and Jerry). They pay $15,000 in interest on the shop's loans and reinvest the remaining $5,000. Their account shows a gain of $5,000. At least they are making some profit.

Or are they? The Molnars could have earned at least $28,000 per year in regular daytime jobs, plus perhaps another $10,000 in spare-time tax accounting (up to their present 70 hours of work per week). The true cost of their labor is therefore $38,000, not $14,000. Because of the $24,000 undervaluation of their own time, they are losing $19,000, not gaining $5,000. Seen another way, they are paying $19,000 a year to have the excitement and independence of running their own business.

Understanding the principles by which a firm should calculate its costs and profits is only one step, although an important one, toward understanding a firm's costs. Now that you have a clearer understanding of exactly what costs are and how they are calculated, it is time to examine the behavior of costs.

To calculate a firm's costs, you really need two pieces of information. First, you must know how much of each input the firm needs to buy to produce its output. Second, you must know what prices it must pay for the inputs it buys, and what prices it should impute to the inputs it owns. By multiplying the input quantities by input prices, you can determine a firm's costs. But how do you know how many inputs the firm will need to buy to produce its output? Clearly, to understand costs, you must first understand the relation between input and output.

Productivity and costs in the short run

Short run and long run

In discussing productivity and cost, economists distinguish between the *short run* and the *long run* because different forces influence productivity, and therefore costs, in the short and long run.

The **short run** is a period of time sufficiently brief so that at least one input cannot be varied in quantity. In the short run, there are both *variable inputs*, whose quantity can be altered, and fixed inputs, whose quantity cannot. For some firms, the short run may be very short indeed: an hour, day, or month. For other firms, such as those in the lumber or mining industry, the short run may last for many years.

The **long run** is enough time, so that all inputs can be varied in quantity. There are no fixed inputs in the long run.

Labor and raw materials are often used as variable inputs in examples, since their quantities can often be fairly easily adjusted. Capital is used to represent the fixed input, since the quantity of buildings and specialized machinery usually takes the longest to adjust. Throughout this chapter, discussions of production and cost are presented in examples using only two inputs. Once you are comfortable with two-input analysis, you will be able to branch out to more complicated situations involving several variables. (And many of you may find the two-input examples challenging enough.) In the short-run analysis presented next, labor will represent the variable input and capital the fixed input.

Productivity in the short run

Productivity simply refers to how much output a firm can get from its inputs. The more productive inputs are, the more output they can produce. Understanding how output changes when inputs are varied, which means understanding how productivity of inputs varies, is crucial for understanding how costs change as output is varied. The reason is that costs of production are largely determined by the number of inputs a firm needs to buy to produce output.

Output or *product* (the terms are used interchangeably) can be viewed in different ways:

✶ **Total product** (TP) refers to total output per unit of time (hour, day, week, year, etc.). It is also called "quantity of output" and "Q."

✶**Average product** (AP) is an output/input ratio, measuring output per unit of some input. In condensed form, Average product = $\dfrac{\text{Total product}}{\text{Quantity of input}}$. Suppose that $TP = 50$, while quantity of input $= 10$. The resulting AP of 50/10 $= 5$ would mean that, on average, 1 unit of input will produce 5 units of output. Another way of stating this output/input ratio of 5 would be that, *on average,* 1 unit of output is produced with 1/5 unit of input. Either way of viewing AP involves the same output-input ratio of 5/1.

✶ **Marginal product** (MP) measures the change in total product resulting from a one-unit change in input. In condensed form, Marginal product = $\dfrac{\Delta \text{ Total product}}{\Delta \text{ Quantity of input}}$, where Δ stands for a small specific change in amount. An MP of 3 would mean that an addi-

tional 3 units of output could be produced by adding 1 unit of input. Another way of viewing an MP of 3 would be that an additional unit of output could be produced with an additional 1/3 unit of input. Either way of viewing MP involves the same Δ output/Δ input ratio of 3/1.

Total, average, and marginal products are just different ways of viewing the same output/input relations. After you work your way through Table 1 and Figure 1, the relationships among these three product measures should be fairly clear to you.

Start with Table 1. The first two columns indicate how many units of the two inputs are used. Column 1 shows that capital is being held constant at 10 units. You know at once that this is a short-run analysis, since there is a constant or fixed input. Labor is the variable input, as column 2 shows, changing from 0 to 10 units. Given the amounts of inputs used, you can calculate total product or output if you know the *production function.*

The **production function** is the underlying technology, which relates inputs to

Table 1 *Calculations of total, average, and marginal product*

1 Quantity of Capital	2 Quantity of Labor	3 Total Product	4 Average Product	5 Marginal Product
(Q_k)	(Q_L)	(TP, Q)	(TP/Q_L)	$(\Delta TP/\Delta Q_L)$
10	0	0	0	
10	1	9	9	9
10	2	32	16	23
10	3	63	21	31
10	4	96	24	33
10	5	125	25	31
10	6	144	24	19
10	7	147	21	3
10	8	128	16	−19
10	9	81	9	−47
10	10	0	0	−81

Short-run production function:

$y = 10x^2 - x^3$ where y = output and x = quantity of labor.

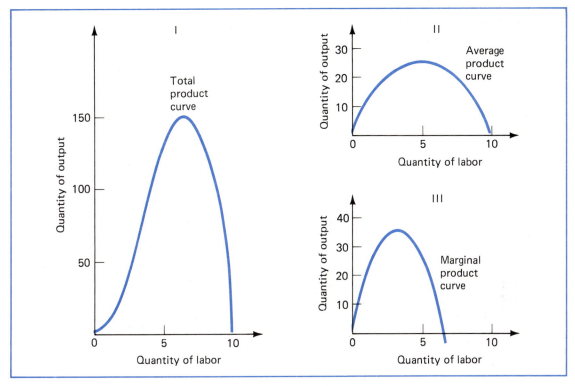

Figure 1   Graphs of total, average, and marginal products from Table 1

output. It is often stated as a mathematical equation. Here you are given a production function of the form $y = 10x^2 - x^3$, where y is total product or output and x stands for the variable input labor. The production function here assumes that capital is held constant at 10 units. If the amount of capital were changed, the production function, and therefore all of the total, average, and marginal figures shown in the table, would have to be recalculated. With the production function and input quantities, you should be able to calculate the total product that would result from the use of different amounts of labor. Try your hand (or, better yet, your hand calculator) at computing total product, and check your answers against those in the table. The total product figures are graphed in Figure 1, Panel I. You can see from the numbers and the graph that total product rises, reaches

a maximum, and begins to decline as more labor is added to the fixed amount of capital.

Once you have calculated total product, average and marginal product are easy to arrive at. All the information you really need are total product and quantity of inputs. Dividing total product by the quantity of the variable input will give you the output/input ratio, or average product. This is calculated in column 4 of Table 1 and graphed in Panel II of Figure 1. Average product will rise, reach a maximum, and then decline as more labor is added to the fixed amount of capital. Marginal product is the change in total product resulting from each one-unit increase in the amount of labor, as shown in column 5 of Table 1 and graphed in Panel III of Figure 1. Just like the average product curve, marginal product will increase, reach a maximum, and then decrease as more labor is used relative to capital.

Once you have grasped the behavior of each individual product curve, you are ready to examine the relations among them. These show up in the relations among the numbers in columns 3, 4, and 5 in Table 1, and are shown graphically in Figure 2.

First think about the relation between TP and MP. The slope of any curve is the change in the vertical/change in the horizontal. The slope of the TP curve must, therefore, be (Δ in output)/(Δ in input). That is the definition of MP. The relation between TP and MP is thus simple: MP is the slope of the total product curve. As long as MP is positive, total product will rise. If marginal product is positive but falling, total product will still increase, but at a slower rate. **When marginal product is zero—as at Point *A*—total product will be at a maximum; and when marginal product is negative, total product will fall.**

All of this may seem obvious to you, but be cautious. Most people are used to thinking about totals and averages, but not marginal figures. People are simply not used to thinking "at the margin," or in terms of small changes. Many of you may be uncomfortable with the idea that total product can rise even though marginal product is falling. That is because you are saying marginal, but thinking total. Remember that marginal product measures the rate of change of output. As long as that change is positive, total product must rise.

Average product (AP) is graphically different from marginal product. It is the slope of a straight line or ray from the origin to a point on TP, as at Point *A* in Figure 2. The ray's slope is the total output divided by the quantity of input, which gives 147/7 = 21 at that point. That slope contrasts with the zero slope of the TP curve itself at Point *A*. Note that the steep-

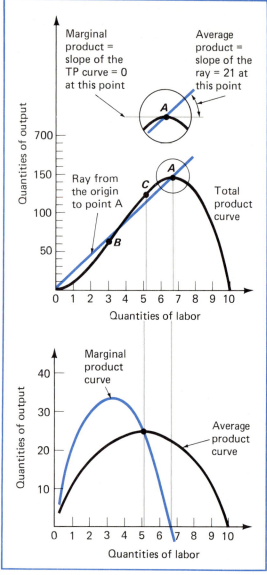

Figure 2   Relationships among the product curves

Total product and marginal product: Marginal product (ΔQ output/ΔQ input) is the slope of the TP curve. As long as MP is positive, TP will rise. Where MP is 0, TP is at a maximum. This is shown by Point *A*. Where MP is negative, TP is falling. MP will reach a maximum (Point *B*) where the slope of the TP curve is steepest.

Total product and average product: AP is at its maximum at the point where a straight line drawn from the origin is tangent to the TP curve (Point *C*).

Average product and marginal product: If AP is rising, the MP must be above it. If AP is falling, MP must be below it. If AP = MP, AP is at a maximum.

est ray to TP would be at Point *B*. That is therefore the maximum value of AP, as shown in the graph below. The two different slopes—of tangents and rays—embody the conceptual difference between marginal and average product.

Marginals and averages The relation between the marginal and average product curves is especially interesting. The relation between any marginal and average figures has certain simple mathematical properties. As an illustration, think of the one marginal-average relation with which you are probably all too familiar: Your grade point average or GPA and your marginal or additional grades. If you take one course and the marginal or additional grade is above your average, your average rises. If you take another course and the marginal or additional grade for that course is lower than your average, your average falls.

This marginal-average relation is clearly seen by comparing the figures in columns 4 and 5 of Table 1, or by examining the graph of these figures in Figure 2. If AP is rising, the MP must be above AP, pulling it up. The MP itself may be rising or falling. What is important is that it is above the average product. If AP is falling, the MP must be below it, pulling it down. What is significant about the point where $MP = AP$? Up to that point, MP was above AP, so AP was rising. After that point, MP falls below AP, so AP declines. If AP rises up to the $AP = MP$ point and declines thereafter, then the point where $AP = MP$ must be the point where AP is a maximum.

The law of diminishing marginal returns
Now that you have had a chance to examine total, average, and marginal products both in numbers and in graphs based on these numbers, the meaning of these product concepts and the relationships among them should be a little clearer to you. But by this time, many of you probably want to know if the numbers in Table 1 were chosen with any purpose in mind. Must AP and MP always rise and then fall? Or could MP and AP first decline and then increase? In other words, is there any reason for the total, average, and marginal curves to be drawn the way they are? As you doubtless suspect, the numbers in Table 1 were carefully chosen to illustrate the expected shape of the product curves. The explanation for these shapes comes from the *law of diminishing marginal returns.*

The law of diminishing marginal returns states that as the quantity of one input is increased, while the quantity of another input is held constant, a point will be reached beyond which additional (marginal) units of input will add less and less to output. In other words, with one fixed and one variable input, a point will be reached beyond which MP must decline, eventually falling below the average. The marginal product curve and therefore the average product curve must have a declining portion. They may increase at first and then decline, as shown in Figure 1, or they may begin to decline from the start, but they must decline at some point.

The law of diminishing marginal returns refers specifically to a situation in which one input is held constant. Therefore, the law of diminishing marginal returns can refer only to *short-run* analysis.

Why does the principle of diminishing marginal returns operate? The answer comes from the changing proportion of inputs. Suppose capital is constant. Now the firm begins to add units of labor. At first, by adding more of the variable input, it finds that it can organize inputs more efficiently, through division of labor or specialization. Each additional unit of input, then, causes output to increase by more than the previous unit. Past some point, however, there may be no more opportunities for specialization. Each unit of labor

Table 2   Effects of additional workers on total, average, and marginal number of meals served

Number of Workers on	Number of Meals That Can Be Served Each Evening	Number of Meals per Worker	Increase in Number of Meals from the Addition of One More Worker
Q Labor	Total Product	Average Product	Marginal Product
0	—	—	
			20
1	20	20.0	
			15
2	35	17.5	
			10
3	45	15.0	
			5
4	50	12.5	

also has less and less capital with which to work. Total product will still increase, but it will increase more slowly with each additional unit of input adding less to output than the units before it.

Consider, for example, the small restaurant that was the case study in the last chapter. Once it is operating, the fixed inputs would be the space bought or rented and the built-in equipment, such as stoves or ovens. The variable inputs would be food, supplies, and labor. Now suppose that when you first open your restaurant you are the only worker. You have to wait on tables, buy food, cook, wash dishes, clean up, figure out bills, and work the cash register. You find that you can serve 20 customers a night.

You decide to hire some help. Now that there are two of you, you can divide up tasks. You do the cooking and cleaning up, while your help waits on tables and works the cash register. With two of you working, you can serve 35 meals a night. (Try calculating the average and marginal product associated with the hiring of the second worker, and check your answers against the figures in Table 2.) A third worker allows you to specialize even further. You concentrate on cooking, another worker clears tables and cleans, while the third worker waits on tables and works the cash register. All of you, by organizing more efficiently, can serve 45 meals a night.

A fourth worker allows even more specialization, and you can now handle 50 meals a night. Notice, though, that while the total meals you can serve has increased, the addition of the fourth worker caused output to rise by less than the addition of previous workers had. Output gains from adding workers are still there, but they are smaller. Should the fourth worker have been added? You really can't tell by looking at marginal product alone. You would need to weigh the increase in cost from hiring the worker against the increase in revenue from serving the additional meals. At any rate, the returns from adding workers clearly diminish in this example.

By now, you know a great deal about productivity in the short run. You have been introduced to three different ways of viewing the relations between output and inputs: total, average, and marginal product. You have seen how to calculate these products, how they behave, and why they behave the way they do. Cost curves may seem to have been left far behind. But as you will quickly see, understanding product curves is absolutely essential to understanding cost curves.

Costs in the short run

Since short-run costs are so closely related to short-run productivity, it is not surprising that for each measure of short-run productivity there is a cost counterpart. Just as there are fixed and variable inputs, there are fixed and variable costs. Just as there are total, average, and marginal measures of productivity, there are total, average, and marginal measures of costs. In this section, the cost measures are defined, and their relation to productivity is spelled out.

The distinction between fixed and variable costs parallels the distinction between fixed and variable inputs. *Fixed costs are the costs associated with fixed inputs, which do not vary with the level of output.* Examples of fixed costs would be rent or payments on bank loans. If a firm decides to shut down and produce nothing, its rent and loan obligations will continue for the life of the lease or the loan agreement. These fixed costs must still be paid even if output drops to zero. Besides the fixed costs that must be paid out of pocket, there are imputed fixed costs of using the firm's resources in the current line of production rather than in an alternative. *Var-*

iable costs **vary with the level of output.** You can probably think of many examples of variable costs, such as wages for production-line workers and payments for energy and raw materials. These costs vary with output, and if output drops to zero, so will the variable costs.

Besides the distinction between fixed and variable costs, you can also divide costs into categories that parallel the productivity measures: total, average, and marginal cost. As you work through the short-run cost concepts, check your understanding of them by examining Table 3. The first five columns of the table, giving input quantities and total, average, and marginal products, are reproduced from Table 1. Given this information, along with the price per unit of the fixed and variable input, all of the short-run costs can be calculated. The cost figures are graphed in Figure 3.

Total cost (TC) refers to the total cost of production. It is the sum of both fixed and variable costs:

Table 3 *Calculation of short-run product and cost figures*

1	2	3	4	5	6	7	8	9	10	11	12
Quantity of Capital (Q_K)	Quantity of Labor (Q_L)	Total Product (TP)	Average Product (TP/Q_L)	Marginal Product (Δ TP/ΔQ_L)	Total Fixed Cost (TFC)	Total Variable Cost (TVC)	Total Cost (TC = TFC + TVC)	Average Fixed Cost (AFC = TFC/TP)	Average Variable Cost (AVC = TVC/TP)	Average Total Cost (ATC = TC/TP)	Marginal Cost (ΔTC/MP)
10	0	0	0		50	0	50				
10	1	9	9	9	50	20	70	5.55	2.22	7.77	
10	2	32	16	23	50	40	90	1.56	1.25	2.28	2.22
10	3	63	21	31	50	60	110	.79	.95	1.75	.86
10	4	96	24	33	50	80	130	.52	.83	1.35	.64
10	5	125	25	29	50	100	150	.40	.80	1.20	.60
10	6	144	24	19	50	120	170	.35	.83	1.18	.68
10	6.67	148	22.1	4	50	133.4	183.4	.34	.90	1.24	1.05
10	7	147	21	−1	50						5.00
10	8	128	16	−19	50						
10	9	81	9	−47	50						
10	10	0	0	−81	50						

Note: Maximum output is reached at Q_L = 6.67. Costs are calculated with price of capital = 10, price of labor = 20.

Total cost = Total fixed cost
+ Total variable cost
$$TC = TFC + TVC.$$

Total fixed cost (TFC) does not vary with output. It is equal to the number of units of the fixed input used multiplied by the price per unit of the fixed input. Since TFC is a constant number, it is graphed as a horizontal line.

Total variable cost (TVC) equals the number of units of the variable input used multiplied by the price per unit of the variable input. TVC increases as output increases, with the rate of increase depending on the productivity of the inputs. When inputs are increasingly productive and total product is rising most rapidly, TVC will be rising relatively slowly. This makes sense because when inputs are increasingly productive, increases in output can be sustained with smaller additional purchases of inputs, and therefore smaller increases in costs.

Columns 6, 7, and 8 in Table 3 show the calculations of TFC, TVC, and TC. Working with the data on input quantities and input prices, try to calculate the total costs yourself, and check your answers against those in the table. The total cost figures from the table are graphed in Panel I of Figure 3. If the relationship between output and total cost is well understood, it is also easier to grasp the relationship between output and both average and marginal costs. **Average total cost** (ATC) is simply total cost divided by output, or:

$$\text{Average total cost} = \frac{\text{Total cost}}{\text{Quantity of output}}.$$

But to see how average total cost changes as output changes, it is helpful right from the start to express it as the sum of average fixed cost and average variable cost, or $ATC = AFC + AVC$:

$$\text{Average fixed cost} = \frac{\text{Total fixed cost}}{\text{Quantity of output}}.$$

Since total fixed cost is a constant number, as the quantity of output increases, fixed cost *per unit* of output, or average fixed cost, must fall. To check this, examine column 9 of Table 3 and Panel II of Figure 3.

Average variable cost is total variable cost per unit of output, or:

$$\text{Average variable cost} = \frac{\text{Total variable cost}}{\text{Quantity of output}}.$$

Since total variable cost equals the number of units of the variable input purchases multiplied by the cost for each unit of input, the expression for average variable cost can be written as:

Average variable cost =

$$\frac{\text{Quantity of the variable input} \times \text{Price per unit of the variable input}}{\text{Quantity of output}}.$$

Forget for a minute about the input price in this expression and concentrate on the remaining quantity expressions: $\frac{\text{Quantity of variable input}}{\text{Quantity of output}}$. Since this ratio is just the average product of the input turned upside down, the expression for AVC can be written as:

Average variable cost

$$= \frac{\text{Price per unit of variable input}}{\text{Average product of the variable input}}.$$

Now you can clearly see that AVC depends on both price per unit of the variable input and on the average product of the variable input. Specifically, AVC will vary directly with the price of the input and inversely with the average product. This makes perfectly good sense. Obviously, higher input prices mean higher production costs. As input prices rise, the whole AVC curve shifts up, and as input prices fall, the AVC curve shifts down.

Higher productivity should also mean lower cost. Average product, after all, indicates how much input is needed per unit

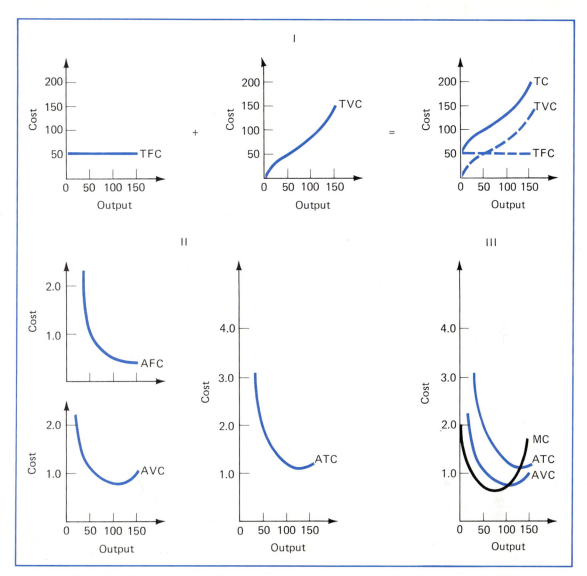

Figure 3   Graphing the Short-Run Cost Curves

Panel I: Total fixed cost is constant, regardless of output. (L) Total variable cost increases with output, at a rate that reflects the changing productivity of input (center). Total cost is the vertical sum of fixed and variable costs (R). Panel II: Average fixed cost falls as output increases (top). Average variable cost falls, then rises, as output rises (bottom). Average total cost is the sum of AFC and ATC. It also falls and then rises (R).

of output. As average product rises, less input is needed per unit of output. Since less input is being bought per unit of output, average costs will be lower. A decrease in AP indicates that more input is needed per unit of output, and since more input is being bought, average variable costs will rise.

The behavior of AVC, then, really depends on the behavior of AP. You already know from the law of diminishing marginal returns that AP may rise and reach a maximum, but then must fall. As AP rises, AVC will fall. When AP falls, AVC will rise. And when AP is at a maximum, AVC will be at a minimum. The relation between AP and AVC should be apparent from comparing columns 4 and 10 in Table 3 and by studying Figure 3.

Panel II of Figure 3 shows how ATC is derived by adding up AVC and AFC. Since AFC gets smaller as the overhead fixed cost is spread over more units of output, the gap between ATC and AVC narrows as output goes up.

Marginal Cost Besides looking at cost per unit of output, it can also be useful to think about the change in cost from producing an additional unit of output. This measure is called *marginal cost.* Marginal cost is concerned only with variable cost, since total fixed costs do not vary with output:

$$\text{Marginal cost} = \frac{\Delta \text{ Total variable cost}}{\Delta \text{ Quantity of output}}.$$

Since the change in total variable cost equals change in quantity of input multiplied by the price per unit of input, the expression can be written as:

Marginal cost =

$$\frac{(\Delta \text{ Quantity of input}) \times (\text{Price per unit of input})}{\Delta \text{ Quantity of output}}.$$

Again, ignore the input price for a moment and concentrate on the quantity expressions. The change in the quantity of the variable input divided by the resulting change in output is just marginal product turned upside down. Thus, we can proceed through the following several steps:

$$\text{Marginal cost} = \frac{\Delta \ Q \text{ input}}{\Delta \ Q \text{ output}} \times \text{Price per unit of input.}$$

Since

$$\frac{\Delta \ Q \text{ output}}{\Delta \ Q \text{ input}} = MP,$$

$$\frac{1}{MP} = \frac{\Delta \ Q \text{ input}}{\Delta \ Q \text{ output}}.$$

Then we can insert $\frac{1}{MP}$ in the earlier equation, thus:

$$\text{Marginal cost} = \frac{1}{MP} \times \text{Price per unit of input}$$

$$\text{Marginal cost} = \frac{\text{Price per unit of input}}{MP}.$$

Or, stated more fully:

Marginal cost =

$$\frac{\text{Price per unit of variable input}}{\text{Marginal product of the variable input}}.$$

Notice the parallel between MC and AVC. MC is input price divided by MP. AVC is input price divided by AP. Again, you can see the relation between production and cost. The law of diminishing marginal returns indicates that MP may rise to a maximum, but then must fall. Therefore, MC must fall to a minimum, but then must begin to rise. Remember that this link between productivity and cost makes sense because productivity is the key to how much input a firm needs to buy. For marginal product, it is the input needed for an additional unit of output. For example, if MP is 5, a firm needs to buy 1/5 of a unit of input to produce an additional unit of output. If MP rises to 10, a firm needs only 1/10 of a unit of input to produce an additional unit of output.

The marginal product–marginal cost relation can be seen by comparing columns 5 and 12 of Table 3, and by studying Figure 4. As long as MP is rising, MC is falling. If MP is falling, MC must be rising. And where MP is at a maximum, with an additional unit of output being produced with a minimum amount of input, MC must be at a minimum.

Finally, Panel III of Figure 3 shows the relationships among marginal cost and both AVC and ATC. You have already seen the relation between AP and MP, and the relation between MC and both AVC and

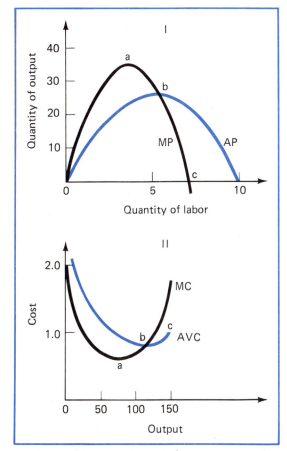

Figure 4   The relationships between product and cost curves

Similarly labeled points correspond to one another. When MP is a maximum (a), MC is a minimum. When MP = AP and AP is a maximum (b), MC = AVC and AVC is a minimum. When MP equals zero (c), output has reached its maximum possible value.

ATC is quite similar. If AVC is falling, MC must be below it, pulling it down. If AVC equals MC, then AVC must be a minimum. If AVC is rising, MC must be above it, pulling it up. The same relation holds for MC and ATC. ATC will decline if MC is below it, rise if MC is above it, and be at a minimum at the point where $MC = ATC$.

This discussion may seem highly abstract. For some students ATC is a theory completely divorced from the real operations of the firm. It is worthwhile to con-

sider for a moment what that ATC curve really represents. Each ATC curve stands for certain combinations of fixed and variable inputs—in other words, a certain technology. The heat and smell and noise associated with actual production are missing, but the results of the use of a particular technology, in terms of cost per unit of output, are effectively conveyed.

Now you know how costs behave in the short run and why. The key to cost behavior is productivity: How many units of input are needed to produce output. Knowing how costs behave as output increases is a key to understanding how firms behave. But all of the analysis so far concerns the short run—situations in which there are both fixed and variable inputs. What happens to costs when firms are freed of the constraints of fixed factors—when they are free to choose among any possible combinations of inputs? For the answer to that question, you need to examine the behavior of costs in the long run.

Productivity and costs in the long run

The kinds of decisions that a firm must make in the long run are substantially different from short-run decisions. In the short run, the firm can vary quantity, but only within the constraint of the fixed factor. If a restaurant wants to serve more meals in the short run, the owners can juggle the amounts of labor and food, and, to a certain extent, the numbers of tables and chairs. All of this change, though, must take place within the limits set by the fixed factors, such as the size of the building and the type of built-in cooking equipment.

But if the managers want to serve more customers in the long run, they can vary the amounts of all inputs. They may lease a larger space or install different amounts and kinds of cooking facilities. In other words, in the long run, a firm is free to choose from among all of the available technologies—from among all of the known ways to combine inputs, none of which is fixed in the long run. By varying the amounts of these factors that are fixed in the short run, it can choose from among all of the existing short-run cost curves.

Derivation of the long-run average total cost curve

The first step for a firm making a long-run decision is to discover the "best" way to produce various output levels. And, of course, the "best" method of production should mean the lowest-cost method of production for a particular output. What the firm needs to develop, then, is a cost schedule or curve showing the lowest cost at which various levels of output can be produced. "Lowest cost" in this context means either lowest TC at each level of output, or lowest ATC at each level of output. The choice of an input combination that will minimize ATC at some output will also minimize TC. It is easier to see what is involved, however, if you focus on ATC.

Such a schedule has to be derived almost a point or section at a time. Select one output level, say 100 units of output. Consider all the possible techniques that could be used to produce this amount of output. Since the short-run ATC curves are shorthand ways of expressing these various technologies or combinations of fixed and variable inputs, graphing these techniques results in a bird's nest of short-run ATC curves, such as Panel I of Figure 5. (For brevity, we will henceforth omit the T for "total" when discussing the short- and long-run cost curves. They will be labeled as SRAC and LRAC.)

In this diagram, one technology or combination of fixed and variable inputs

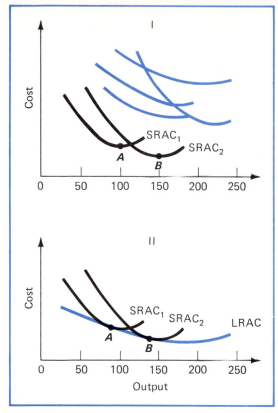

Figure 5   Derivation of the long-run average cost curve

stands out from the others as being the technology that will allow the production of 100 units of output at the lowest per unit cost. This is $SRAC_1$. All other technologies are less efficient in this output range. But you can see from the same diagram that $SRAC_1$ is not the best or least-cost way of producing 150 units. A different technology, using a different amount of the fixed factor, represented by $SRAC_2$, will result in least-cost production.

Identifying the least-cost technology for *all* levels of output involves nothing more than repeated application of the principles for locating the least-cost technology for *each* level. What results is a series of short-run ATC curves, each representing the appropriate technology for a given level of output. Connect all of the points or sections of the short-run curves that represent the most efficient or least-cost technology for given levels or ranges of output, and you arrive at the long-run ATC curve. This is shown in Panel II of Figure 5. Every point of the long-run ATC curve is tangent to some short-run curve at a point representing the least-cost technology for producing the corresponding level of output.

You can think of the long-run ATC curve as a boundary between what is attainable and what is not. It is what the mathematicians call an envelope, or greatest lower boundary for cost. Since the long-run ATC curve was derived by choosing the least-cost method of production for each level of output, it represents the lowest-cost or economically efficient method of production. Any point below the curve is unattainable, given existing technology and input prices. Any point on or above the curve is attainable. Of course, it is preferable to be operating at a point on the long-run ATC curve, since that represents the lowest costs possible.

The term for operating on the average cost curve is **X-efficiency.** It encompasses all actions that achieve the least-cost outcome. *X-inefficiency* occurs when the firm strays above this least-cost level and incurs unnecessary costs.

Tangencies and minimums The long-run ATC curve is not a difficult concept, but there are some technical points about it that require careful attention. First, the short-run ATC curves are not necessarily tangent to the long-run ATC curve at their minimum points. In fact, a short-run ATC curve is only tangent to the long-run curve at its minimum point where the long-run curve is also at its minimum. This implies that a firm may build a certain-size plant (represented by the short-run ATC curve), planning to use it at a level of output that does not represent the lowest per unit cost possible for that plant.

This may at first seem confusing to you or just plain wrong. The explanation is not difficult, but you have to think carefully about it. First, it would be geometrically impossible for all of the short-run ATC curves to be tangent to the long-run ATC curve at their minimum points unless long-run ATC were constant over the whole range of output and were therefore represented by a horizontal straight line. Remember that when two curves are tangent, their slopes must be equal. Any curve tangent to the downward-sloping portion of the long-run ATC curve must also be downward sloping.

Any curve tangent to the upward-sloping portion of the long-run ATC curve must also be upward sloping. When the long-run ATC curve is at its minimum point, any curve tangent to it must also be at its minimum. The least-cost way of producing a given level of output often involves using a plant either above or below its capacity or least-cost point.

You may accept the geometrical explanation for using a plant at other than its least-cost level of output, but still not understand the economic sense of it. Look at Panel I of Figure 6. Why would the firm produce 100 units with the plan represented by $SRAC_1$? Why not use the plant to produce 150 units at $2 less per unit? This sounds reasonable, but the firm is not interested in using a *given plant* (corresponding to a given SRAC curve) at its most efficient scale. It is interested in *choosing a plant* to minimize the cost of a *given output*.

To see the difference, look at Points *A* and *B* in Panel II of Figure 6. They represent two known ways of producing 150 units of output. You can build Plant 1 and use it at its least-cost point, producing the output at $18 per unit. Or, you can build Plant 2 and use it at an output level that is lower than the least-cost point for that plant. Which plant would you choose? Using Plant 2 to produce 150 units of output

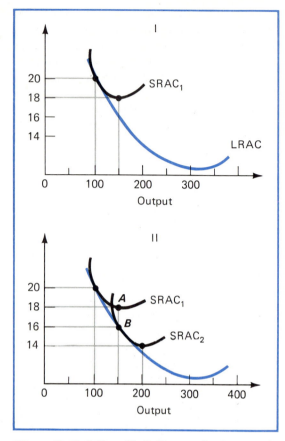

Figure 6 Relationship between short-run and long-run cost curves

seems to involve some inefficiency because you are paying $2 more per unit than if you were using the same plant at its capacity of 200 units.

In fact, however, it is efficient if your goal is to produce 150 units. By building the larger plant, you can produce 150 units at $2 less per unit than you could at the least-cost point of Plant 1. The loss of efficiency ($2) in using the larger plant below its capacity is more than outweighed by the greater efficiency involved in using the larger-scale plant. Remember, a firm's goal is the lowest cost per unit for the amount of output it wants to produce, and not simply to use a plant at the least-cost point.

Choices in the short and long run Now, with the relation between the short-run and the long-run cost curves clearly in mind, you can examine how a producer will make specific choices. Suppose that the producer wants to choose the technology appropriate for an output of 100 units. He or she faces a long-run decision, free to choose any combination of inputs.

The least-cost way of producing 100 units is represented by Point A on the long-run ATC curve in Figure 7. That point stands for the technology—the plant size, equipment, amount and type of labor and raw materials—represented by $SRAC_1$. Having decided, the producer then builds the factory, buys the machines, and hires the labor needed for the chosen technology and output. Once the plant is built and the equipment is in place, the producer is back in the short run, with both fixed and variable inputs. As long as the firm continues to produce 100 units, short-run and long-run efficiency coincide.

But suppose that the firm later decides to produce 150 units. Now it is Point C that represents the lowest-cost method of production. Since Point A and Point C are associated with different short-run ATC curves, they stand for technologies using different amounts of the fixed factor. This means that, in the short run, the firm can-

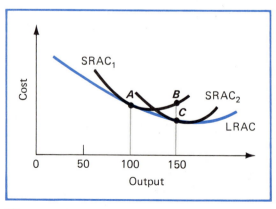

Figure 7 Short- and long-run efficiency

not move from Point *A* to Point *C*. The only way the firm can produce 150 units is represented by a move from Point *A* to Point *B*, changing its variable inputs within the constraints of its fixed inputs. If the firm continues to produce 150 units, it will change the amount of the fixed input as soon as possible, switching from the technology represented by $SRAC_1$ to Point *C* and the technology represented by $SRAC_2$. Movements along the long-run ATC curve can only take place in the long run, when the amounts of all inputs can be varied.

Is it inefficient for the firm to produce 150 units at Point *B* when there is a lower-cost method of production represented by Point *C*? Not in the short run! Given the constraint imposed by the input whose quantity cannot be quickly varied, production at Point *B* is the most efficient way (in fact, the only way) to produce 150 units. In the long run, when the fixed factor can be changed, Point *C* becomes the most efficient way to produce 150 units. So the short-run ATC curves represent short-run efficiency, while the long-run curve represents the points where short-run and long-run efficiency coincide.

You can see that a movement along the long-run ATC curve will occur when the firm chooses a different technology to produce a different level of output at the lowest possible cost. When will the curve shift? The long-run ATC curve is based on two sets of information: the price of inputs and known technology. If either of these changes, the cost curves must shift in easily predictable ways.

If input prices change, the short-run and long-run curves will have to be re-drawn. If input prices increase, the curves will shift up, indicating that output can only be produced at a higher price. If input prices fall or if there is a technological breakthrough, so that inputs can be combined in more efficient ways, then average costs fall at each level of output and the long-run ATC curve will shift down. And remember, if the long-run ATC curve is shifting, the short-run curves must also be shifting. After all, if the curves are tangent, one curve cannot shift without the other.

By this time, you have seen how the long-run ATC curve is derived and what it represents. But why is it shaped the way it is?

Economies of scale: The shape of the long-run ATC curve

Since the long-run ATC curve is U-shaped, just like the short-run ATC curves, you might be tempted to say that the shape of the long-run ATC curve must also be due to the law of diminishing marginal returns. Resist that impulse! Remember that the law of diminishing marginal returns refers explicitly to situations in which more of one input is added while another input is held constant. In other words, it can only be used to explain short-run situations.

What about the long-run, then? A different explanation is needed, that of the concept of **economies and diseconomies of scale.** (The word *scale* here refers to size.)

The long-run ATC curve represents a variety of combinations of fixed and variable inputs—a variety of technologies. Some of the technologies are best suited for lower levels of output, others for higher levels of output. After all, the best way to build a few specialized cars is not the best way to produce hundreds of thousands of automobiles. To invest $500 million in an assembly plant may be the least-cost technology if the firm is planning to spread that fixed cost over hundreds of thousands of cars. If the firm is planning to sell only a handful of cars, it may want to choose a more labor-intensive technology with lower fixed costs.

Since the long-run ATC curve declines to a minimum, and then begins to rise, adopting larger-scale technology must at first cause per unit costs to fall. At some point, though, larger-scale technology will cause costs per unit to begin to rise. Why? Why do long-run average costs decline to a point and then start to increase?

Causes of economies of scale The answer lies in the causes of economies and diseconomies of scale. Economies of scale, corresponding to the downward-sloping or declining portion of the long-run ATC curve, have three major causes: specialization, physical laws, and management.

SPECIALIZATION By specializing at a task, by doing it repeatedly, you can become very fast, skillful, and efficient at it. As long ago as 1776, Adam Smith gave *specialization* center stage in the Wealth of Nations, using the example of a pin factory:

One man draws out the wire, another straightens it, a third cuts it, a fourth points it, a fifth grinds it at the top for receiving the head. . . . The important business of making a pin is, in this manner, divided in about eighteen distinct operations. . . . Each person, therefore, making a tenth part of forty-eight thousand pins, might be considered as making four thousand eight hundred pins in a day. But if they had all wrought separately and independently . . . they certainly could not each of them have made twenty, perhaps not one pin in a day. (Adam Smith, *The Wealth of Nations*, 1776 [New York: Modern Library edition, 1937], pp. 4–5.)

The gains in efficiency come from greater dexterity learned through repetition and the saving in time in not having to switch from one task to another. Through specialization, people are sorted into the jobs they do best. By repetition and learning, of course, their skill increases. This is just as valid for today's modern firms as it was for the 18th-century pin factory. The amount of specialization possible and, therefore, the reduction in average costs that results are usually limited by the size of the firm. The larger the plant, the greater the possibility for more complex machinery and a larger labor force, which allows the production process to be broken into an increasingly refined series of specialized tasks. Thus, the larger the plant, the more specialization and the lower the average costs, up to a point.

PHYSICAL LAWS As the scale or size of a plant increases, physical laws—of volume, temperature, motion, metallurgy, and chemical reactions—often help lower costs. A boiler with ten times the volume of another boiler may require only three times as much fuel. A motor's efficiency may become five times greater as its speed doubles. These engineering relations are an important source of scale economies.

MANAGEMENT Larger scale or size may allow the firm to use more advanced and specialized management techniques. Planning and operations may be carried out more precisely. Opportunities available to management in finance, advertising, innovation, and personnel may be better.

Diseconomies of scale and their causes You already know just from the shape of the long-run ATC curve that increases in plant size can only lower average costs up to a point. **At some level of output, the possibilities for further specialization through increases in size are exhausted. Expansion beyond that point will not cause any further decreases in average costs and may, in fact, cause *diseconomies* of scale to set in. The reason is simply that the three causes of economies of scale—specialization, physical laws, management—have been carried too far.**

SPECIALIZATION can be dull for workers and can lead to resentment and outright rebellion. Short of this extreme, other adverse reactions to specialization can occur.

Workers may grow sloppy; quality may decline; absenteeism may rise. Supervisors may have an increasingly hard time making sure that the work is being done properly. As plant size and specialization increase, all of these reactions may cause costs to increase at some point.

⇒ PHYSICAL LAWS too, may result in size hurting, not helping. At some size, a larger boiler may use less fuel but be harder to control or it may crack more often. More complex machinery may be subject to more metal fatigue, friction, or other problems, so that it needs continual repairs. Almost all physical laws reach such negative ranges. When a factory's continued growth causes enough of them to do so, average costs will rise.

⇒ MANAGEMENT may turn into an increasingly inefficient bureaucracy as a firm grows larger. Supervisors must themselves be supervised by an additional layer of bureaucracy. More and more layers of administrators and executives are added. Organization becomes more confused, paperwork mounts, and top decision makers may get further and further removed from what is really going on. Good managers can overcome many of these problems. But the tendencies toward trouble are there, increasing as size increases. This is true of all organizations, including private firms.

Typical curves From all of these conditions, economists have come to regard the typical cost curves to be as shown in Figure 8. The average cost curve slopes down, reaches a minimum, and then rises. Marginal cost rises, perhaps steeply, cutting through the minimum of the average cost curve. We will see in the next chapter that marginal cost is the central concept in deriving the supply curve.

Although the LRAC curve declines and then rises, it may also have a flat or hori-

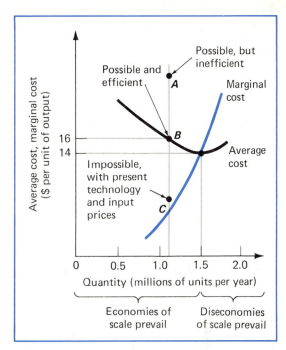

Figure 8   Long-run cost curves for a typical firm: Average and marginal cost

Average cost declines in the range where economies of scale prevail. The firm's natural level of "capacity" is where its average cost is lowest: in this case, 1,500,000 units per year at $14 per unit. At higher levels of production, diseconomies of scale prevail. The marginal cost curve rises sharply above the average cost curve, pulling it up.
    Point A is possible but inferior to Point B. Point C is impossible to attain with present technology.

zontal portion, as shown in Panel I of Figure 9. Here the forces affecting cost balance out evenly, so that average costs are constant. Such a portion of the LRAC curve would be a portion of *constant returns to scale*. It might represent a firm increasing output by building identical plants, all at the same average cost level. Even here, however, the increasing cost of supervising and coordinating the activities of an ever-increasing number of firms may cause costs of management to rise, eventually bringing on diseconomies of scale.

    While all LRAC curves slope down and then up, each industry will have its own specific form of curve, reflecting its own technology. In some industries, the decline of average costs extends up to high levels of output. A firm has to produce a large

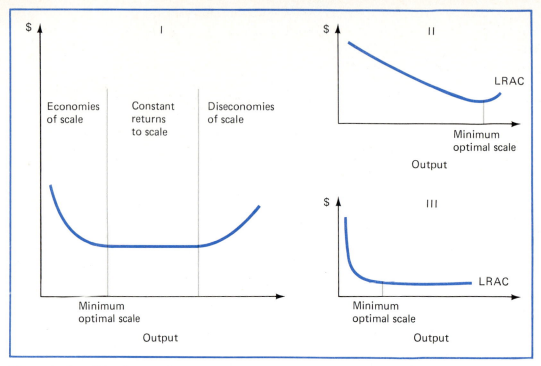

Figure 9 Possible shapes of long-run ATC curves

quantity of output to reach **minimum optimal scale (MOS):** the output where average cost is smallest.

Such a case is shown in Panel II of Figure 9. It is called "natural monopoly," because there is room for only one firm that is large enough to reach MOS. An example is electric service in local markets. One electric firm can supply the entire market at a lower cost than could two or more firms, each with higher average costs because its output is below MOS.

The opposite case is "natural competition." It is illustrated in Panel III of Figure 9. Minimum optimal scale is small, so that many efficient firms can coexist and compete with one another within the market. Good examples of that are farming, printing, and retail shops, where most firms are small and have tiny market shares.

Therefore, the shape of the cost curve can be decisive to the chances for vigorous competition in each market. In research since the 1930s, economists have estimated the MOS in over 40 major markets. A se-

lection of the best recent results is given in Table 4. MOS ranges from as little as 1 percent of the market in fabric weaving and shoes up to 16 percent in canned soups.

MOS sets a floor under the actual firms' market shares, because a firm cannot usually survive if its costs are above those prevailing in the market. For competition to be as vigorous as possible, actual market shares would be driven down to MOS. Any market share above MOS is excess, because it gives no improvement in cost. Moreover, it may reduce competition (as we will show in Chapters 10 and 11).

Therefore, the comparison between MOS and actual market shares is important. Table 4 shows that the largest firms do have market shares well above MOS. They also, on average, have a degree of excess market share. Yet, despite these excess market shares, there is a slight correlation between MOS and market shares. Technology has some influence on the size of firms.

Table 4 *Optimal size and actual market shares of 17 U.S. industries, 1965–1970*

Industry	(1) Minimum Optimal Scale for the Firm, as a Percent of the Total U.S. Market (1965–1970) (%)	(2) Actual Market Shares, 1970 Dominant Firm (%)	(3) Top 3 Firms (average) (%)	(4) Excess Market Share Leading Firm (%)
Automobile	15	55	28	40
Batteries (storage)	2	27	18	25
Beer	6	19	13	13
Bearings	6	18	14	12
Cement	2	12	7	10
Cigarettes	9	28	23	19
Computers	15	66	26	51
Detergents	12	48	27	36
Fabric weaving	1	12	10	11
Glass bottles	5	29	22	24
Oil refining	5	18	8	13
Paints	2	13	9	11
Photographic film	14	65	27	51
Refrigerators	15	24	21	9
Shoes	1	8	6	7
Soup (canned)	16	75	31	59
Steel	3	22	14	19

Sources: F.M. Scherer, *Industrial Market Structure and Economic Performance*, rev. ed. (Chicago: Rand McNally, 1980), pp. 94–119; L. W. Weiss, in R. T. Masson and P. D. Qualls, eds., *Essays on Industrial Organization in Honor of Joe S. Bain* (Cambridge, Mass.: Ballinger, 1976); W. G. Shepherd, *The Economics of Industrial Organization* (Englewood Cliffs, N.J.: Prentice-Hall, 1979), Chap. 11; and various other industrial sources.

Many of the MOS estimates are hotly debated, for they bear on the standing of the leading firms in those industries. Thus, General Motors (automobiles), Eastman Kodak (photographic film), and IBM (computers) each control over half of their markets (as shown in column 2), and they often say that their dominance merely reflects their economies of scale. Yet, Table 4 suggests that scale economies extend only up to about 15 percent of their markets. This highly sensitive point will come up for more discussion in Chapters 10–12. It can be decisive in antitrust actions to increase competition.

The marginal conditions necessary for least-cost production

Only one issue remains to be dealt with in this chapter. To draw the long-run ATC curve, it is necessary to find the least-cost method of production for all of the relevant levels of output. If this least-cost method of production has indeed been found, then a certain relation between the marginal products and prices of inputs must hold.

To look at a two-input case: If a firm is indeed producing at the lowest possible cost, then $MP_K/\text{Price}_K = MP_L/\text{Price}_L$ where K = capital and L = labor. It is easiest to grasp the sense of the equality if you first concentrate on the meaning of a single ratio: MP/price. Marginal product represents the increase in output from a one-unit increase in input. If MP is 10, then the last unit of input gave a return of 10 units of output. If you divide MP by price, what do you end up with? The MP/price ratio represents the return, in terms of additional output, from the last dollar spent on the input. For example, if $MP_K = 10$, and $\text{Price}_K = \$5$, then the last dollar spent on capital resulted in a two-unit increase in output, since $5 bought 10 units of output at the margin.

Suppose that while the $MP_K = 10$, and the $Price_K = \$5$, then $MP_L = 21$, and $Price_L = \$3$. The resulting ratios would be:

$$\frac{MP_K}{Price_K} = \frac{10}{5} = 2 \text{ while } \frac{MP_L}{Price_L} = \frac{21}{3} = 7.$$

In this case, $MP_L/Price_L > MP_K/Price_K$. The last dollar spent on labor gave a return of 7 units of output, compared to the last dollar spent on capital, which gave a return of only 2 additional units of output. The dollars that the firm is spending on its inputs are not being equally "productive." This means that there is an opportunity for the firm to switch some dollars from capital to labor and to increase output without increasing cost.

In this case, if a firm reduces its spending on capital by $1, it loses approximately 2 units of output. Spending this $1 on labor causes an increase of approximately 7 units of output. The switch of $1, then, resulted in a net gain of 5 units of output. As long as the MP/price ratios are not equal, there is an opportunity for such favorable switching of input dollars.

As more and more dollars are switched from capital to labor, what happens to the MP/price ratios, assuming that the price of inputs remains constant? As dollars are switched from capital to labor, the quantity of labor increases relative to that of capital, and the marginal products of capital and labor begin to change. Each unit of labor has less capital with which to work, and the MP_L begins to decrease. Each remaining unit of capital has more labor with which to work, and its marginal product begins to rise.

As dollars are switched from purchases of labor to purchases of capital, the $MP_L/Price_L$ decreases and the $MP_K/Price_K$ increases. Switching dollars from one input to another should continue until $MP_L/$

$Price_L = MP_K/Price_K$. At this point, the last dollars spent on all inputs yield equal returns in terms of additional output. Since there is no further opportunity for favorable changes in input proportions, the least-cost combination of inputs has been achieved.

The MP/price equality can, with a simple regrouping of terms, be written as:

$$\frac{MP_K}{MP_L} = \frac{Price_K}{Price_L}.$$

This looks at the same issue in a slightly different light. This expression emphasizes that a firm should adjust its inputs until the ratios of the marginal productivities of inputs equal the ratios of input prices. The sense of this is fairly easy to grasp. Most firms must take input prices as given. If $Price_K = \$10$, and $Price_L = \$5$, there may be little a firm can do to change the price ratio. What the firm *can* do is adjust quantities of inputs until the last unit of capital is twice as productive as the last unit of labor. A firm is willing to pay twice as much for capital only if it is twice as productive at the margin.

Understanding the MP/price rule for choosing the most efficient method of production can help to illustrate one of the major advantages of a relatively free market system. Suppose that the firm has achieved the combination of inputs at which $MP_K/Price_K = MP_L/Price_L$. Now suppose that labor becomes scarcer relative to demand, so that its price increases. With $Price_L$ increasing, the value of $MP_L/Price_L$ falls, while $MP_K/Price_K$ remains constant. Now, $MP_K/Price_K > MP_L/Price_L$. To restore equality, the firm must increase its purchase of capital and reduce its purchases of labor until $MP_L/Price_L$ once again equals $MP_K/Price_K$.

The increase in the price of the input causes the firm to use less of the input that has become scarcer and therefore relatively more expensive. To the extent that prices really do reflect relative scarcities, the drive of the firm to achieve a balance between input productivity and price will cause increasingly scarce inputs to be used more sparingly.

For example, the price of airplane fuel rose from 11 cents per gallon in 1973 to $1 per gallon in 1980. Since other input prices for airlines rose only about 50 percent, fuel had become relatively much scarcer. The airlines' marginal product/price ratios were now sharply out of line. The airlines responded by making drastic efforts to conserve fuel. That moved them back up their marginal product curves, and *that* would move the ratios between MP and prices back toward equality.

To do this, the airlines switched to lighter seats, rugs, meal trays, and belt buckles. Some stripped the paint off the planes, saving up to 600 pounds per plane. Cargo holds were revamped and wall linings removed. Flight patterns were shifted toward higher altitudes and cruising speeds were reduced. Fuel reserves carried on the planes were cut.

These changes illustrate the wide range of choice—even on planes already built—for responding to input price changes. The same applies to factories and equipment of many kinds. The equal marginal ratios merely show in a formal way the directions that intelligent managers are constantly moving.

Summary

The purpose of this chapter was to introduce you to the concepts of short- and long-run productivity and cost.

1. *Technology* or *the state of the art* encompasses all of the known methods of production.

2. Given technology and input prices, the firm's goal is to choose the method of production that will allow a given level of output to be produced at the lowest possible cost.

3. Economists measure costs using the concept of *foregone alternatives*. Costs calculated according to this concept are called *economic costs* or *opportunity cost*.

4. The opportunity cost of inputs that are bought or hired is calculated by adding up the dollars paid out by the firm. These are the *direct* or *dollar costs* of the firm.

5. *Economic profit* equals revenue minus economic cost.

6. Discussions of productivity and cost must distinguish carefully between the *short run*, a period of time during which at least one input is fixed, and the *long run*, in which all variables can be altered in quantity.

7. Output can be measured in three different ways:
   a. Total product or output.
   b. Average product or output per unit of input.
   c. Marginal product or the change in output from one unit change in input.

8. As the *law of diminishing marginal returns* states, in the short run, as more of the variable input is added to the fixed input, a point is reached beyond which *marginal product* and *average product* must decline.

9. There is an important relation between marginal and average measures. If an average is rising, the marginal must be above it, pulling it up. If an average is falling, the marginal must be below it, pulling it down.

10. For each of the three measures of output, there are corresponding measures of costs:

a. Total cost is the sum of total fixed cost and total variable cost.

b. Average total cost is the cost per unit of output. It is the sum of average fixed cost and average variable cost.

c. Marginal cost is the change in total cost from a one-unit change in output.

11. Short-run costs are determined by the cost per unit of output and productivity, that is, by the amount of input needed to produce total, average, or additional units of output.

The main points concerning *long-run* conditions are:

12. To derive the long-run ATC curve, it is necessary to identify the least-cost method of producing various levels of output. This involves selecting the short-run ATC curve that represents the lowest-cost technology (combination of fixed and variable inputs) for each given output level. When the points or sections of the short-run curves that represent these least-cost technologies are connected, the resulting schedule will be the long-run ATC curve.

13. In the long run, a firm is free to choose any point on the long-run ATC curve, that is, any combination of fixed and variable inputs. Once a point is selected, and the plant and equipment representing that technology are built, the firm is operating in the short run. It can vary its output only within the constraints of its technology. Selection of a new point on the long-run ATC curve can occur only in the long run, when all inputs can again be varied.

14. The long-run ATC curve, and the short-run ATC curves from which it is derived, will shift if input prices or known technological possibilities change.

15. The U-shape of the long-run ATC curve can be explained by economies and diseconomies of scale. As a firm adopts larger-scale technology, average costs will at first drop because of the influence of specialization, physical laws, and management. Expansion beyond a certain point may cause rising average costs because these three influences have been carried too far. A long-run ATC curve may also have a horizontal portion representing constant returns to scale, where forces affecting cost balance out.

16. While all long-run ATC curves decline and then rise, each industry will have a specific shape reflecting its own technology. Average costs may fall off slowly or sharply as output rises.

17. If a firm is producing its output at lowest cost, then the MP/price ratios for all inputs must be equal. If the MP/price ratios are not equal, there is always an opportunity for changes in input proportions that will lower costs and raise profits.

Key concepts

Technology
Opportunity cost
Direct cost, or accounting cost
Imputed or implicit cost
Sunk cost
Economic profit
Short and long run
Total, average, and marginal product
Production function
Total fixed cost

Total variable cost
Average total cost
Average variable cost
Marginal cost
Economies and diseconomies of scale
Specialization
Minimum optimal scale
X-efficiency

Questions for review

1. Two firms both produce identical output. Each firm uses a different technology.
   a. What would be some reasons for the choosing of different technologies?
   b. Is one firm necessarily making a mistake in its choice of technology? Explain.

2. Consider opportunity cost in each of the following situations.
   a. You can either study for an exam or go to a party. You decide to study for the exam. What type of information would you have to know to determine if the opportunity cost of your studying was high or low?
   b. You decide to earn some money this year at school by acting as a go-between for an artist friend of yours and the students on your campus. You will advertise, take orders, pick up the finished items, and deliver them.
      i. Make a list of all the items you would want to include under direct cost and under estimated or imputed cost.
      ii. To determine the price that will give you a fair return for your effort, you need to esti-

mate the opportunity cost of your time. Explain how you would do this, and see if you can come up with a dollar figure representing the value of an hour of your time.
   c. You buy a $20 concert ticket, decide that you really do not want to go, and find that you cannot sell the ticket at any price. What is the opportunity cost of:
      i. going to the concert, although you know that you will dislike it;
      ii. skipping the concert and "wasting" the ticket.

3. Two students are arguing about the concept of economic profit. One claims that to imply that firms should continue to produce with an economic profit of zero is antibusiness. Firms *need* a profit to reinvest in the business and *deserve* a profit as a reward for their effort. The other student claims that, on the contrary, an economic profit of zero means that the firm *has* money for reinvestment and *is* being rewarded for its effort. They ask you to settle the dispute. Do so!

4. Classify the following business decisions as short-run or long-run decisions.
   a. A firm wants to make a seasonal adjustment in output to meet higher Christmas demand.
   b. A group of business people have decided to produce a new product and are attempting to determine the best technology to use.
   c. A firm finds that demand for its product is lower than anticipated, so it is trying to decide the most efficient method of laying off some workers.
   d. Given dramatic increases in fuel prices, a manager must deter-

mine whether the firm's present technology is now outmoded.

5. You own a small business and keep very careful records on inputs, output, and cost. One of your employees, the fourth worker hired, sees that when she was hired, output increased by more than it did when the second, third, or fifth workers were hired. She claims that this proves she is more productive and skilled than the other workers. Show that this may not be true.

6. You find a friend of yours struggling with some of the marginal concepts in the chapter. He presents you with his latest confusion: "If marginal cost, the addition to cost, is declining, then it seems to me that total cost should also be declining. Yet MC can decline, while TC can only increase." Explain clearly (and patiently) to your friend exactly what his confusion is.

7. A long-run ATC curve is derived from tangencies with short-run cost curves. Since the long-run ATC curve represents the least-cost method of production for different levels of output, the tangencies between the long-run and short-run average cost curves must therefore occur at the minimum points on the short-run ATC curves. True or false? Explain.

8. A firm that has adjusted its variable input to meet an unexpectedly high demand for its product finds that it is producing at a point higher than its calculation of long-run ATC for that level of output. Does this necessarily imply inefficient production? Explain.

9. Can the fact that long-run costs decline and then increase be explained by decreases and increases in input prices? Why or why not? If not, what influences *do* explain the behavior of long-run average costs?

10. A firm finds that the addition of its last unit of capital caused output to increase by 15 units, while the addition of its last unit of labor caused output to rise by only 7 units. Since the last unit of capital is obviously more productive than the last unit of labor, can the firm conclude that it should purchase more capital and less labor? Explain.

· 9 ·

Pricing and Output Under Perfect Competition

As you read and study this chapter, you will learn:

- the simple rule for maximizing profit
- the nature of the firm's supply curve
- the derivation of short-run and long-run market supply curves
- the various conditions reached in efficient production in competitive markets

A pair of scissors requires two blades to cut paper, just as it takes two hands to clap. We are now ready to construct the second blade of the microeconomics scissors, by deriving the market supply curve. Working together with demand, the conditions of supply determine the levels of price and output in competitive markets throughout the economy.

As you saw in the last chapter, supply curves reflect cost conditions. In this chapter, we show how the firm compares those costs with prices to determine its rate of production. The result in a competitive market is a supply curve for the firm, which coincides with the marginal cost curve. Then we demonstrate how those individual supply curves determine the market supply curve. Along the way we also discuss shifts in the curves and the various slopes they may have.

The final section notes the efficient conditions that prices and outputs reach in competitive markets. That is an important point of reference for the next several chapters because, as we will see, monopoly leads to inefficiency.

The rules for maximizing profits

From the preceding chapter, you know how the firm minimizes its cost of producing any given level of output. Now we move to the firm's final step: *choosing the output level that maximizes the firm's profits.*

That, in turn, divides into two separate company decisions. The first is *whether the firm should produce at all in this market.* Under some conditions, the firm will close down and shift its resources elsewhere. Second, if the firm does decide to continue to produce, *it must still decide how much to produce.*

Should the firm produce at all?

To answer this basic question, one must use the concept of *opportunity cost.* In the long run, a firm should continue operating in its market only if its total sales revenues are large enough to cover the opportunity costs of the resources its uses. If this occurs, then the firm is covering all of its operating costs and making as high a return on its resources as it could in any alternative use of its resources.

To put the production decision in unit terms, divide total revenue and cost by the quantity of output. A firm will only produce in the long run if:

$$\frac{\text{Total revenue}}{\text{Quantity}} \geq \frac{\text{Total cost}}{\text{Quantity}}$$

or Price ≥ Average Total Cost.

What about the short run? In this perspective, resources cannot be easily transferred to another use, since by definition there are some fixed inputs that cannot be varied in quantity. In the short run, cost does not drop to zero even if production ceases. The fixed costs, such as bank loan payments or rent, must still be paid. Therefore, in the short run, it might be most advantageous for a firm to operate at a loss, if by doing so, it can cover its operating costs and pay off at least some of its fixed costs.

How much should the firm produce?

Profit equals revenue − cost. Therefore, *the rules of profit maximization* must involve the weighing of costs and revenues. To consider the effect of a one-unit change in output on revenue and cost, we must use marginal concepts. If a firm has reached the profit-maximizing point of operation, then a one-unit increase or decrease in output should reduce its profits. The change in profits that results from a one-unit change in output can be expressed as the change in revenue minus the change in cost, or:

$$\frac{\Delta \text{Profit}}{\Delta \text{Quantity}} = \frac{\Delta \text{Revenue}}{\Delta \text{Quantity}} - \frac{\Delta \text{Cost}}{\Delta \text{Quantity}}.$$

The change in cost resulting from a one-unit change in output is *marginal cost,* a concept introduced in the last chapter. The change in revenue resulting from a one-unit change in quantity is called, as you might expect, **marginal revenue.** The change in profit from a one-unit change in output can be expressed as:

Marginal profit = Marginal revenue
          − Marginal cost, or $MR - MC$.

If profits are rising (or losses are falling) from the production of additional units of output, the additional units must be adding more to revenue than they are to cost. The firm must be producing where $MR > MC$. If profits are falling (or losses rising) from the production of additional units of output, the additional units must be adding more to cost than they are to

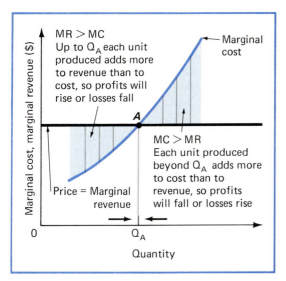

Figure 1   The profit-maximizing level of output

cost: $MR = MC$. To the left of Q_A, $MR >$ MC. In this leftward area, the firm will be adding more to revenue than to cost each time it produces an additional unit of output. Therefore, the firm will be increasing its profits (or reducing its losses) if it increases its level of output. As the level of output approaches Q_A, the gap between MR and MC narrows. Each additional unit of output adds less to profit. Nonetheless, as long as $MR > MC$, the firm does increase profits as it produces additional units, and it should continue to increase output up to Q_A. To the right of Q_A, MC $> MR$. Each additional unit produced adds more to cost than to revenue, driving the firm's profits down (or losses up). If the firm finds itself producing in the region to the right of Q_A, it should reduce output back to Q_A.

It is obvious that producing to the left of Q_A is not profit maximizing. The firm can add to its profits by expanding output up to Q_A. Producing to the right of Q_A is not profit maximizing either. The firm can do better by contracting output back to Q_A. The profit-maximizing point, then, must be Q_A, the level of output at which $MR = MC$. To produce one unit less than Q_A means giving up a unit that added to the firm's profits (or reduced its losses) by adding more to revenue than to cost. To produce one unit more means producing a unit that will reduce the firm's profits (or increase its losses) by adding more to cost than to revenue. It is only at Q_A that the firm is doing as well as it can, in the sense that no adjustment in output levels will improve its profit position.

Remember, though, that the relationship between MC and MR will only tell you whether the firm is maximizing its profits. It will not show the level of the firm's total profits. The gap between the marginal revenue and marginal cost curves does not represent profit. It represents only *potential changes* in profits or

revenue. The firm must be producing where $MC > MR$.

To see this clearly, consider Figure 1, which shows marginal cost and marginal revenue. You already know the shape of the *marginal cost curve*. It first falls and then rises; we will work only with the upsloping portion of this curve. The *marginal revenue curve* may take one of two shapes. It may be horizontal, or it may be downward sloping, depending upon the shape of the firm demand curve. This will be explored in detail later.

For the moment, the MR curve is drawn as a horizontal line. This indicates that the firm always receives the same amount of additional revenue from selling additional units of output. (Either a horizontal or a downward-sloping marginal revenue curve would work equally well to illustrate the point being made.) The marginal revenue and marginal cost curves are combined in Figure 1. The diagram looks fairly simple, but it illustrates one of the most important concepts in microeconomics.

At the level of output marked Q_A, marginal revenue just equals marginal

losses, with no indication of the overall profit-and-loss level. To determine the firm's absolute level of profits, one must know the average or total cost and revenue measures, and not just marginal measures.

To summarize, what rules must a firm follow to maximize profits? *In the short run, the firm should produce if $P \geq AVC$ at the level of output at which $MR = MC$. In the* long run*, the firm should produce if $P \geq ATC$ at the level of output at which $MR = MC$.* Large or small, single proprietorship or giant corporation, a firm must follow these rules if it wishes to profit maximize. Although all profit-maximizing firms follow the same rules, the market outcomes differ greatly, depending upon the market in which the firm operates.

Setting output under perfect competition

The nature of pure competition

The ideal model of competition is *pure competition*. It applies to an "atomistic" market containing 50 or more firms, each of which has a negligible share of the market. Each firm is too small to influence the going market price by any action of its own. Therefore, each firm is a *price taker:* It takes the market price as a given, which it cannot change. Accordingly, the firm's own demand curve is a horizontal line at the going market price. By comparing its costs with that going price, the firm can choose the level of its output that will maximize its profits.

Economists use that pure model of competition as the setting for deriving the market supply curve. Yet, real competition in real industries is a richer phenomenon than the ideal case of pure competition. Some students therefore doubt at first that the pure competitive model and its results are generally valid. Nevertheless, the com-

petitive model is actually a good approximation of what competition does accomplish in the main mass of real markets. *If there is intense rivalry among as few as two firms, the essentials of competitive supply, pricing, and efficiency may still occur.*

To demonstrate that important point, we will first present the substance of competition and then show the basic unity among competitive processes. The competitive assumptions will immediately enable us to derive the supply and efficiency conclusions of this chapter. The concepts also underlie all the rest of microeconomics. Because competition is so important to microeconomics, it needs a careful review at this point to prepare you for the next 12 chapters.

Competition: a process and a zone of choice

Competition is a prime force by which free choice is transmitted into efficient resource allocation.

Effective competition is balanced To be effective, the competitive process needs to be *open and free*, not predetermined, so that effort and skill are needed to compete successfully. The competitors must also be *comparable*. A contest between unequals is not genuine competition. If one competitor has sharp advantages, then the "competition" is not meaningful. The different weight classes in wrestling and boxing recognize this: A bout between a heavyweight and a bantam-weight is punishment, not competition.

Also, true competition is a continuous process. A foot race or a game of Monopoly will end; the competition is over once the prizes are gained. In real life, by contrast, competition in markets means a continuous mutual striving among more-or-less equal firms. If, instead, one competitor gains dominance over the market, then effective competition is replaced by a degree of monopoly.

Rivalry and pure competition may give similar results.

Rivalry Even if there are only two competitors, their **rivalry** may be intense. Though one of the two firms may get the upper hand for a while in a market, the other may soon fight back and equalize its share of the market and profits. Such a rugged rivalry may stir great efforts from the firms and force their prices down close to the levels of their costs. Therefore, effective competition is possible even when there are as few as two or several firms. Each firm would then think and act as if it had little leeway to raise prices or to earn excess profits. If the two firms colluded with each other, they could wield monopoly power. But their intense rivalry prevents any such collusion.

Pure competition, by contrast, guarantees that prices will be forced down to the level of costs. It is the economists' ideal version of competition, an ideal model that has been honed to precision. Like other economists, we will use it to derive the conditions of supply, price, cost, and efficiency.

The analysis of pure competition rests on these four assumptions:

1. There is one identical good sold in the market.
2. No firm has a significant share of the market.
3. All firms adjust rapidly to any changes.
4. There are no hindrances to movement into and within the market. Entry by new producers is free, and changes are frictionless and quick.

For **perfect competition,** there is one further assumption: Each firm knows everything about demand and supply conditions in the market.

Perfect competition is an ideal version, designed to show the analytical outcomes as clearly as possible. Does this mean that it differs from "real" competition, such as rivalry? Not necessarily. *All forms and degrees of competition—including rivalry—lead toward the same basic kinds of economic results.* They narrow the firm's range of choice over its price, forcing it to reduce costs and to adopt new techniques. Though strong rivalry may not always keep prices down exactly to minimum cost levels, it will keep them close to those levels. As long as there is some degree of competition, there is some pressure.

Firm and market demand in perfect competition

In perfect competition, any one firm is so small relative to the market that the amount that it sells has no impact on market price. Whether an individual farmer brings 200 or 2,000 bushels of wheat to market will have no impact on the domestic or world price of wheat. Because a firm in perfect competition can sell as much output as it chooses at the prevailing market price, the **firm demand curve** is a *horizontal line at the level of market price*, as shown in Panel I of Figure 2. Panel II emphasizes that the market price is determined by the interaction of supply and demand forces in the market.

The marginal revenue curve of a perfectly competitive firm is easy to derive. Marginal revenue is the change in total revenue that results from selling an additional unit of output. Firms in perfect competition can sell as many units of output as they wish at the going market price. Therefore, each time a firm sells an additional unit of output, the addition to revenue or marginal revenue equals the market price. The marginal revenue curve, then, is a horizontal line at the level of market price, coinciding with the firm's demand curve. Total revenue (or price × quantity) increases

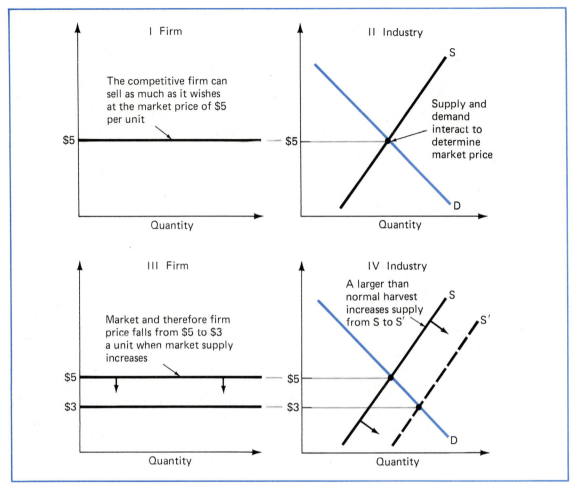

Figure 2 Determination of firm and market price in perfect competition

by an amount equal to market price each time a unit of output is sold. It is represented by a straight line from the origin with a slope equal to $\Delta TR/\Delta Q$, which equals price. With a market price of $5, the firm's MR and TR schedules will be as shown in Figure 3.

Marginal cost

The horizontal demand curve will be superimposed on the firm's cost curves, to locate the output level where profit is greatest. The decisive cost curve is *marginal*

cost because it is the precise measure of opportunity cost to the firm.

The strict definition is simple: *Marginal cost is, at any output level, the added cost of producing one more unit. Therefore, marginal cost is the opportunity cost of the last unit produced.* It shows how cost varies with that unit of output alone. Marginal cost is, therefore, sharply distinct in logic from average cost.

This sharp variation in short-run marginal costs can be illustrated by two examples. First, consider the marginal cost

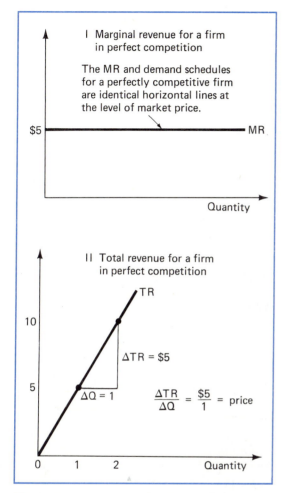

Figure 3   Marginal revenue and total revenue schedules in perfect competition

If market price is $5, the MR schedule is a horizontal line at the level of $5. In perfect competition, then, $P = MR$, as illustrated in Panel I. The TR schedule is a straight line from the origin, with a slope equal to $\Delta TR/\Delta Q$. If $P = \$5$, the slope of the TR schedule will be 5, as is illustrated in Panel II.

of a meal at 3 p.m., when the restaurant is nearly empty. The waiters, cooks, and equipment are already present and paid for. The main extra cost is simply the food itself. So the marginal cost of a meal at slow times might be $1.25. But at 7 p.m., when the restaurant is crowded, an extra meal has much higher cost. An extra waiter and cook may be needed, extra food

ordered, extra tables provided, and so forth. These costs might add up to a marginal cost of $15 per meal at peak times.

Second, consider taking a city bus at 11 a.m. or 5:30 p.m. At 11 a.m., the buses are nearly empty; the cost of carrying you is only a little gasoline, perhaps 3 cents' worth. But at 5:30 p.m., the buses are full, and an extra bus may be needed to carry extra riders. That involves an extra driver and other costs.

The firm's short-run supply curve in perfect competition

To derive the *firm's supply curve*, simply combine the general rules for profit maximization with the particular characteristics of perfect competition. One profit-maximizing rule is that the firm produce the level of output for which $MR = MC$.

Panel I of Figure 4 shows three MR schedules and one MC schedule for a perfectly competitive firm. If the market price is $5, it will be profit maximizing for the firm to supply 100 units, since that is the point at which MR equals MC. The price–quantity supplied combination of $5 and 100 units would therefore be one point on the firm's supply curve. To generate the entire supply curve, simply vary the price. As the MR curve shifts, other price–quantity supplied combinations can be determined.

For example, if the price is $10, the MR schedule would correspond to MR_2 and the firm would be willing to supply 150 units of output. The price-quantity combination of $10 and 150 units would be another point on the firm supply curve. If the market price were $3, the MR schedule would correspond to MR_3 and quantity supplied would be 70 units. Since these price–quantity supplied points will always be the points at which $MR = MC$, all of the profit-maximizing points must lie along the MC curve. Therefore, the supply curve must be the marginal cost curve. If

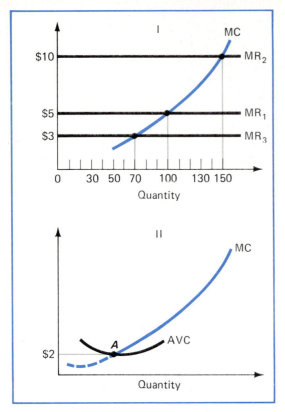

the firm operates at all, the quantity it wishes to supply will be the quantity indicated on the MC curve at the level of the prevailing market price.

However, the competitive firm's supply curve is not the entire marginal cost curve. Remember that it is profit maximizing for the firm to produce in the short run only if $P \geq AVC$. Any quantity for which the corresponding price is less than AVC will not be supplied. As Panel II of Figure 4 shows, *the perfect competitor's supply curve is the marginal cost schedule at or above AVC.* The dashed portion of the

firm's MC schedule in Panel II is not considered part of the firm's supply curve, since the firm will not produce any output at a price lower than its minimum AVC, which in this case is $2.

A more complete analysis

Next we show the profit-maximizing choice in more detail, involving total and average curves as well as marginal ones. Figure 5 presents the conditions for Chapter 7's restaurant *at one time period,* namely 1984. The numerical values for the diagram are in Table 1. The flat (and coincident) demand and marginal revenue curves are derived from the total revenue curve, shown in Panel I. The derivation follows the standard steps, in relating total values to average and marginal values. Average revenue is the slope of the ray through the origin to each point on the total curve. Marginal revenue is the slope of the total curve itself at each point.

Note that the cost and demand conditions are superimposed in both panels of Figure 5. Profit is shown most clearly and simply in Panel I, as the gap between total revenue and total cost. That vertical distance is drawn as a "profit hill." The hill peaks at Point 1, where output is 200,000 meals per year (or 548 meals on the average day). Thus, 200,000 per year is the profit-maximizing level of output. You, the restaurant manager, choose that level, produce it while carefully minimizing the costs, sell the output, and thereby gain profits of $220,000.

The restaurant's choice and its motives are also shown in Panel II. Consider it carefully. Remember that the universal rule is: ***Profits are maximized at the output where marginal cost equals marginal revenue:*** Marginal revenue = Marginal cost. Then the last unit produced is just worth what it cost (in marginal cost) to the firm (in marginal revenue).

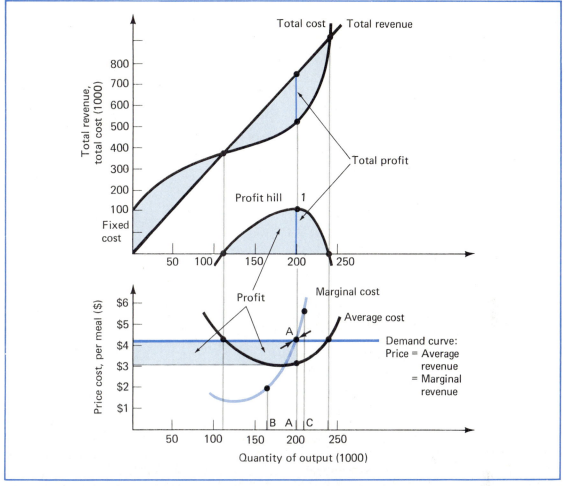

Figure 5   Choosing the output level so as to maximize profits

The total revenue curve has been added in at the top of the figure. Since it is straight, its slope at successive points (marginal revenue) and the slope of the ray from the origin (average revenue, which equals price) are both constant and have the same value. That value is the price, which is shown below as the firm's horizontal demand curve. Such a flat demand curve applies to a perfect competitor, which has to accept the going market price.

Profit is the excess of total revenue over total cost, as shown by the vertical distance in the top panel. The "profit hill" is simply that vertical gap. Below, the average profit per unit is the gap between price (average revenue) and average cost.

Profit is maximized where *price equals marginal cost.* Below that level, marginal output sells for more than it costs. Above that level, the marginal output costs more than its price. Therefore, the firm will move up to, or cut back to, exactly that profit-maximizing level. The resulting profit is the vertical distance in the top panel and the shaded rectangle in the lower panel. It is $1.10 per unit on 200,000 meals, or $220,000.

Under strict competition, marginal revenue is identical to price throughout because the firm's demand curve is horizontal. The demand curve and the marginal revenue curve are the same. Thus, the firm chooses the output level where

Price = Average revenue = Marginal revenue
= Marginal cost.

For competitive firms, therefore, this special condition holds at the profit-maximizing output:

Price = Marginal cost.

Output is set where the rising marginal cost curve cuts the horizontal demand curve.

185

Table 1   *Maximizing profits: The quantities in Figure 5*

Quantity of Output (1000 meals per year)	Total Cost (1000)	Total Revenue (Price × Quantity) ($1000)	Total Profit (Total Revenue − Total Cost) ($1000)	Marginal Cost ($ per meal)	Average Cost (Total Cost ÷ Quantity) ($ per meal)	Price and Marginal Revenue ($ per meal)	Average Profit (Price − Average Total Cost) ($ per meal)	Marginal Profit (Price − Marginal Cost) ($ per meal)
0	200	0	−200	—	—	—	—	—
100	465	425	−40	1.60	4.65	4.25	−.40	2.65
120	480	510	30	1.50	4.00	4.25	.25	2.75
140	495	595	100	1.50	3.54	4.25	.71	2.75
160	515	680	165	1.90	3.22	4.25	1.03	2.35
170	535	723	188	2.20	3.15	4.25	1.10	2.05
180	560	765	205	2.60	3.11	4.25	1.14	1.65
190	590	808	218	3.25	3.10	4.25	1.15	1.00
200	630	850	220	4.25	3.15	4.25	1.10	0
210	685	893	208	5.50	3.26	4.25	.99	−1.25
220	755	935	180	7.10	3.43	4.25	.82	−2.85
230	850	978	128	10.00	3.70	4.25	.55	−5.75
240	1020	1020	0	14.50	4.25	4.25	0	−10.25
250	1270	1063	−207	21.00	5.08	4.25	−.83	−15.75

Note how this occurs in the precise conditions of Figure 5. In Panel II, the 200,000 unit at Point *A* is just "worth it." It costs $4.25 to make that meal (that is its marginal cost) and it sells for $4.25, just enough to cover that marginal cost. The 165,000th unit at Point *B* is definitely worth producing, since it costs only $2.00 to make and it sells for $4.25. So all of the units between 165,000 and 200,000 will be produced because they each return a marginal profit. From 200,001 on up, by contrast, each marginal unit causes a marginal loss (shown in the last column of Table 1). Thus, the 210,000th unit, at Point *C*, costs $5.50 but sells for only $4.25: Its marginal loss is $1.25. Producing more than 200,000 units is foolish.

Starting anywhere *away from* the level where price equals marginal cost, the firm can make more profit by changing to that level. That is clear in both panels of Figure 5. Choosing that level is good for the private interest of the firm. It also brings value (the price reflecting consumer preferences) into line with opportunity cost to the economy (marginal cost). We will return to this price = marginal cost condition later in the chapter.

Profit   At 200,000 units, the average revenue (price) is $4.25 and average cost is $3.15, as shown in Panel II of Figure 5 and in Table 1. Thus, average profit is $1.10 per unit. Total profit is $1.10 times the number of units (200,000), for a total of $220,000. The profit is shown by the shaded rectangle in Panel II. That rectangle corresponds exactly to the vertical profit distance in Panel I. This profit is "extra" profit. Average cost already includes the cost of capital. Here, the firm is lucky enough to make an extra profit of $220,000 per period in the short run.

Now suppose that the market price for meals drops during the slow summer months to $2.50. In this situation, your restaurant can only do a special short-run version of maximizing profits: minimizing its losses. The restaurant still produces where price equals marginal cost. But now it also applies a special threshold crite-

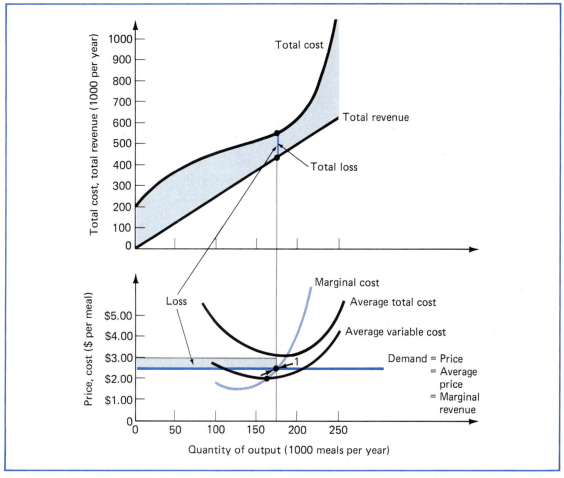

Figure 6 Minimizing losses

Price has now fallen to $2.50 per meal. The total revenue curve has rotated below the total cost curve at every point. No profit is now possible, but at least the losses can be minimized.

In the lower panel, price equals marginal cost at 175,000 meals per year. That is the best output level. At lower output levels, the firm can make marginal profits by expanding. At outputs above 175,000, the restaurant makes marginal losses and should cut back.

The vertical loss *distance* in the upper panel corresponds precisely to the shaded loss *rectangle* below.

rion: ***Price must cover average variable cost.*** If the price equals or exceeds average variable cost, then the firm keeps producing in the short run, until its fixed costs expire. Then all of the costs become variable, and price must cover average total cost. If at any time price is below average variable cost, the firm closes down at once.

Therefore, the competitive firm's supply curve is the part of the marginal cost curve *that is at or above the average variable cost curve.*

This fits both common sense and the familiar business wisdom: (1) to keep pro-

ducing in the short run if the price covers at least your current (or "out-of-pocket") expenses, but (2) to shut down in the long run unless price covers all average costs. It is illustrated in more detail in Figure 6. Average variable cost goes as low as $1.97 per meal. At a $2.50 price, you will definitely stay open during the summer.

How many meals will you supply? The answer is shown by marginal cost, just as before. Where it equals price, losses are minimized. That occurs at a rate of 175,-000 meals per year, as shown by Point 1 in Panel II of Figure 6. Think of it as an av-

Table 2 *Minimizing losses: The quantities in Figure 6*

Quantity of Output (1000 meals per year)	Total Cost ($1000)	Variable Cost (Total Cost – Fixed Cost) ($1000)	Total Revenue (Price × Quantity) ($1000)	Total Profit (Total Revenue – Total Cost) ($1000)	Marginal Cost ($ per meal)	Average Total Cost (Total Cost ÷ Output) ($ per meal)	Average Variable Cost (Variable Cost ÷ Output) ($ per meal)	Price and Marginal Revenue ($ per meal)	Average Profit (Price – Average Total Cost) ($ per meal)	Marginal Profit (Price – Marginal Cost) ($ per meal)
0	200	0								
100	465	265	250	−215	1.60	4.65	2.65	2.50	−2.15	.90
120	480	280	300	−180	1.50	4.00	2.33	2.50	−1.50	1.00
140	495	295	350	−145	1.50	3.54	2.11	2.50	−1.04	1.00
160	515	315	400	−115	1.90	3.22	1.97	2.50	−.72	.60
170	535	335	425	−110	2.20	3.15	1.97	2.50	−.65	.30
180	560	360	450	−110	2.60	3.11	2.00	2.50	−.61	−.10
190	590	390	475	−115	3.25	3.10	2.05	2.50	−.60	−.75
200	630	430	500	−130	4.25	3.15	2.15	2.50	−.65	−1.75
210	685	485	525	−160	5.50	3.26	2.31	2.50	−.76	−3.00
220	755	555	550	−205	7.10	3.43	2.52	2.50	−.93	−4.60
230	850	650	575	−275	10.00	3.70	2.82	2.50	−1.20	−7.50
240	1020	820	600	−420	14.50	4.25	3.42	2.50	−1.75	−12.00
250	1270	1070	625	−645	21.00	5.08	4.28	2.50	−2.58	−18.50

erage of 480 meals per day during the low-demand summer season. Table 2 corroborates the answer. Note the column for marginal profit. Added units make a profit up to about 175,000 meals per year. You move up to 175,000 and stay open. Added meals cause extra losses. The Total Profit column clinches it. Losses are the least possible between 170,000 and 180,000 meals per year. These losses are shown in Panel I of Figure 6 by the vertical distance between the total revenue and total cost curves. That distance is shortest at 175,000 meals per year.

The basic rule is that revenues must exceed corresponding costs. *In the short run, average variable costs are the test. In the long run, all costs are variable, so that average total costs become the minimum test.* Generally, whatever the time period, output is set where marginal revenue equals cost.

Figure 7 shows precisely how the firm's short-run supply curve is the part of its marginal cost curve that lies above average variable cost. At prices below vari-able cost, the firm produces nothing. At higher prices, output is set along the marginal cost curve.

The short-run market supply curve is a summation

The market includes all active buyers and sellers of the good. Within that market are all the firms that might produce and sell at the going price. Our typical firm is one.

Each firm's marginal cost curve is its supply curve. Added up horizontally, these curves form the **supply curve for the whole market. The short-run market supply curve is the summation of the firms' short-run marginal cost curves.** Figure 8 shows the horizontal summation. At low prices, some firms supply nothing, while others supply moderate amounts. As prices rise, some firms begin producing—as price rises above their average variable cost—while the firms already producing raise their levels of production. Since marginal cost curves slope up (reflecting diminishing marginal returns), so does the market

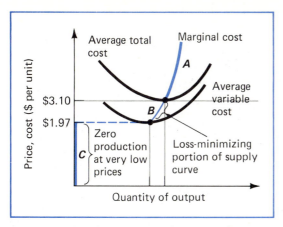

Figure 7 The short-run supply curve of a competitive firm

The supply curve includes Portions *A*, *B*, and *C* in the short run. Price can fall to $1.97 before the firm shuts down immediately. In the *B* range, the firm is taking temporary losses.

supply curve. In short, the shape and position of the supply curve reflect the technology of the industry, as it is embodied in the marginal and average variable costs curves.

Shifts in the firm and industry supply curves

The firm supply curve must shift if its MC curve shifts. Shifts in the MC curve will oc- cur if the variable costs of production change because of changes in either input prices or technology. If, for example, input prices fall, a firm's MC curve will shift down to the right. The firm will be willing to supply more output at every price (or to supply a given level of output at a lower price) because it is profit maximizing to do so.

Various shifts in the firms' MC curves are explored in Panels I and II of Figure 9. The industry supply curve will shift if the firms' MC curves are shifting or if the number of firms in the industry changes. If the number of firms in the industry increases, then more marginal cost curves must be added to arrive at the industry supply curve. The industry supply curve would shift right, showing that more output will be offered at every price. Shifts in the industry supply curve are also explored in Panels III and IV of Figure 9.

Three points about the supply curve should be carefully noted. First, the firm and industry supply curves presented here apply only to perfectly competitive firms and industries because the firms supply

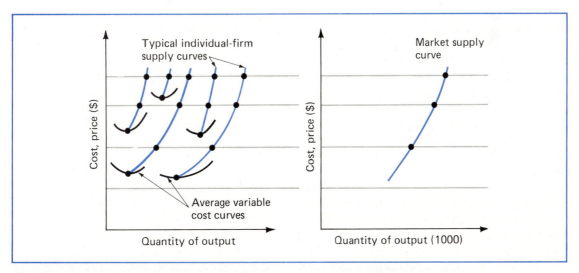

Figure 8 Market supply is the sum of individual firms' supply: Short run

At each price, the firms will act along their own supply curves. Their outputs make up the market's total supply. The market supply curve reflects the shape of the firm's various marginal cost curves. Since they slope up, the market supply curve slopes up.

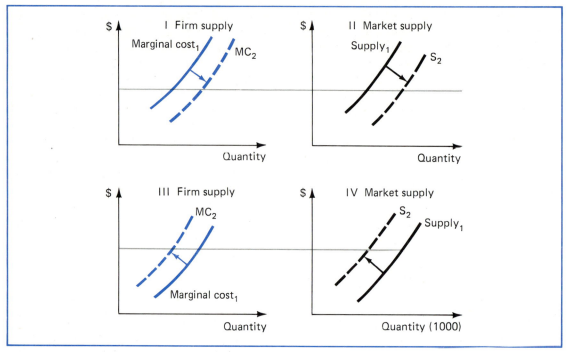

Figure 9 Shifts in firm and market supply curves

In Panels I and II, there has been a decrease in the price of inputs, or a technological improvement. Both the firm's supply surve and the market supply curve shift down.

In Panels III and IV, there has been a rise in input prices, and a decrease in the number of firms. Both the firm's supply curves and the market supply curve shift up.

curve was derived on the assumption of a horizontal MR curve. Since the horizontal MR curve is a result of the specific assumptions of perfect competition, namely that an individual firm is a price taker, the resulting supply curve pertains only to perfect competition.

Second, not all cost changes will affect the firm and industry supply curve. Only cost changes that affect variable and therefore marginal costs can cause the supply curves to shift. If fixed costs increase, the firm's MC or supply curve will not shift. The industry supply curve may shift eventually if the change in fixed costs results in a change in the number of firms.

Third, the firm and industry supply curves discussed here are *short-run* supply curves. Since the firm's MC curves are as-

sociated with a particular-size plant, fixed factors are involved. The industry supply curve is also based on fixed factors, since it represents a fixed number of firms. If the number of firms changes, the supply curve will shift.

Short-run and long-run equilibrium in perfect competition

The short-run and long-run equilibrium conditions for any type of firm can be derived by combining the characteristics of the firm's market with the rules for profit maximization. The rules for profit maximization will, of course, be the same regardless of market structure. It is the different characteristics of each market or industry that will lead to very different equilibrium outcomes.

In perfect competition, the key characteristics to remember are that the firms in the industry are price takers, and that there is freedom of entry and exit. The profit-maximizing rules are that the firms must cover variable costs in the short run and total costs in the long run. Firms must also produce at the point where $MR = MC$.

The three panels in Figure 10 show three possible profit-loss situations for a perfectly competitive firm. Panel I shows a firm taking a loss, with $P < ATC$. Panel II shows a firm making a normal return, with $P = ATC$. Panel III shows a firm making a profit, with $P > ATC$. Which of these situations is compatible with *short-run* equilibrium?

Equilibrium, remember, means a state of rest or balance, a state of stability. For a firm to be in equilibrium, it must be profit maximizing. After all, if the firm is not doing as well as it can, it will certainly have the incentive to make changes. Therefore, for **short-run equilibrium,** the short-run profit-maximizing rules of $P \geq AVC$ and $MR = MC$ must be satisfied. In each of the three situations depicted by the panels in Figure 10, these short-run profit rules are satisfied. Therefore, all three situations of profit, loss, and normal return are compatible with short-run equilibrium. In none of the situations can the firm improve its position. The loss shown in Panel I would not make the firm particularly happy. If $P < AVC$, the firm would immediately shut down. However, as long as $P \geq AVC$, it is best for the firm to continue to operate: It will at least minimize its losses by paying off part of its fixed cost.

In the long run, however, the situation is different. The profit-maximizing rules are now that $P \geq ATC$ and $MR = MC$. Since $P < ATC$ in Panel I, that cannot represent a **long-run equilibrium.**

In Panel III, $P > ATC$. Could this situation represent a long-run equilibrium? To answer that question, you need to think about the specific characteristics of perfect competition. In perfect competition, there is freedom of entry and exit. If the firms in perfect competition are making a profit, with $P > ATC$, other firms will enter the industry. As that happens, the industry supply curve will shift right and market price will begin to fall. Each firm will find its own MR curve or demand curve shifting down in response to the decreased market price, as Figure 11 shows.

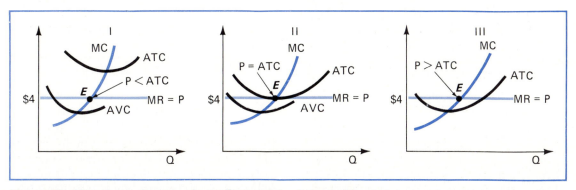

Figure 10   Situations of economic profit, normal return, and loss

At Point *E* in Panel I, *MR = MC* and *P* > *AVC*. The firm is in short-run equilibrium. Panel I does not represent a long-run equilibrium, however. In the long run, losses will cause exit. At Point *E* in Panel II, *P = ATC* and *MR* = *MC*. The firm is in short-run equilibrium. Panel II also represents long-run equilibrium. With *P = ATC*, there is no incentive for entry or exit. At Point *E* in Panel III, *MR = MC* and *P* > *ATC*. The firm is in short-run equilibrium. Panel III does not represent long-run equilibrium, however. With *P* > *ATC*, entry will occur.

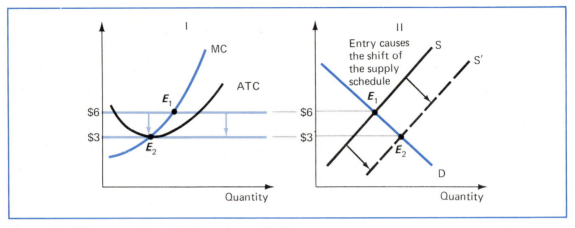

Figure 11   Adjustment toward a long-run equilibrium

At E_1 in Panel I, the firm is making a profit, with price of $6 greater than ATC. Profit attracts new firms, and their entry causes the industry supply schedule to shift to the right, as in Panel II. As the supply schedule shifts right, the market price will fall, shifting the firm's MR or demand curve downward. Entry will cease only when market price equals minimum ATC. This occurs at a market price of $3. At E_2, $P = ATC$ and $MR = MC$. Each firm is maximizing profits and there is no incentive for entry or exit. E_2, therefore, represents a long-run equilibrium.

These shifts will continue as long as $P > ATC$. Since changes are not compatible with an equilibrium, it is clear that economic profits cannot exist in long-run equilibrium for a competitive industry. Only with $P = ATC$ is there no incentive for firms to enter into or exit from the industry. Neither profits nor losses are being made then. Thus, for perfect competition, the two long-run equilibrium conditions are: (1) $P = ATC$, and (2) $MR = MC$.

Because the assumptions about competition are so specific, we can be very precise about the long-run equilibrium outcome in perfect competition. Not only must firms be making a normal return with $P = ATC$, *but ATC must be at its minimum point.* This result stems from the price-taking assumption of perfect competition. Examine Figure 12, which shows a U-shaped long-run ATC curve. Suppose that a competitive firm were operating at Point A. Could this possibly be a stable or equilibrium position? No, it could not. Since price per unit is unchanged by the

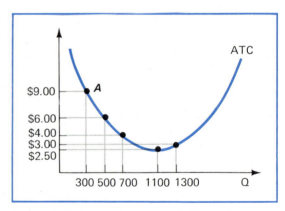

Figure 12   Long-run average total cost

amount the firm produces, the firm has a clear incentive to increase plant size until it is producing at the lowest or minimum ATC. Therefore, in the long run, when the firm can adjust all factors, it will clearly have an incentive to adjust its technology and its output levels until it is producing at minimum ATC. Figure 13 portrays a perfectly competitive firm and industry in long-run equilibrium. Notice how all of

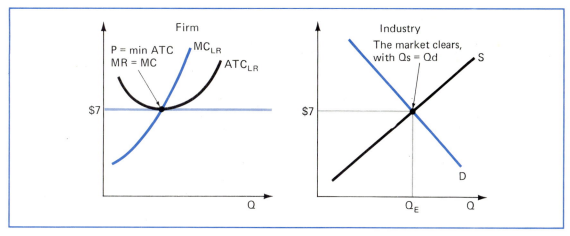

Figure 13   Long-run equilibrium for a perfectly competitive firm and industry

the equilibrium conditions are illustrated in one diagram. At the level of output produced, $MR = MC$, and $P =$ minimum ATC.

Long-run supply

The firm's long-run supply curve
The firm's **long-run supply curve** is its *long-run marginal cost curve* lying above average total cost. That is shown in Figure

14. These cost curves were derived in Chapter 8. Recall that the long-run curve is flatter than the short-run supply curve, reflecting the wider choices available in the long run, when no input is fixed. The same rule applies in setting output. At prices below average variable cost (which is now *identical to average total cost* because all costs are variable in the long run), output is zero. The firm is closed down. Above that price, the marginal cost curve is the supply curve. In short, supply is precisely determined by price and cost.

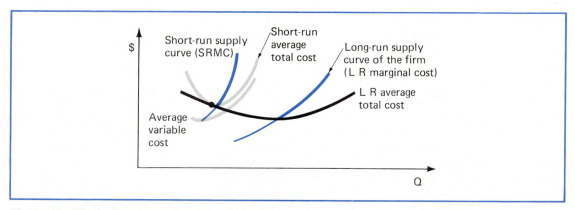

Figure 14   The long-run supply curve of the firm
For a given size of plant, the short-run cost curves show the firm's choices. But in the long run, the firm's supply curve is the long-run marginal cost curve, as shown.

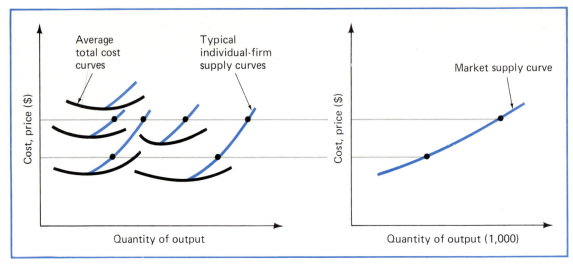

Figure 15 Market supply in the long run
Now the firms' long-run supply curves are more elastic than their short-run supply curves, because adjustments can be made over a larger range of inputs in the long run.

The long-run market supply curve
As in the short run, the long-run supply curve for the market is the horizontal summation of the firms' supply curves. The summation is shown in Figure 15. The long-run supply curve is more elastic, because the firms' long-run marginal cost curves are more elastic. Also, the long run permits the entry of new firms, which augment the supply as price rises. Nonetheless, both curves are derived by the same basic process of horizontal addition.

Efficient allocation under competition
Now consider what the analysis in this chapter has established. The steps have been relatively simple, primarily a horizontal adding up of marginal cost. Yet, the result is profound. In each market, supply occurs as the result of consistent patterns of cost and price. The quantities supplied are precisely governed by the going market prices and the internal costs of all firms in the market. Higher prices induce greater levels of output; lower prices cause production to be cut back. These outcomes are intuitively likely. Here they have been explained by exact, consistent logic.

Moreover, the outcome is in line with *efficient production*. Efficiency is used in economics to define a set of conditions. Several of those efficient conditions have already been defined along the way, in explaining the competitive result. We will now list each of them:

Avoiding unnecessary cost Each firm attains the costs shown by the average cost curve, rather than incurring higher costs. Whatever output level is chosen, average cost is as low as possible. This is termed **x-efficiency**, as noted in Chapter 8.

Optimum scale Each firm also chooses the output level at which average total cost is at its minimum, in the long run. This level is termed optimal scale, for it is the size at which average cost levels are as low as possible.

Allocative efficiency *Allocative efficiency* deals with the pattern of inputs and outputs among all firms and markets. Even if production efficiency and optimal scale are reached in every firm, there might still be too much of some outputs produced and too little of others. The allocation of resources among goods would be inefficient. What is the right pattern of goods? The general answer is: *that allocation in which price equals marginal cost for every firm.* Recall that price represents the value of a good to consumers, shown by what they will pay for it at the margin. Marginal cost is the opportunity cost of the good to the firm. When price equals MC, the firm's own choice is efficient, for the last unit is just worth its cost.

For society as a whole, too, price equals MC defines the best level for each output. Price is the *social* value of the good at the margin: What people will pay for the good is a measure of its value to the general population. Private and social value are identical. As for cost, marginal cost measures the *social* opportunity cost of the last unit of the good. It is the degree of additional sacrifice (in effort, resources, etc.) that the workers must make to sustain the current level of output. When price equals marginal cost, then the value of the added output just equals the sacrifice to produce it.

To clarify efficient allocation, consider a departure from it. Suppose all firms meet the $P = MC$ condition except one, where output is "too small" and price exceeds marginal cost. By expanding production, this firm will create more value (price) than cost (marginal cost). It will

Table 3 *Basic conditions of efficient equilibrium*

Equilibrium Condition	Cause
Short Run	
Price > Average variable cost	A firm will only operate in the short run if it can cover the costs of staying open (the variable costs pay off part of its fixed costs).
Marginal revenue = Revenue cost	Condition necessary for the profit-maximizing level of output.
Price = Marginal cost	Price equals marginal cost for the competitive firm.
Long Run	
Price = Average total cost	*Freedom of entry and exit:* Since firms are free to enter or leave the industry, equilibrium can only occur if there is no incentive for firms to enter or exit. This implies that a normal return (economic profits = 0) is being made by the firms in the industry, since losses would cause exit and profits would cause entry.
Price = Marginal cost	*The condition of profit maximization under competition:* It also equals average cost (the condition of normal return). So price must equal average cost at the point where average and marginal costs are equal, at minimum average total cost.
Marginal revenue = Marginal cost	Condition necessary to achieve the profit-maximizing level of output.
Price = Marginal cost	Price equals marginal cost for the competitive firm.

take resources from uses where they brought no net gain and, in this firm, create a net gain. The total value of production will rise, even if only slightly. When adjustments no longer add net value, then allocation is efficient.

Thus, condition of efficiency will be enforced by competition. Each firm maximizes profits by applying precisely the same $P = MC$ condition that defines efficient allocation for the entire economy. Table 3 (on page 195) summarizes the conditions in detail. If they are reached by all firms, then allocation is efficient throughout the economy.

Limits Neoclassical economists have known the efficiency benefits of a competitive economy for nearly a century. But the process also has various limits, which can cause the outcomes to deviate from social goals:

1. *Distribution.* The distribution of income and wealth may be unfair, even if allocation is efficient.
2. *Technological progress.* The rate at which technology is improved is also largely outside the pure competitive process.
3. *Market prices and costs may deviate from the true social values.* Such deviations would mean that the competitive outcome would not be socially efficient after all. Common examples are the air and water pollution created by some "efficient" factories.
4. *Monopoly.* Competition may be replaced by monopoly in one or more markets. That distorts allocation away from efficiency.

The benefits and limits of the competitive outcome are presented in detail in the chapter on General Equilibrium.

Summary

This chapter first establishes the general rules that all profit-maximizing firms must follow. It then applies these rules to the model of industry behavior known as perfect competition. Short-run and long-run equilibrium conditions for the industry are then derived.

1. A firm should produce in the short run if it is at least covering its operating costs, with $P \geq AVC$. In the long run, a firm will only produce if it can cover its economic costs, with $P \geq ATC$.

2. A profit-maximizing firm should always produce the level of output for which $MR = MC$. If it is producing at a point where $MR > MC$, it should increase output, since each additional unit of output will add more to revenue than to cost, thereby increasing the firm's profit or reducing its losses. If the firm is producing at a point where $MC > MR$, it should decrease its level of output, since each additional unit is adding more to cost than to revenue, thereby reducing the firm's profit or increasing its losses.

3. Competition may be pure or imperfect. But even a two-firm rivalry may approach the results of pure competition, as long as collusion is prevented.

4. The two key assumptions of the model of market structure known as perfect competition are: (1) the firms in the industry are price takers, accepting the market price as given; (2) there is freedom of entry and exit.

5. In perfect competition, an individual firm's demand and marginal revenue curves are both represented by a horizontal line at the level of market price.

6. The short-run supply curve of a competitive firm is its marginal cost curve at or above AVC. The short-run supply curve for the industry is derived by summing horizontally the firm supply schedule. If the firms' MC curves shift or if the number of firms changes, the industry supply schedule will shift.

7. A competitive firm in *short-run* equilibrium will produce with $P \geq AVC$ and $MR = MC$. It may be making a profit, loss, or normal return.

8. A competitive firm in *long-run* equilibrium will be producing at a point where $P = $ minimum ATC and $MR = MC$.

9. The market supply curve is the horizontal summation of the firms' supply curves.

10. The results of changes that lead to disequilibrium can be determined by combining profit-maximizing rules with the characteristics of a specific industry.

11. A long-run supply schedule that allows for changes in the number of firms can also be derived. The slope of the long-run supply curve will depend upon the behavior of input prices as entry and exit of firms occur.

Key concepts

Rules of profit maximization
Marginal revenue
Competition
 rivalry
  pure competition
  perfect competition
Firm demand curve
Firm supply curve
Supply curve for whole market

Firm and industry equilibrium
 short-run
 long-run
Long-run supply curve
Production efficiency
Allocative efficiency

Questions for review

1. Given the information in the following situations, can you determine if the statements are true or false? Explain your answer.

 a. A firm is selling 5,000 units at $5 each. Its total costs equal $20,000. Therefore, the firm must be profit maximizing.

 b. The last unit that the firm produced added $5 to revenue and $3 to cost. The firm should continue to operate.

 c. A firm is selling 1,000 units of output at $3 a unit. Its average total costs are $2,500. The firm should shut down.

 d. The last unit a firm produced added $3 to revenue and $6 to cost. The firm should operate in the short run but not in the long run.

 e. A firm is producing at the point at which $MR = MC$. The firm must be making economic profits of zero.

2. Consider the following list of firms. Which firms would not satisfy the conditions of perfect competition. Explain.

GM	NBC
wheat farmer	A&P
Bethlehem Steel	Harvard
bookstore in	University
your town	local bank

3. Consider the following statements:
   a. A firm in perfect competition can sell as much output as it wishes at the prevailing market price.
   b. There was an exceptionally abundant wheat harvest that year. Every farmer took larger quantities of wheat to market and therefore received a lower price.

   Are these two statements contradictory? Why or why not? Explain.

4. Each of the following statements is incorrect because there is vital information missing. What must be added to each statement to make it correct?
   a. The demand curve in perfect competition is downward sloping.
   b. The supply curve of a perfectly competitive firm is its marginal cost schedule.
   c. If the number of firms in a competitive industry changes, the industry supply schedule will shift to the right.

5. State which characteristics of a perfectly competitive industry will cause each of the following long-run equilibrium conditions. Explain your answers.
   a. $P = ATC$
   b. $MR = MC$
   c. production at minimum ATC

·10·

Monopoly

As you read and study this chapter you will learn:

▶ the varieties of market forms in which monopoly power occurs

▶ the nature of monopoly and its effects on efficiency, equity, and other social values

▶ the possible role of scale economies as a cause of monopoly power

▶ several case studies of monopoly

Whenever friends settle down to play Monopoly, their little board game is much like the endless pursuit of monopoly in real industrial markets. Each player tries to amass as much of the property—real estate, railroads, and utilities—as possible. The player who gets all of one set of properties can force the others to pay much higher rents on them.

The players all strive to monopolize the properties, to extract high profits from them, and, in the process, to bankrupt one another. Eventually one player, the successful monopolist, emerges victorious and the rest are impoverished.

In real industrial life, too, firms strive to gain monopoly power in their markets and to reap its rewards. Pure monopoly—from the Greek word *monopolion*, meaning exclusive sale—has a simple meaning: the control of all sales in a market. Even though a firm has less than 100 percent of the market, it may still have an important degree of monopoly power.

If all firms try to gain a monopoly and yet none of them manages to prevail, then the result is a continuous, healthy competitive process. The aspiring monopolists neutralize one another. When the resulting competition is vigorous, the benefits will be large.

In contrast with competition, monopoly usually causes economic harms. It may distort the allocation of resources, cause waste and inefficiency, and shift wealth unfairly. From the earliest times, rulers have issued countless laws to deal with the harms and distortions caused by monopoly power. Such a serious problem needs careful study. Therefore, this chapter and the two that follow it present the causes and effects of, and the cures for, monopoly in some detail.

This chapter begins by showing the main types of monopoly and competition. Next, we show the distinctive forms that monopoly power takes, and then the main ways by which monopoly can be created. Then, we present the effects of monopoly, contrasting them with the competitive outcomes shown in Chapter 9. Finally, we discuss some case studies of prominent monopolies. They include Standard Oil from 1880 to 1910 and electrical generation in the early twentieth century.

Varieties of monopoly and competition

Pure monopoly is a powerful device for gaining wealth, as we shall soon see. Pure monopolies, however, are highly unusual in modern industry. The polar opposite of pure monopoly is pure competition, where no firm has any control over price. It, too, is unusual.

Most markets lie between these extremes, with some degree—slight, modest, or large—of *monopoly power* (also called

market power). There are many subtle gradations and varieties of monopoly power, but debates in the literature have settled on several main categories. Table 1 lists these classes, with their main features. The table also suggests which parts of the economy each category is commonly found in.

All real markets fit somewhere into Table 1. The categories shade into one another, rather than being sharply separate, so that some industries are on the fence. For example, the automobile industry has features of both a tight oligopoly (with three leading firms) and a dominant-firm case (with General Motors holding about 45 percent of the market). Moreover, each of the categories in Table 1 covers a range of conditions, rather than just one form.

Whether monopoly is complete or partial, the same basic analysis applies. Monopoly produces certain effects, whose strength depends on the degree of monopoly power. When monopoly power is strong, the effects are strong; where it is weak, monopoly power gives only mild effects. Both in this chapter and in the next, therefore, keep in mind that the analysis is relevant to all degrees of monopoly power.

Monopoly and its effects

The first task is to learn to recognize monopoly by its usual forms.

The characteristics of monopoly
Monopoly can exist when the firm's demand curve slopes down, rather than being horizontal as it is for the purely competitive firm. The down-slope gives the firm a range of choice in setting the price for its product. Figure 1 shows both a down-sloping demand curve *(A)* and a horizontal one *(B)*. The firm with Demand Curve *A* can choose Point 1, with its output and price levels. It could also set a

Table 1 **Types of markets, shading over from pure monopoly to pure competition**

Market Type	Main Condition	Familiar Instances
Pure monopoly	One firm has 100 percent of the market	Electric, telephone, water, bus, and other utilities; patented drugs
Dominant firm	One firm has 40–100 percent of the market and no close rival	Soup (Campbell), razor blades (Gillette), newspapers (most local markets), film (Eastman Kodak), hospitals
Tight oligopoly	The leading four firms, combined, have 60–100 percent of the market; collusion among them to fix prices is relatively easy	Copper, aluminum, local banking, TV broadcasting, light bulbs, soaps, textbook stores
Loose oligopoly	The leading four firms, combined, have 40 percent or less of the market; collusion among them to fix prices is virtually impossible	Lumber, furniture, small machinery, hardware, magazines
*Monopolistic competition**	Many effective competitors, none with more than 10 percent of the market	Retailing, clothing
Pure competition	Over 50 competitors, all with negligible market shares	Wheat, corn, cattle, hogs, poultry

Source: W. G. Shepherd, *The Economics of Industrial Organization* (Englewood Cliffs, N.J.: Prentice-Hall, 1979), Chaps. 4, 9, 10. Adapted by permission of Prentice-Hall, Inc., Englewood Cliffs, N.J.
*The phrase (coined by E. H. Chamberlin in 1932) means virtually complete competition, but with a moderate degree of differences among products. See the second main section of the next chapter for discussion.

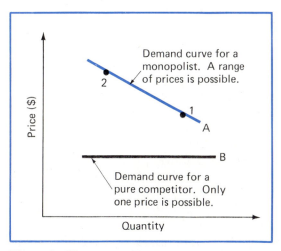

Demand curve for a monopolist. A range of prices is possible.

2

1

A

B

Demand curve for a pure competitor. Only one price is possible.

Figure 1   The monopolist's demand curve slopes down

The monopolist can set the price anywhere that it chooses along its demand curve. A pure competitor, by contrast, has no control over price. When the demand curve is horizontal, only one price is possible.

The monopolist's demand curve shown here is only a sample. Actual cases show great variety, from near-vertical curves to near-horizontal ones. Generally, the less elastic the curve, the higher the firm's degree of monopoly will be.

lower quantity and a higher price at Point 2. All other points along the demand curve are equally available. Meanwhile, the firm in a purely competitive market, with Demand Curve *B*, has no such degree of choice. If it raises its price even a little, it will sell nothing, for its customers will buy from other sellers. If a firm is a pure monopolist, controlling 100 percent of the market, then the market and firm demand schedules will be identical. If, instead, the firm has less than 100 percent of the market, its demand schedule will lie below or to the left of the market demand schedule. For example, in Figure 2, the market demand curve is shown along with the demand schedule of two of the firms in the industry. The firm represented by D_2 clearly has a larger share of the market than the firm represented by D_1.

Ideally, these curves would be known clearly and accurately, so that the degree of monopoly would be obvious. But de-

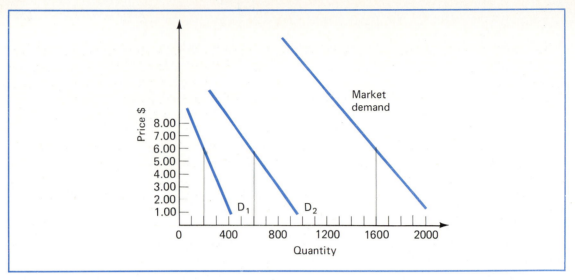

Figure 2 A comparison of firm and market demand

The demand schedules of two firms in this market are compared to the market demand schedule. The firm represented by D_2 has a larger market share, selling a higher quantity at each price than the firm represented by D_1. For example, at a price of $6, the total or market quantity demanded of the good will be 1,600 units. Of this total, 200 units will be demanded from Firm 1 and 600 units will be demanded from Firm 2. The remaining 800 units will be demanded from other firms in the industry.

mand curves aren't casily measured in real cases, as we noted in Chapter 5. So cconomists usually have to rely on other evidence to judge how much monopoly power a firm may hold. The main indicators are:

1. High market share A firm's ***market share*** is measured by its own sales, taken as a percentage of all sales in the market. "The market" is, in turn, defined to include goods that may easily be substituted for each other. A 100 percent share—the highest possible—is pure, total monopoly. A 10 percent share or lower usually gives the firm little market power. *Between 10 and 100 percent, the degree of monopoly power rises as the share rises.* **A market share above 40 percent usually provides substantial monopoly power.**

2. Lack of strong rivals If a firm is far larger than any other firm in its market, then its monopoly power cannot be strongly challenged. By contrast, the pres-

ence of equal or larger rivals would reduce the firm's ability to control the market.

3. Barriers to entry by new competitors Anything that makes it hard for new competitors to come into the market will enhance the market power of the firms already established there. If no ***entry barriers*** existed, even a firm with a 100 percent market share might conceivably have no market power.

4. High profitability Successful monopoly often leads to high profit rates on the firm's capital. Therefore, profit rates—taken together with the other signs of monopoly—often help the economist to evaluate how much market power a firm has. Yet, profitability is not conclusive evidence. Many monopolies fail to show high profits. They may hide their profits by accounting tricks; or they may become inefficient, make mistakes, or fall prey to other problems. Thus, high profit rates are not necessarily an indicator of monopoly power. Nor are they conclusive, since high profits can also come from a company's sheer good luck, its recent innovations, or other causes. *In short, high profit rates can help to confirm monopoly power, but they are not the key proof of its existence.*

In appraising real firms, economists try to consider these and other items. There is no exact formula, and the evidence about monopoly power will rarely be crystal clear. Utilities—with complete, officially protected monopolies—are usually straightforward cases. But the extent of the monopoly power of an IBM, General Motors, or Exxon is often hard to determine with precision. Like the best economists, you must rely on your judgment. Because most ordinary firms have little market power, as we will shortly see, economists concentrate mainly on dominant firms and tight oligopolies.

How monopoly power is created and maintained

There are many ways to gain monopoly power. Most firms try them most of the time, of course, but usually their efforts offset one another. Thus, competition itself tends to prevent monopoly. But when a firm does gain and hold a high degree of monopoly power, one or more of the following methods is usually at the root of it.

1. Mergers to capture a higher market share The firm may simply buy out its rivals, merging with them to get a high combined market share for the new, larger firm. Once unified, the former competitors no longer compete with one another.

2. Economies of scale Economies of scale are present when, because of the industry's technology, a large firm can produce a product more cheaply than a small firm. If the industry's cost curves show large economies of scale, then a firm will reach the lowest average cost at a high market share.

3. Superior innovation or efficiency A firm may capture most of a market by creating new and better products. Older products may be displaced, as when hand-held electronic calculators replaced desk-top electrical calculators in the 1970s. Or the new product may create a wholly new market, as Polaroid did with instant cameras in the 1950s and Xerox did with copiers in the 1960s. In either case, the high market share arises from innovation. Further innovations may help a firm keep its position, especially if its innovation is protected by patent.

Similarly, excellent management may allow the firm to gain and retain monopoly power. By cutting costs and inspiring workers, a firm's managers can cut prices and outsell their rivals. Being more *X-efficient*—producing more outputs from given inputs—the firm earns its monopoly power and profits.

4. Official support Government policies often create or maintain monopoly power.

A. PATENTS are issued for inventions, giving a 17-year monopoly that the owner can exploit to the hilt. This can both provide high profits and be the basis for a lasting monopoly position. Crucial *trademarks*—such as Jell-O, Band-Aid, Kleenex, and Formica—can also have similar effects. They condition people to buy the product just because it has the familiar brand name. Such consumer loyalty allows the firm to charge higher prices without losing customers. In short, trademarks can make the firm's demand curve both higher and less elastic, thereby giving the firm a degree of market power.

B. MONOPOLY FRANCHISES are given to utility companies, excluding all others from competing. Your local electric, gas, telephone, and cable TV companies, for example, are protected by their government franchises. No other firms are permitted to sell those services in your area. Taxi firms, banks, TV stations, and professional sports teams also usually have local franchise protection.

C. GOVERNMENT CONTRACTS often confer market power by making one or two firms the exclusive suppliers for large amounts of specific weapons (e.g., tanks, aircraft, cannon). Most military buying of weapons, for example, involves little competitive bidding among the aspiring suppliers of the armaments.

D. OTHER official supports include the Wagner Act of 1935, which permits labor unions to hold and exert monopoly power in labor markets. Many public enterprises—public schools and the U.S. Postal Service, for example—are also given monopoly power in their markets.

5. Key inputs Some industries rely on key inputs, such as the ores that are crucial for metal industries. By controlling the input, a firm can monopolize all or part of the industry and keep new competitors out. Thus, steel and copper companies have sewn up most of the cheap ore supplies, making it difficult for new competition to enter their markets.

6. Unfair competitive tactics If a firm resorts to unfair methods, it may be able to drive out its competitors and gain monopoly power. "Unfair" action is not a clear-cut category. What's fair in love, war, and rugged competition is often debatable. But firms do often overstep the bounds of vigorous competition in ways that victimize and destroy their rivals.

Altogether, monopoly power has many possible roots. Some of them are praiseworthy, such as economies of scale and innovations. But others have no value at all: mergers, government favors, and unfair tactics, for example. The monopolist, of course, always claims that good reasons

Table 2 *Features and sources of monopoly power*

I. Features of Monopoly Power
1. A high market share, especially above 40 percent.
2. A lack of strong rivals with similar market shares.
3. Barriers to new competition.
4. High profit rates (a supplementary indicator).

II. Ways to Acquire Monopoly Power
1. Merging with competitors, and other actions simply to increase market share.
2. Achieving economies of scale (especially in "natural monopoly" situations).
3. Innovating more rapidly or managing production more efficiently than competitors do.
4. Getting official support for market control from:
   a. Patents on crucial products or techniques.
   b. Monopoly franchises, such as for utilities.
   c. Exclusive government contracts, such as for military weapons.
   d. Others.
5. Controlling a key input, such as a scarce ore or superior location.
6. Unfair competitive actions to harm rival firms.

account for its position. Yet, less praiseworthy reasons for monopoly power may also—or instead—really apply.

Table 2 summarizes the main features and sources of monopoly power. Now we turn to the *effects* of monopoly power, whatever its origins.

The effects of monopoly power

Monopoly can have strong effects on prices, quantities and allocation in the market, the distribution of wealth, innovation patterns, and other economic values—in short, on all of the competitive outcomes discussed in Chapter 9. Table 3 lists monopoly's main effects.

The monopolist's choices *A pure monopolist is the entire supply side of the market.* Therefore, the monopolist's demand curve is the market demand curve itself.

Figure 3 shows the effects of turning a competitive market into a pure monopoly.

Table 3 The main effects of monopoly

I. **Monopoly *harms* economic performance:**
 1. *Efficiency in resource use* is reduced by changes in output and price:
     a. X-inefficiency may occur, raising average costs.
     b. Misallocation may occur, eliminating consumer surplus.
 2. *Equity in distribution* is reduced by monopoly profits (price discrimination may enlarge those profits). Wealth and income are shifted from the many to the few.
 3. *Technical progress* (invention and innovation) is probably reduced. It becomes optional to the monopolist, and perhaps unprofitable because it reduces the value of the monopolist's assets.
 4. *Broader values* may be harmed:
     a. Freedom of choice is reduced.
     b. Democracy is undermined.
     c. Culture and society become more closed and rigid.

II. **There may be offsetting *benefits* from monopoly:**
 1. *Economies of scale* in production and innovation may be achieved.
 2. Large innovations may be made more rapidly.

III. **The *net effects* may go either way, in general and in each case. They require careful study, not mere slogans or assertions.**

At first (in Panel I), the market is competitive; its supply and demand curves intersect to give the equilibrium price and output at Point *A*. Each competitive firm has a horizontal demand curve, though the market demand curve has the slope as shown.

Then a monopolist unites all of the suppliers into one firm. Its demand curve is now identical to the *market* demand curve, sloping down, as shown in both Panels I and II. The monopolist can now choose both the *price* level and the output level: Each price now corresponds to a different level of output. The monopolist's profit-maximizing choice fits the same basic logic as the competitive firm's (or any other firm's): *It sets output at the level where its marginal revenue equals its marginal cost.*

Marginal revenue is crucial to the monopoly outcome. The monopolist's *marginal revenue* curve is now below its demand curve, as shown in Panel II. When

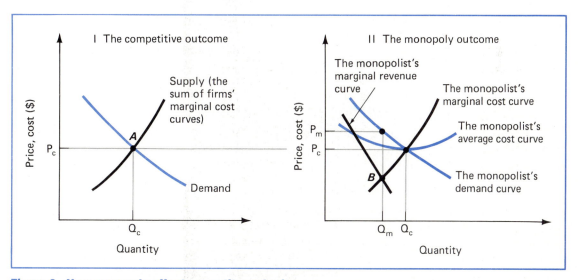

Figure 3 How monopoly affects quantity and price

Supply and demand set the competitive output and price at Point *A* in Panel I. If the market is monopolized by one firm, then the market demand curve is its demand curve. The monopolist now has a marginal revenue curve, as shown. The monopolist now maximizes its profit at Point *B* in Panel II, where its marginal revenue (*not* price) equals its marginal cost. At that output, Q_m, the price is P_m, which is above the competitive price P_c.

demand was horizontal for each competitor, marginal revenue was also horizontal and coincided with demand for each firm. Selling another unit brought in exactly as much revenue as the price itself. But now that there is just one firm, its demand slopes down. To sell more units, the monopolist must cut its price, and *that* reduces the price obtained on all of the units that would have been sold at the higher price.

For example, in Figure 4, the price must be cut from $12 to $11 to sell the eighth unit. That brings the firm an additional $11 for selling that unit (Area *A*). But the price on units one through seven would have been $12. Cutting to an $11 price to sell an additional unit means that the firm gives up $1 on each of those seven units (shown by Area *B*). The *net* gain from selling unit eight is thus $11 minus $7 (Area *A* minus Area *B*), which is only $4. The marginal revenue of the eighth unit is therefore $4, which is well below the $11 price.

The marginal revenue from selling more output is the price of the added unit *minus* the revenue lost by cutting price on the other units. This value must be less than the price on the demand curve. Therefore, the marginal revenue curve always lies below the demand curve.

The marginal revenue curve is easy to locate: The marginal revenue curve of a straight-line demand curve is always a straight line, halfway between the demand curve and the vertical axis. You merely draw two light horizontal lines to the left of the demand curve, mark the halfway points (Points 1 and 2 in Figure 4), and draw the marginal revenue curve through them. Or, alternatively, you draw and divide one horizontal line, find the point on the vertical axis that the demand curve would go through, and then use these two points to draw the marginal revenue curve. With this skill, you can always place the

marginal cost curve roughly correctly, in relation to the firm's demand curve.

Where a monopolist has unified all of the firms in a formerly competitive market, its marginal cost schedule will be the former competitive market's supply curve (as was shown in Figure 3). Remember that this supply curve was the sum of all the competitive firms' marginal cost curves. Since the single monopolist now includes all of those firms, *its marginal cost*

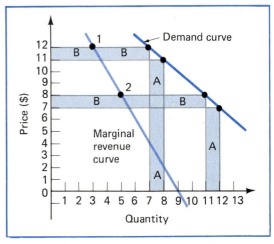

Figure 4   When demand slopes down, the marginal revenue curve lies below it

Marginal revenue shows the net effect on revenue of producing another unit. The revenue from an extra unit is added (Area *A*), but the cut in price for all the other units must be subtracted (Area *B*). The same net calculation can be done for any point along the demand curve. Thus, at an output level of 7, *A* is bigger than *B*, and marginal revenue is positive at a $4 value. But when output is 12, *B* is bigger than *A*, and marginal revenue is negative.

The exact numbers for the two cases shown in the figure are:

Output	Price	Total Revenue	A	B	Marginal Revenue
7	12	84	+11	−7	4
8	11	88			
9	10	90			
10	9	90			
11	8				
11	8	88	+7	−11	−4
12	7	84			

curve is the summation of all the original firms' marginal cost curves.

The monopolist's two curves—marginal revenue and marginal cost—cross at Point *B* in Figure 3, which is thus the monopolist's profit-maximizing output. As always, the firm produces only up to the level at which the extra unit is just "worth what it costs to produce it." That is the commonsense meaning of marginal revenue just equaling marginal cost.

As Figure 3 shows, the monopolist has chosen output level Q_m. The price that results is shown by the point on the demand curve at output Q_m. Consumers will be willing to pay P_m (*m* stands for "monopoly"), so that becomes the monopolists' profit-maximizing price. One might say that the monopolist chooses the output rather than the price; but, in effect, *the monopolist's decisions set both output and price, whereas competitors merely take the price as given.*

Recall also from Chapter 9 that the competitive outcome made prices equal to marginal costs. Price is a measure of the social value of a good, for it shows what people are willing to pay for it. Marginal cost is the true cost—the opportunity cost, the social sacrifice in terms of the resources used—of producing a specific amount of the good. The $P = MC$ equality means that the output of the good is expanded up to the point at which the cost of the resources used to produce the last unit of the good just equals the value that the consumers place on that last unit. This is the general condition of efficiency, since only at this point is the social value of the good equal to its cost.

The monopolist violates that efficient outcome by cutting output and pushing price above marginal cost. In Figure 5 the new monopoly price is much higher than marginal cost. There is economic harm in that disparity. People are willing to pay

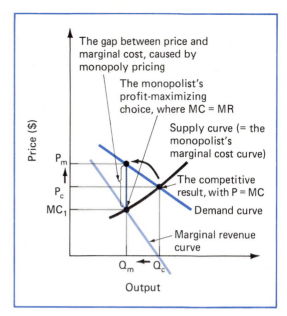

Figure 5   The simple effect of monopoly
The efficient competitive result is where supply equals demand, with Q_c and P_c (c stands for "competitive"). The new monopolist now interferes. It heeds its own marginal revenue curve, setting its output level where marginal revenue equals marginal cost. Output is cut to Q_m and price rises to P_m (*m* stands for "monopoly"). Price is now well above marginal cost, by the distance $P_m - MC_1$. Consumers would pay up to the price P_m to get output that costs only MC_1 to make, but the monopolist won't let them do that. Therefore, output and prices are distorted from efficient levels. (Note: The marginal cost schedule is *not* the monopolist's supply schedule, as you will see.)

more than twice as much as the marginal cost of the good. The value that they place on the good is twice as high as the cost of the resources used to produce the last unit. This is a clear signal that more of the good should be produced. But the monopolist has cut output back, effectively prohibiting sales between Q_m and Q_c. Therefore, it can force people to pay a monopoly price that is well above the real cost of supply. *Price exceeding marginal cost is, therefore, a sign of distortion away from the efficient competitive level. It calls for an expansion of output, but the monopolist prevents that expansion from occurring.*

The severity of this cutback in output depends on the elasticity of demand and the slope of the monopolist's marginal cost

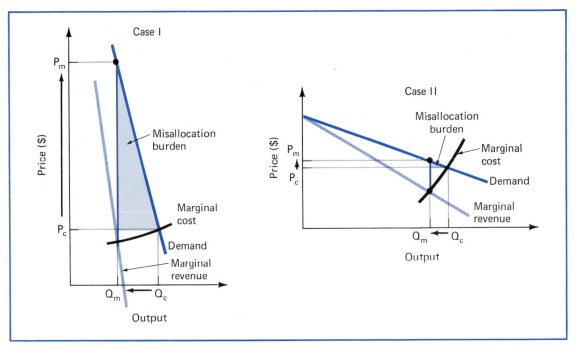

Figure 6 The severity of monopoly's effects depends on demand and cost conditions
In Case 1, because demand is extremely inelastic, consumers can be sharply exploited. The monopolist's sharp cut in output causes price to multiply.
    In Case 2, because buyers apparently have good alternatives to the monopolized product, their demand is more elastic. Also, marginal cost is steep, so that output is not cut back by much. Since both price and output are scarcely changed, monopoly has little effect on allocation.

curve. Compared to elastic demand, inelastic demand gives smaller cuts in output but sharper rises in price. As for cost, the steeper the marginal cost curve, the smaller will be the difference between the monopoly price and marginal cost.

Figure 6 illustrates these conditions. In Case 1, demand is inelastic and marginal cost is relatively flat. Because of these two conditions, monopoly has drastically changed both output and price. The price is four times the original price and five times marginal cost. Output is only about half of the competitive level. When people urgently need an item (a necessity, for example), a monopolist can severely exploit them. In contrast, Case 2 shows only a mild effect: Demand is more elastic, and the marginal cost curve is steeply sloped.

In this case, price is only nudged up—and output down—a little.

A pure monopoly may have a severe, slight, or moderate effect, all with the same 100 percent market share. These are matters of *degree*, depending on conditions. The severity of the effects can be predicted if one knows the underlying conditions of demand and cost. The *logic* of the effects of monopoly is the same in every case.

THE MONOPOLIST HAS NO SUPPLY CURVE Recall that the purely competitive firm faces a horizontal demand curve at the going market price. As that demand curve shifts up or down in response to changes in market price, the firm sets its output at the level where demand intersects the marginal cost curve. The competitive firm's marginal cost curve is therefore also its supply curve.

The monopolist differs. Its demand curve slopes down and is separate from its marginal revenue curve. Moreover, the demand curve can shift in any way—rotating, parallel, bending—rather than be rigidly horizontal. Shifts in the demand curve, therefore, do not trace out a supply curve that coincides with the marginal cost curve. In fact, they do not trace out any supply curve at all.

To verify this conclusion, you can try a series of demand-marginal revenue shifts in a diagram, finding the new profit-maximizing price and quantity combination in each case. You will see that the points are much too scattered to be on any single supply curve. Consider Figure 7. The original demand and marginal revenue sched-

ule, D_1 and MR_1, result in a profit-maximizing price and quantity combination of P_1 and Q_1. Therefore, the firm would want to supply Q_1 at a price of P_1, given the present demand and supply conditions.

Suppose that the demand schedule and therefore the marginal revenue schedule shifted to the left, as shown by D_2 and MR_2. Now the profit-maximizing price-quantity combination results in a lower quantity of Q_2, but the price remains at P_1. Therefore, under different demand conditions, the firm may supply different quantities, Q_1 or Q_2, at a price of P_1. A supply schedule showing unique price-quantity combinations cannot be drawn.

Note that *the monopolist does not raise prices as high as it possibly can.* Instead, it raises prices just to the level that maximizes profits. That rise may be small or big, as Figure 7 illustrates. But it is not the maximum possible price. The maximum price would be at the left end of the demand curve, where the monopolist would sell just one unit.

Monopoly's effects on economic performance There are also other effects of monopoly, such as misallocation, unfair redistribution, X-inefficiency, and a possible slowdown on invention and innovation in a given field. We will now consider these effects one by one, starting with the shift away from the competitive allocation.

MISALLOCATION Because it reduces output, monopoly distorts the allocation of resources. Output is held below the level at which price equals marginal cost. The contrast is shown by Q_m and Q_c in Figures 3, 5, and 6. The cutback in output forces some of the inputs into other markets, where their economic value is less. These distortions ripple through adjacent markets into the whole economy. Monopoly in one part of the economy disturbs the functioning of the whole system. The larger the

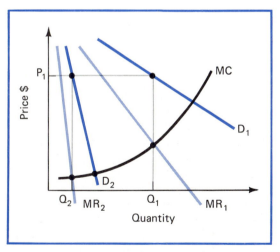

Figure 7 The lack of a unique quantity supplied at a given price

With demand and marginal revenue represented by D_1 and MR_1 the firm will supply the profit-maximizing quantity of Q_1 at a price of P_1. Notice what happens when demand and marginal revenue shift to D_2 and MR_2. The firm will now find it profit maximizing to supply Q_2 at a price of P_1. Given different demand conditions, then, different quantities may be supplied at a price of P_1. Therefore, a schedule representing a distinct quantity for a given price cannot be drawn.

monopolized industry is, and the more severe the direct effects are (as in Case 1 as opposed to Case 2 in Figure 6), then the greater the economic harm will be.

The distortion is called *misallocation.* It is caused by moving resource use away from the efficient pattern. There is a loss of economic value, a loss that shows up as the reduction in **consumers' surplus.** *By forcing price down into line with cost, competition maximizes consumers' surplus,* as shown in panel I of Figure 8. Monopoly's effect can now be seen clearly. By raising the price, as in Panel II of Figure 8, the monopolist eliminates some of this consumers' surplus. Compared to perfect competition, the monopolized market outcome, determined by the marginal revenue–marginal cost intersection, will be a lower output (Q_m instead of Q_c) and higher price (P_m instead of P_c). Note how the con-

sumers' surplus shrinks from *ABC* to *ADE* as market price increases. The total loss in consumers' surplus is made up of two components. The rectangle *EDFC* represents the increase in payments by consumers, in the form of excess profits. It is a redistribution of income from consumers to producer because of the higher price. The remaining portion of the reduction in consumers' surplus, the small triangle *DBF*, represents the welfare loss to society resulting from the resource misallocation that monopoly causes. It is the value that consumers placed on the output that is lost as a result of the monopoly.

Economic welfare is reduced: *The monopolist destroys the economic value shown by the triangular-shaped area of consumers' surplus, by changing the allocation of resources.* Therefore, the burden of misallocation caused by the monopoly is shown

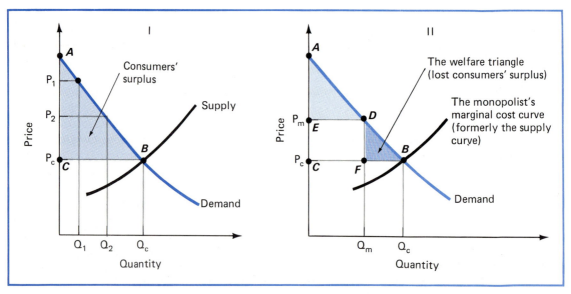

Figure 8 Consumers' surplus and monopoly's destruction of it
Consumers' surplus under competitive conditions is shown by the triangle *ABC* in Panel I. It stands for the difference between the value that consumers place on a commodity, represented by points along the demand schedule, and the market price. Since price under competition equals minimum average total cost, consumers' surplus is maximized under perfect competition.
Monopoly will result in a higher price and lower output, as Panel II shows. Consumers' surplus shrinks from *ABC* to *ADE*. The reduction in consumers' surplus has two components: the redistribution from consumers to producer (the rectangle *EDFC*) and the loss in output *(DBF)*.

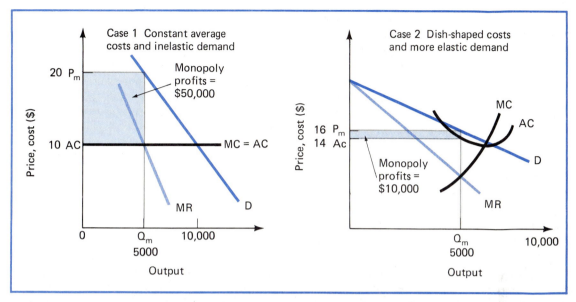

Figure 9   The monopolists' profits may be large or small

Excess profit is the gap between the demand curve (which is the average revenue schedule) and the average cost curve (that is, excess profit per unit) *times* the number of units sold. In Case 1, excess profit is $20 minus $10 = $10 per unit, *times* 5,000 units = $50,000. In Case 2, excess profit is $16 minus $14 = $2 per unit, times 5,000 = $10,000. The shaded areas show the excess profits. These profit volumes are the areas of the rectangles.

by this *"welfare triangle,"* as economists call it.

The **misallocation burden** may be large or small, as illustrated in Figure 6. In Case 1, the burden is large, 40 percent of the monopolist's total sales revenue. In Case 2, the burden is small, perhaps just 1 percent of sales revenue.

UNFAIR REDISTRIBUTION The monopoly may also provide *monopoly profits*, in excess of the normal profits gained by competitive firms. The amount of profits is set by the gap between price and average cost, at the monopolist's level of output, as Figure 9 shows. Total excess profits are calculated by multiplying profit per unit times the number of units sold. In Figure 9, that is $P_m\text{-}AC \times Q_m$. The magnitude of the excess profits depends on the positions and shapes of the demand and cost curves. In Case 1 in Figure 9, because the steep

demand curve is well above average cost at the monopoly output, the excess profits are large. But in Case 2, demand is down close to average cost, so that this monopolist gains only a small excess profit. You can draw other cases, illustrating medium or even zero monopoly profits.

The excess profits—whatever their level—usually represent a degree of unfairness. They redistribute income, transferring money from the pockets of ordinary consumers into the monopolist's till. Many consumers will lose income, while the one (or few) owners of the monopoly will gain sharply. The consumers usually have lower incomes than the monopoly's owners.

Therefore, monopoly tends to tilt the income distribution toward greater inequality. These income flows are capitalized into wealth, as we explained in Chapter 7. A monopoly's stock price will rise to reflect the flow of monopoly profits, and the owners can sell out immediately and put their wealth into other investments. Thus, monopoly creates family fortunes, enriching a few at the expense of many. This shift of wealth is usually quite unfair, since the buyers are ordinary people who can ill afford to pay higher prices to enrich a few monopolists.

X-INEFFICIENCY There is another way in which monopoly may reduce efficiency. Being free from the pressures of competition, the monopoly firm's management may lose some of its tightness and vigilance. Cost controls may not be as strict and productivity may decline because everyone working in the firm knows that the firm is profitable and that it won't go out of business if costs rise.

This internal slack is X-inefficiency. It differs from *allocative* inefficiency among firms and markets (which the welfare triangle shows). *In a monopoly firm, X-inefficiency may cause a simple rise of the cost curves above their lowest possible levels.* Such X-inefficiency can range from small to large.

These effects are defined in a *static* context. (Compare them to the competitive equilibrium in Table 2's summary.) Monopoly also has effects in a *dynamic* context, altering the rate of invention and innovation.

INVENTION AND INNOVATION A monopoly is usually not under pressure to *invent* new products or methods. Nor does it have strong incentives to *innovate:* to apply those new inventions in practice and bring new products to the market. *The monopoly may choose to invent and innovate, but it will do so only at its own pace.* No competitor forces its hand. Even if its capital is outdated or its products mediocre, a monopolist may prefer to protect and continue them rather than to replace them with better ones.

That monopolies often retard innovation has been common knowledge for centuries. The problem has been studied closely and two main lessons have emerged: (1) Monopolists may *invent actively,* so as to know which new ideas are coming. But (2) they usually *innovate* more slowly than competitive firms would. In short, a monopoly usually retards progress.

There may be certain exceptions, however. An innovation may be so big, costly, and risky that a monopolist—with its large size and high degree of security in its market—is better able than a hard-pressed competitive firm to carry it out. Large companies sometimes suggest that such cases are frequent. That is a matter on which judgments vary. Yet note: Even when an innovation does require vast resources to carry out, the monopolist's tendency to retard innovation will still be at work. In short, the monopolist may be able but not very willing.

Another exception can occur when the monopolist is insecure, vulnerable to being dislodged by an innovator. In this case, the monopolist may innovate swiftly because of the fear that the newcomer may do the innovation instead. Yet, the insecurity must be genuine, which may be rare for well-established monopolies. A secure monopolist usually retards progress.

OTHER EFFECTS OF MONOPOLY Monopoly restricts *freedom of choice* for everyone involved except the monopolist. Buyers cannot try other suppliers; they are stuck with this one monopolist, for good or ill. Only those goods that the monopolist offers are available in this market, and they carry higher prices to boot. The former competitors are out of business, or working for the monopolist. Newcomers may be unable to enter the market. If entry barriers are high, only the strongest entrants may have a chance; or perhaps no entrant can survive, so that the choices of former and potential competitors are reduced.

Suppliers also have less choice. Not only are their sales cut back by the monopolist, but they also have less opportunity to offer new products to a variety of firms—there is only the monopolist to sell to in this market. Workers also have fewer choices. They must deal with only the one monopolist in the industry. Everyone—buyers, suppliers, workers, and would-be-competitors—loses freedom of choice.

Democracy is also affected by monopoly. There are fewer firms with less diversity of interests. The monopolist is now a power bloc, with a valuable advantage—and perhaps excess profits and market power—to protect. By supporting friendly candidates, by seeking favorable laws and rulings, and by advertising its interests via the media, a monopoly can use the political process to protect and enlarge its economic position. Even when its actions are mainly subtle, monopoly is likely to undermine democracy.

Culture and society can also be affected. When many markets are monopolized, the economic and social order becomes tight and closed. Society is more stratified and rigid, less open to outsiders and new ideas. Fascism, for example, grew partly out of societies that had market power in many key parts of the economy. In another vein, monopolists can often influence consumers' preferences without challenge from others. An economy of monopolies provides a distinctive and unattractive social content, going against many traditional American values.

Price discrimination

Another special effect of monopoly is **price discrimination.** Its precise definition is: *different price-cost ratios to different customers, rather than one price-cost ratio to all.* In plain English, discrimination means

"charging what the traffic will bear" in each part of the market: "selective pricing," "pricing by market segmentation"—in short, price differences based on the differences in consumers' *demand.*

Monopolists use price discrimination to extract more profit, to improve their market positions, and to defeat their competitors. But all firms try to discriminate—to price selectively *where they can*—and the practice in itself is neither good nor bad. Consider now what it is, how widespread it is, and when it is harmful or helpful to competition and the economy.

Preconditions for discrimination Price discrimination can occur when three conditions hold:

1. Buyers have sharply differing demand elasticities.
2. The seller knows these differences and can separate the buyers into groups based on these differing elasticities.
3. The seller can keep the buyers from reselling the product or service to one another.

Under these conditions, the seller will divide the buyers into two or more groups and then charge higher prices to the buyers who have the less elastic demand. Remember that inelastic demand means a higher degree of urgency or need. Those who would pay more *are made* to pay more. Other buyers with more elastic demand—who have good substitutes or simply can't afford to pay more—are charged less.

The classic instance has been the town doctor who treats all comers, rich and poor. For the same appendectomy, the banker is asked to pay $800, the poor widow $50. Nineteenth-century railroads were also masters at charging what the traffic would bear: typically, 10 cents per ton-mile out on the plains, and 2 cents per

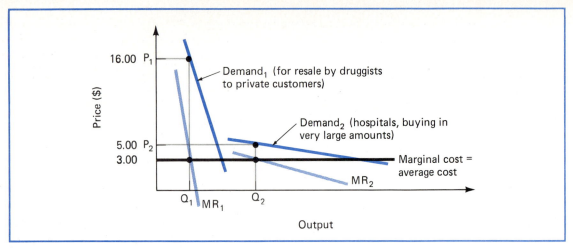

Figure 10 Simple price discrimination

The same drug (with uniform costs) is sold to two groups: one is druggists for resale. Demand is inelastic because buyers merely take what their doctors prescribe. Those sales are priced at $16 per dozen, to maximize profits. Hospitals (Group 2) can shop around and drive hard bargains. Therefore, large-volume sales to hospitals are at $5 per dozen, again maximizing profit on that part of their sales.

If hospitals open drug shops to resell the drug, at any price between $5 and $16, this price discrimination would weaken and perhaps disappear. Would drug firms and druggists oppose this step, by arguments and lobbying for laws to prevent such "unethical" or "hazardous" practices?

ton-mile alongside rivers with competing barge lines. Perhaps the most familiar instance today is half-price movie, bus, train, and airplane tickets for children. The costs are much the same for both children and adults, yet adults pay a much higher ratio of price to cost.

When discrimination occurs, the elasticity of demand—*not* cost—governs prices. A price discriminator will follow the same basic rule as any other profit-maximizing firm: Set the price and output at the level for which marginal revenue equals marginal cost. A single-price firm will be working with the demand and marginal revenue schedules for the entire market. A price discriminator, however, will set price for each group of customers on the basis of the demand and marginal revenue for that particular group.

Figure 10 shows a typical case of price discrimination, using a lifesaving drug as an example. The same drug is sold to two groups: (1) to druggists for resale to individuals, by doctors' prescriptions; and (2) to large hospitals, for dispensing to pa-

tients. The druggists' customers have *low* demand elasticity, for they merely buy what their doctor writes on their prescriptions.

By contrast, the hospitals have *elastic* demand. They can bargain shrewdly, playing off the drug companies against one another to get a low price. Thus, the identical drug, costing perhaps $3 per dozen pills to make, might sell for $16 per dozen to retail druggists and $5 per dozen to hospitals. (In practice, the ratios of price to cost often differ even more sharply.) The inelastic demand results in a higher price to one group, which in this case is the retail druggists.

Many other familiar situations give rise to price discrimination, some of which are listed in Table 4. The critical fact is the differing price-cost ratios among customers. In the drug instance:

$$\frac{\text{Price}_1}{\text{Cost}_1} = \frac{\$16}{\$3} = 5.33 \text{ which does not equal}$$

$$1.67 = \frac{\$5}{\$3} = \frac{\text{Price}_2}{\text{Cost}_2}.$$

214

Table 4 *Instances of price discrimination—and not discrimination*

Good or Service	Consumer Groups	Costs and Prices	How Reselling Is Prevented	How Does This Affect Competition?
1. Prices differ more than costs: DISCRIMINATION				
Movies, airplane trips, train trips	Adults, children	Costs are about the same for all customers, but children pay much less than adults	By letting only children use children's tickets	Usually not much at all
Magazines	Newsstand sales, regular subscriptions, special subscriptions, (to new subscribers, students, etc.)	Costs are about the same, but prices differ sharply among customers	Magazines are bulky and easily damaged; subscriber lists are kept separate	Often it promotes competition; rarely does one magazine dominate the market
2. Costs differ more than prices: DISCRIMINATION				
Bus trips in town	People taking various-length trips	There are uniform fares, but costs differ for different lengths	Tickets are issued only for the ride	Not much for the most part because competition is already excluded by the bus franchise
Electricity	Various times of day and week	Prices per kilowatt-hour do not vary by the time of use, but peak-time costs sharply exceed off-peak costs	Storing electric energy is difficult; reselling is illegal	Not much because competition is already excluded by the utility's franchise
3. Prices and costs differ proportionally: NOT DISCRIMINATION				
Long-distance phone calls	Daytime callers, night and weekend callers	There are higher prices for calls made at peak times; costs at peak times are also higher	Timing cannot be switched	Not much, for the telephone company has an exclusive franchise
Clothing sales	Regular sales, bargain sales	There are low sales prices; the true costs of the clothes are also low, because clothes are excess (recall opportunity costs)	Sales are held only after clothes have lost their popularity	It promotes competition, for the firms rarely have large market shares
Restaurant meals	Luncheon customers, supper and evening customers	At peak-capacity times, costs are higher, even though food costs are uniform; dinner prices are well above luncheon prices	By time of day; meals cannot be stored or resold by those who buy them	It promotes competition by filling restaurant tables at flexible prices, rarely do restaurants dominate their markets

To make price discrimination work, the seller must keep the low-price buyers from reselling the product to the high-price buyers, for such reselling would pull the high price down toward the low price. In all of Table 4's instances, the seller has special ways of preventing the customers from reselling to one another.

Note that uniform prices can be discriminatory if costs differ. For example, the price is 20 cents to mail a first-class letter anywhere in the United States, across town or from Maine to California. Because that uniform price ignores the greater costs of the longer routes, it is discriminatory (though not necessarily bad, and possibly quite good). One judges possible discrimination by comparing *price-cost ratios*, not just prices. Cost differences can justify price differences.

Note, too, that many cases of discrimination are neutral or actually procompetitive, rather than a threat to competition. In fact, many little firms—which hold no market power—compete by selective price cutting. Such price cuts, often called "loss leaders," are common in grocery, drug, clothing, and camera stores. Several items are temporarily offered at discounts, to draw customers in. Once there, the customers may buy other goods that have higher profit margins. Newspaper ads for grocery and clothing sales are often full of such "loss leaders."

Discrimination can be the lifeblood of competition when it is *sporadic* and/or done by *smaller* firms. **Only when it is done forcefully and systematically by dominant firms is price discrimination usually anticompetitive.** That is shown by Figure 11. Indeed, if firms with small market shares try to keep prices systematically out of line with costs, they will lose money and may go out of business. At the other extreme is the utility firm, holding a complete monopoly and selling to many different buyers. It is always tempted to apply deep

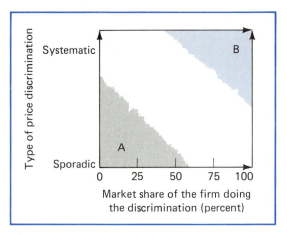

Figure 11 Price discrimination can be procompetitive or anticompetitive

In Area *A*, the discrimination is done sporadically by a firm with a small market share. The result is flexible pricing, which may increase competition. In Area *B*, the firm has a large market share and it practices systematic discrimination. That increases its excess profits and reduces the ability of lesser firms to compete.

price discrimination. That is one reason why utilities in electricity, gas, and telephones need to be regulated by public agencies.

You can discover many cases of price differences in familiar markets. For each case, test (1) whether costs also differ by the same proportion, and (2) whether the discriminator is a dominant firm or a little competitor. Often, systematic price discrimination is a sign that the firm holds market power. Only a firm with a high market share can maintain systematic discrimination in its prices.

Cases of monopoly

Knowing what monopolists are and do, you can now examine some case studies of real-life monopoly power. Though not all of them attained pure monopoly, they illustrate the effects of high degrees of monopoly power. When economists try to evaluate monopoly and its effects, they look especially for raised prices and excess profits, for price discrimination and for X-inefficiency.

Standard Oil

America's most spectacular monopoly has probably been the Standard Oil combine. It was formed in the 1870s by John D. Rockefeller, a relentless, hard-bargaining, tightfisted, puritanical man. It became the Standard Oil Trust, combining a series of Standard Oil companies that were monopolies in their states and regions (thus, Standard Oil of New York, of New Jersey, of Ohio, etc.). For nearly 40 years, this industrial combination controlled between 60 and 90 percent of U.S. oil production—nearly a complete monopoly—and it yielded large monopoly profits. Then, in 1911, a climactic antitrust decision by the U.S. Supreme Court divided Standard Oil into its 33 parts, many of which were regional monopolies.

By the 1930s, competition had set in throughout the oil industry, though the successor oil firms have often tried to avoid open price competition. (The present descendants include Mobil—formerly So-cony-Mobil, the Socony being *Standard Oil Co. of New York*; Standard Oil of Ohio; of Indiana; of California; and other firms. Standard Oil of New Jersey was the main successor. It changed its name to the anonymous-sounding "Exxon Corporation" in 1971.)

Standard Oil probably raised oil prices by over 30 percent on average, after driving out or merging with its competitors. Its profit rates were over 60 percent on capital before 1911. That is an exceedingly high rate, as Chapter 7 showed. The flow of monopoly profits totaled over $1 billion by 1911, creating an immense Rockefeller family fortune, which was soon applied in other industries. The profits were extracted from competitors and customers, shrinking their wealth.

Standard Oil used price discrimination to weaken its small rivals. It cut prices selectively in one area after another, often forcing single small competitors to go out of business or to sell out to Standard Oil at reduced values. In many cases, it needed only to threaten to cut prices to get its way. Though some economists deny that Standard Oil actually killed off small rivals by using price discrimination, the selective pricing certainly helped reduce their ability to compete.

Opportunities for others to do business in the industry were sharply curtailed. Standard Oil also corrupted legislators, railroads, and other businesses. Indeed, some of its growth came from forcing the railroads to pay Standard a sum of money for every barrel of *competitors'* oil that the railroads shipped!

Standard Oil strongly displayed most of the classic features of monopoly. It was widely hated and feared, and the final antitrust action came after a nationwide groundswell of discontent and legal attacks. The modern distrust of the oil industry has deep roots in the Standard Oil Trust.

Electric companies

In the decades after Thomas Edison invented the electric lamp and the technology of electric distribution in 1879, electric companies grew and spread from local to regional systems. There was an early period of competition in many cities, but most electric companies soon merged and gained exclusive franchises in their service areas. These combinations mainly reflected large economies of scale—the downslope of average cost curves—that gave "natural monopoly" conditions (one set of wires per town is much cheaper than two). Until these companies eventually were regulated in the 1920s and 1930s, they behaved as monopolies generally do. Many of them set price levels to earn high rates of return. Price discrimination was rampant, tailored to customer groups' demand elasticities. The management of electric utility companies often became slack, sheltered as it was by monopoly.

During 1910–1940, as electric systems grew and broadened, regulation also spread. It gradually reduced the utility firms' profit rates toward the cost of capital and limited the more obvious kinds of discrimination. But some price discrimination persists even today in the 170 private electric systems and in various public ones, too. For example, electricity prices are usually uniform rather than varied to fit differing costs at peak times during the day and off-peak times at night and on weekends. Management also retained a degree of X-inefficiency in many electric firms up through the 1960s. Yet, since 1965, pressures from rising oil prices and new technology have forced utility companies to become more efficient. Therefore, on the whole, electricity firms have exhibited some of the normal monopoly behavior, even though regulation is supposed to prevent it.

Summary

1. Monopoly power is an ancient and continuing problem.
2. Pure monopoly and pure competition are both unusual. Most markets have a mixture of monopoly and competition, ranging from dominant firms down to monopolistic competition. Each market's degree of competition is usually a matter of debate.
3. Monopoly usually hurts economic performance. The monopoly restrains trade in the market by reducing output and raising price. This causes the allocation of resources to be distorted, as shown by the welfare triangle.
4. Monopoly may also encourage slack management and slow innovation. It enriches a few at the expense of many. It shrinks freedom of choice, and its concentration of power can undermine healthy democracy.
5. There may be economies of scale or large innovation that offer social benefits.
6. Natural-monopoly conditions resulting from substantial economies of scale may make competition impossible. Yet, the economic harms of monopoly still occur even when there are gains from reducing costs. The economic task is to compare the harms with the possible gains. Often a firm will gain much more monopoly power than scale economies can justify. In practice, monopoly's effects have occurred in many industries, often mildly but occasionally severely.
7. Price discrimination, which causes differences in price-cost ratios, is often practiced sharply by monopolists. When it is done systematically by dominant firms, it reduces competition. But done sporadically by lesser competitors—as, in fact, it frequently is—price discrimination can promote competition.

Key concepts

Monopoly power or market power
Market share
Entry barriers
Natural monopoly
X-efficient and X-inefficient
Consumers' surplus
Welfare triangle

Misallocation burden
Price discrimination

Questions for review

1. a. Consider the following list of firms. On the basis of your own knowledge of firm and industry characteristics, classify each according to the market types found in Table 1. If possible, compare your classifications with those of other students in the class.

    i.   General Motors
    ii. A & P
    iii. Wheat farmer
    iv. U.S. Steel
    v.   Local clothing store
    vi. Procter & Gamble
    vii. Time-Life Publishing Company
    viii. Michigan Consolidated Gas

    b. Now try to find one example of each of the six market types listed in Table 1 in or near the town or city in which your own school is located.

2. Total revenue is maximized at the point where marginal revenue equals zero. A friend of yours is convinced that this must, therefore, be the profit-maximizing point. Prove to your friend why the profit-maximizing rules cannot hold at the point where total revenue is maximized. Explain to your friend the difference between maximum revenue and maximum profits.

3. Explain what information, if any, each of the following statements gives about the degree of market power the firm may possess.

    a. A firm is the sole supplier of a newly developed product and has 15 years left on a 17-year patent.

    b. A firm has shown a rate of return significantly higher than the average for manufacturing for a five-year period of time.

    c. A firm exists in a market with no entry barriers.

    d. There are no good substitutes for the product produced by a particular industry, so that the market demand curve is very inelastic.

    e. A firm's demand curve lies well below the market demand curve.

    f. There are 20 firms in the market.

4. A friend of yours feels that monopoly power always causes harm. Another friend disagrees, claiming that monopoly power and profits are usually fair rewards for superior performance. To help clarify the issues, draw up a list of ways in which a firm can acquire monopoly power. Briefly explain how each item on your list can help a firm gain monopoly power. Determine whether each specific path to monopoly will involve any social benefits.

5. One problem of monopoly is that consumers are prevented from receiving as much of a particular good as they want.

    a. What is the signal that output is restricted? Explain.

    b. Why is output lower under monopoly than under competition?

6. Suppose that the following statements appear in students' answers to exam questions. Would you give credit for the statements? Why or why not? If not, write a brief explanation for the student showing what was wrong.

    a. X-inefficiency refers to a firm that is too small to achieve economies of scale.

    b. Monopoly will probably show a better performance in terms of the rate of innovation than in the rate of invention.

    c. Monopoly power will usually result in a redistribution of income from consumers to the monopolist.

    d. Misallocation resulting from monopoly power will be larger when demand is relatively more inelastic.

7. Price discrimination is a common form of behavior for firms with monopoly power.

    a. Name three instances of price discrimination that you have personally experienced.

    b. Explain the characteristics used to group customers according to elasticities. Explain how these characteristics would cause different demand elasticities.

11

Degrees of Competition

As you read and study this chapter, you will learn:

▶ the characteristics of dominant firms and their effects

▶ how oligopoly interdependence may affect pricing behavior

▶ how monopolistic competition may cause slight deviations from competitive outcomes

Between pure competition and pure monopoly lies the domain of partial competition. It includes the great mass of industrial activity in the modern economy. Whether tiny or huge, simple or complex, most industries are partially competitive rather than at one extreme or the other.

You can readily appreciate from your knowledge of economies of scale that technology and demand shape the structure of firms in a particular industry, and this structure, in turn, may influence both the behavior of individual firms and the economic performance of the industry as a whole. In this chapter, we make the underlying logic more explicit and apply it to cases between pure competition and pure monopoly. In this middle range, the conditions are mixed and the lessons about them are often debatable. Such difficulties make the field a lively one, full of disputes.

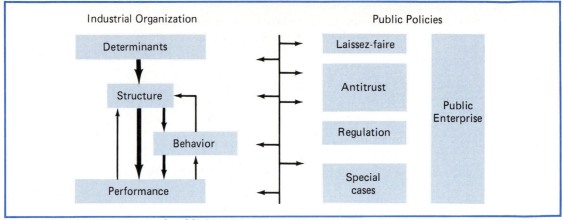

Figure 1 The underlying logic of industrial organization and public policy

The typical industry is on the left-hand side. Causation runs mainly downward, as shown by the thick arrows, from determinants to structure, behavior, and performance. On the right-hand side are the public policies (covered in Chapter 12) that may be taken toward industries with monopoly power. The arrows in the middle go in both directions because policies not only apply to industries but are also affected by them.

Before we discuss this middle range, we should note that this chapter is your first step into a specialized field of economics. Chapters 1–10 were not specialized; they were concerned with the basic theory and facts of economics, which all economists share. But economics has some ten main "applied" fields that deal with specific topics.

"Industrial organization and public policy," which includes the detailed study of markets and policies, is one of these fields. The basic concepts of the industrial organization field are shown concisely in Figure 1. On the left side, each industry is seen as having (1) its own basic underlying conditions, which may shape (2) the industry's structure (its degree of concentration and its barriers against new competition). That structure, in turn, influences (3) the behavior of firms in the industry, and their behavior finally affects (4) how well the industry performs. To show how these concepts are applied to practical cases, we give two contrasting illustrations in Table 1. The fast-food industry is highly competitive, while the automobile industry has been dominated by a few large firms.

Economists have come to divide the degrees of competition into three main categories: dominant firms, oligopoly (from the Greek word for "several sellers"), and monopolistic competition. They were presented in Table 1 of Chapter 10. Although the three categories shade into one another at their edges, each of them has its distinctive concepts. For example, *dominant firms* commonly take unilateral actions toward their little competitors. *Oligopoly* involves several leading firms instead of one, and these several firms interact in complex ways. **Monopolistic competition** is different from them both, for it involves firms that have only a small degree of monopoly power and little chance to earn excess profits. We will examine each of these categories in this chapter.

The dominant firm

Definition of dominance

Market share A firm is said to be dominant when it has over half of the sales in the market and is more than twice the size of the next largest firm. Note that the dominance is defined primarily by market share. The higher the dominant firm's market share, the closer it comes to being a pure monopoly. To that extent, the firm's demand curve slopes up, perhaps steeply.

Table 1 *Two case studies of partial competition*

	Fast-Food Restaurants	**Automobile Industry**
Determinants	The technology gives limited economies of scale, so that minimum efficient scale is reached by the typical local fast-food restaurant.	Economies of scale are significant, requiring plants to have at least an 80,000-car-per-year capacity. Firms need to have at least two lines of car models.
Structure	Low concentration and easy entry.	Medium to high concentration; the largest four firms have about 75 percent of the U.S. market. High entry barriers, except against imports.
Behavior	Flexible pricing; little price discrimination.	Oligopoly pricing, with close interaction among U.S. firms. Mutual reliance on frequent model changes.
Performance	Little excess profit; efficient operations; rapid innovation.	Substantial excess profits (before import pressure during 1978– 1981). Inferior arrangements for quality control and for worker incentives. Narrow innovation and neglect of small fuel-efficient designs before 1976.

At high market shares, the dominant firm's demand curve approaches the slope and position of the entire market demand curve.

That slope gives the dominant firm a distinct marginal revenue curve, which lies below its demand curve. The dominant firm therefore acts like a pure monopoly, even though its power over the market is less than complete. There is some competition from the small competitors, but it is usually not severe. Mainly, the dominant firm just sets its profit-maximizing decisions unilaterally, given the degree of monopoly that its demand curve provides.

Entry barriers An entry barrier is any condition that makes it difficult for a firm to enter a market for the first time, so as to become a new competitor. Such entry barriers can reinforce the market power that the dominant firm derives from its market share. There are several types of causes of entry barriers. One is product differentia-

tion, which arises from heavy advertising and from trademarks of brand names. Thus, new entry into the beer, detergent, and toiletries markets is difficult because advertising has wedded many consumers to familiar brands such as Budweiser, Tide, and Right Guard.

Barriers are also caused by large economies of scale, which can force a new entrant to raise large amounts of expensive capital to come in at "minimum efficient scale" where average costs are lowest. Barriers can also come from other causes, such as the need for crucial ores or special skilled workers, which the dominant firm has and new entrants can't get.

Instances and effects of dominance

Dominant firms are unusual because a high market share is hard to capture and maintain. Yet, the firms that do get market dominance often become household names. Notice the familiar company names in Table 2. The computer, car, razor blade, film, or detergent that you buy, the soup you sip, and certain other widely used goods are likely to have been made by dominant firms. Their names and brands are well known precisely because the firms are dominant, producing a large share of the goods in their markets. Many local markets also contain dominant firms. Your local newspaper is probably one, and so perhaps is the biggest local bank, lumberyard, taxi company, and hospital. Judging carefully, you may be able to discover several others, especially if your city is not large.

Dominant firms usually have two effects on prices, similar to those of pure monopoly (recall Chapter 10): (1) They raise the level of their prices, often (though not always) gaining excess profits; and (2) they engage in price discrimination. These traits are normally weaker than would occur under pure monopoly, for dominance is a diluted form of monopoly. The remaining firms do provide a degree of competition. Yet, the patterns are usually similar to what pure monopoly causes.

EXCESS PROFITS arise approximately in the pattern shown in Figure 2. Profitability is commonly measured by the rate of return on equity capital. Market shares are given on the horizontal axis. The statistical pattern has emerged in repeated testing; though there are exceptions, higher market shares correlate closely with higher rates of return. Dominance usually yields progressively higher excess profits, above the cost of capital.

PRICE DISCRIMINATION is also common. Controlling half or more of the sales in the market, dominant firms can often segment the market and set varying price-cost ratios for distinct customer groups. The discrimination will be weaker than it would be under pure monopoly, but the patterns will be similar. For example, General Mo-

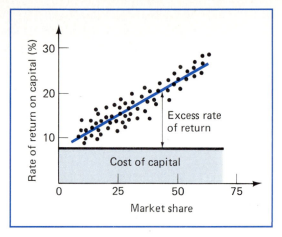

Figure 2   Market shares correlate with rates of profit

Economic theory predicts that companies' market shares are correlated—though not perfectly—with their rates of return. This has been affirmed in statistical testing of large U.S. corporations and other groups of firms. Each dot is for one large company, showing its average market share and rate of return during 1960–1969. There is some variation around the main pattern, caused by a variety of other influences.

Source: W. G. Shepherd, *The Economics of Industrial Organization* (Englewood Cliffs, N.J.: Prentice-Hall, 1979).

tors was recently making a profit of over $3,000 per car on its Cadillacs, but only $100 on its small Chevettes. Demand elasticity is low on Cadillacs because buyers will often pay extra for the status they give. But for Chevettes (which face stiff competition from domestic and imported subcompacts), demand is highly elastic. To take another example, IBM has set much higher price-cost margins on its small machines, where competition has been *weakest*, than on its largest computers. And Campbell Soup is said to price its standard tomato soup close to cost, while setting higher price-cost margins on its clam chowder and other fancy soups. These few examples merely illustrate the same result.

Possible causes of dominance

Economies of scale Dominance is often said to reflect the economies of scale arising from modern technology. The dominant firms themselves invariably argue that there is only room for one or two effi-

Table 2 *A selection of leading instances of dominant firms, oligopolies, and monopolistic competition*

1. Dominant Firms	Markets	The Firm's Average Market Share (%)	Entry Barriers
IBM Corp.	Computers, electric typewriters	60	High
Western Electric Corp.	Telecommunications equipment	95	High
Eastman Kodak Co.	Photographic supplies	60	Medium
Procter & Gamble Co.	Detergents, toiletries	50	Medium
Boeing Corp.	Aircraft	55	High
United Industries	Aircraft engines	50	Medium
Campbell Soup Co.	Canned soups	85	Medium
Gillette Corp.	Razors, toiletries	60	Medium
Wall Street Journal	Business newspapers	65	High
Washington Post	Washington, D.C., area newspapers	84	High

2. Oligopolies	Sales Revenue, 1977 ($ million)	4-Firm Concentration Ratio in Relevant Markets (%)*
Artificial fibers	1,003	80
Automobiles	76,518	84
Flat glass	1,577	90
Batteries	666	87
Glass bottles	3,664	54
Cereal breakfast foods	2,497	89
Newspapers	13,055	90+
Chewing gum	567	93
Cigarettes	6,377	95
Steel	15,331	55
Oil refining	91,688	55
Bearings	2,567	56
Beer	6,652	64
Cement	3,042	56
Fabric weaving	6,325	42

3. Monopolistic Competition	Sales Revenue, 1977 ($ million)	4-Firm Concentration Ratio in Relevant Markets (%)
Movie theaters	2,606	30
Poultry	5,746	16
Yarns	3,846	19
Commercial printing	9,359	18
Knit fabrics	3,169	20
Sheet metalwork	4,863	10
Costume jewelry	816	23
Retail shops	723,134	6
Restaurants	28,470	24
Wood millwork	3,928	14
Dresses	4,188	8

Source: W. G. Shepherd, *The Economics of Industrial Organization* (Englewood Cliffs, N.J.: Prentice-Hall, 1979), Chapter 10, updated using various sources. Adapted by permission of Prentice-Hall, Inc., Englewood Cliffs, N.J.

*The 4-Firm concentration ratio is the share of the market's sales made by the largest 4 firms in the industry.

cient firms in the industry. Therefore, the cost curve shapes you learned in Chapter 8 now become crucial. If scale economies are actually small in those industries (as in Panel I of Figure 3), then the market is *naturally competitive* because there is room for many efficient firms. In that case, any dominance would merely reflect sheer market power. But if economies are larger (as in Panel II), the dominance might be caused by—and therefore provide for—lower average costs.

The issue is clear and important, but the facts are a matter of intense debate. Measuring cost curves is difficult. Technology is usually not simple and rigid, so that costs can't be read off easily from simple formulas. The best research was summarized in Chapter 8. The key question is: Are the dominant firms larger than the optimal scale ("minimum efficient scale")? It turns out that most dominant firms are indeed larger than scale economies seem to require. In some small local markets, such as newspapers, scale economies may indeed be large enough to require high market shares. The markets are small because

they are local. Even a modest amount of scale economies will therefore make the firm bulk large in the market, like a medium-sized frog in a small puddle. Yet, the research has not yet reached definitive answers, and conditions can change. As research continues, this consensus—that scale economies do not cause or justify the actual degree of concentration in many national industries—may, of course, be revised.

Yet, there is a contrary view: Modern business has to be big to be efficient. For many decades, some business observers have said that large factories and whole firms are the natural form for mass production and national sales. That may have been true during 1890–1940, at least in some industries, but countertrends toward a smaller optimal scale have quietly set in since the 1940s in many industries.

There are three main reasons for this reversal:

1. The *industrial mix* has changed. There has been a broad shift from "heavy," relatively crude industrial processes to

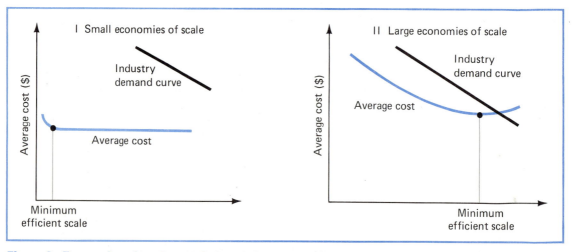

Figure 3 Economies of scale vary between large and small

In Panel I, small economies of scale cause minimum efficient scale (MES) to be only 3 percent of the market. As many as 33 companies can coexist efficiently in such a naturally competitive market. In contrast, Panel II shows an instance where MES is 90 percent of the market. A dominant firm is sure to exist in that case.

more complex, delicate products involving high technology. From such typical products as cast-iron bridges, bricks, and battleships around 1900–1910, the economy's array of products has shifted toward computers, antibiotics, missiles, and stereo sets. The more refined products often require close controls and small-scale assembly, rather than the more crude mass production that could turn out simple industrial products. Therefore, the newer goods are often best produced in smaller factories and firms.

2. *Technology* has shifted broadly in favor of smaller-scale power sources and controls. The power to drive production comes nowadays not from large steam engines but from small electric motors, applied precisely. Small, powerful computers permit exact controls on production, even in small plants. Trucks traveling on the highway network can link numberless small factories much more efficiently than the earlier system of railroads and waterways. In earlier decades, the transport system typically involved a few big factories along the major railroad lines. That favored concentration, rather than a dispersal among many small plants and companies. The telephone system, too, has fostered small-scale efficiency by making close coordination possible even among many separate small firms.

3. *Workers' attitudes* are now more independent, less easy to regiment on a large scale than around 1880–1920, when immigrants were flooding into the labor force. Now, under the pressure of import competition, there is a trend toward more worker responsibility and more flexible work arrangements. These conditions also favor smaller scale.

In light of these trends, we can consider the origins of those firms that have held dominant positions since 1900. Some of them can still be considered dominant in their markets, though many have faded. At least several main causes helped create these firms.

Mergers When two or more competitors combine to form one firm, that is a *horizontal merger* (called "horizontal" because the firms were previously side-by-side competitors). In the three great waves of mergers that we noted in Chapter 7, dominant firms were created, especially in the first wave during 1890–1901. Hundreds of large firms were created, many with 80 or 90 percent of their markets. Usually, these mergers only provided market power, not any true economy of scale.

Many of these instant dominant firms dwindled or collapsed under the pressure of new competition or owing to their own incompetence. Yet, others persisted, some of them even down to the present. Prominent cases of such merger-created dominant firms include U.S. Steel (1901–1910), American Tobacco (1900–1915), United Shoe Machinery (1890–1960), and General Electric (1900–1930).

Patents and trademarks Patents are official monopolies issued by the government to inventors. They protect new inventions during a 17-year period, so that the inventor can gain a high reward in selling the new product. The economics of patents are discussed in Chapter 16. For now, note that many dominant firms originated with one or more crucial patents. Major instances (with their periods of dominance) are the Aluminum Company of America (1895–1950), Gillette Company (1903 to the present), Kellogg's in corn flakes (1890–1930s), Xerox Corporation in copiers (1961–1975), Polaroid Corporation in

Newspapers: Dominance and Scale Economies

The true markets for most newspapers are limited to their cities and surround-ing areas. Within these markets, it is common for one firm to have high mar-

Dominant firms in selected newspaper markets 1980–1981

Metropolitan Areas	Circulation of Copies, 1980–1981 (12-month average)	Newspapers' Share of Market (%)
Des Moines, Iowa	107,095	
Register, Tribune*	106,803	99.7
New Orleans, Louisiana	245,480	
Times-Picayune, States-Item*	238,230	97.0
Miami, Florida	331,843	
Herald, News*	312,765	94.3
Milwaukee, Wisconsin	442,151	
Journal, Sentinel*	398,491	90.1
Kansas City, Kansas-Missouri	562,000	
Star, Times*	503,910	89.7
Atlanta, Georgia	385,513	
Journal, Constitution*	341,562	88.6
Washington, D.C.	616,493	
Post	517,989	84.0
St. Louis, Missouri	519,718	
Post-Dispatch, Globe-Democrat*	435,405	83.8
Phoenix, Arizona	391,688	
Republic, Gazette*	317,511	81.1
Austin, Texas	139,201	
American-Statesman	111,113	79.8
Akron, Ohio	192,175	
Beacon Journal	139,978	72.8
Pittsburgh, Pennsylvania	658,552	
Press, Post-Gazette*	411,207	62.4
Baltimore, Maryland	548,790	
Sun	328,417	59.8
News American	137,645	25.1
Los Angeles, California	1,516,102	
Times	690,749	45.6
Herald Examiner	119,245	7.9
Chicago, Illinois	1,596,593	
Tribune	657,951	41.2
Sun-Times	637,381	39.9
Boston, Massachusetts	1,095,072	
Globe	410,015	37.4
Herald American	191,202	17.5

Source: American Newspaper Markets, Inc., *Circulation '81/'82* (Malibu, Cal., 1981).

*Newspapers whose names are separated by commas are owned by one firm (e.g., the Des Moines *Register* and *Tribune*).

ket shares. The table presents a selection of such dominant firms, plus a few with lower market shares.

These are familiar papers, some of them civic-minded and long established. They vary in tone, political slant, and quality; most of them are highly profitable. In any event, they are all dominant firms holding a high degree of market power. Since many of their owners also own local television and radio stations, their market power in the entire local media market is often very great.

These newspapers are survivors from earlier eras in which most large cities had three, four, or more newspapers. What has caused the decline in numbers of newspapers? The main causes are rising economies of scale in printing and delivery, and the tendency for advertisers to cluster their spending in only one paper. Even the largest "second" newspapers have been squeezed, such as the venerable *Washington Star*, which folded in 1981.

instant photography (1948–1980), and many medical drugs since the 1940s.

Monopolizing tactics, including price discrimination By sheer tenacity and various tactics, a number of commercial geniuses have built up dominant firms. As we saw in the last chapter, John D. Rockefeller and Standard Oil is a leading instance, involving price discrimination. Others include Eastman Kodak in photographic film (1895 to the present), General Motors in automobiles (1930–1950), IBM in computers (1955 to the present), and United Fruit in bananas (1890–1960).

Scale economies Economies of scale have sometimes been important at the beginning of an industry, when one firm got a firm foothold. It is less usual for scale economies to preserve a dominant position in a mature industry. Among the few present-day examples are newspapers in many cities. Yet, such cases are often debatable, for often there are small competitors whose existence suggests that the scale economies are not conclusive.

Oligopoly

Concentration and leading firms

The economist's basic criterion in defining oligopoly is **concentration,** and the usual practical measure of it is the *concentration ratio*. That ratio is the combined share of the market's sales that is held by the largest four firms in the market.* For example, if market shares in the United States automobile market are General Motors 45 percent, Ford 20 percent, Chrysler 10 percent, and Toyota 4 percent, then the four-firm concentration ratio is 79 percent.

Concentration obviously can vary continuously from near zero for a purely competitive market all the way up to 100 percent when there are only four firms or fewer. One therefore speaks of concentration in numerical terms, such as 35, or 62, or 93 percent. Table 2 shows some of this

---

*In the United States, concentration is reported only for the top 4, 8, 12, and 20 firms because the Census Bureau is forbidden to disclose facts that could reveal individual companies' conditions. Three-firm concentration ratios would be valuable to have, but—it is claimed—two of the three firms might get together, share their data, and learn the market share of the third! So no three-firm ratios are published, and scholars must make do with four-firm ratios.

variety. But economists divide this continuous range into several approximate categories, in order to clarify certain distinct features. They usually apply the phrase *tight oligopoly* to markets whose four-firm concentration is above 60 percent or so. By contrast, *loose oligopoly* occurs when concentration is in the range of about 20 to 40 percent. When concentration is below 20 percent, economists usually define the market condition as monopolistic competition. That is treated in the next section.

The typical oligopoly has several leading firms plus a fringe of little competitors. Those leading firms are rarely equal in size, as in Panel I of Figure 4. Instead, they normally taper down from the biggest one, as in Panel II of Figure 4, with each firm substantially smaller than the next. It is often not exactly clear where the oligopoly firms end and the fringe firms begin. Nonetheless, the key economic feature of oligopoly is the presence of a group of leading firms. This leads to two distinctive conditions.

Interdependence One of the distinctive conditions about the oligopoly group is the *interdependence* among its members. They must be constantly aware of one another's actions, planning their own moves carefully and ready to react to one another's tactics. Therefore, oligopoly is permeated with strategy. Actions cannot be simple unilateral steps, as they are in pure competition, pure monopoly, or dominance. These strategic conditions will be presented later in this chapter.

Tight oligopoly is often like a chess game or a war. Each firm's choices hinge on what it expects the others to do, in response to its actions or in following their own strategies. Like a chess player or a general plotting a military campaign, an oligopolist often needs to think three or four moves ahead—in short, to have a strategy. The oligopolist tries to anticipate its rivals' reaction to its own actions. Its own choices, therefore, often depend crucially on what its rivals' policies are likely to be. Moreover, each of the other firms

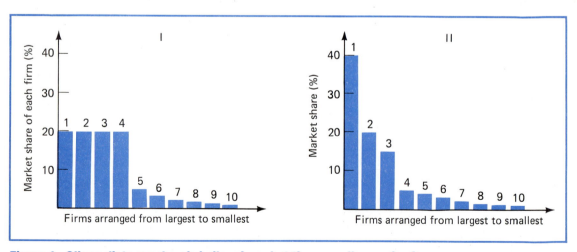

Figure 4   Oligopolists may be of similar sizes, but they usually vary in size
Panel I shows a tight oligopoly with four equal-sized firms. In Panel II, by contrast, the oligopolists have sharply varying sizes, even though their total concentration, 80 percent, is just the same as in Panel I.
    The tapered pattern in Panel II is far more common in actual oligopolies than is the equal-size group in Panel I.

The Schumpeterian Process

The strongest argument that big business is highly competitive has come from one of the most colorful and erudite of economists, Joseph A. Schumpeter (1883–1949). An Austrian, he was a young diplomat with a stable of horses in Egypt, a politician, and then, after fleeing Hitler in 1933, the reigning economic theorist at Harvard for 16 years. Deeply conservative, he sought to defend capitalism, even its monopolies. His striking image of "creative destruction"—published in 1944—was and is a dramatic dissent from the prevailing view of neo-classical economists.*

Competition and progress go together, he said, but in a series of temporary monopolies. The Schumpeterian version of competition is almost the exact reverse, point by point, of the neo-classical equilibrium analysis. At each period of time, each market might be dominated by one firm, which earns monopoly profits. But these high profits attract other large firms, one of which will innovate and displace the first dominant firm. The new dominant firm then thrives, but it too is pushed aside.

This cycle of "creative destruction" continues: innovation, dominance, monopoly profits, new innovation, a new dominant firm, and on and on. As time passes, the average degree of monopoly profits might be small—surely smaller than the innovators hoped. Meanwhile, the cycle might generate benefits of technical progress far exceeding any costs of marginal misallocation which are caused as market power comes and goes.

Capitalism, Socialism and Democracy (New York: Harper & Row, 1944).

must think strategically too, so that the whole process is complex and thoroughly problematic.

Oligopoly thus differs from all other market forms. Under monopoly, dominance, pure competition, and (as we will soon show) monopolistic competition, each firm merely finds and achieves its profit-maximizing levels of price and output. It ignores any possible responses by specific other firms.

Variety Oligopoly's other distinctive trait is its variety. It embraces a remarkable diversity of conditions. *Concentration* may range from 20 percent on up. The leading firms may be about *equal* to one another in size or, instead, even more strongly *different* than in Panel II of Figure 4. The *products* may be "homogeneous" (like cement and lumber) or "differentiated" (like electrical generating plants and brands of cereal or beer). *Entry barriers* to the market may be high, medium, or low.

Oligopoly's main lines Since oligopoly embraces such a wide variety, there can be no single economic "model" for it. Economists have only been able to develop several general lessons and methods for showing oligopoly's main lines. These concern:

1. The oligopolists' conflicting incentives, either to compete or collude with one another.
2. The contrast of outcomes between tight and loose oligopoly.
3. The central tendency that usually emerges under oligopoly.
4. Ways to explain why oligopoly prices are often rigid over long periods of time.
5. Whether economies of scale have been the main cause of oligopoly concentration.

Conflicting incentives can make oligopoly unstable

Each firm in an oligopoly has mixed incentives toward its several rivals. Depending on how the balance tips, a firm may fight, or cooperate, or reach some mix of actions toward its fellow oligopolists.

Competing Each firm could compete intensely against its rivals, seeking every way to defeat them and maximize its own profits. Of course, an aggressive firm must expect sharp retaliation from the others. Its own hostile actions may force the others to respond in kind, even if they were not equally hostile and aggressive in the beginning.

Colluding Yet, collusion is also attractive. Each oligopolist knows that if all the firms in the industry cooperate, they can maximize their total profits. At the extreme, they might make as much total profit as if they were united in a single complete monopoly. Such "joint profits" will greatly exceed the sum of the individual profits that firms make when they are fighting one another. For example, three beer companies agree to hold prices at $2.70 per six-pack, well above the average cost of $2.30 per six-pack. Sales are 37.5 million six-packs, which yields them excess profits of $50 million each, or $150 million in total. If they had competed fiercely, the price might have been driven down to $2.45 per six-pack, raising the sales to 60 million six-packs. The result would provide them only $3 million apiccc in excess profits, for a total of $9 million.

As with these firms, so with the common run of oligopolists: The incentive is to cooperate, not compete. The rewards from cooperation and collusion depend largely on how concentrated the market is.

The higher the concentration, the stronger are the firms' incentives and opportunities to cooperate successfully and thus to maximize their joint profits. If there are only two or three firms, this urge to collude is strong and often compelling. Yet, even when concentration is low, the incentive to collude is still present. Oligopolists can always gain by setting up a price-fixing ring and raising the price—*if* they can prevent price cutting.

But often they cannot suppress the urge to compete. Even if the oligopolists do raise price so as to achieve maximum joint profits, each firm still has the contrary incentive to compete. Once the high collusive price is set, each firm could gain by secretly cutting its own price just below the jointly agreed upon price. The slightly lower price will take away large amounts of sales from its rivals, and so this one firm's profits will increase. As soon as other firms discover why they are losing sales, they will be under pressure to cut their own prices or at least to try to penalize the "chiseler." Cooperation may well collapse and a price war may break out.

Accordingly, oligopolists' collusion is often unstable, breaking apart from its own inner tensions. Thus, in the example of the three beer firms, one of them could gain $10 million in profits by cutting price to $2.65 per six-pack *if* the other two stay at the $2.70 price. For instance, the price cutter could raise its sales to 20 million six-packs; at a profit of 35 cents per six-pack, the firm's excess profits would now be $70 million.

All price-fixing firms share this temptation to cut the price. But they also know that the other two will probably retaliate. The situation mingles rewards for both price cutting and price fixing.

Oligopolistic industries often veer between being restrictive and stagnant when cooperation holds, and being aggressive and progressive when competition breaks out. Oligopoly frequently is like Dr. Jekyll and Mr. Hyde. Or, rather, it is like a person who, constantly torn between the temptation to sin and belief in a moral code, resists at some times but gives in at others. There is always the tension between opposing choices.

Each oligopolistic setting provides several possible outcomes. The specific results of each one are usually *indeterminant*—that is, they cannot be predicted in advance. The structures are too diverse, and the attitudes of the firms' managers are varied and unpredictable. Thus, the outcomes vary. In one oligopolistic industry, the firms will settle into snug cooper-

ation and act like a monopoly with high prices and little innovation. In another oligopoly, the firms will engage in endless warfare, with low prices and frantic innovation. A third oligopolistic industry will alternate between the extremes.

Despite this variation of specific cases, there are some predictable basic patterns that favor collusion. When the following three conditions occur, collusion is likely to stick.

1. Similarity of the firms' conditions If the firms have similar demand conditions and/or similar cost conditions, they will be more able and more likely to cooperate. Their interests will coincide, and they can have more confidence that cooperation will last. That very confidence will deepen their mutual trust and make collusion among them more likely to succeed.

For example, if there are three oligopolists in the copper industry with identical marginal costs of 68 cents per pound, then they may easily agree on 97 cents per pound as the best price. But if their costs differ—at 51 cents, 63 cents, and 82 cents—they will have trouble setting one price. At a 97-cent price, the lowest-cost firm (with its 51-cent marginal cost) would wish to cut price perhaps to 68 cents, while the highest-cost firm (with marginal cost at 82 cents) would fight such a move. In short, differences breed discord, whereas similarity breeds cooperation.

2. Familiarity over time Each firm's managers get to know the other companies as time passes, and they learn to judge and predict one another's behavior more accurately. Misunderstandings become less likely, and mutual trust grows. The oligopolies in older industries tend to have a clubbier, more comfortable atmosphere. When new managers take over in one firm or another, things may be less stable for a while. But further experience tends to restore mutual understanding.

3. Concentration. The likelihood of cooperation varies closely with the *degree of concentration*. Higher concentration breeds more collusion, for two main reasons. First, collusion is easier when there are fewer firms controlling the bulk of the market. The few firms can organize, understand, and enforce their mutual agreements more thoroughly. Moreover, the leaders—having most of the market—face little pressure from those small fringe firms that are outside the price ring. Those fringe firms' price actions can have only a mild effect on the leading firms' market share. Second, price cutting by any renegade oligopolist is easier to discover and penalize when there are only a few firms. If there are only three firms, the other two will quickly know that the third firm is the chiseler. In contrast, if there are 15 or 20 firms involved, any one of them or several—or all—will be more sorely tempted to chisel, since each one can expect to succeed for a longer time before being discovered.

Types of collusion

The kinds of collusion that may occur in oligopolies range from tight, explicit collusion to informal, loose arrangements.

Explicit, formal collusion If price fixing is legal, the price fixing in tight oligopolies can be so complete that it approaches the level that a pure monopoly would achieve. *Cartels* may be formed. A cartel is a formal organization created by companies to manage their cooperation. It fixes prices and enforces penalties against members who violate the agreement. The cartel may also set output quotas, control investments, and pool profits. Most cartels have existed in Western European countries and certain international markets, such as OPEC in the world oil market.

Price fixing has been against the law since about 1900 in most U.S. industries, under Section 1 of the Sherman Act and various state antitrust laws (see Chapter 12 for details about antitrust). The U.S. antitrust laws, therefore, shift the margin of choice away from collusion and toward competition in most U.S. oligopolies. But there is some hidden price fixing, nonetheless, done through secret meetings, phone calls, and other covert ways. Indeed price fixing is a way of life in many industries, as the leading business magazines and newspapers have occasionally noted. Table 3 presents some typical instances, drawn from a wide variety of markets. Each year, scores of antitrust cases turn up many more examples.

Tacit collusion Price fixing can also occur in a milder form, called *tacit collusion*, or parallel pricing, or price signaling. The oligopolistic firms do not conspire directly or sign binding agreements, mainly because it is against the law to do so. But a firm can give indirect hints and signals of its preferred price levels. Then all the other firms simply go along with the same price changes. Often, a cooperative price is reached, just as if formal collusion had occurred.

One version of this tacit collusion is called *price leadership*. In it, one firm periodically judges the best new joint-maximizing price for them all and then sets that price. The others simply follow the leader, quickly matching its price. The pattern then is: long periods of stable prices, punctuated by simultaneous price jumps, usually led by the same firm. Such lockstep, stair-step pricing strongly suggests some degree of tacit collusion. In practice, prices usually do not rise in such a starkly rigid form. Instead, the firms often shift their prices at about the same time, to

Table 3 *Typical instances of price fixing in recent years*

Product	Geographic Scope	4-Firm Concentration (combined share of the largest 4 firms) (%)	Number of Conspiring Firms
Bedsprings	National	60	10
Self-locking units	National	97	4
Women's swimsuits	National	65	9
Carbon steel sheets	National	69	10
Commercial baking flour	Regional	50	9
Gasoline	Regional	45	12
Liquid asphalt	Regional	56	20
Book matches	National	77	10
Concrete pipe	Regional	100	4
Linen supplies	Local	49	31
Plumbing fixtures	National	76	7
Class rings	Regional	95	3
Tickets	Regional	97	3
Baked goods	Regional	46	7
Industrial chemicals	Local	90	5
Armored-car services	National	99	3
Vending machines	Local	93	6
Ready-mix concrete	Local	86	9
Wrought-steel wheels	National	85	5
Metal library shelving	National	60	7

Source: George A. Hay and Daniel Kelly, "An Empirical Survey of Price Fixing Conspiracies," *Journal of Law and Economics*, 1974, pp. 13–38. © 1974, The University of Chicago Press.

about the same levels. The economist then has to judge whether tacit collusion has really occurred, or if instead the shifts largely reflect changes in costs.

Tight oligopoly crystallizes such indirect cooperation much more fully than does loose oligopoly. When the few rivals control nearly all of the industry, tacit collusion can often be nearly as complete as with a full-blown cartel (or even with pure monopoly). Loose oligopoly, in contrast, has too many "leading" firms, and their collective market share (that is, the concentration ratio) is less than 40 percent. Thus, loose oligopoly is usually a scene of chronic strife, often degenerating into flexible, competitive pricing action.

The contrast is not absolute, however. Tight oligopolies often undergo bouts of fierce competition when collusion collapses, and loose oligopolies can sometimes be effectively collusive. But the general contrast is valid. It marks out tight oligopoly as a special problem, even where price fixing is illegal.

The central tendency under oligopoly

The central tendency in oligopolistic markets is for firms to converge on identical prices and product features. Collusive prices under tight oligopoly is just one part of this fundamental tendency. We now explain this central tendency in broader terms.

The customers in a market are often distributed along a range: of geographical areas, of product types, or of time periods. Typically, the distribution has a central cluster with two tails, as shown in Figure

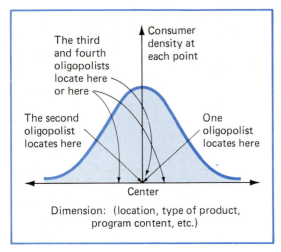

The third and fourth oligopolists locate here or here

The second oligopolist locates here

Consumer density at each point

One oligopolist locates here

Center

Dimension: (location, type of product, program content, etc.)

Figure 5   Under tight oligopoly, the firms cluster at the center of the market

Customers are arrayed along a dimension, such as geographical location or type of product. Most of them cluster in the middle. Two oligopolists will choose the exact middle, back to back. A third and fourth firm will also probably crowd into the center. Only as more oligopolists arise will they possibly locate in the other parts of the distribution, catering to the variety of customers.

5. For example, a country town is spread along the main road, with a clustering of population at the center.

If there are just two competitors ("duopolists"), they will locate at the exact center of the distribution. Thus, two gasoline stations, restaurants, bookstores, department stores, or banks will usually be found close to each other at the middle of town. In practical terms, they will both locate at the main intersection downtown. Equally, two television networks will tend to produce the same sort of mass programs, aiming for the center of the distribution of program preferences. The two political parties, Republicans and Democrats, tend to offer similar programs to voters, rather than take radically opposed positions. Therefore, duopoly exhibits a strong tendency for the two oligopolists to adopt uniform positions at the center of the market.

This tendency continues even when there are three or more oligopolists, though it weakens as the oligopolistic group gets bigger. Consider what happens if other firms enter the market. A third oligopolist would also move to the middle of the market, for that is where it can hope to attract the most demand. Additional firms, however, might begin to move away from dead center to seek out special customer groups. For example, a fifth TV network might specialize in the arts, popular sports, or news. That is, indeed, what has happened as specialized cable and satellite networks have emerged since 1978, offering all-day sports and news coverage. Radio stations have also specialized as the old network dominance has been diluted. Every city has several types of popular music stations, each specializing in one "sound" rather than all offering the same music.

Rigid prices: kinked demand curves

Oligopoly tends toward rigid prices, changed relatively infrequently (as noted just above). For example, steel and automobile prices in the 1950s and 1960s followed a distinct stair-step pattern: constant for 12 months, and then raised uniformly by all firms in August of each year. An ingenious analysis to explain this rigidity—which economists call the "kinked" demand curve, because the curve, indeed, has a kink in it—was developed in the 1930s and is still the most widely accepted single model of oligopoly. It is particularly valuable for showing the kind of pricing dilemma that oligopolists face once an industry-wide price has been established.

Its general form is illustrated in Panel I of Figure 6. Panel II gives more details about how it is derived. Its logic can be grasped by putting yourself in the oligopolist's shoes. Suppose that you run an oli-

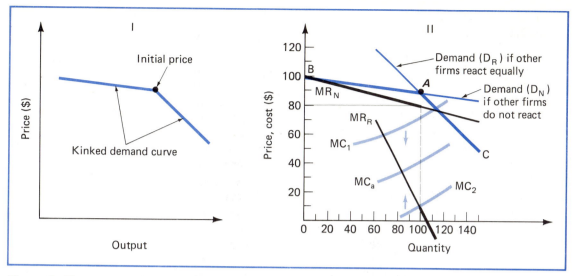

Figure 6   The conventional kinked demand curve for a timid, pessimistic oligopolist

gopolistic firm and are trying to determine the results of changing your price. As in a chess game, your strategy—your choice of a price—depends crucially on the reactions of the other firms in the industry. In fact, you can't determine the demand curve for your firm until you make some assumptions about your rivals' responses. Panel II of Figure 6 illustrates one possible set of such assumptions. Note that the figure doesn't indicate what the rivals will do, only what the firm *expects* them to do.

For example, if your rivals do *not* change price when you do, you will lose a lot of sales to them if you raise the price, and gain a lot of sales if you lower it. In other words, you will face a relatively *elastic* demand curve, such as D_N in Panel II of Figure 6. On the other hand, suppose that your rivals match all of your price changes. Then raising your price won't lure customers away from your rivals. Your demand curve will be relatively *inelastic*, such as D_R in Panel II. Table 4 illustrates these conditions.

Which assumption do you make? Will your rivals match your price changes? Suppose that you take a timid, pessimistic approach. After all, it's better to be pessimistic and pleasantly surprised than to be

optimistic and find things turning out worse than you had anticipated.

Therefore, you start at the current price and output level, represented by Point *A* in Panel II of Figure 6, and ask yourself what the worst reaction of your rivals could be to an increase in your price. Clearly, it would be simply to leave their price unchanged. Then, with your own higher price, you would lose a lot of sales to your rivals. The gain from a higher price would be more than outweighed by a loss in sales. In other words, if you raise your price, you perceive that you will be operating on a portion of the elastic demand curve or D_N, such as the *AB* portion: An increase in price results in a substantial drop in quantity.

Now suppose you begin again at Point *A* and consider a price *cut*. Here the worst response of your rivals would be to match your price cut. Now you're stuck with a lower price, but hardly any increase in quantity sold. After all, your lower price won't help you to draw customers from your rivals if they, too, are charging the new lower price. If you lower your price, then, you expect to be operating on a portion of the inelastic demand curve or D_R, such as the *AC* portion: A reduction in

Table 4 *An illustration of the kinked demand curve*

I. With the Conventional Kink: A Pessimistic Oligopolist

Increasing Price				Cutting Price			
Price	Units Sold	Total Revenue	Marginal Revenue	Price	Units Sold	Total Revenue	Marginal Revenue
$100	0	$ 0		$90	100	$ 9000	
			98				$ 6
98	20	1960		86	105	9030	
			94				−2
96	40	3840		82	110	9020	
			90				−10
94	60	5640		78	115	8970	
			86				−18
92	80	7360		74	120	8880	
			82				−26
90	100	9000		70	125	8750	

II. With the Reverse Kink: An Optimistic Oligopolist

Increasing Price				Cutting Price			
Price	Units Sold	Total Revenue	Marginal Revenue	Price	Units Sold	Total Revenue	Marginal Revenue
$110	75	$8250		$90	100	$ 9000	
			$46				$78
106	80	8480		88	120	10560	
			38				74
102	85	8670		86	140	12040	
			30				72
98	90	8820		84	160	13440	
			22				68
94	95	8930		82	180	14760	
			14				64
90	100	9000		80	200	16000	

price results in only a small increase in quantity sold.

Your pessimistic assumptions about your rivals' reactions result in a *kinked demand curve*, BAC in the diagram. The kink occurs because you expect a relatively elastic demand curve at prices higher than Point A and a relatively inelastic demand curve at prices below Point A. If you sketch in the marginal revenue curve for this kinked demand curve, you discover another oddity. As you jump from the relatively *elastic* demand curve segment to the left of Point A to the relatively *inelastic* demand curve part to the right of Point A, you must also jump from the corresponding *elastic* marginal revenue curve segment down to the *inelastic* marginal revenue curve part to the right. To do this, you travel down an actual discontinuity in marginal revenue, shown by the vertical dashed line at output Q_0 from $80 down to $10. (Try drawing this yourself to verify the result.)

With the demand and marginal revenue schedules sketched out, you're ready to apply the $MC = MR$ rule of profit maximization. But now you encounter a serious problem. Suppose that marginal cost lies *within* the area between MC_1 and MC_2, such as MC_a in Panel II. You can't apply the $MC = MR$ rule in the usual way, since there is no marginal revenue curve in the interval between $80 and $10. Because the marginal cost curve MC_a does not intersect the MR curve, a policy of no action is best. The producer will remain at Point A. Thus, even when changing costs sharply shift the MC curve, the oligopolist is not likely to change its price and output levels.

The kink can clarify the long periods of rigid prices that occur in some oligopolies. It also helps one understand why oligopolists often maintain the same pattern of market shares without changes over long periods, as, for example, when the four leading U.S. meatpackers kept constant market shares from 1890 to 1920.

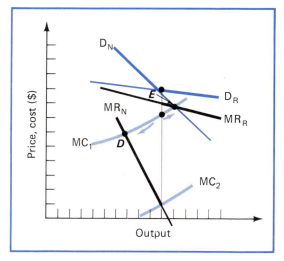

Figure 7   The reverse kinked demand curve for an aggressive, optimistic oligopolist

trate the importance of attitudes. An old, familiar group of rivals may have learned to coexist and avoid price changes; each fears to upset the applecart. That situation gives the usual kink, which we explained first. But a brash newcomer, or a change of attitude by one of the firms based on aggressive optimism, can upset the equilibrium. The reverse kink shows that. The resulting sequence of moves among the firms can vary, but a stable equilibrium will recur only when no firm has a reverse kink.

It is important not to take the theory of the kinked demand curve *too* literally. The managers of oligopolistic firms do not spend their time staring at diagrams of discontinuous marginal revenue schedules. But their choices come out *as if* they did this sort of analysis. The theory's value comes from the fact that it illustrates the kind of interdependence that oligopolists face. The effects of future price changes can never be anticipated with certainty, since rivals' reactions are often unpredictable. By illustrating this interdependence and uncertainty, the kinked demand curve is useful for understanding oligopoly.

Economies of scale: a cause of oligopoly?

Oligopolistic concentration is not strongly influenced by economies of scale. The situation differs only in degree from that presented for dominant market shares. Oligopoly includes more cases where market shares of the leading firm are not much above the levels that scale economies make necessary. Thus, many oligopolists in medium and small markets have market shares of 10 or 15 percent, while minimum efficient scale is 8 to 12 percent. "Excess" concentration, therefore, is often not large.

Yet, there are many cases when oligopolists have a larger market share than required for efficiency. Often the biggest oligopolist has a market share of 30 to 40

But kinked demand curves can lead to other conclusions. Suppose the oligopolist has an aggressive and optimistic attitude. It expects the *best* reactions to its price changes, not the worst: Its rivals will match its price rises but not its price cuts. That will cause the *reverse* kink to hold, as shown in Figure 7 (Table 4 gives the numbers for it). For price rises, the firm expects not to lose much quantity. For a price cut, the firm expects to gain a sharply higher quantity.

Now marginal cost equals the expected marginal revenue at both Points D and E in Figure 7. These points both differ from the original price output levels. Therefore, thinking positively, the firm will now definitely change its price, away from the original level, choosing either Point D or E. Though we cannot predict which way the optimistic oligopolist will go—whether it will cut or raise its price— the firm *will* change its price and, therefore, also force its rivals to change one way or the other.

Note that these two contrasting results based on pessimism and optimism illus-

percent, well above the MES of 10 or 15 percent. Therefore, on the whole, much of the concentration found in oligopoly markets is not required or justified by the economies of scale.

Monopolistic competition

The lower ranges of loose oligopoly shade into another market type, called ***monopolistic competition.*** It has low levels of concentration, but each firm has a slight degree of monopoly. Therefore, economists treat this market structure as a highly diluted form of monopoly, in which firms' demand curves have only a slight downward slope. No firm's market share is more than 10 percent.

The distinctive features of monopolistic competition are as follows:

1. There is some *product differentiation,* which means that consumers can develop preferences among the sellers. This slight degree of market power

gives the firm's demand curve a slight downward slope, as illustrated in Figure 8. The product differentiation can occur either (1) because the products themselves *differ physically or in brand images* (like various brands of bread, jewelry, or shirts); or (2) because of the sellers' *locations* (as when a local grocery store, hotel, or restaurant is convenient to a neighborhood).

2. There is *free entry* into the market. New firms enter whenever any excess profit (above the normal competitive rate) is being made in the industry.

3. There is *no interdependence* among individual firms. No firms have large enough market shares to influence the rest of the market. Each firm merely feels the competitive pressure from all of the many other firms in the market.

These conditions are common among retail outlets and in other markets, as shown in the third group of markets in Table 2. A typical case of monopolistic competition is a grocery or clothing store, with

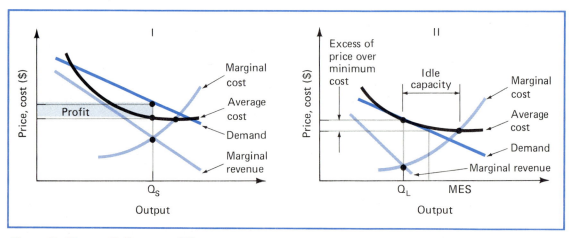

Figure 8   Monopolistic competition

Demand is highly elastic. Profits may occur (Panel I). But soon demand is forced down until the average cost curve just touches the demand curve (Panel II). There is no extra profit, but price is above minimum average cost, and there is idle capacity.

some loyal clientele in its neighborhood but steady competition from many other stores farther away. The firm's demand is highly, but not infinitely, elastic. Because the demand curve is nearly flat, the firm has only a little room for choice.

In the short run, the situation in Panel I of Figure 8 may hold. The demand curve may lie above the average cost curve. That permits the firm to earn short-run excess profits, as shown when it chooses the output Q_S. But then free entry takes its toll. New firms, seeing that excess profits are being made, enter the market, and that forces down this firm's demand curve until it is just tangent to the average cost curve.

In Panel II, the demand curve is nowhere above the cost curve, so that no excess profits are possible. The firm can just survive at output Q_L—where marginal revenue equals marginal cost—barely earning the competitive rate of profit. The power of monopolistic competition eliminates long-run excess profits, and inelastic demand can result in no excess profits.

Yet, monopolistic competition does cause two deviations from the efficient results of pure competition (recall Chapter 9). *First*, cost and price will both be slightly higher than under perfect competition (which settles at MES in Panel II of Figure 8). This difference is shown by the higher price and by Q_L being less than MES. This added cost is not just a dead loss, for consumers benefit from the extra price they pay. For example, the local grocery store may charge higher prices, but to its neighborhood customers, the extra convenience can be worth the extra cost of shopping there. Or perhaps brand preferences are at work. For example, suppose that a restaurant has a better menu than the other restaurants in town. Some customers will be willing to pay more for these meals, along the demand curve shown in Figure 8. They pay a higher price, but they also get meals that they like better than those in the other restaurants.

The *second* deviation is idle capacity. Because output Q_L is less than MES, some of the firm's capacity (the amount MES − Q_L) stands idle most of the time. In practical terms, most retail shops have near-empty aisles for much of every day; most restaurants would like more customers than they have.

You can see these two distinctive features—idle capacity and extra pricing "for convenience"—in many stores that you deal with. Monopolistic competition is a special analytical case, but a familiar phenomenon in many day-to-day businesses.

Patterns and trends in real markets

You can now interpret the main patterns and trends of industrial structure in the U.S. economy. Recall the examples in Table 2, which were merely a selection to illustrate the main types of markets. Now it is time to consider the whole patterns and trends of industrial structure in the U.S. economy.

There are three main kinds of conditions to consider: (1) the aggregate share of total output produced by the largest firms in the economy (such as the share of the 50, 100 or 200 largest firms); (2) the degree of concentration in individual markets; and (3) conglomerate firms that operate in many markets.

Aggregate concentration

Aggregate concentration is the share of national output produced by the largest firms in the economy. All of the biggest firms are added together, to see how much of all U.S. economic activity is held in a few hands. This kind of concentration has little to do with competition, for it merely

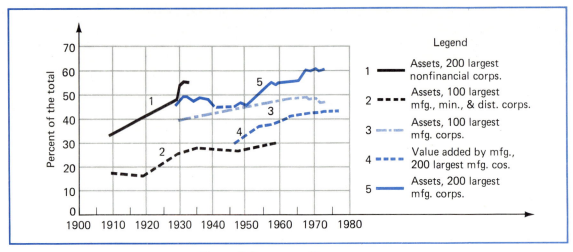

Figure 9   The scope and trends of large U.S. corporations
One can measure the largest firms' share of total assets or value added in the manufacturing and financial sectors. The trends have been up, though perhaps tapering off in recent years, and possibly even declining.

Source: Shepherd, *The Economics of Industrial Organization*, 1979, p. 114, and U.S. Census Bureau data.

totals up all kinds of companies, most of which do not compete with one another. If their total share is high, then big business may exert power over the economy. If their share has been rising, that might show that corporate power and control have been increasing in the entire economy.

The actual levels and trends of the largest 100 or 200 *industrial* firms are shown in Figure 9. (Data for the entire economy have not been prepared by economists, because there is no single correct measure to use.*) Large firms evidently hold substantial shares of total industrial assets and economic activity, but there is no spectacular dominance by just a few firms. The broad trend in the shares, which was upward after 1945, has been tapering off since the 1960s, perhaps even declining in the 1970s.

Concentration in individual markets
Because there are thousands of individual markets, which range from wheat and coal to steel, automobiles, newspapers, telephone service, banking, and restaurants, and the evidence about them is incomplete, economists cannot be precise about the degree of monopoly in the whole economy. Yet, close study over several decades has clarified the main patterns.

The Census Bureau defines about 440 manufacturing industries in the United States, and it reports their four-firm concentration ratios about every fourth year. Using these and other sources, a recent study has classified U.S. markets into four categories: pure monopoly, dominant firm, tight oligopoly, and all others.* The "all others" category includes loose oligopoly, monopolistic competition, and pure competition, all of which together can usually be regarded as very close to the fully competitive situation.

---

*Thus it is not technically meaningful to add up the assets of manufacturing companies with the paper assets of banks and insurance companies. If one added up all the companies' sales together, then retailing firms would be overemphasized because they have large sales volume but little capital or employment.

---

*William G. Shepherd, "Causes of Increased Competition in the U.S. Economy, 1939–1980," *Review of Economics and Statistics* (to be published 1983).

To test the trends over time, the study made estimates for three widely spaced years, 1938, 1958, and 1980. These estimates are summarized in Table 5 and Figure 10.

There are two main lessons from this study: *First,* **the economy contains a wide variety of market conditions. *Second,* there has been a marked rise in competition in the economy.** Pure monopolies were about 6 percent of national economic activity in 1939, but their share had shrunk to 2 percent by 1980. Dominant firms shrank almost as sharply, from 5 percent to a 2 percent share of national income in 1980. Tight oligopolies had no less than 36 percent of national income in 1939 and 1958, but then shrank sharply to 19 percent in 1980.

Taken altogether, these three categories of market power have decreased dra-

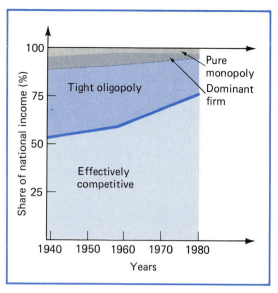

Figure 10   The trend of competition in the U.S. economy 1939 to 1950

In 1939, just over half of all national income arose in markets that were effectively competitive (they were either loose oligopoly, monopolistic competition, or pure competition). The competitive share rose to 56 percent in 1958, and then to 76 percent in 1980. Much of the rise occurred in the 1970s.

Table 5   *Trends of competition in the U.S. economy, 1939–1980*

Sectors of the Economy	National Income in Each Sector 1980 ($ billion)	The Share of Each Sector That Was Effectively Competitive		
		1939 (%)	1958 (%)	1980 (%)
Agriculture, forestry and fisheries	55	91.6	85.0	86.4
Mining	25	87.1	92.2	95.8
Construction	88	27.9	55.9	80.2
Manufacturing	460	51.5	55.9	67.9
Transportation and public utilities	164	8.7	26.1	39.1
Wholesale and retail trade	262	57.8	60.5	93.4
Finance, insurance, and real estate	211	61.5	63.8	94.1
Services	245	53.9	54.3	77.9
Totals	$1,510	52.4	56.4	76.3

The Share of Each Category in Total National Income

1. Pure monopoly	38	6.2	3.1	2.5
2. Dominant firm	36	5.0	5.0	2.8
3. Tight oligopoly	283	36.4	35.6	18.0
4. Others: effectively competitive	1,153	52.4	56.3	76.7
Total	$1,510	100.0	100.0	100.0

Note: Totals may not match because of rounding.

matically. Production by monopolies, dominant firms, and tight oligopolies shrank from nearly half of national income in 1939 to less than one quarter in 1980. Correspondingly, the effectively competitive share rose from just over one half to 76 percent of the economy. This rise in competition has affected nearly every sector, as is evident in Table 5. As you can see from Table 6, the two main causes for this sharp rise in the competitiveness of the economy have been *import competition* and *policy actions* (to be explained in Chapter 12). These causes have acted with special force in the 1970s. Some major industries, however, have retained a high degree of monopoly.

Altogether, the shift toward increased competition has affected most of the economy and appears unlikely to be reversed. Much of it came unexpectedly in the 1970s, after decades in which U.S. industrial structure had gradually grown more monopolistic and more stable.

Conglomerate firms

Conglomerate firms operate in *many* markets, rather than in just one. They range from firms with two product lines to highly diversified enterprises with hundreds of branches and thousands of products. Such diversified enterprises have long existed. The British East India Company in the 17th to 19th centuries, for example, was a large and powerful conglomerate, operating in cloth, spices, minerals, and many other products. Modern conglomerates are sometimes quite small. But some of them are very large and own a string of subsidiaries with high market shares. ITT is one such conglomerate; among other activities, it owns Continental Baking ("Wonder Bread"), lumber, Avis (car rental), and Sheraton Hotels. RCA—with TV-set production, Hertz car rental, NBC, and many other lines—is a second example.

In fact, virtually all large firms are diversified to some degree, making a main

Table 6 *Leading cases of rising competition in the U.S. economy*

1. *From Imports and Foreign Competitors*

Automobiles	Oceanic fishing
Steel and products	Motorcycles
Cameras	Television sets
Copiers	Tires
Shipbuilding	Aircraft
Typewriters	

2. *From Deregulation*

Airlines	Radio broadcasting
Air freight	Long-distance telephone service
Railroads	Banking
Stock markets	Bus travel
Some telephone equipment	Trucking
Television broadcasting	

3. *From Antitrust Actions*

Aluminum	Automobile rentals
Metal cans	Certain professions
Film processing	Some professional sports
Motion pictures and theaters	Electrical equipment
Cement	Telephone equipment
	Photographic supplies

line of products but also stretching into other fields. Though it is not usually regarded as a conglomerate, General Motors makes automobiles *and* buses, locomotives, trucks, and scores of other products. Many chemical and food companies are highly diversified within their broad sectors. Thus, the DuPont company makes thousands of chemicals; General Foods sells hundreds of disparate food products; and General Electric makes many types of electrical equipment.

Some conglomerates are only holding companies, which act mainly as financial supervisors and sources of capital for the operating firms they own. At the other extreme, many conglomerates exert tight management control over all of the detailed production activities of all their subsidiaries.

The distinction between *established* diversified firms and *new* conglomerates is also important. The older diversified firms were created decades ago and have become part of the established industrial structure: blue-chip firms that are accepted by bankers and other large firms. New conglomerates, in contrast, are regarded as upstarts and threats, for they often try to take over solid blue-chip companies against their will. Since the business press usually reflects the interests of the old-line firms, it often portrays the new conglomerates as dangerous and unreliable hucksters.

Yet, these newcomers often provide the new blood that is needed to stir up the staid ways of the business establishment. Scores of conglomerates were formed by hundreds of rapid mergers during the "gogo" stock market boom of the 1960s. Many of these soon fell apart, performed poorly, and were dismantled by the late 1970s. Yet others have been highly efficient and innovative.

Conglomerates are mainly neutral in their impact on competition and perfor-

mance. One great economic benefit is that conglomerates often "take over" sluggish firms and then improve their efficiency. Just the threat of being taken over against their wishes will keep many firms' managers working harder to be efficient, so as to avoid an actual takeover. Since the managers naturally fear losing their jobs after a takeover, they often put up stiff resistance to the merger.

Each month you can find several dramatic takeover attempts reported in the financial press. The target company may escape, but even so, the trauma will usually change its attitudes drastically. Henceforth, the firm will tend to operate more efficiently, so that no other firm is tempted to take it over and make it even more profitable.

On the other hand, three harmful economic results can be caused by conglomerates. *First*, conglomerates often make mistakes, bungling their mergers and supervising their subsidiaries poorly. For example, the Penn-Central Railroad merger in 1970 was a spectacular failure, partly because the officers were busy trying to juggle real estate and other diversified projects. Whole trains got lost from time to time, and operations became confused. This type of wreckage affected scores of firms in the 1970s, and new fiascos still occur frequently.

Second, many conglomerate firms are distant absentee owners of their far-flung operations, with little local awareness or sense of responsibility. A fine local business, once it is bought out by a conglomerate based in a distant metropolis, is often shut down or moved away with little concern for how these decisions will affect the local community.

Third, some large conglomerates can exert power on local governments to get tax and other privileges. The firms can negotiate to pay lower taxes or obtain subsidies, under a threat to move their operations elsewhere. When the firms operate in many international markets, they can often exert the same pressures on small countries.

Yet, on the whole, most conglomerates are neither so sinister nor so virtuous as is often claimed in popular discussion.

Summary

This chapter covers the middle range of industry structure lying between pure monopoly and pure competition. The main points in the chapter are summarized below.

1. Degrees of competition can be divided into three major categories: dominant firms, oligopoly, and monopolistic competition.

2. A firm is said to be a dominant firm when it has over one half of the sales in its market and is more than twice the size of the next largest firm. Its demand curve is close to having the position of the entire market demand curve.

3. A dominant firm's position is usually protected by *entry barriers* that make it difficult for new rivals to enter the market. Such barriers might be due to heavily advertised *product differentiation*, which weds consumers to familiar products, or to substantial *economies of scale*, which require large amounts of capital and a large market share for efficient production. Other causes of dominance are *mergers*, and *patents, and trademarks*.

4. *Oligopoly* refers to an industry dominated by two or more rivals of approximately equal size. The key to oligopoly is *interdependence*. Each firm is aware that the actions of other firms will have an impact on its own market

position. Oligopoly is usually measured by the *concentration ratio*, which represents the percentage of sales accounted for by the largest firms in the industry, usually the top four firms.

5. Oligopoly embraces such a wide variety of structures that no one "model" of oligopoly has been developed. Some of the general lessons regarding oligopolists' behavior are:

   a. Oligopoly has conflicting incentives, to both compete and collude. Collusion is more likely when firms have similar demand and/or cost conditions, when firms' managers are familiar with rivals' behavior, and when there is a high degree of concentration.

   b. Types of collusion range from tight and explicit forms, such as price fixing, to more informal, looser arrangements, such as price leadership.

   c. In oligopoly markets, there is a tendency for firms to converge not only on identical prices but on similar product features as well.

   d. In oligopoly, each firm's choices depend on what it expects the others to do. The oligopoly must therefore develop a *strategy*, to anticipate its rivals' reactions to its own actions.

   e. Because of the uncertainty arising from the firms' interdependence, oligopoly tends toward rigid prices, changed relatively infrequently. One theory developed to explain these rigid prices is the theory of the *kinked demand curve*. The kink arises from the fact that the firm expects to have an elastic demand if it increases its price (because other firms will not increase their prices) and a relatively inelastic demand schedule if it lowers its price (because other firms will lower theirs).

f. Studies show that economies of scale are not a universal cause for oligopoly. There are many cases where oligopolistic firms have a larger market share than required for efficiency.

6. *Monopolistic competition* refers to markets in which firms have a small market share (less than 10 percent) and a differentiated product that gives the firms' demand schedules a slight downward slope. Freedom of entry and exit exists for these markets and there is no recognized interdependence among the firms.

7. Because there is freedom of entry and exit, a monopolistic competitor may earn only a normal return (economic profits = 0) in the long run, as was true for perfect competition. Under monopolistic competition, however, average total cost and equilibrium price will be higher and quantity lower than under perfect competition.

8. Studies of the U.S. economy show that there has been a noticeable rise in the degree of competition in the economy during the 1938–1980 period. The cause of this has been both an increase in import competition and policy actions, including antitrust actions and deregulation.

9. Conglomerate firms, which operate in more than one market, have become an increasingly familiar part of the economy since the 1960s. Although they can produce harmful economic results, such firms seem, in general, to be fairly neutral in their impact on industry competition and performance.

Key concepts

Dominant firms
Oligopoly
Concentration
Tight oligopoly
Loose oligopoly
Interdependence
Price fixing
Monopolistic competition
Conglomerate firms

Questions for review

1. Given what you know of their markets, classify the following firms as dominant firms, oligopolies, or monopolistic competitors. State the reasons for your decisions.
   a. U.S. Steel
   b. Local family-owned restaurant
   c. Procter & Gamble
   d. Ford
   e. Kodak (film market)
   f. The largest local newspaper
   g. Budweiser
   h. Campus-area movie theater

2. Consider the following statement and determine whether it is true or false. Explain your answer.

   Even if the technology of a certain industry involves substantial economies of scale, new firms need not be at a competitive disadvantage. After all, both old *and* new firms would need to reach a high level of output to achieve minimum efficient scale.

3. Classify each of the following statements as true or false. Explain your answers.
   a. Firms in an oligopoly will have no incentive to break a price-fixing agreement as long as the agree-

ment results in higher profits than each firm would have in the absence of any joint action.

b. According to the theory of the kinked demand curve, an oligopoly with a pessimistic view would expect to face an inelastic demand if it increased its price and an elastic demand if it lowered its price.

4. As its name implies, monopolistic competition is an industry structure that shares characteristics of both monopoly and competition. In what ways is monopolistic competition similar to competition? In what ways is it similar to monopoly?

5. Explain how the combination of the *characteristics* of monopolistic compe-

tition and the general rules for profit maximization will lead to the existence of idle capacity in monopolistic competition.

6. Consumers pay higher prices under monopolistic competition than they would if the industry were competitive. Yet, society gets something in exchange for these higher costs and prices. Explain.

7. Many judge that the existence of conglomerate firms is close to neutral in terms of impact on industry performance. What are two of the possible benefits and two of the possible harmful effects of conglomerates?

◄ 12 ►

Policies Toward Monopoly Power: Antitrust

As you read and study this chapter, you will learn:

▶ the origins and standards of antitrust policy

▶ the economic elements of antitrust cases

▶ the three specific parts of antitrust: toward existing concentration, mergers, and price fixing and other actions

When European economists discuss what is special about the United States economy, they frequently mention its large size and abundant natural resources. But even more distinctive than these, they often say, is "your touching faith in competition, as shown by your antitrust policies." They also point to our treatment of the main public utility industries, where we regulate private companies rather than convert them to public ownership. Indeed, antitrust and regulation are unique American experiments, and they are the country's main defenses against monopoly power.

Antitrust policies promote competition throughout most sectors of the economy. Price fixers are punished and anticompetitive mergers are stopped. Regulation sets limits on utility prices. These policies are the focus of intensive debate because they deal with urgent, complex problems whose stakes run into many billions of dollars.

To their critics, U.S. antitrust and regulation policies appear to be weak, deceptive, or even harmful. However one judges these policies, they deserve to be studied closely, for they can decisively affect the nature of the competitive, market-based economy.

After briefly summarizing the origins and economic standards of antitrust policy in the first section, we devote the rest of this chapter to discussing antitrust policy. The main lines of actual antitrust policies are discussed in the second section. The third section considers the three specific parts of antitrust: toward existing concentration, mergers, and price fixing. Throughout, we have space to present only the basic patterns of this complicated subject.

Origins and standards of U.S. antitrust policies

Before presenting U.S. antitrust policies one by one, we need to review their origins so that you will better understand their nature. The policies have been hammered out over decades of turbulent political action, and they remain the focus of intense battles. With such mixed origins and continuing pressures, the three policies—antitrust, regulation, and public enterprise—are naturally imperfect rather than ideal. The task is to discover what these policies are really doing to the economy.

Three waves

There have been three major waves of policies toward business. The first came in 1885–1915, as antitrust policies and regulatory agencies were begun. Then, during 1933–1950, a second wave occurred, especially as airlines, telephones, and electricity came under regulation. Finally, in 1965–1975, the third wave created a battery of agencies regulating safety and health. Figure 1 includes some of the main antitrust and regulatory parts of these waves.

Each wave reflected the public's discontent with recent business performance and its belief that new actions were needed. Many of the actions were inadequate, went too far, or applied the wrong incentives. Some of the faults were corrected after each wave, when efforts were made to trim back the policies.

The most crucial formative period for policies was 1890–1910. Before 1890, there had been a scattering of rules and laws dealing with the early forms of business, mostly at the local and state level. In cities, the gas and water utilities were controlled in various ways, often under city ownership. The charges for using turnpikes and canals presented problems of monopoly pricing, met in diverse ways by the various states.

Upon this localized scene the U.S. industrial revolution burst with great force during 1865–1900. The railroads spread across the country, forming monopolies in some regions and charging discriminatory prices ("what the traffic would bear"). Stirred by the Civil War and the railroad boom, heavy industries grew rapidly. Gold rushes, land rushes, the invention of electric light systems and telephones, the dramatic growth of the oil industry during 1870–1890—these and other new developments created an industrial transformation of the growing country. Moreover, the high financiers—especially J. P. Morgan—were busy forming "trusts" in many industries by merging scores of little firms into big ones.

The 1880s brought rising public agitation about these changes. Farmers organized to fight price gouging by the railroad monopolies. They and other citizens increasingly denounced the new industrial trusts. Amid sharp political debates, there

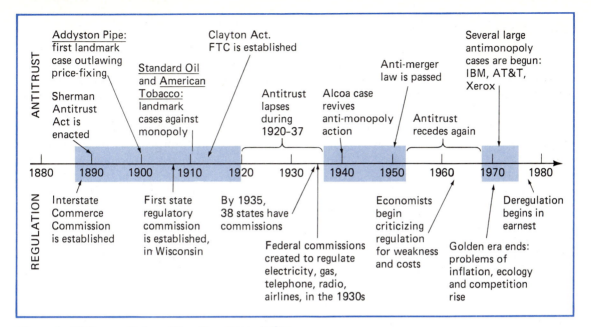

Figure 1   Main events in antitrust and regulation

The figure shows a timeline from 1880 to 1980. Above the line (ANTITRUST):

- Sherman Antitrust Act is enacted
- Addyston Pipe: first landmark case outlawing price-fixing
- Standard Oil and American Tobacco: landmark cases against monopoly
- Clayton Act. FTC is established
- Antitrust lapses during 1920-37
- Alcoa case revives anti-monopoly action
- Anti-merger law is passed
- Antitrust recedes again
- Several large antimonopoly cases are begun: IBM, AT&T, Xerox

Below the line (REGULATION):

- Interstate Commerce Commission is established
- First state regulatory commission is established, in Wisconsin
- By 1935, 38 states have commissions
- Federal commissions created to regulate electricity, gas, telephone, radio, airlines, in the 1930s
- Economists begin criticizing regulation for weakness and costs
- Golden era ends: problems of inflation, ecology and competition rise
- Deregulation begins in earnest

followed two kinds of policy action. *First,* regulation was established, starting with the Interstate Commerce Commission in 1887 to regulate the railroads. Then state regulatory commissions were created from 1907 on, to regulate electricity, telephones, and railroad traffic within the states. These steps accepted the *private* ownership of the basic utility operations, thereby turning against the public ownership of the railroads and city utilities that was already common in other countries.

The regulatory commissions were supposed to control the private utilities strictly, permitting only "fair" rates of return and "just and reasonable" prices (i.e., without too much price discrimination). By the 1930s, most of the states had their own regulatory commissions, and new federal commissions had been created to cover *interstate* operations in the main utility sectors.

Second, **antitrust policy** was created in 1890 to reduce monopoly in the rest of the economy. It was called "antitrust" because it was aimed against the creation of industrial trusts (which were combinations of firms to fix prices). The Sherman Act of 1890 outlawed both monopolizing by one firm and collusion among competitors. After some delay, the law was applied firmly to price fixing in 1899 and to monopolies in 1911. As further enlarged in 1914 and 1949, the U.S. antitrust laws became a uniquely thorough method for stopping industrial monopoly and price fixing.

Yet, antitrust and regulation have had checkered careers since 1920, reflecting the larger economic trends and political swings. Antitrust has veered between great waves of action (in 1938–1952 and 1968–1980) and relatively inactive periods (the 1920s and 1952–1968). Regulation took a long time to get established, with full coverage and powers being reached only in the 1950s. At most times, both antitrust and regulation have been sharply criticized, by business for being too harsh and "antibusiness," and by others for being too weak and "probusiness."

The selections of people to run the agencies are made under political pressure, often resulting in mediocre appointments. The agencies' budgets are also political decisions. Often the strongest lobbying is done by the very companies that the policies are supposed to control. In these and other ways, the companies may influence policy as much as policy influences the companies' actions.

That is what is meant by those two-way arrows in the middle of Figure 1, Chapter 11. Actual policies evolve in a rugged political setting, often under intense pressures from many sides. Therefore, one must expect antitrust, regulation, and public enterprise to be imperfect and limited. We will show, nonetheless, where they have often come close to sound economic results.

Public enterprise has not been fully eclipsed. It has continued in the U.S. Postal Service, many hundreds of city electric and transit systems, thousands of city water works, and still other cases to be noted in Chapter 13. Yet, it has scarcely been tried at all in manufacturing and finance. This is a sharp difference between the United States and many other countries. Since 1945, foreign experience with public enterprise has included all economic sectors.

Standards of efficient policies

Economists judge policies by a simple standard called "cost-benefit analysis." It is merely a specialized version of the fundamental economic comparison we have pointed out repeatedly in earlier chapters. Recall that each economic action provides benefits, usually in the form of a good that people will pay for. The same action will also incur costs—the effort and resources needed to produce the good. Efficient economic decisions will carry production until the marginal benefits just equal marginal costs, as we stressed in Chapter 9. The marginal unit is just worth its cost.

Public policy choices face exactly the same criterion of efficiency: *Each action should be carried out up to the level where its marginal benefits just equal its costs.* But here the benefits are the *public's* benefits that arise when monopoly's effects are prevented: greater efficiency, lower prices, more rapid innovation, and other desirable goals. If the action is wise, then the public reaps these benefits through the improved performance of the economy.

But there are also policy costs to consider. They are mainly incurred by the public in paying for the agency to take the action. Agencies use resources (in staff members' salaries and other costs) in applying their policies. For example, the antitrust chief considers whether to prosecute five bakers in St. Louis for fixing the prices of their bread. The case will cost $10,000 to carry out (in working time, travel, etc.), and it will only improve conditions in one small market. Ideally, the official weighs the benefits and costs, at least approximately, in such a marginal case. In practice, the judgments may be faulty or the agencies may be given either too many or too few resources.

This kind of cost-benefit comparison is the correct basis for appraising antitrust, regulation, and public enterprise. We will show what the agencies have been doing, which is fascinating in itself and full of human drama. But the ultimate economic task is to judge which policies have been carried too far or not far enough, in light of their probable costs and benefits. The specific sums are rarely easy to measure, so that careful judgments have to rely on reasonable likelihoods rather than actual numbers. For example, was the recent large antitrust case against AT&T worth its cost? Should the regulation of long-distance telephone service, railroads, banking, even of electric service, be withdrawn? In these and scores of other cases, the student can practice the kind of cost-benefit thinking that is the test for rational policies.

U.S. antitrust: Forms and coverage

Antitrust policies deal with anticompetitive conditions that arise in the broad range of ordinary markets. As we showed in the preceding chapter, firms are always tempted to eliminate the annoyances of competition by merging with each other, fixing prices, or other tactics. Competition often needs a helping hand, or even sharp antitrust actions, to be effective.

Since 1890, it has been illegal to monopolize markets, or to fix prices, or to deal abusively with one's competitors. These antitrust laws seek to keep competition effective, so that markets will be both efficient and fair. Like any laws, antitrust laws have to be enforced, by prosecuting and penalizing those who violate them. The laws and the enforcement are quite imperfect in practice, as we will shortly show. Yet for all its faults, American antitrust policy stands out as the world's great policy experiment in trying to maintain competitive markets.

U.S. antitrust policies offer fascinating lessons about the economics of competition. Our aim in this chapter is not to convey the details of policy; they are often minor and confusing, and they change frequently. Rather, we wish you to learn how antitrust policies produce economic results. Then you can judge the value of competition and of antitrust itself.

Antitrust policy is pervaded by controversy, and many of the issues are debated intensely. The policy toward price fixing has always been strict; the treatment of mergers has been mixed; while the treatment of dominant firms and tight oligopoly has mostly been mild. Are these policies right, or should they be changed? If changed, should it be toward stricter or gentler enforcement? You will need to keep an open mind and to think independently about these issues. Basic economic concepts can clarify the main points of the debates, but they do not lead to definitive answers.

The agencies and laws

Antitrust policy consists of (1) *agencies* that enforce (2) *laws*. There are two enforcement agencies: (1) the Antitrust Division of the Department of Justice; and (2) the Federal Trade Commission, an independent agency created in 1914. Until the late 1930s, they were tiny agencies with minuscule budgets and a few score staff members. During the second policy wave, they grew to about 300 lawyers each by 1950, and then stabilized. They expanded again after 1970, during the third policy wave. Their budgets for antitrust enforcement were $4 million each in 1950, and still below $12 million in 1970. By 1981, their budgets for antitrust enforcement had grown to about $40 million each. Yet they were still tiny compared to an economy of $2 trillion and a total federal budget over $600 billion.

These resources are thinly spread. Many major industries are dealt with by just a few lawyers and economists. Many other sectors, especially new industries, are given only passing attention. A single big case can engross a sizable share of the whole agency's resources. At the top, the agencies are run by political appointees, who are usually in office for only three years or less. Most significant actions take between five to fifteen years to run their course. Therefore, policies often lack sustained guidance.

The setting for the agencies includes (1) the rest of the government and (2) private antitrust resources. Though they are nominally free from outside interference, the agencies are subject to various pressures. Their budgets are settled by the executive branch and Congress. Firms try to use officials in the executive branch (in the White House, Defense Department, and elsewhere) and members of Congress to influence the agencies. Actions can be appealed to the appellate courts and the U.S. Supreme Court, either to reverse decisions or merely to delay the process.

On the private side, the defendant firms often deploy large resources to resist or manipulate the policy efforts. The private antitrust bar includes about 10,000 lawyers. Large firms can routinely apply 5, 10, or 20 times as many lawyers and experts to a case as the public agencies can. This fits their large stakes in the outcomes, often running into hundreds of millions of dollars. They may spend up to the total amount of profit that is at stake in order to win the case.

Private antitrust suits—by one firm against another—often trigger or supplement actions by the public agencies. Each year there are over a thousand such private cases, in a great variety of markets. In theory, they should neatly fill in any gaps in public policies. In practice, private cases often are lacking precisely where they are most needed.

Because they are so small, the two antitrust agencies mainly try to develop a series of precedent-setting cases, rather than to pursue and catch every firm that might be breaking the antitrust laws. We will present some of those landmark cases in the third main section of this chapter.

The laws are broad and powerful, so that even the two tiny agencies can have some strong effects. The Sherman Antitrust Act, passed in 1890, is the country's basic antitrust law. It has two main sections, which are summarized in Table 1. Section 1 outlaws conspiracies to "restrain trade." It mainly applies to explicit price fixing, which was discussed in the preceding chapter. Section 2 outlaws "monopolizing" or "attempts to monopolize"; that is,

Table 1 *The basic U.S. antitrust laws*

1. **Restraint of Trade** (Sherman Act, Section 1)
   Collusive actions, such as price-fixing, market-rigging, and sales-allocating schemes, and other restrictive actions, are all forbidden.
2. **Monopolizing** (Sherman Act, Section 2)
   Both monopolizing and *attempting to monopolize* a market are illegal.
3. **Mergers** (Clayton Act, Section 7, amended in 1949)
   Any merger that may substantially reduce competition in any market is illegal.
4. **Other Actions That Are Prohibited:**
   a. Interlocking directorates (one person serving on the boards of two competing companies).
   b. Price discrimination that harms competition (Robinson-Patman Act of 1936).
   c. Exclusive and tying contracts (Clayton, Section 3). (If good A can only be bought by also buying good B, then the two goods are "tied.")
   d. "Unfair" methods of competition (FTC Act, Section 5). These are unspecified in the law but would include abusive or extreme actions.

firms that clearly try to dominate their markets.

History

After a shaky start, the Sherman Act was applied firmly against price fixing in 1897 in the *Addyston Pipe* case (the case is summarized in the third main section of this chapter). That strict prohibition of price fixing is still enforced. No longer able to collude with each other after 1897 because of this new precedent, many firms simply merged. Figure 2 charts the waves of mergers and antitrust actions since 1890. The pattern of action and response is clear. Each new wave of mergers stirred anxiety in the populace that corporate power was being enlarged. Antitrust officials then renewed their efforts.

First came Theodore Roosevelt's "trust-busting" campaign, actually carried

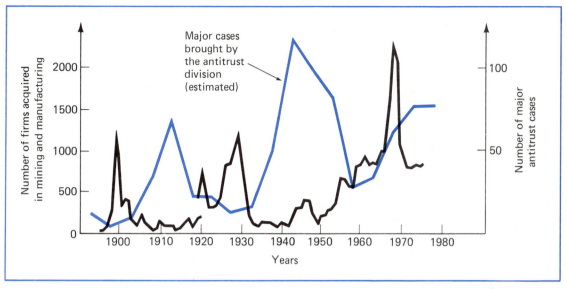

Figure 2 The pulses of merger and antitrust activity

The three merger waves—of 1897–1901, the 1920s, and the 1960s—have been dramatic and turbulent. Antitrust actions have also come in three distinct waves, as shown by the number of cases (weighted for importance). To some extent, the actions have been a response to the mergers and other industrial events.

Source: Mergers: W.G. Shepherd, *The Economics of Industrial Organization* (Englewood Cliffs, N.J.: Prentice-Hall, 1979). Antitrust: adapted from Richard A. Posner, "A Statistical Study of Antitrust Enforcement," *Journal of Law and Economics,* 13 (October, 1970), pp. 374–381.

through mainly during William H. Taft's presidency in 1909–1913. The Standard Oil Company and the American Tobacco Company were each divided into several companies, and several other firms were required to sell off a plant. For example, Standard Oil was separated back into its original regional monopolies, while American Tobacco was divided into three firms in 1913, which are still operating—American Tobacco, Liggett and Myers, and P. Lorillard.

Because the Sherman Act is so terse and broad, business interests soon demanded more details about exactly which actions were illegal. Under Woodrow Wilson's "progressive" approach, the Clayton Act in 1914 was written to try to cover those details, though only a few specific offenses were spelled out. The Federal Trade Commission was also created at that time to enforce the law.

Antitrust then went into hibernation during the "Roaring Twenties," even as the second great merger boom mounted to its peak in 1929. The balance of antitrust actions actually favored mergers and cooperation among firms. But the Crash of 1929 and the Great Depression of the 1930s renewed pressure to act against what was seen as rising corporate power. The second deep antitrust wave, from 1938 to 1952, touched many dominant firms. Thus, the aluminum monopoly (Alcoa: the *Al*uminum *C*ompany of *A*merica) was challenged in 1937, and two new competitors were finally added in 1950. The monopoly in metal cans (American Can Company and National Can Company) was subjected to restraints by a court decree in 1950. The dominant National Broadcasting Company (NBC) was required to sell one of its two radio networks in 1943, thereby creating the American Broadcasting Company

(ABC). Movie companies were forced by the *Paramount Pictures* decision in 1948 to sell their movie-theater chains. There were also major cases against some tight oligopolies, including the leading cigarette companies.

The pace of antitrust actions slowed again from 1953 to 1968. The only exception was the application in 1962 of strict new limits against mergers among competitors. On other antitrust fronts, little was done to reduce market power or to stem conglomerate mergers during the "go-go" merger boom of the 1960s.

After 1968, the antitrust pulse quickened, especially with several large cases alleging that IBM, Xerox, AT&T, and the big cereal companies had monopolized their markets. Then in 1981, the Reagan administration reduced the reach of both antitrust agencies. Efforts to lessen market dominance were trimmed, especially at the FTC. The AT&T case was settled and the IBM case was dropped. Merger rules were relaxed, resulting immediately in a merger boom in 1981. Only price fixing was to be pursued as strictly as before.

After all these fluctuations, antitrust enforcement has settled into a mature state of moderation, part of the industrial and social fabric, but beset by sharp debates about its value and wisdom. Conservatives regard antitrust as mainly a harassment of businesses, doing little good in an economy that is already strongly competitive. By contrast, many liberal experts describe antitrust as weak and poorly managed, a token effort that leaves much monopoly power untouched.

These are old, old issues, always lively and sharply argued. They are also big-league issues because billions of dollars and high degrees of innovation are often at stake. The 10,000 antitrust lawyers are continually engaged in studying and litigating, and at any time there are many hundreds of cases in progress. Many of those cases are brought by private firms, alleging that they have suffered from antitrust violations by other private firms (by being overcharged for goods, by being driven out of business, etc.). Often a firm's fate is affected more deeply by an antitrust case than by any conditions out in the market itself. Almost every issue of the economics and legal journals—and of *Fortune, Forbes, Business Week*, and the *Wall Street Journal*—has articles discussing these topics. The conflicts of evidence and views are often dramatic.

Antitrust criteria

An economist must try to see through the legal details of antitrust to discern its (1) economic criteria and (2) economic effects. Table 2 presents the main antitrust criteria that have evolved in the courts since 1890, in hundreds of precedent-making cases and decisions.

The wording of the statutes sounds broad and conclusive, but the laws have come to be applied only within "reasonable" limits—following what the lawyers call a "rule of reason." In practice, "reasonable" means what the courts will accept, and the limits of enforcement often move as the courts change and as the country's political momentum shifts. For example, the Supreme Court under Earl Warren in the 1960s tightened the criteria against mergers and dominant firms. The "Burger Court" of the 1970s and 1980s has drawn back the margin of antitrust enforcement, toward more moderate treatment of mergers and of the pricing tactics used by dominant firms.

Throughout, one pivotal issue has emerged: the definition of the market. *The two sides usually offer sharply differing definitions of the true extent of the market.* The plaintiff (an agency or a private company

Table 2 *The main economic patterns of antitrust policy*

1. **Toward Existing Structure** (mainly Sherman Act, Section 2).

    Firms with market shares above 60 percent, high barriers to entry, and high rates of profit are to be sued. If market power is high and seems to have economic costs, the court then weighs possible economies of scale and the danger that an antitrust conviction will harm a broad range of the company's stockholders. Although its decision on the case will usually reflect all these factors, the court's formal opinion will usually cite only the market power and any abusive actions by the firm.

    If the firm is convicted, the remedies and penalties applied to it will usually be only moderate (such as levying fines or setting limits on the firm's future actions), rather than requiring the firm to sell part of its capacity.

2. **Toward Mergers** (Clayton Act, Section 7).

    *Horizontal mergers** of firms with a combined share above 10 percent of the market will usually be challenged by the Antitrust Division or the FTC. If the degree of concentration in the industry is rising, and if the merger would not give demonstrable economies of scale, the courts will usually stop the merger.

    *Vertical mergers** of firms with more than 10 percent each at their stage of the industry will usually be stopped.

    Conglomerate mergers will usually be permitted unless they unite two firms that are dominant in their own markets.

3. **Toward Price Fixing and Other Such Actions** (Sherman Act, Section 1).

    All efforts to fix prices will be prosecuted if they are discovered. This is true even if the firms have only a small share of the market. Most firms will be convicted, as long as there is tangible proof of the collusion. Most forms of market splitting (where firms divide up the sales in the market) and other explicit collusion will also be sued and convicted.

    Tacit collusion is exempt from prosecution, unless it becomes very thorough and obvious.

*Horizontal mergers are between competitors in a market (e.g., between General Motors and Ford). Vertical mergers are between firms at different stages in the chain of production (e.g., between a steel company and the firm supplying its iron ore).

claiming to be a victim of monopoly) urges a narrow definition, which gives the defendant firm a high market share. The defendant claims instead that the market is much larger, so that its share of that market is small. The court's decision on this point often governs the rest of the case, for if it accepts a large market, then harmful market power could not exist. Generally the Warren Court defined markets narrowly, whereas the Burger Court has accepted broad market definitions.

Precedents

Policy is applied by bringing individual cases, which the agency lawyers develop, bring to trial, and try to win. Some of the cases become vast, involving scores of lawyers, years of preparation, and millions of documents, as we will soon show. Many others are compact and clear, taking only a year or two from the violation to the final decision. The courts' decisions in these cases set precedents, which then govern subsequent cases. We will present various landmark cases in the third main section.

The precedents all reduce to fairly simple patterns, as shown in Table 2.

Toward existing structure The threshold criterion for prosecution has become (1) a 60 percent market share, (2) *plus* some evidence that the firm intended to gain dominance or has been unfair. Since any firm with a market share below 60 percent will almost certainly be acquitted, no cases are brought against firms in that range. Even with a market share above 60 percent, a firm can argue that its position arose from "superior skill, foresight, and industry" (that is the usual legal phrase), so that it deserves its dominance. Judges are often persuaded by that argument. IBM had particular success with it, winning a series of cases since 1968. Market shares even above 60 percent often go untouched for decades because the antitrust officials expect that any suit against the firm would fail in the courts.

Mergers

HORIZONTAL MERGERS will usually be stopped if the resulting firm would have more than 5 percent of the market. Thus, a merger between Ford and Chrysler automobile companies (with market shares of 20 and 10 percent) would almost certainly be prevented. A merger of two 8 percent firms will be permitted if they can prove that they would thereby achieve economies of scale.

VERTICAL MERGERS will usually be stopped if the firms have more than 5 percent each of their markets. For example, Ford was stopped from buying Autolite, a firm that sells 20 percent of automobile batteries (mostly to the auto companies). Such a merger would have excluded other battery companies from a fair chance to sell batteries to Ford. However, Ford would be permitted to build up its own battery company, if it wished, by creating new capacity.

CONGLOMERATE MERGERS are left mostly untouched, especially if they involve small firms and small market shares. Thus, a tire company might buy a bakery, and then a railroad might buy the tire company. Since no market shares are increased in any market, an antitrust challenge to the merger would probably not occur. Only if each of the firms has a large share of its market *might* the merger be challenged.

Price fixing Price fixing is treated most strictly. The courts will not permit a defense of it on the claim that is was "reasonable." The agency merely needs to show at trial that the price fixing occurred, even without proof that its effects were strong. The courts will then usually convict it *per se* (that is, guilty "in itself").

PRICE DISCRIMINATION Little firms often accuse bigger ones of hurting them by price discrimination. The damage can occur if the larger firm makes selective price cuts, drawing customers away from an efficient small firm and thereby driving that firm out of business. Standard Oil, IBM, Xerox, and hundreds of other firms have been accused of this practice. But convictions on such charges are unsure, and the penalties are usually light.

Economic effects

The economic effects of these policies are debatable, but they probably have been as follows. A few major dominant firms have been reduced in size, mainly in actions taken before 1950. Tight oligopoly has not been touched, effectively challenged, or changed. Many horizontal mergers have been forestalled since 1962, though hundreds of mergers from 1890 to 1962 had already led to substantial concentration in many industries. Price fixing has mostly been driven underground, probably eliminating a large share of it. Yet, as we noted in the previous chapter, secret collusion does continue routinely in many industries and in a variety of tight oligopolies.

Altogether, antitrust policies have probably kept U.S. industrial concentration and the extent of price fixing much lower than they would otherwise have been. If antitrust were abolished, a large merger boom would immediately occur, raising concentration sharply in many industries. Formal price-fixing cartels, with official staffs and binding contracts preventing price competition, would be created in thousands of markets. Therefore, antitrust has created important economic benefits, which continue quietly because antitrust itself continues.

Yet, the economic effects of antitrust have also caused some imbalance. Dominant firms are now largely free to set prices internally over large shares of the market. Thus, General Motors sets prices for some 45 percent of the U.S. automobile market and 85 percent of the locomotives market. But the little rivals of dominant firms (say, two firms with 6 percent market shares each) can neither meet to fix their prices nor merge with each other. Though they would affect only 12 percent of the market, they would be pounced upon by the antitrust agencies.

In cases like this, the law is gentle to the big and strict toward the small. Once a firm has gained dominance, it is largely immune from antitrust actions, free to do things internally that lesser firms cannot do among themselves. Ideally, antitrust would be equally strict toward dominant and little firms.

Antitrusts's ultimate effects are *debatable*, then, perhaps promoting efficiency on the whole, but perhaps also lacking balance. The effects are also *limited*, for antitrust reaches only to part of the economy. As Table 3 shows, most utilities, local markets, newspapers, professions such as the law and medicine, all labor unions, all patents, much weapons production, and most public enterprises are exempt from antitrust. The antitrust domain is, therefore, the core of national manufacturing industries and trade, altogether less than half of the U.S. economy. Meanwhile, various other policies directly reduce competition in many markets. They are summarized in Part 2 of Table 3. On the whole, antitrust's reach is far from complete. And even where it does reach, its resources are usually stretched thin.

Think of antitrust as *interacting with industry*, not standing above it exercising lordly powers. Like any other policing

Table 3 Departures from antitrust: Exemptions and policies that reduce competition

1. **Exemptions**
   Much local and statewide activity: construction, shops, repairs, services.
   Labor unions at all levels.
   Utilities and urban services: electricity, gas, telephone.
   Social services and health services: schools, hospitals.
   Public enterprises: many electric, transit, and water systems at the local and regional levels.
   Farm and fishery cooperatives: dairy cooperatives.
   Many military suppliers: aircraft, tanks, ships, ammunition, etc.
   Baseball and, to a lesser degree, other professional sports.
   Newspapers' joint publishing arrangements in many cities.
2. **Policies That Reduce Competition**
   Tariffs and other barriers to international trade, such as quotas and agreements to limit imports.
   Patents: they provide a monopoly for 17 years.
   Banking regulation that prevents new entry in many banking markets.
   Price raising for certain farm products (milk, tobacco, etc.) is enforced by the U.S. Department of Agriculture.
   Shipbuilding and shipping: price fixing is enforced by the Federal Maritime Commission.

agency, antitrust officials are influenced by industry, by Congress, by the executive branch, and by swings of popular attitudes. Policy choices are often political, mistaken, rash, or too cautious: in short, thoroughly human, fallible, and changeable. Yet, the basic economic effects—against price fixing and mergers—remain relatively steady.

Specific parts of antitrust

Antitrust actions toward existing concentration

Defining the market The court decisions in cases involving an existing concentration of power usually hinge on the market

Is Antitrust Necessary?

Antitrust has severe critics, even apart from those businesses that would simply like to be free of its constraints. In recent decades, the attacks have come from two opposite sides.

Free-market liberals believe that nearly all markets are highly competitive. Only governments create lasting monopoly, they say. Any private market power will quickly be wiped out by new competition. Schumpeter's sequence of temporary monopolists (recall the box in Chapter 11) gives a similar result.

Accordingly, a minimal antitrust policy is needed, merely to stop blatant price fixing. Dominant firms, mergers, tacit collusion, price discrimination, and all other restrictions will not harm competition. Antitrust actions against them are useless or make matters worse.

Another group, whose most prominent spokesmen are John K. Galbraith and Lester Thurow, regards large firms as so efficient and innovative that efforts to divide or limit them are futile. If economies of scale and innovation are large, then antitrust should leave large firms untouched, even if their monopoly power is strong. Antitrust should also leave lesser firms free, for they are innocuous, and it is unfair to punish them for doing what large firms are free to do. If not abolished, antitrust should at least be pruned severely. Some degree of price controls or public ownership may be needed for the more powerful large firms.

These and other views all pivot on the same underlying economic conditions: the economies of scale, the effects of monopoly power, the sources of innovation, and the speed at which monopoly is eroded by market forces.

share of the leading firm. That, in turn, depends on the relationship between the firm's sales and the size of the market. Therefore, defining the market is a crucial step.

As Chapter 4 already noted, the market's true size depends on the extent of substitution among goods. That degree of substitutability is measured by the cross-elasticity of demand. We presented that concept in Chapter 4. Now we will show how the concept is applied step by step in antitrust decisions.

The relevant market The concept of "the" market rests on the choices made by consumers, as they compare substitutable goods. These choices are usually made along two main dimensions: the *kind* of good being exchanged (the "product type") and the *geographical area*. We will now consider those two dimensions in turn, just as the courts do in typical antitrust cases.

Consider *product types* first. The market should include those goods that are substituted freely. Thus, the newspaper market might include magazines and/or TV and radio broadcasts. But most buyers of newspapers will buy the newspaper even if its price rises (or if other goods' prices fall). Therefore, newspapers are in their own separate market because there does not appear to be much substitution between newspapers and television.

Likewise, the *geographical area* of the market will be defined by the choices that consumers make. Thus, most people just buy the local paper, while some also, or instead, buy the Chicago *Tribune* or New York *Times.* Yet very few Boston *Globe* readers will shift to the Cleveland *Plain Dealer* or Des Moines *Register,* even if the *Globe's* price triples. Therefore, the *Globe* is in a separate geographical market from the others, even if its product type (newspaper) is identical. In the last chapter, we presented a number of such local newspaper markets.

Both of these elements involve cross-elasticities of demand, but such elasticities are rarely calculated. A reasonable, careful judgment about the main scope of the market is usually all that the judges have to go on. In antitrust cases, the defendant firm invariably claims that the market is large (e.g., a defendant newspaper might try to include all newspapers in all cities within 200 miles, plus all magazines sold in that area). The plaintiff claims, to the contrary, that the real market is much narrower (e.g., solely the local newspaper market).

When the case has been argued and the evidence presented, the judges then have to decide what the "true" market is, as best they can. Any economics student is free to second-guess them, and it is widely agreed that the judges have often been mistaken. Section 2 cases against established market power offer fascinating tests of one's ability to use economic tools to judge the scope of the market sensibly.

Economies of scale   The other key question in a Section 2 monopolization case is whether there are large economies of scale. If the dominant firm can show that it has gained important economies of scale, most judges will acquit it, even if the rest of the case against the monopolist is airtight. Economies of scale are not included in the letter of the antitrust laws, but judges are usually persuaded by them nonetheless.

Of course, whether economies of scale really exist is usually highly debatable from case to case. The defendant will claim that the economies are large, while the plaintiff will usually present experts who say that they are small or nonexistent. Once again, the *logic* of the issue is clear, but the *matters of degree* are uncertain.

Two basic concepts—the extent of the market and of possible economies of scale—are central for understanding the antitrust actions taken toward dominant firms. The agencies try to pick those cases where the degree of monopoly is high, compared to what the economies of scale might require. The agencies also naturally focus their efforts on large firms in major industries, where a single case might yield a large economic gain. Often, too, several private firms have already sued the dominant firm, claiming that it has damaged them. These private suits often stir (or embarrass) the agencies into taking action.

Leading cases   Leading cases are summarized in Table 4. Two recent cases show the current issues and define the scope of current precedents.

UNITED STATES V. INTERNATIONAL BUSINESS MACHINES CORPORATION*   This was the big IBM case, filed in 1969. After a marathon trial from 1975 to 1981, it was finally dropped by the Reagan administration in January 1982. It had become a mammoth case, with hundreds of lawyers preparing the IBM defense, against about ten lawyers on the Antitrust Division side. The Antitrust Division's side of the case took 726

---

*These and other antitrust cases can be looked up in two main sources. For past cases, the decisions are in the standard volumes of Supreme Court and appeals court decisions. For current cases, the *Antitrust and Trade Regulation Reporter,* issued biweekly, gives details of the events as they unfold.

Table 4 *A selection of leading antitrust cases against established dominance*

Case	Origin of Dominance	Year of Decision	Alleged (%)	Market Share Defendant's Version (%)	Final Decision (%)	Result of Case
U.S. v. Standard Oil (oil)	1870s	1911	90	60	90	Convicted. Separated into about a dozen regionally dominant firms.
U.S. v. American Tobacco (cigarettes)	1890s	1911	90	90	90	Convicted. Separated into three firms.
U.S. v. Alcoa (aluminum)	1903	1945	90	30	90	Convicted. War plants sold in 1950 to two new firms (Reynolds and Kaiser).
U.S. v. Du Pont (cellophane)	1920s	1956	70	18	18	Acquitted because market held to be broad.
U.S. v. IBM (computers)	1952–1955	1982*	70	33	—	The case was withdrawn.
FTC-Xerox (copiers)	1961	1975†	90+	~50	—	A compromise, giving access to some Xerox patents.
FTC–Du Pont (titanium dioxide)	1970s	1981	55	42	55	Acquitted. Dominance credited to innovation.
U.S. v. AT&T (telephone equipment and service)	1880s	1982†	100	below 50	—	With conviction likely, the case was settled by compromise.

*The case was withdrawn.
†The case was settled by compromise.

trial days and 104,000 pages of transcript; IBM's lawyers called 856 witnesses and cited 12,280 exhibits.

Yet, the economic question at the heart of the case was simple: Did IBM have too much monopoly power? The suit alleged that IBM had held 60 to 70 percent of the computer market since 1955. Also, the suit alleged, IBM engaged in various anticompetitive acts during the 1960s, such as predatory pricing against certain successful competitors (those actions are discussed in that part of the third main section dealing with pricing tactics). IBM

had also gained large monopoly profits on its equity capital—18 percent for more than 25 years.

IBM's defense rested on a market definition that included all equipment used with computers in any way (display units, typewriter terminals, office equipment, etc.). IBM also included most other products made by firms that produce computers. Honeywell, for instance, makes computers plus various other industrial equipment; IBM included all of that other Honeywell equipment in the claimed computer market. In a market defined that broadly, IBM had a market share of only about 35 percent in the 1960s, well below the traditional 60 percent legal threshold.

IBM also argued that its market position arose from the superior "skill, foresight, and industry" that it had shown in developing computers, rather than from unfair pricing and tactics. At the most, IBM said, it had competed vigorously, but hard competition should not be penalized. IBM claimed to be the most innovative computer company, and to have achieved large economies of scale. Its high profit rate, it said, was merely the financial reward for efficiency and innovation.

Reagan officials accepted IBM's arguments, which fitted with their general policy of letting dominant firms alone unless they could be proved to have committed severe abuses. In dropping the case, the officials argued that conditions in the computer industry had changed sharply since the 1960s.

The case left this informal precedent: *Dominant firms are free to compete with extreme force, even if they drive other firms from the market. If their actions are not clearly abusive, and if the case lasts so long that the industry can be said to have changed, then the firm will be acquitted.*

THE FTC-XEROX CASE Xerox Corporation attained a complete monopoly of plain-paper photocopying in the United States during 1961–1970. It held crucial patents, developed many others, and practiced extensive price discrimination. The FTC challenged this monopoly in 1972. After private negotiations, the FTC and Xerox reached a compromise settlement in 1975 (moving much faster than the IBM case!). Though the Xerox case was not argued or decided formally in public hearing, the issues were discussed in detail.

The FTC defined the market as *plain-paper copiers only*. There are coated-paper copiers too, but the copies they make are rather different in feel and desirability. Since coated-paper copies are regarded as inferior to plain-paper ones, they would not be substitutable. Therefore, plain-paper copiers were said by the FTC to be "the" market. Xerox had 100 percent of the plain-paper market until 1970, and about 85 percent of it in 1974 (IBM, Eastman Kodak, and others had entered by then).

Xerox's price discrimination showed that it had the intent to eliminate competition by making sharp discriminatory price cuts on products where it faced competition. On products where its market power was higher, Xerox set much higher price-cost ratios. The FTC further claimed that Xerox realized few scale economies, was not an innovative leader after 1965, and made high monopoly rates of return averaging above 27 percent during the 1960s.

In its defense, Xerox defined the market as *all* copying during the 1960s, which would have given it a market share of only 65 percent, and all copying *and reproducing* (mimeographing, etc.) in the 1970s. On that basis, Xerox's market share was probably well below 50 percent by 1973. Xerox also pointed out that the crucial patents it held were perfectly legal and binding. Therefore, it said, its large market share, pricing, and high profits were justified. Xerox also claimed that those profits, which dwindled below a 20 percent return on capital by 1973, merely reflected Xerox's scale economies and fruitful innovations.

You can judge for yourself by direct experience whether plain-paper copies are closely substitutable for coated-paper copies and/or other reproducing processes. Consider their physical features, plus speed and convenience. Most coated-paper copies have had a shiny surface, a gray shading, and a chemical smell. It is debatable whether these make coated-paper copies inferior to plain-paper copies. Would you expect the cross-elasticity between these methods of reproduction to be high? The claims about scale economies and innovation cannot be proved or disproved, for the facts are unclear and experts' opinions vary.

A moderate compromise was reached in 1975, giving Xerox's rivals the chance to license some of Xerox's extensive collection of patents on copier technology. Little new U.S. competition has emerged since then, but new Japanese products marketed by the Canon and Savin companies since 1975 shrank Xerox's share of plain-paper new-machine sales to less than 50 percent by 1981.

This sample of just two cases cannot show the full variety and lessons from actions against dominant firms. But it does reflect several common features of these cases. The cases can be extremely lengthy, for they are complicated and intensely debated. Indeed, the defendant usually gains by delay and can stall action by many procedural tactics. Even the most basic issues can be made to seem complex during the legal contest, as each side's lawyers strive to win. The details of these cases proliferate, often into scores or hundreds of volumes of testimony, reports, and data.

Under current decisions, dominant firms can expect to continue without challenge, even if their market shares are well above 60 percent. Only if the firms are clearly abusive or inefficient may they be convicted of monopolizing. And even then, the penalties may be light. Since 1913, the courts have rarely required divestiture (that is, the selling off of part of a firm to reduce market share). Severe competition by dominant firms now appears to be largely immune to antitrust policy.

Antitrust policies toward mergers

There are usually at least 1,500 mergers a year in the United States. The antitrust agencies challenge about 30 per year and usually win about two thirds of those cases. The court precedents for merger policy were set mainly by a series of landmark cases in the 1960s.

Leading cases Leading cases are summarized in Table 5. The precedents from these cases probably forestall thousands of other mergers because the potential partners expect that their projected merger would be prevented. We will present four of those landmark cases, to show how merger policies have been formed.

U.S. V. VON'S GROCERY COMPANY (1966): A HORIZONTAL MERGER There were no effective laws against mergers until 1949. After 1910 or so, the dominant firms in perhaps ten major industries knew that any further mergers would probably precipitate a major Section 2 case. But otherwise firms could merge with impunity, even though they could not collude to fix prices.

In 1950, this merger loophole was closed by the Celler-Kefauver amendment to the Clayton Act. There was a pause of six years, until a merger came along to test the law. That merger (between two steel companies) was stopped, and then others involving shoe companies and banks were prevented. Finally, in 1966, the Von's Grocery decision set the strict rules for horizontal mergers. That strict precedent held until 1981, when Reagan administration officials announced a loosening of the rules.

For a case with such a large precedent, Von's Grocery involved remarkably small firms. Two small Los Angeles grocery-store chains had tried to merge in the 1950s: Von's, the third largest chain, and Shopping Bag, the sixth largest. After the merger, their combined share of the Los Angeles grocery market would have been only 7.5 percent. Concentration in the Los Angeles market was declining, and entry barriers in it were low. The merger would

Table 5 *A selection of leading antitrust cases against mergers and price fixing*

Case	Year of Merger or Price-fixing	Year of Decision	Market Share Held by the Merging or Price-fixing Firms (%)	Action Taken
Horizontal Merger				
Brown Shoe—Kinney Shoe (shoes and shoe retailing)	1957	1962	20	The merger was prevented.
Von's Grocery—Shopping Bag (grocery stores in Los Angeles)	1959	1966	8	The merger was prevented.
Vertical Merger				
Du Pont—General Motors (paints and fabrics)	1920	1957	30	Du Pont's was required to sell its shareholding in General Motors.
Conglomerate Merger				
Procter & Gamble—Clorox (bleach)	1958	1967	55	Clorox was restored as a separate firm.
ITT and various firms (hotels, baking, car rental, insurance, etc.)	1960s	1971	"leading"	ITT chose to retain Hartford Fire Insurance and to sell several other firms.
Price-fixing Cases				
U.S. v. Addyston Pipe & Steel Co. (cast-iron pipe)	1890s	1899	30	Conviction and fines.
U.S. v. Socony-Vacuum (gasoline)	1930s	1940	35	Conviction and fines.
Electrical Equipment Cases (heavy electrical equipment)	1930s–1950s	1960	over 90	No defense: fines and several brief jail terms.
U.S. v. General Electric and Westinghouse (turbine-generators)	1963–1975	1976*	over 90	Compromise. The scheme for tacit collusion was renounced.

*The case was settled by compromise.

therefore not have eliminated much competition.

Yet the Supreme Court stopped the merger. The majority opinion stressed the need to prevent concentration and preserve vigorous small competitors. It was willing to promote low concentration, even

down to preventing this small merger. If the Court was wrong, the harm would be slight. Each grocery chain, after all, was still free to grow by setting up new stores or buying them a few at a time.

The Court's minority in this case complained bitterly, saying that since the market was already highly competitive, the merger was harmless or even beneficial. Was the decision wrong? Opinions are still divided. Most scholars now think that the Von's Grocery precedent might have been too strict, but not by much.

U.S. V. DU PONT (1957): A VERTICAL "MERGER" The Du Pont chemical company began as an explosives maker. During World War I, it made enormous profits, some of which it used in 1919 to buy about one quarter of the stock of the General Motors Company. In the following decades, General Motors bought most of its paints, glues, and seat cover fabrics from Du Pont. The Antitrust Division sued Du Pont in 1949, claiming that this vertical link between the two companies had excluded other paint and fabric firms from a fair chance to sell their products to General Motors. The Supreme Court agreed in 1957, forcing Du Pont to sell its shares and end the link. Since then, General Motors has broadened its purchases sharply. The case did increase competition in the market.

FTC V. PROCTER & GAMBLE (1967): A CONGLOMERATE MERGER When Procter & Gamble bought Clorox Chemical Company in 1958, P&G was the largest household products firm. It did not sell bleach, but it had been planning to enter the bleach business. Some of its products were related to bleach, and P&G management had considered making a direct entry—by building a new factory to produce bleach—before deciding to enter by buying out the Clorox Company instead. Clorox itself was the dominant bleach firm, with a long-established share of 49 percent of the national market. Clorox's share in the Mid-Atlantic region was as high as 71 percent, compared to 15 percent for Purex, the next largest bleach producer.

The merger would clearly have subtracted a leading new "potential entrant"

into the bleach market: P&G itself. That would have reduced competition and, by itself, probably led the FTC to stop the merger. Yet, the FTC (later affirmed by the Supreme Court) instead cited P&G's advertising advantages as the main grounds for preventing the merger.

The FTC and the Court stressed that P&G would be able to give Clorox overwhelming advantages in advertising and distributing its bleach. P&G was the nation's largest advertiser (spending over $175 million on advertising in 1967), and its discounts and market power were likely to entrench Clorox further as the dominant bleach firm. A "toehold" acquisition by P&G of a small bleach company (say, Purex or smaller) would not have encountered this objection and would likely have been allowed. The loss of a potential competitor would have been more than offset by the increase in the small firm's ability to compete vigorously.

ITT's CONGLOMERATE MERGERS During the 1960s, the International Telephone and Telegraph Corporation bought up a series of large firms that were leaders in their markets: Continental Baking ("Wonder Bread," etc.), Avis (car rentals), Levitt (house builders), Sheraton Hotels, Canteen Corporation (dispensing machines), and others. The Antitrust Division sued ITT in 1969, saying that ITT's large financial resources would help to entrench these leading firms even more, thus reducing competition. By contrast, smaller "toehold" mergers—in which ITT bought firms with 10 percent market shares or less—would have promoted competition by building up little firms to compete more effectively with the market leaders.

ITT settled the case in 1972 by selling off some of the firms. Because the case was not tried and brought to a decision, it did not set any clear precedents for other conglomerate mergers. Still, the case emphasized that conglomerate mergers with leading firms may be challenged and even stopped.

These cases convey some of the fascinating variety and drama of actions against mergers. Sometimes the agencies go too far, fighting mergers that are neutral or even economically desirable. The courts, too, are fallible, often shifting the policy rules too far one way or the other. The basic issue is always: *What conditions—in the form of low market shares and low entry barriers—will ensure effective competition and efficient production at an adequate scale of production?*

Where scale economies are large, mergers may merely help to achieve them. But where the economies are small (recall Table 5), most mergers are purely a means to gain monopoly power, for they give little or no gain in efficiency. The economic task is to set the limits on mergers carefully, so that no more competition is sacrificed than scale economies make necessary. Presently, the policies may be roughly correct, setting a fairly strict standard of skepticism toward claims of scale economies.

Even if merger policies err toward being too strict, the harm is usually slight, for firms can always *grow internally*, instead of by mergers. They can build their own new factories, thereby increasing the industry's capacity and competition. The internal growth may take longer and incur some added costs. But it is possible, and it *increases* competition rather than reducing it. So merger policy is relatively easy to apply, because (1) it only stops new conditions, rather than trying to change long-established positions; and (2) it leaves internal growth as a good alternative.

The contrast is sharp between strict merger policy and weak actions toward existing monopoly. It is easy to see why this difference has evolved. Section 2 cases are hard to win, because of (1) complexity, (2) severe resistance and delay, and (3) the reluctance of judges to tamper with large successful firms. Yet there is an awkward gap between the 10 percent ceiling on mergers and the 60 percent safety level for dominant firms. To be economically consistent, the two criteria should be brought closer into line.

Policies toward price fixing and other actions

Price fixing The agencies probably catch little of the price fixing that goes on in oligopoly markets. Even so, the range of cases and convictions is remarkably wide. In a recent six-month period, cases in the biweekly *Antitrust and Trade Regulation Reporter* (which your college library may have) included: Korean wigs, ready-mix concrete, Hawaii package tours, paper labels, timber, Utah egg dealers, steel products, construction firms, bakeries in El Paso, liquid asphalt, plumbing supplies, and scores of others. Even tight oligopolies frequently indulge in elaborate price fixing.

U.S. V. ADDYSTON PIPE AND STEEL COMPANY (1899) In this first landmark case, six producers of cast-iron pipe in the region including Ohio and Pennsylvania had divided up their markets and operated a bidding ring. To prevent competition, they arranged to rotate the contracts among them, designating for each time who would make the lowest bid. Such a bidding ring ensures cooperation among the sellers and gives the buyers no real choice. Though the six firms held less than half of the markets, their price fixing was convicted as illegal *per se* by William H. Taft, then an Ohio judge. Thereupon, the firms soon merged with each other to fix their prices internally, and legally!

THE ELECTRICAL EQUIPMENT CONSPIRACY (1960) Sixty-one years after *Addyston* made price fixing flatly illegal, this spectacular case showed that price fixing had been a way of life for decades in seven major markets for heavy electrical equipment (generators, transformers, switch gear, etc.). Producers of heavy electrical equipment had run secret bidding rings, using formulas based on phases of the moon to rotate orders among themselves. Executives met in hotels, motels, cabins, bars, and other secret retreats. The cloak-and-dagger operations often degenerated into wrangling, but they did raise prices by 20 percent or more for long periods on many billions of dollars of equipment. Some 29 companies, including General Electric and Westinghouse, and scores of their officers, were involved. There were fines and damage suits by customers, and some officials served brief jail sentences. The whole set of penalties, however, was not generally regarded as severe.

THE GENERAL ELECTRIC–WESTINGHOUSE CONSENT DECREE (1976) Even after the electrical equipment manufacturers were caught and penalized in 1960, the industry's tight oligopoly structure remained a basis for tacit collusion. Competition did break out vigorously in 1960–1963. Then, in 1963, General Electric set up a new pricing method, based on simple formulas, which it published in full. Finally GE promised to give any new price cut retroactively to all other purchases made during the *previous* six months. That amounted to a heavy penalty on itself for cutting its prices. Therefore, it was a form of pledge to its rival that it would rarely cut prices.

Moreover, GE pledged to publish all of its price offers and orders.

Thus, GE surrendered all of the secret competitive tactics by which oligopoly pricing can be kept flexible and sharply competitive. This can be illustrated by imagining that GE and Westinghouse have both sold 15 turbines in six months for $20

million each. But GE wishes to get a major new contract for 5 turbines by bidding only $18 million each. The retroactive price cut (to $18 million each on the 15 earlier turbines) costs it $30 million, besides the $10 million on the 5 new turbines. That extra $30 million penalty will discourage GE from making the price cut at all. Moreover, Westinghouse would know exactly what GE would do, so the chances for avoiding competition are high. GE's main rival, Westinghouse, immediately copied GE's plan, down to the precise numbers.

Therefore (as GE memos show was intended from the start), the two companies now had a firm basis for mutual trust and tacit collusion. For many years after 1964, there was no price cutting or flexibility in this industry. Competition had been tacitly eliminated. Only later, after 1970, when a large utility customer (American Electric Power Company) sued GE and Westinghouse, did the Antitrust Division intervene with its own case. Eventually, in 1976, the firms agreed to drop the plan and restore competitive pricing. But there was no trial, conviction, penalties, or payment of damages.

This major industry shows how tight oligopoly poses sharp problems. Tight oligopoly can result in straight price fixing, which often can be caught, proved, and penalized. Even after such treatment, however, the temptations to collude still remain, on a more informal but nearly as effective basis. Changing the industry's structure into loose oligopoly by dividing the leading firms into smaller units usually seems to be too drastic a treatment. But without a structural change, the tendency to collusion will probably remain.

Price discrimination A leading firm can often reduce competition, not by cooperating with its rivals, but instead by taking actions that harm them. Such actions are designed to victimize and exclude competitors. When dominant firms act this way too severely, they can reduce competition.

Some price discrimination does just that, especially when a dominant firm makes deep selective price cuts. Remember that price discrimination can *promote* competition when it is done sporadically by firms with small market shares. Only when it is done systemmatically by dominant firms is discrimination *harmful* to competition. Standard Oil's selective pricing before 1900 often had this effect.

For another example, IBM's new 360 line of computers in the 1960s was threatened at two points: by GE "time-sharing" computers and by computers designed for scientific uses. IBM rushed out two costly stop-gap models to meet that new competition, at prices that did not cover IBM's costs. Such loss-making models succeeded in stopping the competitors, helping drive both GE and RCA from the market altogether. The episode illustrates how a dominant firm can selectively defeat competitors who have superior products by setting prices that are below cost.

There are no recent cases on predatory actions that offer clear precedents and rules. Indeed, judges in the 1970s have generally acquitted "predatory pricing," even when little firms were sharply damaged by the larger firms' tactics. If a dominant firm's selective price cuts don't take price levels below the levels of marginal cost, they will probably be exonerated, regardless of the impact on other firms.

The economic argument for acquittal usually runs as follows: As long as price is not cut below marginal cost, any efficient rival should be able to survive the price cuts. The selective price cuts should be welcomed for providing products to customers at low prices, while weeding out inefficient producers.

On the other hand, even if price does not go below marginal cost, it may go be-

low average cost. The smaller firm would lose money and perhaps face bankruptcy. A dominant firm can usually weather such hard times better than its small rivals. Also, large firms can harm little efficient rivals in many ways, with pricing as only one of their weapons. For example, the large firm can announce a new line of products just when a small firm brings out a new product. That will induce customers to hold off buying the small firm's offering. Or the large firm can merely threaten to cut prices deeply, causing fear and fluctuations for small rivals.

At any rate, marginal cost is usually hard to measure as a basis for judging if the price cuts have been abusive. Thus, a dominant firm's whole strategy can be damaging even if the prices do not go clearly below marginal cost.

Summary

1. U.S. antitrust developed in thousands of fascinating cases since 1890. U.S. antitrust policies are a unique effort to get economic benefits with minimal public cost and interference in industry. Antitrust is an imperfect human activity, as fallible officials and judges process a stream of cases, many of which have confusing details.

2. The two antitrust agencies are small, compared to their economic tasks. The aims of antitrust are both efficiency and equity: to promote competition as far as it is consistent with scale economies, and to promote fair conditions and outcomes.

3. If antitrust works, then competition is more effective and will be more productive, open, and fair. Accordingly, direct control of firms will not be needed.

4. Antitrust policies have been mainly gentle toward existing market dominance, but strict toward mergers and price fixing. This causes some imbalance and unfairness, letting dominant firms do individually what their little rivals cannot do together.

5. Yet, the whole effect of antitrust has been toward much less concentration and price fixing than otherwise would have occurred. The U.S. economy is much closer to the ideals of free competitive markets because of antitrust policies.

Key concepts

Antitrust policy

Questions for review

1. a. What is the major criterion by which public policies should be judged?
   b. Describe the agencies responsible for enforcing antitrust policies.

2. a. Which type of merger is least likely to be challenged (horizontal, vertical, conglomerate)?
   b. What determines whether a merger should be challenged?

3. Price fixing and price discrimination are two offenses which are likely to be treated quite strictly by the courts. True or False? Explain.

4. How can cross-elasticity and economies of scale be used to determine the outcome of antitrust action?

5. Describe some of the potential harms and benefits of conglomerate mergers.

13

Policies Toward Monopoly Power: Regulation and Public Enterprise

As you read and study this chapter, you will learn:

▶ the economic reasons and criteria for regulation

▶ four economic issues of regulation: marginal-cost pricing, effects on efficiency, new competition, and deregulation

▶ economic criteria for public enterprises

▶ several case studies of actual public firms

When you switch on a light or mail a letter, you are dealing with the subject matter of this chapter. Electricity is a classic case of a natural monopoly, placed under public regulation. The U.S. Postal Service is a public enterprise because it, too, is both a natural monopoly and has certain social purposes.

In these cases and others, competition is not efficient. Instead, the public lets the supplier have a monopoly, and then it regulates its prices. The supplier may also be put under public ownership. These approaches rest on several clear economic concepts, which we present in this chapter. But, in practice, the problems are often complex, and the results are debatable. We present some of those issues too.

In the first section, we discuss the economic regulation of prices. Then, in the next section, we present public enterprise.

Regulation of utilities

In some markets, one or several firms are given an exclusive franchise and then supervised by a regulatory commission. The commission has powers to scrutinize the firm and to control its prices. Such price regulation has covered a series of public utilities and several oligopolies (such as airlines). It is a distinctively American approach, combining a maximum of private ownership with some degree of public control. It is supposed to achieve economies of scale in cases of **natural monopoly**, while keeping the monopolist's prices down toward costs.

The economic objective of **regulation** is shown in Figure 1, for electricity service, for example. There are large economies of scale, with the average cost of electricity declining to the output level Q_1. The demand curve for electricity intersects the average cost curve at that same output level. The regulators now set the price of electricity at P_1, and so consumers demand—and receive—the output level Q_1. No excess profits are earned by the firm, capacity is fully used, and electricity is supplied at the lowest possible cost. The economies of scale are achieved, while price is held down to the level of cost.

At its best, regulation does apply such controls, briskly and fairly. The economic task has two parts. One is to set price levels, so that the firm does not earn excess profit and exploit its customers. The other part is to set a price structure that is "just and reasonable," among the variety of customers. The monopoly will try instead to set discriminatory prices, along the lines shown in Chapter 10. Economic efficiency requires aligning prices with marginal costs instead. Remember that the alignment of price and marginal cost brings value into line with sacrifice at the margin.

The ideal commission does these two tasks with a minimum of cost and delay.

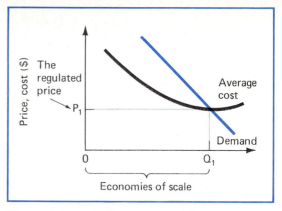

Figure 1   Regulation of a natural monopoly
The large economies of scale are shown by the decline of the average cost curve in the output range of zero to Q_1. The market demand curve passes through the average cost curve at its minimum point at output level Q_1. By setting the maximum permitted price at P_1, the regulators prevent the firm from earning excess profits. Output Q_1 is produced, and the economies of scale are achieved.

And when natural monopoly conditions fade away, then the regulation and the franchise should be withdrawn, so that competition can take over the job.

Yet, regulation may, instead, go wrong. It may become a captive of the industry. It may be applied where natural monopoly conditions do not exist. It may be slow, ineffective, and costly, and it can have inefficient side effects. Regulation now covers industries with only about 6 percent of national income and 15 percent of total investment. Yet, it raises important and complicated issues. And regulation is highly controversial: Is it a charade, as some experts suggest? Sluggish? Highly effective? A captive? A cause of waste? Since 1960, criticism of regulation has been rising, and, in fact, as we noted in Chapter 11, in the 1970s, several major sectors were *deregulated*.

Patterns of regulation

What is to be regulated?   Ideally, regulation is applied to natural monopoly, as shown by the down-sloping average cost curve. The firm's resulting monopoly power could be enhanced if (1) the good is a "necessity," with highly inelastic demand (such as for electricity, water and telephone service); and (2) users are physically connected to the supplier (as by wires or pipes). In those cases, consumers would be especially vulnerable to exploitation and harmful price discrimination.

These conditions are all matters of degree. Economies of scale are often moderate rather than extreme; industries do not divide neatly into natural competition and natural monopoly boxes. Moreover, technology often changes, so that the econo-mies of scale grow or recede. Today's natural monopoly may soon be naturally competitive. Therefore, the proper scope of regulation is often uncertain and changing, rather than clear.

Commissions There are 4 main federal regulatory commissions and nearly 50 state regulatory bodies. They are summarized in Table 1. There are usually three to seven commissioners, who hear and decide issues brought before them by the regulated firms, by customers, by the commission staff, or by other parties. Commission resources vary from scant to large. Housekeeping and peripheral tasks (such as

Table 1 **The main federal commissions and five selected state commissions**

Commission (year established)	Number of Members	Number of Staff Members	Budget, 1979 ($ million)	Jurisdiction
Federal				
Interstate Commerce Commission (1888)	11	1,770	29.4	Railroads, trucking, buses, water shipping, oil pipelines, express companies, etc.
Federal Energy Regulatory Commission (1920, 1935)	5	1,191	22.8	Electricity, gas, gas pipelines, oil pipelines, water power sites
Federal Communications Commission (1934)	7	1,785	32.8	Telephones, television, cable television, radio, telegraph, CB radios, ham operators, etc.
Civil Aeronautics Board (1938)	5	708	13.5	Airlines (passenger and cargo), other carriers. (The CAB is scheduled for abolition in 1983.)
State				
California	5	522	12.2	Electricity, gas, telephones, railroads, buses, trucks, airlines, water supply, warehouses, cable TV, sewage, etc.
Colorado	3	72	1.0	Electricity, gas, telephones, railroads, buses, trucks, airlines, oil pipelines, water supply
Georgia	5	57	0.8	Electricity, gas, telephones, railroads, buses, trucks
New York	5	343	12.8	Electricity, gas, telephones, oil pipelines, water supply
Wisconsin	3	140	3.2	Electricity, gas, telephones, railroads, buses, trucks, taxis, airlines, oil pipelines, water, sewage

Source: Federal Energy Regulatory Commission, *Federal and State Commission Jurisdiction and Regulation* (Washington, D.C.: Federal Power Commission, 1980).

safety at railroad crossings and the licensing of small operators) absorb much of the resources of some commissions.

Commissioners are political appointees. Usually they are politically active lawyers, either ambitious young ones or older ones on the way out. Since the more talented commissioners usually rise to higher positions elsewhere, they are in regulatory office less than three years, with little time to develop or change basic policies. Staffs tend to be bureaucratic, cautiously adjusting among the conflicting interests of firms, customers, and other groups. Like antitrust, the process is run by lawyers, who use adversary procedures to turn out decisions meeting legal criteria. The formal legal powers of the commissions are usually large, but the duties and criteria are vague ("fair," "just and reasonable," the "public interest," etc.).

Background The concept of the "independent regulatory commission" was developed in 1885–1910 in the hope of applying expert, honest, nonpolitical control to the problems of natural monopoly. The "utility" firms themselves often lobbied to be put under regulation, since it gave them a monopoly franchise and might be manipulated to serve their own interests. The Interstate Commerce Commission (ICC) was the first federal commission, established in 1888, though it did not gain real powers until after 1910. Wisconsin Progressives started the first state-level commission in 1907. Other state commissions followed, and by the 1930s, most states had regulatory bodies of some sort. The other federal commissions date mainly from the 1930s. Their coverage and activities have evolved with practice and do not fit a uniform pattern.

Until 1944, most commissions were ineffective, stalled by debates over the value of company assets. The firms claimed that the *current* value of assets must be used in setting "fair" profits; but that would have mired regulation in endless, obscure controversies over what the current values really were. In 1944 a landmark Supreme Court decision made the original accounting cost of assets the standard basis for setting profits. This has provided a relatively firm footing for commissions to set strict controls on profits.

A few commissions have applied strict regulation, during some periods. Others have been passive or vigorously procompany. Only in the 1960s did the Federal Energy Regulatory Commission, Federal Communications Commission, and the Civil Aeronautics Board begin to assert firm control over rate levels, rate structures, and the scope of the monopoly held by an individual firm.

Before 1968, there was something of a golden age for most regulated sectors (except railroads). Growth was achieving economies of scale, costs were steady or falling, and the problems to be solved were rather simple. Since 1968, however, severe problems have battered both firms and regulators. These include rapid inflation, ecological impacts, multiplying fuel prices, consumer activism, nuclear power, and antitrust challenges. Regulation has come under great stress, and some commissions have been forced to go deeply into price structure and competitive issues.

Thus far, the 1970s and 1980s have been a watershed, with Congress removing some regulatory controls over airlines, air freight, railroads, trucking, telephones, cable television, banking, and natural gas. The debate and flux continue.

Evolution Most utility sectors evolve through a four-stage process, as shown in Table 2. Stage 1 is the birth of the industry. Stage 2 is rapid growth. Stage 3 brings stability, and the industry matures. Stage 4 is a reversion to natural competition, when regulation is no longer needed. These utilities are natural monopolies only during the first three stages, when there are large economies of scale. These economies then shrink, which allows competition to exist. Therefore, natural monopoly conditions will usually justify regulation only for a finite period.

Regulation also evolves. It is usually promotional at first, to boost the industry's growth and penetration of the market. Then, in Stages 3 and 4, it often tries to protect the firm from new competition. Deregulating is frequently a difficult process, resisted by the commission *and* by the regulated firms. Therefore, regulation often fits the natural monopoly conditions poorly. Also, the real scope of effective regulation is often different from the area that, by the legal definitions, is supposed to be under control. Even when a commission reaches the right fit, the conditions may soon change and go out of alignment.

Process Commissions hold open hearings on issues put before them and then render decisions. In the typical rate case, the firm announces a new, higher set of prices and asks the commission to approve them.

Hearings are scheduled at which the company makes a detailed case for its request, often using expert witnesses as well as company officials. The commission staff then presents a rebuttal, presumably representing the consumers' interests. The staff usually urges setting a lower rate of return and price level, and perhaps a different structure of prices. Other parties may also join in. The hearings often take months, and the ensuing decision may come as much as a year after the original request. The commission usually grants a fraction of the request (half is on the basis of its collective judgment.

The procedures provide due process, with an open forum for all interested parties. Each cites criteria and facts that would favor it. The outcome is usually a compromise among the conflicting interests, stated in terms of some criterion or mix of criteria (fairness, efficiency, etc.).

Decisions on price levels and structures

Commissions deal with three main kinds of economic issues: price level, price structure, and the scope of competition.

Table 2 Life-cycle stages of typical utilities

	Birth of the Industry	Rapid Growth	Maturity	Reversion to Natural Competition
	Stage 1	Stage 2	Stage 3	Stage 4
Manufactured gas	1800–1820	1820–1880	1880–1920	1920–1950
Natural gas	1900–1930	1930–1950	1950–	
Telegraph	1840–1850	1850–1916	1916–1930	1930–
Railways				
All	1820–1835	1835–1910		
Passenger			1910–1935	1935–
Freight			1910–1960	1960–
Electricity	1870–1885	1885–1960	1960–	
Street railways	1870–1885	1885–1912	1912–1922	1922–
Telephone	1875–1880	1880–1947	1947–	
Airlines	1920–1925	1925–1965	1965–	
Television	1935–1947	1947–1965	1965–	
Cable TV	1950–1955	1955–		

Source: W. G. Shepherd, *The Treatment of Market Power* (New York: Columbia University Press, 1975), p. 228.

Price level is the conventional topic, refined by decades of practice to a traditional litany of issues. The elements are summed up in the following equation:

$$\text{Permitted rate of return} = \frac{\text{Profits}}{\text{Invested capital}}$$

$$= \frac{\text{Total revenue} - \text{Total cost}}{\text{Invested capital}}.$$

The commission decides what the firm's "rate base" is (its amount of capital invested in the business). Next, it decides what rate of return is "fair," usually in the range of 7–11 percent. Then the firm is allowed to set price levels that will generate enough sales revenue to provide the fair rate of profit on the rate base. Hence, this approach is often called "rate-base regulation."

If the commission permits higher output prices, that will raise total revenue, increase profits, and therefore raise the rate of return. The company wants maximum profits, while the commission tries to hold profits (and prices) down to much lower levels.

The basic choice is shown in Figure 2. The utility firm is assumed to have built the right level of capacity; the demand curve cuts both the average and marginal cost curves as close as possible to the minimum of average cost. Therefore, *a price set at marginal cost will give economic efficiency.* **Marginal-cost pricing** will also avoid excess profits and will achieve the lowest possible average cost.

The utility would prefer a higher price. To maximize its profits, it would like to set output at Q_m, where its marginal cost just equals its marginal revenue. The price would then be P_m, and profits would be maximized and high (note the large Excess profit rectangle in Figure 2). Since the regulatory commission instead tries to limit price to P_c, there is inherent conflict between the regulators and the firm.

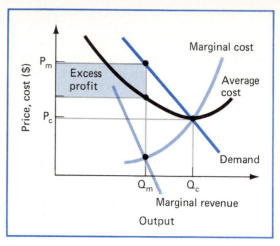

Figure 2   The basic economics of utility regulation

Capacity (the bottom of the average cost curve) is roughly in line with demand. The utility firm would like to set output at Q_m and charge P_m, making excess profit, as shown. But the regulators try to set price at P_c, which gives the utility enough total revenue to cover its total costs. The utility is required to produce Q_c, which is the amount that people want to buy at the regulated price P_c.

In practice, the commissions' decisions usually have no clear rationale. Yet, beneath the process lie some remarkable economic issues.

Some ceiling or "permitted" rate of return is to be set by the commission, but its level is controversial. The laws usually require a fair rate of return, neither too high (unfair to customers) nor too low (unfair to the firm's shareholders). It should also be efficient, by several possible criteria: It should equal the cost to the firm of its capital (the "cost-of-capital" criterion). And/or it should be high enough to attract just the optimal amount of new investment (the "capital attraction" criterion). And/or it should be in line with the risk-return conditions in other industries (the "comparable returns" criterion).

These three criteria all relate to the same basic concept of efficient allocation of capital. But they are not precise as guides to real conditions. "Fair" rates of return usually lie between 6 and 12 percent, but the correct level for each case can be debated endlessly without arriving at a definitive answer. The commission simply applies its judgment and picks a figure or range, such as 10.25 percent or 9.5–11.0 percent.

Then the value of the **rate base** is fixed by the commission. The firm's invested capital includes (1) fixed capital, at various possible depreciation rates; and (2) other assets, including a range of short-term and liquid assets. Some or all of this is allowed in the rate base, in what can be a complicated judgment by the commission.

Total costs may also be reviewed, to make sure that they are necessary and not inflated—in our terms, to assure that they are "X-efficient." The specific price level then follows fairly directly, since it is the price change needed to let the firm's profit rate go up to the permitted ceiling rate.

These price decisions usually ignore two complications. First, demand may be elastic. Since price changes will alter the amounts consumed, the net revenue change may not be a simple matter at all. Second, future conditions may change, so that the new price schedule turns out to yield profits either above or below the permitted rate of return. Indeed, actual profit rates often do rise above the permitted ceilings.

The decisions are usually only a prediction about the price level that will actually result in the optimal or reasonable profit. Moreover, beneath the veneer of arcane debates about criteria, they are usually just a compromise. Such rough-and-ready decisions must be made, and the regulatory outcomes may even turn out to be reasonably close to the ideal solutions.

Price structure is supposed to be "just" and "reasonable," in the standard legal wording. Price discrimination by these firms is likely to be very sharp; they have a complete monopoly, and they sell to a wide variety of customers (in homes, in shops and factories of all sizes) who usually have very different demand elastici-

ties. Some degree of discrimination may be efficient; but that is a very complex issue, beyond the scope of this chapter. Generally, optimal pricing would contain much less price discrimination than the firm would prefer.

Instead, the proper criterion for prices is cost—specifically, marginal cost. For each specific customer group, price should be set as close to marginal cost as possible. That will bring the utility into line with efficient allocation in the rest of the economy.

The structure of costs may be quite complicated. The regulatory task is to bring prices at least roughly into line with that cost structure, while avoiding discriminatory patterns. Overhead and joint costs (costs incurred supplying all customers) often make marginal costs unclear. Also, most regulated utilities have marked fluctuations in demand, such as the peak loads for electric and telephone service during business hours, and off-peak levels during nights and weekends. These fluctuations cause marginal costs to vary sharply, being high at peak times and low at off-peak times. Therefore, the efficient price structure will also need to have marked differences—by seasons, by day, and by time of day, as we will analyze shortly. The topic can grow difficult, obscure, and frustrating in actual hearings.

Until recently, most commissions have allowed firms to decide most of their price structures. The firms, in turn, have tended toward (1) discrimination or (2) flat across-the-board price changes that, being uniform, minimize complaints among customer groups. Since about 1965, price structure has received closer attention from some commissions.

Four economic issues of regulation
As noted, the four main economic issues of regulation are: setting prices in line with

marginal costs, the inefficiencies that regulation may cause, competitive pricing, and deregulation.

Marginal-cost pricing   Regulated firms usually have a variety of outputs, differing by physical features (size, weight, design) or by conditions of supply. Seemingly uniform products can differ sharply in costs. For example, the cost of a kilowatt-hour of electricity at midnight will differ from that of one at noon. More generally, off-peak production usually is cheaper than production at peak-load times. That is shown by the typical daily load curve in Panel I of Figure 3. Output peaks during the day, and then falls to low levels during the off-peak night-time hours. The best equipment is

run continuously, giving low costs at off-peak times. That corresponds to low marginal cost in Panel II. But at peak times, costly extra capacity must be started up and used, at high marginal costs. Therefore, peak-load marginal costs are commonly a multiple of off-peak costs.

But remember that *price should equal marginal cost*. If price diverges sharply from marginal cost, then allocation is inefficient. Therefore, utility regulators should strive to get utility price structures into line with marginal costs. That calls for *peak-load pricing*, with prices set much higher at peak times than at off-peak times. In Panel II of Figure 3, the efficient prices are P_o and P_p, with outputs at B and C. A single uniform price P_u would in-

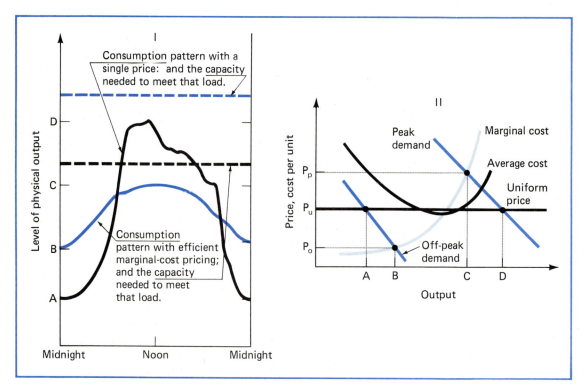

Figure 3   Load patterns, demand, and cost in utility pricing
The letters *A* through *D* are aligned between the two diagrams. The load fluctuates sharply between Levels *A* and *D* if a uniform price is charged at all times. That uniform price is P_u in Panel II. It results in the black-line load curve in Panel I. But if prices are set equal to marginal cost during the peak and off-peak times (P_p and P_o), then the load pattern will be smoothed: It is reduced to *C* at peak times and raised to *B* at off-peak times, as shown by the blue-line load curve.

stead lead to too much quantity demanded at *D*, while cutting off-peak outputs to Level *A*.

Such marginal-cost pricing is socially efficient, and often the regulated firm would gain greatly from adopting it. For example, setting prices too low for peak outputs could encourage too much load on the system at peak times and threaten the whole utility system with collapse. Indeed, marginal-cost pricing often lies in the same direction as price discrimination, at least for parts of the utility's output. For example, low-cost bulk power may go to large users who have high elasticity of demand. Both cost and demand would then call for a low price.

Yet, cost and demand conditions often diverge, so that the regulators must force the firm to follow efficient, marginal-cost pricing. Setting high prices at peak-load times is especially important. But it is often hard to enforce because it usually requires higher prices for the periods when the system seems to be "most urgently needed." Also, rate-base regulation may encourage the regulated firm to add more capacity than is efficient. In the great mass of regulated outputs, marginal-cost pricing is both correct and reasonably practical to accomplish.

Nevertheless, before 1965, these lessons were largely ignored, for utilities were eager to raise their growth by means of promotional pricing, which is often discriminatory. Peak-load output was usually priced low, at average costs or even at zero (for local telephone calls, for example). The new scarcities and stresses that have arisen since 1965 have made marginal-cost pricing seem wise, even urgent, both to many regulators and to the firms themselves.

Electricity prices used to ignore high peak-load costs almost entirely, thereby encouraging people to use electricity out to Level *D* of Figure 3. This, in turn, required

the companies to build too much capacity to meet those overstimulated peak-load levels. Local telephone pricing has been even worse. By charging a *zero* price for local calls, the firms have encouraged too high a level of use. That is shown more precisely in Figure 4, where calls at level Q_1 have a true marginal cost that is very high. Thus, when you call a friend at 4 p.m. and chat for a half hour, the true cost may be a dollar or more, although the call's value is low, as shown by the demand curve. But since you pay nothing extra, you (and millions of others) make the calls, and the system absorbs those extra costs.

Long-distance prices reflect marginal costs more closely than do local-service prices. The price differences are familiar and can be seen in the front pages of any telephone directory. Prices during business hours are often double or triple the off-peak (night-time and weekend) prices. Therefore, marginal-cost pricing has been routine in certain utility services, even though it has been avoided in most others.

In the 1970s, there were new efforts to shift toward marginal-cost pricing. In electricity, perhaps a third of the companies have adopted time-of-day pricing. A typical time-of-day price schedule is shown in Table 3 for Wisconsin Electric Power Company. Peak times are defined rather roughly as 7 a.m. to 7 p.m. Monday to Friday during the seasonal hot-weather peak in July–October, when the heavy use of air conditioners strains the whole electric system's capacities and makes marginal cost very high. Off-peak hours are 7 p.m. to 7 a.m. and weekends. During November–June, the 7 a.m. to 7 p.m. hours are an in-between category, neither peak nor off-peak.

Notice that peak-load prices of 8.2 cents per kilowatt-hour are set far above the off-peak price of 1.3 cents per kilowatt-hour. The in-between period has an inter-

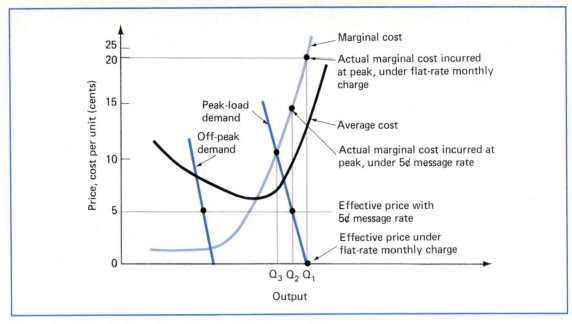

Figure 4   An illustration of local-service telephone pricing

Users pay a flat monthly fee (such as $11 per month) and get unlimited free calls. At that zero price per call, they use service out to level Q_1. At Q_1, the marginal cost of service is high, and the inefficiency is shown by the gap between price and marginal cost.

The efficient peak-load price is where demand intersects marginal cost, giving output level Q_3. A "message rate" may be set, such as 5 cents per call. But it still ignores peak–off-peak cost differences. It would give the output Q_2, with still a large gap between price and marginal cost.

Table 3   A time-of-day price structure for electricity (Wisconsin Electric Power Co.)

Class of Service	Residential–Time-of-Use	
Effective in AVAILABILITY	All Areas Served	

To residential customers contracting for electric service for domestic purposes for a period of one year or more.

RATE

Customer Charge, including one meter	$5.00 per month Billing periods	
Energy Charge per kWh	July–October	November–June
On-peak energy*	8.20¢	5.20¢
Off-peak energy†	1.30	1.30

Meter Charge

The monthly meter charge for each meter in excess of one shall be $2.50.

*Residential on-peak energy usage is the energy in kilowatt-hours delivered between 7:00 a.m. and 7:00 p.m. Central Standard Time, Monday through Friday, including holidays.
†Residential off-peak energy usage is the energy in kilowatt-hours delivered during all hours other than during on-peak hours.

mediate price—5.2 cents per kilowatt-hour. These prices fit the cost patterns shown in Figure 3. Even if they are not fine-tuned to fit marginal cost closely, these peak-load prices do at least fit the main patterns of cost. Therefore, they give a practical instance of efficient pricing under regulation.

Despite some progress in this direction, much pricing of electricity, gas, and telephone service is in the old uniform-price patterns that ignore marginal costs. Many economists, therefore, continue to criticize those policies. They have also studied the cost and demand conditions intensively and have developed detailed proposals for revised prices.

The effects of regulation on costs Standard regulation lets the firm charge prices that will cover its costs plus a "fair" profit. This "cost-plus" approach may permit or even encourage X-inefficiency in the firm. If its monopoly power is sufficient, the firm can raise prices enough to cover its costs even if they are greatly inflated. This is reinforced by the firm's interest in providing high-quality, reliable service, which usually entails extra costs. It is difficult to set the socially efficient level of quality and reliability, and the cost-plus-profit basis of regulation may induce the firm to choose too high a level of quality and cost.

In the total cost part of the basic regulatory equation, both the prices and the amounts of the inputs may be raised because of regulation. That is because the firm gets the profits whether it keeps input costs down or not. This problem of "cost-plus" inefficiency has long been familiar in military weapons buying by governments. Under regulation, it is more subtle but still chronic. There are two main limits on it: (1) the professional standards of the industry (managers and engineers presumably apply good sense and technical criteria to what is needed in their system); and (2)

scrutiny by the commission (from the start, regulators and courts have recognized the need to guard against possibly extravagant or unnecessary costs). In practice, the controls have usually been weak. The firm's expenses are often listed and looked over in some detail, but little can be done to challenge or rectify dubious cases.

Investment may also be too large under regulation. The conventional method of rate-base regulation encourages the firm to increase the value of the rate base itself. Normally, the permitted rate of return is set a little above the cost of capital. The firm's shareholders, therefore, gain a little (or a lot) of profit from each extra bit of capital included in the rate base.* The process probably works subconsciously, but it encourages the firm to use more capital than is economically efficient.

The rise could come about in two ways: (1) Actual investment could be higher. In choosing new technology, the firm would lean toward more capital-intensive methods. Capacity to meet peak loads might also be higher because of the rate-base effect. This would give the firm more security from embarrassing breakdowns at peak times. (2) Accounting choices would be made so as to maximize the recorded value of assets. Depreciation methods would be the main item to be adjusted, toward writing down the assets' value slowly. The firm may permit overcharging in the prices of the equipment it buys.

The whole rate-base effect has never been accurately measured, and, of course,

---

*Suppose that the cost of capital is 7 percent and the permitted rate of return is 9 percent. Then every additional $100 million in the rate base will increase net profits by $2 million (that is, $9 million return minus $7 million cost of capital). Capitalized at a 10:1 ratio, that $2 million might equal $20 million in added stock value to the shareowners.

the firms deny that it occurs at all. It probably does shift the margin of choice by some degree in most regulated utilities.

Cream skimming and competition   All utility industries have some markets that can be supplied competitively. The regulated firm, however, naturally wishes to encompass them in its exclusive franchise. Indeed, the rate-base effect encourages it; the firm wants to add to its rate base the capital in the adjacent market. Meanwhile, other firms want to get in to compete against the utility.

The key point is that the newcomers are often naturally attracted to the most lucrative parts of the regulated firm's market, where the price-cost ratios are highest. Since there is price discrimination, the entrants usually fasten first onto the "creamy" markets. This "cream skimming" (the British call it "picking the eyes out of the market") is regarded as an acute threat by the regulated firm. The firm will claim that the cream skimming strikes at the "system integrity" of the utility, for the creamy parts are necessary to support the skim parts. With the cream gone, either (1) the whole system will go bankrupt, or at least, (2) prices for most consumers will have to rise.

The regulated firm, therefore, resists any and all competition. If competition is permitted nonetheless, the original firm demands the right to meet the competition by selective price cutting. But if that is permitted, the price cuts may be deep and predatory enough to keep out competition, while still maintaining a discriminatory price structure. The commission thus gets drawn into setting *floors* on specific prices as well as *ceilings* on the firm's whole price and profit levels. And it must usually rely on cost figures prepared by the regulated firm itself.

This baffling problem stems from the basic sources of natural monopoly: overhead costs and economies of scale. These conditions make the regulation necessary, and yet the natural monopoly basis does not extend throughout the system. Competition can, and probably should, enter into some parts. But which parts, how far, and on what competitive terms, must be decided somehow by the commission. Often the conditions are highly complex and changing, and the pressures are intense. Moreover, since commissions are usually imperfect and short of resources, their treatments, too, are often inefficient. They may give the utility firm too wide a franchise or be slow to let in new competition.

The difficulties are widespread in postal service, airlines, railroads, telephones, banking, electricity—anywhere that a commission has to supervise a firm with an exclusive franchise. Cost and competitive conditions vary by gradations, rarely fitting into neat boxes. Regulators are forced to cope with these severe problems as best they can.

Deregulation   In extreme cases, regulation should be withdrawn entirely. Such *deregulation* often looks attractive, compared with the regulatory effects we have just reviewed. But it must be done with care and sophistication. Since 1975, deregulation has been extensive in parts of the transport, broadcasting, and telephone sectors.

The hardest task is to balance between (1) letting new competition in and (2) withdrawing controls on prices. If the controls are removed before competition is effective, the utility firm has a bonanza: It holds monopoly power but is constrained neither by competition nor by regulation. Naturally, the utilities call for such a "freedom to compete," even though it would be premature and lead to the usual social costs of monopoly. The opposite error is to let competition in but keep rigid controls on the original firm. Then the firm may be limited too tightly.

Airlines provide the leading case study of deregulation. The economies of scale in airline service are moderate, permitting effective competition on most of the hundreds of airline routes connecting pairs of cities. Yet from its creation in 1938, the Civil Aeronautics Board (CAB) protected the market positions of the 12 original airlines. New airlines were not permitted to enter, nor, with rare exceptions, were existing airlines permitted to move into new routes. Moreover, the CAB permitted the airlines to set ticket prices and then enforced those prices against any competitive price cutting.

During 1960–1975, a series of economic studies showed that these rigid policies were causing inefficiency. A shift to open competition would reduce ticket prices, increase the variety of choice, and improve the efficiency of scheduling flights. The CAB reversed course in 1975 and began permitting new entry and flexible pricing. In 1978, a law was passed to abolish the CAB by 1983.

Airline competition quickly became intense, bringing precisely the improvements predicted by economists. Two possible disadvantages have turned out to be mild. One is that the large airlines have withdrawn from many of the small-city routes, because the sparse traffic does not fill their large aircraft. Yet, small commuter airlines have sprung up to help fill that gap. The other is the heavy use of special discount fares (e.g., "super-savers") that involve price discrimination and could be anticompetitive. Yet, in fact, most of the discounting is procompetitive because the airlines now usually lack dominant market shares.

This remarkable deregulation process has been managed well by the CAB, which has relaxed regulatory limits in balance with the rise of competition. Deregulation has also begun in such other sectors as telephone service, railroads, trucking, and broadcasting.

Public enterprise

A public enterprise is owned by the state, on behalf of the citizenry. It can be identical to private firms in every respect, other than having private stockholders. It uses inputs to produce outputs, and it keeps thorough accounts of costs, revenues, and profits. But despite these parallels, the public firm need not maximize its profits as a private firm does. It may pursue other goals, and so its economic performance may differ sharply from that of a private firm. Therein lies the fascination of public enterprise, for it offers a wide variety of possibilities and outcomes.

Coverage and purposes

The main lines of public enterprise in the United States and Western Europe are indicated in Figure 5. The United States differs from other Western economies chiefly in the low share of public enterprise in its utilities, industry, and finance. Otherwise U.S. patterns are not peculiar. The typical pattern in Western economies is (1) *utilities*, entirely or mainly publicly owned; (2) *finance*, one or several public banks; (3) *insurance*, large social insurance programs; (4) *industry*, several major industries under partial public ownership; (5) *social services*, mainly under public ownership; and (6) *distribution*, with little public enterprise.

Public enterprise exists in many parts of the U.S. economy. There is a great variety of forms and behavior, as suggested by

Figure 5 **The share of public ownership in major sectors in selected countries, 1978**

Industrial Section

(Privately owned: ○ Publicly owned: ◔ 25% ◑ 50% ◕ 75% ● All or nearly all)

Country	Posts	Tele-communi-cations	Electric-ity	Gas	Railways	Coal	Airlines	Motor industry	Steel	Ship-building
Austria	●	●	●	●	●	●	●	●	◕	na*
Belgium	●	●	◔	◔	●	○	●	○	○	○
Britain	●	●	●	●	●	●	◕	◑	◕	●
France	●	●	●	●	●	●	◕	◑	◑	◑
W. Germany	●	●	◕	◑	●	◑	●	◔	◔	◔
Holland	●	●	◕	◕	●	na	◕	○	◔	○
Italy	●	●	◕	●	●	na	●	◑	◑	◕
Spain	●	◔	○	◔	●	◑	●	○	◕	◕
Sweden	●	●	◑	●	●	na	◑	○	◕	◕
Switzerland	●	●	●	●	●	na	○	○	○	na
United States	●	○	◔	○	◔	○	○	○	○	○
Yugoslavia	●	●	●	●	●	●	●	●	●	●

Note: *NA: not available. The proportions shown are often approximate.
Source: Adapted from *The Economist,* March 4, 1978, p. 93.

Table 4. They range from conventional utility cases, such as the Tennessee Valley Authority, to industrial and service areas, over into certain subsidy programs, and into important *social* enterprises such as public schools and universities, mental hospitals, the courts, and prisons. Yet, these public enterprises tend to be a phantom presence in the United States, not recognized for what they really are.

There are many reasons for creating public firms, but the most valid normative reason is that the enterprise can serve some social purpose that a private firm would ignore or violate. This social purpose usually falls under the following headings:

1. *Social Preference.* A society (city, state, or country) may simply prefer public to private control, especially for certain prominent sectors. Such cultural preferences seem to explain much of the great variation in Figure 5.

2. *Inadequate Private Supply.* A new industry or project may seem too large and risky for private firms to invest in. They will demand government guarantees, grants, or other subsidies. It may seem wiser to put the unit under direct public ownership.

3. *Salvaging Firms.* The public often "rescues" failing firms by buying out their

284

Table 4 *Local, state, and federal public enterprises in the United States*

1. **Localities**	**Extent of Public Enterprise**
Utilities	
Transit (bus, subway, trolley commuter lines)	All large cities
Water and sewage	Virtually all large cities
Garbage disposal	Most cities
Electricity	Over 1,000 smaller cities; several large cities, including Los Angeles
Ports	Port of New York Authority (transport and urban facilities); New Orleans, ocean ports
Airports	All large cities
Social Units	
Schools	All cities and towns
Libraries	Virtually all cities and towns
Parks, golf courses, pools	Virtually all cities
Sports stadiums	Many cities
Museums	Many cities
Zoos	Several large cities
Cemeteries	Most cities and towns
2. **States**	
Prison facilities	All states
Insurance services	Unemployment: all states
	Workman's Compensation: 18 states
Parks	Most states
Liquor retailing	16 states
Electricity	All Nebraska, a large share of New York
Toll roads, bridges, and tunnels	29 states
Health care	Mental and old-age institutions
3. **Federal**	*(Expenditures)*
Electricity	Corps of Engineers, $1,420 million; Bureau of Reclamation, $618 million; Tennessee Valley Authority, others
Postal service	$17,700 million expenditures; $784 million subsidy
Lands	Forest Service: $834 million
	National Park Service: $364 million
Commodities stockpiles	Value about $700 million
Transport	Alaska and Panama Canal railroads; military air and sea transport services; St. Lawrence Seaway
Loans and guarantees	About 100 agencies, includes housing, farming, rural electricity and telephones, Export-Import Bank, Small Business Administration
Insurance	Many agencies: banks, housing, crops, shipping, foreign investment, stock markets, veterans life and annuity insurance, old-age pensions
Health care	Medicare, Medicaid, veterans' hospitals
Industry	Various: Government Printing Office; military production, etc.

Sources: For figures, U.S. Government, *Budget* (Washington, D.C.: U.S. Government Printing Office), Appendix volume.

capital and supporting their rehabilitation. There are always new candidates for such salvage operations. Some are valid. But they tend to burden the public with sick industries that absorb large subsidies.

4. *External Impacts.* Public firms may allow for outside social harms or benefits that private firms ignore. In the extreme, the service may be a *pure public good* calling for a full subsidy (see Chapter 17).

5. *Sovereignty.* A country may take over the local branches of large international firms in order to neutralize their power.

The typical public firm, therefore, has a **social element** *to serve, which is apart from its usual commercial goals of producing its services efficiently and selling them at prices that fit cost and demand conditions.* For example, a local bus line is supposed to provide reliable service throughout the city, on a more extensive schedule than a strictly commercial bus line would provide.

The social element is usually debated intensely, both its nature and its extent. What social element is provided by the Postal Service, for instance? And does it require daily deliveries, including Saturday? Should "junk mail" be subsidized? If so, to what extent? You may have noticed the ongoing controversies over Amtrak's services, library hours, parks, Medicare, and city sports stadiums used by professional teams. Quieter debates continue constantly about city services, public schools and universities, airports, golf courses, state liquor stores in 16 states, and all other public enterprises. In every case, the questions are: What is the valid social element? How much of it should the public pay for?

Subsidies and efficiency

The public pays by means of subsidies, which come from government tax revenues. The subsidy can be of any amount, ranging from 100 percent to zero. Thus, the public schools are subsidized totally from taxes, while local water supply is paid for by the users. Most public universities are in between, supported partly by government subsidies and partly by students' tuition payments.

The subsidy ought to be fitted precisely to the social element of the public firm. *A small social effect requires little or no subsidy, while a large social element might justify a total subsidy.* Total subsidy means that the direct users pay nothing; the taxpayers pay for it all.

There are two dangers from subsidies to public firms. One is that the subsidy will simply be too large, giving the users an undeserved free ride. Should library users, or local golfers on the public course, or bus riders, or students at public universities be subsidized heavily? Does the service meet a special social need? Are the users really needier than the cross section of tax payers?

The second risk from subsidies is that they will weaken the enterprise's incentives to cut costs. Whenever costs can be covered without effort, the firm may let them rise. The subsidy can become a self-creating device. Public firms as diverse as city transit, the Postal Service, and Medicare are regularly accused of such wasteful and demoralizing subsidies.

These dangers are real, and they have no universal solution. Society must struggle along with its public enterprises, trying to fit the subsidies to the true social element and trying to avoid wasteful incentives. If the political process works well, it may supervise the firms effectively and trim their subsidies to just the right patterns. Public enterprises can go beyond the narrow limits of profit to serve genuine public needs. But this capacity needs constant control to keep the firms from wasteful mistakes.

Efficient pricing Public enterprises come under the same rules for efficient pricing that private firms do. Their prices should be aligned with their marginal costs (including social costs), just as for regulated utilities. Many public firms do, in fact, adopt efficient price structures, carefully measuring marginal costs and setting prices in line with them. The task is easier because the firms are not subject to the special biases—from monopoly power and cost-plus-profit regulation—that privately owned utilities have.

Yet, many public firms set inefficient prices, and governments often fail to press the firms to improve their policies.

4. Public enterprises commonly have a social element, as well as commercial operations. Any public subsidy needs to be fitted to this social element. The danger is that the subsidy will diverge from that level, and that it will sap the firm's incentives for efficiency.

5. The actual performance of public enterprises ranges from excellent to poor. Good performance usually requires careful supervision and clear economic guidance.

Key concepts

Natural monopoly
Regulation
Marginal-cost pricing
Deregulation
Public enterprise
Social element

Summary

1. Regulation is a unique U.S. policy. It attempts to limit private firms to zero excess profits and to efficient price structures. There are economic guidelines for these decisions, but the commissions often have to make rough decisions and compromises.

2. Marginal-cost pricing is usually the correct guide for efficient pricing, but it often conflicts with the utility's preferences. Peak-load pricing is being increasingly applied in electricity and telephones.

3. Regulation may induce various kinds of inefficiencies. It may also need to be removed as the sector evolves back toward natural competition. But that transition requires a delicate balance between competition and control.

Questions for review

1. a. What is meant by *rate-base regulation?*
   b. What are some of the difficulties inherent in setting prices through rate-base regulation?

2. The price of phone calls usually varies with the time of the call. Explain how this price variation could encourage an efficient allocation of resources.

3. First-class mail users pay 65% of all postal revenues, although lower-class mail (advertising, newspapers, magazines) weighs far more. Do first-class mailers therefore subsidize bulk mailers? Explain.

4. What is the extent of public enterprise in the United States? How does it compare with foreign countries?

5. Are public firms in the United States justified? Explain and give some examples to support your answer.

14

Input Markets

As you read and study this chapter, you will learn:

▸ the firm's precise choices in buying inputs

▸ conditions governing the demand for and supply of inputs

▸ the effect of monopoly upon input choices

▸ the causes and meaning of economic rent

You have probably seen schematic drawings of the human circulatory sytem, with its miles of large and small blood vessels. One half of the system is arteries, through which fresh blood is pumped to tissues in all parts of the body. The other half is veins, which bring the used blood back to the heart for further circulation. These two complex sets of blood vessels coexist in the complete system.

In the same way, the economic system contains two complicated sets of markets—input markets and output markets—both of which are necessary to complete the system. Output markets were explained in Chapters 4–13. Now we present the other great half of the system, input markets. They too are important, for the factors of production must be priced and chosen for economic activity to occur. They determine such conditions as: wages, which range from less than $3 per hour for some workers to over $350 per hour for others; decisions affecting $5 trillion of capital; and land prices ranging from $1 to $1 million per acre.

Labor, capital, and land are priced and hired in numberless input markets every day. We explain that process in this chapter. Later chapters consider the individual factors more fully: labor in Chapter 15, capital in Chapter 16, and natural resources in Chapter 21.

We begin in the first main section with the individual firm's demand for inputs. By deciding how to use each input, the firm is completing its whole set of profit-maximizing decisions. The second main section of this chapter treats the supply of inputs and the market-wide outcomes, and also presents the concept of economic rent.

The demand for inputs

To present input pricing clearly, it helps to begin with purely competitive factor markets. The first task is to explain how much of an input is used at each price of the input.

The level of input use
The critical assumptions are three:

1. The firm is a profit maximizer in its decisions about inputs as well as outputs.

2. The firm is also a price taker in all *input* markets, where it buys its labor, materials, capital, and other inputs. Because those markets are perfectly competitive, the supply price of each input to the firm is the given market price, regardless of how much the firm buys.

3. The firm uses only one variable input. Other factors are fixed during the analysis. For example, labor might be the variable input, while capital and land are fixed during the period being considered.

The firm will follow this profit-maximizing rule: Use the input up to the level at which the added *cost* from one more unit of the input just equals the added *revenue* from the output that the last unit of input produced. *More precisely, the firm uses the input at the level where the cost and revenue of the marginal unit of input are equal.* The key comparison is between cost and benefit at the margin.

To see the decision clearly, we need to discuss its parts one by one. Half of the choice rests on the cost of the input. Since the firm is a price taker in the input market, it can buy as much of the input as it wants at the going market price. Every time it uses another unit of input, therefore, the addition to cost is simply the price of the input. Input price is often referred to as the marginal cost of the input. However, do not confuse the marginal cost of the input with that of output. They are not necessarily the same. For example, if a unit of input costs $10, that is the marginal cost of the input. If that unit of input can produce two more units of output, the marginal cost of the output will be $10/2 or $5.

Marginal revenue product
The other half of the comparison is *marginal revenue product (MRP),* the dollar value of the output produced by the marginal unit of the input:

$$\text{Marginal revenue product} = \left(\begin{array}{c} \text{Marginal product of the input} \end{array} \right) \times \left(\begin{array}{c} \text{Marginal revenue of output} \end{array} \right).$$

The relationship between the quantity of an input and its marginal revenue product is called the *MRP curve.* The shape of the MRP curve depends on both the MP and MR curves. The marginal product schedule may at first slope upward, but will then

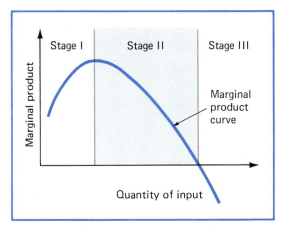

Figure 1   Three stages of the marginal product curve

Stage I is associated with rising marginal product, Stage II with declining marginal product, and Stage III with negative marginal product. Stage I is characterized by too little of the variable input relative to the fixed input for efficient production. The *fixed* input is being wasted. Stage III is characterized by too much of the variable input relative to the fixed input for efficient production. The *variable* input is being wasted. Only in Stage II are both inputs being used in efficient amounts relative to each other. Therefore, profit-maximizing firms will only produce in Stage II, where marginal product is declining.

reach a maximum and begin to decline, as in Figure 1. The eventual decline of the marginal product curve is explained by the *law of diminishing returns*. If a firm uses a fixed input and a variable input, at some point further additions of the variable input will add less and less to output. A firm will normally want to operate in the area of diminishing marginal productivity.

As Figure 1 shows, the marginal product schedule may include three stages. In Stage I, marginal product is rising. In Stage II, marginal product is declining, and in Stage III it is negative. There seems to be something good about increasing marginal productivity, so the intuitive reaction might be that firms will choose a level in the range where the marginal product is increasing. But in this case, intuition is wrong. With a little thought, you can see why.

Start by thinking about Stage III. Obviously, no firm will produce in Stage III, where the marginal product of the variable input is negative. There is so much of the variable input relative to the fixed input that more of the variable input actually makes total output decline. Now consider Stage I. While Stage III was characterized by too much of the variable input, Stage I has so little of it that much of the fixed input is wasted so that its marginal product may even be negative. While Stage III is associated with wasteful amounts of the variable input, Stage I is associated with wasteful amounts of the fixed input. Only in Stage II are both inputs being used in efficient amounts relative to each other. In the long run, therefore, a firm will only produce in Stage II, where the marginal product schedule is downward-sloping. This means that when the marginal revenue product schedule is being derived, only the downward-sloping portion of it is relevant in general.

The next question in determining the shape of a firm's marginal revenue product schedule is what the firm's marginal revenue schedule will look like. As you saw in earlier chapters, the marginal revenue schedule can take one of two general shapes. For a *perfectly competitive firm*, the marginal revenue schedule will be horizontal. For an *imperfectly competitive firm*, such as a monopoly or an oligopoly, the marginal revenue schedule will be downward sloping.

As Figure 2 shows, the marginal revenue product schedule for a competitive firm is the product of the downward-sloping portion of the marginal product schedule and a horizontal marginal revenue schedule. For a competitive firm, this is often called the **value of marginal product** schedule. For an imperfectly competitive firm, the marginal revenue product schedule is the product of the downward-sloping portion of the marginal product schedule

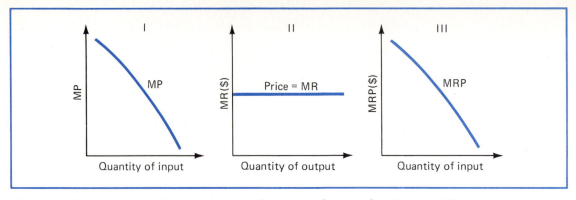

Figure 2   Deriving the marginal revenue product curve for a perfectly competitive firm
For a perfectly competitive firm, the marginal revenue product schedule is derived by multiplying the declining portion of the marginal product schedule by the constant marginal revenue. The result is a declining marginal revenue product schedule.

and a downward-sloping marginal revenue schedule, as shown in Figure 3. The result in both cases is a downward-sloping marginal revenue product schedule.

Now that both the change in cost and the change in revenue from using an additional unit of input have been derived, that information can be used to determine the profit-maximizing level of input use.

The profit-maximizing level of input use

In Figure 4, the price of the input has been added to the diagram of the marginal revenue product curve. To the left of Point A, each unit of input adds more value than it

costs: MRP exceeds the price of the input. The blue shaded area shows the net addition to the firm's profits from hiring those inputs, whose value exceeds their costs. The firm will hire those units, since doing so increases its profits (or reduces its losses).

Beyond Point A, the input's MRP has fallen below the input's price. Since each added unit of input now costs more than it adds to the value of production, it causes net financial losses to the firm, as shown by the gray shaded area to the right of Point A. The firm will not use any inputs to the right of Point A.

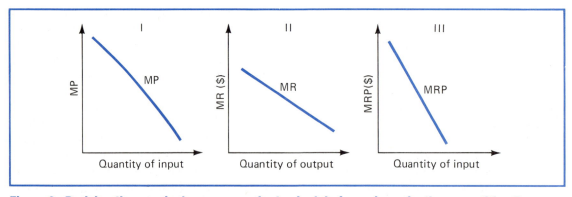

Figure 3   Deriving the marginal revenue product schedule for an imperfectly competitive firm
For an imperfectly competitive firm, the marginal revenue product schedule is derived by multiplying the declining portion of the marginal revenue product schedule by a declining marginal revenue schedule. The result is a declining marginal revenue product schedule. The marginal revenue product schedule will decline more sharply than it would if the firm were completely competitive.

292

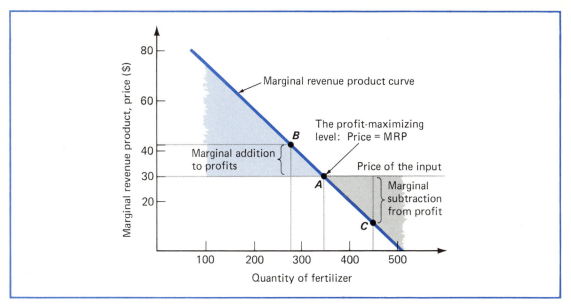

Figure 4 The profit-maximizing level of the input: _MRP_ = input price

At Point _A_, the price paid for the marginal unit of input just equals its marginal revenue. At lesser amounts, such as _B_, the MRP exceeds the price. At higher amounts, such as _C_, the input's price exceeds its MRP. Profits will be reduced by using more inputs than at _A_.

At precisely Point _A_, the firm has gotten the maximum net profits that the input can provide, while avoiding the net losses: _The input's MRP equals its price._ Marginal value equals marginal cost for this input. That condition is precisely analogous to the marginal-revenue-equals-marginal-cost rule for the firm in maximizing its profits in choosing its _output_ level.

Deriving the firm's demand schedule for an input

Using the profit-maximizing rule of marginal revenue product equals input price, the firm's demand schedule for the input can be derived. The analysis holds only if we assume that the firm is a price taker in the input market, and uses only one variable input.

A firm's demand schedule for an input will show the amount of the input that the firm will wish to purchase at different input prices. Taking the input price as given, the firm will wish to purchase the profit-maximizing amount of the input. In Figure 5, for example, at a price of $10 per unit of input, the firm would want to adjust the quantity of input it uses until the MRP equals the input price of $10. The firm would wish to purchase 170 units of the input at a price of $10, and Point _A_ would represent one point on the firm's demand schedule for the input. To generate additional points on the firm's demand schedule for the input, simply vary the input price and locate the quantity that will equate marginal revenue product and price. At a price of $25 per unit of input, the profit-maximizing quantity of input would be 130 units. That price-quantity combination of $25 and 130 units of input, Point _B_, would represent an additional point on the firm's demand schedule for the input. At an input price of $45 per unit, the profit-maximizing quantity of input would be 80 units. Point _C_ would be yet another point on the firm's demand schedule for the input. As the input price changes, the new price-quantity combination will always lie at some point on the firm's marginal revenue product schedule. The firm's demand curve for the input is

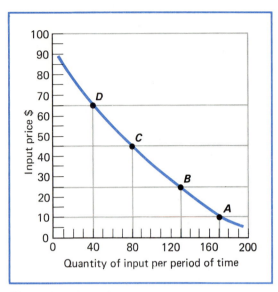

Figure 5 Derivation of a firm's demand schedule for an input

simply the marginal revenue product schedule.

The demand schedule for inputs also slopes downward. This implies that a firm will find it profitable to use more of the input as its price falls. In Figure 6, as the price of a variable input falls, the firm's marginal cost schedule shifts to the right, reflecting the lower costs of production. The profit-maximizing point, the new marginal revenue–marginal cost intersection, will shift from Point A to Point B. The firm will now find it profitable to produce more output.

If more output is to be produced, more input must be purchased. Thus, the demand schedule has a downward slope, indicating that the quantity of inputs demanded will rise as their prices fall.

Elasticity of demand for an input

The extent to which the quantity demanded of the input will respond to a change in input prices can be measured by the elasticity of demand for the input. Three conditions make the demand for the

input relatively elastic or responsive to changes in input prices:

The input accounts for a large percentage of total costs Suppose that the price of an input falls by 50 percent. That sounds like a big change. However, the impact on quantity demanded when the input accounts for 2 percent of total costs will be quite different from when it accounts for 70 percent of total costs. The higher the percent of total costs the input accounts for, the more important it is in the total cost picture and the bigger the shift in marginal cost from a given percentage change in input price. This will make the profit-maximizing level of output and, therefore, the demand for input more responsive to changes in input price.

The demand for output is relatively elastic As input price falls and the marginal cost schedule shifts to the right, the profit-maximizing price of output will also fall. The more elastic the demand for output, the larger will be the increase in the profit-maximizing quantity that will accompany a given change in price. The larger increase in the demand for output will cause a larger increase in the demand for input for that given price change. Therefore, the more elastic the demand for output, the more elastic the demand for an input will be.

Substitution is easy A third condition is the ease of technical substitution. In the long run, a fall in the price of the variable input will cause a substitution of the variable for the fixed factor. If the technology of the firm allows one factor to be easily substituted for another, there will be relatively larger change in the demand for the input when its price changes.

However, substitution of variable for fixed factors cannot explain elasticity along a given input demand schedule. The

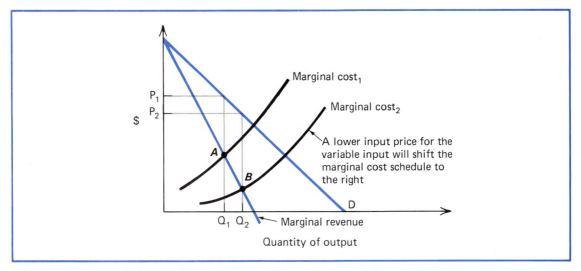

Figure 6   A change in input price will change the profit-maximizing level of input use

Originally, the firm finds it profit maximizing to produce Q_1 at a price of P_1. When the price of the variable input falls, the marginal cost schedule shifts right. The profit-maximizing point is now **B**, which represents a higher level of output, Q_2. To produce the higher level of output, more of the variable input must be bought. This explains why the demand schedule for the input is downward sloping, with more input being purchased at lower input prices.

reason is that as such substitution takes place, the marginal product schedule, from which the demand schedule for the variable input was derived, will also shift, as a result of changes in the quantities of other inputs. Ease of technical substitution only helps to determine the overall change in the demand for the input as its price changes, not elasticity along a given demand schedule with other inputs fixed.

Shifts in the marginal revenue product schedule

Since the marginal revenue product schedule is derived from the marginal product and marginal revenue schedules, it will shift only if either the marginal product schedule or the marginal revenue schedule also shifts. For example, if the demand for output changes because of a change in consumer income, taste, or population, the marginal revenue schedule for output and, therefore, the marginal revenue product schedule must shift as well. If the marginal

product schedule shifts because of a change in technology, the marginal revenue product schedule will also shift. Remember that a change in the price of the variable input will simply cause a movement along the existing input demand schedule, at least in the short run. In the long run, a change in the price of the variable input may cause the input demand schedule to shift because of changes in the amount of the fixed factor used, which will cause a shift in the marginal product schedule.

Comparison of input use of a perfect competitor and a firm with monopoly power

As you have seen, the marginal revenue product schedule is derived from both the marginal product schedule and the marginal revenue schedule. For a perfectly competitive firm, the marginal revenue schedule is a horizontal line at the level of market price. For a monopolist, the marginal revenue schedule slopes downward and lies below or to the left of the firm's

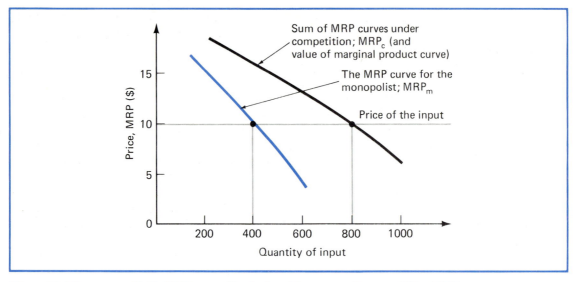

Figure 7 The monopolist's MRP curve lies below the summed competitive MRP curve

The sum of the competitive firms' MRP curves is shown by *MRP*ᵪ (c for competitive). This is also called the value of marginal product curve. But the monopolist has a marginal revenue curve lying below its demand curve. Those MR values are used (rather than competitive price) to derive the *MRP*ₘ curve, which therefore lies below the *MRP*ᵪ curve.

demand curve. These differences in the marginal revenue schedules of perfect competition and monopoly lead to important differences in the allocation of resources.

In Figure 7, MRP_c represents the sum of the marginal revenue product schedules of the firms in a perfectly competitive industry. MRP_m represents the marginal revenue product schedule for an industry in which the firm or firms have monopoly power. Since the marginal revenue curve for such an industry would lie below the demand curve, its marginal revenue product curve will lie below the competitive marginal revenue product schedule, which would coincide with the industry demand curve. The resulting competitive schedule is often referred to as value of marginal product. Since the marginal revenue product schedule represents the firms' demand for inputs, you can see that monopoly power reduces the amount of inputs that firms in the industry will wish to buy at a

given input price. In Figure 7, competitive firms will purchase 800 units of the input at a price of $10 per unit. The monopolistic firm will purchase only 400 units of the input at the same price. The reason is, of course, that the downward-sloping marginal revenue schedule of the monopolist, which lies *below* the demand schedule, reduces the value or return to the firm of an additional unit of input.

The key result is that *monopoly power reduces the amount of inputs used by an industry,* compared to the amount of inputs used under competition. This reduction in input use is consistent with the monopoly restriction of output that was explained in Chapter 10. Obviously, if less output is to be produced under monopoly, smaller amounts of the input are needed. Note, too, that the reduction in production of output and in input use under monopoly is not due to any conscious decision on the part of the monopolist to restrict output. Both a competitive firm and a monopolist compare marginal costs and marginal benefits in determining production levels. Both set marginal revenue equal to marginal cost to determine output levels, and marginal revenue product equal to the price of the input to determine input use. Because of the differences in the marginal revenue schedules, however, the same rules lead to quite different results.

Taken altogether, the analysis also provides the link between consumers' final demand and the firms' demand for inputs. Consumers express their preferences and spending power in their demand curves, which, working with supply, set the market price. Those market values then transmit back to give MRP its specific values. If consumers' demand rises, that will usually increase the output's price and cause MRP to shift up. Final demand, therefore, influences the demand for inputs. For example, when consumers' preferences change to smaller cars or more formal clothes, then the demands for inputs to make those goods will rise. Such adjustments are routine, linking all outputs and their inputs.

Recall that the demand for inputs is a "derived demand," arising from the final demand for goods. We have now shown how the input demand is derived. It may proceed back through many stages—for example, from a refrigerator to the sheet steel for its surface, to iron, to the iron ore and coal used to smelt it. At each point, the same link exists between the demand for the firm's output and the firm's demand for its inputs.

Supply and equilibrium in input markets

Now we turn to the supply of inputs and to the equilibrium results that occur in input markets. First we explain why input supply curves slope up. Then we discuss the supply-demand equilibrium and, finally, economic rent, a key concept.

The supply of inputs

At the market-wide level, inputs conform to the general rule that *supply curves slope up*. But the causes differ from those in output markets, where supply curves reflect up-sloping marginal cost curves of firms.

To understand input supply, remember that the individual competitive firm faces a horizontal supply curve of each input. The firm buys such a tiny share of the whole market's supply that its own actions do not affect the input's market price.

But for the whole market, the supply curve is rarely horizontal. Instead, increasing amounts usually can only be obtained at higher prices. There are two main reasons for this up-slope in the supply curve.

1. Opportunity Cost: The input must be bid away from valuable alternative uses To get larger amounts, higher prices must be paid to draw the input from increasingly valuable alternatives.

For example, more trained mechanics may be needed. The first 1,000 of them can be obtained by offering salaries of $20,000 per year. To obtain the next 1,000 mechanics, however, it may be necessary to offer annual salaries of $25,000 to get them to leave well-paying jobs in other industries. The next 1,000 must be attracted away from specialized aerospace jobs that pay $30,000. Therefore, they must be paid at least $30,000. This feature alone would cause the supply curve to slope up.

2. Direct Cost: It may be increasingly costly to produce the input Small amounts may be obtained by simple, cheap processes, but larger amounts may require expensive methods of production. Therefore, the supply curve may slope up to reflect these increasing direct costs of production.

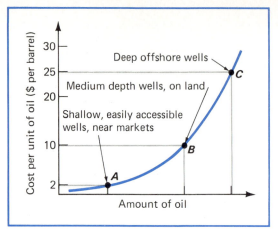

Figure 8   Increasing direct costs can make an input's supply curve slope up

The cheap, easy sources are tapped first, as at Point *A*, where oil only costs $2 per barrel to find and extract. To get the amount at Point *B*, wells must be drilled deeper, in less accessible locations. Costs are therefore higher—$10 per barrel. Obtaining the amount of oil at Point *C* involves much higher costs, for expensive rigs to drill deep wells out in the ocean. A price of $25 or higher will induce companies to incur those costs.

The best examples of this are natural resources, such as coal, ores, water, and fertile land. Each exists in a variety of qualities and locations. Some are easy and cheap to use: easily accessible oil, water flowing in nearby rivers, thick coal seams near the surface, the best-quality land nearest the cities. They are used first, at low cost, as shown for oil by Point *A* in Figure 8. Then, to get more supply, the more difficult sources must be tapped, at the higher costs shown by Point *B*. Still higher costs are incurred for still higher quantities, at Point *C*, which represents very deep offshore wells. Since the costs of extracting the oil are so high at this point, oil will be supplied only at high prices.

The point also applies to other resources—for example, to the recruitment of a specialized labor force to operate a new enterprise. Training the necessary labor may be increasingly costly. The first trainees may well have innate talent, and so their training will be rapid and cheap. Further candidates are likely to be less talented and therefore costlier to train.

These two conditions—opportunity costs and rising production costs—give the supply curves their characteristic positive slope. The degree of slope will vary from case to case, but the same logic applies to them all. If the firm operates in both a competitive output and an input market, the contribution of each input to the process of production is easy to determine. In that case, each input is paid an amount equal to the value of its marginal product. As you know from the earlier discussion in this chapter, the value of marginal product represents the inputs' marginal contribution to revenue. The input payment is set at precisely what the input is worth to producers. Therefore, competitive markets tend to pay inputs what they contribute to revenue at the margin.

Market equilibrium   As in any market, the equilibrium price and quantity for each input are determined by the interaction of the supply and demand forces. Figure 9 illustrates the equilibrium result for one input market. The demand and supply

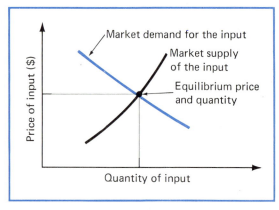

Figure 9   Equilibrium in an input market

As with output markets, the equilibrium price and quantity in input markets are determined by the interaction of supply and demand forces. While the demand and supply schedules for an input have the same slopes as do the demand and supply schedules for output markets, remember that the explanations for the slopes differ markedly.

schedules for the inputs have exactly the same basic appearance as do the demand and supply schedules for output markets. But remember that the explanation for the slopes of the schedules, and for the derivation of the curve, is different for input and output markets.

Economic rent

One special feature of supply is **economic rent.** To explain it, we begin with the polar case of perfectly inelastic supply. Then we show how economic rent occurs when supply has varying degrees of elasticity.

Perfectly inelastic supply When a good's supply is perfectly inelastic—with a vertical supply curve—the same quantity of it will be supplied regardless of the price. The price depends strictly on the level of demand, as in Figure 10. The amount, Q_1, will be supplied when the price is as low as P_1 or even zero. If demand shifts up, the price will rise (as to P_2 and P_3), but quantity will stay at Q_1.

In such a case, all payments to the input's owners are *economic rent*. They are not cost or profit. ***Economic rent is a payment in excess of the price needed to elicit supply.***

Rent is common for inputs, especially natural resources. Urban land is the economists' traditional instance of perfectly inelastic supply and, therefore, of pure economic rent. Each plot of land in a city is merely an area upon which buildings and valuable activities can be located. The economic uses of such land generate value, which, in turn, give rise to demand for the land itself. As the density of economic activity rises, the demand for the land also rises. That causes the price of the land to rise, as to P_2 and P_3 in Figure 10.

Therefore, urban land prices (which provide economic rent) reflect economic density. Within a city, the more densely

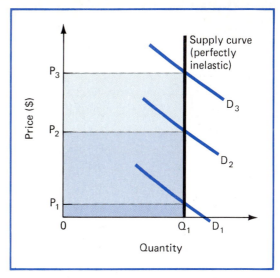

Figure 10   When supply is perfectly inelastic, all payments are economic rent

Because the same quantity, Q_1, will be supplied at all prices, such as zero, P_1, P_2, or $P3$, the actual price is determined by demand. All payments are economic rent; the total rent payments for each price (P_1, P_2, P_3) are shown by the shaded areas below those prices.

used central land costs more than peripheral land. Over time, a rising density of use will raise prices (and economic rent) on all land.* Each city has contours of land values, with high prices at the center and lower prices at the edges.

The analysis applies to any good that is in fixed supply. All payments to it are economic rent.

When supply has a degree of elasticity In general, supply is up-sloping but not perfectly inelastic. The payments to the input provide both *economic rent* and *transfer earnings.* **Transfer earnings are payments that are necessary to elicit supply;** in competitive markets, *transfer earnings are identical to cost.* For example, with lumber, in Figure 11, the supply curve slopes upward,

---

*Economic rent is not to be confused with "rent" for leasing apartments, automobiles, and the like. A rental rate is merely a periodic payment for a service. It need not contain any element of true economic rent.

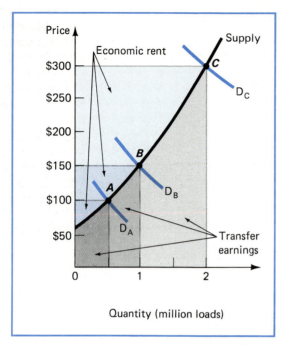

Figure 11 Separating economic rent and transfer earnings

The height of each point on the supply curve represents the dollar payment required if the lumber is to be supplied. Summing all such heights, the area under the supply curve represents total transfer earnings. The areas *above* the curve but *below* the going price represent economic rent. Transfer earnings are shown below the curve, for various prices; economic rent is shown above the curve for various prices.

starting with the most accessible and suitable areas for harvesting lumber (at Point *A*), and then moving to less and less accessible and productive forest land (at Points *B* and *C*). Successively higher costs of harvesting the trees must be incurred as the quantity of lumber increases. Therefore, higher prices must be offered to lumber suppliers to elicit more lumber.

Any payments above those transfer earnings are economic rent. For example, if a particular load of lumber will be supplied for $100, but the going market price is $300, then the supplier of that load receives $200 in economic rent.

Figure 11 shows how the total payments to this input can be divided between transfer earnings and economic rent. Suppose that the equilibrium market price-and-quantity combination is $150 per load and 1 million loads, as at Point *B*. The supply schedule shows that the 500,000th load will be offered at a price of $100, which is its cost of production. Because market price is $150, the 500,000th load receives transfer earnings of $100 plus economic rent of $50. The 750,000th unit will be supplied only at a price of $125, and so the market price of $150 provides it with $125 in transfer earnings and $25 of economic rent. The 1 millionth unit (supplied at the going price of $150) earns no economic rent at all; the $150 is all transfer earnings.

In general, since the height of the supply curve shows the cost of supply, the area below the supply curve represents transfer earnings, which cover the suppliers' costs. The area that is above the supply curve and below the horizontal line representing the market price is the total economic rent received at that market price. It is shaded blue in Figure 11. Some units obtain large economic rent, while others get little, and the last unit supplied receives no rent at all.

If demand increases to level D_C the equilibrium price will rise to $300, as shown. The quantity supplied will rise to 2 million. As before, the last unit supplied (now the 2 millionth) receives only its transfer earnings, with no economic rent. But the price rise enlarges the economic rent gained by other units. The 500,000th unit's economic rent rises to $200, the 750,000th unit's rent to $175, and so on. The total additions to transfer earnings and economic rent are shown by the shaded areas in Figure 11.

When demand rose to D_C, the original suppliers of the first 1 million loads did not change their choices or behavior. But their economic rent rose substantially. Such rises in economic rent are often called **windfall gains,** for they occur with no added effort or contribution by the owners of the inputs. Recent examples have come from the rises in real estate and in oil prices during the 1970s. The holders of those assets simply gained extra value without altering their own decisions or activities.

Taxing economic rents

Land is both a fixed factor, which earns economic rents, and a large share of the value of all assets. Therefore, it has always attracted interest as a source of taxes. In the pure case, since its supply curve is vertical, all payments to it are economic rent, as in Figure 12.

If a tax were set to take Area I, or even the entire shaded area, the land would still be supplied and used. The price paid by

the users would be as high as before (P_1), reflecting the land's economic value as an input. But the state would simply take some or most of the owners' rent. Nothing in the economy's efficient production choices would be changed, and the government would have more tax revenues. Moreover, the tax is easy to apply, for the land is immobile and visible.

These points became the heart of a crusade in the 1880s by an amateur economic thinker named Henry George. A tax on land would make an ideal source of revenue, he urged. Land values rose merely because cities grew. Since landowners contributed nothing to deserve that rise in rent, he argued that taxing away this newly created rent was both efficient and fair. The tax might even cover all of government's costs, at a time when public spending was far less important than it is now. Hence it was called a "single tax."

An effective orator, George was nearly elected mayor of New York in 1886. But a conservative reaction set in and George's single-tax movement faded. Nonetheless, a Henry George Society still exists in New York, and economists have always accepted the core logic of his argument. Indeed, his argument was derived directly from the marginal utility theory, which economists were developing at that time.

However, the single tax does have practical defects. As we noted earlier, there is usually a mingling of land and building values. Since both rent and cost are often present, separating them is usually difficult, even though in principle it could be done. Another practical limit is that nowadays the land tax would not be able to provide all of the national budget. Land's relative importance has dwindled, as capital has expanded and government budgets have multiplied a hundredfold. The "single tax" could no longer cover much of total public spending.

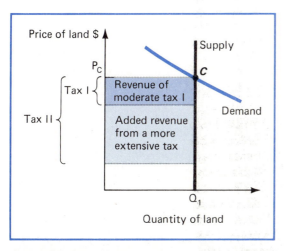

Figure 12   Taxation of rent from land
If land is a fixed factor, its supply curve is vertical, as shown. This would be likely for land in towns, where the amount in a given area is fixed. The equilibrium price is P_c. If Tax I is levied, the government will receive the revenue shown by Area I. The steeper Tax II would yield the total shaded area. Yet, even though the owner would be receiving a much lower net payment for the land, he would still supply the land in the same amount, Q_1.

Yet, the tax on economic rent *has* become a major part of modern public finance, as local property taxes. Levied by virtually every city, these taxes on residences and businesses are usually set at between 0.5 and 1.5 percent of the value of property. The revenues are usually over half of the city budgets.

Who provides the value of production?

Now we advance to one of the most divisive economic issues in the history of economics: Which factor provides the most value in the production process?

The basic problem is readily apparent. When a person spins wool by hand and then knits a sweater from it worth $50, the labor has provided most of that $50 value. But complex modern production is not so easily dissected. Consider a row of gleaming new $8,000 cars emerging from an assembly plant. Labor, capital, and land were used together to produce the cars, and each provided some of the $8,000 value. But exactly *how much* of the value did each factor add?

That question poses an explosive issue, for each factor's owners naturally think that theirs is the most important one. Economists have debated the issue for over three centuries, and their diverse views are shown in Table 1. Gold, land, industry, capital, and labor have each been credited at some time with being the main source of value.

The issue has great importance in labor negotiations. Workers regard their labor as the main source of value and claim high wages as their due. The company managers see their factories and equipment as the crucial factor of production and resist wage increases to gain higher profits on the invested capital.

The issue arises even in your classrooms. Whose efforts cause learning to occur? Teachers often feel that their lectures, labs, and office hours have instilled the knowledge. Students instead often give the credit to their own hard work.

In such cases, all inputs contribute, but how much? If all markets are competitive, then each firm buys its inputs at competitive prices. Therefore, it is paying

Table 1 *Alternative views about the most productive factor*

Person or Group	Main Period	Primary Source of Economic Productivity
Mercantilists (Western Europe)	1650–1750	Gold
Physiocrats (France)	1750–1780	Land (in agriculture)
Adam Smith (Britain)	1770–1789	Industry and trade; also land to an extent
Industrial spokesmen "Manchester Liberal" economists (Britain) Austrian capital theorists	1800–1890	Capital
Karl Marx (Western Europe)	1850–1883	Labor (capital merely embodies the labor that made it)
Neoclassical economists (Western Europe and U.S.A.)	1870–present	All factors share in productivity according to their marginal revenue product

each factor an amount equal to its marginal revenue product. Since MRP is each factor's contribution to production, *the payment for each factor is set precisely at the economic value that it adds to production.*

Under competition, these payments to the factors use up all of the firms' sales revenue, so that there is no surplus money that could be given to any factor. A well-functioning competitive market system, therefore, tends to pay all inputs approximately what they contribute to production at the margin. Input choices are efficient, and the division of payments among inputs has a definite basis.

Yet, this basis is narrow, and what is efficient may not be fair. The narrowness and possible unfairness will be discussed later, when we present the general equilibrium outcomes for the whole economy. The effect of monopoly on labor incomes will be considered sooner, in the next chapter.

Summary

This chapter deals with the demand for and supply of inputs. Its main points are the following:

1. The theory of input markets is based on three assumptions: the firm is a profit maximizer; the firm is a price taker in the input market; and the firm uses only one variable input in addition to its fixed inputs.

2. The addition to cost from using an additional unit of input is the price of the input.

3. The addition to revenue from using an additional unit of input is the product of the addition to output resulting from the additional unit of input (the marginal product) and the addition to revenue from the sale of this output (the marginal revenue). The product is called marginal revenue product.

4. A firm will use an input up to the point at which the last unit of input adds as much to cost as to revenue. This is the level of input use at which the price of the input equals marginal revenue product.

5. The firm's demand schedule for an input is the marginal revenue product schedule for the input.

6. The demand for an input will be more elastic: The larger the percentage of total costs that the input accounts for, and the more elastic is the demand for output.

7. A monopolized industry will purchase less of an input than would be the case if the industry were competitive.

8. While an individual firm is assumed to be a price taker in the input market, increased supplies of the input to the *industry* are likely to be available only at higher prices.

9. *Transfer earnings* are the minimum payment that the owner of the input must receive if the input is to be offered for sale. *Economic rent* is the payment to the owner of the input over and above what is necessary to prevent the owner from transferring that input to another use. An increase in the economic rent paid to the owner of the input is called *windfall gains.*

10. If a firm operates in output and input markets that are both competitive, each input's contribution to output is measured by its value of marginal product.

11. A tax on economic rent does not affect the supply of an input offered for sale.

Key concepts

Marginal revenue product (MRP)

Value of marginal product

Economic rent

Transfer earnings

Windfall gains

Questions for review

1. Which of the following statements is true? Explain your answer carefully.
   a. For one variable input, the price of the input and the marginal cost of output are the same.
   b. If marginal revenue product is greater than the price of the input, the firm must be making a profit.
   c. The profit-maximizing level of output must occur at the point where the marginal revenue product equals input price.

2. Indicate which of the following changes will cause a firm's demand schedule for an input to shift.
   a. The firm purchases more of the input.
   b. The price of the input falls.
   c. The price of a substitute for the firm's output falls.

3. Explain why monopoly power will influence the allocation of resources to a particular industry.

4. Why is a tax on pure economic rent more desirable than a tax affecting transfer earnings, from the point of view of resource allocation?

· 15 ·

The Economics of Labor and Unions

As you read and study this chapter, you will learn:

▸ how people choose their jobs and their amounts of work

▸ how wage and employment levels are determined in the market

▸ the varieties of occupations and pay rates

▸ how monopoly elements (unions and monopsonies) alter the competitive wage and hiring levels

According to the book of Genesis, human life began in idyllic surroundings. In the Garden of Eden, the soil was rich, food was abundant, and the living was easy. After yielding to temptation, however, Adam and Eve were banished from that land of plenty, doomed to wrest their food from the soil with suffering, and to eat their bread with sweat on their brows. Simply put, they now had to work for a living. Unfortunately for us, this curse has extended to all of their offspring. Since that day, work has been the lot of humankind.

Economists have always recognized labor's great importance in the economic process. Work absorbs a large share of most people's efforts, time, and emotions. Work is not only how people "make a living." It also defines much of each person's success and sense of personal worth.

Labor is also a prime productive force in the economy, applied in millions of factories and stores. Like any other commodity, labor is bought and sold every day. There are many types and grades of labor, all being sold at market prices. The whole economic process allocates labor, as people choose jobs, employers hire workers, and wage rates adjust.

Yet, because labor directly affects human welfare, it is not just another commodity like gravel or zinc. If you keep labor's special importance in mind, you will better understand the urgency of its social role. Policies toward labor—especially toward minimum wages, unions, and job discrimination—evoke strong reactions, and rightly so. They matter because work matters.

In the first main section of this chapter, we analyze the supply of and demand for labor. This is based on marginal productivity theory. The second main section discusses the varieties of labor. Finally, the third section analyzes departures from competitive conditions: unions and their effects, and employers' market power.

Labor supply, demand, and market outcomes

The basic unit of labor is the hour of work, in which skills and/or force are applied as part of a production process. The degree of effort and skill is assumed to be constant, so that each kind of labor-hour is a standardized input. Labor-hours are bought and sold on labor markets, with outcomes that are determined by supply and demand.

On the supply side, people have to decide whether to work at all, at what job, and for how many hours. On the demand side, firms have to decide how many labor-hours to buy. As these two sides of labor markets interact, the wage rates and quantities of labor hired are determined throughout the economy.

The marginal utility of work

Work is productive effort, done for a reward. Some work is interesting and satisfying, a source of *utility*. But work can also be hard, unpleasant, and, often, boring. The negative side of work is called *disutility*—the opposite of utility, or pleasure. Disutility embraces all the things that can make a job unpleasant.

The task is to explain (1) how people choose among jobs, and (2) how much work they will choose to do in those jobs at varying wage rates. The decisions depend largely on how much satisfaction or dissatisfaction the work brings, and that, in turn, depends on two elements: the person and the job.

Panel I of Figure 1 shows how the nature of the job may cause different amounts of satisfaction. The three curves illustrate how one person may view three different jobs, apart from whatever wages are paid. The average hours worked per day are plotted on the horizontal axis; *marginal utility* (the addition to job satisfaction) from each additional hour worked is on the vertical axis. Curve 1 represents a truly unpleasant job, which causes displeasure (negative utility) from the first moment.

Curve 2 represents a job that would give some satisfaction or enjoyment to the person who does it, for at least the first five hours or so. But the law of diminishing marginal utility applies, and the additional hours worked bring disutility. Curve 3 represents a highly enjoyable job. Only after 15 hours a day does disutility set in. For each person, then, different jobs will yield different amounts of satisfaction.

The three curves can also be viewed from a different perspective. As in Panel II of Figure 1, the curves could represent the same job as viewed by three different people. Person 1 dislikes the job entirely; the second person gets some utility from the

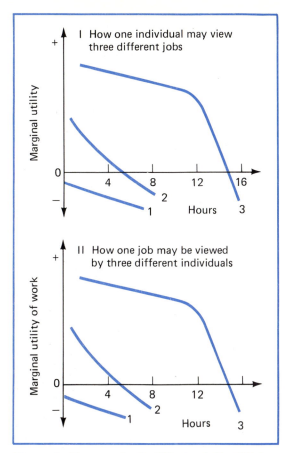

Figure 1 The marginal utility (and disutility) of work

Panel I represents the varying amounts of marginal utility (or satisfaction) that a person may derive from three different jobs. Job 1 brings no positive satisfaction for any of the hours worked. Job 2 satisfies up to the 5½-hour mark. Job 3 satisfies up to the 15th hour worked. Note that all of the jobs involve declining marginal satisfaction, with each hour worked bringing in smaller additions to satisfaction or larger additions to dissatisfaction.

Panel II shows that while different jobs may yield a person varying amounts of marginal utility, the same job may yield varying amounts of marginal utility to different persons. Person 1 receives only dissatisfaction from the job. Person 2 receives some positive enjoyment from the job, at least up to the 5½-hour mark. Person 3 enjoys the job the most, receiving increases in enjoyment for the first 15 hours worked. Note, however, that for each person, each additional hour worked causes smaller increases in satisfaction or larger increases in dissatisfaction.

minishing utility applies: There is decreasing satisfaction from additional hours of work. At some point, because people have to sleep, eat, and relax as well as work, extra work brings disutility.

Each rational worker aims to maximize the utility or satisfaction gained from a job by balancing the benefits of work (the enjoyment and the pay) against the cost (the disutility). Two decisions must be made simultaneously: which job to take and how long to work at it.

The choice of a job

Each person rules out many jobs because their disutility more than offsets the pay. People's job choices also reflect their own specific skills and preferences. Such talents can be innate or they can be acquired or developed through training. These skills are first discovered and developed in high school. Some students are attracted to specific jobs, such as auto mechanics, cooking, or carpentry, and may pursue vocational training or go directly to work. Those who attend college go through a further sorting process, deciding about future work on the basis of their interests and aptitudes. The job selection process leads people into the jobs that they are relatively best at—the jobs for which they have a *comparative advantage.*

Of course, in actually choosing a job, you have to consider not only your skills and interest but also how much it pays. You might get your greatest satisfaction from painting, but if no one will pay for your masterpieces, you will have to paint for a hobby and find another line of work. The wage rate you will accept depends largely on how interested you are in the job. The greater your interest, the lower the pay you may be willing to accept.

But wage rates also affect the *number of hours* people work.

job; while the third person would happily do it for 15 hours a day.

In all cases, even given the differing natures of jobs and people, the law of di-

Individual labor supply schedules

Each person has a supply curve of labor showing the amount of work she or he would choose to do at differing rates of pay. Normally this curve will slope up, as it does in Figure 2, because a higher rate of pay is necessary to overcome the increasing marginal disutility of work.

As Figure 2 shows, the elasticity of labor supply may differ from one person to another. Bentley has a more elastic supply curve than Angelos. A wage increase from $7 to $10 makes Bentley willing to work 3¹/₂ hours more, while Angelos would only be willing to work for another hour. A person whose time available for work is limited, such as a parent of young children or a full-time student, would tend to have a relatively inelastic supply schedule for labor. An increasing wage rate would not induce that person to work many more hours.

Some jobs have fairly inflexible hours: You must work eight hours a day or refuse the job. Other jobs offer more flexibility.

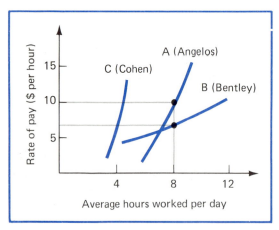

Figure 2 Individual supply curves of labor

The supply curves all slope up in this range of pay. Higher rewards induce longer hours, by offsetting the marginal disutility of work. Viewed differently, higher pay rates make the marginal hours of leisure more expensive because each extra hour of leisure results in more and more income lost that could have been earned.

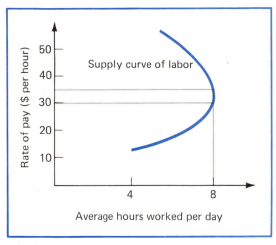

Figure 3 A backward-bending supply curve for labor

At higher rates of pay, a person's supply curve for labor may bend backward. The *price effect* increases work effort by increasing the opportunity cost of an hour of leisure. The *income effect* reduces work effort by increasing a person's ability to purchase leisure. If the income effect overcomes the price effect, higher pay will reduce the number of hours worked, and the person's labor supply curve will bend backward.

In this diagram, pay rate increases up to $30 cause the person to work longer hours, and the price effect is dominant. Increases from $30 to $35 per hour result in constant work effort; the price and income effects just balance. Pay rates higher than $35 per hour cause the person to work less, and the income effect is dominant.

Since workers' preferences and needs are so diverse, a range of jobs with flexible schedules is needed to match the variety of individual preferences.

Price and income effects

The labor supply curves in Figure 2 all slope upward. Yet, it is possible for labor supply curves to become vertical and then slope backward, as shown in Figure 3. As pay rises, people may choose to work *fewer* hours. The reason for this reversal of slope is the dual operation of a **price effect** and an **income effect.** As wages increase, the opportunity cost of an hour of leisure also increases. If wages are $5 an hour, substituting an hour of leisure for an hour of work means a sacrifice of only $5. If wages rise to $10 per hour, the opportunity cost of an hour of leisure would rise to $10.

The increasing cost of leisure resulting from higher wages is referred to as the *price effect*. The wage rate is, in fact, the price of leisure. As this price rises, people tend to work more and "consume" less leisure. This helps to explain the upward-sloping portion of the labor supply curve: Higher wages mean more work and less leisure because the cost of leisure is high.

However, the *income effect* also operates here. As wages rise, so does your income. With this rising income, you can afford to consume more of all goods, including leisure. For example, if you are paid $15 per hour for 8 hours of work per day, 5 days per week, 48 weeks per year, you earn $28,800 per year. A wage increase to $20 per hour would give you $38,400 a year, an increase of $9,600. If you feel that $30,000 is about all you really need, you might trade off some of the increased pay for increased leisure, by working only 7·½ hours per day.

Thus, as the rate of pay rises, the price effect increases the cost of leisure, while the income effect increases one's ability to purchase leisure. If at some point the income effect overcomes the price effect, then a person works less for more money, and the supply curve bends back.

Virtually everyone's labor supply curve reaches a range of backward slope at sufficiently high wage rates. For most people, that range occurs well above the wage rates they can actually get for their skills. Therefore, only the positive-sloped portion is relevant for their actual choices.

The market supply curve of labor

To obtain the market supply curve of labor, all persons' labor supply curves are added horizontally. Figure 4 shows how the summation is done. The backward-bending parts of most people's curves occur at high rates of pay, well above the prevailing wage rates. Since most people are responding to wages on the upward-sloping portion of their supply curves, the market *summation* of individual curves usually slopes up rather than back. In Figure 4, for example, the market supply curve still slopes up, even though Person B's supply curve bends backward at wages above $12 per hour.

The market supply for specific kinds of labor will slope up, not only because of the shape of the individual supply curves, but also because new people will be attracted to work in the industry as the wage rate rises. If the pay for secretaries is increased, other things being equal, people who are already secretaries may work more. Salespeople and clerks—or even teachers or pipefitters—may also decide to become secretaries. Moreover, the higher pay can attract workers from other locations. Rising wages in Houston, for example, have drawn new workers from as far away as Michigan and Maine. The upward slope, then, represents both longer hours and more employees.

The balance between work and leisure, decided by millions of workers, yields the overall pattern of participation in the entire labor force. Such overall patterns are called *labor force participation rates*. They strongly affect the operation of the entire economic system.

Figure 5 shows the participation rates for people of various age groups and marital status. The participation rate is the share (up to 100 percent) of each group that works for pay. On the horizontal axis, the main working years are about ages 20 to 65.

Over 90 percent of the men between ages 20 and 65 work for pay. Whether women work depends crucially on their marital status. Most unmarried women (single, divorced, or widowed) have paid jobs. About 40 percent of married women

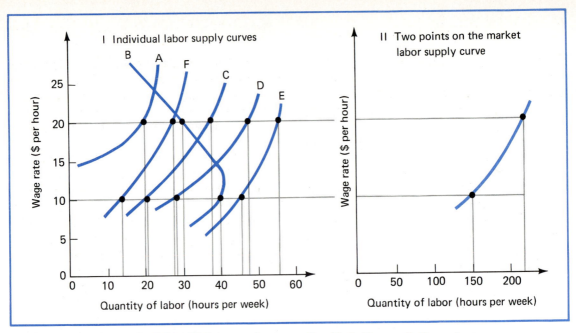

Figure 4   Summing up individual labor supply curves to obtain the market supply curve

Labor markets usually consist of hundreds or thousands of people. Here, the labor supply curves of only six people are summed to show how the *market* supply curve for labor is derived. At a pay rate of $10 per hour, the six people will work for a combined total of 148 hours. At $20 per hour, the same six people are willing to supply 220 hours of labor. By adding the combined labor-hours these people will offer at various wage rates, the entire market supply curve can be obtained.

Figure 5   Labor force participation rates by age for men and women by marital status, 1970

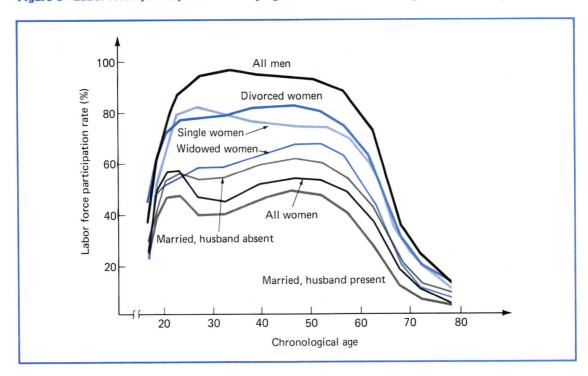

work outside the home, but fewer work during the child-rearing years of 25 to 40. The average rate for all women has risen from about 50 percent in 1970 to about 60 percent in 1980.

The overall supply of labor to the economy involves the decisions of a complex variety of people in many circumstances. Their decisions about work are not made unilaterally, however. What people can actually achieve in terms of hours of work and pay rates depends not only on their own preferences, but also on the demand for labor.

The demand for labor

The demand for labor is, like the demand for any other input, a *derived demand*. It derives from the demand for the output that the input helps to produce. Firms will hire workers only up to the point at which the value added by the workers to output is equal to their wages cost. As with other inputs, the firm's demand curve for labor is the *marginal revenue product curve: the amount of output that one additional unit of labor can produce (the MP) times the additional revenue from the additional output (the MR).**

The *height* of the firm's MRP curve for labor, in Figure 6, depends mainly on two conditions: (1) the amount of other inputs used; and (2) the price of the output. If the amount of other inputs is increased—for example, by giving the workers bigger and better machines to work with—then the marginal product curve of labor shifts up, and so must the marginal *revenue* product curve. If the market demand for output increases, so that the marginal revenue curve for the output shifts up, the mar-

---

*Remember that the MRP curve represents the demand curve for an input if the firm is a profit maximizer, a price taker in the input market, and uses one variable input.

Figure 6   Contrast of a firm's demand schedule for labor with one variable input and with several variable inputs

For one variable input, the marginal revenue product schedule is the demand schedule for labor. For more than one variable input, the demand schedule for labor will be more elastic than the marginal revenue product schedule because substitution among the variable inputs will cause a larger change in the quantity demanded of inputs in response to changes in input prices. As wages fall below W_1, the firm will substitute labor for other inputs, causing larger increases in the quantity demanded of labor. As wages increase, the firm will substitute other inputs for labor, causing larger decreases in the quantity demanded of labor.

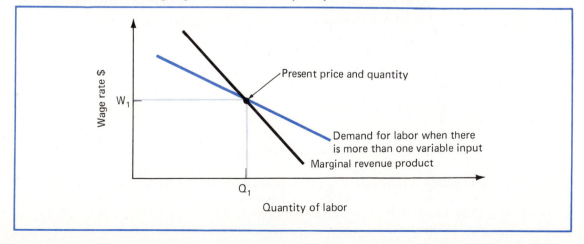

ginal revenue product curve must also shift up and to the right. Finally, the downward *slope* of the marginal revenue product curve reflects the law of diminishing marginal product.

Remember, though, that the firm's demand curve for labor is the marginal revenue product curve only for cases in which labor is the only variable input. It is interesting to see what happens to the demand for labor when there is more than one variable input.

Figure 6 shows the firm's marginal revenue product schedule, the demand schedule for labor if there is one variable input. The curve slopes downward, indicating that the firm will hire more labor as wages decrease. The reason for this, as you saw in Chapter 14, is that as the price of a variable input falls, the firm's marginal cost schedule shifts down and to the right. This causes the profit-maximizing level of output—the point at which marginal cost equals marginal revenue—to increase. To produce more output, the firm must hire or buy more inputs.

When there is more than one variable input, there is another reason for the firm's demand for labor to change: substitution among inputs. As wages fall, for example, labor becomes relatively cheaper compared to other inputs. The firm would, therefore, try to substitute labor for its other variable inputs in the short run. When wages fall, the firm will hire more labor, *both* to produce more output *and* to substitute for other inputs. The total change in demand for labor, then, will be greater in the case of several variable inputs, assuming that the firm's technology permits substitution among inputs. For decreases in the cost of labor, the firm's demand for labor will lie to the right of its marginal revenue product schedule.

If wages rise, the firm's marginal cost schedule will shift to the left. The profit-maximizing level of output falls and will

cause the firm's demand for labor to fall. If the firm uses more than one variable input, the firm will also attempt to substitute other inputs for the relatively more costly labor. Again, the total change in demand for labor will be greater in the case of several variable inputs, assuming that technology permits substitution among the inputs. For increase in wages, then, the firm's demand curve for labor will lie to the left of the marginal revenue product curve, indicating larger decreases in the quantity demanded of labor.

Since both increases and decreases in wages will lead to larger changes in the quantity demanded of labor when there is more than one variable input, the resulting demand schedule will be more elastic in the case of several variable inputs. The degree of elasticity will depend on the ease of technical substitution. The easier the substitution, the more elastic the demand for labor will be, all other conditions being equal. This contrast between the marginal revenue product schedule as the demand schedule for the input in the case of one variable input and the more elastic demand schedule for labor in the case of several variable inputs is shown in Figure 6.

In some cases, a market supply or demand schedule can be derived by summing up individual supply or demand schedules. For labor, however, the derivation of the market demand schedule for labor through a summation of the firms' demand schedules for labor is not strictly accurate. The reason is simply that changes in labor costs may cause industry output and, therefore, prices to change, resulting in shifts in the firms' labor demand schedules. For example, suppose that labor costs fall. This will cause the marginal cost schedules of all firms in the industry to shift down, resulting in an increase in industry output. As industry output increases, the industry price for the firms' output will fall. This fall in output price will cause the firms' demand schedules for output and, therefore, the marginal revenue schedules to shift down. As the marginal revenue schedules shift, the firms' demand schedules for labor will also shift. If a change in labor costs can cause the firms' demand schedule for labor to shift, a summing up of existing labor demand schedules will not accurately reflect the total quantities of labor that the firms in the industry will use at different prices.

While the market demand schedule for labor cannot be derived from a horizontal summation of the firms' demand schedules for labor, the factors that will influence the firms' demand for labor will obviously also influence the market demand for labor. For example, increases in labor productivity or in the demand for the firms' output will shift the firms' demand schedules for labor to the right, and also shift the market demand for labor. Increases in the number of firms operating in the industry will also cause a rightward shift in the market demand schedule for labor.

Equilibrium between supply and demand

Once the market supply and demand curves for labor are derived, the equilibrium quantity and wage in that labor market can be determined. The intersection of supply and demand is the equilibrium point at which the market clears. In Figure 7, for example, the market equilibrium occurs at a wage of $9.25 and quantity of 9,000 labor-hours. The equilibrium quantity of 9,000 hours of labor per week reflects both the number of people working and the average number of hours that they each work. At wages higher than $9.25, there would be an excess supply of labor, with unemployed workers bidding the wage level down. At wages below $9.25, there would be an excess demand for labor, with eager employers bidding wages up. In both cases, the wages would be

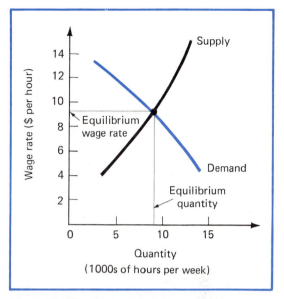

Figure 7   The demand for and supply of labor in each market determine the equilibrium wage rate and the amount of labor hired

Market equilibrium is reached at the point where the market clears, with the quantity supplied of labor just equal to the quantity demanded. In this diagram, equilibrium is reached at a wage of $9.25 per hour with 9,000 labor hours purchased. At higher wages, the excess supply of labor would bid the wage down. At wages lower than $9.25, the excess demand for labor would cause the wage to rise.

pulled back toward the equilibrium wage of $9.25.

The important distinction between changes in supply and demand and changes in quantity supplied and quantity demanded still holds. A change in wage levels (the price of labor) will cause changes in quantity supplied and quantity demanded, shown by a movement along the supply or demand schedules for labor. A change in supply or demand refers to a *shift* in the entire supply or demand curve. A change in technology or in demand for output would cause a shift in the *demand* schedule for labor. A change in people's work preferences or in the size of the labor force would cause a change in the amount of labor offered at every wage, shifting the labor *supply* schedule. Some possible shifts

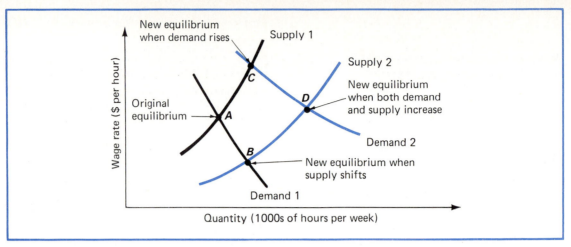

Figure 8 Shifts in the demand for and supply of labor

If the *supply* of labor increases, the supply curve will shift to the right from Supply 1 to Supply 2. The new equilibrium at Point B will show a lower wage rate and a higher quantity of labor hired than the original equilibrium, represented by Point A.

If the *demand* for labor increases, the demand curve will shift to the right, from Demand 1 to Demand 2. The new equilibrium (Point C) will show a higher wage and higher quantity of labor hired than the original equilibrium.

If both the supply of and demand for labor increase, the equilibrium quantity of labor hired will increase, but the net effect on the wage rate is uncertain, depending on the relative size of the shifts. The wage rate will fall if the supply shift dominates and rise if the demand shift dominates. In this diagram, the demand shift dominates, and there is a slight increase in the wage rate.

and their impact on the labor market's equilibrium outcomes are shown in Figure 8.

Like other supply and demand schedules, the labor supply and demand schedules have elasticities that reflect underlying market conditions. The elasticity of demand for labor will depend on both the elasticity of demand for output and the importance of labor costs as a percentage of total costs. As Chapter 14 showed, the elasticity of demand for an input such as labor will be greater the more elastic is the demand for output and the larger is the percentage of total costs for which labor accounts.

The elasticity of the supply of labor will depend on both the responsiveness of present workers to wage increases and the ease with which new workers can be attracted to the particular labor market. The more willing present workers are to increase the amount of work they do as wages increases, the more elastic the supply of labor will be. Moreover, the easier it

is for new workers to enter the job market, the greater the elasticity of supply will be. For example, consider the supply of neurosurgeons. Because access to a medical school education is limited, the increase in the supply of doctors in response to a wage increase is restricted. Training to become a neurosurgeon is a lengthy and costly process, and not many people have the talent for it. All of these factors tend to make the supply of neurosurgeons relatively inelastic. This is particularly true for short-run elasticities because workers cannot easily shift into this profession from other fields.

In contrast, the supply schedule for part-time waiters is relatively elastic. The flexibility of hours would attract many people; the training period is short and not costly to the worker. Since the specific skills required to wait on tables are not numerous, there can be shifts to such a job from other occupations, like clerking in a store, or simply from new additions to the labor force. The nature of the job, then, in terms of the skills required and the length and cost of training, is a major determinant of the elasticity of supply.

Differences in labor skills

The actual variety of jobs in any modern economic system is staggering. The standard system of job classifications divides jobs into ten main classes, as shown in Table 1. Each of these main classes contains a great diversity of jobs in terms of specific

skills, physical and mental effort, and job conditions. There are *blue-collar jobs* that deal directly with production, such as drill press operators and farmers. *White-collar work* is done mainly in offices.

Variations in pay rates

With these job variations in mind, consider the basic wage patterns and trends in the U.S. economy, as presented in Table 2. Though white-collar jobs pay better than blue-collar work on the whole, skilled

Table 1 **Varieties of jobs**

Category	Specific instances
White-collar workers	
Professional, technical, and kindred workers	Physicians, dentists, editors, osteopaths, engineers, lawyers, chemists, teachers, pilots, architects, accountants, etc.
Managers and administrators, except farm	Buyers, purchasing agents, sales managers, school administrators, public administrators, bar managers
Sales workers	Insurance agents, brokers, and underwriters, real estate agents and brokers, sales clerks in retail stores, peddlers
Clerical and kindred workers	Bank tellers and cashiers, bookkeepers, billing clerks, mail handlers, postal clerks, file clerks, typists, etc.
Blue-collar workers	
Craftsmen and kindred workers	Electricians, plumbers, automobile mechanics, TV repair workers, carpenters, bakers, sheetmetal workers, printers, upholsterers, etc.
Operatives, except transport	Meat cutters and butchers, gas station attendants, laundry workers, welders, packers and wrappers (except product), etc.
Transport equipment	Truck drivers, delivery workers, taxi drivers, bus drivers, chauffeurs
Laborers, except farm	Construction laborers, freight, stock, and material handlers
Farmers, farm managers, and farm laborers	
Service workers, except private households	Janitors, cooks, waiters, waiters' assistants, dishwashers, fire fighters, security guards, nurses' aides, orderlies, hairdressers, policemen, etc.

blue-collar workers earn more, on average, than salespeople and clerks. In fact, a good plumber may earn more than the average college professor. One of the most noticeable features of the table is the impact of skills on pay rates. The pay gap between unskilled and skilled work, for both white-collar and blue-collar jobs, is large.

Around the average earning figures, shown in Table 2, lie infinite variations in earnings, caused by a particular worker's age, experience, specific company, region of the country, and, of course, productivity. Although many factors influence pay for both individuals and different lines of work, two main causes of wage differentials are the costs of training and the scarcity of talent. These factors are examined in this section of the chapter. Monopoly power of either the buyer or seller of labor can also influence levels of power. This issue is examined in the third main section of this chapter.

Investment in human capital: The cost of training

Labor is not just the use of raw, muscular force. Labor is, in fact, the use of *human capital,* the talents and skills created by

Table 2 *Broad and specific variations in incomes*

Category	Median yearly earnings, full-time workers, 1980
White-collar	
Professional and technical workers	$19,656
Managers and officials	22,100
Clerical workers	11,960
Sales workers	14,664
Blue-collar	
Craftsmen and foremen	$17,368
Operatives	12,480
Nonfarm laborers	9,100
Private household workers	3,848
Other service workers	9,360
Farm workers	7,696
Specific occupations	
Physicians and surgeons	$82,000
Executives	76,000
Lawyers	47,000
Dentists	46,000
Airline pilots	44,000
Electricians	34,000
Economists	31,000
Automobile workers	24,900
Accountants	24,000
Insurance salespeople	21,000
High school teachers	20,000
Computer programmers	18,000
Typists	11,000
Retail salesclerks	10,500
Unskilled labor	7,400

Source: U.S. Labor Department and Census data, adjusted from 1970 information; *Medical Economics* (for physicians and surgeons); and various other sources. Most figures are approximate and do not include nonsalary benefits.

Investing in College

You are a costly bundle of human capital already, on the way to becoming even more valuable. Consider the average child of a middle-income family who goes to a four-year public college. The average family's direct costs for that average child are $85,000, in 1980 prices. The table shows the detailed estimates from a recent study.

Besides the direct family investment there are other costs. Public schooling from kindergarten through senior year of high school costs about $1,000 per year, or about $13,000. Moreover, the earnings forgone while at college may be about $7,000 per year, or $28,000 in total. On top of all these expenses are the lost earnings of parents who choose to stay home with their children. For example, for a parent who stays home until the child is ten years old, giving up a $10,000 yearly job, the opportunity cost is $100,000. (Of course, if both parents work, day-care expenses must be calculated into direct costs.)

All of these direct and indirect costs add up to an average expenditure of about $230,000 by the time the student graduates from college. Studies after college or on-the-job training and experience will increase the total amount of that investment even more.

Average investment in a child by graduation from college

Category	Amount (in 1980 prices)
1. *Direct family costs*	
Housing	$24,711
Food	17,931
Transportation	12,027
Public college for 4 years	9,784
Clothing	5,686
Medical	3,716
Childbirth	2,485
Educational materials	1,020
All other expenses	7,726
Total	$85,086
2. *Public schools cost*	19,500
(13 years at $1,500 per year)	
3. *Earnings forgone by student while at college*	28,000
(4 years at $7,000 per year)	
4. *Earnings forgone by parents while raising child*	100,000
(10 years at $10,000 per year)	
Total	$232,586

Source: Family costs from Thomas B. Espenshade, *Raising a Child Can Now Cost $85,000*, INTERCOM, 8, no. 9 (Washington, D.C.: Population Reference Bureau, September 1980).

investment in people. Each person is born with certain unique qualities, or talents. Talent is a raw material that is made more productive by education and training. Each person is like a complex machine, with productive skills built up by a long process of economic investment. The investing begins at birth, continues with feeding and sheltering, then expands with schooling and specialized training.

The economic theory of human capital suggests that people will invest in schooling and/or other types of training up to the point where the marginal return to training, measured in terms of future income gains, equals the marginal cost of training. Those costs include both the direct costs (the cost of tuition at a college or university, for example) and indirect costs, such as the income given up to receive more schooling. This theory suggests that talented people will invest more in education, since their marginal returns are likely to be higher; it also predicts that those who have access to cheaper funding (because of affluent family backgrounds, for example) will invest more in training.

These predictions generated by the theory of human capital are confirmed by actual data. The effect of educational investment on later earnings is shown in Figure 9. Workers with a high school education had earnings well above those who had only completed the eighth grade. College graduates' earnings were much higher still.

The extra earnings are a form of return from the added educational investment in human capital. Economists have investigated the rates of return on this investment. A representative recent set of results is given in Table 3. These results fit the predictions of economic theory. Grade schooling provides rates of return above 20 percent. Higher grades provide decreasing marginal returns, but postcollege work still produces an average return on invest-

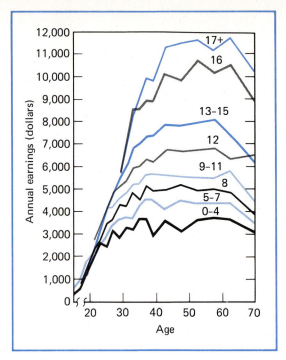

Figure 9   Age profiles of earnings of white, nonfarm men 1959 (annual earnings classified by years of age, for indicated schooling groups)

NOTE: Figures on curves indicate years of schooling completed.

Source: Jacob Mincer, *Schooling, Experience and Earnings* (New York: National Bureau of Economic Research, 1974), p. 66.

Table 3   *Estimated rates of return to investment in human capital: Various levels of education*

Additional year of schooling	Private rate of return in the form of higher income
8th year	22%
11th year	16%
12th year (senior year of high school)	16%
16th year (senior year of college)	12%
17th and higher years	7%

Source: J. T. Addison and W. S. Siebert, *The Market for Labor: An Analytical Treatment.* Copyright © 1979, Scott Foresman and Company. Reprinted by permission.

ment of over 7 percent. This is comparable to the returns earned by most other forms of capital. Therefore, the process of education and training resembles other kinds of productive investment.

To view people as the embodiment of valuable investment does not demean them. The analysis of human capital merely recognizes the economic truth that skills are costly to develop. A skilled population is a valuable resource. The productivity of labor—for each person and for all of us collectively—reflects the investments made in human capital, both today and in the past.

Since investment in human capital is costly, the pay that workers receive must compensate them in the long run for the training that they acquire. If the benefits of an occupation do *not* equal the costs of preparing for it, the supply of workers will soon decrease. Consider a specialized doctor who has trained until age 35 before opening a medical practice. Assume that the doctor's true costs of postcollege training (including forgone earnings) were $240,000. Between age 35 and retirement at 65, the doctor would need to earn at least $240,000/30 = $8,000 more each year than other college graduates, plus interest on the investment, to offset those additional training costs. After all, many people are unwilling to undertake additional training now unless they feel that it will "pay off" in higher income later. Therefore, the higher income can be interpreted as a necessary incentive to induce candidates to undertake training.

The doctor may, in fact, earn much much more than that extra $8,000 a year. If, instead, he or she earns $50,000 extra per year, only a small fraction of it would be explained by the cost of training. Other factors must be at work.

Scarcity of talent

Scarcity is a theme that underlies most economic analysis, and wage determination is no exception. For any given level of labor quality—involving skill, strength, and creativity—greater scarcity, repre-

sented by the height of the supply curve, will result in higher pay. Increasing scarcity results in a leftward shift of the supply curve, which will cause the equilibrium wage to increase. How much wages will rise depends on the elasticities of labor supply and demand. The more inelastic supply and demand are, the larger is the wage increase that an increasing scarcity of labor will bring. A greater elasticity of supply and demand will result in smaller wage increases as labor grows relatively scarce.

The influence of labor scarcity can be seen in any number of everyday situations. Picking tomatoes requires effort and endurance, but because the supply of tomato pickers is ample relative to demand, wages are low. The talent of a John McEnroe, a Bruce Springsteen, or a Luciano Pavarotti is rare, and these performers earn enormous salaries. If there were 200 people with talents identical to Bruce Springsteen's or Luciano Pavarotti's, these men might earn much lower wages.

There is a *natural scarcity* of many talents, although training and hard work can enhance average abilities. *Artificial scarcity* can also occur, when people or organizations deliberately exclude qualified or potentially qualified people from a certain job market. The medical profession is often accused of doing this, by limiting medical school enrollments to hold down the number of doctors. Some 50 professions—from the law and dentistry to hairdressing and undertaking—are "protected" by state licensing laws, which help to limit the number of people in these professions. Of course, licensing restrictions do more than keep the supply of labor low. Few consumers would want to be attended by incompetent dentists or doctors.

You can see that many factors such as productivity, training costs, workers' preferences, demand for output, and scarcity interact to determine prevailing wage rates in each job market. As individuals work their way through the educational process, they consider various job possibilities in the light of their own skills, the possibilities for enhancing present skills or acquiring new ones, and differences in wage rates. On the basis of these factors, they begin to make job-related choices. If the supply of labor in a particular labor market is high relative to demand, wages in that market will fall. Fewer people will be attracted to that line of work, and the supply and demand imbalance will disappear. If the demand for labor in a certain job market is high relative to supply, wages will rise. New entrants will be attracted to that job market, and the shortage of labor will correct itself.

Up to this point, the discussion of labor markets has focused on situations in which no group of suppliers or demanders of labor—neither the employees nor employers—controls the labor market. Yet there are important cases in which this assumption does not hold. Workers (the suppliers of labor) can join together to form monopolies such as unions on the supply side of labor markets. Buyers of labor services may hire such a large percentage of the workers in a given labor market that the firm becomes a monopoly on the buying side, which economists call a *monopsony*. These two types of departures from the competitive functioning of labor markets are examined in the next main section.

Departures from competitive market outcomes

Labor markets usually include hundreds or thousands of workers, making these markets inherently competitive on the supply side. No one worker can exert any market power. Yet, if workers can form **unions** or other associations, they may be able to control some of the supply side of the labor market. The group can then behave like any other monopoly, limiting the quantity of labor supplied while raising its price or wage rate. The labor monopoly may also seek other goals, such as improved work conditions, and greater stability of employment.

To maximize its control, the union commonly seeks to unify all the local unions into one industry-wide union. The union can then apply the strategy that works best: dealing with the weakest firms first, for example.

Barring entry by nonmembers can be crucial. Each worker has conflicting motives toward the union. The worker can gain increased wages by joining and supporting the union. Yet, it is also possible to gain from having a successful union but *not* joining it. Such "free riders" get the higher wages but don't have to pay the union dues or sacrifice their incomes by supporting a strike. Unions at one time tried to negotiate a *closed shop,* with only union members eligible for hiring. Closed shops have been illegal, however, since the Taft-Hartley Act of 1947. Another approach is the *union shop.* In this case, nonunion members may be hired if they agree to join the union within a specified time (union shops are illegal in 20 states).

If the union fails to limit the labor-market entry of nonmembers, support for the union dwindles. Each worker relies on the *others* to support the union. The company, of course, would like to have no union at all. Failing that, it would prefer its own company union or an *open shop* in which union membership is not required for employment. Unions have less control over the labor supply in an open shop and therefore tend to have much weaker bargaining strength than unions that can restrict the hiring of nonmembers.

Labor's control over a particular market is reflected in the elasticity of demand for the union's labor. An industry-wide closed-shop union would have a relatively inelastic demand for its members, since the industry has no legally available substitutes for union labor. That gives it more ability to raise wages by restricting the quantity of labor supplied. In contrast, an open-shop union would face a more elastic demand because its members can be replaced by the hiring of nonmembers. The high elasticity means that wage increases will result in a relatively large decrease in the number of union members employed.

Leverage: The power to inflict economic damage Once a union controls the labor supply in a particular market, the extent of its power to extract better pay and work conditions depends largely on its ability to inflict economic damage on the employer. This damage occurs as work stoppages or *strikes*. A successful strike stops production. The struck firm loses sales and, therefore, profits, perhaps experiencing large financial losses. Customers of the struck firm lose, too, especially if it produces a crucial good or service. The suppliers of inputs to the struck firm also lose sales, and their profits decrease. The disruption often spreads further. Stores that sell to the workers suffer, since striking workers have less money to spend (even though they usually receive some strike pay from the union) and therefore buy less. Since local government tax revenues are cut along with the strikers' income, local services can also be affected. Disruption from a large-scale strike can be severe and widespread.

The greater the possible disruption from a strike, the more seriously an employer will view a strike threat. The larger, therefore, will be the gains that the union can force the employer to yield. To maximize the threat of a strike, the union will choose the most favorable time to strike, the time that will most adversely affect a firm's production. The very threat of a strike may be sufficient to gain the union's demands, or the employer may refuse to give in, and the strike may occur. Whether the strike occurs depends largely on the employer's weighing of the costs of the strike against the costs of giving in to the union's demands.

Employers' losses from a strike depend on the ease with which striking workers can be replaced. This depends on several factors. First is the specific role the striking workers play in the technology of production. Highly skilled workers, such as operators of giant oil refinery equipment and hospital staff doctors, play crucial roles. By contrast, unskilled or low-skilled workers, such as tomato pickers and janitors, are generally easy to replace because there is a large and readily tapped reservoir of available workers. Thus, unskilled workers rarely win important strikes.

Second is the effective cohesion of labor. If labor sympathy for the striking workers is strong, or if the union can enforce a complete shutdown and block replacement workers, the union's leverage will increase. Finally, the union's leverage is affected by the ability of firms to relocate production, both immediately and in the long run. "Multinational" firms that have parallel production facilities abroad can often break a strike merely by shifting their production to a foreign plant. A nationwide firm can shift production to new plants in less unionized parts of the country. In general, the ability of firms to threaten job losses by shutting down plants and permanently relocating production can eliminate a union's leverage.

Yet, employers and unions must consider not only how a strike will damage them, but also how it will hurt others. A doctors' strike threatens the sick. A strike against a canning firm harms vegetable growers, whose crops may rot in the fields.

A telephone strike stops communications throughout the nation, affecting nearly everyone. All of the groups harmed by a strike will pressure the employers to come to terms.

In general, the union's leverage and the likelihood that it will prevail increases with the amount of damage that a threatened strike poses to all the parties that might be affected by it. When the threat of damage becomes especially severe, however, as with special groups such as doctors, nurses, police, teachers, and fire fighters, the groups are often forbidden to strike by law. Or society believes that they have a duty not to endanger others by striking. The group members themselves may consider strikes unethical or "unworthy" of them.

The choice, then, of whether to use the strike as a bargaining tactic depends both on the calculations of the economic damage of the strike and on the labor organization's view about whether the strike is an appropriate bargaining tool.

The choice of goals and methods Given whatever degree of control and leverage it has, the labor group must choose its economic goals and tactics. The demand curve for its labor is down-sloping. The union can obtain higher wages for its members, but doing so will reduce the number of workers hired. The union's desire to raise wage rates will clash with its dislike of cutting the numbers hired.

In this dilemma, the elasticity of the demand curve for labor is crucial. If the demand curve is highly inelastic, wages can be forced up to high levels without reducing the number of jobs by very much. A highly elastic demand curve will, by contrast, leave little room for wage rises; even a small increase may drastically reduce the number of workers hired.

Most unions are not just profit-maximizing monopolies. They have a range of other goals, and their costs are not clearly defined. Therefore, economists usually set aside the profit-maximizing approach and, instead, compare the likely results of unions with the competitive market outcome.

To clarify unions' choices, we divide the discussion into two parts, reflecting two kinds of unions and their characteristic strategies: (1) *industrial unions*, which try to enroll all workers and then set higher wages for them; and (2) *craft unions and professional organizations*, which mainly attempt to reduce the supply of labor in their trades.

The typical *industrial union's* choices are shown in Panel I of Figure 10. In this case, the wage that will maximize the total payment to labor is higher than the competitive equilibrium wage. In Panel I, the levels W_1 and Q_1 represent the competitive equilibrium determined by the intersection of the supply and demand curves at Point A.

To determine the wage that will maximize the wage bill, one needs to examine marginal revenue. As long as the addition to labor revenue (which is the union group's marginal revenue) is positive, the wage bill increases as employment rises. Thus, just as with sales revenue, *total labor revenue* (W × Q) *is also maximized where marginal revenue is zero*. In Figure 10, the wage bill will be maximized at a wage of W_2 with Q_2 workers hired. The result is clearly a wage higher than the competitive level, but with fewer workers hired. As Panel I shows, employment will decrease from Q_1 to Q_2 workers. The total amount of dollars paid to workers is now the rectangle $OW_2\,BQ_2$, an increase from the competitive outcome.

The precise effects depend on the elasticities of both demand and supply. Inelastic demand (e.g., for "crucial" workers, who cannot easily be cut back) will result in a sharp wage boost for union labor, as

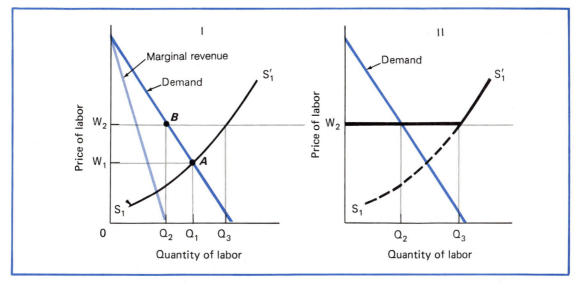

Figure 10   The possible effects of unions on wages and employment

In Panel I, competitive supply and demand conditions would result in an equilibrium wage of W_1 with Q_1 workers hired. The union, however, may try to maximize the total wage bill by bargaining for W_2 with Q_2 workers hired. The wage bill B (OW_2BQ_2) is larger than at Point A (OW_1AQ_1).

Panel II shows the supply curve perceived by the firm if the union negotiates a wage of W_2. The firm may hire as many workers as it wishes at the wage of W_2, up to a quantity of Q_3 workers. The supply curve of labor to the firm, therefore, becomes a horizontal line at the level of W_2. The actual number of workers hired will be determined by the firm's demand curve for labor. To obtain more than Q_3 workers, the firm must offer higher wages.

was noted above. At any rate, some workers will be unemployed at the new wage rate. Those not employed in that industry will eventually be absorbed elsewhere. Still, some workers (the amount Q_3 minus Q_2) will seek jobs here and not get them.

Of course, at a wage of W_2, more workers want the job than at W_1. The amount Q_3 shows how many would work at the wage of W_2, but only Q_2 will actually be hired. Since the union controls the supply of workers, however, the firm no longer perceives its supply curve for labor as S_1 S_1' as shown in Panel I. Rather, once the union negotiates a wage of W_2, the firm sees its labor supply curve as a horizontal line at the W_2 level, as shown in Panel II. Up to Q_3, the negotiated wage is higher than the supply curve, so that the firm can hire as many employees as it wants at the wage of W_2. To reach levels above Q_3, the

firm will have to offer higher wages to attract more workers.

Alternatively, the union may seek to set even higher wages in the interests of a smaller group of workers—perhaps those with seniority. Total incomes will be smaller, but the remaining workers will have higher wages. Or the union may aim for a wage rate below W_2, to give wage gains to as many workers as possible. Typically, a union will not have a single precise goal. Rather, it will grope, estimating and compromising its objectives as it goes, in an uncertain environment. Yet, the likely range of those choices can be shown conceptually, as in Panel I of Figure 10.

Craft unions and professional groups   Unlike industrial unions, craft unions and **professional groups** do not usually have to rely on the threat of strikes and similar actions

323

to achieve their goals. Craft and professional workers—plumbers, doctors, morticians, lawyers, electricians—usually sell their services to a mass of small-scale personal buyers. It would be inefficient to try to negotiate with so many employers. Instead, these service workers try to control labor market conditions by restricting or reducing the number of workers who can enter their fields. Craft unions require apprenticeship training before membership, and then tightly limit the number of apprentice positions. Thus, they effectively control the number of members. Professional groups such as legal and medical organizations often restrict entry into their professions by limiting the number and size of accredited professional schools.

The effect of this scarcity is wage levels that are higher than competitive levels. The excess supply of workers shows up as the number of people who try to get into the *training programs* but cannot. Because fewer people can enter the field, there is no unemployment among those who do succeed in getting in.

Now compare the two approaches to labor market control: supply restrictions and threats of strikes. They have similar results compared to the competitive market: A higher wage rate; fewer workers hired; and other workers who cannot get the job they want. Nor are the two approaches mutually exclusive: A craft union will often both restrict entry and threaten to strike.

Raising demand It is sometimes argued that unions may indirectly increase the demand for members' services, offsetting to some extent the restrictive effects of their actions. If a greater sense of security and participation causes union members to work harder and more efficiently, their marginal product curve—and therefore the demand curve for labor—will shift to the right. For professional groups, strin-

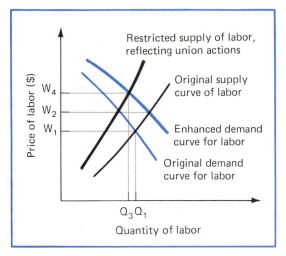

Figure 11   Union actions may raise the demand for labor

Though it restricts supply, the craft union may also take actions that increase the demand for its members' labor. The net effect of this decrease in supply and increase in demand will be higher wages. The effects on the quantity of labor hired are uncertain. Employment will rise if the demand shift dominates and fall if the supply shift dominates. In this example, the supply shift dominates, and the quantity of labor hired decreases slightly from Q_1 to Q_3.

gent quality requirements may increase the public's confidence in the quality of services, thereby increasing the demand for these services.

The shifting out of the demand curve is shown by the "enhanced" demand curve in Figure 11. Both the supply reduction and the demand increase will increase wages above the competitive level. The net effect on the quantity of workers hired will depend on the relative size of the supply and demand shifts. If the supply decrease dominates, the equilibrium quantity of labor will fall below the competitive level. If the increase in demand for labor dominates, the equilibrium quantity may lie above the competitive quantity.

So far, the interferences with competitive labor market outcomes that we have discussed all come from the labor or supply side of the market. The market power, however, may be concentrated on the buyer or employer side of the market. This is discussed in the next few sections.

Monopsony and competitive supply

Monopsony occurs on the demand side of labor markets when there is only one buyer of labor. The key difference between a monopsonist and a competitive buyer of labor is found in the slope of the supply curve that each type of firm faces. Since the monopsonist firm is the only buyer of labor in the particular market, the labor supply curve faced by the firm *is* the industry supply curve. Therefore, the monopsonist faces an *upward-sloping* supply schedule of labor. This upward slope indicates that the monopsonist can hire more workers only if it will pay a higher wage to all workers. *The marginal cost of the labor curve, therefore, lies well above the supply curve for labor.* The gap between the marginal cost of labor curve and the labor supply curve represents the amount by which the wages paid to previously hired workers increases.

The monopsonist follows the same general rule as other profit-maximizing firms: Hire the input up to the point where its marginal revenue product equals its marginal cost. The result of monopsony is that the firm pays each worker an amount *less than the marginal revenue product of the last worker.* The monopsony condition drives a wedge between the wage rate and labor's value to the employer. Not only the wage rate but also the quantity of workers used will be lower than in a competitive situation.

Pure monopsony is unusual. Even a pure *monopolist* seller may not be a *monopsonist* as an employer. Thus, an electric utility may have a monopoly on the provision of electricity to a particular area but be only one among many employers of skilled electricians in the area. On the other hand, a *competitive seller* may have

monopsony power in hiring. For example, a furniture company may have only 3 percent of the national furniture market but still be the one big employer in a small "company town."

More commonly, monopsony power is only moderate, with two or three firms dominating the hiring in a labor market. If the oligopsony power creates extra profits, workers are likely to organize to recapture some of the surplus for themselves. The result is a labor market in which both the supply and demand sides are controlled. This situation is called a **bilateral monopoly.**

Bilateral monopoly

When both the suppliers and buyers of labor have some degree of market power, each side hopes to use that power to reap extra benefits for itself. The result, of course, is a continuing struggle between the two sides for the largest share of the financial pie. The firm wants to pay a *low* wage rate; the union wants to obtain a *high* wage rate. The gap in between is the zone of contention.

Figure 12 illustrates the union-monopsonist battleground. The monopsonist tries to equate MRP and the marginal cost of labor, hiring Q_2 workers. It would like to pay W_2, the absolute minimum wage necessary to obtain Q_2, indicated by Point M on the supply curve for labor. The union, on the other hand, seeks the highest possible wage (W_3) for Q_2 workers, indicated by Point U on the MRP (or demand curve) for labor.

The gap between W_3 and W_2 becomes the battlefield. Each side tries to get a wage as close to its goal as possible, but will settle for nothing less than its minimum condition: W_3 for the firm, and W_2 for the union. Both sides know the range of dispute, with the union demands at the top end of the bargaining range and the company's counteroffers at the bottom. Each

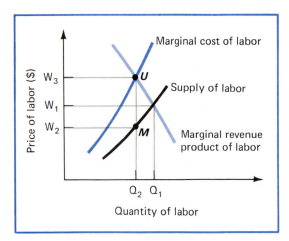

Figure 12   Bilateral monopoly between a union and a monopsonist

The monopsonist wishes to pay the low wage of W_2. The union seeks the higher wage of W_3, knowing that the monopsonist would pay it if it were forced to do so. The actual outcome depends on factors such as bargaining strength and the economic climate.

side also knows the other's strengths and weaknesses. The outcome depends on the relative bargaining power of the two sides, and so the stage is set for industrial strife, with threats, bluffs, and intense bargaining. All of the conditions that give the union its degree of leverage will now come into play. The union may threaten and actually carry out a strike.

The results depend also on the firm's ability to withstand union pressure and apply pressure of its own. The firm's power to make and carry out threats depends on such conditions as the inventories that can be sold during a strike, easy access to other workers who can replace strikers, and the firm's financial resources.

By chance, the outcome could be the same wage rate as a strictly competitive market would have given, such as W_1 in Figure 12. W_1 is close to the middle of the bargaining range set by W_2 and W_3, so that it would result from roughly equal power between union and management sides.

The effects of labor groups on workers' incomes

Many of the unions and professional groups formed during the last century have become powerful, often winning large raises. Yet, the wage increases might have occurred even without union activity.

Have unions raised wages in general significantly above what they might otherwise have been? The difficulty lies in separating out the unions' unique effects from the many other economic changes occurring at the same time.

Research indicates that unions' effects are substantial. During the 1960s, the consensus is that unions raised their members' wages by about 25 percent, compared to wages received by nonunion workers. The more recent detailed patterns shown in Tables 4 and 5 suggest that the effects have continued. Despite some variations, union wages were 19 percent above nonunion wages in 1977 (Table 4). Also, wages rose faster during 1970—1979 in unionized than in nonunionized industries (Table 5).

At the bottom of the job scale, the gains from unionization are marginal at best. These unions tend to be fairly weak because demand for their members is highly elastic, as already noted. In the middle range of the wage scale, unions appear to do best (1) when they are industry-wide, and (2) when they face firms that have monopoly power as sellers. Toward the top of the job scale, some craft unions and professional groups have raised their members' incomes by large amounts: doctors and lawyers are prime examples, along with electricians and plumbers.

On the whole, then, many labor groups have directly raised their members' wages, more so in skilled than in unskilled jobs. But these *direct* effects have also created *indirect* effects that reduce other workers' wages. Throughout this chapter,

Table 4 Comparing wages for union and nonunion workers in major sectors, 1977

Industry	Average Weekly Earnings, Union	Average Weekly Earnings, Nonunion
Mining		
Construction	$296	$339
Manufacturing	343	230
Durable goods	243	234
Nondurable goods	252	250
Transportation, communications, &	227	214
public utilities	293	267
Wholesale trade	255	263
Retail trade	228	175
Services	250	206
Public administration	279	258
All industries	262	221

Source: U.S. Department of Labor, *Earnings and Other Characteristics of Organized Workers, May 1977* (Washington D.C.: U.S. Government Printing Office, 1979), p. 32

you have seen that the wage-raising effects reduce the level of hiring in the industry, so that some workers become unemployed. They then seek work elsewhere, shifting the labor-supply curves down in the other industries that they enter. The result is to reduce wages in *nonunionized* industries.

This indirect reduction of nonunion wages needs to be compared with the direct raising of union members' wages, in judging whether union activity has raised the general level of wages in the economy. The net result depends on the elasticities of supply and demand in the various industries. Shifts clearly do occur, but their relative amounts are still debated.

It is also relevant to consider the amount of work time lost by strikes, to place in perspective the impact of union activities. In most years, strikes actually occur in less than 4 percent of negotiations. Strikes have cost about 30–50 million lost workdays each year during recent decades. This, however, has been a tiny fraction of all working time, never above 1 percent and usually below $\frac{1}{2}$ of 1 percent. About 4 percent of the work force is involved each year in strikes, but most

Table 5 Unionization and wage rises in selected industries, 1970–1979

Industry	Percent Unionized	Percent Wage Increase, 1970–1979
Railroads	99	130
Basic steel	98	150
Major vehicles	98	115
Cigarettes	95	124
Laundries	29	89
Knitting mills	26	83
Clothing stores	11	75
Banks	8	62

strikes last less than two weeks. Moreover, the number of major strikes (those involving 10,000 or more workers) has been declining steadily since 1970, when there were 34 in the United States. In 1978–1981, there were on average only 11 such strikes each year.

Summary

This chapter has explored the functioning of labor markets, examining influences on both the supply of and demand for labor. The key points of the chapter are summarized below.

1. Workers try to maximize the satisfaction gained from their work by balancing the benefits of work (enjoyment and pay) against the cost (dissatisfaction).

2. Even given the differing natures of jobs and individuals, working more hours will, at some point, involve decreasing satisfaction. Therefore, people usually need the incentive of higher pay to put forth more work effort.

3. There are two opposing influences on a labor supply curve: a *price effect* and an *income effect*.

4. To obtain the market supply curve of labor, individual labor supply curves are added horizontally. Since most are on the upward-sloping portion of their supply curve, the market summation of individual curves usually slopes up rather than back.

5. On the demand side of the labor market, firms will hire labor up to the point where the contribution to the value of output of the last worker hired (or marginal revenue product) equal the wage cost.

6. The intersection of the market supply and demand curves for labor will determine the equilibrium wage and quantity of labor hired in a particular market. Therefore, to understand wage differences from one labor market to the next, it is necessary to examine how supply and demand conditions in the various labor markets differ.

7. One important factor in explaining wage differences is the investment in human capital embodied in each worker. Higher amounts of training or investment in human capital are correlated with higher earnings.

8. The scarcer a particular type of labor is, in relation to demand, the higher the wage it will receive. While there is a *natural scarcity* of many talents, *artificial scarcity* may also exist.

9. There are important cases in which labor markets depart from the competitive model. Suppliers of labor can form employees' organizations such as unions to gain some monopoly power. Buyers of labor may have a monopoly on the buying side of the market, or *monopsony*.

10. A labor union's power depends on two key factors: its *control* of the labor supply, and its *leverage* or ability to inflict economic damage on the employer through such actions as strikes.

11. A monopsonist will hire labor up to the point where the marginal cost of an additional worker just equals the marginal revenue product. The result is that wages and the quantity of workers hired are forced below the competitive level.

12. In a bilateral monopoly, both suppliers and buyers of labor have some monopoly power. The result is a

struggle between the two sides for the larger share of the financial pie.

13. The actual effects of labor unions on workers' income is unclear, although some unions have made fairly significant gains for their workers.

Key concepts

Marginal utility
Price effect
Income effect
Blue-collar jobs, white-collar work
Human capital
Unions
Professional groups
Monopsony
Bilateral monopoly

Questions for review

1. Does the principle of comparative advantage apply equally to the selection of part-time jobs and lifetime jobs? Explain.

2. Two doctors graduate from medical school together and set up a joint practice. Over the years, as their real income rises, one doctor works longer and longer hours, while the other doctor takes longer and longer vacations. Using the concept of the labor supply curve, explain why this different behavior might occur.

3. Discuss the impact of each of the following on the demand and/or supply curve for labor.
   a. A firm modifies its assembly-line techniques in a way that makes labor more productive.
   b. A union manages to gain a wage increase for its members.
   c. The cost of capital increases relative to the cost of labor.

4. List three jobs that you consider to be relatively high paying and three that you consider to be relatively low paying. Try to identify some of the factors that would contribute to the wage differentials among these specific occupations.

5. What is meant by the statement that the monopsony condition will result in workers being paid "less than they are worth." Illustrate and explain.

6. Using a diagram, show the bargaining range that might exist in a bilateral monopoly.

7. Define the terms *price effect* and *income effect*. How do they interact to determine the amount of work that a person is willing to do?

8. How do the strategies of industrial unions differ from those of craft unions or professional organizations?

9. What determines the likelihood of a successful strike by an industrial union against a company? What advantages do the union and the employer enjoy against each other?

10. In which of the following types of jobs might a union provide the most gains for its members? Why?
    a. janitors
    b. dentists
    c. electricians
    d. steel workers
    e. carpenters
    f. waiters
    g. apple pickers

11. Which of the following statements are true and which are false? Explain your answers.
    a. Strikes are a major cause of lost work time in the United States's economy.

b. In the late 1970s, wages were higher in non-unionized industries than they were in unionized industries.

c. Between 1970 and 1979, the income of railroad workers, most of whom are unionized, rose faster than the income of bank clerks, most of whom are not unionized.

d. The number of major strikes that occur each year in the United States is on the rise.

e. The effect of strong unions is to raise wages throughout the economy.

f. Skilled labor is in a more advantageous position than unskilled labor when it comes to collective bargaining.

Capital, Investment, and Technological Change

As you read and study this chapter, you will learn:

▶ how firms decide how much capital investment to undertake

▶ what the determinants of the returns to capital are

▶ how the market values capital assets

▶ how innovations occur

To explain capital, we begin with running shoes. A shoe is a piece of capital: long-lasting and a source of improved human efficiency. Almost any shoes will do for a beginner, but a serious runner will usually invest in a more expensive, specialized pair. The higher cost will be justified by the benefits (speed, comfort, pizazz) gained in race after race.

Indeed, runners invest in more than shoes. They buy special shorts, tops, warm-up suits, key holders, complex timing watches, and so on. And as these pieces of capital wear out, they need to be replaced, just like industrial capital. Running equipment may be scant compared to golfers' club sets and motorized carts or to football equipment. Even so, runners' investments exhibit many of the essential features of capital.

This chapter explains the nature of that capital, of the returns to capital, and of investment choices that create capital of all kinds, from running shoes to factories. There are two general forms of capital: *real* or *physical capital,* such as machinery and buildings; and *money* or *portfolio capital,* such as bonds and stock certificates. These two kinds are sharply different in some respects, but they are related, and their quantities are governed by similar kinds of investment choices that compare costs, returns, and risks. Therefore, we offer an integrated coverage of the basic issues, pausing where needed to point out the differences between real and money capital.

In the first main section, we present the nature of real capital and the basic investment choice. Next, in the second main section, we analyze the return to capital, focusing on risk and return. We also contrast interest and profit. Then, in the third main section, we show how the values of assets respond to various influences in markets. We also explain how capital markets direct industrial activity throughout the economy. We conclude by reviewing the main ways in which technological progress alters capital and its productivity, in the fourth main section.

Capital and investment decisions

What is capital?

All physical capital shares several characteristics. First, it is *productive;* it aids labor in production, so that total output is higher than it would be without capital. Second, capital is *made by people.* It is not a natural resource but a product of human effort. Third, capital *lasts over time* rather than being used up immediately. Fourth, capital involves a *present cost* to create the capital goods, but then it delivers a stream of *future values* by improving production.

Therefore, capital results from investment, which creates a set of equipment and other productive facilities. Production is diverted from present consumption

goods to produce capital goods, which then raise the capacity to produce both kinds of goods in the future. **The process occurs over time, with an initial commitment of resources (the investment), followed by a period of higher productivity (the return on the investment) while the capital lasts.**

As always in economics, there is a comparison of cost with benefits. The cost is the sacrifice of present consumption as the capital is produced and installed. The benefit is the increase in the value of production that the capital brings about. For investment in capital to be efficient, the benefits must exceed the costs.

How capital aids production can be seen in several examples. At the simplest, a worker can drive nails and break stones more effectively with a hammer than with a rock or a stick. The hammer may cost a carpenter $10 to buy, but over years of use, it saves labor time and reduces the carpenter's cost by a larger amount. Similarly, a computer that requires $20 million of resources to produce may cut its owner's costs by $10 million per year for many years.

The benefits created by capital reflect the *productivity of capital* in use. They are called the *return to capital.* Returns are necessary if the capital is to be provided in the first place. If the return to capital is too low, then the benefits do not justify the cost incurred in creating it.

Actual capital and investment

The real capital of an economy is a complicated array of productive facilities, from computer chips to bulldozers, printing presses, oil rigs, and office buildings. It comes in nearly infinite varieties and can be seen almost everywhere that production occurs. Besides durable items like machinery, capital includes the inventories of parts and finished products that businesses need to maintain their production.

On the consumer side, too, capital is extensive and familiar. Houses, furniture, appliances, even clothes, are "consumer durable goods," which is one category of capital. Besides these physical forms of real capital, the investment in human skills also creates human capital, which we discussed in the previous chapter.

About one sixth of national output is spent yearly on investment in business capital. Approximately half of the investment replaces worn-out or obsolete capital. The rest is new investment, which adds to the capital stock. Because investment decisions are crucial to future production, we must now analyze them.

The decision to invest

The decision to invest is a commitment to the future.

Whether to invest The firm has first to decide whether to invest at all. The cost is the outlay to acquire and install the capital. The benefits are the future stream of net returns (or profits) gained from selling the goods that are produced by using the capital. Future returns must be discounted for time, to reflect the fact that present dollars are more valuable now than future dollars. Panel I, of Figure 1 illustrates the effect of discounting where the *constant money stream of benefits translates into a decreasing stream of present values of benefits.* The present values are obtained by the formula

$$\text{Present value} = \frac{\text{Future value}}{(1 + r)^T}$$

where r is the interest rate used to discount future values and T is the number of years into the future. The more distant benefits are discounted more heavily, be-

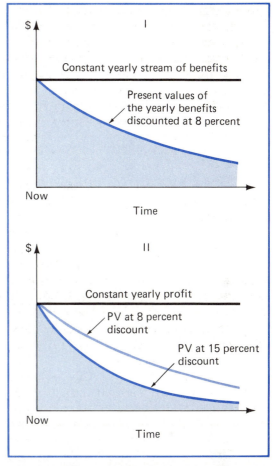

Figure 1   Discounting future payments to present values

In Panel I, discounting for time reduces the present value of a future payment below its nominal value. The effect of discounting increases as the interval increases. The sum of the present values, shown by the shaded area, is the total present value of the entire stream.

In Panel II, a higher rate of discount reduces the present value even further, leaving a smaller shaded area representing present value.

cause the yearly discounting process operates over more years. A $1 million profit expected next year has a present value of $920,000 when discounted at 8 percent; the $1 million expected in the 10th year has a present value of only $463,200; after 15 years only $315,200, and so on. These discounted present values (shown by the shaded area in Panel I) are summed to obtain the total benefits (or profits) from this amount of investment. The total PV from Period 1 forward is:

$$\text{Total present value} = \frac{\text{Profit}_1}{(1 + r)} + \frac{\text{Profit}_2}{(1 + r)^2}$$

$$+ \frac{\text{Profit}_3}{(1 + r)^3} + \cdots + \frac{\text{Profit}_n}{(1 + r)^n}.$$

If the stream continues at a constant level for an indefinite number of periods, then the formula becomes much simpler:

$$\frac{\text{Total}}{\text{present value}} = \frac{\text{Yearly profit}}{\text{Discount rate}} = \frac{\text{Yearly profit}}{r}.$$

Thus, a $1 million yearly stream discounted at an 8 percent rate has a total present value of $12.5 million. A higher discount rate gives a lower present value; for example, if r is 15 percent, then PV is $6.7 million. In Panel II, of Figure 1, the higher discount rate leaves a smaller shaded area.

This calculation of total PV is called *capitalizing the value of future benefits.* It will be used often in this chapter.

As for the firm's choice, the expected total PV must be at least as great as the cost of the investment, or else the investment will not be worth undertaking.

How much to invest Where investment returns are high enough to warrant some level of investment, the firm must decide *how much to invest.* The firm compares the cost and benefits of alternative amounts of investment. It arrays its investment projects from the most profitable to the least profitable. The task is to select the optimal level of investment, which is the level that will *maximize the firm's profits in the long run.* The array is based on the *rates of return* expected from the investment levels, as in Figure 2. The rate of return for each project is the interest rate *that will just*

equate the capitalized value of an investment's future profits with the investment's initial cost. It is called the *internal rate of return* of the investment project. For example, a $10 million investment might generate $3 million yearly in profits for an unlimited number of years. By the simple equation

$$\text{Investment cost} = \frac{\text{Yearly profit}}{\text{Rate of return } (r)}$$

we have

$$\frac{\text{Investment}}{\text{cost}} = \$10 \text{ million} = \frac{\$3 \text{ million}}{r}.$$

Transposing the $10 million and r terms, we get

$$r = \frac{\$3 \text{ million}}{\$10 \text{ million}} = 30 \text{ percent.}$$

The project, therefore, has a rate of return of 30 percent. At an interest rate of 30 percent, it will just break even. For comparison, suppose that a $13.8 million investment yields a yearly profit of $3.78 million. Its internal rate of return is ($3.73) ÷ ($13.8 million) = 27 percent. If the profit stream is for a finite period, the calculation is only a bit more complicated.

The firm ranks its possible investment projects according to the rates of return they offer, starting with the highest, as in Figure 2. What the projects accomplish often varies widely, but the investment decisions all reduce to the same basic financial terms: their dollar amounts and their rates of return. Thus, the best project requires $15 million and has a 23 percent rate of return; the second best also costs $15 million, and has a 20 percent rate of return; and so on.

Together these projects comprise an investment opportunities schedule, showing the *marginal returns on investment* (MRI). The marginal return on investment is the rate of return provided by the incremental dollar of investment; here it is ap-

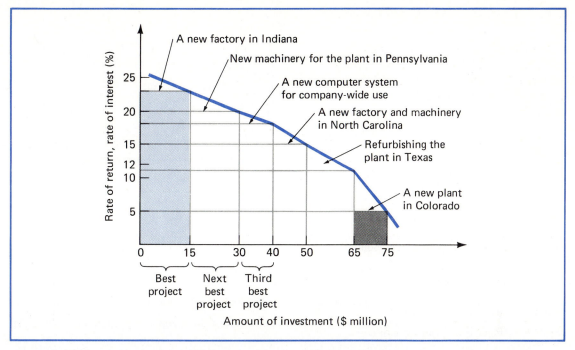

Figure 2   The productivity of capital, shown by the returns on investment projects for a typical large firm
The firm's possible investment projects are arranged in descending order of yields, starting with the best one at the left. The range of possible yields is typical of many firms' actual prospects.

proximately shown by the return to the marginal project. Thus, the firm's marginal rate of return on investment in the $50–$65 million range, where the Texas project is on the margin, is 11 percent.

For simplicity, the MRI curve is usually drawn as a smooth curve, as in Figure 3. Smooth or not, the curve shows the marginal returns available to the firm at various investment levels. Knowing this curve of possible *benefits* from investment, the firm has half of the information it needs to select the **profit-maximizing level of investment.** The other half is the *costs* of investment.

The cost of capital   *The cost of real investment is the opportunity or market cost of the funds that are committed to the investment.* By spending its funds on capital, the firm forgoes the returns that could be obtained on the money in other ways during the life of the investment. These alternative re-

turns may be measured by the rate of interest paid in financial markets, if financial investment is the most profitable alternative to real investment. The firm in Figure 3 could have put the funds into interest-bearing bonds rather than into real capital. The cost of capital is, therefore, the forgone rate of interest. To get the benefits of the investment projects, the firm must incur the economic cost of not earning interest on the funds. If it does not have funds, it must raise them on the market and pay the market rate of interest.

This **cost of capital** (CC)* in the simplest case, then, is the market interest rate. Figure 3 illustrates a 12 percent rate: All investment by the firm will cost it 12 percent a year. Because the cost of capital is

---

*The "cost of capital" here is the cost of the funds used to purchase capital goods, not the price levels of the capital goods themselves (such as $150,000 for a machine).

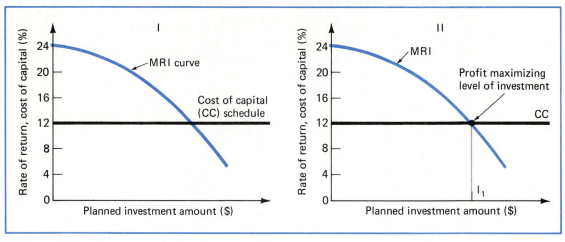

Figure 3　The returns and costs of investment

In Panel I, the marginal returns to investment curve is down-sloping, while the cost of capital is shown as constant rate of interest.

　　In Panel II, the profit-maximizing level of investment is at I_1, where the marginal returns to investment just equal the marginal cost of investment.

constant in this case, both the average and marginal cost of capital are equal at all investment levels.

Profit-maximizing investment A firm that has all the needed information can perform the basic benefit-cost comparison at the margin. All projects whose rates of return exceed the cost of capital will be carried out, for they add net profits. Projects whose returns are below the cost of capital will be avoided. *Therefore, investment will be set at the level where the marginal return equals the marginal cost of capital.* That is level I_1 in Panel II of Figure 3, where MRI cuts the CC curve. At that level, the internal rate of return at the margin (which equates the capitalized value of future profits with the investment's initial cost) equals the market rate of interest. The firm's profitability on the marginal investment is equated to the general cost of capital as measured by the market interest rate. The firm thereby avoids investing too little or too much.

　　Changes in the returns or the cost of capital will usually alter the firm's profit-

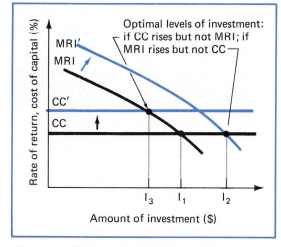

Figure 4　Effects of shifts in investment returns and costs

If the cost of capital rises, CC will shift up, causing the optimal investment level to fall to I_3. But if the returns to investment rise while the cost of capital stays unchanged, investment will rise to I_2.

maximizing level of investment. A rise in the MRI schedule will increase the level of investment whose returns exceed their cost, such as to I_2 in Figure 4. A rise might occur if the market's growth unexpectedly increases or if the firm develops new innovations. As for CC, a rise in the market interest rate will raise CC and shift down the margin of profitable investment. In Figure 4, a rise of r to 15 percent reduces the profit-maximizing level of investment to I_3.

In general, firms' investment opportunities and the cost of capital interact in this way to set investment levels in markets throughout the economy. A deterioration of investment prospects (shifting MRI curves down) reduces investment; an improvement in prospective returns raises investment. A rise in r induces firms to invest less; a fall in r evokes increased investment.

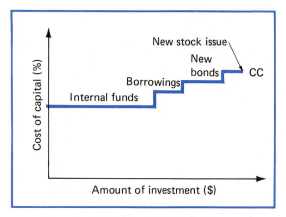

Figure 5   The firm's cost of capital curve may slope up

The firm arrays its sources of capital in order of increasing cost. Internal funds from retained earnings are cheapest, followed by borrowings and bonds, and then new stock issues.

Market demand and supply for capital

Demand   *Each firm's MRI curve is its demand curve for capital.* MRI expresses the benefits of investment to the firm. Individual demand curves can be summed horizontally to obtain market demand curves for capital, providing the prospective returns to any one firm appear to it to be independent of the investment undertaken by others.

Supply   The supply of investment funds to the firm is embodied in its CC curve. The simplest case is a horizontal line at the going interest rate.

But the supply of capital to the individual firm may be upward-sloping rather than horizontal. A firm has two sources of funds. One is *internal funds,* which arise when the firm reinvests its own profits. Such funds may superficially appear to be costless to the firm, but they have an opportunity cost equal to the rate of interest that could have been obtained by investing the funds outside the firm. *External funds,* obtained from lenders and investors outside the firm, have an explicit price. The cost of external funds is, therefore, the di-

rect interest and dividend payments that must be made to bondholders and stockholders to acquire their funds.

External funds customarily have a rising marginal cost. The two kinds of external funds are *debt* and *equity.* Debt involves interest payments for loans and bonds. Interest payments are recorded as business costs and are tax deductible. Equity capital involves common stock that is paid dividends. Because dividends are paid out of profits, they are not a cost and are not tax deductible. The cost of equity capital is thus higher than the cost of debt.

In obtaining funds, the firm arrays its sources from the cheapest to the costliest, as in Figure 5. Usually it must pay lenders or investors at higher incremental rates to obtain more funds, partly because of **risk.** Therefore, the CC schedule slopes up, as illustrated. The slope and position may differ among firms, but the same basic analysis applies to them all.

To simplify matters, the firm's CC schedule can be drawn as a smooth curve, as in Figure 6. This curve crosses the MRI schedule and determines the profit-maxi-

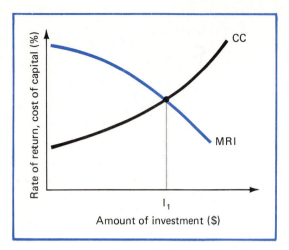

Figure 6   The profit-maximizing investment choice

When CC slopes up, the optimal investment choice still follows the same logic, with the outcome here at I_1.

mizing level of investment at I_1. The underlying logic of the choice is the same whether CC is up-sloping or horizontal.

The supply of funds to an individual *firm* varies according to how much funding it can generate internally and the terms on which it can arrange debt and equity financing on the market. For any given *industry*, the supply curve is similarly composed of an internally generated portion and a higher-cost portion representing outside financing. For a given firm or industry in sound financial health, the cost of equity or debt financing may, over a wide range, be independent of the amount of funds raised. But the supply of capital to the *economy as a whole* is obviously not independent of the amount raised, since savers cannot supply limitless amounts of new funds at the going rate of interest. The supply of funds as a whole is a complex matter, dependent on the level of national income and the elasticity of saving to changes in the rate of return. The MRI for the entire economy is also complex, since the return to investment in any one industry depends on overall prosperity, which,

in turn, is linked to the rate of investment in other industries. The determination of total investment is one of the central concerns of macroeconomics, the study of the economy as a whole.

The return to capital

When we examine the return to capital more thoroughly, we find that it contains several distinct economic elements: (1) *the pure interest rate on invested capital*, which would be earned if investment had no risk; (2) a *risk premium*, which is an additional return required to reward investors for risky investment; and (3) any remainder, which is *economic profit*.

Because risk is a key concept, we discuss it next. Then we consider interest and profit separately.

Risk and return

When funds are invested, the owner bears some risk about the outcome. Since risk is normally viewed as a hazard, investors must be rewarded with extra returns to bear the unpleasantness. There is, accordingly, a **risk-return relationship,** which is a basic feature of investment decisions. To analyze it, we must first define risk.

Risk   Taking risks means accepting a probability that things will turn out badly. Life is permeated with risks, whether you are crossing a busy street or choosing a career. Some risks are voluntary, such as in skydiving. Others are unavoidable. For example, you must choose *some* occupation, and any such choice incurs risks.

For firms and investors, risk is financial: the probability of losing the value of the investment. Investment decisions involve committing funds to make profits. But the profits are not guaranteed. There are varying degrees of risk that the outcome will be worse than expected.

Risk is a matter of *probability* of loss. It is often expressed in percentage terms that reflect the odds. Thus, a project's probability of failure may be 1 percent (one in a hundred), which may be regarded as a low degree of risk. A higher percentage, such as a 10 percent or 50 percent likelihood of loss, would indicate a higher degree of risk. The familiar betting odds can be stated as probability values; "even odds" means 50 percent risk; 10 to 1 odds against a loss means a 9 percent risk.

Financial risks are also of both kinds, voluntary and involuntary. *Voluntary financial risk* is undertaken when a firm or investor selects a high-risk investment instead of a low-risk alternative. *Involuntary risk* is faced by every firm with funds to invest: *Some* choice must be made, and all alternatives involve some risk, however small. The risk may be of *commission,* as when a risky investment collapses, causing the capital to lose its value. Or the risk may be of *omission,* as when the firm mistakenly misses a chance to make a large gain.

For example, a firm with $60 million to invest may choose the "riskless" alternative of putting the funds in government bonds, whose money value will stay constant. But this may mean passing up other investments that, though they carry a slight risk of loss, offer some chance of a $30 million capital gain. Therefore, the seeming "riskless" choice (the bonds) actually bears a risk of sacrificing the $30 million in capital gain.

The simple analysis of risk focuses on the risk of loss, as a matter of probability. The future outcomes are dispersed around their most likely values, in what is called a *probability distribution.* For example, the two investments in Figure 7 may be most likely to return a $3 million profit each year if one could make only one best estimate for each one. But the possible outcomes can be much higher or lower.

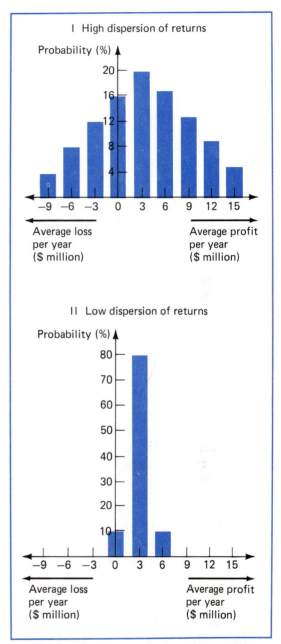

Figure 7 Dispersions of likely profits from two differing investments

The probability of each profit or loss level is the percentage likelihood that it will occur. Thus, in Panel I, a $3 million loss is expected to occur 12 percent of the time. In Panel II, a $3 million profit is 80 percent likely.

The dispersion of expected results is much wider in Panel I than in Panel II, even though the average expected value ($3 million) is identical in both.

In Panel I of Figure 7, the likelihood of an actual loss is the sum of probabilities of incurring a $3 million, $6 million, or $9 million loss—which is, respectively, 12 percent plus 8 percent plus 4 percent (the shaded bars), which equals 24 percent in total. By comparison, another project might also have a $3 million yearly profit, according to the best estimate, but with much less dispersion in its probability distribution, as in Panel II. Here there is no probability of an actual loss. Therefore, the risk exposure is much less in this project than in the first.

One definition of *risk is the share of the probability distribution that falls in the range of financial losses.* For any given level of expected profits (such as the value of $3 million in both panels of Figure 7), a wider dispersion will result in a larger probability of loss because the shaded portion that falls in the loss range will be larger. Therefore, *risk is commonly associated with the degree of variation in returns around their average expected value.*

The risk-return relationship   Because risk is unpleasant, people usually will accept it only if they expect compensating rewards. For example, steeplejacks and oil-drilling workers usually get higher pay than people who have safe jobs. Similarly, in investment choices, the reward for risk bearing is a higher-than-average level of expected return.

Consequently, economists and financial analysts apply the concept of a *risk-return relationship: Investments with higher risks must offer higher average returns.* Most investors are *risk averse*—they dislike risk and must be compensated for bearing it. Only the prospect of an unusually high reward will induce them to accept danger. Exceptions can be found, of course, but they *are* exceptions.

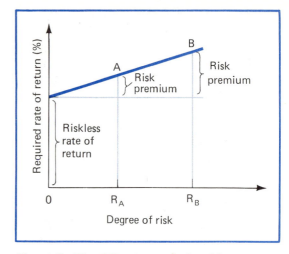

Figure 8   The risk-return relationship
As risk rises, investors require a risk premium in compensation. The riskless rate of return is expected to be earned, on average, by all investments. The total rate of return includes both the riskless rate of return and the risk premium.

Accordingly, there is usually a positive relationship between risk and expected returns. In Figure 8, risk is on the horizontal axis, from zero to high degrees of risk. The required rate of return is on the vertical axis. As risk increases, so does the rate of return that the investor will require.

At zero risk, the required rate of return will be 10 percent, as shown. That rate of return would be available without appreciable risk by investors on short-term U.S. government securities. At higher risk levels, higher rates of return are required. The difference between these rates of return and the **riskless rate of return** is the *risk premium:* the reward for bearing risk. In Figure 8, a risk level of R_A involves a specific risk premium, as shown; the higher risk level of R_B requires a risk premium twice as large. These premiums reflect the general preferences of investors between risk and returns, as expressed by their actions in financial markets.

Alternative outcomes along the risk-return relationship are equivalent to one another for the average investor. At each point, the risk premium offsets the disadvantage of the risk. Therefore, the riskless return is as attractive to the average investor as Point A with R_A risk or Point B with R_B risk.

Of course, *individual* investors and firms may have differing risk-return preferences. Some dislike risk intensely; others are only mildly averse to it. Extremely risk averse investors will tend to choose lower-risk investments, toward the left, unless they are compensated by very high returns. Those more willing to accept risk will make choices more toward the right, without demanding a big risk premium.

Regardless of these variations, the basic risk-return relationship is a central part of investment decision making, both for firms and for investors.

Risk-return patterns can be observed in actual financial markets. Risk itself is difficult to measure, because it deals with future probabilities. Those are inherently unknowable with precision, as are all future conditions. One measure of risk is to be found in the ratings of bond quality that are made by the two major investment analysis companies, Moody's Investors Service and Standard & Poor's Corporation (S&P). The ratings reflect the estimated probability of default on the bonds, which would reduce or eliminate their value. In making the ratings, the two firms assess many features of the companies and governments that issue bonds: their stability, prospects, profitability, and other conditions. They then assign the bonds a rating ranging from "high quality" to "speculative," as follows:

The ratings reflect judgments, not mechanical formulas. They are widely accepted as useful practical indexes of risk.

They also directly affect the interest rates that must be paid. A B-grade bond will have to offer a rate of interest higher than the rate on an Aaa bond, precisely because the B bond carries more risk of loss. U. S. government long-term bonds have the lowest yields because they have the lowest risk.

Diversifying One way to reduce risk is to choose a single low-risk investment, such as a U.S. government or Aaa bond. Another way is to *diversify*, by choosing several investments that, though they individually have risk, will tend as a group to offer stability. Known colloquially as "not putting all your eggs in one basket," diversifying deserves explanation.

The fundamental principle is the *law of large numbers*: The larger the sample drawn from a random distribution of possible outcomes, the more likely it is that the sample's average value will equal the total distribution's average value. In short, there is safety in numbers. *The yield on a diversified selection of investments will tend to be close to the average yield of all assets in the market.* It will be higher than the yield on a single risk-free investment.

With the risk-return relationship clarified, we now turn to the analysis of interest and profit.

Interest

Interest is a contractual payment to compensate lenders for the use of borrowed

	High Quality		Investment Grade		Substandard		Speculative
Moody's	Aaa	Aa	A	Baa	Ba	B	Caa to D
S&P	AAA	AA	A	BBB	BB	B	CCC to D

capital. The borrower obtains the funds either as *loans* from specific lenders (such as banks) or by selling *bonds* to the market. The borrower pledges to pay a fixed amount of interest per year to the lender (or bondholder). Calculated as a percent of the loan (or bond's) initial value, the money payment is the rate of interest.

For example, a firm may borrow $30 million either by taking a loan from a bank or by selling $30 million worth of bonds. If the rate of interest is 10 percent, the firm will have to pay $3 million in interest each year besides having to pay off the $30 million borrowed. Any failure to pay that $3 million will place the firm in legal default and perhaps ultimately in bankruptcy.

The interest rate that a firm pays reflects the going rates of interest in financial markets as a whole. Those rates, in turn, reflect the productivity of real capital, the pattern of consumer and business saving, the government deficit, the state of the business cycle, and a host of other macroeconomic variables.

Variations among the rates that different firms must contract to pay should be interpreted as risk adjustments. The risk-free rate of return is pure interest. Any excess beyond this is compensation for the likelihood of default.

Profit

The total return to the owners of a firm—sole proprietors, partners, or corporate stockholders—is all called profit. As noted, profit has three components: (1) a pure or riskless rate of return, (2) a risk premium, and (3) economic profit (the remainder).

The first two components of profit (riskless return and risk premium) are similar to the components of interest paid on loaned capital. They *must* be paid if investors are to supply equity capital. Thus, a firm might have $178 million in net in-

come after taxes, but the riskless and risk components account for $82 million of it. The remaining element—economic profit—would be $96 million. Economic profit is large when the firm is successful, but low or negative when the firm is in difficulty.

Economic profit can be subdivided into two further components of its own. First, it is *a return on entrepreneurship and innovation* by the firm's managers. Creative policies develop new products and put the firm into new lines. For such excellence, part of economic profit is an appropriate reward.

Second, the firm may hold *monopoly power*, and *part of the profit may be a payment for that advantage.* The size of that element will depend on the firm's degree of monopoly power. For example, Firms A and B have identical profit rates of 25 percent on equity capital. Yet, Firm A is highly risky and has no monopoly power, while Firm B has little risk, strong entrepreneurship, and much monopoly power. Actual cases offer endless variations.

Total profits are available for the shareholders' benefit. Part of profits is usually paid out to shareholders as *dividends;* in recent years, the dividend pay-out ratio has averaged between 30 and 50 percent. The rest of profits are *retained earnings*, which are reinvested in the firm. They enlarge the firm's capacity to produce, increasing its earning power. Therefore, retained earnings usually increase the value of the stock, by making it more likely that its price will rise and provide a capital gain when it is sold. In contrast, dividends provide direct money benefits to shareholders.

Total corporate profits have a long-term growth trend, but fluctuate with the business cycle. Their pattern in recent years is shown in Figure 9. The share of profits paid out in dividends declined dur-

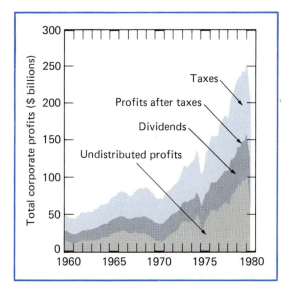

Figure 9   The trend of total corporate profits

Profits have grown as the total value of production has risen. The share of profits paid out in dividends has declined, while the share of undistributed profits (retained earnings) has risen.

Source: Federal Reserve Board, *Historical Chart Book.*

ing the 1970s from about 50 percent to about 30 percent.

The value of assets

There are well-developed markets for all kinds of physical and portfolio capital. Each item of capital commands a value or price in the market. That value can change, as economic forces alter the equilibrium price. Both physical and portfolio capital can undergo price changes. No matter how solid a factory may be or a gilt-edged bond certificate may look, its market value can rise or fall, perhaps sharply.

We now show how economic processes determine those **asset values.** The processes are driven by **expectations** and apply both to real and to paper assets. They

enable the stock market to function as a system of control that limits the actions of all corporations in the economy.

But first we show how sharply asset values do, in fact, fluctuate. We focus on stocks and bonds, but pay some attention also to real assets.

Fluctuations in asset values

Stocks are the most widely known fluctuating asset. Each corporation issues stock, which is then bought and sold by private investors in stock markets. The price of each company's stock at each moment reflects the supply and demand for that stock. They, in turn, reflect (1) the company's specific conditions (its profits, future growth, etc.), and (2) general shifts in the whole stock market (when the whole market is rising or falling, all stocks are affected).

Over 1 million corporations' stocks are traded, but the largest several thousand firms are the main focus of the major stock exchanges, as noted in the box on page 344. Several stock market averages have been developed to measure stock price swings: Figure 10 shows two of them. The "Dow Jones Industrial Average" covers just 30 leading firms, while the NYSE Composite Index is broader, covering all 1,900 stocks traded on the New York Stock Exchange. These indexes can be followed virtually minute by minute each weekday, as they respond to market changes.

The fluctuations are substantial. Between January 1973 and September 1974, the NYSE average fell from 63 to 36, a drop of 43 percent. It then rose by even more; between late 1974 and late 1979, it more than doubled (the 30 firms in the Dow Jones average did not rise as much). Then the NYSE index fell again by 22 percent between November 1980 and March 1982.

The Main Parts of the Stock Market

Decisions to sell or buy stock are made by millions of investors. Most transactions are carried out through stockbrokers, acting in one of these major stock markets:

but only 200,000 or so hold $1 million worth or more each. Most of the remaining investors hold less than $5,000 worth of stock apiece. These are the "small" investors. "Institutional" inves-

Stock Exchange	Number of Companies Included	Main Types of Firms Included	Volume of Shares Traded on an Average Day
New York Stock Exchange (New York)	1,900	Largest and next largest firms, banks, utilities, etc.	50,000,000
American Stock Exchange (New York)	800	Large and middle-sized firms in all sectors	5,000,000
"Over the counter" market	3,500	Small firms; new and risky firms	27,000,000

The price of each transaction is publicly noted. Any broker can obtain it almost instantly. The stock prices and trading volume for about the leading 3,000 companies are published the next day in the *Wall Street Journal;* other papers focus on the larger firms.

About 20 million people own stocks,

tors (large private holders, insurance companies, pension funds, bank trust departments, etc.) now make over 70 percent of all stock transactions. These professional investors' operations also vary in size. Perhaps the largest 300 of them make over one half of all stock-market transactions.

Many *individual* stock prices moved much more sharply, however. Four examples are given in the two panels of Figure 11: Sears and Polaroid dropped by 70 percent or more, while Time Inc. dropped by 60 percent and then quadrupled, and Holiday Inns rode an even steeper roller coaster. Many more such cases can be found in standard stock market reference sources.

A swing in the stock market can change asset values by hundreds of billions

of dollars. Thus, the total value of all corporate stocks fell by several hundred billion dollars during January 1973–September 1974, then rose by about $600 billion during 1974–1979, and dropped $200 billion during 1980–1982. These changes have a very large impact on the wealth of over 20 million stock owners.

Bonds also fluctuate in value. Because bonds provide fixed interest payments, they have long been regarded as having stable asset values. Yet, sharp changes in

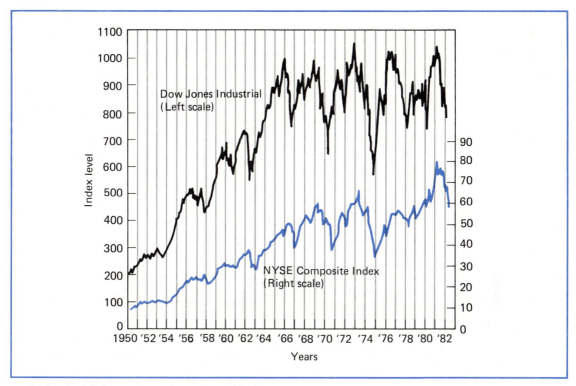

Figure 10   Movements in two stock market averages
The Dow Jones Industrial Average covers 30 leading industrial firms, while the NYSE Composite Index includes all stocks traded on the New York Stock Exchange. Their movements are largely parallel, but there was some divergence during 1979–1982. Both indexes indicate the sharp fluctuations that occur.

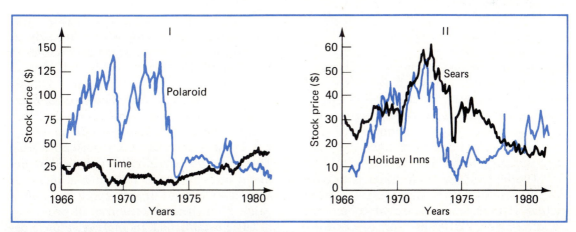

Figure 11   Selected stocks, showing sharp changes
These four stocks have shown sharp price changes since 1965. Values have changed by as much as a multiple of 5, often in short periods. The changes reflect conditions internal to the firms, as well as various industry-wide factors *and* changes in stock markets as a whole.

bond values have occurred since 1965 (for reasons that will be explained shortly). The prices of many bonds fell by over 40 percent during 1977–1982.

Real assets (for example, machinery, office buildings, houses, oil tankers) also fluctuate in value. Office buildings provide a good illustration. The demand for office space can increase sharply. Because the supply is fixed in the short run, such booms raise the rents and prices of existing buildings. New construction then occurs, sending rents and building prices down again. The physical characteristics of existing buildings do not change, but their prices do.

The forces causing such large changes in values are strong and pervasive. Superficially, one can cite shifts in demand and supply as the causes. But what causes those shifts? The answer is a single crucial phenomenon: expectations.

Expectations govern asset values

Expectations about future returns and interest rates are the main determinants of asset values. They are forward looking and reflect human judgment about the probabilities of future events. The market values of assets differ from accounting values, which are based on past expenditures.

Expectations affect prices through the process of investment choice. Each asset (real or portfolio) offers a flow of expected benefits. These benefits are capitalized, by discounting them for time. If risk is high, a risk premium is also appropriate, and the future values are discounted not only for time but also for risk.

The logic of asset valuation is universal: It applies both to physical capital (which is used to produce real goods that may be sold at a profit) and to portfolio capital (which is held to receive interest or dividend payments and possible capital gains).

In the simplest case, the future benefits are a constant stream continuing for an indefinite period. Then the simple formula for capitalizing the stream to a present value can be applied. The discounting rate is the going rate of interest for assets with the given degree of risk. To illustrate, consider again the asset providing a $3 million yearly profit flow, at a time when the market rate of interest on assets bearing that degree of risk is 10 percent. The present value (PV) is

$$PV = \frac{Yearly\,profit}{Interest\,rate} = \frac{\$3\,million}{10\,percent} = \$30\,million.$$

Because 10 percent is the opportunity cost of the capital, this investment must pay a rate of return at least as high. Therefore, the market rate of interest sets the "required rate of return" on the asset. And that, in turn, sets PV, as you can see.

The present value is, in fact, what the asset is now worth. The value will change if either element in the ratio changes. A rise in expected profit levels will raise the asset's value proportionally. For example, if expected profits jump to $4 million yearly for any reason, the asset's value will rise to $40 million (which is $4 million ÷ 10 percent).

Interest rate changes will also affect the asset's value. Suppose profits stay at $3 million, but the interest rate doubles to 20 percent. The asset's value will sink to $15 million (which is $3 million ÷ 20 percent). If the interest rate then falls to 5 percent, the asset's value will *rise* to $60 million (which is $3 million ÷ 5 percent).

These asset values are not capricious. They are the equilibrium values that demand and supply in capital markets will actually yield. At its creation, an asset's value is governed by the cost of providing it. Once established, its market value is dependent on expected returns and interest rates. Fluctuations in asset values can be very sharp, not only in stocks but also in bonds, productive capital, and other assets (gold, paintings, cattle, houses, etc.). Sufficiently unfavorable changes can reduce an asset's value to zero, even though its physical and legal characteristics are unchanged.

Bonds and stocks

Now consider bonds and stocks specifically in more detail. *Bonds* offer two kinds of future yields: a stream of *interest payments* plus a possible capital gain (or loss) in selling the bond.

For simplicity, we consider only very long term bonds, which will be redeemed in 25 or more years. That interval is so long that the current prices are virtually unaffected by the future redemption value. Such bonds are free to fluctuate widely in price.

They do fluctuate. The recent rises in interest rates have driven bond prices sharply down. In a typical case, a $10,000, 40-year bond was issued in 1965, paying $550 per year (5.5 percent interest at the start). The rise in the interest rate to 11.5 percent has caused the bond's price to fall to $4,800, with an effective interest yield of the same 11.5 percent (which is approximated by $550 ÷ $4,800). Thousands of other bonds' prices have moved similarly. Of course, if the bond is bought now at $4,800 and held while interest rates fall to their 1965 levels, then it could be sold for $10,000 and provide a capital gain of 108 percent (which is [$10,000 − $4,800] ÷ $4,800).

Stocks are slightly more complicated to analyze because their dividends are subject to change. The most common expectation is that a firm's dividends will grow as the firm's sales and profits grow. The expected future dividends are estimated by beginning with the recent year's dividend payments and then factoring in a growth factor, which can be labeled *g*.

To illustrate, suppose that AT&T's recent dividend is $6.00 per year, and that this dividend is expected to grow at 5 percent per year. The expected AT&T dividend in any future year (designated as Year *T*) is then the original dividend plus a factor for 5 percent growth during the interval from now to Year *T*. For example, the expected dividend next year (when *T* is 1) is $6.00 $(1 + g)$ = $6.00 (1.05) = $6.30. The cumulative growth in the dividend level by the fifth year will be

$$\begin{aligned}
\text{Expected dividend in Year 5} &= \$6.00\,(1 + g)^T \\
&= \$6.00\,(1 + g)^5 \\
&= \$6.00\,(1.05)^5 \\
&= \$6.00\,(1.2763) \\
&= \$7.66.
\end{aligned}$$

Suppose that the growth factor *g* is constant: The firm's future growth in profitability and dividends is expected to continue steadily. Then *g* can be included in the simple present-value formula as follows:*

$$\begin{aligned}
\frac{\text{Present value}}{\text{of the stock}} &= \frac{\text{Current dividend}}{\text{Interest rate} - \text{Growth factor}} \\
&= \frac{D}{r - g}.
\end{aligned}$$

The greater the expected rate of dividend growth (g), the greater will be the stock's value (for any given levels of D and r). That is logical because a stock is simply the right to the stream of dividends; more dividends means that the stock is more valuable.

In the example, if the interest rate is 15 percent, then the present market value of AT&T stock would be

$$PV = \frac{\$6.00}{.15 - .05} = \frac{\$6.00}{.10} = \$60.$$

---

*The proof for this role for the *g* factor can be found in standard texts on managerial finance.

Sometimes the current *dividend yield* on a stock (dividends as a percent of the stock's current price) is below the market rate of interest. In the above illustration, the current $6.00 dividend pays only 10 percent on the current $60 value of AT&T stock, while the interest rate is 15 percent. But that simple comparison neglects the growth factor. Because dividends are expected to rise, the current yield is below the expected total rate of return. The rise in dividends will cause the share's price itself to rise by 5 percent yearly over time, so that it can be sold for a capital gain. The stockholder's total return, therefore, includes *both a dividend yield based on* r *and a capital gains yield based on* g.

The choice process equalizes returns

The process of investor choice will bring returns on stocks into line with those on bonds. This is known as the **equalization of returns.** *The process tends to equalize rates of return throughout the capital markets (portfolio and physical).* If equilibrium is reached, all investments of equivalent risk offer equivalent returns. And among investments of differing degrees of risk, all rates of return will differ just enough to provide compensating risk premiums.

Three levels of knowledge

The equalizing process does not, of course, operate with steel-trap finality. Markets are often out of equilibrium. Thus, there are many opportunities to make unusually high (or low) returns. But to make high returns one must have superior knowledge on three levels:

1. *Real conditions:* within firms (new products, planned growth, etc.) and financial markets.
2. *Financial effects:* expectations about how the firms' financial performance (profits, dividends, rates of return, etc.) will be affected by the real conditions.
3. *Timing:* how far *other* investors have already acted. It is crucial to act *before* others do; otherwise the potential gains are all discounted away in advance. Timing is crucial.

Therefore, it is not only *what* you know but *when* you know it that matters. You must not only know the firm and its financial prospects. You must also outguess the rest of the market by acting before other investors have reaped the possible gains.

For example, suppose that the Eastman Kodak Company develops a new type of camera and film, which will probably raise its growth rate of profits and dividends from 5 to 10 percent per year. An investor needs to know that real and financial information, but the third category can be even more important. Specialists working for large investors will learn of Kodak's plans almost as soon as they are made. By buying Kodak stock immediately, they can drive up the price many months before the actual innovation occurs and becomes well known.

Other investors, especially small investors, will tend to act too late. Indeed, the Wall Street adage is "Sell on good news" because the stock's price has probably been driven up *above* its new equilibrium level by the time any good news about a company reaches the newspapers.

Stock markets as a control system

By performing well, a firm's managers create growth in profits, which usually leads to rising stock prices. Investors, acting on expectations, bid up stock prices when firms' prospects improve or bid them down when prospects worsen. Their assessments of the future cause stock prices to change *now*.

The stock price is, in fact, a crucial index of the firm's expected performance, for three reasons. First, it reflects the firm's whole performance as a profit maximizer, as judged by skilled financial investors. Second, it looks ahead to discount future prospects into an immediate present value; there is little or no delay in applying the appraisal to present money values. Third, the stock price is of great practical concern to the firm's managers. They wish to keep investors satisfied by performing well, so that the stock's price rises and will provide capital gains to the firm's shareholders. If managers' performance levels suddenly drop, the lowered expectations will cause the stock's price to fall and thereby cut the value of the owners' investment. That stirs stockholder discontent and may ultimately jeopardize the managers' jobs. In the extreme, if stock prices fall too far relative to the value of physical assets, the firm will be bought up by outsiders and either reorganized or merged into another firm.

For these reasons, the stock market limits managers' performance. It pressures them to eliminate inefficiency, forcing costs down to the minimum possible levels on the average cost curves. It keeps them from resting on their laurels, for the market discounts results ahead of time, based on expectations about future achievements.

To the extent that it is rapid, informed, and powerful, the stock market is a system of control. Nearly all significant firms in the United States are under this baleful eye. Even if the firm issues no more new shares, the trading of existing shares maintains the pressure.

Stock markets also supply funds to businesses for investment. That role is important, but it has been shrinking since 1960, as firms have relied increasingly on internal funds and bonds rather than new stock issues. But even if stock markets provided no new funds at all, they would still exercise their control function over corporate managers throughout the economy.

Capital and technological change

The use of physical capital is closely related to technology. The current technology is embodied in the forms of capital itself. As technology changes, new forms of capital are produced and installed, replacing the old. The new possibilities for raising productivity are put into practice by investment decisions. The resulting changes in the productivity of capital have caused much of the economic progress in modern economies in the last two centuries, and in the future, they may be the only escape from increasing resource scarcities.

Trends of capital and productivity

The growth of total national output occurs partly because of simple growth in the labor and capital inputs, but it largely depends on *the progress of knowledge and skills that make both capital and labor more productive.*

Total output can grow more rapidly than the growth in inputs. To illustrate, if inputs grow at 1 percent per year while output grows at 3 percent, then **total factor productivity** (TFP) rises at 2 percent per year; the inputs have become 2 percent more productive each year.

In fact, TFP has probably risen at just under 2 percent annually during the last century. Though 2 percent yearly may not seem to be a high rate of gain, it cumulates over decades into very large increases. For example, 2 percent growth raises $1,000 in 100 years to $7,236. And 3 percent would raise the final total to $19,184! Even a small rise in technological progress can eventually provide a large yield.

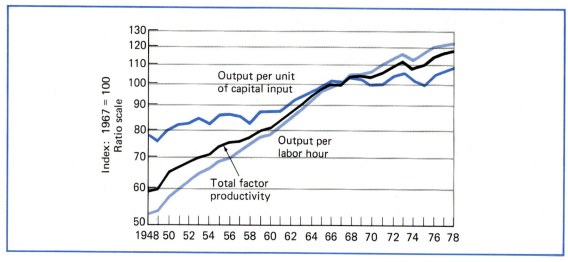

Figure 12 Productivity in the private domestic business economy 1948–1978

Sources: U.S. Department of Labor, U.S. Department of Commerce; Conference Board.

Economists therefore study productivity trends closely to discover what causes the gains and how they could be raised further. Trends for the decades since 1948 are summarized in Figure 12 and Table 1. The amount of output per unit of labor and capital rose, as Figure 12 shows. Output per hour of labor more than doubled, from 50 in 1948 to 120 in 1976. Output per unit of capital rose more slowly, from 78 to 107. The disparity partly reflects the fact that capital per worker was rising; by using an increasing amount of machinery, workers became more productive.

Table 1 *Growth rates in total factor productivity in the U.S. economy, by sectors, 1948–1976*

Sectors				Average Annual Rates of Growth for the Entire Period (percent)	
	Output	Capital	Labor	Total Factors (a weighted average of capital and labor growth)*	Total Factor Productivity (output growth minus total factor growth)
Farming	0.9	1.1	−3.9	−2.1	3.0
Mining	1.7	0.7	−0.3	0.1	1.7
Construction	2.6	5.0	1.4	1.6	1.0
Manufacturing	3.3	3.0	0.6	1.2	2.1
Transportation	2.1	0.7	−0.5	−0.3	2.4
Communications	7.1	5.8	2.0	2.8	4.2
Electricity and gas	5.8	4.3	0.9	2.7	3.0
Distribution	3.8	3.4	1.3	1.6	2.1
Financial	3.6	5.5	2.1	3.5	0.1
Services	3.7	3.8	1.7	3.8	1.6

*The weights are based on the relative shares of the factors in total costs.

Source: John M. Kendrick and Elliot S. Grossman, *Productivity in the United States: Trends and Cycles* (Baltimore: The Johns Hopkins University Press, 1980), pp. 36–46. Copyright © 1980 by The Johns Hopkins University Press.

Table 2 *The main sources of rising productivity in the U.S. economy, 1948–1976*

	Contributions to the Growth of Real Gross National Product (expressed as an addition to the yearly growth rate)
Growth rate of real gross national product (corrected for inflation)	3.9%
Increase in the volume of labor and capital inputs (growth rate)	1.0%
Increase in the productivity of factors (growth rate):	2.9%
Advances in knowledge	1.4%
Formal R&D activity	0.85%
Other sources of advances	0.55%
Changes in the quality of labor	0.6%
Other changes (in the composition of industry, economies of scale, etc.)	0.9%

Source: Kendrick and Grossman, *Productivity in the United States*, p. 16.

But that was not the only influence. Both capital and labor were improving in quality. Capital was embodying better technology, and labor was becoming better educated and more skilled.

The resulting trends differed strongly among sectors of the economy. Look especially at the TFP column of Table 1. The most rapid rises were in communications, electricity and gas, and farming; TFP growth was slowest in finance and construction. Within the manufacturing sector, more detailed measures show that there was rapid TFP growth in textiles, electrical machinery, and chemicals, but slow TFP growth in such older industries as metals, machinery, and furniture.

In general, the causes of productivity growth lie in the improving quality of both labor and capital. That is indicated in Table 2 for 1948–1976. Of the total 3.9 percent yearly growth in total output during 1948–1976, only 1.0 percent was caused by the expansion of capital and labor. The remaining 2.9 percent increase in TFP was due to other causes, mainly advances in knowledge.

The trends of technology and productivity growth are the crucial sources of economic progress. We now consider their main forms and components.

Forms and components of technological change

The progress of technology is a series of individual innovations, whose development is divided into several economic stages. Once you understand them, you can analyze both the causes and value of individual innovations and the entire flow of technological change.

First, recognize that progress comes from economic effort. To develop new technology requires inventive skills and new investments, which are commonly designated as research and development (R&D).

Though R&D is mostly done by private firms, over half of all U.S. R&D expenditures are paid for by the federal government. Much of the government-sponsored R&D is for military and space programs, although some also goes for civilian products.

These R&D resources create progress in the ***invention-innovation-imitation sequence.***

Invention, innovation, and imitation Technical change can be divided into three phases:

Invention is the creation of the new idea. The act is intellectual: the perception of a new condition, of a new connection between old conditions, or of a whole new area for action. Inventions, large or small, involve new ideas that can be refined for practical use. *Invention* is usually a lonely activity requiring intensive mental exploration. Eccentric thinkers are often best at this, although large-scale "team research" may be necessary for some large and complex inventions.

Innovation brings the idea to practical use. The innovator builds production facilities and brings the new product or process to the market. This often (although not always) displaces products or processes in general use. *Innovation is a business act.* The entrepreneurship involved in the financing, arranging of complex engineering details, and taking of risks goes beyond the management of old processes. Though many innovations are small and safe, some require extraordinary skills.

Imitation then follows as the innovation is copied by others. Economists call this the *diffusion* of the innovation across the market. Imitating is usually easier and safer, though less creative, than invention and innovation. The imitator merely copies, often when the innovation has become safe and routine.

Process and product innovations Technical changes divide into two main kinds: process and product innovations. *Process* in-novations alter how given products are made (examples: a new way to use a drill press, or to organize a factory, or to smelt a metal). *Product* innovations create a new good for sale (examples: a digital watch, a new kind of toothpaste, a new type of automobile, or a larger model in a line of electric motors).

The two kinds of innovation are distinct in concept, though they are often mixed together in actual cases. They call on different resources. Their incentives and effects often differ sharply. Each can vary from trivial differences to radically new approaches.

Decisions to innovate
Since innovation requires investment in R&D and new capital, the decision to innovate resembles the decision to invest.

For *product innovations,* the incentive to bring a new product to market arises from the expected return from marketing the product. If the firm predicts that a new product will yield profits higher than the returns available from alternative uses of its funds, the product will be developed and marketed.

A *process innovation* that lowers the costs of production in an industry will be adopted by new firms that enter the industry. But existing firms may not immediately adopt the new technology. The old methods may be *technologically* obsolete, but they are not *economically* obsolete unless the firms can no longer cover the variable costs when using the old technology.

Some existing firms may be on the point of replacing worn-out machinery or equipment. They would replace their present methods with capital embodying the innovative technique. Yet, other firms would find it profitable to continue to use their existing production facilities until their variable costs are above the total cost of the new technique.

As the new, lower-cost technology spreads, the marginal costs of production and, therefore, the profit-maximizing price will fall. When the market price falls below the average variable cost of the firms using the old technology, those firms can no longer cover their variable costs, and the old technology becomes *economically obsolete*. This occurs when the average total cost curve of the new technology falls below the average variable cost curve of the old technology. At this point, firms with the old technology will make larger losses by continuing to operate than by shutting down. Therefore, all firms must eventually either adopt the new technology or go out of business.

Sources of change: Induced and autonomous *Induced inventions* occur from the hope of making money. Without that cash stimulus, they would happen later or not at all. Much commercial R&D activity fits this type. Teams of scientists in company laboratories, working under budgeted plans, seek inventions that will pay off for their companies: no payoff, no inventive effort.

In contrast, ***autonomous innovations*** arise spontaneously from the ongoing growth of knowledge and technology. Discoveries in one area often make an advance in another area inevitable, which, in turn, permits or causes progress in still other fields. For example, the automobile became possible only after the discovery of oil and the development of the internal combustion engine and rubber tires.

The patent system

The distinction between autonomous and induced changes can be crucial to economists in assessing public policies to promote technological change. The U.S. *patent system* is a long-established institution whose purpose is to promote inventive activity. It grants a 17-year exclusive monopoly right on an invention to the first person to file for a patent on it. The patent monopoly offers the inventor a high reward for being first.

About 70,000 patents are issued yearly, and many industries (including drugs and electronics) are strongly influenced by the race for patents and by the profits from the resulting patent monopolies. Most other countries also have patent systems, with similar terms and effects.

A patent system is economically efficient if its *benefits* (from speeding up inventions) exceed its *costs* (from monopoly restrictions on the patented goods). But the system imposes net social costs if all inventions are *autonomous;* inventions would occur even without the incentives provided by patents, but the social costs of monopoly are imposed. Only if inventions are mainly *induced* might the social benefits of the patent exceed its costs.

Therefore, the patent system's value is highly controversial. The economic appraisal depends on (1) what share the induced inventions are among all inventions; (2) whether the induced inventions are important or trivial; and (3) how much they are speeded up by money rewards. Only if the three answers are (1) large, (2) important, and (3) substantial does a patent system have a clear economic justification.

Summary

Capital is one of the most interesting factors in economic production. Some of its dimensions you will want to understand and remember are:

1. Real capital is produced and used to increase the efficiency of production over a period of years. Portfolio capital is paper securities (bonds and stocks) held for their expected money returns.

2. Actual capital is highly diverse, both in company assets and in consumer assets.

3. In decisions to invest, expected future returns are discounted to present values. Prospective rates of return are compared with the cost of capital in selecting profit-maximizing levels of investment.

4. The returns to capital contain a riskless component, a risk premium, and economic profit from other causes.

5. Rates of return usually are systematically related to risk.

6. Asset values fluctuate to reflect expected returns and interest rates.

7. Capital market decisions tend to equalize the rates of return on all assets.

8. Stock markets supervise and reward corporate performance.

9. Technological change is embodied in capital investment.

Key concepts

Real (physical) and money (portfolio) capital
Productivity of capital
Return to capital
Capitalizing the value of future benefits
Internal rate of return
Profit-maximizing level of investment
Cost of capital
Risk
Risk premium
Risk-return relationship
Riskless rate of return
Asset values
Expectations
Equalization of returns
Total factor productivity
Invention-innovation-imitation sequence
Induced and autonomous innovations

Questions for review

1. Which of the following can be classified as capital? Explain your choices.
   a. farm tractor
   b. coal
   c. football stadium
   d. 18-wheeler truck

2. Explain how a firm would derive a schedule showing the benefits of various investment projects. What is this schedule called?

3. a. How is the cost of capital investment projects determined? Is capital investment financed by internal funds costless?
   b. How would the firm use cost-benefit information to determine which investments would be most profitable?

4. Explain how each of the following would affect a firm's rate of investment.
   a. A technological breakthrough that will substantially lower investment costs requires the purchase of new equipment.
   b. The market rate of interest falls.

5. a. Would an economist view the total return on capital investment as profit?
   b. What factors determine how much profit a firm receives from an investment?

◄17►

General Equilibrium

As you read and study this chapter, you will learn:

▸ how general equilibrium unifies the parts of the economic system

▸ the specific conditions of an efficient general equilibrium, and the meaning of the "Invisible Hand"

▸ how changes ripple out through the economy

▸ the five kinds of gaps and limits on the efficient equilibrium

Since the 1870s, the unifying concept of microeconomics has been *general equilibrium*. It reduces the great variety of entire economic systems to the simplicity of a few clear, logical relationships. Having mastered those ideas separately in the previous chapters, you can now learn them as an integrated whole. Seeing the system as a whole is one of the economist's special skills.

But there is more. Not only may a general equilibrium exist. It may also generate an efficient allocation of resources, if the markets in the economic system are competitive. That property was stated briefly in Chapter 9; now it is time to develop it more fully. Efficient allocation has been demonstrated and refined by a century of neoclassical theorists, from Leon Walras and Alfred Marshall on. Yet that efficiency does not guarantee paradise, for it often has gaps and limits.

To understand efficient allocation and its limits, you need first to grasp the interrelatedness of markets in the economy, which the first section of this chapter shows. The second section presents the conditions of efficient allocation and discusses how the system adjusts to changes.

The last section reviews the limits on the competitive outcome and explains how social cost may diverge from private cost. Then the possible failures of the competitive process are shown in turn.

The general process toward equilibrium

Thus far, the book has offered partial-equilibrium analysis, which deals with decisions made in separate markets. In *general equilibrium,* the analysis widens to embrace the whole economy. Because the process of allocation operates throughout the economic system, the analysis has to be equally inclusive. All of the elements of general equilibrium have already been developed in earlier chapters. Now we combine them to derive the general patterns.

"General" means interrelated *In the analysis, as in the economy, every part is ultimately related to every other part.* Some markets are more closely interrelated than others, of course. Close relationships occur for many substitutes and complements. For example, coal and oil, beef and pork, automobiles and gasoline, tools and lumber, all interact closely. Changes in one such market can strongly affect the other market's outcomes. Yet, many other parts of the economy are only faintly related; New York real estate and San Francisco labor markets, for example, or beef and sulfuric acid. Yet, ultimately, they can all interact to some degree, for they all draw on the common pool of inputs and go to the same broad variety of consumers.

Any change anywhere will cause *ripple effects* to spread through the economy, like waves across a pool. Changes are transmitted among markets and sectors, binding the whole system together. If many changes occur at the same time, the

ripples may cross and interact, so that the whole set of repercussions in the economy is mixed and seems unclear. Yet, each ripple has its own logic and can be analyzed as a distinct sequence. The economist is skilled in following such effects clearly, with a sure touch for their direction and degree of impact. We will see in the second main section that even distant repercussions can be traced. For now, the basic lesson is that ripple effects are the process by which the economy absorbs changes and adjusts to them throughout its parts.

Adjusting toward equilibrium The adjustments do not just occur randomly; they pull outputs and prices systematically toward the equilibrium patterns. The process and the interrelationships were first defined rigorously by Leon Walras in the 1870s (see the adjacent box). At each point, there are basic conditions of demand and supply that define the conditions for allocation throughout every part of the economy. The economy will adjust production toward those conditions rather than oscillate aimlessly.

MARKET CHOICES PROVIDE THAT PULL TOWARD EQUILIBRIUM If a market price is high enough to permit the firm to gain excess profits, for example, then new firms may enter the market, increase supply, and thereby drive the price down toward average cost. Each unit only maximizes its own interest. But the whole set of resulting actions causes prices and quantities in the market to adjust. The markets are cleared in each time period, so that there are neither physical shortages nor leftover surpluses. Since all goods are sold at the going price, production flows smoothly to consumers. The equilibrium conditions can continue, period after period.

The whole self-correcting process can be vigorous and thorough. If even a small gap remains, either the sellers or the buy-

General Equilibrium and Input-Output Analysis: Walras and Leontief

Although the classical economists dealt with the economic system as a whole, it was neoclassical economists who first envisioned the economy as a system of interrelated parts, thus providing the basis for a detailed analysis of general equilibrium.

The leading neoclassicist was Leon Walras (1834–1910), whose *Elements of Pure Economics* presented a comprehensive set of formulas representing all parts of the economy. By reducing the economy to a complete mathematical system, Walras was able to show precisely the fundamental processes and conditions lying beneath the great variety of the economy. And by stressing the interrelationships among markets, Walras clarified general equilibrium as the set of conditions toward which market choices adjust. Despite later refinements, Walras's analysis is still the core of modern microeconomics.

In the 1930s, Wassily Leontief (born 1906) developed the practical embodiment of Walrasian analysis, which he called "input-output analysis." Leontief, who left Russia in the 1920s, created a research organization at Harvard to process the large volumes of data that input-output tables reflect.

In later decades, he refined and enlarged the analysis, and by the 1960s, the government-issued tables presented hundreds of sectors. Leontief's work in conceiving this approach and implementing it won him a Nobel Prize.

LEON WALRAS

WASSILY LEONTIEF

Table 1 *Conditions of efficient allocation*

1. *Markets*. All markets are cleared, with no shortages or surpluses. All resources offered for sale are used.
2. *Households*
    a. In choosing among consumer goods 1 through *n*, each household reaches these conditions:

$$\frac{\text{Marginal utility}_1}{\text{Price}_1} = \frac{\text{Marginal utility}_2}{\text{Price}_2} = \ldots = \frac{\text{Marginal utility}_n}{\text{Price}_n}$$

    for goods that it chooses to consume.
    b. In choosing how hard to work, people reach the level where the marginal utility of income just balances the marginal disutility of work.
3. *Firms*
    a. The firm's output is set at the level where

    Price = Marginal cost = Average cost (at its minimum).

    b. Input choices are made—among inputs 1 through *n*—so that:

$$\frac{\text{Marginal product}_1}{\text{Price}_1} = \frac{\text{Marginal product}_2}{\text{Price}_2} = \ldots = \frac{\text{Marginal product}}{\text{Price}_n}$$

    and each input is used until its marginal value product equals its price.

ers—or both groups—will take action in their own interest, pulling the outcome into an equilibrium that is part of the entire economy's general equilibrium.

When it works well, the process is therefore spontaneous and automatic. No centralized knowledge or coordination to discover the correct values and require firms and consumers to meet targets is required to make it happen. People on Nebraska farms interact independently with others in New York offices and Seattle neighborhoods, for example, and their choices tend to harmonize in a general equilibrium.

Conditions and processes of general equilibrium

In general equilibrium, resources are allocated in definite patterns throughout the economy. *If the markets are competitive, that allocation will reach a special set of conditions that economists call efficient.* They include the price-cost conditions that Chapter 9 showed for individual markets.

They also include the input pricing conditions presented in Chapter 14. Now we assemble them all to show how they obtain across the whole general equilibrium system.

These conditions of **efficient allocation** are the analytical core of microeconomics. Though they are stated precisely here, they need not always hold exactly in every part of a real economy. They define the conditions that the economy is adjusting toward, whether they are reached precisely or just approximately.

The conditions
A competitive setting is necessary to obtain an efficient allocation of resources. To be competitive, markets must have many sellers, operating independently of one another and preventing any one firm from dominating. New competitors can enter quickly and easily.

In this setting, the decisive microeconomic results are *marginal*. They are reached by households maximizing their utility and by firms maximizing their profits. As they choose and adjust in individual

358

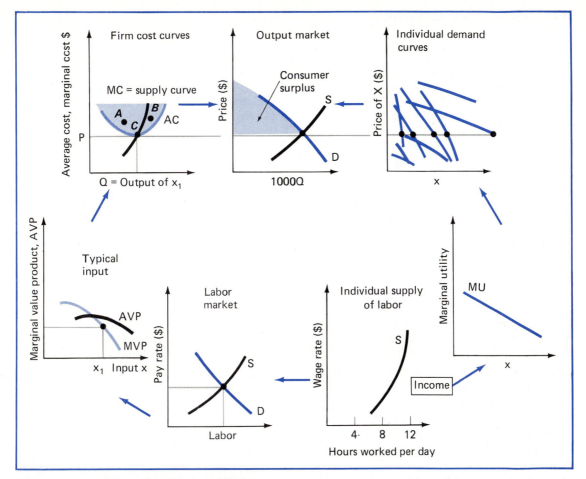

Figure 1   A summary of general equilibrium

As before, the inputs and outputs flow clockwise (recall Figure 1 in Chapter 1), while the money to pay for them flows counterclockwise. But now we see how each set of decisions involves the underlying technology (suppliers) and preferences (consumers).

Start with the output market at the top, where demand and supply come together. Demand is the sum of individual demand curves (to the right), which reflect each consumer's marginal utility (below) and income level.

Meanwhile, supply is the sum of firms' marginal cost curves (to the left), which, in turn, reflect the technology embodied in the firms' marginal and average cost curves (below). Costs also reflect the prices determined by demand and supply in input markets, such as for labor (bottom center). Finally, those labor prices govern the household incomes that flow back into the demand side on the right.

The system is therefore complete, and all parts are related to the rest. Since all of the decisions are made at *the margin*, marginal conditions are crucial.

markets, these decision units determine prices, costs, and output and input levels throughout the system. The whole outcome is governed by *marginal* choices, which tend to align values and costs everywhere in the economy.

Table 1 and Figure 1 summarize the main conditions. The conditions all fit together, and in doing so, adjust mutually toward a general equilibrium. Changes in

one market will change the values in other markets, and further waves of change will then ripple through the system. The whole process of adjustment to these changes will move the economy toward these **marginal conditions.**

The conditions are familiar to you, of course, since they are merely the partial conditions presented in earlier chapters. But this whole is more than the sum of those parts. *The parts of the economy interact and adjust, and increased output in one part usually requires reductions in other parts.* Those are the special features of the general equilibrium system. In making all the changes and interactions that continue throughout the economic system, not only does one household or firm move toward equilibrium, all of them do.

Efficient allocation in competitive markets If markets are competitive, then the resulting allocation of all those resources, among all their uses throughout all of the markets, will usually be drawn toward efficient patterns. Firms in all of the competitive markets act to reach the same long-run condition: *Price equals marginal cost at the lowest level of average cost.* That condition was explained in Chapter 9, where we discussed partial equilibrium in a single market, but it holds generally, across all markets. *Marginal cost is true cost*, opportunity cost, the real measure of sacrifice. *Price is value*, showing what consumers will pay for the marginal unit of

the good out of their own limited funds, in free choices between this and other goods.

Therefore, if price equals marginal cost then all resources are used efficiently throughout. Sacrifice and value to consumers are everywhere brought into line at the margin. Any distortion of such an efficient pattern—for example, with fewer computers than the optimum but more X-ray machines, as in Figure 2—would be inferior. In the computer market, price would exceed marginal cost: Computers might sell at a price of $10,000 but have a marginal cost of only $7,000. Since the computers would cost $3,000 less than their value at the margin, producing fewer of them would sacrifice that extra value. X-ray machines might now cost $14,000 each to make, but sell for only $11,000, as before. Producing the marginal X-ray machines would be wasteful, for their cost would exceed their value.

Both markets would be distorted from efficient outcomes, and the total value of GNP would fall below its potential level. The greater the distortion, the more GNP

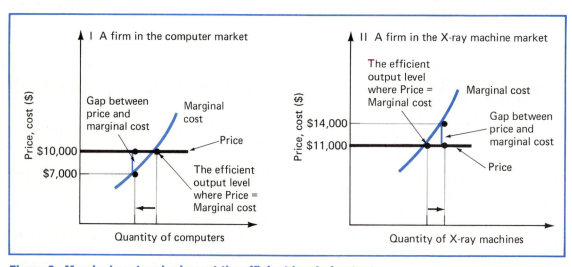

Figure 2   Marginal cost and price set the efficient level of output

The distortion arises from having too few computers and too many X-ray machines. In this situation, computers cost only $7,000 to make, at the margin, but they are worth $10,000 each, as shown by the price. X-ray machines are worth only $10,000, as before, but their marginal cost is $14,000. By moving to the levels where price equals marginal cost, there would be a net gain in welfare.

would be reduced. A simple switch of resources and production levels back to the efficient marginal conditions would again raise GNP to its maximum.

Efficient allocation is a powerful result, with large economic benefits. It maximizes national output for any given amount of inputs. Because resources are scarce, they need to be used sparingly. Consider work, for example, an input that involves personal sacrifice. When millions of people rise at 5:30 a.m. for the dawn shift at the factory, or when they endure the eighth daily hour of heavy lifting, nonstop typing, or tomato picking, they are making real sacrifices. Other inputs are also costly. For example, ores are dug, transported, and smelted, using complex capital equipment. All of these operations entail sacrifices—opportunity costs—which are embodied in the costs of the goods themselves. To waste such resources causes needless pain and effort, often of great magnitudes, measured in billions of dollars. By minimizing society's whole sacrifice in production, efficient allocation makes a substantial contribution.

Behind the simple price equals marginal cost equation lie all of the other equimarginal conditions: in input choices, consumers' ratios of marginal utility to price, and so on. They, too, would be violated by any distortion in output levels. Therefore, efficiency is a pervasive array of conditions, touches all decisions in the economy, and interacts to bind them together. Such a set of conditions sounds impossibly theoretical, but it has real meaning even in the imprecise workaday world. These ideal conditions help economists to define any large distortions that occur and to show what changes would improve economic efficiency.

The invisible hand The process works in a self-activating way, as Adam Smith noted over 200 years ago:

As every individual, therefore, endeavours as much as he can both to employ his capital in the support of domestic industry, and so to direct that industry that its produce may be of greatest value: every individual necessarily labours to render the annual revenue of the society as great as he can. He generally, indeed, neither intends to promote the public interest, nor knows how much he is promoting it. . . . He intends only his own gain, and he is in this, as in many other cases, led by an invisible hand to promote an end which was no part of his intention.

The phrase *Invisible Hand* has become overused, and some economists go too far in worshiping "The Hand" and its efficient work.

Yet the process does have power. Millions of people, each acting selfishly—as consumers, workers, managers, and resource owners—may pull resources toward their best allocation, throughout the economy. A harmonious social result may arise from all of these purely private motivations. No single authority arranges it, but everybody unwittingly helps make it happen. Billions of decisions are made individually every day, and yet the whole set of markets may keep adjusting toward efficient allocation.

The process is resilient, not brittle or unstable. Disturbances are absorbed, as the process adjusts toward the next efficient equilibrium. Even where competition is not complete or other gaps arise, the basic integrity of the process remains. It also induces workers, managers, and other participants in the economy to apply great effort and care in their activities. As Adam Smith suggested, a competitive economy can be a powerful engine of economic affluence. The process is not universal; as we will see, it has gaps and limits. But where the Invisible Hand does reach, it is a strong organizing force.

Ripple effects

Now consider more closely how changes spread from market to market. The process can be seen clearly by using an *input-output table* of the economy. A recent such table for the U.S. economy is given in condensed form in Table 2. Over 200 million people and 14 million enterprises interact in many thousands of markets. Here, they are summarized by a selection of 15 of the total 85 sectors, arrayed both at the side and at the top of the table.

As you read each row stretching across the table, the numbers show how much sales volume flowed *from* each industry to each of the other industries that are listed across the top edge of the table. *Reading each column vertically*, you can find where each industry's inputs came from, among the industries listed on the left-hand edge. Try tracing such flows for petroleum refining, following the shading of rows and columns. Most of its *output* went to chemicals ($1,800 billion), transportation ($1,999 billion), and wholesale and retail trade ($1,375 billion), as expected. Its *inputs* came mostly from crude petroleum and natural gas ($11,556 billion). Try tracing the flows for lumber products, iron and steel, and others. Once you have grasped the basic logic, the table is simple to use.

The input-output table is suggestive in three ways: (1) It helps you to visualize the many directions in which each industry relates to others, both in getting inputs and in selling its outputs. (2) It also helps you to see how any change may affect three, five, ten, and even more additional rounds of change. For example, suppose that the boll weevil cuts cotton production in half. Less cotton will flow into the textile indus-

Table 2 *Input-output table of the U.S. economy 1967: selected sectors (amounts in $ million)*

Industry Code Numbers	Industry Code Numbers	Oil and Gas 8	Raw Chemical 10	Lumber Products 20	Paperboard Containers 25	Chemicals and Products 27	Petroleum Refining 31	Iron and Steel 37	Other Metals 38
8	Crude petroleum and natural gas	374	—	—	—	49	11,556	—	—
10	Chemical mining	—	61	—	—	608	—	26	3
20	Lumber products (except containers)	—	1	3,492	13	55	2	74	76
25	Paperboard containers and boxes	—	1	24	109	116	75	18	16
27	Chemicals and products	164	27	160	141	4,407	623	392	184
31	Petroleum refining	33	3	106	30	1,800	1,831	116	48
37	Iron and steel	120	18	43	32	184	8	6,017	340
38	Other metals	—	2	3	20	322	41	859	6,723
49	General industrial machinery	86	—	11	2	70	65	344	89
59	Motor vehicles and equipment	—	—	5	—	16	3	121	46
65	Transportation and warehousing	146	15	429	227	611	1,389	1,420	539
68	Electric, gas and water utilities	172	44	124	45	699	462	822	427
69	Wholesale and retail trade	175	16	441	151	543	303	934	726
70	Finance and insurance	93	9	79	17	100	250	182	116
71	Real estate and rental	2,429	40	109	96	543	630	80	153
	TOTAL	15,031	1,027	12,905	6,031	23,182	26,975	31,723	20,870

Source: *Survey of Current Business*, April 1979.

tries. From those industries, in turn, less output will flow to still others such as wholesaling and retailing. Meanwhile, the cotton industry will *buy* fewer inputs—machinery, gasoline, fertilizer, and so on—from other industries. Those industries, in turn, will buy fewer of their inputs from still other industries. So both the rows and the columns help you to see how changes ripple through the economy.

Moreover, the system does not change aimlessly. The repercussions follow definite patterns, which economic analysis can often clarify. Therefore, (3) the table also helps you to visualize that the responses to changes will usually pull the economy toward the efficient patterns. To see this clearly, consider some big and little practical examples of ripple effects. Always

note the *net* changes—the shifts that *did* occur compared to what would otherwise have occurred.

Oil prices Let the price of oil rise sharply, as it did during 1973–1974 and 1979–1980. Then costs and, therefore, prices are likely to rise in all sectors of the economy that use oil heavily, such as gasoline and oil fuels, petrochemicals, plastics, electricity, and asphalt. If demand has any elasticity, consumers will respond to higher prices by buying less of the goods. How sharply output will fall depends on demand elasticities. Sales revenue may rise or fall, again depending on the elasticities. The rise in oil prices will also cause a fall in demand for complementary goods, such as automobiles. Thus, the industries sup-

| | | | | | | | | | ← FINAL DEMAND → | | | |
General Industrial Machinery	Motor Vehicles and Equipment	Transportation and Warehousing	Utilities	Wholesale and Retail Trade	Finance and Insurance	Real Estate and Rentals	Intermediate Outputs, Total	Personal Consumption Expenditures	Federal Government Purchases	State and Local Government Purchases	Total Final Demand	Total Production (Intermediate plus Final)	
49	59	65	68	69	70	71							
—	—	26	2,521	—	—	165	14,692	—	—	—	339	15,031	8
—	—	1	—	—	—	6	838	2	—	31	189	1,027	10
22	43	2	1	92	—	29	12,118	259	30	4	787	12,905	20
14	47	26	3	571	—	4	5,841	73	34	21	191	6,031	25
13	61	46	56	215	1	301	18,797	504	1,752	113	4,385	23,182	27
30	73	1,999	275	1,375	92	720	14,105	10,194	1,078	292	12,870	26,975	31
845	103	261	41	37	—	62	30,395	4	290	2	1,328	31,723	37
308	673	66	11	42	—	37	19,752	15	8	—	1,119	20,870	38
514	297	135	37	69	—	22	4,844	—	303	13	2,956	7,800	49
41	12,157	71	3	99	—	116	15,464	15,822	1,002	731	28,276	43,740	59
71	716	5,228	563	1,235	115	1,096	32,172	11,396	3,324	985	20,653	52,823	65
52	195	342	6,888	2,415	392	436	21,370	13,935	344	1,599	15,952	37,321	68
257	926	1,629	202	3,382	598	1,612	42,551	109,367	1,397	384	120,815	163,365	69
32	114	781	219	2,474	8,701	3,574	21,934	25,267	54	403	25,818	47,711	70
100	192	1,360	155	8,608	1,961	3,654	38,798	70,868	292	618	74,456	113,253	71
7,800	43,740	52,825	37,321	163,365	47,752	113,253		490,660	90,804	88,315	795,388		

plying their inputs will have to cut back. Moreover, asset values will change in many industries and consumer markets (for example, house prices will fall in some towns where automobile workers live, but rise in others where oil workers live).

It is also possible to trace *geographic* ripples. Thus, for example, changing New York real estate prices can affect the level of employment in San Francisco. As New York office prices rise, some firms will move their headquarters elsewhere, driving up office prices in an ever-widening circle around New York. Certain firms will relocate farther west, driving up rents there and inducing still other firms to shift, ultimately, to San Francisco. The effect is reinforced because rising house prices in New York will also induce some New York residents to move to other towns. That ripple will also encourage firms to locate westward, eventually reaching San Francisco.

Day in, day out, the economy accommodates an endless series of ripples among sectors and locales. Predicting them, tracing them, factoring each one out from the host of others that are occurring, these are standard economic skills. *Logic* is involved, in deciding which things are affected and in which directions, up or down. *Matters of degree* are also involved, in weighing which changes are largest and most important. For example, the price of cold-rolled steel has only a minor effect on the price of dog-racing tickets (and vice versa), but it significantly affects the price of automobiles. One learns to focus on the main changes, so as not to get lost among the lesser ones.

Limits on competitive efficiency

Remarkable though it is, the market system may not provide a completely satisfactory outcome. The Invisible Hand may fal-ter, so that there are gaps in its results. These limits have long been recognized and studied. Sometimes their effects are minor, but often they have great force, causing large economic losses.

Market failures fall into five main classes, which we present in this section. In other chapters and in your own daily life, you will come to learn the many cases where they crop up and pose difficult choices for society, causing endless troubles that are major issues in the political process. One must understand them to judge their causes and cures.

External costs and benefits

Thus far, we have assumed that all prices and costs in the market are identical to the true social values and costs. If that holds true, then *prices* as used in consumer decisions will equal the ultimate social worths of the goods. The *costs* of private firms would also exactly reflect true social sacrifice.

But if external effects occur, then private values will no longer equal social values, and markets will cause inefficiency. For example, an automobile model may cost $5,000, including $950 worth of steel. At that price, it is bought and sold by many thousands of people. Yet, the making of that steel may have created water pollution and smoke that, per ton of steel made, costs other people $100 to clean up or to cure the medical harm. The steel companies do not have to pay those extra costs. Moreover, each car may release fumes that, when breathed, cost $50 worth of health damage to others. The **external costs** are $150 per car. The private parties—steel and automobile firms, and car drivers—act strictly on the private cost and price, which total $5,000 per car. Yet, the true **social cost** for producing and using each car is $5,150. The dollar difference may seem small here, but the logic, as illustrated in Figure 3, is clear.

Illustrations of Ripple Effects in the Economy

1. A series of military crises abroad causes U.S. officials to triple military spending for tanks, armored cars, and hand weapons. Consequently, production and prices rise for heavy metals, explosives, paint, motors, and other inputs for weapons. Costs also rise for other goods using those materials. Profits and stock prices of weapons companies rise, making their shareholders richer. The opposite happens for most other companies using those inputs, for higher costs squeeze their profits. Real estate values rise in the weapons-producing areas (parts of Texas, California, etc.).

2. The demand for large automobiles falls, while demand for small imported cars rises. Some 200,000 U.S. automobile workers are laid off. Production of automobile parts also falls, and workers in those markets also lose jobs. As the laid-off workers' incomes fall, the towns they live in suffer economic declines. Retail shops close, property values decline, and some of the population moves to look for better jobs. The stockholders of automobile and automobile parts firms undergo capital losses as the value of their shares falls.

3. The electronics industry (computers and related applications) encounters explosive growth. The wages for computer engineers and programmers rise sharply, attracting workers from other industries. That forces wages up in those other industries, raising their costs. Suppliers of electronics components also have a boom, as do those suppliers' suppliers. Their shareholders achieve capital gains. A series of adjustments toward electronics products, inputs, and workers' skills takes place.

4. An inefficient steel plant in Youngstown, Ohio, is closed down, putting 6,320 people out of work. Steel production goes down, and steel prices are slightly higher. Demand and prices of inputs fall off. Shipments of goods to and from the town are sharply cut, reducing jobs and incomes of railroad and trucking workers. Unemployed workers in Youngstown spend less for most items, reducing their quantities and prices. House prices drop, especially as people begin moving elsewhere. Local stores suffer and some fail. The cutbacks spread to other locales, whose products were used in Youngstown. Since virtually all activities in Youngstown are cut back, the ripple effects elsewhere cover a wide variety of products and locales.

Social and private values diverge whenever there are such external effects (often called "spillover effects"). *Since only the "internal" costs—or market costs— matter to the private actors, they have no incentive to take external costs into account.* Such external costs have been widespread, and despite the vast environmental

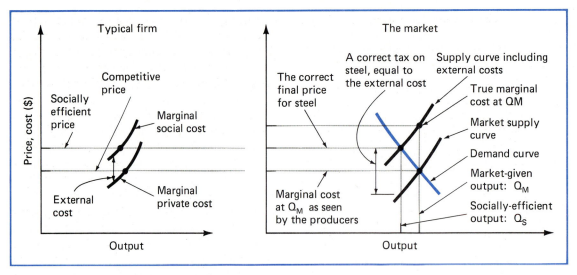

Figure 3 Adding external costs to private costs

Private costs are those incurred by the firm. They help determine how much the firm produces. But other costs may also be incurred, which are external to the firm's own interests. Pollution may occur, which is costly to others. This results in price (marginal benefit) being less than marginal cost at the market-given output. The marginal resources allocated to steel have opportunity cost in excess of the benefits they produce for steel buyers.

The full social costs—private costs plus external costs—are illustrated here. They may give a socially efficient level of output and price that differs from the market levels.

cleanup program in the United States since 1968, many such costs continue.

Whenever there are external effects, the competitive allocation will stray from the efficient patterns. In Figure 3's example, external costs will mean that the market output is too large and market price is too low, compared to the socially efficient levels. Such distortions from true social values will not be self-correcting, since the external costs are simply ignored by buyers and sellers acting through the market. If firms or car drivers need not pay for the harmful waste or smoke emissions they inflict on others, then the damages will occur. Allocation will be distorted from the socially efficient patterns.

The logic is simple but sound. You can now analyze and portray a class of deviations—or market failures—that competition will not correct. Indeed, competition will pressure firms to ignore external costs to survive.

Some familiar examples of both external costs and *external benefits* are given in Table 3. External costs may need to be reduced by social action: taxes, rules, limits, or others. Otherwise private choices will yield far too much of them to be efficient. Of course, because thousands of external effects are small, people let them pass as minor gains or irritants. But where external benefits are large—parks, schools, national defense, highways, lighthouses, courts, or police, for example—then the market process may fail altogether.

In such cases, special measures are needed to encourage production and consumption. Those extreme cases are called "social goods," for the benefits are large and widespread throughout society. Private markets will not provide them, because the sellers cannot confine the benefits just to the buyers. After all, anyone is free to go to a park, drive the streets, and enjoy the security of the nation's military

Table 3 Several examples of external costs and benefits

1. *External Costs*
   a. *In Production*
      Pollution of air and water by factory smoke and
      toxic wastes.
   b. *In Consumption*
      Fumes from automobiles; highway accidents,
         caused by reckless driving of automobiles.
      Loud music played in apartment buildings.
      Forest fires caused by careless campers.
      Nonsmokers' lung cancer, caused by smoke
         from others' cigarettes.
2. *External Benefits*
   a. *In Production*
      A lighthouse, whose beams are seen by all
         ships.
      Schooling, which provides an educated
         electorate and cultural support, as well as
         private skills.
   b. *In Consumption*
      Inoculation of one person against contagious
         disease gives added protection to others.
      A neighbor's beautiful garden and lawn, visible
         to others.

defenses. To sell them for private use would be absurd. Therefore, some or all of their cost must be met by public budgets, as we discuss in Chapters 18 and 20. Public goods are not just fringe matters. Some of them are central to a productive economy and a healthy society.

Distribution may be unfair

The Invisible Hand does not assure that income and wealth will be fairly distributed. *Fairness* is a matter separate from the allocation of resources. *Equity is, therefore, apart from efficiency.* Even if competition gives an utterly efficient allocation, distribution may be utterly unfair.

To illustrate the point, imagine a society in which a few rich aristocrats live in opulence while the mass of peasants suffers grinding poverty. Then suppose that an "industrial revolution" occurs, trans-

forming the aristocrats into affluent business owners while the peasants are herded into factories as common laborers to toil at subsistence wages. The resulting economic outcome may be highly competitive and an efficient allocation of resources, but the unfair distribution between rich and poor may be no better than it was before. It may even be worse. Whether it be worse, better or the same, the Invisible Hand does not assure that the outcome will be fair.

Yet, the competitive outcome might be fair because wages are aligned with **marginal productivity.** Remember that in competitive markets each input (land, labor, capital, materials, etc.) is used up to the point where its marginal value product just equals its price. *Therefore, it seems, inputs are paid just what they are worth.* If the marginal value product of mill hands or assemblers is $3.50 per hour, then that is what they will be paid. That is all their labor is worth, and thus, perhaps, all they deserve to get. The same holds for interest as a payment to owners of capital, for the pay of presidents of companies, for the price of farmland—indeed, for any input into the competitive economy. *Each input gets paid no less, and no more, than what it adds to the value of production at the margin.*

The logic seems impeccable, and it does reflect one general standard of fairness: "Rewards should fit contribution." Some 19th-century Manchester school economists carried the point to extremes, using it to defend low wages for workers and high profits for capital. Each input, they said, deserved exactly what it got in the capitalist system, no matter how unfair the disparities may have seemed by other standards, including need, equality, and the avoidance of destitution. Further, the economists said, attempts to alter the market outcomes would be self-defeating, for they would distort the system and cause more economic harm than good.

Most economists now do not accept that extreme view because people's skills and opportunities are often unfairly governed by their families' status, rather than by their own efforts and talents. Some children get much more help up the economic ladder—in schooling, job connections, and inheritances—than do other children. Furthermore, some children can be said to have an unfair advantage if they have by genetic chance inherited superior talents. Thus, the marginal revenue product of a ditchdigger or of a senior vice-president may be the outcome of an unfair process, with some people having greater privileges and help than others. Differing pay and wealth might be fair if every person had precisely fair chances all along, and if every person's rewards fitted his or her efforts.

Technological progress may not be at optimum rates. This possibility was presented in Chapter 16.

Cultural values are not necessarily provided

A competitive economy can be bleak. Competition itself is ultimately divisive, pitting people against one another to struggle endlessly in anonymous markets. Competition provides no mercy, no safety net, no relief from the pressure. Coldhearted, aggressive competitors will commonly do better economically than kind and sensitive people. Children may be sent into factories and mines to do degrading work for low wages—conditions that were widespread in the 19th century. The creative and performing arts (music, drama, painting, and others) will exist only if they can sell at a profit in the marketplace. Otherwise, cultural activities may be provided by non-profit enterprises, if at all. Such enterprises are largely outside the private market system. Free-market capitalism may give progress and diversity or harshness and desolation; a favorable outcome is not assured.

Cultural health in a competitive system is, therefore, an open question. The heyday of competitive capitalism in Victorian Britain and the Gilded Age in the United States, for example, both inflicted cultural and social damage and brought certain economic and cultural gains. Indeed, the cultural effects—both harms and benefits—of a competitive system may ultimately outweigh the importance of its economic impacts. On the other side, one benefit of a competitive economy is that thorough competition makes political democracy healthier, by avoiding large concentrations of economic power.

All of these harms and benefits make it complex to judge the cultural results of a market economy. The main lesson here is that *healthy social and cultural conditions are not guaranteed by a competitive economy; they may, instead, be limited or prevented by it, or be simply independent of it.*

Monopoly

Effective competition may be prevented in some or all markets, as we discussed at length in earlier chapters. **Monopoly power** may arise in two main ways; (1) There may be large economies of scale, (2) or one firm may simply seize a monopoly position.

Economies of scale If minimum efficient scale (the low point of the average cost curve) is reached at a small share of the market, then there is "natural competition." But if economies of scale prevail up to firm sizes that give a large share of the market, then the first firm to grow can undersell the others and take over much or all of the whole market. Such "natural monopoly" conditions make competition—and its spontaneous efficiency—impossible.

Monopolizing Even if scale economies are lacking, an aggressive firm may simply be able to buy out other firms or to use unfair tactics to gain a monopoly. Indeed, every competitor in every market seeks to capture a higher market share for itself, but competition among these firms prevents any one firm from gaining dominance. Yet, sometimes a firm does attain a dominant position or even a pure monopoly. When this occurs—even if only a partial degree of monopoly is gained—the precise competitive results are distorted.

We need not recapitulate all of monopoly's effects here. Allocation is usually distorted away from efficient patterns to some degree, and innovation and equity may suffer. Against those probable losses, there may be gains from achieving lower costs because of economies of scale. The outcome is a matter of degree, of comparing the costs and benefits.

Natural resources

Competition may have special effects on **natural resources.** The resources of this planet fit on a spectrum from *renewable* (like crops and fresh air) to *nonrenewable* (like iron ore and oil), which, once used, are gone forever. *Competitive markets can give the best economic use of these resources, conserving them, so that we use them neither too fast nor too slowly.* That remarkable point—that free-market choices by resource owners tend to conserve many resources, not waste them—is presented in detail in Chapter 20.

Yet, there are three exceptions to this rule:

1. Common-property resources are available to more than one owner Whoever captures them can keep them. Fish and game animals are examples of such common-property resources. *The rate of use of these resources in a competitive setting will be too rapid.* Each user has an incentive to take the resource as fast as possible, because otherwise it will be taken by others. In total, all users will deplete the resource

faster than is optimal. Hence, many great shoals are "overfished" under open competition. (That, too, is why the "Save the Whales" campaign is trying to prevent the effects of economic incentives on a common-property resource, the whales.) And the hunting of deer, elk, and other game animals has to be limited by seasons and licenses. Otherwise, the animals will be reduced in numbers and possibly become extinct.

2. External effects among resource users can distort their use (this is one class of external costs). For example, careless farming on a high slope can cause rapid runoffs of water, which then wash off valuable topsoil from other farms down below. The topsoil loss is external to the farmer on the upper slope. External effects can also affect air, water, and other resources, as Table 3 illustrated.

3. Permanence Free markets are particularly effective at solving short-run problems needing marginal (that is, small) adjustments. The same also holds true for most resources. The owners look ahead to use their resources efficiently now and for the foreseeable future. Market prices rise to reflect emerging scarcities.

But what of virtually permanent actions, where the effects last many centuries? Here, the competitive calculus may not give optimal results. For example, nuclear-power plants operate for only about 30 years and then must be closed down and sealed off for some 24,000 years—virtually forever by human time scales. If people could see the future better, they might build no such perpetual mausoleums, with their stores of nuclear material; or, instead, they might build more of them, if technology will make it easy to store the wastes or neutralize the radiation. There is simply no reliable current guide to those future choices. The next 24,000 years may bring unimaginably different conditions and needs, or they may settle down into grinding scarcity. At any rate, free-market choices may be too short-sighted in such long-run global matters.

These five main limits on the Invisible Hand could reduce the domain of true free-market efficiency to a few small zones, rather than the entire economy. Or perhaps the domain is nearly complete, at least in some economies at some times. Economists have found that the limits do affect some sectors more sharply than others. All of the limits lead to lively controversies in practice.

Summary

1. The study of general equilibrium combines all of the marginal conditions reached by consumers and firms in competitive markets. Together, these conditions define efficient allocation throughout the system. When it works well, the market system adjusts spontaneously toward the efficient allocation and, once in equilibrium, holds to it.

2. The key equimarginal condition for each firm is price equals marginal cost, at minimum average cost. When this occurs, all of the arrays of marginal utilities and marginal productivities are brought into line with their prices. Inputs are paid the value of their marginal products, and that may give a fair distribution.

3. Economic changes cause ripples to spread among sectors and regions. An input-output table helps one to visualize and trace these successive changes. Big and small changes can be traced through several or more rounds of adjustments.

4. If private values diverge from social values, then the Invisible Hand gives distorted results. There are five main

causes of such market failures: (1) There may be external costs and benefits, which markets ignore. At the extreme, public goods will be entirely lacking. (2) The distribution of wealth and income may be unfair, even if allocation is efficient. (3) There may be a bleak culture and unhealthy social conditions, or cultural richness, or other results. The outcome is indeterminate. (4) Monopoly may occur, either via scale economies or simple monopolizing. (5) Natural resources may be used inefficiently in some situations. If resources are owned on a common-property basis, have external effects, or involve truly permanent changes, then competitive free-market choices may distort their use.

Key concepts

General equilibrium
Ripple effects
Efficient allocation
Marginal conditions
Invisible Hand
Market failures
External costs
Social cost
External benefits
Fairness
Marginal productivity
Monopoly power
Natural resources

Questions for review

1. *Is* every market related to all of the others? Try to give three instances of pairs of markets that are utterly *unrelated*. Then try to show that they are related, after all.

2. An earthquake shakes Los Angeles, knocking down hundreds of buildings and injuring 2,000 people. Trace the effects this might have on real estate prices near steel mills throughout the United States, on construction workers' wages in Los Angeles and Louisiana, and on the value of medical supply companies' common stocks.

3. "Price equals marginal cost is just a simple equation." Explain why it is also of profound importance.

4. Production of plastic pipes involves standard-shaped cost curves. Draw them, with average cost reaching a minimum of $1 per foot. Also draw supply and demand curves, intersecting at $1 per foot. The factories pour toxic wastes into nearby streams, whose cleanup costs are 50 cents per foot of pipe. Draw that extra cost in the cost-curves diagram and the supply-demand diagram. Show how the private prices and outputs depart from the socially efficient ones.

5. Define an efficient allocation under general equilibrium. Next, define a fair distribution, by any standard you prefer (or perhaps a combination of several standards). Will the efficient outcome be fair, either necessarily or by chance?

6. You are ambitious and hard-working, looking forward to a career that may eventually pay you $70,000 per year or more. Would that income be fair? Explain.

7. What good things do a decent society and rich culture provide? Which of these will a competitive economic system assure? Which of them might it not assure?

8. One day General Motors merges with Ford, Chrysler, and Volkswagen. In what directions would this probably change the prices and outputs of automobiles, steel, rubber, Detroit real estate, buses, and airline services?

9. The price of lobsters has gone from $4 to $13 per pound in recent years. How might competitive harvesting of this resource explain that rise?

· 18 ·

Public Finance

As you read and study this chapter, you will learn:

- the nature of social goods and external effects
- how to analyze public spending decisions using cost-benefit analysis

- how to analyze the effects of taxes on distribution and incentives
- the main pattern of actual spending and taxation

When economics first took modern shape in the 19th century, it was called "political economy." The two-word name is fitting because two great parallel processes together shape the performance of the economic system. One is the *economic* process itself, with all of the technical conditions of allocation that you now know. The other is the *political* process, which proceeds continually in cities, states, and the federal government.

Economic groups try to advance their own interests in these two processes, both individually in the market system *and* collectively by trying to exert political pressure. One result of all these efforts is a set of government rules, spending programs, and taxing policies. They have widespread effects because government takes over 30 percent of total GNP in the United States. Some of those policies have been mentioned in Chapters 1–16, but an extensive analysis of their nature has awaited this chapter.

Public finance—the study of spending and taxation by governments—is an especially challenging microeconomic subject. Good policies can often be defined, as we show in the first section, using well-established economic concepts. Social cost, social goods, and cost-benefit analysis are crucial concepts that can clarify even the most intricate problems. They all involve the familiar comparison of marginal costs with marginal benefits.

With these concepts in place, we discuss in the second section how economists analyze three fundamental subjects: *Incidence:* Who really bears the burdens of taxes? *Incentives:* How do taxes and subsidies change people's working habits? And *distribution:* How might the structure of taxes affect the distribution of wealth and income?

Though optimal social policies can be analyzed abstractly, they may not be applied in practice. Indeed, governments' actual regulatory, spending, and taxing decisions may be thoroughly inefficient and misguided. No government is perfect, and many are abject failures. History gives many examples of flawed government from Nero to Richard Nixon, from Boss Tweed to many present city councils. In fact, many governmental follies are visible in the daily news reports. Few subjects are more hotly debated than pollution controls, military budgets, welfare spending, and taxes on property and income. The actual trends presented in the third section of this chapter are the outcomes of intense, incessant struggles at all levels of government.

Economic concepts of optimal public policies

Governments have economic effects through three main powers: rule making, spending, and taxation. *Rules* are of many types, covering a variety of conditions, such as monopoly power, labor unions, pollution, and hosts of lesser matters such as speed limits and housing safety codes. *Spending* and *taxes*, however, are the core topics of public finance. They deal with the *budgets* of governments: how they take in money from the populace, via taxes, and how they spend money in public programs that provide goods and services to the populace.

Economists traditionally assign three main purposes to the public sector: **Efficiency,** the use of spending and taxes to improve the allocation of resources; **equity,** to improve the fairness of the distribution of wealth and income; and **stabilization,** the use of the budget to reduce economic fluctuations. All three are often closely mingled in the rough and tumble of actual budgetary actions in Congress, in the state legislatures, and in every town and city.

Moreover, the three goals can be in conflict. An efficient program may cause unfairness and instability, or a fair redistribution of wealth by taxes may hurt incentives for efficiency, and so on. These conflicts among goals may be important in some cases but minor in others. Over large areas of choice, the goals may be in harmony rather than in conflict.

In any event, economists try to keep the three goals clear as concepts. Each is valuable, and each can be served by good fiscal policies.

Social goods

Government policies are necessary because private markets often fail to reach optimal conditions. The main causes of such *market failure* are social goods, external effects, inequitable distribution, common-property resources, and monopoly. Table 1 gives examples of these market failures. Ideally, government policies will correct these problems by applying the principles

Table 1 *Categories of market failures*

Categories	Examples
1. *External effects:* External costs and benefits are ignored by private decision makers.	
a. *External cost:* Private choices cause output to be too large, compared to the optimum.	Pollution of the air and water by toxic wastes, smoke, etc.
b. *External benefit:* Private choices cause output to be too small, compared to the optimum.	Too small levels of: an educated electorate and worker skills (that could be provided by public schools); national defense; parks; police; lighthouses; public health actions against contagious disease
2. *Inequitable distribution*	Departures from criteria of fairness; e.g., large payments to nonproductive people, low payments to hard-working and/or needy people
3. *Open access to common-property resources:* Private actions cause excessive depletions of the resource.	Oceanic fish, lobsters, oysters, salmon, whales, etc.
4. *Monopoly:* Output is restricted; price is raised; innovation is retarded; etc.	Postal service; water and sewage; urban transit systems; courts; fire fighters
5. *Others*	
An unfair distribution of wealth and income	Extremes of wealth and poverty
An exclusion of some people from adequate health care, insurance or other needs	"Uninsurable" people; sick people unable to afford minimum health care
Hazardous jobs and products	Workplace fatalities; dangerous toys; carcinogenic products
Other hazards that a "decent society" protects its citizens against	Mass unemployment
"Nonmarket" values: There is no price tag possible, so the market will not produce them, although society may value them.	Justice; freedom from degrading and dangerous activities

of efficient resource allocation to the public sector.

A ***social good*** differs from a private good in one crucial respect: Consumption by one person does not reduce the supply available to others. ***Social goods are nonexclusive (or nonrival) in consumption. Private goods are exclusive:*** If Jones buys and uses a loaf of bread, chair, automobile, or house, each item is unavailable to everyone else. But a social good (such as a park, a road, and fire protection) is simultaneously enjoyed by many or even all citizens.

A classic instance of a social good is national defense. The military defense of the country provides a unified service. That service cannot be sold piecemeal to individuals to fit their personal desires. Instead, all citizens share alike in the resulting level of national security. A private market, by contrast, might generate various private armies for certain wealthy groups, but there would be no efficient country-wide system, and thus no true "national defense." The same logic applies, in lesser degree, to such things as public parks, police and fire protection, and public roads. Private markets would supply little or none of them.

Because a social good is consumed nonexclusively, many or all users of the good can be "free riders." Once a social good is provided, more people can use it. All users will, in fact, wish to be free riders, to use it without paying. For example, people will expect to have free access to a park or to police protection, once they are in operation. But when all people are free riders, none of them makes any payment for the social good. There is no economic expression of demand for the good.

Therefore, because social goods will not be supplied by private markets at all (or they will be undersupplied), they are a social (governmental) responsibility. The government must then decide (1) *whether* to supply the good at all, and (2) exactly *how much* of it to provide. The question of *whether* is important: Many possible social goods should not be provided at all. But the question of *how much* is the more complex issue, for which economists have prepared the following method.

For social goods, demand is summed vertically To fit the unique character of social goods, economists have developed a distinctive analysis of the demand for them. People still have their private preferences for these goods, in choosing between them and all others. Thus, people's willingness to pay for parks, schooling, and national security can be represented by individual

demand curves. These demand curves show how much people would each be willing to pay (if they were required to pay) for varying amounts of each public good. Figure 1 illustrates the case of police protection in a city. People's demands may vary, as shown, rather than be rigidly identical. Thus, Alpha's demand is much above Beta's, because Alpha has (1) stronger preferences for police services and/or (2) more money to pay for them.

But these demands are not summed up horizontally, as individual demands for private goods are (recall Chapter 6). Instead, they are summed up *vertically*, as shown in Figure 1, because the good cannot be consumed separately. You do not take a public park home for your own use, the way you do a tomato or a pair of shoes. The park is open to all, whether you use it or not. Therefore, the desired quantity of the public good, say, a park or road system, has to be the same for all. **Only the summation of what people are willing to pay gives the basis for judging how much of the public good should be provided.** That summation is done vertically, as shown in Figure 1. Then the efficient amount is given by the intersection of the demand curve with the supply curve (Point *A*). At that point, marginal benefits just equal marginal cost. At a higher quantity, marginal costs would exceed marginal benefits; the extra output costs more than it is worth.

The supply curve's rising slope reflects the added costs needed to obtain larger amounts of the good. That is perfectly conventional.

Ideally, public officials would discern people's demands, add them up, lay on the supply curve, locate the intersection of total demand and supply, and thus neatly fix the optimal level of each public good. The right amount of spending for defense, public parks, schools and public universities, welfare programs, and the thousands of

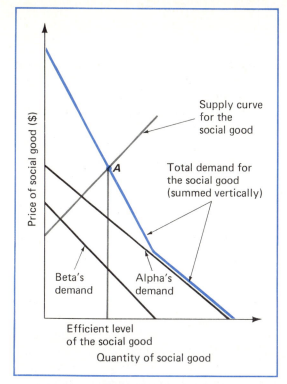

Figure 1   Summing the individual curves vertically for a public good

Public goods are available to more than one person, perhaps to many, in contrast to private goods. Therefore a vertical summing of individual demand curves is logical, as shown for the two people in this illustration. The question is not how much they would each buy at each price, but rather *how much the two persons together would be willing to pay for each level of public goods.*

other public goods could be decided clearly and precisely. Efficient conditions could be found and achieved.

The ideal process is not possible in practice, for two main reasons. *First, people are likely to misrepresent their true demand.* The public good is nonexclusive: If some people can pay for the good, other people can enjoy it for free. This is the free rider problem, as we noted earlier. Everyone would like to be a free rider, claiming to have little demand for the public good, but using it nevertheless when it is supplied. If people know their statements about their demands will commit them to pay a certain price, they will understate their true levels of demand. Other people,

they hope, will pay for the public good. But, of course, if all people claim that their demands are low, then the public good may not be produced at all.

Conversely, if citizens' answers do not affect how much they have to pay, they will be induced to overstate vastly the value of the public good to them. Yes, they will say, we should have enormous parks, fine schools, superb roads, and so on (so long as I'm not paying for them).

Both approaches to discovering demand are therefore wrong; One understates demand, the other overstates it. For ordinary private goods, by contrast, people's actions in markets directly express their willingness to pay.

Second, people may be unsure about their preferences, even if they try to give honest answers. They are accustomed to deciding about ordinary goods' prices and purchases scores of times a day. But they are rarely asked to set a money price on parks, schools, national defense, roads, and the like. People want them, in some degree, but they will often be unable to express consistent demand curves.

Altogether, social goods routinely stir exaggerated claims about people's needs and wishes. But no neat metrical process, involving economists taking polls, drawing demand curves, and finding the demand-supply intersections, can be used to decide their optimal levels. Instead, there is a political process to thrash out the choices, in a loose sequence of public debate and compromises among interest groups. The outcomes are inherently controversial, for (1) various groups have opposing interests, (2) people are often rewarded for misrepresenting their attitudes, and (3) the underlying true conditions are often unsure and changeable.

External effects

Between private goods and pure social goods lies a band of goods that are private but also have **external effects.** Such goods are partly social in nature, because the external effects create social values that the market process will ignore.

A simple instance of the divergence was given in Chapter 17: Pollution caused in producing steel is not a cost that the steel company must pay, but it results in real cost to society. Though the company can and does ignore the cost of pollution, society cannot. Public policies are often applied to allow for such external effects; pollution-control programs are one example. *But the policies are appropriate only if their costs are less than the external costs that they are designed to prevent.* If the steel company pollution's external costs are $20 million, then a pollution control program costing more than $20 million would be wasteful. In short, an external effect invites corrective public action but does not require it; the issue is one of cost.

External effects occur whenever production has repercussions beyond the seller and buyer of the good. The externalities can be either **costs** or **benefits,** as illustrated in Table 1. They are often called *social* costs and benefits to separate them from the strictly private costs and benefits that are covered by private market choices.

External costs, such as pollution, have often been severe in industrial areas. London, Pittsburgh, and scores of other cities were shrouded in thick and unhealthy smog. Despite cleanup efforts since 1950, air pollution persists in places as diverse as Gary, Indiana, Los Angeles, and New York City. Chemical wastes at hundreds of dumping sites are another large problem. There are many other external costs, including noise, traffic hazards, and even such subtle effects as those a large new building causes when it blocks the sunlight and views of nearby buildings.

External benefits arise when a good provides value to people who do not have to pay for it. Thus, a beautiful house and lawn or a handsome office building gives pleasure to people passing by. The owners pay for them, but the benefits are also available to others. External benefits are often less obvious than costs, but they can be important.

These external effects range from small to large, compared to the size of the private benefits and costs of goods. Ideally, the external element could be analyzed separately, by adding up the external benefits vertically. The private demands, meanwhile, would be added horizontally to form the market demand curve. In practice, however, such a two-part arrangement is difficult to apply.

Now we turn to the general methods for setting the levels of public expenditure for public goods or external effects.

Public expenditure: Cost-benefit analysis
Public expenditure requires choices among a large array of possible projects, whose total is far more than the public resources available. To allocate those scarce resources efficiently, economists rely mainly on **cost-benefit analysis.** Before presenting that set of tools, we need to show how spending is to be allocated among alternative projects and between social and private goods.

Allocating spending among goods Suppose that there are two social goods, A and B (they might be military and civilian programs, highways and welfare, schools and police, or any other pair). Their benefits are known, as illustrated in Figure 2 by curves showing the marginal benefits of successive dollars spent on A and B. Those curves slope down, to reflect the diminishing marginal utility of these goods. Dollars

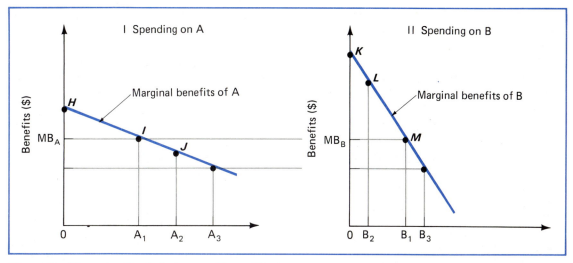

Figure 2   Allocating funds between alternatives

Let *A* and *B* be alternative social goods. The marginal benefits of each alternative are shown in Panels I and II; the downward slopes reflect declining marginal benefits.

An efficient choice sets spending so that the marginal benefits of spending on the two goods are equal. That condition is reached at A_1 and B_1. Total benefits ($OHIA_1$ plus $OKMB_1$) are maximized. For larger total spending, both levels increase, but the equality of marginal benefits is still needed, as at A_3 and B_3.

The same logic applies to allocations between public and private spending. If *A* were public and *B* were private goods, solutions such as A_1B_1 or A_3B_3 would be efficient; A_2 and B_2 would be inefficient.

not spent on *A* can be spent on *B*; therefore, the opportunity cost of a dollar spent on *A* is the marginal benefit lost by not spending it on *B*.

An efficient choice will allocate spending between *A* and *B*, so that the marginal benefits from each social good are equal. Thus, the levels A_1 and B_1 will be set, as shown, with $MB_A = MB_B$. The sum of total benefits is measured by the areas $OHIA_1$ for Good *A* and $OKMB_1$ for Good *B*. Those total benefits from both goods will be maximized when A_1 and B_1 are chosen. Any other selection (as at A_2 and B_2) will reduce the total benefits. The benefits area, A_1IJA_2, gained by spending A_1–A_2 more on Good *A* is much smaller than the benefits area, B_2LMB_1, lost by spending B_2–B_1 less on Good *B*.

If total spending is changed, then the amounts spent on *A* and *B* will also change, but the marginal benefits must still be equal. If spending increases sharply, the new efficient equilibrium might be at A_3 and B_3; the marginal benefits are lower than MB_A and MB_B, but they are equal.

We have shown how a given spending level is allocated. What if the spending level is variable? The analysis also shows what level should be chosen. **The guiding principle is that *the opportunity cost of public spending is the benefit lost by taking resources away from private projects in the economy*. The goal is now to maximize the total of *public and private benefits*. The solution involves allocating dollars until the marginal public and private benefits are equal.** This corresponds to the choice among social goods, and Figure 2 can illustrate the outcome. But now Good *A* is assumed to be private goods, while Good *B* is public goods. For any given level of total economic resources, the efficient allocation is reached when marginal private benefits from *A* equal marginal social benefits from *B*: A_1B_1 or A_3B_3 would satisfy that criterion.

Cost-benefit analysis for specific projects
Cost-benefit analysis is a formal method for deciding the efficient size of public projects. It was developed in the 1930s to analyze projects to dredge waterways and to build dams for flood control. Refined in the 1950s, it became in the 1960s the formal basis for all federal budget appraisals (under the name of "planning-programming-budgeting analysis," or PPB). The enthusiasm for it has receded, yet cost-benefit analysis is still a valid basis for framing the issues. Its core is sound and simple, though there are difficulties that keep it from giving definitive solutions. We present the technique and the problems.

THE CATEGORIES OF COSTS AND BENEFITS
The first step is to define and measure all of the costs and benefits of a project. These values are of the following main categories: *tangible or intangible* and *direct or indirect*. *Tangible* benefits and costs can be measured in the market, using dollar figures from actual transactions. *Intangible* values are real but not readily assessed in money terms. For example, education raises students' future earnings, which is a tangible benefit; it also gives the intangible benefits of greater understanding and a richer life.

Direct costs and benefits are closely related to the project's main purpose, while *indirect* values are by-products or tangential. The distinction is meaningful, even though it is hard to define rigorously. For example, a university may directly provide education, but it indirectly adds to research and technological progress, and it also increases the prosperity and the quality of life of the town where it is located.

These categories are illustrated in Table 2 by costs and benefits for irrigation

projects, education, and space research. Typically, some values can be estimated, but others can only be surmised. **Still, *the crucial first step is to include all significant kinds of costs and benefits, so that the comparison is complete, even if imprecise.*** Omission of any main class of costs or benefits can bias the evaluation and lead to major errors in policies. For example, the foregone earnings of college students are a large opportunity cost; ignoring it would encourage an overexpansion of public campuses, absorbing some students whose efficient choice is to take paying jobs. Conversely, one might ignore the research and new technology created by university faculty. That would understate total benefits and cause too little to be spent on education.

THE ANALYSIS The purpose is to maximize the net social benefit from each project. That result occurs when marginal benefits equal marginal costs. Stated simply:

Net social benefit
  = (Total social benefit) - (Total social cost).

When net social benefit is maximized, spending is at the level where

  Marginal social benefit = Marginal social cost.

The result is illustrated in Figure 3 for any typical project. All costs and benefits are included, even though some may be estimated rather than precisely known. The efficient level is *OA*, where marginal costs and benefits are both at the level *AE*. Total costs are *OBEA*. Total benefits include consumers' surplus in the amount *BCE*, so that the total benefits *OCEA* exceed the total costs *OBEA*.

Alternative levels are inefficient. Level A_1 is too small, for it fails to achieve the net benefit *DEF*. Level A_2 is too high, for it causes the loss of *EGH* in net benefits. Note how the logic parallels the marginal cost-benefit choices that have recurred

Table 2 Illustrations of the main categories of costs and benefits

Costs	Benefits
IRRIGATION PROJECT	
Tangible: Direct: Cost of pipes, channels, and other facilities	Increase in farm output
Indirect: Diversion of water from other uses	Reduction in soil erosion
Intangible: Direct: Loss of wilderness area	Beautification of the area
Indirect: Destruction of wildlife	Preservation of rural society
EDUCATION EXPENDITURE	
Tangible: Direct: Teachers' salaries, cost of campus facilities, books, and related items	Increase in students' future earnings
Indirect	Reduced costs of preventing crime, because added skills reduce crime rates
Intangible: Direct: Foregone leisure time	A richer life, with greater understanding
Indirect	A more intelligent electorate, greater political stability
SPACE RESEARCH	
Tangible: Direct: Costs of inputs (workers, equipment, fuel, etc.)	As yet unknown
Indirect: Diversion of talent and research from earth-based problems	The generation of new technology (discovering resources, flight, communications, etc.)
Intangible: Direct: Pollution of space	Fascination of discovery; knowledge of the universe
Indirect	Gain in world prestige; military advantages

Source: Adapted from Table 8–2 in R. A. Musgrave and P. B. Musgrave, *Public Finance in Theory and Practice* 3rd. ed. (New York: McGraw-Hill, 1980). ©McGraw-Hill Book Company, 1980. By permission.

throughout the discussion of microeconomics in this book.

Matters of degree are also important, as Figure 4 illustrates. If costs are underestimated, then the true cost curve lies above the apparent cost curve. The correct level is at A_3, less than half of A. If instead, benefits are overestimated, then the true benefits curve lies below, and the correct level, A_4, is even lower. Indeed, virtually none of this project should be done. Such contrasts occur frequently in practical cases, including irrigation, education, and space research. The project's advocates foresee large benefits and small costs; its critics expect costs to be large and benefits small. Whether the project should be large or terminated, then, turns on the correct amounts in the cost-benefit calculation.

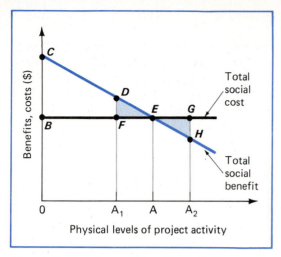

Figure 3   Simple cost-benefit analysis

The efficient level for the project is *A*, where both the marginal benefits and the marginal costs of the project are the amount *AE*. Level *A₁* is too small because it would forgo the net benefits *FDE*. Level *A₂* is too high because it incurs the unnecessary net loss of benefits shown by *EGH*.

DISCOUNTING   The costs and benefits occur over time, rather than instantly. Though most of the costs are immediate, the benefits often stretch out over many years. For example, the construction of a public university classroom building requires cur-

rent spending, but the building's benefits will only be realized during many future decades.

Such future values must be discounted because future benefits are less valuable than current benefits. The same is true of costs. The future values must be converted to *present values*. The discounting is similar to the discounting of private values done by private firms (in Chapter 7).

The discounted value depends on (1) the duration of the time interval and (2) the discount rate. For example, a $1 million value 10 years hence discounted at 5 percent has a present value of $613,900; for a 20-year interval, it is $376,900; for 20 years discounted at 10 percent, the present value is only $148,600. The most common error is to discount future benefits at too low a rate. That can cause a project's benefits to be sharply overstated and encourage too much spending on the project.

The correct discount rate is a matter of debate, but the consensus is that it should be at the interest rates prevailing in the private economy, with possibly an

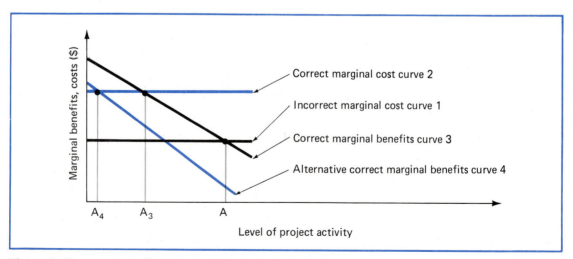

Figure 4   How wrong estimates can affect the outcomes

If officials believe that Curves 1 and 3 are correct, then amount *A* appears to be efficient. But if Curve 2 is correct (rather than 1), then the efficient level is much smaller, at *A₃*. If, moreover, Curve 4 is the correct representation of benefits (rather than Curve 3), then the efficient choice is at the low level of *A₄*.

adjustment to reflect social values. Private interest rates are usually much higher than those at which governments can borrow funds. Private rates would, therefore, apply a tighter standard to public projects, sharply reducing the efficient level of spending.

For example, for many years the Army Corps of Engineers used the interest rate on government borrowings (then about 3–5 percent) as its discount rate in justifying the building of hundreds of dams. But those projects took capital from the private sector, where it could have earned perhaps 10–12 percent on average. Since the opportunity cost of the capital was the forgone 10–12 percent rate, the Corps should have used a discount rate in that range. That would have shown that scores of the dams were an inefficient use of resources and should not have been built.

WHO SHOULD PAY: GENERAL TAXPAYERS OR SPECIFIC USERS? Even if the efficient level is defined, there is still the question of who should pay for the public service. Funds can come from *general tax revenues;* or the *users* can be charged for some or all of the costs; or both sources can be used, in some ratio.

General tax funds are the best source to use when the benefits are widely spread. Such universal social goods include military defense, police and fire protection, public health programs, and schools. The costs are shared because the benefits are shared.

At the other extreme, because *many social goods are used only by specific groups of people, those groups ought to bear the financial burden.* Examples are airports, water supply, harbors, many state and national parks, and certain roads. "User fees" or "earmarked taxes" are often charged to cover part or all of the costs. The fees may be general (e.g., a gas-oline tax that pays for building and maintaining roads) or specific (e.g., a park permit or a toll charged for crossing a bridge).

Naturally, each user group tries to get its social good included in the general budget to minimize its own payments. Often, as a result of impassioned argument, deceptive data, or political muscle, such groups get their way. Therefore, many narrowly used public programs are financed out of general tax revenues, even though they benefit small groups of affluent people. Only when the recipients are poor and unable to pay is there a good reason for drawing on the general budget.

In practice, public funding is a patchwork of many varieties, with many departures from what seems appropriate. Moreover, the actual levels of many programs are also sharply inefficient. The political process is not perfect, and it often gives inefficient and unfair outcomes. Details on major public policies will be given in the third main section of this chapter and in Chapters 19 and 20.

Alternatives to public spending and taxes

Often a social need can be provided by means other than public spending and taxes. Four such alternatives follow.

Rules and fines rather than spending or taxes Social action can often rely on the setting of rules rather than on direct spending and taxes. For example, pollution can be reduced by declaring certain levels of it to be illegal, with fines imposed on violators. Firms would then adjust their profit-maximizing choices toward lower pollution levels. If, instead, the government gave money to the firms for cleaning up, or provided tax incentives to them, the dollar cost to the public budget might be much greater.

Setting such limits correctly is an important task, for which economics provides

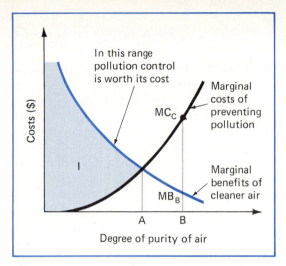

In this range pollution control is worth its cost

MC_C

Marginal costs of preventing pollution

Costs ($)

I

Marginal benefits of cleaner air

MB_B

A   B

Degree of purity of air

Figure 5   Costs and benefits of preventing air pollution

One solid line shows the marginal social benefits of clean air. It is high at the left, where pollution is intense; but as pollution recedes (toward the right), the *marginal benefits* of cleaner air decline to low levels. The *marginal costs* of preventing pollution follow the opposite pattern: They rise sharply as efforts are made to filter out the last few degrees of pollution (to the right).

Given these curves, the efficient level of cleanliness of air is at Point *A*, where marginal cost just equals marginal benefit. At a higher pollution level, the marginal damages of pollution are above the cost it would take to prevent them. The shaded area I is the net gain from reducing pollution to Point *A*. To get the air cleaner than it is at Point *A* would cost more than the damage it would prevent. At Point *B*, for example, the marginal cost of clean air *(MC_c)* is far above the marginal social benefits of the clean air *(MB_B)*.

a clear analysis, as illustrated in Figure 5. "How much pollution" is a matter of degree, with higher levels imposing ever-higher marginal costs on society. But the costs of preventing pollution are also real, and they rise too, even at the margin, as pollution is reduced toward zero. Thus when automobile emissions were first attacked by law after 1965, it was relatively easy to prevent about half of the fumes and particles. Small adjustments in engine design were cheap and effective. But stopping the last 20 percent of harmful emissions (at the right-hand end of Figure 5) is far more costly, requiring major design changes and costly apparatus. The same is true of most factory smoke and chemical wastes.

The economic task is to compare marginal benefits and costs, to stop pollution only as far as it is worthwhile to do so. That balance is reached at Point *A* in Figure 5, where the marginal benefit of preventing that last bit of pollution equals the marginal cost of doing so. Reducing pollution even further would require using resources that cost more than the extra benefit they give.

Some students resist the idea that the pollution below *A* is economically acceptable: All pollution is bad, they say. Possibly, but when the marginal cost of stopping it is much higher than the extra benefit, the economist can only conclude that stamping out every trace of pollution makes no economic sense. To do so is too costly. Of course, the locations of the cost and benefit functions are often debatable.

Differing estimates of relative costs and benefits imply different policy actions. There is little wonder that the issue is controversial. For example, officials in the Reagan administration have argued that the marginal costs of pollution control are understated and the marginal benefits are exaggerated.

Another problem arises *when the costs of action are borne by different groups of people from those who gain the benefits.* For example, air pollution may hurt all people living in New York City, but the costs of cleaning it up might fall on factory owners and truck owners living elsewhere. Efficiency requires that a cleanup occur up to the correct margin, shown by Point *A* in Figure 5, but the factory and truck owners will resist the program. New Yorkers will advocate it, naturally. In such cases, there are political difficulties in achieving the efficient result. Yet, the economist's main task is still to define that efficient outcome.

These issues are perfectly general, applying to all external effects. A balance is usually needed between the marginal benefits and costs of the public action. But now comes a subtle point: The costs of correction are equally valid, whether they are borne by the government budget or by private firms. If stopping factory smoke requires expensive new furnaces, that cost matters whether the companies or the government pays for it. Therefore, the cost curve in Figure 5—as well as Point *A*, the efficient level—applies regardless of who pays the costs.

Once Point *A* is known, the government can require companies to meet it. If enforced, that simple law gets the desired result without requiring public spending. The government could, instead, try methods that absorb public funds: To reach Point *A*, it could guarantee loans, provide tax breaks, or even buy new furnaces for the factories. But the government can minimize the taxpayers' burden by simply imposing the efficient rules.

Private sources Often the public service can in fact be supplied by private firms who see the need, design the service, and find a way to sell it. Thus, private "health maintenance organizations" arising since 1970 may obviate the need for more expensive public medical programs. Even where a social element remains, it can often be met by a limited subsidy rather than by a total public subsidy. Thus, public universities usually draw only part of their funds from governments. They rely on private tuition and fees to cover the private values that they provide to students.

Insurance pooling Risks of accident, disease, loss of work, and other calamities can be covered by government programs. But often private insurance schemes can be developed to cover most or all of such risks. As long as the pooling permits the system as a whole to meet its costs, coverage can be extended to include even people with high risk levels.

Charity and other not-for-profit suppliers When private firms fail to provide goods that have external benefits, government action may not be needed if special not-for-profit firms fill the gap. Until recent times, churches and charities provided most social assistance to the poor and helpless. Though often meager and demeaning, such charity support was frequently important. Even with the enlargement of public programs in recent decades, many not-for-profit firms still exist, including hospitals, cooperatives, the Red Cross, YMCA-YWCA, cultural organizations, and United Way groups.

These so-called third sector groups now make up a substantial part of the economy. Moreover, they cover some of the most distinctive social activities in our culture. In many sectors, they provide services that make public spending unnecessary.

Altogether, these four categories cover many social needs in ways that avoid public spending. The art of public finance lies in *minimizing* public spending while attaining efficient and fair social results.

Categories of spending and taxes

We conclude the first main section of this chapter by setting forth the standard categories of public spending and taxation. They provide background for analyzing tax impacts in the second main section and the major patterns of public finance in the third main section.

Spending Governments spend money on thousands of different items, from battleships to teachers' salaries to welfare payments. These items divide into two main categories:

PURCHASES Governments buy labor, products, and services. The money is spent to obtain costly items. Thus, people work for governments and receive salaries. Companies sell governments such products as police cars, foods, aircraft, garbage trucks, desks, and all the rest. Governments buy such services as the building of schools and the paving of highways.

TRANSFER PAYMENTS This category is distinct from purchases, because **transfer payments** simply provide money to people who are in certain categories. The people do not supply any work, product, or service in return. To qualify for transfer payments, people must be poor, elderly, sick, or in some other category specified by the programs. The payments simply transfer funds from taxpayers to recipients. Of course, the recipients then spend the funds on goods and services that they choose.

Purchases provide governments with the supplies they need to function. Transfer payments, on the other hand, are meant to provide needy people with the funds they need to function—to spend as they choose.

Taxes A tax takes money from a person or organization by a government. **Taxes** can be imposed at many points in the economic process, such as on sales, income, property, or imports. Actual taxes present a wide variety. Yet, all taxes divide into two basic categories.

PERSONAL TAXES are based on the taxpayer's personal ability to pay. The leading example is the personal income tax, levied on the yearly flow of income. Most personal taxes are *direct* taxes, coming directly out of personal income.

IN REM TAXES ("taxes on things") are levied on objects or activities, such as sales, purchases, transfers of property, or the holding of property itself. These taxes are not based on the taxpayer's personal ability to pay. Most *in rem* taxes are *indirect* taxes, being imposed at various points in

the economy rather than directly on the people who will finally bear the burden of the tax.

For example, a sales tax is an *in rem*, indirect tax. As we showed in Chapter 5, its burden depends on the relative inelasticities of demand and supply. An income tax is direct, coming straight from the pocket of the person who pays it.

Taxes: Impacts on distribution and incentives

We now discuss three effects of taxes: (1) on who bears the burden of the tax, (2) on incentives to work, and (3) on distribution. Economists have developed standard analyses of each topic, using supply, demand, and other concepts that you have now mastered. Their logic is straightforward, even though the matters of degree are often complex.

Incidence: Analyzing who bears the burden of taxes

Each tax dollar must come ultimately from someone. But that burden is often difficult to trace. For example, though you may pay $4 in sales tax when you buy $100 worth of textbooks, the $4 may ultimately be paid not by you but by others: perhaps the bookstore, or the publishing companies, or still others. For another example, private landlords usually pay real estate taxes on their apartment buildings. Do student renters end up paying those taxes indirectly?

These are matters of **incidence,** the real burden of taxes. Incidence matters because tax burdens can be heavy, and where they fall is often highly uncertain. Tax burdens are often *shifted* from one group to another. Because personal income and wealth taxes cannot be shifted very much, their incidence falls directly on the payer. But since sales taxes and taxes on businesses may be shifted extensively, economists have studied their incidence in great detail.

In Chapter 5 we presented the main technique for analyzing the incidence of a sales tax. As you may recall, the tax is added to the supply curve of the good, as was shown in Figure 7 of Chapter 5. This shifts the market equilibrium from Point *A* to Point *B*. Output shrinks from 100 to 80. As for price, the consumer now pays $35 for each unit, which is more than the original $30 price before the sales tax was imposed. But the seller only receives $25 per unit, after turning over the $10 in tax to the government.

Therefore, in this case, the burden of the tax falls equally on the sellers and the buyers. Buyers pay $5 more per unit; sellers receive $5 less. This illustration was designed to show that the burden can fall on both groups. But the perfectly equal division it depicts is a fluke; the burdens of most taxes will be unevenly divided between sellers and buyers, perhaps even falling entirely on one group or the other.

What determines the outcome? How can the division of the burden be discovered? We presented the analysis of incidence in detail in Chapter 5. The basic answer is: *The burden depends on the relative elasticities of demand and supply*.

At the extreme, if either demand or supply is perfectly inelastic, then buyers or sellers, respectively, will bear the entire burden of a sales tax. More generally, the relative incidence of burdens reflects the relative inelasticities. Both demand and supply may be inelastic or elastic, but the burden will fall more heavily on the side that is *relatively less elastic* than the other.

This fact has long been recognized by tax officials, who have always sought inelastic items to tax. Inelasticity means, by definition, that there is little response of quantities. Therefore, the tax yield will be relatively high.

Examples of heavily taxed items with inelastic demand are such necessities as gasoline today and salt and spices in the Middle Ages, and such habit-forming items as liquor and tobacco. Though governments often claim to be taxing liquor and tobacco to discourage drinking and smoking, a primary reason for such taxes is that demand for these things is inelastic. As for inelastic supply, land is a prime instance, because it cannot be moved. Therefore, it is not surprising that most cities rely heavily on real estate taxes on land values.

Incidence also affects the equity of taxes. If the burden falls on people with low incomes, the tax may be unfair. One intriguing example is real estate taxes on apartments. Does their burden fall mainly on renters or on landlords? The tax is usually reflected in higher rents, so that renters pay at least part of the tax. But the exact shares depend on relative elasticities.

Taxes also affect efficiency by changing quantities and prices. If the original conditions were efficient, then taxes distort them and cause total output to shrink. Of course, the opposite may occur. The original conditions may have been inefficient, with prices not equaling true social values. If the tax just nicely corrects those original distortions (e.g., reaching Point *A* in Figure 5), the tax itself is *efficient*.

Incentives: How taxes may affect choices

Economists have long studied how taxes change people's individual choices. They have focused most closely on the *incentives to work*. Taxes may discourage people from working, by taxing away the money they are paid for their work. It is a perennial issue, and, indeed, it seems obvious to many people that taxes discourage work by cutting the rewards for it. Improving the economic incentives for effort has been a main theme of the Reagan economic program. But economic analysis shows that the ***incentive effects*** are not obvious at all. Taxes may encourage work, discourage work, or not affect it at all.

The actual effect depends on each person's supply curve of labor, a curve that we discussed in the chapter on labor. Two contrasting cases of supply curves are shown in Figure 6, for Ludwig and Jewett. The amounts each will work per day are related to the wages they can obtain. Imagine that both Ludwig and Jewett are paid $8 per hour and that they both happen to work an average of 7 hours per day.

Now suppose that a 25 percent tax on income is imposed, so that their net pay after tax is only $6 pcr hour. That after-tax income is shown by the horizontal line at

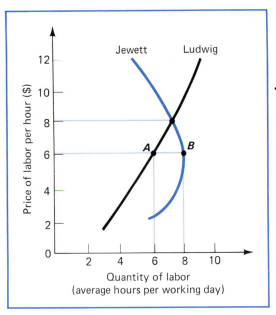

Figure 6   Analyzing the effects of a tax on incentives to work

At a wage rate of $8 per hour, both workers choose to work for 7.0 hours per day, on the average. A 25 percent tax would reduce their take-home pay to $6 per hour. In response to that tax, Ludwig cuts back to 6 hours per day, while Jewett increases to 8 hours per day.

If the original wage rate were $4 per hour, the 25 percent tax would lead both workers to reduce their hours of effort. But if Jewett's original wage rate is $10 per hour, even a 50 percent tax would cause him to increase his hours.

$6, which cuts the labor supply curves at Point *A* for Ludwig and *B* for Jewett. Evidently, the tax leads Ludwig to work less but Jewett to work more. The general conclusion is easy to grasp: The effect of an income tax upon the incentive to work depends on the shape of the labor supply curve. Depending on the curve, the effect may be positive, negative, or neutral.

Many students find it easier to understand Ludwig's response than Jewett's. Ludwig works less because he is paid less. But Jewett's response can be explained by recalling the *price and income effects* from Chapters 6 and 14. As the net wage rate falls, it makes work less attractive at the margin (the price effect). But it also cuts the income that the worker receives for a given amount of work (the income effect). If the person needs the income desperately enough, the income effect will overcome the price effect, causing that person to work more. Jewett is such a case for wage rates over $5, as shown by the bending back of his supply curve above the $5 level.

But notice that Jewett's curve slopes upward at wage rates below $5 per hour. Therefore, if the original wage rate is $4 and the 25 percent tax cuts the net wage to $3 per hour, both Jewett and Ludwig will cut their work times. This makes the whole effect of taxes on people even less predictable because the same person may respond differently at differing wage levels.

Altogether the work-incentive effects of taxes are an open issue, even if the tax rates are high. Thus, even a 50 percent rate would lead Jewett to work more, if the original wage rate were $10 per hour. The same logic also applies to any other kind of effort that taxes might discourage, such as inventing, investing, or the creative arts. It also holds for estate taxes, where the parents' efforts to provide wealth for their children might be cut by taxation.

Taxes may either discourage or encourage effort. The outcome is a matter of degree. Despite its obvious importance to the whole work burdens and productivity of the populace, the issue has not been settled by factual research. Economists have not been able to determine which way the actual effects go, on balance. As in other areas, the logic is clear, but the magnitudes are difficult to unravel.

Tax friction Nevertheless, taxes do clearly alter the choices of many taxpayers. Even if some people work more, many others probably work less. Some people shift toward barter and more do-it-yourself projects. Other choices are also disturbed. For example, people buy more houses because the interest paid on mortgages is tax deductible. Business managers may spend more because they are on tax-deductible expense accounts. Every day millions of choices are shifted because of tax effects.

Economists call the resulting distortions of choices *tax friction.* This friction subtracts from national output because it disturbs the efficient conditions that tax-free market choices would have given. Many of the disturbances are small, but together they can add up to significant totals.

Economists have tried to devise "costless" or "frictionless" taxes that won't alter any choices. But the search has been discouraging. Virtually all taxes are keyed to the levels of what is taxed: income, sales, property values, and so on. The closest to an ideal frictionless tax is the so-called lump-sum tax, which is levied simply on a person or enterprise. It is carefully *not* based on any economic magnitude. Rather, it is just a dollar amount taken either once-for-all or at some interval. Thus, a tax of $500 per year on each adult person would be a lump-sum tax. It would not specifically alter people's choices about work. But, of course, even this lump-sum tax would cause friction by

making people poorer and therefore leading them to change some of their choices.

Perhaps even better in principle is a tax on pure *rent*. When any good is in perfectly inelastic supply, then all payments to it are rent. A tax on pure rents to land would be nearly frictionless, for it would not affect the supply of land. To that extent, taxes on land values are superior to other taxes because they do not distort choices at the margin. But land taxes do have practical problems because most land has capital improvements, whose supplies *are* disturbed by property taxes.

Distribution: The effects of taxes and spending

We now arrive at one of the most basic features of public finance: how it affects the distribution of income and wealth. At each moment, the population is arrayed along a spectrum between low and high economic status, between poor and rich. Each person's status is determined by such *economic* forces as the income from work and the inheritance of property from parents. The state also affects this status by its *policies*, in applying taxes that take money away and spending programs that provide money or valuable services.

In short, taxes and spending have an incidence on the whole distribution of income and wealth. This is a larger topic than the incidence of sales taxes between sellers and buyers, discussed above. Now the basic question is whether each tax or spending item moves income up or down.

Progressive and regressive incidence The crucial concepts are progressivity and regressivity. A *progressive tax* falls more heavily on the rich than the poor. A *regressive tax* is the opposite, taking more heavily from the poor than the rich. Spending programs follow the same logic. Economists also speak of the incidence of taxing and spending taken together: Does the whole budget tend to shift money and benefits down the income scale or upward? Even if one specific tax is regressive, the net effect of all taxes and spending may be progressive.

The term *proportional* is the key to defining progressivity and regressivity. A proportional tax takes the same percentage share of income, no matter what the level of income is.* A constant 15 percent tax rate, for example, is proportional. It is illustrated in Figure 7 by Line *A*. The horizontal axis is the amount of money income. The vertical axis is the tax rate, as a percentage of income. The flat-rate 15 percent proportional tax is a horizontal line, for the percentage rate does not change as income changes. The *marginal* tax rate out of each additional dollar of income is identical to the *average* tax rate out of all income. Both are constant at 15 percent.

A progressive tax takes a rising share of income, as income rises. Line *B* in Figure 7 illustrates such progressivity, using recent actual rates of the U.S. federal income tax as they apply to a single person. The tax rate rises by steps: The first $2,300 of income has a zero rate; the next $1,100 pays a 14 percent rate; the next $1,000 a 16 percent rate. Then the rises get steeper; between $14,000 and $41,500, the rate rises from 26 percent to 49 percent. The rises continue on up to a maximum 70 percent rate for income above $108,300. These rising rates contrast with the constant rate of the proportional tax.

The rising tax share as income increases shows a "progressive incidence." Progressive incidence tends to reduce inequality, by making after-tax incomes more equal. Neutral incidence leaves in-

equality unchanged: Everyone's income is scaled down by the same degree.

The progressive stair-step rates in Figure 7 are called *marginal tax rates* because they show what share is taken out of each marginal increase of income. There is also an *average tax rate* at each level of income. With a proportional tax, the marginal and average rates are identical throughout, as at 15 percent in Figure 7. But the average rate diverges from the marginal rate when progressivity occurs. Below a $2,300 income, both rates are zero; but by $3,400, the marginal rate is 14 percent and it is pulling up the average rate. The average rate lags below the marginal rate, for it also includes the earlier zero rates on income below $2,300. The same principle holds throughout, because the average rate includes all earlier rates, while the marginal rate applies strictly to the last dollar.

Note that even when marginal rates are 50 percent, the average tax bite may still be substantially lower. For example, at a taxable income of $85,000, the marginal rate is 50 percent. But the tax actually paid would be $40,000, which is an average of 47 percent. In short, the high marginal rate may have a large bite, but the taxpayer's whole sacrifice may remain less sharp on average.

Now consider the case of *regressive taxes*. They take a lower percentage of income as income increases, as illustrated in Figure 8. Several major taxes are, in fact, regressive. Sales taxes, which are typically 4 to 8 percent of the sales dollar as levied by most states and some cities, fall on people's consumption expenditures. Those purchases are a bigger share of income for poor people than for the affluent. Thus, a New York family with $7,000 per year may have to spend it all on consumption items, paying the 8 percent sales tax on all its income. A $100,000 New York family might spend "only" $30,000, saving the rest. The

---

*Strictly speaking, the structure of a tax can be considered separately from its effect on actual after-tax incomes, that is, from its incidence. But economists commonly use the term *incidence* for both meanings.

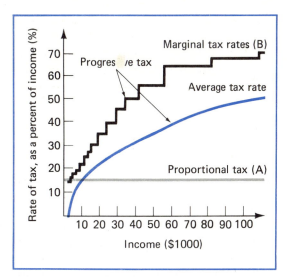

Figure 7   Proportional and progressive tax rates

The proportional tax is a constant percentage income, regardless of level. A proportional tax at a 15 percent rate is shown by the horizontal line.

A progressive tax imposes steeper rates as incomes rise. The marginal rates follow a rising stair-step pattern. The average rate of tax actually paid is below the marginal rate, as shown. The progressive tax rates shown are the recent U.S. federal income tax rates for a single taxpayer. The taxable income is the amount after all deductions.

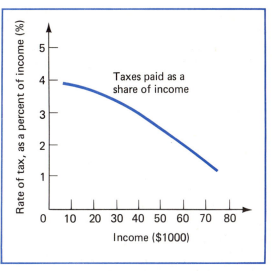

Figure 8   A regressive tax

The sales tax is levied at, say, 4 percent of sales. Families with low incomes spend virtually all of their income on consumption goods, so that the 4 percent tax takes away about 4 percent of their incomes. But more affluent families spend a smaller share of their income on retail items, so their sales tax payments are a smaller share of their incomes. A $60,000 family spends "only" $30,000; the 4 percent tax on that $30,000 yields $1,200 in taxes, which is only 2 percent of the $60,000 income.

resulting $2,400 that it pays in sales tax on its $30,000 of purchases is only 2.4 percent of its income, compared to the 8 percent paid by the $7,000 family.

Other regressive taxes include gasoline taxes, liquor taxes, and real estate taxes. Each falls *proportionally* more heavily on the poor than on the rich because, on average, these items loom larger in the budgets of lower-income people. (Note: Renters also pay real estate taxes, but only indirectly in their monthly rents. The owners pay the taxes directly, but pass at least some of the tax on in higher rents.)

Public spending programs also have an incidence on the distribution of income by providing money and other benefits unevenly along the income scale. Some programs are tied firmly to income tests, so

that they go to poor families. Examples are income supplements for the poor, and public housing that is provided at below-cost rents to families with low incomes. Such programs are progressive because they tend to equalize the distribution of income. Other programs are regressive because their benefits go mainly to upper income people. Farm policies, for example, have channeled large payments to large-scale farmers, most of whom are already prosperous.

In sum, the basic logic of incidence is straightforward. Society can tax and spend in ways that move money and benefits up or down the income scale. Logically, too, economists can define an *optimum incidence* of these policies, reflecting any given set of social goals. But when one tries to apply such broad judgments in practical details, there are two problems to solve:

1. *How much* progressive redistribution would be optimum is highly controversial.
2. The optimum policies will involve careful *balancing* among various kinds of taxes and spending.

The task is often complex because the goals are controversial. Moreover, the actual incidence of policies is often hard to discover because people manage to escape or twist the policies in unexpected ways. Also, the policies are not created by benevolent wizards; they evolve instead in an imperfect democratic political process.

Economists have defined the main features of a "good" tax system as follows:

1. The distribution of tax burdens is fair, by whatever criteria the society chooses.
2. Taxes are chosen and designed to minimize friction, which reduces the economy's efficiency.
3. The system is understandable to taxpayers and run at as low a cost as possible.

With these goals in mind, you can now approach the actual patterns of taxes and spending.

Major patterns of public finance

Among all the varieties of spending and taxes, there are several important trends and patterns. We present first the trend of total spending and then the composition of spending and taxes. In the process, we will also explain such technical features as indexing and tax expenditures. We save for a later chapter a review of how progressive the incidence of taxes and expenditure really is.

Economic policies apply rules and controls, as well as taxes and spending. Those rules and controls are too varied for a full survey, but some of them will be shown in the three case studies in Chapter 20.

Trend and share

The expanding economic role of governments is reflected in the trend of total U.S. public expenditure in Figure 9. A rise in the dollar totals was inevitable: As the population grew, national output increased, and prices rose. To put that dollar growth in perspective, Figure 9 shows total government spending as a share of gross national product (or GNP). That share was below 20 percent of GNP until 1940. It rose sharply after 1940 because of World War II and the large military expenditures due to the "cold war" of the 1950s. Then the 1960s brought major "Great Society" welfare programs, the space race to put people on the moon, and the Vietnam War. These ventures swelled spending, leading after 1980 to the Reagan administration's efforts to reduce the size of government. In short, there have been specific forces and conditions at work in the United States, causing both the rising trend and a series of changes. Yet, total government spending since 1953 has only risen from 28 to 33 percent of total economic activity. Less than one third of GNP now passes through the hands of governments in the United States. Actual government purchases of goods and services have remained at about 20 percent of GNP since 1952.

Is that "high" or "moderate"? By international standards (see Table 3), the United States is below the middle range of industrial economies in this respect. The relative affluence of many of these countries permits them to afford high levels of various public services. However, the sim-

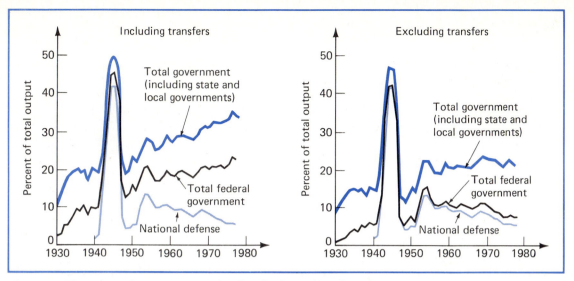

Figure 9   The trend of government spending in the United States

Before 1930, total public spending was below 10 percent of GNP. Programs to cure the Depression raised it toward 20 percent, and then World War II increased it sharply to nearly 50 percent. Since 1950, total spending has risen from about 25 to about 33 percent. Yet, public purchases of actual goods and services have stabilized at about 20 percent of GNP.

ple comparisons offered in Table 3 do not indicate whether in each country all the public programs are close to their efficient levels. Social needs differ sharply from country to country, because of differences in social structure, military needs, geographical size, and natural resources. Also, national preferences differ about what society should provide for its people.

Table 3   *The relative size of the public sector in selected countries*

Country	Tax Revenue at All Levels of Government, as a Percent of GNP (1980)
Sweden	56
Netherlands	55
France	45
United Kingdom	43
Canada	39
Switzerland	36
West Germany	30
United States	28
India	20
Japan	18

Sources: Tax revenue: International Monetary Fund, *Government Finance Statistics Yearbook*, Vol. V, 1981. GNP: International Monetary Fund, *International Financial Statistics*, December 1981.

Table 3 suggests little more than that the United States' share of GNP is lower than that taken by governments in other industrialized Western countries. The reductions in certain nonmilitary programs by the Reagan budget cutters in 1981–1984 will reduce the share slightly. In the 1940s, Colin Clark argued that any rise of public spending above 25 percent of GNP would cause severe economic problems. The experience of most western economies has belied that warning. Public expenditure can go too far and may be wasteful in many cases, but no general law seems to hold. One must look instead at the parts, to see if they are efficient and fair.

Composition: Local, state, and federal shares
The growth of spending by the three main levels of government is shown in Figure 10. Until the 1930s, spending by local governments was more than half of the total, while spending by the federal government was slight (except during World War I). The ruling conservative doctrine regarded federal programs as unnecessary, even reckless. All true needs could be met lo-

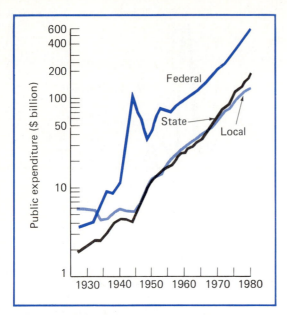

Figure 10 Public spending by the three U.S. levels of government

Local expenditure was originally the largest. Then federal spending rose sharply and has continued to grow. State spending has played an intermediate role.

cally, it held. Income taxes played a minor role, since they were held to invade personal freedoms.

Local spending has continued to be important throughout modern times. Its main purposes are basic ones: schools, streets, utilities, and personal safety. The tie between taxing and spending is close, for the funds stay in the locality. Yet, there has been a growth of local programs paid for mostly by the federal government, including aid to the poor, urban renewal, and health care.

State spending has traditionally been the least important, but since 1965, it, too, has expanded strongly. "Revenue sharing" has channeled back substantial amounts of federal funds to the states, which the states can use as they wish.

Altogether, since 1940, federal spending has been the dominant share, but local and state spending have been keeping pace

since 1965. Thus, issues of public policy are important at all levels.

Purchases and transfer payments

Most public spending goes to buy work, products, and services. Such *purchases* from private markets cover an endless variety of items, such as workers' skills of various types, military weapons, school buildings, asphalt for roads, garbage trucks, and gasoline for police cars. The flow of these items now totals 20 percent of GNP, as shown in Figure 9.

Transfer payments have risen sharply since 1965, as Figure 11 shows. The rise reflects partly the growth of "Great Society" programs designed to relieve poverty and urban problems. Social Security payments and other pensions also rose after 1968, when Congress "indexed" them to the consumer price index. When price inflation occurs, these payments automatically rise.

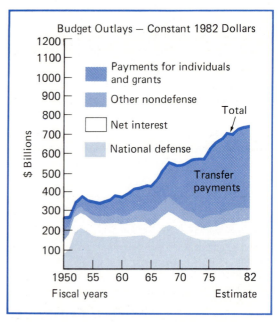

Figure 11 Transfer payments and other federal government outlays 1950–1981

The main transfer payments are in the upper part of the trends in the figure. Their share has grown since the early 1960s.

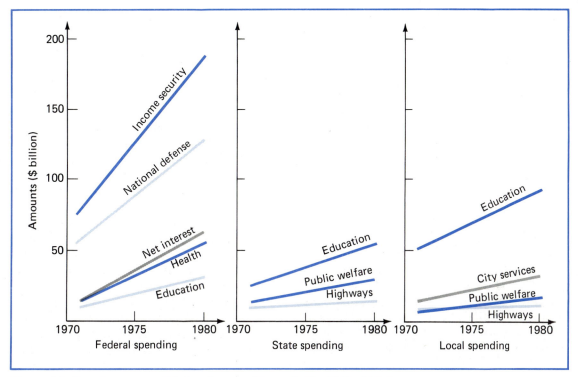

Figure 12   Local, state, and federal expenditures in the United States

However wise these growing transfer payments may be, they do not take goods out of the private economy—they only shift money to different consumers. Transfer payments, therefore, are less important than purchases in altering the capacity and composition of national production.

The variety of spending programs

Figure 12 indicates the diversity of the main spending programs at the three levels of government. Federal programs range from agriculture to space, military defense, highways, welfare payments, and Medicare. State spending is mainly for education and roads. Local spending goes primarily to schools, roads, and local services.

Several important programs are not shown in the budget. They are financed "off-budget," out of so-called trust funds with money from earmarked taxes. One such off-budget item is the federal highway program, which is paid out of gasoline taxes. Another is large loan-guarantee programs to farmers and to cities for pollution-control equipment. Their inclusion would appreciably alter the federal budget.

The loan guarantee programs need a special word. Perhaps they seem like a costless method for the government to induce people to make investments that it wants. Thus, to promote city development, the government guarantees loans to companies locating in the desired cities. The firms get the loans at lower interest rates, cities get the factories and jobs, and with luck, the loans are paid off. There is no direct public expenditure.

However, three defects mar this neat logic. One is economic: The loan guaran-

395

tees actually do have a significant opportunity cost. Each government must pay to borrow money at going interest rates (governments currently issue over $1,500 billion in bonds). The more it borrows or guarantees, the more the government draws funds away from private uses and from other worthy public purses. Since that raises the cost of funds, the government must pay higher interest rates. This increase is the cost of the "costless" guarantees. It can be large, even though it is indirect.

The other two defects are practical. Usually, the guarantee program spreads to cover a variety of loans unrelated to the purpose of the program. Thus, the Federal Farm Loan programs in the 1970s made loans for golf courses, condominiums, and shopping malls. Many other such programs become windfalls for interest groups. Finally, some of the loans don't change behavior even though they formally go to firms making the correct investments. If the worthy investment would be made

even without the loan, as is often the case, then the loan guarantee is a waste.

Taxes

Turning to taxes, one also finds great variety and uncertain effects. The main lines are given in Table 4 for federal, state, and local taxes. Federal income and Social Security taxes have become dominant now at 60 percent of all taxes and 20 percent of total GNP. Next are the various sales taxes, and then property taxes. The corporation profits tax is highly valuable over the business cycle, supplying between 10 and 25 percent of federal revenue. The estate tax, which is intended to reduce the impact of inherited wealth, continues to represent only 2 percent of federal taxes and less than 1 percent of all taxes.

Tax expenditures ("loopholes") We need also to discuss *tax expenditures.* The standard tax rates do not, in fact, apply to everyone. There are many exceptions and special provisions, so that taxpayers'

Table 4   *Taxes and revenues at the local, state, and federal levels (% billions)*

	1932	1950	1970	1980	
				Amount	Percent
Local					
Property tax	4.2	7.0	33.0	64.1	29.9
Sales and gross receipts tax	0.26	0.48	3.1	9.3	4.3
Individual income tax	—	0.64	1.6	4.1	1.9
Other	1.7	8.0	51.4	137.0	63.9
State					
Sales and gross receipts tax	0.73	4.7	27.3	58.3	25.9
Individual income tax	0.07	0.72	9.2	29.1	12.9
From federal government	0.22	2.3	19.3	51.2	22.8
Other	1.5	6.2	33.1	86.4	38.4
Federal					
Individual income tax	0.41	15.7	90.4	181.0	42.0
Corporate income tax	0.60	10.5	32.8	60.0	13.9
Sales and gross receipts tax	0.73	7.8	18.3	25.5	5.9
Other	0.90	6.1	64.1	164.8	38.2

Sources: *Statistical Abstracts,* various years; *Historical Statistics; Census of Governments.*

Table 5 *The main federal tax expenditures*

	Amounts (in billions)	
	Corporations	Individuals
Lower tax rate on capital gains	$ 1.0	$ 22.3
Deductibility of state/local taxes paid		17.7
Deductibility of medical and health costs		15.7
Investment tax credit	15.4	3.1
Exemption of contributions to pension funds		15.1
Deductibility of consumer and mortgage interest payments		14.9
Exemption of Social Security and similar benefits		14.2
Deductibility of charitable gifts	1.0	8.0
Lower corporate tax for smaller firms	6.9	
Exemption of state-local bond interest	4.7	3.0
Other	13.5	25.7
Total	$42.5	$139.7

Source: U.S. Office of Management and Budget, *Special Analysis of the U.S. Budget for 1980.* The totals shown are of dubious validity because of interactions among the loopholes shown, which would change the amounts of some if others were eliminated.

guidebooks to federal income taxes run over 100 densely printed pages. These loopholes reduce the standard rates for various groups. Some exceptions reflect a variety of valid social and economic purposes. But others merely reward affluent people who can exert political leverage. At any rate, these special provisions reduce the true progressivity of taxes.

The technical term for them is "tax expenditures." The phrase reflects that standard tax revenues are "expended" by reducing what certain groups would have to pay. Thus, each taxpayer receives a $1,500 deduction from taxable income per child. The tax expenditure for this deduction, multiplied by the 60 million children in the United States, deducts $90 billion from income. Since the average tax rate on that income would have been about 20 percent, some $18 billion in potential taxes is left in certain taxpayers' pockets.

Certain local and state bonds receive another large tax expenditure, because the interest they pay is exempt from federal taxes. This helps cities to issue bonds for local schools, roads, hospitals, and the like, since they do not have to pay the going market rates of interest. However, it has grown into a large windfall for affluent people. Though anyone can buy any of the billions of such tax–exempt bonds issued annually, only those people in marginal tax brackets over 45 percent gain from doing so. Below an income of about $40,000, the after-tax yield from a taxable bond is better than that from a tax-exempt bond. But the comparison of after-tax yields reverses at higher income levels, and thus at higher marginal tax rates. Accordingly, high-income people can put most of their assets in tax-exempt bonds and avoid nearly all federal income taxes. On balance, the benefit to cities must be compared to the regressive effects on distribution.

Tax expenditures are indirect, and their amounts can often only be estimated. The main tax expenditures are shown in Table 5. All are "loopholes," but all are also legal and many have valuable effects. Economists insist that they involve real costs, much as if the public money were actually spent directly. The $180 billion of tax expenditures in 1980 needs to be included in any evaluation of public finance.

SUMMARY

The policy issues in public finance are often complicated, but economists have developed several basic concepts and analyses to clarify them.

1. A social good is nonexclusive in consumption. The total demand for such a good is a vertical summation of the individual demands. This total demand interacts with supply to determine the efficient amount of the public good.

2. A public interest arises when economic decisions create external effects. The effects can be costs or benefits.

3. Other economic reasons for public policies include common-property resources, monopoly, and unfair distributions of wealth, income, and opportunity.

4. Under efficient policies, the marginal benefits per dollar spent on alternative public programs and on private goods will be equal.

5. Cost-benefit analysis is a method for defining the efficient amount of specific public programs. It equates marginal social costs and benefits. It does not tell who should pay for the program: the beneficiaries or the general taxpaying public.

6. Spending divides into purchases and transfer payments. Taxes are of personal and *in rem* categories.

7. The incidence of an *in rem* tax usually depends on the relative elasticities of demand and supply.

8. Taxes may affect incentives to work, to invent, or to do other activities. The direction of effect depends on the shape of the individual supply curves of effort.

9. Tax friction is the loss of production that occurs when people alter their decisions so as to lighten their tax burdens. Such friction is the real economic cost of taxation.

10. A progressive tax takes a rising share of income as the taxed variable increases. Therefore, the tax falls more heavily on the rich than on the poor. A regressive tax is the opposite, taking disproportionally more from the poor.

11. Actual taxes and spending take about one third of GNP in the United States. They make up a complex patchwork at the local, state, and federal levels. Tax expenditures are amounts that would have been collected in taxes if special exceptions had not been made.

Key concepts

Efficiency, equity, stabilization
Social good
External effects: costs and benefits
Public expenditure
Cost-benefit analysis
Transfer payments
Taxes
Incidence
Incentive effects
Tax friction
Progressive and regressive taxes
Tax expenditures

Questions for review

1. a. Give five examples of a social good.

   b. Why are private markets likely to supply few social goods?

   c. Ideally, how would a government determine how much of a public good should be provided to its citizens? What are the two chief drawbacks to this ideal process? Explain.

2. a. What is the rule that will lead to maximum net social benefit from each public project? Explain.

   b. Why must future benefits and costs be discounted when calculating the costs and benefits of a project?

   c. Should the private sector interest rate or the rate at which the government can borrow funds be used to determine the appropriate discount rate? Explain.

3. a. Define: regressive tax, progressive tax, proportional tax. Give an example of each.

   b. If a country's tax system is regressive, does its budgetary policy shift money from the poor to the rich? Explain.

· 19 ·

Inequality, Poverty, and Discrimination

As you read and study this chapter, you will learn:

- why income and wealth are unequally distributed in the United States
- why some people are poor despite our high standard of living
- how discrimination affects economic inequality
- how taxation, government spending, equal opportunity laws, and the minimum wage affect the distribution of income

At its best, the market economy rewards skill, hard work, and creativity. However, it also penalizes people who are unable or unwilling to behave in economically productive ways. Most Americans seem to accept this as fair in some sense. At least it is free from corruption.

But basing incomes on marginal productivity does not produce equality. Labor skills are unequally distributed, and the ownership of land and capital is even more unequal. Thus, even if income were strictly based on productivity, it would be unequally distributed. Discrimination only reinforces a tendency already built into the market economy. Deliberate government policies alleviate inequality, but they do not eliminate it.

This chapter is divided into three main parts. The first describes the income and wealth distribution in this country and outlines some of the reasons for inequality. The second discusses the impact of discrimination based on race and gender. The third analyzes various government policies that are meant to make the income distribution more equal.

Income differences and their causes

In this section, we look at economic inequality and its basic causes.

The degree of inequality

The basic patterns are shown in Table 1. The U.S. population is arranged from the lowest to the highest levels of wealth (what people own) and income (what they earn). One can compare the shares of income and wealth held by the poorest one fifth of the families with those of the richest one fifth. The same families, roughly speaking, will be found at the same positions on the wealth and income scales. Wealth provides access to income, and the two are closely related.

As Table 1 shows, wealth is much more unequally distributed than income. That has long been true. A relatively few families can accumulate much wealth, but

most scrape by with little or no net assets. In recent years, the richest 1 percent of families have held about 25 percent of all private assets. Taking just corporate securities (stocks and bonds), the top-ranking 1 percent of the population held 57 percent of the value of all personally held securities in 1972. The richest 5 percent of the populace held nearly 70 percent. The top 100,000 families held over $3 million in assets each. Their average wealth was $15 million per family. Such wealth permits families to combine a very high level of consumption with continued growth in wealth, while work is a matter of choice. The very rich can live in a state of affluence that the ordinary citizen cannot easily imagine. The richest 5 percent of the populace are largely free from financial anxiety. Their lives differ sharply from the lives of those at the bottom of the income and wealth scale.

At the lowest end of the income distribution are the approximately 10 percent of families that live in poverty. They receive only about 2 percent of total income, and they hold less than none of the assets because they are in debt. The average income of the top 10 percent of families is about 15 times as large as the average income of

Table 1 *The distributions of income and wealth in the United States*

Population groups	Income share 1978	Average income, $ 1975	Wealth share* 1962	1972	Average wealth, $ 1962	1978
Bottom fifth	5.2	5,222	0.2		169	
2nd fifth	11.6	11,649	2.1		1,776	
3rd fifth	17.5	17,574	6.2		5,245	
4th fifth	24.1	24,203	15.5		13,112	
Highest fifth	41.5	41,677	76.0		64,289	
Highest 5%	15.6	62,666	—		—	
Highest 1%	—	—		24.1		438,230
Highest 1/2%	—	—		18.9		693,942

*Wealth is defined as net worth (assets minus debts).
Source: *U.S. Statistical Abstract*, 1980; and U.S. Congress, House Committee on the Budget, *Data on the Distribution of Wealth in the United States*, September 26, 29, 1977.

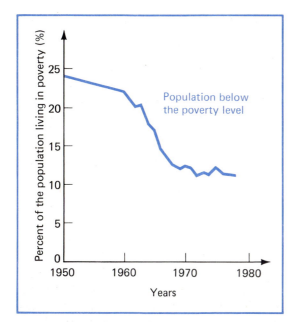

Figure 1 The level and trend of poverty in the United States since 1950

About one in ten American families lives in poverty, a total of about 25 million people. The percentage of Americans living in poverty is slowly declining, although the 1970s brought little change.

Source: U.S. Statistical Abstract, 1980, p. 464.

the bottom 10 percent. Having no net assets, the average poor family is subject to financial insecurity from job loss, sickness, and accident.

Trends In the 20th century, there has been a trend toward a more equal distribution of wealth and income but it has been slow. The extremes of income narrowed slightly from 1920 to 1950, but have scarcely changed since then. The inequality of wealth narrowed distinctly during 1930–1949, but there has been little change since 1949.

Mobility Within the distributions of wealth and income, there is some mobility. In particular, there is a surprising degree of *upward* mobility. **The dominant characteristic**

of great wealth in the United States is that it is usually created rapidly. By a spectacular success, the founder of a dynasty builds up immense wealth in a decade or two. One of our cultural myths is that wealth is accumulated slowly, by saving from income over a lifetime or two. But, in fact, most great wealth has come into being quickly, created by innovations, discoveries, monopolies, patents, and luck.

Once it is created, wealth tends to persist. Approximately 50 percent of the largest fortunes derive from inheritance, not from new wealth. This persistence of wealth provides stability rather than change. Such families as the Rockefellers, du Ponts, and Mellons have been wealthy for generations. Families with long-established wealth are at the top of the social structures in New York, Philadelphia, Boston, and most other large cities, except in the oil-rich Southwest.

At the lower economic levels, poor families are caught in a continuing cycle of poverty, poor education, and inferior jobs. Although children often move up the ladder, and some make large leaps, most people who are born poor stay poor.

Poverty Although "poverty" has no fixed definition, a series of thorough government studies has led to a general agreement on an income standard below which people are clearly living in poverty. By that measure, poverty continues to be a major problem in the United States.

Figure 1 shows the extent and trends of poverty in the United States over the past 30 years. There is a long-term downward trend, though there was little change in the 1970s. About 25 million Americans, just over 10 percent of the population, still live in poverty. Such poverty translates into a hard, grinding life, often marked by family strain and hopelessness. Coexisting as it does with the high affluence of part of the populace, such poverty is very divisive socially.

The poor are not a single homogeneous category. There are several distinct groupings of poor people.

Over 30 percent of *black families* have incomes that fall beneath the poverty line. They suffer from high unemployment rates, especially among the young. Over half of poor blacks live in families headed by a woman. *The elderly* account for nearly one fifth of all those living in poverty. They often have inadequate pensions, or none at all. Though many are able and willing to work, they cannot find jobs. *Single-parent families* are a special category, accounting for about half of all poor people. The strain on the parent in such cases is severe. She or he must struggle to earn a living and to manage the household. The children often lack adequate emotional support and guidance, which hinders their own development. *Farmers* are a heterogeneous lot, but about one sixth of them are poor, especially those on small farms in the South. Other categories of poverty include people living in economically depressed regions, people with low intelligence and skills, and immigrants who face language problems and discrimination. Altogether the poor constitute a diverse group with widely varying characteristics, although these often overlap in specific individuals. Thus, a black family on a small southern farm, with grandparents living in but no father at home, is especially likely to be poor.

Poverty is a major problem that tends to be transmitted across generations. It is partially alleviated by special public programs such as ADC (Aid to Dependent Children) grants, food stamps, and Medicaid and Medicare. After allowing for the benefits of such programs, only about 6 percent of families remain below the poverty line. Yet, nearly every city and large town has a sizable group of poor people;

New York alone has over a million. Because of the diversity of its causes, poverty is unlikely to yield to any single cure.

Technical causes of apparent inequality

Economists have long known that some of the apparent inequality in the distribution of total wealth and income stems from purely technical aspects of how it is measured. These sources of inequality need to be filtered out, to arrive at the true degree of economic inequality.

Age and life cycles   Earnings usually rise with age, in the life-cycle pattern of increasing wages. Thus, in 1978, families whose head was below 28 years of age had incomes averaging $12,500, while those with heads aged 45 to 54 averaged twice as much ($25,400). A 20-year-old clothing salesman may make only $10,000 now, but he might expect to make $30,000 by the time he is 45. A junior executive makes $18,000 and has few assets at age 25. But her 50-year-old counterpart makes $70,000 and has $200,000 in assets. The younger person has a good chance to reach the older colleague's level. To assess true inequality in income and wealth, one should compare people *of the same age.*

Regions   Because of differences in climate alone, regions differ in costs of living. The warmer climate in the South and Southwest and on the West Coast makes housing and clothing costs lower. Such factors can make a 30 percent difference in living costs. Also, cities are generally more costly to live in than towns or farms. Among cities, too, there are sizable differences in costs. Manhattan is a much costlier place to live than Muncie, Indiana.

Family size   The adequacy of a family income is affected by the size of the family. For example, if there are just two adults, an income of $15,000 will be much more adequate than if there are seven children plus a grandparent in the family.

The economic forces shaping the income distribution

Some factors that cause inequality improve economic efficiency, some are neutral, and others cause inefficiency.

Causes improving efficiency Talent and effort are the two main personal characteristics that affect equality. Both influence the distributions of income and wealth, but neither is the dominant cause of inequality. Effort is almost neutral in its effect on the inequality of wealth. Many people in low-wage jobs work long, hard hours, but their intensive effort often produces income barely above the poverty level. Immigrants are the classic example of unusually hard workers. Yet, their strong efforts commonly elevate them only from the lowest levels of income to the lower middle classes. Effort alone, then, does not explain much of the total disparity in wealth and income.

Creative talent is probably more important than effort in explaining inequality. Many large, rapidly created fortunes have come from major innovations, such as instant photography by Edwin Land and xerography by Chester Carlson. These people captured some of the extra value created by their genius (and efforts), but some of the benefits were also passed on to consumers. Thousands of lesser fortunes have arisen from patented inventions and from the creative building of businesses. Yet, such purely creative activity has probably not been the major source of wealth. Many of the most creative people, including inventors, have worked for a salary for firms or public agencies. Their contributions have not made them personal fortunes; instead, the benefits have gone mainly to others.

Luck Luck operates capriciously through people's genes, location, timing, and other factors beyond personal control. Examples of "lucky" wealth are stock market winnings and successful commodity speculation. Much oil industry wealth is also a matter of luck. On the negative side, personal accidents, floods, droughts, and speculative disasters frequently separate people from their assets and income. Even if one could magically create perfect equality today, differences in luck would restore a large degree of inequality tomorrow.

Causes reducing efficiency People have found many ways to exploit their fellow humans. Economists recognize several methods by which economic power has enriched some people at the expense of others: A good example is monopoly power.

Monopoly not only reduces economic efficiency, it also impairs equality. It shifts income and wealth from the average citizen to a few people who hold unusual amounts of capital. One fairly reliable estimate of the monopoly effect on distribution suggests that 20 to 40 percent of the private wealth held by the top 5 percent of families probably came from monopoly power. Many large family fortunes can be traced back to the exercise of market power in some particular industry. Such instances include the Rockefellers (oil), the du Ponts (chemicals), and the Mellons (oil, aluminum). Some of the wealth acquired in this way was later given to universities, which were named for the "robber barons" whose money built them. Examples include Stanford University (Leland Stanford—western railroads), Duke University (James B. Duke—the American tobacco monopoly), Vanderbilt University (Cornelius Vanderbilt—railroads), Carnegie-Mellon University (Andrew Carnegie—steel; Andrew Mellon—oil and banking), and Rockefeller University (John D. Rockefeller—oil).

Discrimination

Discrimination involves the differential treatment of people on the basis of superficial, easily perceived differences. Despite the ugly connotations of the word, not all discrimination is undesirable. For example, employers routinely discriminate among job candidates on the basis of their past experience and recommendations from former employers; readers select books according to their expectations of the contents.

Discrimination is unfair or undesirable if the perceived differences do not in some sense objectively justify the differing treatment. For example, race, sex, and ethnic background in themselves have no systematic effects on worker quality. Therefore, discrimination based upon such criteria is economically harmful.

Employment discrimination

When women, blacks, Hispanics, native Americans, and other groups are subject to job discrimination, it undermines equal opportunity. The discrimination has two elements—exclusion from employment, and low pay. First, people are *excluded from certain jobs:* They are not permitted to apply, or are not hired when qualified, or are hired only in trivial numbers. Second, even if hired, they are *paid less for equal work,* relegated to inferior status, and not promoted in a timely manner.

In practice, employment discrimination of both types has been common in many markets. The earnings differential between men and women, as illustrated in Figure 2, reflects both the exclusion of women from a wide range of jobs (a trend that did not begin to decline until the 1960s) and sharp differences in pay rates. Until the 1970s, women were simply kept out of most heavy work, skilled craft jobs, and management positions. Women's "place" was said to be that of clerk, tele-

phone operator, salesgirl, grade school teacher, and cleaning lady. Blacks are still confined largely to the menial, unpleasant jobs. So are Hispanics and native Americans. The pay for these groups is 30–60 percent below that of white males.

Discrimination has eased somewhat since the 1960s, more than had seemed possible before then. Yet, the total gains have been small. Job inequalities not based on skill or experience still exist, and minorities and women are often only a token presence in many of the upper-level jobs (such as managers, financiers, doctors, and lawyers).

Part of the inequality is caused by inadequate skills, which many minority people have because of poor schooling, the ab-

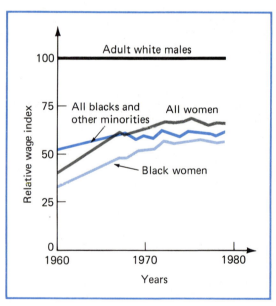

Figure 2   Relative earnings of various groups within the U.S. population 1960–1978

Earnings by adult white men are the standard of comparison; they are set at an index value of 100. Women and blacks have been paid at just about 60 percent of the income levels of white men. Black women are paid even less. The gaps narrowed moderately during the 1960s but remained steady during the 1970s.

Source: Data from *U.S. Statistical Abstract*, 1980, p. 424; calculations based on average weekly earnings.

406

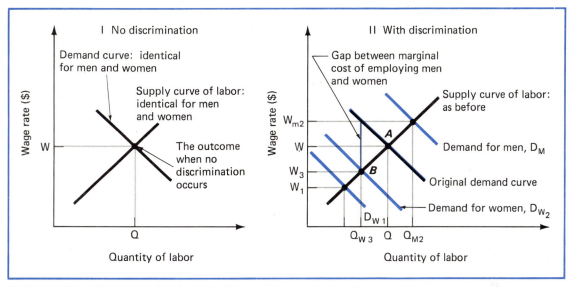

Figure 3　The effects of job discrimination on wages and employment levels

When opportunity is equal (Panel I), supply and demand curves are identical for women and men. They are hired in roughly equal numbers at the same wage rate.

　　Discrimination (Panel II) shifts in the demand curve for women, causing them to endure lower wages and a smaller level of employment. Men are now favored with more jobs at higher pay. The marginal cost of male labor is now W_2; of female labor, W_3. The gap between W_2 and W_3 is large, as shown. It reflects the inefficiency, as well as the unfairness, caused by discrimination.

sence of past incentives to gain skills, and the lack of adequate family financial support. The problem of inadequate skills will take time and resources to correct, although its importance is often less than is claimed. Many skills can be learned quickly on the job, if there are adequate incentives. Although exclusion from employment and lower pay are conceptually distinct parts of job discrimination, the problem can be usefully analyzed without separating the two effects.

　　The analysis of discrimination begins with simple supply and demand curves for labor in a typical job market. But now there are two groups of workers, women and men, seeking work as, say, construction supervisors. Assume that the women and men are equally qualified (that is, their marginal revenue products are identical), and that their supply curves are also the same, as shown in Panel I of Figure 3.

Therefore, with no discrimination, they would be hired in identical numbers and paid the same wages (Point A in Panel II). The selection process between women and men would be random and sex-blind.

　　But if women are regarded as "unsuitable," the demand for female labor shifts in. If the decline is severe, as with the labor demand curve D_{W_1} in Panel II, then fewer women will be hired, and only at a dramatically lower wage, W_1. This often happens when women are deemed to be "out of place" in risky or unpleasant jobs, or in complex "responsible" jobs like running an investment bank, piloting an airline jet or double-bottom oil tanker, or presiding over a government agency.

　　A lesser degree of discrimination would move the labor demand curve for women in moderately, perhaps to D_{W_2} in Panel II of Figure 3. In that case, the results at Point B are less severe for the

407

women, but in equilibrium, women laborers receive less pay, and fewer are hired.

The demand for male workers shifted out when the demand for women shifted in, moving to Demand Curve D_M. This gives a new equilibrium for male labor, with more jobs and a higher rate of pay. To draw the extra men away from other jobs, where their marginal revenue product would be higher, the firms in this industry must bid up their wages. The new equilibrium is at a higher number of male workers, Q_{M2}, and a higher wage, W_{M2}.

Accordingly, men take jobs from women *and* the men's wages rise while the women's wages fall. Such a shift would cause sharp protests if it were to happen suddenly. In practice, however, it usually occurs gradually and by tradition, so that it is less visible and controversial. Sometimes, indeed, the effect gradually dwindles as time passes. But lost jobs and lower pay do occur. Exclusion can be complete or virtually so; and pay rates may differ a lot.

Discrimination is both inequitable and inefficient. This can be seen in Figure 3 by comparing men's wages with the cost of hiring more women. Men are being paid the wage W_{M2}. Yet, the marginal man could be replaced by an equally productive woman at a cost of W_{M3}, which is only about half of W_{M2}. The marginal costs of labor are thus out of line with the marginal products. This distortion causes the discriminatory economy to produce less than would be possible with equal opportunity.

This disparity of wages might be expected to trigger corrective actions by competitive firms: They would hire the women, reduce their own costs, and gain extra profits. Such a process does occur in some degree, but it has not eliminated the main patterns of discrimination. When discriminatory attitudes are ingrained in the culture, they can resist the inducements of the profit motive.

Firms that exclude women and minorities often say that the excluded workers are simply not qualified. Thus, if all executives are white males, they explain that they could not find qualified women and blacks for these high posts, and that it would take decades to locate and train new candidates. For lower-level jobs on the production line, the minority applicants are often said to be unreliable and disobedient.

If that were true, the lower demand curves D_{W_1} or D_{W_2} in Figure 3 would reflect the lower marginal revenue product of such groups, and would not be the result of unfair discrimination against them. The firm might regret the results, but it would be discriminating on relevant economic grounds. In practice, some minority workers *are* technically less productive because of poor schooling, work habits, and so on. The key questions are: Is the quality difference truly present? How severe is it? How easily can it be overcome? Often the distinction is illusory or quickly remediable by on-the-job training.

Discrimination in housing

Minority groups have long been excluded from affluent neighborhoods and confined to ghetto areas of the major cities. Such discrimination in housing is sometimes subtle, but usually effective. Although it has declined since the 1950s, it is still widespread. The main economic elements are straightforward, and supply-demand analysis can clarify them.

Consider a typical neighborhood housing market without racial discrimination, as illustrated in Figure 4. The equilibrium price and quantity of housing exchanged are determined by the intersection of total demand for and supply of housing. The resulting quantities are divided so that Q_W houses are sold to whites and Q_B to blacks, on the basis of relative demand.

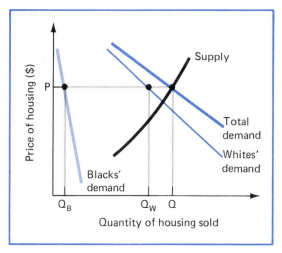

Figure 4 Housing sales without discrimination

With no discrimination in the housing market, Q houses are sold at a price of P. Q_B houses go to blacks and Q_W go to whites. Sales reflect buying power regardless of race.

Now suppose that racial discrimination against blacks occurs. That results in two separate supply curves for housing, contingent on the buyer's race. The supply to blacks is represented by Curve S_{B_1} or S_{B_2} in Figure 5; the supply curve to whites is S_W.

If exclusion is complete, then supply to blacks is S_{B_1} and the quantity exchanged is zero at all prices. Such a supply curve coincides with the vertical axis. Even at the highest price they would be willing to pay (at Point A), blacks cannot buy any housing in this neighborhood. Meanwhile, whites can buy housing at Point B. That gives a lower equilibrium price compared to the no-discrimination case because the discrimination has ruled out blacks as buyers. That lower price is endured by the *sellers* of the houses to keep blacks out. It is a price the white neighborhood will pay.

However, the temptation to sell at a price as high as A may finally stir some neighbors to sell to blacks after all. Some

limited supply for black buyers may emerge, as in S_{B_2} in Figure 5. A few houses will be sold at Price C, which is above the price to white buyers at B. Once the rigid color line is broken in this way, market forces may drive the two prices together, and discrimination will be squeezed out as Prices B and C converge.

Discrimination is both unfair and economically inefficient. The effects are not always recognized because such practices are traditional and ingrained.

Public policy and income distribution

Poverty is deeply rooted and surprisingly resistant to political solutions, but four main types of public policy have been di-

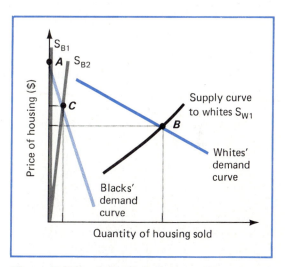

Figure 5 Discrimination changes the amounts and prices of houses sold

Discrimination shrinks the supply of housing to blacks, perhaps all the way to zero, as shown by S_{B_1}. Owners will not sell even if blacks offer a high price, at Point A. The supply to whites is now the same as total supply was before, so that the price whites have to pay goes down to B.

If some supply is offered to blacks, as shown by S_{B_2}, the price C results, where supply and demand for blacks are in equilibrium. Blacks can buy, but at a higher price than whites. Owners may then supply more houses to blacks, to get the higher price. This will tend to close the gap between C and B.

rected at changing the income distribution: progressive taxation, transfer programs, equal opportunity programs, and minimum wage laws. The first two have been discussed generally in Chapter 18. Only their effects on inequality are examined here. The last two policies are introduced and evaluated in this section.

Tax policies

Recall that *progressive taxes* take a higher *percentage* of income as income increases. Taxes could significantly even out the income distribution if they were sufficiently progressive.

A *regressive* tax takes a *lower* percentage bite as income increases. It accentuates existing inequality. Several major taxes do appear to be regressive, chiefly property, sales, and excise taxes. The regressivity occurs because the poor tend to spend a higher *percentage* of their incomes on housing, cigarettes, and other taxed consumption goods.

Finally, *proportional* taxes take a constant percentage of income or wealth and do not affect inequality.

The burden of taxes is ultimately borne by individuals. It is customary to define that tax incidence in terms of *disposable income**, which is what remains after taxes are netted out of gross income. There are three main types of taxes. Income taxes are the largest ($214 billion in 1980), but sales taxes ($93 billion) and property taxes ($64 billion) are also substantial.

Each household's disposable income is simply:

$$\frac{\text{Disposable}}{\text{income}} = \frac{\text{Gross}}{\text{income}} -$$

$$\left(\frac{\text{Income}}{\text{taxes}} + \frac{\text{Sales}}{\text{taxes}} + \frac{\text{Property}}{\text{taxes}} + \frac{\text{Other}}{\text{taxes}} \right).$$

---

*This is a somewhat different concept of disposable income than that used in national income accounting.

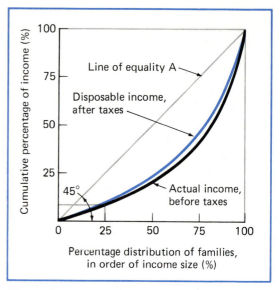

Figure 6   A Lorenz curve showing the degree of inequality

With households arranged in order of their incomes, a perfectly equal distribution of income would give Curve A. The "lowest" 25 percent of families would have 25 percent of the income, and so on. Actual pretax incomes are unequal, as shown by Curve B. The lowest 25 percent of families have only 10 percent of total income, etc. Taxes tend to equalize incomes slightly, as illustrated by Curve C, which is above Curve B.

The specific tax bite on each household will vary with many factors: income levels, amounts of goods bought, taxable property owned, and the tax rates being applied. The tracing of tax burdens is a highly complex matter, depending on elasticities and patterns of property ownership that are not accurately known. Income and property taxes are straightforward and their effects are fairly well known; for sales taxes, the estimates are less precise; and for other taxes, the effects can only be estimated.

If they were known perfectly, a "Lorenz curve" could be drawn, like that in Figure 6. The population is arranged along the horizontal axis in order of increasing income. The vertical axis is the cumulative share of their incomes, starting with the lowest income groups. If incomes were perfectly equal, the distribution would be the straight line *A*. Any inequality will cause the actual distribution to lie along a curve below *A*, such as *B*.

Now suppose that Curve *B* is the actual distribution of income before taxes. Each household in that distribution is at one point along the horizontal axis. Then taxes are deducted, leaving disposable income. The resulting distribution of that disposable income is Curve *C*, again with each household located somewhere along the horizontal axis. If the net burden of taxes is progressive, then Curve *C* lies above Curve *B*, reflecting a more equal distribution of disposable income than of gross income. If taxes are instead regressive, then the disposable income curve would lie below Curve *B*.

Many studies of tax incidence in the United States and other countries have been done in recent decades. They involve varying assumptions about the shifting and incidence of various indirect taxes, and their results are not uniform. Table 2 and Figure 7 present the results of one major study, showing patterns that have probably changed little since the study was undertaken.

As expected, *federal taxes* are broadly progressive, as shown by the rising line (*B*) in Figure 7 and line 6 in Table 2. The regressive effects of the federal excise taxes on cigarettes and gasoline (line 4) and of the payroll tax (line 5) are outweighed by the progressivity of the income tax (line 1). State and local taxes are regressive, as shown by the down-sloping line (*A*) in Fig-

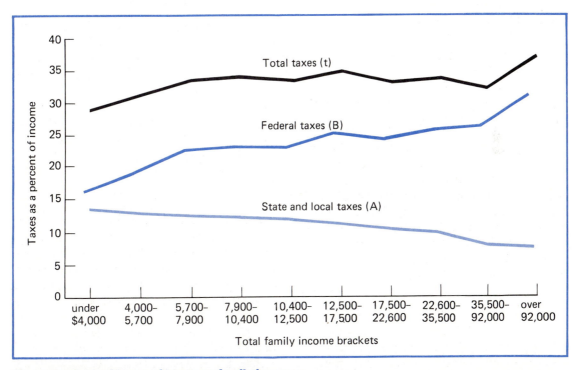

Figure 7   The incidence of taxes on family incomes

The estimated taxes taken from incomes are shown (as percentage shares) on the vertical axis. State and local taxes are regressive on the whole, as shown by Line *A*. Federal taxes are moderately progressive (Line *B*). Total tax incidence appears to be mildly progressive, especially at the lower and upper ends of the income scale.

Source: Musgrave and Musgrave, *Public Finance in Theory and Practice*, p. 267.

Table 2 *Taxes as percentage of total family income, 1968*

Taxes	\$4,000	\$4,000–\$5,700	\$5,700–\$7,900	\$7,900–\$10,400	\$10,400–\$12,500	\$12,500–\$17,500	\$17,500–\$22,600	\$22,600–\$35,500	\$35,500–\$92,000	\$92,000 and over	All Brackets
	Under					**Income Brackets**					
Federal Taxes											
1. Individual income tax	2.0	2.8	5.9	7.1	7.9	10.1	10.6	12.7	14.8	18.5	9.9
2. Estate and gift tax	—	—	—	—	—	—	—	0.6	2.0	2.7	0.4
3. Corporation income tax	5.1	6.1	5.0	4.0	4.3	4.6	4.8	5.1	5.3	6.6	5.0
4. Excises and customs	2.5	2.8	3.1	3.0	2.9	2.7	2.1	1.1	0.9	0.6	2.3
5. Payroll tax	5.5	6.3	7.0	6.9	6.7	6.1	5.2	4.2	1.5	0.6	5.2
6. Total	15.2	17.9	20.8	21.6	21.6	23.4	22.6	23.8	24.5	29.1	22.7
State and Local Taxes											
7. Individual income tax	—	0.1	0.3	0.6	0.7	1.1	1.4	2.3	1.6	1.3	1.0
8. Inheritance tax	—	—	—	—	—	—	—	0.2	0.6	0.8	0.1
9. Corporation income tax	0.4	0.5	0.4	0.4	0.3	0.4	0.4	0.4	0.4	0.5	0.4
10. General excise tax	3.4	2.8	2.5	2.3	2.2	2.0	1.7	1.0	0.5	0.3	1.8
11. Excises	2.7	3.0	3.3	3.0	2.9	2.5	1.9	1.0	0.8	0.6	2.1
12. Property tax	6.7	5.7	4.7	4.3	4.0	3.7	3.3	3.0	2.9	3.3	3.9
13. Payroll tax	0.2	0.5	0.8	1.0	1.0	1.0	1.1	1.2	0.2	0.1	0.8
14. Total	13.4	12.5	11.9	11.6	11.1	10.6	9.7	9.1	7.1	6.9	10.3
All Levels											
15. Total	28.5	30.5	32.8	33.1	32.8	33.9	32.4	32.9	31.6	35.9	33.0

NOTE: Items may not add to totals because of rounding.
SOURCE: Adapted from Richard B. Musgrave and Peggy Musgrave, *Public Finance in Theory and Practice*, 3rd ed. (New York: McGraw-Hill, 1980), pp. 267 and 275.

ure 7 and by line 14 in Table 2. Excises (lines 10 and 11), which are sales taxes, are highly regressive, as expected. Property taxes (line 12) are also regressive; they largely reflect taxes on houses, which are the only substantial assets that most lower-income families own. For higher-income families, housing is proportionally less important, and so property taxes take a smaller share of their income.

The combined effect of all taxes appears to be nearly proportional over the wide middle range of incomes, where over 70 percent of households are located. Toward both ends of the scale there is a higher degree of progression.

Public expenditures

Government spending, particularly transfer payments, can also have a significant redistributive effect. Recall that such expenditures can be considered progressive, regressive, or proportional, depending on which groups benefit most as a percentage of their incomes. For example, such programs as welfare payments, public housing, Medicaid, and food stamps are clearly progressive. Other expenditures are less progressive.

The value of many *specific* benefit programs can be assigned to income groups with a high degree of confidence. Transfer payments are the largest item, at a level of 7 percent of total income, followed closely by public education. General benefit programs are not so readily assigned, because their benefits are widely spread. Figure 8 presents one careful estimate of the incidence of benefits. The benefits appear to be much more progressive than the burdens (taxes), especially at the low end of the income scale, where transfer payments are highly concentrated. (The effects of these upon work incentives are considered in the adjacent box.)

The combined incidence of taxes and benefits ("Net" in Figure 8) is also highly progressive at lower incomes, thanks almost entirely to benefits. At about $8,000 income (in 1968), there is a crossover from net benefits to net burden. The poorer families receive net benefits; the richer families bear a net burden. Restated in current incomes, the crossover might be at about $20,000 income. Above that level, the progressivity is slight.

In short, public programs do markedly add to the real incomes of the poor as a group, but the degree of progressivity in other income ranges is mild. The poor are helped, but there is only a moderate tendency toward leveling down the affluence of the rich.

Equal opportunity programs

The 19th century brought economic opportunity to millions of immigrants in the United States, and legal freedom for the slaves. But women's opportunities were reduced on the whole, and those of native Americans were nearly obliterated. After the 1870s, segregation severely limited the opportunities of most blacks.

During the first half of the 20th century, economic discrimination against these groups remained strong. Only in the 1960s did government policies begin strongly to promote equal opportunity. The 1964 Equal Opportunity Act made job discrimination on the basis of sex or race illegal and created the Equal Employment Opportunity Commission (EEOC) to enforce fair hiring practices. After several years of experimenting, the EEOC centered its actions on large firms, to get a maximum economic effect for the least number of cases.

The EEOC usually reached compromises with discriminatory companies, requiring payments of money to minority

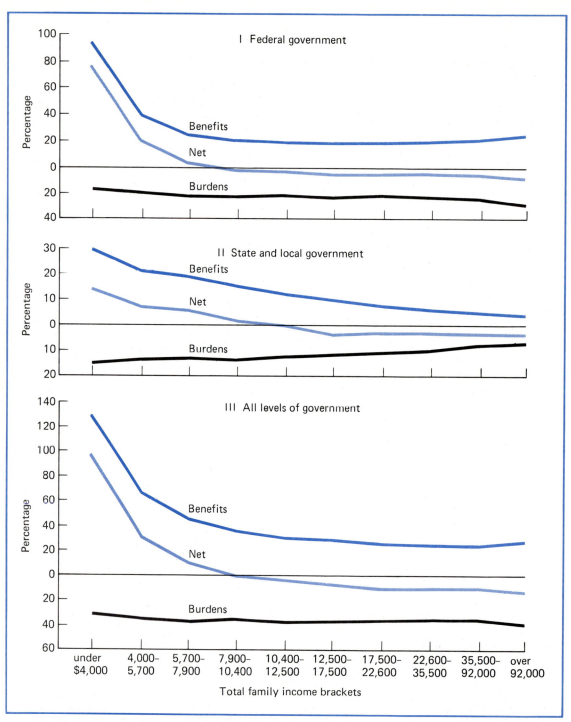

Figure 8   Tax burdens and expenditure benefits as a percentage of total family income
Source: Musgrave and Musgrave, *Public Finance in Theory and Practice*, p. 275.

Welfare Payments and Incentives to Work

Few redistributive policies have raised more difficult economic issues than income maintenance programs for the poor (popularly called welfare). They include cash grants for Aid to Families with Dependent Children, as well as Medicaid, food stamps, subsidized housing and other benefit programs. Though they have grown rapidly since 1960, they have been common for many decades both in the U.S. and elsewhere.

The incentive problem they raise is fundamental. Because they are aimed at helping the poor, the benefits are confined to people below certain income levels. Any earnings which raise the family's income above that income ceiling are under a steep implicit tax, because they result in the loss of large benefits. Hence welfare may produce disincentives to work.

One version of the problem is illustrated in the figure. Earnings from work are measured on the horizontal axis; the total income received (earnings plus welfare benefits) are on the vertical axis. Earnings, therefore, trace out a 45° line, because they are earned and kept.

If $6,000 is a minimal income, society may supplement lower earnings so as to bring them up to that level. Panel I illustrates such a supplement program. The worker receives at least $6,000 even if earnings are zero. But notice that the supplement implicitly taxes below $6,000 at a 100 percent rate: The $6,000 is received even if no

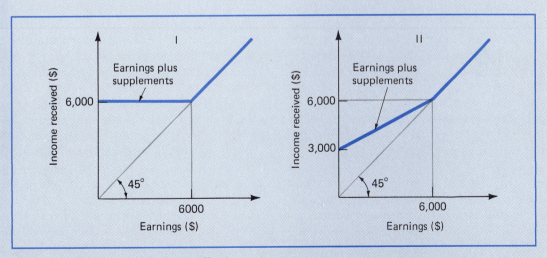

Income support and implicit tax effects

In Panel I, a worker is guaranteed at least $6,000, regardless of his or her wages. Implicitly, income is taxed at a 100 percent rate up to the $6,000 level. In Panel II, the worker receives in transfers one-half the difference between $6,000 and his or her wages, up to an income level of $6,000. The implicit tax rate is only 50 percent.

work is done. This disincentive may have strong effects for workers whose lack of skills limits them to jobs in that range.

One alternative is to lower the income threshold, say to $3,000. Then the disincentive no longer operates in the $3,000–$6,000 range. But people genuinely unable to obtain work will now undergo hardship because they will receive only $3,000.

Alternatively, the supplement can be only partial, providing 50 percent of the difference between earnings and $6,000, as in Panel II. Then the implicit tax is only 50 percent. But many families will still fall below $6,000, and there is also a disincentive from the 50 percent implicit tax rate.

This approach is often called a "negative income tax." The progressive tax rate on higher incomes is simply extended below a threshold income level, to provide partial subsidies to poor people.

All welfare programs face the same central dilemma: *The disincentive effect varies directly with the degree of assistance provided.* As long as aid is based on an income test, there is an implicit tax. The greater the aid, the steeper the implicit tax, with its possible disincentives.

The effects of disincentives are not precisely known, but research has suggested that primary earners (e.g., the head of the household) are not sensitive to them. Secondary earners (e.g., working children) are more responsive, enough to cause significant declines in total earnings because of the disincentives.

and female employees to compensate them for having been underpaid in the past, and new programs to increase minority and female employment. The payments were only a crude way to offset the previous low pay. They missed all potential employees who had *not* been hired. Yet, the whole effort did substantially improve opportunity, especially for women. Meanwhile, individual cases piled up by the thousands, entailing long delays. Here the gains that the EEOC could obtain were small and specific, rather than large and broad. On the whole, the EEOC allocated its small resources fairly effectively, trying to get the largest total gain in opportunity.

Minimum wage laws

We presented an analysis of the effects of minimum wage laws in Chapter 5. They raise wages for some people but leave others unable to get the jobs they would prefer. The specific effects depend mainly on the elasticities of demand and supply of labor. Here we merely summarize the probable effects as of 1982. The Reagan administration has proposed sharp changes in the law, which could alter the effects.

The law's coverage has large gaps. Exemptions include household workers, trainees, farm workers, students, outside sales workers, all workers in retail and service shops with annual sales below $325,000, and handicapped workers. The law, therefore, does not affect about 10 million nonsupervisory workers. Many of those exempted are in the classic low-wage jobs, such as migrant farm workers and teenagers. Moreover, millions of other legally covered workers are, not, in fact, affected because their employers ignore the law.

Thousands of immigrants (both legal and illegal) toil in sweatshops at subminimum pay, unable to request legal wages and afraid to report their employers for fear of losing their jobs.

Altogether, 3 million workers are paid at the minimum wage level. About 3.9 million receive less, under legal exceptions. And probably 3 million more are paid less than the minimum illegally. The best estimates are that only about 5 million workers' wages are actually raised by the law. The increase probably averages about 35 cents per hour, which is about $700 per year. Perhaps half a million workers are forced to take other jobs because their marginal product is below the minimum wage rate. Another 100,000 workers may be unable to find work at all because of the wage floor. Those negative effects of the law fall most heavily on teenagers and unskilled workers:

. . . teenagers have more to lose than to gain from higher minimum wages; they appear to be forced out of the better jobs, denied full-time work, and paid lower hourly wage rates. . . . If one of the goals of minimum-wage legislation is to eliminate sweatshop low-wage jobs, for teenagers the law appears to be counter-productive.*

Adult women, by contrast, "are the main beneficiaries of increases in the minimum wage. . . . A higher minimum brings adult females from the part-time into the full-time labor force, forcing even lower-wage teenagers out into the part-time jobs that they have vacated."†

Yet, high unemployment rates among youths, especially black males, may not be caused by the minimum wage, though one frequently hears arguments to that effect. Instead, many of these youths live in poor urban areas, where jobs simply do not exist at any wage rate.

All told, the law probably improves incomes by about 10–12 percent for 3 million low-wage workers; it reduces wages marginally for about half a million other workers; and it may price about 100,000 workers out of jobs altogether. Therefore, the effects of the law have been mixed.

Summary

Equity in distribution is a complicated subject, with many unexpected, sophisticated issues that ultimately cannot be wholly resolved. These main points should be remembered:

1. Actual distributions of wealth and income in the United States are markedly unequal, though less so than in most comparable countries. Wealth is much more unequal than income, and much of the inequality is transmitted from generation to generation. The degree of inequality has been declining gradually.

2. Poverty is focused especially among minorities, single-parent families, small farmers, and old people. Inheritance is a substantial element in inequality.

3. Some inequality has been caused by differences in effort and creativity. But large fortunes arise primarily from other "instant" causes, including luck.

4. Discrimination has strongly affected the economic position of women and blacks and other minorities. It reduces efficiency as well as equity.

*Edward M. Gramlich, "Impact of Minimum Wages on Other Wages, Employment and Family Incomes," Brookings Papers on Economic Activity, No. 2, 1976, Washington D.C. p. 409.
†Ibid., p. 462.

5. Government taxes and spending can have a progressive, neutral, or regressive effect.

6. Actual taxes are moderately progressive, with the basic progressivity in the federal income tax nearly offset by regressivity in sales, gasoline, liquor, cigarette, real estate, and other taxes. Government spending is more clearly progressive, mainly because of programs to aid the poor (welfare, food stamps, Medicare and Medicaid, etc.), which have grown since 1960.

7. Policies to equalize opportunity have had some effect. Minimum wage laws have probably helped lower-income workers on the whole, especially women. But teenagers and certain other poor groups have been hurt by them.

Key concepts

Discrimination
Benefit programs

Questions for review

1. Compare the economic inequality of two families: The Smith's income is $15,000 per year; the Jones's income is $50,000 per year. What factors would have to be taken into account before you can make an accurate comparison?

2. Use supply and demand analysis to explain how job discrimination against minorities will affect the wages and the numbers who are hired of both minority and non-minority workers in a given labor market.

3. Explain why discrimination in hiring that is not related to differences in productivity is economically inefficient.

4. The Federal income tax is progressive. Can it be assumed, therefore, that the net effect of taxes in the U.S. is a greater equality in income distribution than would otherwise be the case? Explain.

5. How do government expenditures affect the equality of income?

· 20 ·

Education, Social Regulation, and the Military

As you read and study this chapter, you will learn:

- how educational policies pose issues of efficiency and equity
- how simple cost-benefit analysis can clarify the effects of policies to control pollution and industrial hazards
- how military policies—purchasing, arms levels, and the draft—can be improved along economic guidelines

Consider how far you have come in microeconomics. You first mastered the analysis of demand and supply. Next came costs, market outcomes, and supply in competitive markets. The effects of monopoly followed, and then the main inputs, capital, labor, and natural resources. Finally, you learned the main lines of public finance and studied poverty and discrimination. Now you are prepared to apply this training to three difficult economic problems facing society. These problems are the education of the young, the protection of safe living and working conditions, and national defense.

These three complicated cases can be clarified using basic economics. Indeed, the cases are a test of your skill at this analysis. They also test your maturity and sense of balance, for there are no simple answers. It is rarely clear what the strictly best policies are, for they often must strike a balance among several goals and interest groups. Economists often show the effects of each policy, so that society can make informed choices.

Education, our first case, has been your own main job for the last 12 to 15 years. It is crucial both for each student and for the whole structure of society. We will show the main private and social elements that education contains and the questions of fairness that it poses. The first section of this chapter may lead you to see the economics of your college activity in new ways.

The second section discusses the protection of the environment from pollution. The great environmental cleanup in the United States since 1965 has applied several kinds of rules and incentives. Some of them have been effective, others not. We will show their nature and effects.

Then we take you through the remarkable economics of military spending. The Department of Defense spends over $160 billion per year. We show how the process departs partly from the conventional conditions of market efficiency, so that a degree of inefficiency is likely to occur. We also use simple theory to show why the arms race continues. It appears probable that there is too little competition among the armaments suppliers and too much between the United States and Soviet Russia! Finally we turn to the military draft showing why a volunteer army is usually more efficient.

In all three cases, the problems involve both the concepts of competition and monopoly and of public finance. Some of the social elements arise because monopoly conditions have strong effects. Indeed, the public programs themselves are often monopolistic in ways that limit people's choices and stifle their incentives for effort. Therefore, one must analyze monopoly and incentives both in these cases and in the budgets themselves. The *design* of the policies is as important as their *size*.

Economics of education

Educating the young has always been a leading social task. Some societies mainly teach religion and obedience to their children. Others try to instill creativity and independent thinking. All industrial societies now absorb most of their youths' time from the age of five to the mid- or late teens in primary and secondary schooling. Most young adults then take paying jobs, but a minority go on—as you have—to college, and a few more take advanced studies.

Although education differs sharply from country to country, it has the same economic features everywhere. It adds skills, which make people more productive. It sorts people into work that fits their skills, along the lines of comparative advantage (recall the brief discussion in Chapter 2). It instills traditions and methods, so that citizens can be stable members of society. Some teachers also do creative research, which helps to improve technology and enrich the culture. Altogether, education creates large economic values, ranging from technical productivity in factories and offices to the progress of knowledge itself. What you may have regarded as merely schoolwork is, in fact, part of a crucial economic process.

Education's various values divide into two classes: private and social. Each student gains *private* benefits by learning how to think more maturely and to do certain specific job-related tasks. Later, these benefits can be translated into higher pay on the job. Since the additional amounts of pay go only to the worker, they are strictly private. The *public* benefits are often more subtle.

We will now analyze both categories.

Private benefits of education

If there were no formal schooling, children would still develop productive skills as they matured. But effective schooling raises the levels of those skills and thus provides higher productivity.* That, in turn, usually results in higher incomes for the educated person. These incomes are received and enjoyed privately. In exchange for spending all those years in school, you will eventually attain higher pay during your working life. Moreover, your jobs will probably be more pleasant, and you may understand the meaning of life more fully and be better able to cope with the complexities of modern existence.

Public benefits of education

There are three main types of *public benefits* which people's education may provide to other people rather than just to themselves. **First, universal public schooling provides everybody with the *basic skills*** for work and self-care. It enlarges the pool of productive workers and provides a variety of skills and mobility in labor markets. Because workers are more effective and intelligent, industry becomes more efficient and profitable. It can provide goods to consumers at lower cost. The whole society benefits, not just those who invested in an education.

Without schooling, many people would be unable to cope with the complexities of society. Some might turn to crime and violence; others would simply require public assistance. Indeed, many do both of these things now, and better schooling might well reduce their numbers. Society might relieve the economic and social burdens of crime by supplying better education to these citizens.

Second, schooling provides a *stable electorate*, reasonably well informed and able to function in an effective democratic process. Because people understand public issues better, they will deal with them more intelligently. Extremists are less dangerous to the fabric of a well-educated, skeptical society. The sense of decency and cohesion is deeper, and the ability to resist specious political claims is stronger.

Third, the greater productivity of the population provides a larger economic base for the *taxes* that finance *adequate public services*. Although education yields higher *private* incomes for people, these incomes are the economic base for meeting social needs. If productivity were lower, society would have fewer resources for all of the programs covered in Chapter 18, including education. Therefore, partly as a circular matter, education enlarges the scope for efficient public spending in the future.

These main public benefits are hard to measure precisely because they are so complex. Much of their value in forming the basic productivity and stability of the populace is provided in grades 1 to 12. That justifies subsidizing schools at those levels with public funds, perhaps with a total public subsidy.

For education at the college level, however, the public benefits may be relatively weaker when compared to the large, private career rewards. True, there is much valuable research done at universities, which gives public benefits that justify public funding. Moreover, the career system generates many of the future leaders in politics and society. Also, the taxes on the careerists' later earnings may have especially high yields for the public purse.

Nonetheless, the balance between private and public benefits in higher education is tilted toward the private side. Therefore, the economic case for full public subsidies is weaker at the college level than it is at the grade-school and high-school levels.

---

*Skills can also be acquired in other ways: at vocational schools or through on-the-job training, for example. Here we focus on the net addition to skills and income above the gains from those alternatives.

Table 1 *Enrollments in public and private schools: High school and college levels, 1930–1985 (in millions of students)*

	1950	1960	1965	1970	1975	1980	1985*
High School							
Public	5.7	8.5	11.6	13.3	14.3	13.3	12.1
Nonpublic	.7	1.0	1.4	1.3	1.4	1.5	1.4
College							
Public	1.4	1.8	4.0	6.4	8.8	9.1	9.0
Nonpublic	1.3	1.4	2.0	2.2	2.4	2.5	2.4

Source: *U.S. Statistical Abstract*, 1980, p. 143.
* Projected levels.

Actual expenditures on education

These broad conditions are reflected in the actual finances of education. Along with sharp rises in the total spending on education during 1955–1975 has come a major rise in the public share in the educational sector. Table 1 and Figure 1 indicate the scope of this change.

Most education is *public* education, by federal, state, and local sources: Nearly nine tenths of all students go to public grade and high schools. Over two-thirds of college and advanced students go to public institutions.

Public schools for grades 1–12 are financed virtually entirely by tax revenues, as if they were pure social goods. Some schools charge various fees for books and equipment, but these are usually minor. These virtually total subsidies seem to ignore the private benefits that the schooling provides. Other reasons, such as fairness or practicality, apparently explain this complete reliance on public funds.

In higher education, public campuses have grown rapidly since 1960, from 57 to 68 percent of all spending at this level. Enrollment figures in Table 1 show the shift even more sharply. While student ranks in private colleges have only risen by about 500,000 since 1965, they have grown by 5.1 million at public campuses, more than doubling the 1965 level. Two causes are behind this rise. First, there has been a

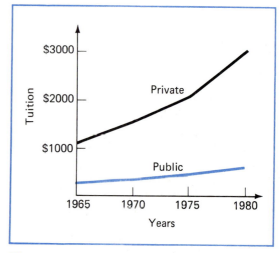

Figure 1   Trends of tuition at private and public colleges and universities

vast boom in capacity, especially at new two-year community colleges. Second, there is the effect of relative prices: Because heavily subsidized public colleges have become much cheaper than less heavily subsidized private colleges, public campuses have absorbed nearly all of the growth in students. In 1980, as Figure 1 shows, while private-college tuition averaged about $3,000 per year, it was only $600 at public colleges and $380 at two-year public campuses. Although the difference is not large compared to the total opportunity cost of college (recall Chapters 2 and 14), it is important enough to decide many students' choices. Private colleges have rightly seen subsidized public colleges as a severe form of competition in education markets.

Because the baby boom of 1948–1955 was followed by smaller families during 1960–1968, school enrollments first mounted and then declined. The shrinkage will have major effects on colleges in the 1980s. Enrollments at many campuses had already become smaller during the 1970s, and several private colleges have gone bankrupt. Others may follow as the demand for college education shrinks further. Only as enrollments gradually rise again after about 1990—as is predicted—will education regain its normal condition of moderate growth. In the meantime, you are observing and participating in a system that is in the throes of contraction.

College funds come mainly from government subsidies, as shown in Figure 2. Taking both public and private colleges together, student payments have produced only about 20 percent of all funds. Direct government funds have covered about half of total costs since 1950. Moreover, since private gifts to colleges are tax deductible, the tax revenues of the federal government are reduced by donations to colleges. This provides a "tax expenditure" that benefits college students at the expense of other taxpayers. There is thus extra support for many colleges besides what they obtain from the direct flow of public expenditure.

Moreover, research is important at many larger campuses. On average, it absorbs about 10 percent of college spending. Much of those funds comes as grants from various branches of the federal government. Altogether, over half of higher-education costs are publicly subsidized in these direct and indirect ways.

Public schools and the issue of choice

Because public schooling in grades 1 to 12 is fully subsidized, it has eliminated nearly all competition by private schools. For most students, the local school system is a monopoly, the only available place to go. This gives a mixture of economic effects. There are major *social benefits* from having neighborhood-based schools that are available to all youths: cohesion, mutual adjustments among diverse people, and a shared sense of identity and social values. No children are excluded because they lack funds.

But there are also *social costs.* Neighborhoods themselves are often ethnic or economic enclaves that inhibit people from mixing with the residents of other such enclaves. The neighborhood school can thus reflect and help perpetuate not diversity but rather the divisions in society.

Moreover, school quality often correlates with neighborhood incomes. Impoverished neighborhoods tend to have poor schools, affluent towns good ones. At the extremes, rich neighborhoods often spend

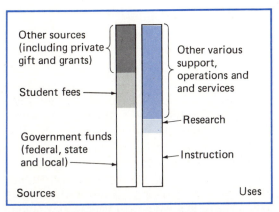

Figure 2 The basic finances of colleges and universities

Among the sources of funds, direct government support (federal, state and local) provides nearly half. Next come student tuition and fees, and then private gifts and grants.

The money goes mainly for instruction. But research also takes a large portion, along with food and buildings. (How does your own campus budget compare with these patterns?)

three or more times per student than poor neighborhoods. Even in the middle ranges, the better schools often have double the resources of the poorer schools. In many poorer school districts, this frequently translates into inferior buildings, inadequate equipment, and a sense of hopelessness. The disparities are caused primarily by the practice of financing schools from local property taxes. The richer neighborhoods naturally can draw on higher tax revenues.

Given those systematic differences in resources, the monopoly nature of the local school systems is important. Though the whole pattern allows for a healthy neighborhood-school cohesiveness, it can also lock children into unequal opportunities. Not only do most students have no choice among schools, but their school usually reflects an underlying economic inequality. Therefore, educational opportunity is often highly unequal, so that poor people have much worse chances for developing their talents. Even if the worst "blackboard jungles" in urban ghettos were remedied, there would remain strong inequalities of opportunity among other neighborhoods.

Two main economic cures have been proposed to provide more equal educational opportunities. *One is to reverse the disparities in resources* by channeling extra resources into schools in poor neighborhoods to offset the inequalities inherent in the neighborhoods themselves. Such specially financed schools could indeed improve students' learning and opportunities, as some practical cases have shown. But the weight of experience is that the political process will not provide the extra funds. Affluent neighborhoods always feel hardpressed just to pay for their own schools; they never think they have a surplus to help pay for other districts. Therefore, the underlying neighborhood inequalities can be expected to prevent a significant

shift toward high-quality schools in lower-class areas.

The other proposal is to attack the monopoly aspect of public schools: Let people have free choice among schools, so that consumer preferences can take effect. As a result, poor students could choose good schools in other districts, rather than be confined to their poor local schools. The poor schools would have to improve or else close for lack of students. Each student would be given a "voucher," good for enrolling at any school (public or private). Each voucher would be paid for by the government. The voucher would be no more costly than the present average public expenditure on schooling for children. The best schools would draw excess physical demand—shown by a waiting list of students applying to get in—and would be able to expand, while poor schools would be under financial pressure to improve. New schools could be opened, and, if good enough to draw students, they would offer more choice.

In short, free choice would operate in a setting much like a free competitive market. The public monopoly would be ended, so that families' preferences could take effect. There would be flexibility and variety, as new schools opened where demand was greatest. Fairness would be assured by giving equal-value vouchers to all, so that even the poorest child could try the same schools that are now available to the wealthy.

The approach is based firmly in neoclassical economic concepts of consumer choice, competitive processes, and efficient allocation. Its strongest advocates are classical liberal economists, such as Milton Friedman. With their vigorous endorsement for over 15 years, the method has had some practical testing. Several pilot studies have been done in school districts, with favorable results. Indeed, much of the schooling in the Netherlands is already on a similar basis. There new schools can be set up and receive public funds if they can attract enough students. In this setting, Dutch schools actually do offer variety and good quality.

Yet there are limits on the free-choice approach. A voucher is of little use if the only decent school is 20 or more miles away. Even for a three– or four–mile trip, the time and costs of travel could be a large barrier to many poor children, while affluent families could afford to transport their children to the best schools. There would also be severe problems of adjustment in the short run: The best schools would immediately be oversubscribed, so that some method of rationing the excess demand would have to be applied.

Both approaches address a real problem—inquality and monopoly in the public schools—but in opposite ways. The voucher plan had a certain vogue in the 1970s, but that has faded more recently. In general, equal educational opportunity is no longer seen as a major route for social reform in the United States, now that the bright hopes of the 1960s have dimmed. **Economists can agree that the monopoly element of schools aggravates the problems of unfairness and inefficiency in the present system of schooling. Yet, the political process seems more likely to maintain those problems than to solve them.**

Financing public colleges: Efficient? Fair?

Finally, we turn to an important economic feature of college education: whether their financial basis is efficient and fair. Public colleges and universities are highly subsidized: The price (tuition and fees) often covers less than one fourth of total costs. On some public campuses in New York and California, the subsidies are virtually complete. In recent years, efforts to raise the fees to significant levels have caused near-riots on some of those campuses. "Universal education," it was said, would be undermined.

The subsidies pose two main economic questions: Is it efficient to let public college compete on a cut-price basis? Is it fair to channel subsidies from taxpayers to college students' families?

Efficiency If all schools were strictly private, the market outcome would be a variety of schools of differing quality. They would be priced at various levels to cover their costs. For a minimal education, students could try a low-cost local school. For top-quality schooling, they could pay much more at one of the best colleges (if they qualified for admission). On this basis, prices would fit costs at each college, and no campus would be subsidized. The actual array of colleges in the United States shows much of this variety, ranging from small-town junior business colleges to the top public and private universities.

Fairness But there is an important departure from such an efficient market outcome. Public campuses get subsidies, which are often substantial. The economic result is illustrated in Figure 3, for a simplified case with just one standard quality of education. Panel I shows the demand for places at public colleges, given whatever prices are charged by private campuses. The supply of such places, at public colleges, at the prevailing real costs (of teachers' time, buildings, libraries, etc.) is shown by Curve S_1. At a cost-covering price set at P_1, the number of students shown by level Q_1 will choose to attend those public colleges. Meanwhile, in Panel II for private colleges, similar demand and supply curves result in a price of P_A and Q_A number of students.

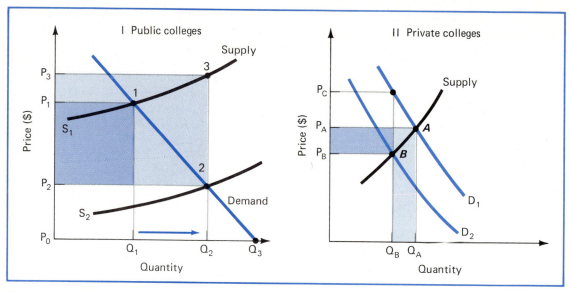

Figure 3 Subsidizing public-college education has mixed benefits

The subsidy shifts down the supply curve in Panel I. Enrollment increases from Q_1 to Q_2. The tuition charge is only P_2, even though the true cost is P_3. (If tuition were cut to zero, with a total subsidy, as many as Q_3 students would enroll.)

The subsidy is the shaded rectangle $P_2 P_3 32$ (which equals $Q_2 \times P_3 - P_2$). Some of the subsidy goes to make it possible for students from poor families to attend college. But part of the subsidy (shown by the smaller, darker box) goes to students whose families were willing to pay the full original price of P_1. That subsidy is a windfall gain that does nothing to improve educational equality.

Private colleges, meanwhile, face a reduction in demand from D_1 to D_2 in Panel II. At the new equilibrium, fewer students attend even though the price has fallen to P_B.

Now suppose that subsidies are introduced. The supply curve for public colleges shifts down to S_2 in Panel I because the lowered price for public colleges draws students away from private campuses. More students (at Q_2) will choose these bargain-priced campuses because demand has some price elasticity. The students whose families could not afford P_1, but can afford P_2, are those lying between levels Q_2 and Q_1. Those added students are drawn away from many other lines: jobs, vocational courses, and private colleges. The subsidy does make college education more widely available. A total subsidy, at a zero price of P_0, would have brought in even more students, to the level Q_3.

Meanwhile, private colleges now find that their demand curve has shifted inward because the price of a close substi-

tute (namely, public colleges) has been cut, drawing away some of their students. Private-college demand is now D_2 in Panel II, and the new outcome at B gives P_B and Q_B: fewer students and some lowering of price. The cutbacks from A to B reflect the closing of marginal, high-cost colleges. The private colleges maintain that they are faced with unfair competition, for they have much less access to direct public subsidies. They do get some moderate, indirect public support because donations to them are tax deductible. Those "tax expenditures" are not trivial, and they do encourage people and firms to donate more funds to private colleges (and public colleges) than they otherwise would. But that indirect benefit to private colleges falls far short of the direct subsidies provided to public colleges.

Are the subsidies efficient and fair? Economic analysis shows several separate effects, as follows.

CLOSURE OF PRIVATE COLLEGES   By forcing some private campuses to close, the subsidies withdraw resources from them whose value was $Q_A - Q_B \times P_A$ (the shaded vertical rectangle in Panel II of Figure 3) *plus* $P_A - P_B \times Q_B$ (the horizontal shaded rectangle). At Q_B, the original customers of private colleges thought that the value of the colleges' services was as high as P_C, as shown. Some of those students have now migrated to public campuses. But the disparity between P_B and P_A indicates that cost is now out of line with value at the margin (the margin being level Q_B).

FINANCIAL PRESSURE ON PRIVATE COLLEGES   Since the remaining private colleges now take in only a revenue (or price) of P_B per student, their funding is reduced. Their total revenues are $P_B \times Q_B$ which is much smaller than their former revenues of $Q_A \times P_A$. They will have to reduce costs, and possibly services and quality, too.

AT PUBLIC COLLEGES, VALUE AND TRUE COST ARE SEPARATED   The true cost at public campuses is now P_3 on Supply Curve S_1 (the supply curve still reflects opportunity costs, even though subsidies have altered the price paid by students). P_3 is the private payment per student (P_2) plus the subsidy ($P_3 - P_2$): Together they just cover the average total cost for the education of Q_2 students.

Note that the marginal value of public-campus education is now down to P_2, reflecting people's preferences and their ability to pay. Meanwhile, the marginal cost of education is much higher (at P_3) than the marginal value. This large deviation between price and marginal cost—between value and sacrifice at the margin—reflects an inefficient allocation. Students are receiving services that cost three times as much as they are valued at the margin.

AN UNNECESSARY SUBSIDY   But the cost of this result is a large subsidy, whose total amount is shown by the shaded rectangle P_2P_332. That amount reaches into many billions of dollars. Much of that subsidy goes to unneeded students' families, who were already able and willing to pay the original price of P_1 to the public college. Since those Q_1 students now only have to pay the bargain price of P_2, they get a subsidy shown by the shaded rectangle $P_2 - P_1 \times Q_1$. That functionless subsidy simply goes into their pockets without changing any of the Q_1 students' choices. In Figure 3, the wasted subsidy is nearly half of the total subsidy paid to the public colleges, as you can see by comparing the two shaded areas.

To reach a judgment on the whole matter, economists would consider efficiency first and then equity. *Efficient allocation is disturbed by driving the wedge between price and marginal cost.* The deviation is not small: "Too many" students are drawn to public campuses, compared to the costs of serving them and to the best alternative uses of their time. And private campuses are cut back from their efficient levels.

Some amount of "dynamic" efficiency may be recouped, however, if the added public-college students (between Q_1 and Q_2) become much more productive than they would otherwise have been. Their later productivity could offset some of the distortion that is caused in the current allocation. How large these relative benefits might be is not known.

The equity effects are much clearer. The subsidy is large and indiscriminate, going to all public-college students whether needy or not.

Economists point out that scholarship programs based on need would be more efficient and fair than the present broad subsidies given to public colleges. Tuitions would be set to cover the full cost of education, but scholarships would be provided fully—up to the direct costs of college *and* forgone income—for poor students who are qualified and can show definite need. The scholarship aid would flow only where it would provide equal educational opportunity. It would avoid the current inefficiency and functionless subsidies, while getting all of the possible gains from giving access to college for poor but talented students. And the cost of scholarships would be a small fraction of the present subsidies.

Despite this clear analysis, the traditional subsidies continue. Yet, there has recently been some revision toward better patterns, because the taxpayers' willingness to pay for education receded in the 1970s. The result has been a moderate shift toward higher tuitions and larger scholarship programs in some states. But this shift is short of what microeconomic analysis calls for.

Social regulation: Protecting the environment, workers, and consumers

Since 1960, there has been a rapid growth in two kinds of social regulation: abating pollution and protecting the safety of workers and consumers.* Because these policies have costs and effects, they raise economic issues. Amid much criticism, the

---

*They differ from the "economic regulation" that we presented in Chapter 13. There, the regulation controls prices, profits, and the ability of firms to enter and compete in markets. The aims are to prevent monopoly's bad effects while obtaining economies of scale.

Social regulation, by contrast, deals only with *social* aspects of production: pollution and safety, at work and in the design and use of consumer products.

policies have made some progress. We present them together here, for they involve the same basic kinds of **cost-benefit analysis.** First, we take up environmental issues. Then we discuss worker and consumer protection.

Environmental issues and programs

The environment can be harmed in many ways: the pollution of water and air, the destruction of wilderness and underground water sources, the infliction of loud noises in cities. Industrial factories often cause the damage, but normal life in crowded cities also creates numberless external effects. Correcting those problems is a leading area for political action, as Chapter 18 has noted.

Until the 1960s, most economists regarded such environmental problems as minor and of no lasting impact. The few serious ones—such as polluted rivers, and smog in cities such as Pittsburgh (where street lights were often kept lit all day through the 1940s) and Los Angeles—were regarded as a regrettable but small price to pay for economic progress. Efforts to prevent or cure the pollution were said to be too costly and likely to cause barriers to industrial growth. Business interests held more sway than in the 1970s and 1980s, and had little interest in limiting themselves to reduce pollution.

When the environmental movement took hold in the later 1960s, economists developed the analysis of the economic causes of pollution and showed how to design efficient cures. The economic remedies are reasonable, simple, and clear for many pollution problems, but the political problems are often quite complex. Accordingly, many policies have been inadequate or unnecessarily costly.

Over $500 billion has been spent since 1968 in cleaning up pollution in the country. The yearly totals of cleanup costs have risen from about $25 billion in 1972 to $61 billion in 1981. A further $619 billion of costs are projected for between 1982 and 1988 (in 1981 dollars), even with no new laws, according to estimates by the Council on Environmental Quality. These cleanup costs have been estimated to raise the inflation rate by 0.2 percent, to raise unemployment rates by 0.2–0.4 percent, and to slow national productivity growth by about 10 percent. Because large costs are involved, the United States may face difficult choices between the quality of life and economic growth.

Policies have been set mainly by the Environmental Protection Agency (EPA), which was created in 1969. The EPA has had only modest powers and funds and has been slow to develop effective tools. The main methods available to it are summarized in Table 2, with examples. Despite much criticism, both fair and unfair, the EPA has reduced some kinds of pollution. Its techniques have also improved, moving gradually from just issuing rules toward using economic incentives. Certain states have also taken specific cleanup actions. Congress has provided various financial subsidies, trying to encourage pollution abatement. These actions have brought improvements in some types of pollution and in some areas.

Yet, much pollution remains, as Figure 4 indicates. Large areas of the country still have severe air and water pollution. Acid rain—caused by sulfur dioxide and nitrogen dioxide—has increasingly sterilized lakes, harmed forests, and contaminated groundwater. Over 30 cancer-causing air pollutants have not been regulated at all.

In short, the cleanup process has been expensive, of doubtful effect, and incomplete. It is important to make further efforts efficient, lest their cost become astronomical. But many pollution-control programs have been criticized for being wasteful. The policies have relied mainly on rules rather than cost-benefit analysis, and microeconomists have been among their sharpest critics. During 1977–1982, some EPA programs began to incorporate economic incentives more effectively.

Pollution control, therefore, poses sophisticated economic issues, which are evolving under debate in hundreds of in-

Table 2 *Alternative solutions to pollution*

Types	Examples
Persuasion	
Public appeals	Requests for reducing pollution.
	Exposés of actual pollution.
	Threats to enact laws.
Rules and Fines	
Sets permissible levels; imposes fines for violation	Equipment standards limiting factory effluents.
	EPA standards for automobile emissions.
	Rules requiring "scrubbers" on electric-utility smokestacks.
Direct Incentives: Taxes and Subsidies	U.S. subsidies to cities for better sewage-treatment capacity.
Market-type Solutions	"Bubble" treatments.
	Marketable pollution permits.

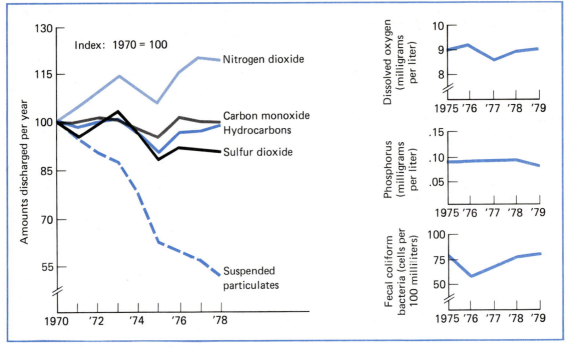

Figure 4 Changes in and persistence of pollution
Source: *U.S. Statistical Abstract.*

dustries and thousands of locations. Amid the variety of pollutions and remedies, several main points of economic analysis are now well agreed upon.

The main problems lie in (1) defining the criteria that should guide the policies; and (2) designing actual policies that achieve these goals efficiently, with a maximum benefit from given costs.

Cost-benefit issues

Economists insist that cost-benefit analysis is the best basic framework for analyzing pollution and its cures. The main economic elements are usually of the cost-benefit kind that is illustrated in Figure 5. We now present those issues in more depth.

The level of cleanliness (of avoiding pollution) is shown on the horizontal axis,

with rising levels toward the *right*. To stop pollution means to move to the right, toward a zero level of pollution. The benefits of doing so include the lives that are saved and the health damage that is avoided (recall Chapter 18). Businesses also often benefit from having better water and air resources available to use in production. Thus, a wood-pulp mill might require large amounts of clean water. If only polluted water is available, the mill will have to build a filter plant, at some cost. The extra cost would raise its total cost of production. Therefore, having clean water is a direct economic benefit.

In Figure 5, we assume that these benefit values can be measured reliably, to compare with the costs of reducing pollution. We also assume that those costs are minimized for each level of cleanup achieved, by applying the best pollution-abatement methods. The efficient control of pollution occurs at Point *A*, where the marginal benefits just equal the marginal costs. The logic is clear because departing from Point *A* is demonstrably inefficient.

A serious problem arises if the costs are paid by one group of people but the benefits go to another group. Then the issue of efficiency is mixed with the question of fairness. This problem is avoided if costs are assigned to the beneficiaries, either precisely or approximately. Where this is not done, cost-benefit analysis has less validity as a method.

Some observers also criticize cost-benefit analysis for allegedly understating the health benefits of clean air and water. The benefits usually involve values of people's lives based on their productivity; that productivity, in turn, is measured by their incomes. Thus, a 50-year-old person now earning $60,000 per year would be project-

ed to earn at that rate for 15 more years, for a lifetime value of 15 × $60,000 = $900,000. The present value of this income would, of course, be lower after discounting future incomes.

This method for valuing lives has limitations, however. *First*, it assigns a zero value to a person who works at home rather than at a paid outside job; the true value of his or her work is ignored. *Second*, it assigns a low or zero value to retired people and young children because they do not hold paying jobs. And *third*, its income criterion assigns low values to janitors and high values to executives: Though possibly efficient, it conflicts with the ethical concept that all people's lives are inherently of equal value.

Past government decisions have frequently set low values on human lives, often in the range of just $20,000 to $40,000. Yet the problem is a *matter of degree*, not

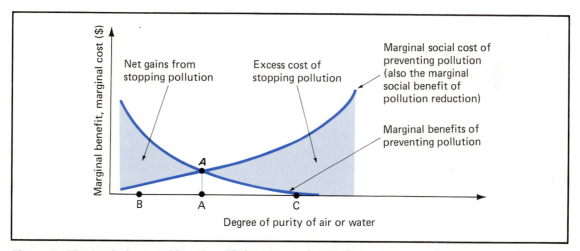

Figure 5   The basis for reaching the efficient level of pollution

Small amounts of pollution cause little social harm because they are assimilated by nature and do not build up in people's bodies. But rising pollution (to the left) causes a rising marginal degree of harm, as annoyance turns to sickness and eventually to death from high pollution.

Meanwhile, the marginal costs of reducing pollution become extremely high to the right, in trying to eliminate the last traces of pollution. But at the left-hand end, the marginal costs are low because the worst degrees of pollution can be reduced relatively easily.

At point *A*, the marginal costs of stopping pollution are just equal to the marginal social gains. Pollution levels above *A* are too expensive to correct efficiently. Pollution levels below *A* cause more harm than it would cost to prevent them.

of logic. The need is for better estimates, rather than for rejecting the cost-benefit approach altogether.

Indeed, human lives are frequently valued in private insurance cases, where settlements have commonly been in the range of $250,000 to $800,000, depending on age and occupation. Such values indicate the order of magnitude that can usually be assigned to saving lives by regulating pollution and safety.

In sum, any rational policy will have to compare costs and benefits. It will (1) include all costs and benefits fully, rather than omitting or understating some of them; (2) weigh all risks properly (risks of harm to people, firms, etc.); and (3) make sure that future interests are properly weighted. Doing that can satisfy the main criticisms of cost-benefit analysis. For many purposes, the debate is primarily about the categories and the amounts, not the basic logic.

Now we turn to specific policies to reduce pollution. They have mainly involved physical rules and limits, which we will discuss first. Only recently have economic incentives been explicitly introduced into the policies.

The use of rules to limit pollution

Congress has largely controlled the standards of clean air and water that the EPA has tried to enforce for factories and automobiles. Timetables have set targets for successive years. Costs are given little standing as guidelines for EPA decisions. Instead, the EPA has relied extensively on the following approach: The "best available control technology" is required in new equipment, as long as it is "feasible"—that is, its costs will not put a large share of the industry out of business.

These two methods—permitted levels of pollution and "best (feasible) technology"—can fit cost-benefit outcomes but

only by chance. Instead, they may go to either extreme, Even where they happen to hit the right degree of purity, these methods lack proper incentives for firms to reduce pollution efficiently.

Moreover, the controls have mainly applied to *new* equipment, such as machinery and automobiles. That has (1) too sharply raised the cost of new equipment, discouraging innovation and reducing productivity; and (2) ignored possible major gains from reconditioning old equipment and automobiles.

The EPA has relied on setting physical standards for air and water quality in geographic areas. Factories are then required to reduce their emissions by certain percentages. They must install low-emission equipment in new factories. In areas already meeting the standard, complex rules permit only certain "increments" of new pollution. The rules and procedures are often time-consuming. Two cases—automobile emissions and the steel industry—illustrate the main economic issues.

Automobiles In 1970, Congress set a schedule of automobile emission standards to be met in a detailed timetable of successive years. The main harmful emissions were to be reduced by 90 percent by 1975. The benefits were not measured precisely; 90 percent was simply set as the target. The true harms caused by the emissions were not known, even approximately, and they were still largely unresearched.

In practice, the targets have frequently been moved back, though by 1981, a large share of harmful auto emissions had been eliminated. Two features of this program were especially debatable on economic grounds. One was the rush to require costly catalytic converters on U.S.-made cars after 1974. Cheaper methods for reducing emissions were developed by Japanese automobile companies at much lower cost, using many small changes in engine design. Moreover, a large proportion of the catalytic converters on U.S. cars have been disconnected or ruined by misuse, while the Japanese cars could not be so easily changed to permit emissions.

The costs of emission controls reached $40–$110 per year for 1981 model cars. Did the benefits justify the costs?

In appraising the benefits and costs of emission controls, one crucial point is that automobile pollution is not evenly spread. Its harmful concentrations occur only in certain large cities, while virtually all auto emissions elsewhere—more than half of total emissions that occur—are dispersed harmlessly in small towns and open spaces. Therefore, at least half of emission-control costs are unnecessary.

Conversely, the existing controls still leave pollution levels relatively high in the main large cities. If pollution-dense zones could be defined, then the controls could be confined to cars operating in them. The rest could be free of the extra costs. Or possibly there could be pollution taxes on cars operating in high-density urban areas.

Yet, actual policy has instead forced *all* new cars—and *only new cars*—to meet engineering emission-control standards. The alternate, more precise approach was regarded as impractical, since cars move freely among areas. Moreover, inspection programs have not been implemented, even though they could cheaply identify the worst polluters and enforce repairs.

The United States has stopped a large share of automobile emissions, but in inefficient ways. If pollution is to be reduced further, it is important to apply more efficient methods.

Steel In recent years, the steel industry has made good progress in complying with federal pollution standards. As of 1981, some 87 percent of steel plants complied with pollution standards (in most other industries, compliance is between 10 and 25 percent).

The EPA has relied mainly on rules and fines in a series of negotiations with this industry to press the companies to invest in cleaner technology. Industry officials say that the new equipment adds 25 percent to the volume of its investment needs, even though the average cost of steel is raised by less than 3 percent. Since imported Japanese steel is now available and competing strongly at lower prices than many U.S. firms can match, the U.S. companies find it natural to blame pollution control for the loss of steel production and jobs. "Cleaner air costs jobs" is the apparent dilemma.

But the real issues go deeper. For decades, the industry has been so sluggish in adopting new technology, that U.S. firms are now paying Japanese firms to show them how to improve their efficiency. If the U.S. industry had been more innovative and efficient during 1930–1970, the current cleanup could easily be funded while still letting the industry meet Japanese import competition. (The Japanese firms already meet high standards of pollution control in Japan.) Because of the U.S. industry's failures, the EPA rules now do seem to impose difficult choices on steel factories in some parts of the country. One solution might be to provide public funds to help finance the pollution-control equipment, along with other actions to rehabilitate the industry.

In short, this case involves more than simple rules or subsidies. Pollution control needs to be included in a larger approach to industrial innovation in the steel industry.

The use of incentives

Though many economists have urged that more **economic incentives** be applied, little of that has yet been done. There is increasing experimentation with three specific methods: the "bubble" concept, "marketable permits," and taxes on emissions.

The bubble concept   The EPA has begun applying a "bubble" concept in some cases since 1977. This approach applies to firms that have several or more pollution-emitting plants in an area which is treated as a single unit or "bubble." They are allowed to adjust among those sources of pollution, as long as their total emissions are within permitted levels. The method lets firms decide how best to reduce their emissions. Otherwise, the agency would have to reduce emissions from each factory, stack by stack, which would make it harder for each firm to design efficient ways of reducing its total pollution. By 1981, over 80 "bubbles" had been established, and the practice was spreading rapidly.

Marketable permits   Some economists regard marketable permits as even more promising. They are specific emissions rights, which can be bought and sold. They work as follows: Suppose a 33 percent reduction is deemed appropriate, based on a full cost-benefit analysis, in an area with 150 factories that pour out 15,000 tons of pollution daily. The agency first establishes severe fines for firms that pollute at levels higher than their permits. Next it prints permits for 10,000 tons daily. It then either (1) gives or sells these to the existing polluters in proportion to their emissions; or (2) gives them to citizen groups or cities in the area that suffer from the pollution; or (3) sells them off to all comers at auction.

If enforcement is complete, pollution should drop to the 10,000-tons-a-day rate, but the 150 firms could adjust by the least-cost methods. Complex, burdensome rules would be avoided. If method 2 were chosen, the factory owners would have to pay to the sufferers of pollution a dollar amount that approximates the social costs that the pollution inflicts. Therefore, this method would come closest to a complete economic treatment of pollution by making the *external* costs of pollution an *internal* cost to the polluters. Moreover, the victims of pollution would be compensated for their losses.

Under methods 2 and 3, citizen groups or government units could buy and reserve some of the rights, thereby forcing even lower levels of pollution. This would allow people to cut the pollution they dislike directly. It would also force the foes of pollution to consider the real costs of the cleanup, by testing what they are willing to pay. (But note that poor people who suffer from pollution could not afford to purchase pollution rights.)

If marketable permits are accurately priced and backed by strict enforcement, the results are close to an economic ideal because they let decisions be controlled by marginal costs and benefits. Those who know best (managers) and care most (citizens groups) could act without relying on a bureaucracy.

Taxes on emissions are a more direct method and one also favored by many economists. Such "effluent fees" are simple to use and apply economic incentives to reduce pollution. The agency's main task is to set the tax at a level that will reach the right outcome. In Figure 6, the tax would be set at T_A per unit of pollution, which equals both the marginal cost and the marginal benefits of pollution control in equilibrium. That would make the external cost of pollution an internal cost to the polluting firm. The firm would then be willing to spend up to that amount to reduce the pollution. Therefore, firms would respond by reducing pollution to level P_A, making their own best choices about how to do so most efficiently.

The logic of these several methods is clear, but putting them into practice could

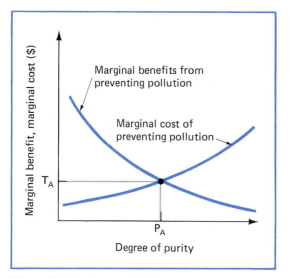

Figure 6   Setting an efficient pollution tax

The efficient level of pollution is at P_A in this illustration, because that is where marginal costs and benefits are equal. A tax set at the value T_A would then confront the polluters with the social cost of their actions: The external cost would become an internal cost to the firms. They would then have the incentive to spend up to that amount so to avoid the tax. They could do so in the most efficient way.

1970s. Pollution taxes are especially appropriate for emissions that cause widespread, long-distance problems like acid rain. "Bubbles" and marketable permits are better suited to localized pollution problems. Though precise optimal outcomes are difficult to predict, these methods do give strong incentives, with little bureaucratic involvement. That fits the economists' usual preference for price signals rather than regulations.

In any event, these three methods require monitoring the companies' pollution levels. When companies are few, these costs will be low. But when hundreds or thousands of companies are involved, the monitoring costs may overwhelm the economic advantages of these incentive schemes. Therefore, the best practical control of pollution will vary from industry to industry. These choices, too, can be guided by comparing the costs and benefits of alternatives.

be complex. Since the marginal values are rarely precisely measurable, some guesswork is necessary. Because the numbers are debatable, companies resist, and the taxes, fines, and enforcement could become entangled in debates and lawsuits.

Nonetheless, each of these methods can improve on the rigid rules of the

Programs protecting worker and consumer safety

Since 1970, three federal agencies have been created to promote safety in the workplace and in consumer products (joining the Food and Drug Administration (FDA), which was created in 1906). As summarized in Table 3, the new agencies are a response to real problems. Over 100,000

Table 3   New federal agencies for worker and consumer protection

Agency (year created)	Budget 1981–1982 ($ million)	Staff Members	Formal Purpose
Occupational Safety and Health Administration (OSHA) (1970)	$193	3,260	To protect safety and health on the job
National Highway Traffic Safety Administration (NHSA) (1970)	$141	825	To reduce traffic accidents, by requiring better design of motor vehicles
Consumer Product Safety Commission (CPSC) (1972)	$58	899	To reduce product-related injuries to consumers

people are killed each year by industrial, consumer, and other accidents; over 5 million people a year undergo injuries that disable them for more than one day. The costs in treatment, lost work, and suffering are large. Millions of workers are still exposed to significant risks of accidents and such health hazards as lead, vinyl chloride, cotton dust, coal dust, and arsenic. Many consumer products also are hazardous. From automobiles, motorcycles, and bicycles to foods, medicines, poisons, ladders, cribs, and children's toys, there is a variety of products that can harm people. The question is how much public protection is needed.

Like the FDA earlier, OSHA, CPSC, and NHSA have had the usual history: Created to solve large problems, the agencies have grown rapidly, made some mistakes, stirred opposition, and, since 1980, been trimmed back. Often criticized as harmful bureaucracies, they have experimented with a variety of methods, just as the EPA has. Economists have urged them to use cost-benefit criteria. Instead, they have often sought to provide extreme, absolute degrees of protection that deliberately ignore costs.

Costs and benefits The basic economic issues are identical to those involved in protecting the environment, as illustrated in Figure 5. But it is the degree of safety from bodily harm that is measured on the horizontal axis in Figure 7. Providing safety incurs economic costs, which rise at the margin. Reducing the worst hazards gives high benefits, but attaining near-absolute protection often gives only small marginal benefits. The valuation of the benefits from safety is done as before, by estimating the benefits of avoiding the suffering, lost production, and other impacts. For example, a worker who loses his or her legs not only suffers personally, but also must pay for

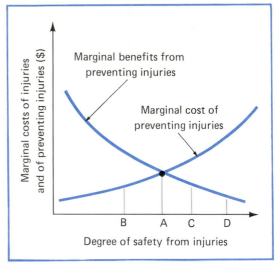

Figure 7 Marginal costs of injuries and of preventing injuries

The conditions correspond to those in Figure 5. *A* is the efficient level of safety protection. *B* is too little protection, while *D* and *C* are too much, by cost-benefit criteria.

artificial legs, wheelchairs, and other assistance.

The marginal costs of protection rise, as shown in Figure 7. Cheap protection such as guardrails, hard hats, goggles, and the like may sharply reduce risks, as at Point *B*. But reducing risk down to very low levels, as at Point *C*, may require that machines and factory layout be redesigned. Therefore, an effort to provide, absolute safety, like absolutely clean air or water, can be exceedingly costly.

The efficient degree of risk is at Point *A* in Figure 7. Ideally, OSHA, CPSC, and NHSA would design policies to reach that point in each case they handle. For example, NHSA would require only this amount of crash protection (seat belts, bumpers, reinforcements, etc.) in cars. Similarly, the FDA will require foods to meet only these marginal conditions of safety, and if a guardrail near steel furnaces fits Point *A*, OSHA will not require more protection than that.

Yet the laws creating FDA, OSHA, and CPSC stressed the *benefits* of worker and consumer safety but gave little attention to *costs*. For foods, *any* risk of causing cancer would require a ban. For OSHA and CPSC, the greatest "feasible" protection was mandated; cost was a limit only if it would be large enough to force many or most firms out of business. Later Supreme Court rulings have upheld this willingness to enforce safety even if it imposes costs that exceed benefits. Thus, the laws appear to call for Point *C* or *D*, if that is necessary.

In practice, the agencies have usually followed that priority. They often make no explicit effort to locate the efficient degree of protection corresponding to Point *A*. Instead, OSHA, for example, requires that all producers adopt the safest technology now available. It has also set levels for toxic fumes and dusts—such as benzene, asbestos, arsenic, lead, and cotton dust—that require changes in machinery. These standards have been accused of being too tight by cost-benefit standards.

Cotton dust is a good example. It causes byssinosis (brown lung disease) in cotton-mill workers. When it is present at levels of about 200 micrograms per cubic meter, about 13 percent of workers will contract the disease. In 1978, OSHA set limits on cotton dust, requiring firms to reduce the levels substantially. These standards mean that it will cost about $135,000 to avoid each case of brown lung disease. The benefits have been calculated at only about $20,000 per case, suggesting that the rule is too strict. Alternatively, the same degree of protection could have been reached much more cheaply by requiring employers to pay workers at least $20,000 (or up to $135,000) if they contract the disease. The Reagan administration sought in 1981 to relax standards such as these, in line with their new cost-benefit emphasis. But through 1982, the Supreme Court has upheld the stricter approach. Consumer safety protection by CPSC has followed similar lines, with no close reliance on cost-benefit comparisons.

Military spending

The U.S. military system is the biggest single spending program in the country. Figure 8 shows its size and main trends. Much military spending goes to pay for personnel: officers, soldiers of all ranks and skills, and people in many other job categories. The rest goes to buy weapons and materials, ranging from pencils to complete missile systems. These items now make up over 70 percent of all purchases by the government.

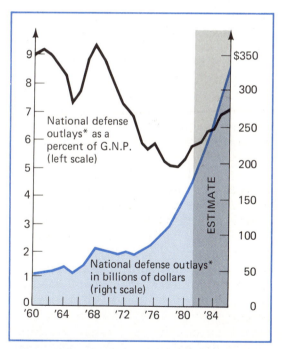

Figure 8   Trends and projections of U.S. military spending

*National Defense includes outlays by the Defense Department, the Energy Department, the General Services Administration, and the Selective Service System.

Source: Office of Management and Budget.

The Pentagon is also a large owner of capital. Besides its own bases, inventories of armaments, and transportation networks, it owns 149 manufacturing plants and over 100,000 items of industrial equipment. Military spending also plays a large role in total U.S. research and development (R&D). It pays for over half of all R&D carried out in the United States, and in certain key industries—aerospace, aircraft, and related technology—it buys nearly all of the R&D that is done.

This huge flow of money for arms, people, and technology poses three main economic issues: (1) How can waste be avoided in producing the supplies? (2) How much military spending is appropriate, neither too little nor too much? (3) How can a volunteer military force be arranged, so as to avoid the costs of a military draft? We will treat each issue in turn.

Avoiding waste in producing military goods

Wartime procurement always entails urgency and, therefore, an unavoidable element of waste. In peacetime, however, the Pentagon could ensure that its materials are supplied efficiently, at minimum cost. Like conventional buyers in private markets, it would seek the lowest-price sellers for each item. The goods would be made at minimum cost, and the price for each would cover only that cost, including the cost of capital.

In practice, less than 10 percent of military purchases are made under such competitive market conditions. Most of those competitively acquired goods are simple ones like foods, clothing, and furniture. The other 90+ percent are bought after considering only a few suppliers and picking one. The terms are negotiated rather than set by impersonal markets, and often the military services end up paying much more than they originally contract for.

In sum, most weapons purchases are made outside the standard conditions of efficient competitive markets. The main deviations are shown in Table 4. They reflect an unusual set of conditions found in military weaponry. Each new weapon (e.g., an aircraft, tank, ship, warning system) requires new designs and testing. In developing the plans, the Pentagon officers usually deal with only a few firms. Those firms may compete strenuously to win the crucial first contract. But the winner anticipates having the whole production run—of M1 tanks, B1 bombers, missiles, Trident submarines, or whatever. The supplier-buyer relation tends to become fixed and intimate, as in any bilateral monopoly or oligopoly.

At any time, the whole flow of complex armaments involves scores of such situations. They evolve and change, but the Pentagon and the main suppliers continue in a pattern of working relationships. The leading 20 suppliers in 1967 through 1977 remained mostly the same. President Eisenhower called this pattern of interests the "military-industrial complex." Retiring military officers frequently take jobs with the companies, and company leaders are often appointed to high policy positions in the Pentagon.

This complicated set of relationships between firms and military officials gives some genuine social advantages. Officers know the companies well. Plans are made under conditions of close cooperation. The companies are supported in business, so that they are ready to meet wartime emergencies. There is a high degree of continuity and mutual understanding.

But there are also economic and social costs. The planning of new weapons is often imbued with optimism, as company officials anticipate and offer to the military officers the kinds of weapons that fit their preferences. The focus is often on getting the highest technical quality of weapons,

Table 4 *Contrasts between conditions in competitive markets and many weapons markets*

Competitive Markets	Many Weapons Markets
Many small buyers	One buyer (DOD)
Many small suppliers	Very few large suppliers of a given item
All items small, perfectly divisible, and in large quantities	One ship built every few years, for hundreds of millions of dollars
Free movement in and out of the market	Extensive barriers to entry and exit
Prices set in line with marginal costs	Prices proportional to total costs
Prices set in line with marginal utility	Any price paid for the desired military performance
Market shifts rapidly to changes in supply and demand	7–10 years to develop a new system, then 3–5 years to produce it
No government involvement	Government is regulator, specifier, banker, judge of claims, etc.
Selection based on price	Selection often based on politics, or sole source, or "negotiation"; only 8 percent of dollars awarded on price competition

Adapted from J. S. Gansler, *The Defense Industry*. Copyright © 1980 by Jacques S. Gansler. Used by permission of the MIT Press, Cambridge, MA.

with little regard for cost. As new weapons develop from mere ideas to early designs, both the firms and the military become committed to the need for producing the new weapon.

Meanwhile, the hopeful companies make ambitious proposals. To "buy in" and get the first contract, they often make deliberately low bids, even though they expect to have to ask for higher payments later as production occurs at higher costs. Their *marginal* cost for new orders is low when they have a small backlog of orders, and they need only cover *variable* costs in the short run. Yet, the contract payments must eventually cover the companies' average *total* costs.

So each supplier has an incentive to set low prices in its bids when it is short of orders. Later, when production is under

way and costs turn out to be higher than predicted, the military has only the one supplier. It then often must acquiesce in the cost overrun and cover the extra costs. But that overrun will frequently be ascribed to changes in the weapon's design and to the weapon's high technical quality.

Most of the buying decisions are made by middle-level officers trained as engineers, who know little about economic efficiency. The contracts are usually on a "cost-plus" basis: The supplier is paid for its production costs plus a fee for its efforts. Thus, for a 300 fighter-plane order the military may pay $2.4 billion ($8 million apiece) for the $2.1 billion of costs plus a $300 million contractor's fee for carrying out the production. If costs had been $1.5 billion or $3.5 billion, the $300 million fee would still have been the same.

In such "cost-plus" contracts, the supplier has no incentive to minimize costs once the contract is signed. Some contracts even tie the size of the fee to the level of the costs themselves, so that larger costs yield a larger fee. In these cases, the contractor is directly induced to increase the use of resources by raising the level of the costs. But even a neutral "cost-plus, fixed-fee" contract departs from sound private-market standards.

Such cost-plus contracting has long been recognized as inefficient, but it remains standard for the Pentagon. The weapons are said to be too new, and complex for a price to be specified in advance. And the initial competition for the contract, which forces the winner to offer a low bid, is itself a second main cause of inefficient allocation, for it makes it seem that the weapon will be much cheaper than it inevitably turns out to be. Many current weapons systems would not have been chosen if their true costs had been known in advance. When a firm offers to build for $1.9 billion a nuclear warship that will eventually cost $4.5 billion, it encourages the Navy to purchase the ship. The military can refuse to pay the higher costs when the production is completed, but often the supplier can argue that important new features were added to the weapon's design by the Pentagon, so that the firm should not be responsible for the excess costs. If the military officials do force the supplier to undergo large financial losses on such contracts, they may bankrupt the company and lose its capacity to produce weapons in the future.

This economic process continues, generating new families of weapons systems, which frequently cost over 50 percent more—and occasionally over 200 percent more—than was planned. In each case, there is argument about the true cause of the cost increase; each case has its unique features. But there is no doubt that an element of cost inflation exists.

Pentagon officials concede that much inefficiency occurs. The best economic estimates are that the waste is in the range of 10–20 percent of total military purchasing. That would be about $7–$15 billion yearly in recent years. As a contributory factor, the military leases over $200 billion of buildings and equipment to suppliers at virtually no cost. In this setting, the military preference for high technical reliability rather than minimum cost inevitably leads to significant excess costs.

The main economic causes of the problem have been well known and studied for years, but a cure would require reorienting the basic thinking and techniques of the thousands of officers responsible for the military's purchases. Though economists may continue to argue for more efficiency, there is little probability of change.

Efficient military levels and the arms race

Military expenditures take a significant share of total world production. At over $650 billion, the total spending on armed forces in 1981 was 6 percent of worldwide economic activity. In the same year, the international trade in weapons was $120 billion. This accelerating global arms race absorbs large flows of scarce resources and raises the risks and impacts of warfare, with its severe economic disruptions.

The economics of the arms race derives from both budgetary overstatement and oligopolistic competition. We discuss them in turn.

Military estimates Economists and others have long discussed the tendency for the military to overstate its economic needs. To provide military security, the Joint Chiefs of Staff naturally prefer a big army and navy and a large stock of weapons, capable of meeting all likely threats. Each report of the Soviets making better planes, tanks, submarines, and missiles raises pressure to provide the same to our military services. To attain absolute security, we would have to devote all national production to military ends, and that still might not be enough.

For economists, military needs are a matter of degree. An efficient policy would provide the total of weapons at which the marginal benefits (in enhanced national security) equal the marginal costs. Within that total, each weapons system and type would also be provided just up to the efficient margin.

Therefore, trade-offs have to be made at two levels: between military and civilian needs, and among military choices (such as submarines, B1 bombers, M16 rifles, and footsoldiers). The natural role of military officials is to request everything they might need, and that of the government to reduce the levels to those consistent with efficient total allocation.

Ideally, those optimum marginal conditions could be identified and the military budget nicely calculated in total and in all its parts. In practice, the benefits of weapons and personnel are mostly matters of conjecture. Admittedly, some direct calculations can be made. For example, given the known Soviet armored capacities, how many tanks, artillery, and other forces would be needed to "win" a certain type of war in Europe?

These and other practical "scenarios" for prospective military actions are modeled repeatedly by Pentagon planners, using many assumptions. The analyses give some practical estimates about the weaponry needed to achieve specific objectives. Moreover, data about Russian weapons budgets are analyzed thoroughly to suggest what the adversary's future weapons might be.

Yet, even complete weapons data could not anticipate the unpredictable "human" factors. Military actions may arise from unexpected sources, and random events may lead to growing armed conflict in many places. The combat may recede or recur at any time. Moreover, the process is partly circular: U.S. military preparations influence Soviet actions, which, in turn, influence U.S. actions.

Therefore, economists are not able to provide conclusive measures of the "right" level of military spending. But they have been able to clarify the most disturbing weapons issue of all: the dynamic process that causes the international arms race.

Dynamics of the arms race The arms race is a competitive process leading to excessive production and deployment of weapons. It occurs for the following reasons, largely related to the fact that the U.S.-Soviet relations are a form of oligopoly.

Because U.S. and Soviet policies are partly interdependent, one cannot define the efficient level of U.S. armaments without considering Soviet actions. The United States cannot realistically expect to attain perfect security, for such a high level of U.S. armaments would threaten the Soviets. The Soviets would react either by expanding their armaments to restore equality, or by taking some desperate action to remove U.S. superiority. The same logic holds for the United States.

Therefore, the two superpowers are locked in a need to reach approximate parity. Neither can seek clear superiority without causing the other to redress the balance. Exactly the same logic applies to any pair of adversary countries (such as Pakistan and India), and to groupings of allies. The result has been a continuing arms race, leading to over 50,000 nuclear weapons, the vast yearly spending on weapons, and the large international weapons trade.

Concerning this process, economists offer three lessons: *First,* efforts by one superpower to gain superiority over its rival are irrational and ultimately dangerous to all sides. *Second,* a stable condition of peace requires both some guarantee against surprise attack and some assurance that any nuclear action will cause severe damage to all. But *third,* an absolute guarantee against nuclear actions can also be costly. By neutralizing the risk of nuclear war, it makes conventional warfare, without fear of escalation, more practicable. The nuclear threat itself is horrific, economists note, but it has prevented direct warfare between the two superpowers. That has probably prevented large amounts of conventional war costs and destruction that might otherwise have occurred.

Yet, the arms race continues, with its large opportunity costs. The economic burdens increase the severity of other world economic problems. Moreover, those armaments are likely to be used sooner or later, causing even more loss. Even limited warfare can severely disrupt the economic systems of both adversaries. Indeed, just the risks of future war can discourage productive long-term investments.

The economic basis for a volunteer army

A recurring urgent issue of public policy is whether young people should be subject to a military draft in peacetime. One doctrinaire position is that everyone has a patriotic duty to serve the country. Another is that drafting people is immoral, since forced military service is a form of involuntary servitude.

The most common argument on behalf of the draft in preference to a volunteer army is that the draft is cheaper than the alternative ways of staffing the armed forces. Because draftees cannot decline to serve, their wages are much lower than those that would be needed to raise a volunteer army of the same size and quality. Proponents of the draft frequently argue that the government cannot afford a volunteer army. Generals often argue this way (although the general staff itself is all volunteer!).

Do you find this argument persuasive? If you do, read on, and see if your views are influenced by economic analysis.

Why don't you want to be drafted, even though being a peacetime soldier is not a hazardous occupation? Presumably, you think that you have better things to do. The cost to you of being drafted is the value to you of the next best thing you could do with your time; that is, your *opportunity cost.* If you are in college, your time must be quite valuable because you are paying a large price to be there, in terms of tuition and the earnings you are foregoing. Those neither in college nor in the military are in civilian jobs, earning rates of pay that correspond to the value of their productive work. If they are taken from jobs that pay $15,000 to serve in the army at $6,000 per year, the true cost of their time is still $15,000.

An economist would calculate the true cost of an army of drafted soldiers not according to the dollars that they are actually paid in wages (such as $6,000 apiece), but according to what the same draftees would have to be paid to attract them into the army voluntarily. This value based on a full payment measures the opportunity cost of their time. Of course, this calculation attaches a far higher cost figure to the draft army than the actual dollars paid by the army to its draftees. But since draftees are forced to serve, their pay has little to do with the economic value of their time.

The draft does not save money. It simply reassigns the true costs of military service, away from taxpayers and onto the conscripted youths. The youth who could earn $15,000 per year is taxed $9,000 per year by the draft.

That the draft subtracts from civilian production was recognized over 200 years ago by Benjamin Franklin. In opposing the impressment (the forcible drafting) of sailors, he stated the economic principle clearly and even estimated the size of the hidden tax:

But if, as I suppose is often the case, the sailor who is pressed and obliged to serve for the defence of this trade at the rate of 25s. a month, could have £3. 15s., in the merchant's service, you take from him 50s. a month; and if you have 100,000 in your service, you rob the honest part of society and their poor families of £250,-000. per month, or three millions a year, and at the same time oblige them to hazard their lives in fighting for the defence of your trade.

To show the economic effects precisely, we use the standard analysis of supply and demand for labor in the armed forces. Like any other line of work, the military services have a supply of potential workers, as illustrated in Figure 9, using hypothetical numbers. The number volunteering for military work depends on the rates of pay offered. There is also a demand curve, reflecting the value of the work done. The curve slopes down in line with the law of diminishing returns. The 500,000th soldier adds more value to natural defense than does the 3 millionth or 5 millionth soldier.

The equilibrium at Point A provides the correct number of soldiers. The marginal soldiers contribute a value (demand) which just equals the cost of paying them (supply). Beyond that level, the value of additional soldiers would be less than

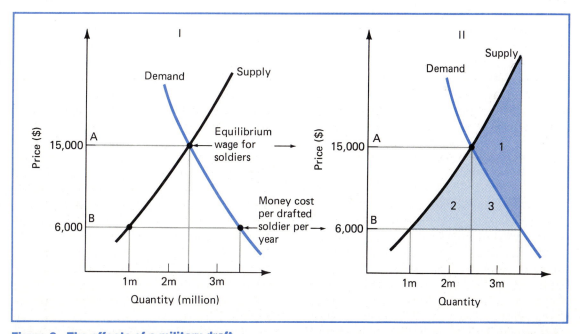

Figure 9   The effects of a military draft
A volunteer army succeeds when there is an equilibrium of supply and demand, at a cost per soldier of $15,000 per year. If there is a draft, the cost per soldier appears to be only $6,000 per year (covering room and board and a small rate of pay). But the real cost to society also includes the net loss of production value, if the drafted soldiers had been in civilian jobs. Area 1 shows that loss: it is subtracted from the national output. The drafted soldiers lose even more heavily. Their loss of income is all of the shaded areas, numbered 1, 2, and 3.

their cost. At Point A, the pay rate is high enough to sustain a volunteer military of 2.5 million total workers, earning $15,000 on average. Workers make free choices between civilian and military jobs. Thus, opportunity costs guide the decisions, and the nation's total production is maximized.

The effects of a military draft are readily contrasted in Figure 9. Military expenses are kept low, at level B, just $6,000 per year (covering costs plus a small wage). Only 1 million workers volunteer to serve at that low rate of reward. Meanwhile, it appears to the military management to be worth hiring 3.5 million soldiers at that low price. The resulting "shortage" of 2.5 million soldiers seems to make some kind of military draft necessary. But the draft would be unnecessary if the equilibrium price of A were paid.

Note how this diagram shows clearly the major points made. The suppression of military pay to B causes military officers to want a larger army: The value contributed to the military by the soldiers (shown by the demand curve) is above $6,000 in the range between 2.5 and 3.5 million soldiers. Therefore the use of those soldiers (at a *money* cost of $6,000) appears to be justified. But the drafted soldiers (between the 1 million volunteers and the 3.5 million total) would otherwise have held civilian jobs; the value they would have produced in those jobs is shown by the supply curve, which lies far above the $6,000 level of money costs for drafted soldiers.

The economic losses caused by the draft are shown in Panel II. The drafted soldiers lose all of shaded areas 2 and 3. They would have been paid their value in civilian jobs, which is shown by the supply curve. Instead, they are only paid $6,000. The entire economy loses the civilian production of those workers between A and B. It does gain the added military value

shown by the demand curve between A and B. But the loss is more than the gain. The shaded area 1 shows that net loss.

In short, supply-demand diagrams show more precisely the relative gains and losses from the draft. They can also illustrate the effects of various elasticities of the curves. For example, if you redrew Panel II with supply much less elastic and demand more elastic, the draft's economic cost would become much larger.

Only during a war, when the military needs preempt civilian ones, does a military draft fit the criteria for economic efficiency. But that is partly because the situation is unusual and out of equilibrium. In normal peacetime conditions, where markets and free choices function reasonably well, a military draft is economically inefficient.

Since 1972, the army has been staffed on a volunteer basis, in line with this economic logic. But during 1978–1982, there were calls to revert to a draft, and steps to reinstate it were taken in 1980, at the urging of military officials seeking to reduce their budgetary requirements for military pay. Those favoring a draft note two defects of the volunteer forces. *First,* **the volunteer recruits are drawn heavily from the ranks of the poor.** *Second,* **there is a high rate of turnover in many of the more skilled military jobs.** Many young recruits sign on for the bonuses and pay, obtain their training, and then go to better-paying civilian jobs instead of reenlisting. For them, the military is a vocational school, not a career. That raises the services' training costs, while leaving them with fewer reliable, long-term professional members in positions requiring special skills.

Therefore, the "deterioration" of military personnel—combined with budget pressures and rising tensions over Afghanistan, the Middle East, and Central America—led to a reversion toward the draft.

Reinforcing it was a wish to "prove our resolve" by showing our "willingness to sacrifice."

Economists do not deny the *logic* of these points, but they insist that in these *matters of degree*, the opportunity costs of the draft are large, and proper economic incentives (i.e., improved levels and design of payments to soldiers) could solve the problem. Any desired size and mix of personnel can be achieved by making the economic incentives sufficiently high.

Consider the two asserted problems: low skills among ordinary soldiers, and an excessive rate of turnover in skilled positions. Economic research has shown that the supply of labor for these positions is price elastic: Higher wages will induce a higher quantity of workers. The elasticities are large enough to indicate that higher salaries have a strong degree of drawing power. Indeed, because of those elasticities, the present low military wages are deterring volunteer soldiers.

The problem arises in the archaic military pay system. Rather than being paid for the type of work they do, members of the armed forces are paid in line with their rank and length of service. Those holding the same rank and seniority are usually paid at the same rate, no matter how skilled their job.

This contrasts radically with the wage patterns prevailing in the private economy. There, pay is governed mainly by the marginal revenue product. Pay is aligned with productivity (at least approximately), in line with skills and scarcity. As the relative scarcity of each category of workers changes, wages adjust accordingly. Therefore, wages largely fit and respond to opportunity costs.

This is not true in the military pay system, in which all personnel can rise through a standard pay scale (grade E-1 up to E-9) regardless of the nature of their work. Many soldiers in low-skill jobs are now overpaid for the value of their work; many skilled workers—trained at great expense to the military service—are underpaid and therefore leave.

The needed reform is to set different pay grades in line with skill levels. Thus, supply clerks might be in grades E-1 to E-6, while radar technicians might be in grades E-3 to E-9. There would still be equal opportunity for promotion, but differences of pay would reflect skills.

The pay differences would be fitted to private-market wage differentials. Reenlistment bonuses could also be designed to induce soldiers with scarce skills to remain. By correctly designed incentives that reflected true economic scarcities, the military could achieve any desired mix of skills and other attributes.

Concurrently, military pensions could be revised. The current system encourages all soldiers to serve 20 years and then retire at a substantial pension. An efficient system would selectively encourage the scarcer workers to remain and retire at the ages common in the economy. Such a system could provide fully for old-age security, while encouraging the needed variety of skills, and at a much lower level of total cost.

Altogether, an efficient, selective pay system could make the voluntary approach work, probably at a *lower* total budgetary cost than in the present basis. ***The need is simply to align pay rates with the basic economic conditions of marginal productivity, scarcity, and opportunity cost.*** A draft superimposed on the rigid pay system would simply compound the economic inefficiency and eliminate free choice on a large scale.

Summary

1. These cases illustrate the main issues in public finance.

2. Benefits need estimating and costs need measuring. Then efficient choices can try to reach the efficient margins, even if only approximately.

3. Those simple criteria remain valid, but special care is also needed in designing the inner nature of the programs and the kinds of economic incentives they apply.

4. Commonly, the treatments also involve issues of competition and monopoly.

5. Moving toward a more competitive market basis (as in schools, pollution, and military hiring) can often clarify choices and activate the right incentives.

6. Even the simple analysis in this chapter has shown that some inefficient public programs have arisen and persist. Several of them are on a grand scale, and their wastes run into many billions of dollars each year.

Key concepts

Social benefits
Social costs
Cost-benefit analysis
Economic incentives

Questions for review

1. a. Describe the *voucher* system for education.
   b. What are some of its costs and benefits?

2. Describe one possible method by which pollution by private firms can be regulated. Will this method balance the marginal costs and the marginal benefits involved in controlling pollution? Explain.

3. a. How do the wage patterns in the military differ from those in the private sector?
   b. How does this difference tend to create inefficiency in allocating military labor?

· 21 ·

Natural Resources: Concepts and Policies

As you read and study this chapter, you will learn:

▸ the economic concepts of natural resources and conservation

▸ how to define the optimal rate for using natural resources

▸ conditions under which private markets may optimize resource use

▸ the main issues in agricultural economics and farm policies

▸ how prices and elasticities can avert future resource crises

You have undoubtedly seen photographs of Earth taken by the lunar astronauts. There is Earth, a sphere glowing blue and white and floating in the dark void of space. It is a beautiful, haunting sight, which no human being had ever seen before the 1960s.

You may also have noticed how small and lonely Earth looks. Until 1969, humans had always been on or near Earth's surface. There, the planet seems enormous, with its endless shining seas and vast plains. Now, Earth can be seen and understood for what it is: "Spaceship Earth" holding limited amounts of resources and room. Some of its precious resources are, in fact, being used up by the growing demands of industrial growth: topsoil, water supplies, metal ores, coal, sulfur and other minerals, gas and oil—especially oil. Acid rain as strong as vinegar now falls on forests and lakes, and toxic wastes are reducing the purity of many rivers. The depletion of natural resources has become a leading economic problem, especially in the United

447

States. When the resources are gone, what then? Economic doomsdays have been forecast for the next century, even as early as the year 2020, fewer than 40 years away.

This resource problem is one that economists have long studied. Adam Smith, Ricardo, Malthus, and other early economists were deeply concerned about the inevitable depletion of resources by economic growth. In fact, that is how economics came to be dubbed the "dismal science": It contemplated a dismal future of growing scarcities under the pressure of rising population and production. In the mid-to-late 1800s, however, industrial growth boomed, science produced many highly productive inventions, and vast pools of oil and lodes of minerals were discovered. Science seemed able to banish scarcity. Economic growth might well go on forever, it seemed. The "conservation movement" struggled against a prevailing industrial optimism.

Events since the mid-1960s have dispelled much of that optimism, and the adequacy of natural resources is now widely regarded as an economic threat to future growth and social stability in the world. This chapter presents the fundamental economic concepts, expanded from the brief discussion of conservation in earlier chapters.

We first present the tools for determining the optimal rate of using exhaustible resources. Using these concepts of conservation, we then take up a specific problem: America's farm policy. Finally, we discuss the likely future course of energy prices.

Basic concepts

Natural resources come in many kinds, as Table 1 shows. Some are abundant, like sunlight and seawater. Others are renewable and can be efficiently harvested vir-

Table I *The main types of natural resources*

Nonrenewable
  Fuels (coal, oil, gas), land, ores, chemical deposits
Replaceable at great cost
  Soil, wilderness, certain rivers and lakes
Renewable
  Other rivers and lakes; urban fresh air
Self-renewing
  Forests, fisheries, other "crops"
Virtually inexhaustible
  Rural fresh air, solar energy

tually forever: forests and farm crops, for instance. Still other resources, such as oil, ores, and coal, are strictly exhaustible. Once used, they are gone forever.

Should the exhaustible resources be saved, rather than used? If they should be used, how rapidly? Such issues appear to be complicated, involving many special features. No single best rate of use applies to all kinds of natural resources. Each one needs careful study.

Yet, two major concepts are fundamental to them all: economic rent and conservation. **Economic rent is a payment made to an input that would be supplied even if no rent were paid.** Most natural resources are paid an element of economic rent, as growing demand causes their prices to rise. ***Conservation*** is the other main concept involving natural resources. We now explain its meaning and uses.

Conservation: Reaching the optimum rate of use

The term "optimum" here implies *social* efficiency: the best net use of resources for society as a whole, over the relevant span of time. The general meaning of allocative efficiency was presented in Chapter 16. Essentially, it requires that all resources be used in each time period up to the point where their marginal benefits just equal their marginal costs. Natural resources provide a special case within this general rule.

However, costs and benefits must be very carefully defined when they are applied to natural resources of limited amounts. The economic aim is to use efficiently—and equitably, both *within* each generation of people and *among* generations as the decades and centuries pass—each physically limited, depletable resource. Efficient use will yield the maximum net value for the resource over time, according to several factors we will discuss. Equity involves difficult problems because the resources used up by present generations are denied to future generations. Since the future inhabitants of the world are not here now to urge that resources be saved for their use, present generations may selfishly consume these limited resources *too rapidly*.

Conservation does not equal preservation Yet, the hoarding of resources for future use can err on the other side, toward *too slow* a rate of use. The goal is to strike the right balance between present and future. To define this goal, you can best begin by recognizing that each resource is an asset, a physical stock, that may have economic value. It can be held in its present form or used at some rate, either for present consumption or for investment.

Decisions about the use of resources are basically judgments about their future worth, either as left in their natural state or as converted to some other form. Physical *preservation* is only one alternative among the ways to conserve a resource. The efficient use of a natural resource often requires that it be used up. The economic task is to define the efficient rate of usage.

One common fallacy is to regard the present resource base as a fixed inventory that, once exhausted, will leave society with no means of survival. A related fallacy is that physical waste equals economic waste: that it is wasteful to use materials in ways that make them disappear. This attitude can lead to devoting $10 worth of work to "saving" a few cents' worth of paper, scrap metal, or bottles. *Neither hoarding nor physical recovery is synonymous with conservation.*

Consider a decision on the use of iron ore. It can be kept in the ground for future use, or it can be mined, smelted, and fabricated to create new productive machinery *now*, with a consequent expansion of economic capacity to produce. Though it is physically destroyed or altered in creating the machinery, the ore's economic value is enhanced. Some rate of current use for that purpose is clearly justified.

The *logic* is clear; only the matter of *degree* is to be determined. The economist's task is to distinguish such productive uses of resources from those that deplete them "too fast." How can that **optimum rate of use** be determined?

The optimum rate of use can be defined precisely as a matter of logic, even though it is often difficult in practice to determine the exact values for each resource. *The optimum rate is the speed of usage that will maximize the net present value of all future uses of the resource.* Consider the case of an ore that must be mined and processed. Its net present value is found by the following steps:

1. Predict the *physical amounts of usage over future years*, under what you think is the best set of methods for mining and processing the ore. As illustrated in Panel II of Figure 1, the probable best approach would be to use the resource at a constant rate until the year 2100, when all of the known reserves of it will be gone

2. Predict the *prices at which the resource will sell*. In Panel II of Figure 1, a rising trend of prices is predicted.

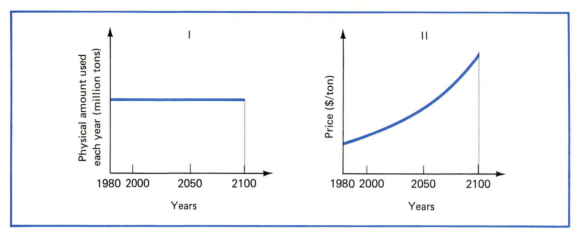

Figure 1   Two steps in choosing the optimum rate of using a resource

3. Multiply the prices times the physical volumes to obtain *the flow of future values from using the resource.* They are illustrated in Panel I of Figure 2. But these flows are not the final basis for setting optimum resource use because they ignore the element of time.

4. Therefore, you must discount the future values by some reasonable rate of time discount. This will probably be an interest rate in the range of 5 to 20 percent, although the best rate of dis-

count may be highly debatable, as we will soon see. Panel II of Figure 2 illustrates the effect of using some reasonable rate of discount. The result is a single figure summing up the total present value of the total future time-discounted values from using this resource. That is given by the area under the solid line in Panel II of Figure 2. But even this is not the final answer. You must also allow for the costs of obtaining and using the resource.

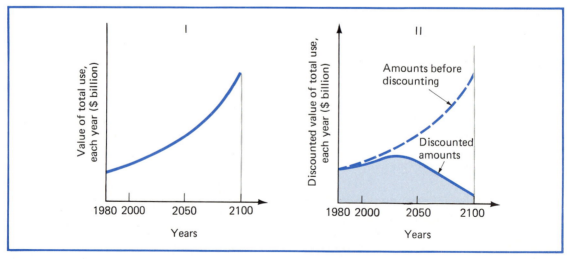

Figure 2   Calculating the discounted value of future use of the resource

5. Thus, you must next *estimate the future costs of extracting and preparing the resource* between now and the year 2100. That involves guesses about the increasing physical difficulty of mining the ever-depleting resource in deeper and deeper veins. You must also guess how far the future progress in mining methods may offset some or all of that increasing physical difficulty. Perhaps new lasers or conversion techniques will sharply reduce the costs. Or, instead, rising fuel costs may sharply raise the costs of mining and processing the resource. Panel I of Figure 3 shows an estimate of these future costs.

6. Then you must *discount the future costs for time*, just as you discounted the values of the resource flows. You will, of course, use the same discount rate, whatever it is, on both the costs and benefits. The result is illustrated in Panel II of Figure 3.

7. Now you can *subtract the discounted costs from the values* of the resources, to obtain the **discounted net present value** of the resource from that plan. That step is also illustrated in Panel II of Figure 3. Let us suppose that the re-

sulting figure is $500 billion. That measure of the net present value is precise, even though many of the elements going with it —the reserves, the future prices and costs, the "correct" discount rate, and so on—were guesses. Altering those values would change the final sum. Yet, since those estimates are the best you can do, the final figure is significant.

8. But there is still one more step: *You must compare this value with* alternative *reasonable plans for using the resource*, to be sure that this first plan really does give the highest net present value. Thus, you try various alternatives, as in Panel II of Figure 4. Plan *B* has a longer, slower period of use, lasting until the year 2200. Plan *C* uses it all by the year 2050. Plan *D* starts at a slow rate but then accelerates. Plan *E* starts fast but tapers off.

The net present values of each plan are shown in Panel II of Figure 4, using the same price, cost, and discount assumptions (for simplicity, we have omitted the intermediate calculations). Suppose that the net discounted present values for each plan are: Plan *B* $600 billion, Plan *C* $460

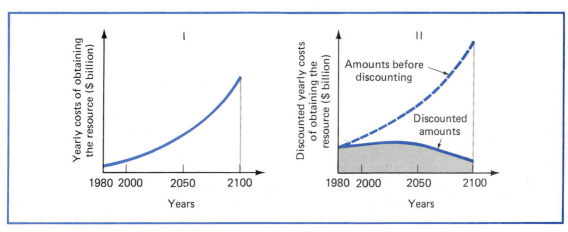

Figure 3   Calculating the discounted costs of obtaining the resource

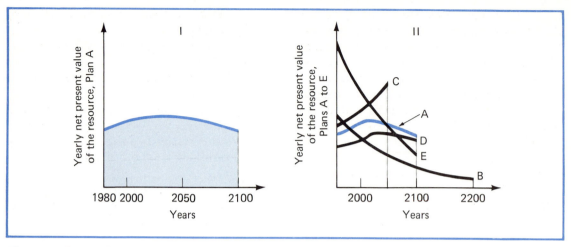

Figure 4   Comparing final present values for alternative uses of the resource

billion, Plan *D* $480 billion, and Plan *E* $680 billion. Evidently Plan *A* was not the optimum, for its $500 billion is exceeded by both Plan *E*'s $680 billion and Plan *B*'s $600 billion. Plan *E* is the optimum rate, at least until further calculations reveal a better one.

Note that Plan *E* uses the resource rapidly now, before the time discounting of distant years begins to weigh heavily. Note, too, that the process is similar to the profit-maximizing calculations made in the appendix to Chapter 7. Whenever future plans are compared, an economist calls for time discounting of future values.

Finally, note that the optimum rate of resource use merely compares costs and benefits. Here, there were some complex elements and a long time horizon. But the basic reliable concept is the same as always: Define costs and benefits correctly and then compare them.

Five determinants of the optimum rate

Now consider which parts of this process are most decisive. There are five main elements determining the optimum rate for each resource: current prices compared with future expected prices; the rate of interest; the costs of finding, using, and renewing the resource; predictions about future technological change; and the ethical weights used to compare the needs of present and future generations.

1. Present and future prices   Prices directly indicate economic scarcity and, thus, relative value. If a resource's price is expected to rise sharply above its present level, that tilts the choice toward holding the resource for its later, more valuable use. Conversely, if a resource's price is expected to drop steeply, then it might as well be used more copiously now. The falling expected price indicates that its future value will be small. Therefore, saving it is not economically valuable. The expected future price trends are, of course, only estimates, which require judgment. These are not official sources or infallible predictions.

2. Time discounting and the rate of interest   When people discount the future sharply compared to the present, they are assuming high interest rates. That encourages using resources faster now, rather than holding them for future use. Comparisons like those in Figures 1–4 are usually highly sensitive to alternative interest rates. Thus, a higher rate of interest would have made Plan *C* relatively more attractive, for it would have cut the later discounted value of the other plans more sharply.

Consider another example: A fine stand of walnut trees may promise to sell for $700,000 in 1999, compared to just $200,000 in 1983. At an interest rate of 10 percent, the 1999 sum has a present value in 1983 of $152,340; the trees should be kept standing until 1999. But if the interest rate rose to 15 percent, the present value in 1983 of the 1999 sum of $700,000 would fall to $74,805; then, the trees should be harvested without delay.

In general, higher interest rates favor a faster present use of resources. Low interest rates favor a slower rate of use, over a longer time span.

3. **Direct costs of finding and harvesting the resource** Resources do not rise spontaneously out of the ground, smelt themselves, or carry themselves to market. There are usually costs of discovering, mining, converting, planting, harvesting, or transporting them. These direct costs often influence how rapidly the resource is exploited.

For example, the search for oil and gas proceeds just up to the margin at which the value of finding them is balanced by the cost of the search. Fishers take their ships out only so long and so far as the marginal cost of catching the fish equals the marginal value of what they can catch. Farmers use their soil only to the margin where the extra crop's value justifies the cost of the extra resources used. American settlers pushed out into virgin land only so far, in each decade, as the marginal value

of the land justified the costs of clearing and planting it.

This general principle is clear and powerful, applying to all resources and all periods. The analysis takes a very specific form in dealing with resources that are cropped, such as fish, trees, and farm crops. *The optimum yield in each period is a balance between the sales value of the crop and the costs of raising and harvesting it.*

In Figure 5, the rounded curve shows how crop yields respond to increasing cultivation. Variable inputs are grouped together on the horizontal axis. Although they provide a rising total crop yield, the familiar diminishing marginal returns set in immediately. Eventually, at Point *B*, they grow strong enough to cause even total returns to fall. If this were fishing for

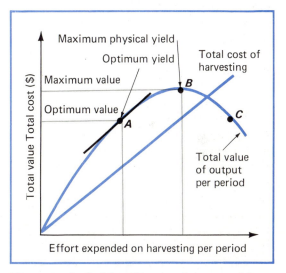

Figure 5 **Optimizing the use of a renewable resource**

By harvesting more intensively, the fishers can catch more fish—but only up to Point *B*. Beyond that level, they reduce the total catch by overfishing.

But *B* is not the economically efficient level. That is reached earlier at Point *A*, where the marginal value of extra fish just equals the marginal cost of catching them. Therefore, the efficient level of fishing effort stops short of that necessary for the maximum physical crop of fish. This principle applies equally to other harvested resources, such as grain and lumber.

cod, for example, Point *B* would show the maximum physical catch. Heavier fishing (to the right of Point *B*) would deplete the schools of fish and reduce the total catch, as at Point *C*.

The optimum level of harvesting this renewable resource is precisely at Point A, *where the marginal value of the extra yield of fish just equals the marginal cost of catching them.* (Remember, marginal cost is the slope of the total cost curve; marginal revenue is the slope of the total revenue curve. At Point *A*, the slopes of the total cost and revenue curves are equal.) Notice that *the optimum yield at* A *is below the maximum possible physical yield.*

Think of every crop in this fashion, comparing costs and revenues from harvesting efforts at the margin. In this light, "maximum yield" is not a desirable goal. The optimum level is less than that.

4. Future technological change The best present use of a resource usually depends on its present alternatives, which can change as time passes and technology advances. The future uses of the resource, therefore, depend on future conditions, which can often only be guessed at.

For example, oil's value has risen sharply because there are few good substitutes for it as a fuel for many machines. But fusion power might be developed to replace oil for many uses, such as generating electricity and fueling industrial ovens and boilers. Accordingly, oil would be less scarce and, therefore, less valuable in the future. The present value of oil, gas, or coal hinges on such predictions about future technology. Major technical advances can deflate the value of resources by making them less scarce.

Predicting technology changes, although notoriously difficult, is an essential part of making choices about resources.

Often, estimates of future technology sharply conflict. Thus, some experts foresee breakthroughs in fusion and laser technology that will radically reduce the cost of energy from the next century on. Other experts expect the opposite: The breakthroughs will not occur; nuclear energy's problems will intensify; and energy scarcity will become increasingly severe.

Energy is only a dramatic instance of the element of gambling and uncertainty that occurs in all predictions of future technology, as in metals, foods, and forestry. The predictions are constantly being revised in the face of innovations and new information. But it is often virtually impossible to predict technology beyond 20 years into the future.

5. Ethical weights among generations How strongly should our present interests weigh, compared to those of our children and their successors? Each generation inherits certain resources, uses some of them, and passes the remainder on to the next generation. The present generation is no exception: It is shrinking the resources available to future generations though innovations are also opening up other opportunities. What is a fair balancing of **intergeneration choices,** between our interests and those of our numberless unborn successors?

According to careful estimates, in the year 2100, there will perhaps be 11 billion people, compared to 4.5 billion now. This larger population will need resources even more urgently than we do. Yet, most of the oil and gas will be gone, farmland will be further eroded or put to urban uses, and the stocks of ores and many other resources will be much smaller than they are now. The extent to which current use is irresponsible or excessive—or, possibly, slower than optimal—depends on the ethical weights used to compare our needs with those of the people who will be alive then.

There is no definitive way to formulate or apply those weights. Roughly speaking, *giving a higher weighting to the interests of future generations means using a lower rate of time discount.* At the extreme, we might weight future people's needs so much more heavily than our own that a *negative* rate of interest would be suitable in assessing the present values of resources. Then the present value of using 100 billion barrels of oil in 2001 or 2050 or 3050 would exceed the value of using that oil now.

More normally, a *positive* rate of discount applies, but it may be high or low. If we apply a high rate, we will use up resources relatively rapidly, leaving less of them for future generations. They may then curse us for our extravagance. But, being long dead, we will not have to suffer for having served our preferences rather than theirs. Indeed, we will have had it easy. That is the problem in attaining an optimum rate of use among generations: Each generation can ignore posterity with impunity.

Private markets can optimize the use of resources, except. . .

Now return to the general case of a resource that is privately owned. Economists offer a clear, optimistic lesson about the conservation of such resources: *Private markets operating with reasonably complete knowledge and rationality can meet the social criteria for conserving resources over time.* The owners will be guided both by their profit-maximizing motivations and by the objective conditions prevailing in financial and industrial markets. These will tend to reflect precisely those social valuations of time preference, productivity, and expected innovation that deter-

mine the optimum usage rate. Moreover, it is in the interests of the resource owners to seek out accurate information on these magnitudes and to apply them in their own decisions. Therefore, the private market disposal of natural resources can optimize their use.

This result holds only for competitive markets. Monopolists will usually hold the rate of resource use *lower,* by restricting output and raising price in the present. That will lean toward too-slow use, rather than toward using resources too quickly. Yet, because even monopolists will want to maximize the value of resource use in the long run, the restrictive effect may distort their choices only slightly.

Altogether, then, when there are rational choices in private markets, the prices of natural resources will tend to anticipate future scarcities. The logic applies to all resources: land, oil, minerals, coal, gas, and the rest. Their market value moves with changes in the expected stream of future rents, which, in turn, reflect the expected shifts in demand and supply. Therefore, if people's expectations about future prices should rise, they will quickly bid up the capital value of the resource. Prices rise in anticipation of coming shortages. That price rise acts, in turn, to reduce the usage of the resource, if demand is at all elastic.

Therefore, the rising scarcity leads to (1) a rise in price ahead of the actual shortage; (2) possibly a cutback in the quantities used; and (3) windfall capital gains for the resource's owners. Such "forward pricing" acts to smooth the onset of rising scarcity: The rising prices reflect and enforce the present need to conserve the resource more stringently.

To this degree, the owners and users of resources will act in accord with the genuine social costs of their use of resources (unless there are externalities). Further, as unexpected changes occur in these predicted future scarcities, the prices of resources will adjust quickly and automatically. Therefore, both the present and future scarcities, even if they are changing and uncertain at each point, may be reflected as fully as possible in the prevailing prices and rates of usage. This will occur spontaneously, without conscious or detailed social planning. In short, economists conclude: The "Invisible Hand" extends to conservation.

Limitations and biases However, this optimum result depends on strict conditions, which may not be met. Six such cases follow:

1. COMMON-PROPERTY RESOURCES Some resources are not individually owned. Thus, no price for using them can be levied by a specific owner. As a result, they are available at a zero price to whoever captures them. That can lead to competitive overuse and destruction, as each user maximizes its own profits by taking the resource rapidly. Fish are one example. Oil and gas in an oil field that can be tapped by different landowners who own plots of land above the oil field are another. Each user is oblivious of the conditions shown in Figure 5, which reflects the total use of the resource. Since the competitive user considers only its own interests and is aware that the resource will dwindle, the incentive for rapid removal is increased.

The net effect is often a race to capture the resource. If the resource is harvestable, as fish are, the process will exceed the optimum rate and possibly reduce the total catch or even render the species extinct (at the right end of Figure 5). If the resource is a fixed stock, such as oil, the current rate of extraction will be raised well above the optimum. Moreover, the oil field itself will be harmed: As the separate owners drill many wells to get the oil out faster, the excessive numbers of wells will cause the underground pressure to fall, thereby raising the costs of extraction.

The corrective to this problem is to create a monopoly: to unify the control of each such resource in one owner, so that the optimum technical pattern and rate of usage can be designed and applied. Here, monopoly is clearly preferable to competition. Of course, society should also prevent the monopolist from causing the harms that we reviewed in Chapter 10.

2. DISCOUNTING AND MYOPIA The private rate of discount may be too high. As Figures 2–4 illustrated, this encourages a current rate of use above the optimal rate. The high rate of discount gives more weight to the present generation's interests than to those of future generations.

Actual rates are more likely to be above the correct social rate of discount than below it. Ultimately, perhaps, a negative rate of time preference should be applied to some intergeneration choices. If population and income levels continue to grow, and technology fails to provide new methods, then the pressure on resources may far exceed anything now imagined. Therefore, in the long run, it might be optimal for us to put more value on future than on present use. At any rate, the social rate of time preference may be lower, perhaps much lower, than the rate established by private choices in private markets.

3. INADEQUATE FORECASTING Present users may simply fail to foresee future developments. This may reflect insufficient research or an inability to discern future change. There may be close interactions among the uses of resources that are not presently apparent to the various users. And some users may simply be careless or

irresponsible in their judgments. In any case, the result would be resource use that deviates from the optimal patterns.

4. POLITICAL INFLUENCES   Specific taxes and other incentives may encourage an overly rapid use of resources. In fact, the use of almost every resource is affected by artificial incentives. There are special tax provisions for the extraction of almost all natural resources such as oil and ores. The use of land surrounding cities has been intensified by special tax provisions that favor suburban developments as investment tax shelters. Farm policies affect the extent and intensity of cultivation. Maritime policies affect the exhaustion of oceanic fish resources. These incentives usually induce a more rapid use of resources, even to the point of extinction.

5. EXTERNAL EFFECTS   There are important externalities in the uses of many resources, so that private users ignore major social costs of their actions. This affects both the rate of withdrawal of natural resources and the degree to which the common environment of air, water, and habitat is degraded. Recognition of such externalities would require a slower and altered use of resources. The failure to do so has led to environmental damage from land, air, and water pollution.

6. DISTRIBUTION   Finally, private market decisions are based on the existing distributions of wealth and income. Since resource users vote with their dollars, market demand will more strongly reflect the interests and preferences of the wealthy. This may conflict with broader social criteria. Some impacts, such as congestion and pollution, may affect the poor more acutely than the rich. And the poor have a greater need for common recreational space and facilities. Thus, an "unfair" distribution can result in undesirable outcomes.

Agricultural economics

Agricultural economics emerged in the 1920s as the leading branch of applied economics: Agricultural economists actively measured real demand and supply curves, estimated economies of scale, and even showed a dynamic cycle in farm prices and outputs. But agricultural economics is more than a technical field. It must grapple with some of the most dramatic issues and dubious public policies that are found in any sector. To present them, we begin with the basic conditions of farming.

Basic conditions

Agriculture is the growing of crops and livestock. Crops are sown, weeded, and harvested. Livestock are bred, raised and fattened, and sold. All of this occurs on a thin layer of topsoil, varying from a yard or more deep in the richest Iowa land to a mere few inches or less on the western ranges. To understand agricultural economics, one must recognize several main features of the agricultural sector.

Variety The agricultural sector embraces a great variety of conditions. Figure 6 indicates the main kinds of production, each with its own conditions of demand and supply. There are sharp differences among, for example, western cattle grazing, Florida orange growing, Virginia tobacco farming, and potato growing in Maine and in Idaho. Each uses special combinations of inputs (soil, fertilizer, equipment, etc.). Each has its particular regions, climates, sensitivity to weather, and classes of consumers.

Rising productivity Despite its old-fashioned aura, the agricultural sector in the United States has had rapid progress, with productivity rising more than twice as fast as in the economy as a whole. This high

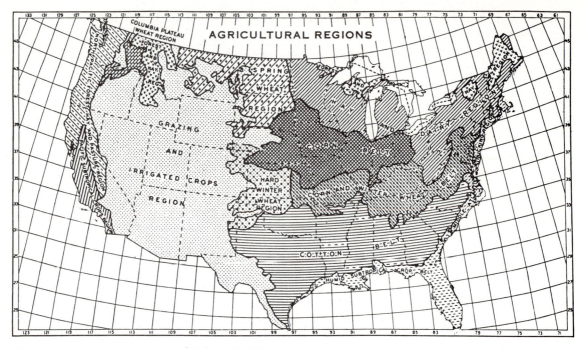

Figure 6 The main patterns of U.S. agriculture
Only the main types of crops and livestock are shown. Even so, it is evident that there is much variety within the agricultural sector.

productivity reflects rich soil and a favorable climate. But the advance of agricultural technology has also been a major cause.

The rising efficiency of agricultural technology reflects three main causes. First the improvement in capital inputs. Farm machinery has grown larger and more complex. Each unit of capital can produce a larger volume of output with about the same labor. Thus, a big combined harvester-thresher-baler can handle triple the volume that machinery of the 1940s could do, but still needs only one person to operate it. The equipment both raises efficiency and substitutes for labor.

The second cause is improved fertilizer, insecticides, and chemicals for livestock. In recent decades, much more and better fertilizer has been used, yielding higher crops and permitting more crop cycles during the year. Chemical insect and bacteria killers have also

become widely used for ground and tree crops. Heavy doses of medicines and specially prepared chemical feeds are now routine for livestock.

The third main cause is better *breeding*. Since the 1920s, there have been major genetic improvements in crops that have given faster growth, hardier plants, better resistance to diseases, and larger yields per plant. Livestock breeding has also become more efficient and produced better animals.

Since these gains are continuing, agricultural productivity may continue to advance at unusual rates. Yet, there are two main limits to this advance: increasing energy scarcity, and the loss of topsoil and water.

Energy scarcities Farming has come to rely heavily on commercial energy sources. Heavy equipment requires gasoline and oil; fertilizers and insecticides are made by energy-intensive processes. This trend was efficient when farm wages were rising faster than oil prices, for the changes substituted a cheaper factor (energy) for an increasingly expensive one (labor). But the sharp rise in energy prices since 1970 has reversed the comparison. Therefore, two sources of rising farm productivity (capital and chemicals) are being cut off by changed scarcity conditions. Simple relative prices, reflecting relative scarcities, are now moving farm technology away from energy-intensive methods.

Topsoil and water The loss of topsoil and water sources is also likely to limit future agricultural gains in productivity. Natural soil forms slowly by the continual growth and mingling of plants and bacteria. Human cultivation endangers that process by breaking the ground cover and applying chemicals. That, in turn, exposes the soil to erosion by wind and water.

Yet, by the best estimates, a century or so of cultivation has dissipated about one-half of the nation's topsoil. On average, the loss is at more than 6 tons of topsoil per acre per year. The total annual loss from all U.S. farms is approximately 6 billion tons, equivalent to peeling an inch off the state of Missouri.

The rate of loss has recently been increased by the heavy use of chemical fertilizers, weed-killers, and insecticides. In the short run, these chemicals have increased crop yields. But they undermine the natural fertility of the soil, replacing it with artificial chemical nutrients. The soil itself becomes sterile and grainy and is easily eroded. As a result, topsoil is lost both by physical erosion and by the depletion of its natural fertility.

Artificial fertilizing reaches diminishing returns in the long run, as the soil deteriorates. Yet, in the short run, farmers have been induced to increase their profits by using fertilizers heavily. Indeed, they have had little choice, since when some farmers adopted the method, all of them had to follow suit to remain competitive. The resulting farming methods reflect a short-range view of land values, using high rates of time discount.

Since 1973, the increased scarcity of energy has been making chemical fertilizers less economical, by raising their prices. Yet, much topsoil is now dependent on the continued use of those fertilizers. Therefore, the long-run role of chemical fertilizers in the use and conservation of land is in doubt.

At any rate, the remaining topsoil is vulnerable to substantial further erosion. The increasing scarcity of topsoil will, in turn, accentuate the future increase in farm prices.

Water poses a different problem, for it is usually not owned by specific users. It gathers in the underground aquifers that make up the "water table." As a common-property resource, it is open to competitive overuse by farms, factories, and towns. One user can sink a well, install a large pump, and drain the water supplies that are needed for many miles around. On a larger scale, huge irrigation projects in western states have already substantially lowered water tables and are raising the likelihood of permanent depletion and water shortages. The problem has grown acute in the Great Plains, in south-central Arizona, and in the San Joaquin Valley in California.

With the basic problems of soil and water in mind, we now turn to the specific economic issues that have troubled farming and inspired a variety of dubious government policies.

Farm policies

Farm incomes are often unstable from year to year, for two main reasons. One is weather. Drought or hail can destroy a crop one year; good weather can give a bumper crop the next year. The second reason is the inelasticity of demand and supply for most farm products. As we saw in Chapter 5, shifts in those inelastic curves can cause marked changes in prices, which, in turn, cause farm incomes to fluctuate sharply.

Everyone agrees that, ideally, farm incomes should be more steady. The first programs to stabilize farm incomes were started in the 1930s, using the logical idea of a buffer stock or "ever-normal granary." Thousands of storage bins were built in the farming areas for use as reservoirs. The long-run equilibrium prices and quantities were estimated. In good years, the government bought and stored enough crops to keep prices up to the long-run level. In bad years, the bins were emptied of enough crops to make up the gap, thereby holding the price to the long-run equilibrium level. The cost of the bins and storage was small compared to the benefits of stabilizing farm incomes. The program worked well for grains, powdered milk, eggs, and several other crops.

But then the program was altered to serve another purpose: *raising and holding the price above the long-run equilibrium level.* The "price supports" raised farmers' incomes by increasing their total and net revenues. But they also hurt consumers by raising the long-run prices that they would have to pay for the foods, clothing, and other products made from farm outputs. By raising prices above equilibrium cost levels, the price support program caused inefficient allocation.

Besides being inefficient, the programs were also inequitable because they mainly benefited the farmers with the largest levels of output. The higher crop price is multiplied times the quantities sold. Since small farmers produce less, they also benefit less, even though they are the truly

needy farmers. The benefits have flowed mainly to the big, already-prosperous farmers. Altogether, price supports have reflected political clout, rather than the use of clear, rational economic tools.*

This perversion of the original programs from *income stabilizing* to *price raising* has had several predictable economic effects. *First,* as Figure 7 illustrates, the higher price has led farmers to produce more over the long run and consumers to buy less. The resulting physical surpluses were enormous in the 1950s and 1960s. The Agriculture Department has had as much as $10 billion tied up in surplus stocks, at a yearly cost of $3 billion for storage, spoilage, and interest. After 1970, many of the stocks dwindled as farm prices rose and made price supports less necessary and less politically acceptable. Yet, the prices of several important farm outputs are still supported, including milk, cheese, eggs, tobacco, peanuts, sugar, and California oranges.

A *second* effect has been to raise the price of farmland. By making crops more valuable, price supports have made the land itself more valuable. That explains some of the surge in land prices, which has raised prices per acre more than 12-fold since 1950. These benefits are strictly a rise in economic *rent*, which farmers get for doing nothing more than their normal work. That rent is shown by the shaded trapezoid in Figure 7. Indeed, one could say that the benefits have gone to the land or to land ownership, not to farmers as such. In any event, these benefits, too, have gone mainly to large-scale farmers, most of whom were already prosperous.

Since the surpluses were a costly and embarrassing defect of the price-support

---

*For a thorough treatment of these issues, see Geoffrey S. Shepherd and Gene Futrell, *Marketing Farm Products*, 7th ed. (Ames, Iowa: Iowa State University Press, 1982).

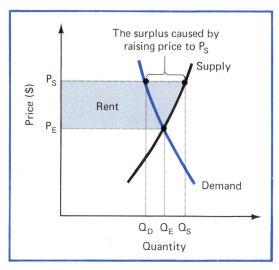

Figure 7   The main effects of raising farm prices

Long-run equilibrium is reached at P_E and Q_E. The supported price P_s results in consumers buying Q_D while farmers produce Q_s. The difference $(Q_s - Q_D)$ is a physical surplus. Although it is "only" about 30 percent of the crop (because both demand and supply are inelastic), the yearly surplus can become enormous as the years pass.

program, efforts were made in the 1950s to reduce them while still keeping farm prices up. To reduce output, farmers were paid to take some of their land out of cultivation and put it in a "land bank." This was costly, the more so because farmers naturally set aside their worst land. Moreover, they tilled the remaining land more intensively because their other inputs (equipment, labor) were little changed. Accordingly, total production was little reduced. The land bank, a clear case of economic waste and a costly failure, was abandoned in the 1960s.

Surpluses were also channeled into school milk programs and giveaways to needy foreign countries. But such "Food for Peace" types of foreign aid depressed farm prices and farm incomes in those countries receiving the foods, thus harming farmers and undermining the prospects for agricultural progress in those countries.

Certain farm prices were also raised indirectly. For example, the land permitted for growing tobacco has been rigidly limited since 1938. That has raised tobacco prices and enriched landowners by raising the price of the land far above its economic value. The same is true of peanut acreage. About 40 other crops (from dates and grapes to California oranges) are under "marketing orders." When their prices threaten to fall below target prices in bountiful crop years, the Agriculture Department buys the surplus and destroys it.

Such waste could be avoided and needy farmers could still be helped—but only by avoiding any effort to change farm *prices*. The efficient treatment would simply identify the needy farmers and raise their incomes by direct payments. The payments would be based on an appraisal of the farmers' true degree of need, just as welfare programs are mainly confined to those who are genuinely in need. The payments would, therefore, flow mainly to small-scale farmers, as in Appalachia and parts of New England. Little or nothing would go to the big commercial farmers on the plains, who are not needy.

Being relatively focused, the payments would be much less costly to the public purse than programs based indiscriminately on prices and outputs. They would avoid enriching already-rich farmers and would not raise farm prices. They would also avoid needless economic rents and windfall gains from rising land prices.

The only drawback is that direct payments might encourage people to stay on farms that are too small and/or barren to justify farming. Such marginal farms should, by strictly economic criteria, be abandoned or merged into larger farms. Direct income payments might tend, instead, to encourage a permanent class of small operators on inefficient farms.

Yet, that mistake could easily be avoided. The direct payments could be kept low enough to encourage inefficient farmers to migrate to towns. Or specific relocation grants could be provided to encourage marginal farmers to shift toward more productive jobs and locations.

By contrast, actual farm programs based on farm prices have had sharply inefficient and unfair results. Poor marginal farmers have received little benefit, and the prices of farms have been driven beyond their reach. Since the 1930s, that has forced many small farmers off the land.

The whole topic illustrates how economic analysis can clarify complex situations, even with simple tools. It also shows how policies can continue in error long after their economic faults are exposed.

The economics of energy

The modern economy uses vast amounts of energy in farms, factories, homes, and transportation. Moving from a primary reliance on wood in the early 19th century, to coal and finally oil in this century, economic expansion has absorbed rapidly growing volumes of energy. The 1970s saw an abrupt end to a long period of energy abundance in which coal, oil, and gas were discovered in ever growing amounts. Industrial economies are having to make severe adjustments to cope with the rising energy scarcity. Energy economics has become an urgent topic.

Basic trends

We begin by adopting a large perspective, for the current issues are best seen as small parts of fundamental shifts. The modern dependence on fossil fuels—especially coal, oil, and natural gas—is a brief episode in human history. Since they took 300 million years to form, these resources will not be replaced in any meaningful degree. Even the vast reserves of coal will largely be gone in a few centures.

As for oil, the United States will probably pass its peak rate of production in the 1980s; world production will probably peak by 1995, as Figure 8 shows. Indeed, the Middle East oil kingdoms expect to exhaust most of their reserves in about 30 years. If you are 20 years old now, the decline may begin by your 40th birthday; when you are 65, some 80 percent of all recoverable world oil reserves will have been consumed. Economic growth will have to be sustained somehow on a shrinking flow of oil.

The economic use of fuels begins with the easiest and cheapest sources and then moves to less accessible costlier reserves. That exactly parallels the use of the best farmland first, the best hydroelectric sites, and every other natural resource. As the best coal is used up, shafts must be sunk to deeper veins. Similarly, oil and gas must be sought in ever more inaccessible places. *In short, the use of fuels proceeds up a rising scale of costs.*

The present array of sources ranges from shallow Mideast oil wells to expensive, capital-intensive solar equipment. As the actual prices of fuels rise, the margin of production from these sources shifts to the right. If oil sells for $20 per barrel, shale is not worth processing to produce oil. But if the price of oil rises to $40, then massive oil shale mines and processing plants may become economic. *The whole issue turns on the future opportunity costs of alternative fuel sources.*

Note that the rising scarcity of fuel is a matter of degree. Fuel reserves are not a single pot that contains a definite amount. The *physical* presence of fuels is ultimately a given: Whatever is there is there. But, *economically,* there is a wide spectrum of choices, moving from cheap fuels to very costly ones. Rather than "run out" all at

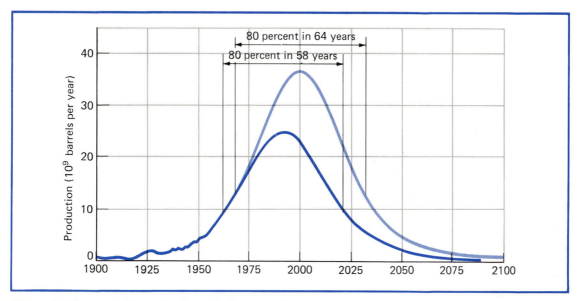

Figure 8   The probable path of world oil production

The cycle of world oil production is plotted on the basis of two alternative estimates of the amount of oil that will ultimately be recovered. Even by the larger estimate, 90 percent of the recoverable oil will be used by about 2030. Even a marked slowing in consumption will only postpone the scarcities by a few years.

Source: Adapted from M. King Hubbert, "The Energy Resources of the Earth," *Scientific American*, September 1971.

once, the world will move to increasing scarcity, which will take the form of rising energy prices. We explained that process in the first main section of this chapter. The world has been "running out" of the best energy sources for a long time. This process will continue, probably pushing energy prices even higher—unless technology creates new, cheaper sources.

Indeed, energy prices do not rise only when the supply dwindles. Investors will realize the coming scarcity and try to buy the reserves now, which in itself will send up prices. *In short, the market anticipates the physical shortages, building the expected future price increases into the current price of fuel.* That ensures that fuel prices will rise as soon as future scarcity is adequately perceived. On both sides of the market, economic processes make price trends reflect and anticipate true long-run scarcities.

In retrospect, then, the fuel gluts of the 1950s and 1960s —when oil and gas prices

stayed at relatively low levels—were a marked oddity. They reflected the brief flooding of world markets by vast new Middle Eastern oil reserves. There were also bright hopes for cheap nuclear power. But those were just fluctuations around the trend. Though they did lull many shortsighted analysts into believing that fuels would always be abundant and therefore cheap, the 1970s brought an abrupt return to the reality of advancing scarcity.

Since most fuels can be substituted for one another in at least some uses, the rise in oil prices naturally induced a parallel rise in other fuels, including coal, gas, nuclear fuel, and even firewood. All of these fuel price rises caused windfall gains for the owners of the fuels, as rising prices were capitalized into the value of the fuel reserves. There was also a worldwide cartel in nuclear fuels from 1969 to 1974, which attempted to fix the price of uranium above competitive levels. But the net effect of that cartel is debatable, for by

1973, rising oil prices were already causing uranium prices to rise strongly.

Indeed, even OPEC's price fixing may not have raised the price of oil much higher than it would have been pushed by market forces. The rising scarcity of fuels would have caused oil prices to rise naturally in any event, as owners and investors bought reserves in anticipation of future price rises.

OPEC seemed to force the price up sharply during the Arab oil embargo in 1973–1974, and the Iran-Iraq war seemed to cause another sharp rise in 1979–1980. But they may have had little real effect. One concludes that the underlying pattern was as shown in Figure 9. If it is valid, then OPEC merely moved oil's price up in

1973–1974 a little earlier than it would have risen from the other causes. The rest of the rise has not been caused by OPEC. Other experts blame all of the price rise on OPEC and suggest that conflicts within OPEC will cause oil prices to fall back to $20 per barrel or below.

Seen in perspective, rising oil scarcities probably increased oil prices strongly after 1970, perhaps as much as MacAvoy suggests. The debate is not about the size of OPEC's vast oil revenues, but about how those money flows are defined: either as rents (if oil prices would have risen anyway) or as monopoly profits (if OPEC has raised the prices artificially). The debate is even more important for what it leads us to expect about future oil prices: If the long-term trend is up (reflecting a rising global scarcity), then further rapid rises are likely.

But if OPEC's price fixing has been the real force raising oil prices, then OPEC might not be able to raise them further or even to maintain present price levels. If the sharp differences among OPEC countries causes them to disagree about the joint-maximizing price (recall Chapter 11's analysis of collusion), their price-fixing efforts might collapse altogether, or at least stabilize at a much lower price level. Most likely, the true answer involves a mixture of these two points of view.

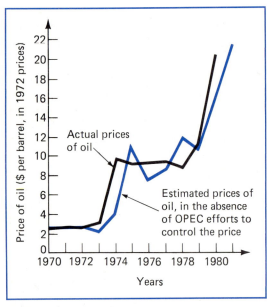

Figure 9   Has OPEC really raised the long-run price of oil?

MacAvoy's projection suggests that OPEC did not affect the long-run upward trend in oil prices, but only moved it ahead in 1973–1974. However, other specialists suggest that OPEC intensified the rise, even if it was not the sole cause. The price of oil is stated here in constant 1972 dollar values, in order to filter out the effects of general inflation.

Based on Paul W. MacAvoy, *Crude Oil Prices: As Determined by OPEC and Market Fundamentals* (Cambridge, Mass.: Ballinger Publishing Company, 1982). Reprinted with permission.

The search for oil   Whatever its causes, the steep rise of oil prices has stimulated the search for more oil deposits. Much of the effort has been focused on the ocean floors, via hundreds of large oil rigs, but discovery has also moved into remote regions. The search for gas has also been spurred by the removal of some controls on the price of U.S. gas. These added efforts have brought some results. But the marginal returns to exploration continue to decline. That is inevitable, for the cheapest, most accessible sources were exploited decades ago. Moreover, the more remote oil and gas reserves are also costlier to transport to the market. For example, oil and gas pipelines from Alaska are large-investment projects, which have had to overcome severe problems of climate and terrain.

All of this perfectly fits the logic of rising long-run scarcity, but ultimately, of course, no discovery, however fast, can increase the amount of fuel in the ground by so much as a gallon. It only confirms the reserves' existence sooner and makes it possible to convert them to human uses more rapidly. Indeed, a rapid discovery and use rate may *violate* the long-run conservation of fuel, which would call for it to remain stored in its natural forms to be used later. That choice, in turn, depends on the long-run prospects for alternative fuel sources, such as solar energy, nuclear power, fusion processes using plain water, and ocean tides. Those future trends are mostly unknowable now. Only if other sources are going to be cheap and abundant would the rapid discovery and use of oil be efficient now. If, instead, the prospects for new technology are dim, then oil prices should rise more rapidly now, causing the use of new oil to be postponed rather than hastened.

Future world resources

Fuels are not the only resources that appear to pose severe long-run economic hazards. Other threatened resources include many ores, chemicals, topsoil, animals, and water sources. All of these are threatened by population growth and economic growth.

The population on the earth has risen to nearly 5 billion people, from only 1 billion in 1830. Despite a recent decline in the growth rate, especially in the industrialized economies, the world's population is certain to continue to rise substantially; the only question is how far. The answer depends on the *replacement-level birth rate*. It is about 2.2 children per woman, which is above current levels in industrial countries but well below current levels in the more populous developing countries. Even if a replacement-level rate is achieved, a momentum factor will operate to keep the population rising for several decades more.* Accordingly, the following outcomes can be predicted:

If the world attained replacement fertility in:	World population would then stand at:	And world population could be expected to stabilize eventually at:
2000–2005	5.9 billion	8.4 billion
2020–2025	8.4 billion	11.2 billion
2040–2045	12.0 billion	15.1 billion

World population will almost certainly double because replacement fertility cannot be reached by the years 2000–2005. Indeed, few experts are confident that it will ever be attained. Even if it is reached as soon as 2020–2025, population will still grow to 2.5 times the present 4.5 billion.

To feed, shelter, and clothe the added population will strain the world's resources of space, housing capacity, and food production. Moreover, the added population will add to the demand for products using fuels, ores, chemicals, and other exhaustible resources.

To accentuate this pressure, future populations will want higher real incomes than people today have. Even if real in-

---

*The numbers of young people coming into the age of fertility in developing countries are so much larger than the numbers of people at older ages that, even if couples have only enough children to replace themselves, total births will continue to outstrip total deaths until the disproportion in the number of people in the childbearing ages disappears. This could take a century or more in countries where population growth has been very high. The size of the population will be far larger than when fertility dropped to the replacement level.

comes per capita increase by only 1 percent per year and population stabilizes at the "low" level of 8 billion, total production will need to rise by more than 100 percent by 2020 and by an another 100 percent by the year 2050.

This growth will have to occur despite shrinking natural resources. As some resources become more scarce, their relative prices will rise, perhaps drastically. Nations lacking those resources will face rising economic pressure. International tensions may become severe, with chronic conflicts over the control of valuable oil, ores, fish, chemical, and agricultural resources. Already there have been conflicts over ocean fishing rights, fertile land, and oil fields. Seizure of land and resources has been a common cause of warfare throughout human history, and the pressures for such wars will intensify. It is a dismal prospect: increasing international stress as resources dwindle and population rises.

Yet, economists have largely rejected this doomsday view, for reasons that reflect the very nature of economics. The doomsayers rely mainly on engineering models, with fixed relationships among the causes and effects. They assume that certain key resources, including oil and ores, would continue to be used at past rates. Projected forward by 40 or 50 years, those rates truly could not be sustained, and some sort of collapse seemed inevitable.

But the models left out the key role of *prices* and *elasticities*. Rising scarcities will be reflected in rising prices. Both demand and supply may respond to the changing relative prices, so that the rates of physical usage do not charge ahead at a constant rate. On the contrary, as the oil price rises of the 1970s showed, the demand for fuels has substantial elasticity, especially in the long run. Such elasticities may be reasonably high for most or all of the crucial resources.

Therefore, economies are likely to adjust their resource use, softening the impact of resource scarcities. Rather than rush blindly into radical physical shortages, the economies are likely to absorb the changes gradually and minimize their impact. The doomsday predictions were therefore said by most economists to be too pessimistic: The disasters are conceivable but not likely. There will be soft landings, they said, not crashes.*

Summary

The main points have been:

1. Each resource has an optimal rate of use, which maximizes the net present value of all future uses. This rate reflects a discounting of benefits and costs. Market choices may reach the optimal rate.

2. Common-property resources will be used too rapidly by free-market activities. Other possible causes of non-optimal use include wrong discount rates and external effects.

3. Farm policies usually cause inefficiency when they attempt to raise prices rather than to stabilize farm incomes.

4. The rise in energy prices in 1970 reflected both long-term shifts and, possibly, OPEC's raising of oil prices.

---

*Julian Simon goes further, arguing that added population will increase the capacity to produce and to solve global problems. He also predicts that technology will adjust to resource scarcities and maintain the long-term growth of per capita incomes. The view rests on optimistic expectations of new technology and human capacities, in the tradition of technological optimists who "refute" the Malthusian predictions. See Julian L. Simon, *The Ultimate Resource* (Princeton, N.J.: Princeton University Press, 1981).

5. Future resource scarcities may cause world-wide crises within several decades. But price changes and elasticities can make for smooth rather than disruptive adjustments.

Key concepts

Conservation

Discounted net present value

Optimum rate of use

Intergeneration choices

Questions for review

1. a. What is the rule for determining the optimum rate of use of an exhaustible resource?

   b. List the five main elements which determine the optimum rate of use of a resource. Discuss how each of them influences the optimum rate of use.

2. Explain how each of the following may interfere with the most efficient use of resources:
   a. common-property resources,
   b. political influences,
   c. distribution of wealth and income.

3. Farm programs have moved from income stabilization to price raising. Discuss two economic effects of this change in goals.

4. Using economic analysis, explain how an increase in oil prices could lead to an increase in the cost of firewood.

Glossary

accounting cost See *Direct Cost*.

accounting profit See *Profit*.

allocative efficiency Is achieved when price equals marginal cost for every firm.

antitrust Policies that deal with anticompetitive conditions that arise in various markets.

assets Assets include two categories: current assets are mainly cash, accounts receivable, and inventories; fixed assets are the real plant and equipment that the firm has built up over the years.

average fixed cost See *Fixed Cost*.

average product See *Total Product*.

balance sheet A financial statement that lists the firm's assets and liabilities (or claims against its assets).

bilateral monopoly A market in which both buyers and suppliers have market power. In labor markets, a bilateral monopoly would be a monopsonist (demand side) facing a union (supply side).

bracket creep When the share of personal income taken by the government in taxes increases because of increases in nominal (but not real) income.

capital Human-made inputs to the process of production. Physical capital includes such tangible capital as buildings, machinery, roads, and telephone systems. Human capital refers to the skills and talents of the labor force. Money capital refers to assets such as stocks and bonds which are sold to finance the purchase of physical capital.

capitalism Refers to economic systems in which capital is mainly privately owned rather than owned by the government.

cartel An association of producers which sets prices and enforces penalties against members who violate the agreement.

circular flow Interconnections of selling, consuming, and producing which tie the sectors of the economy together, so that events in one sector affect the economic system as a whole. The real flows of goods and services are matched by money flows moving in the opposite direction.

classical economics A school of economic thought characterized by its insistence that national wealth is the capacity (resources, labor, and capital) to produce goods or material products.

closed shop See *Labor Union*.

competition Pure competition is an industry model based on the assumptions that: a) there is one identical good sold in the market; b) no firm has a significant market share; c) firms adjust quickly to changes; and d) there is freedom of entry and exit. Perfect competition adds the assumption that firms and consumers know prices throughout the market.

concentration ratio The combined share of a market's sales that is made by the largest firms in the industry. Concentration ratios are reported for the top 4, 8, 12, and 20 firms in each industry.

conglomerate firm A firm which operates in more than one market. Conglomerates range from firms with two product lines up to highly diversified enterprises with hundreds of branches and thousands of products.

conglomerate merger See *Merger*.

consumers' surplus The difference between the value which the consumer places on a good and the price which the consumer must pay for the good.

cooperative An enterprise owned by its customers or suppliers, with profits channeled back to its owners.

corporation A firm that issues voting stock which investors can buy and sell.

cost-benefit analysis A method of allocating scarce resources efficiently by equating marginal social costs and benefits.

council of economic advisers (ceo) A three-member group, appointed by the president with the consent of the Senate, that is responsible for advising the president on economic policies.

cross-elasticity of demand $\dfrac{\%\Delta Q \text{ of Good 1}}{\%\Delta P \text{ of Good 2}}$ Measures how the quantity demanded of one good responds to price changes of another good. A positive cross-elasticity indicates that the goods are substitutes. A negative cross-elasticity indicates that the goods are complements. Complementary goods are those used together such as cars and gasoline.

demand The entire price-quantity relationship; the entire demand curve.

dependent variable A variable which is influenced by changes in another variable. In an equation relating expenditures and income, expenditures is the dependent variable, being influenced by changes in income.

diminishing marginal effect The effect of any good or input tapers off as more of it is used.

diminishing marginal returns (law of) States that when additional units of one input are used, with other inputs held constant, a point is reached beyond which marginal product begins to decline.

diminishing marginal utility As the amount of a good consumed by an individual increases, marginal utility falls.

direct cost / explicit cost / accounting cost Direct, explicit, and accounting cost are the same: that part of a firm's cost that can be calculated by adding up the dollars the firm pays out. Direct costs include the purchase of raw materials and equipment, wages paid to hired employees, rent, interest, and utilities.

diseconomies of scale See *Economies of Scale.*

distributions Graphs that show how such economic variables as income and wealth are spread among the population.

disutility Displeasure, as indicated by negative marginal utility.

dividends Payment of some of the accounting profits to shareholders by the firm.

dominant firm One firm has 40–100% of the market and no close rival.

economic analysis A system of concepts and logical hypotheses developed over more than two centuries in debates among economists.

economic cost A firm's economic cost is the opportunity cost of production. Economic cost is the sum of all direct and imputed (implicit) costs, thereby including a value for all scarce resources used in production.

economic model A precise formal statement of one or more economic relationships.

economic profit See *Profit.*

economic rent A payment to an input in excess of the payment necessary to elicit supply.

economic system Each economy is a system in which the production and distribution of goods are organized around soci-

ety's wants. Modern economic systems range from freemarket capitalism, in which most choices are made in private markets, to controlled economies in which choices are determined primarily through economy-wide plans.

economies of scale/diseconomies of scale Refers to the decrease in long-run average total cost which can accompany increases in output. Economies of scale result from specialization, physical laws, and management.

Increases in long-run average total cost accompanying increases in output are referred to as diseconomies of scale.

Economies and diseconomies of scale explain the U-shape of the long-run average total cost curve.

efficiency Efficiency in the use of resources is achieved when a given level of output is produced using the least amount of inputs. Economic efficiency in production is referred to as the least-cost method of production.

elasticity A measure of the responsiveness of one variable to a change in another variable.

elasticity of demand See *Price Elasticity of Demand.*

elasticity of supply Elasticity of supply: $\frac{\%\Delta Q \text{ supplied}}{\%\Delta \text{Price}}$ measures the relative responsiveness of quantity supplied to changes in price. Because price and quantity supplied are directly related, supply elasticity will be positive. If elasticity is greater than 1, supply is said to be elastic, with quantity supplied being relatively responsive to changes in price. If elasticity is less than 1, supply is said to be inelastic, with quantity supplied being relatively unresponsive to changes in price. In most cases, supply elasticity will differ from one point on the supply curve to another.

enterprise Enterprises or firms are the basic units of production, converting inputs into outputs. An enterprise may consist of one local plant (factory or office) or up to hundreds of plants.

equilibrium   A condition reached when all influences balance one another out, so that there is no pressure for further change.

equity   The net worth of the firm, equal to assets minus liabilities.

explicit cost   See *Direct Cost.*

exports   Goods and services produced in one country and sold to another country.

external effects: costs and benefits   External effects—either costs or benefits—occur whenever an action has repercussions which the actor need not take into account. In such cases, social costs and benefits (costs and benefits to the entire society) will differ from private costs and benefits.

factors of production   See *Inputs.*

fixed cost/average fixed costs   Costs of production which do not vary with the level of output. Examples of fixed costs include rent and bank payments. Fixed costs exist only in the short run. Average fixed cost refers to fixed cost per unit of output.

flow   Processes or values occurring over a period of time. Income per year or sales per month are examples of flows.

general equilibrium   Refers to equilibrium of the entire economy. General equilibrium analysis examines the impact of a change in one sector of the economy on the economic system as a whole.

horizontal merger   See *Merger.*

household   Any unit in which people make decisions about work, consumption, the disposal of personal property, and other personal activities. Households consume, as opposed to enterprises, which produce.

human capital   See *Capital.*

implicit cost   See *Imputed Cost.*

imputed cost/implicit cost   The estimated or implicit value of scarce inputs for which there is no market transaction. Their value is equal to the return they would get in their best or highest paying alternative use.

incidence   See *Tax Incidence.*

income effect   As the price of a good changes, purchasing power changes, so consumers must adjust the quantity demanded of all goods. In labor markets, the income effect refers to the increased ability of workers to purchase leisure as the wage rate increases.

income elasticity of demand: normal good and inferior good   Income elasticity measures the responsiveness of quantity demanded to changes in income. A positive income elasticity indicates that the good is a normal good, with quantity purchased increasing as income increases. A negative income elasticity indicates that the good is an inferior good, with quantity purchased decreasing as income increases. If the value of income elasticity is greater than 1, the good is said to be a normal good with an income-elastic demand, meaning the quantity demanded is relatively responsive to changes in income. If the elasticity value is between 1 and zero, the good is said to be a normal good with an income-elastic demand, meaning the quantity demanded is relatively unresponsive to changes in income. Income elasticity can vary with income levels.

income statement   A statement showing the firm's revenue and the division of its revenue into costs, taxes, dividends, and retained earnings.

independent variable   A variable which causes change in another variable. In an equation relating expenditures and income, income is the independent variable, influencing the level of expenditures.

industry   A set of producers making similar products.

inferior good   See *Income Elasticity of Demand.*

inflation   An increase in the general level

of prices. Inflation has many causes. Cost-push inflation results from increases in input costs. Demand-pull inflation results from an expansion of demand. Expectational inflation results from the fact that when people expect inflation, their behavior (such as negotiating a wage increase or a long-term contract) is altered in ways which will cause the inflation rate to increase.

innovation See *Invention/Innovation/Imitation.*

inputs (or factors of production) Items used in the process of production. The three traditional classes of inputs are labor (physical and mental effort), capital (human-made aids to production), and land (natural resources).

intercept The point at which a straight line touches the vertical axis.

internal rate of return The interest rate that will just equate the capitalized value of an investment's future profits with the investment's initial cost.

invention/innovation/imitation Technical change can be divided into three phases: (1) invention-the creation of a new idea; (2) innovation-making practical use of the idea; and (3) imitation-diffusion of the idea as it is copied by others.

invisible hand A phrase coined by Adam Smith, who believed that the guiding of economic choices by self-interest would lead to the right amount and mix of output.

labor force participation rate The percent of each group of the population that works for pay.

labor monopolies See *Labor Union.*

labor union An association of workers formed to gain some control over the supply side of the labor market.

In a closed shop, only union members may be hired. In a union shop, nonunion members may be hired if they join the union within a specified time. In an open shop, union membership is not required for employment.

linear equation The equation for a straight line representing the relationship between two variables. The general form of the equation is $y = a + bx$, where y is the dependent variable, x is the independent variable, a is the intercept of the line and b is the slope.

long run A period of time long enough for all variables to be altered in quantity.

macroeconomics Deals with issues involving the entire economic system, such as the general level of prices and the total amount of output and employment.

marginal analysis Most economic choices involve marginal changes. Marginal means (to be most precise) adding just one more unit. A decision "at the margin" compares the benefits and costs of changing a level slightly.

marginal cost The change in total cost resulting from a one-unit increase in output.

marginal cost pricing The setting of price equal to marginal cost at a level of output corresponding to minimum average total cost. Marginal cost pricing is one criterion which regulatory agencies could use to set prices of regulated firms.

marginal product The change in output resulting from a one-unit increase in the quantity of the variable input.

marginal product/price ratio Represents the increase in output resulting from the last dollar spent on the input.

marginal revenue The change in revenue resulting from a one-unit change in output.

marginal revenue product The increase in revenue resulting from the use of the last unit of input. It equals the marginal product of the input multiplied by the marginal revenue of output.

Value of Marginal Product is the term used to refer to the marginal revenue product of a perfectly competitive firm.

marginal utility The change in total utility or satisfaction resulting from a one-unit change in the consumption of a good.

marginal utility/price ratio The change in total utility or satisfaction resulting from a one-dollar change in the amount spent on a good.

market A grouping of buyers and sellers who exchange a specific good at a particular price.

market equilibrium The price at which the quantity supplied and quantity demanded of a good are equal.

market failure Markets fail to reach optimal conditions because of the interference of such conditions as social goods, external effects, inequitable distribution, common-property resources, and monopoly.

market power/monopoly power A firm with market power (monopoly power) has some degree of control over prices. This is indicated by a downward-sloping demand schedule for the firm. Firms with market power range from monopolistic competitors who have a slight degree of market power to pure monopolists who have 100% of the sales in a market.

market share A firm's share of the market is measured by its own sales, taken as a percentage of all sales in the market.

merger The joining of two or more separate firms into a combined firm. The three main kinds of mergers are: (1) Horizontal merger: a merger of firms in the same market; (2) Vertical merger: a merger of firms at different but related steps in the production chain; (3) Conglomerate merger: a merger of firms which do not operate in related markets.

microeconomics The branch of economics that concentrates on the details of the economy, on parts of the whole.

minimal optimal scale (minimal efficient scale) The lowest level of output necessary to achieve minimum average total cost.

minimum wage The lowest wage which is legally permissible. The minimum wage is a form of price floor.

money capital See *Capital.*

monopolistic competition A market structure in which there is a low level of concentration, free entry, and product differentiation which gives each firm a slight degree of monopoly power.

monopoly In pure monopoly, one firm has 100% of the market. A degree of monopoly or market power exists if the firm's demand schedule slopes downward.

In the case of a natural monopoly, scale economics permit the efficient operation of only one firm in the market.

monopsony Occurs when a firm purchases or hires such a large percentage of inputs in a given market that the firm becomes a monopoly on the buying side of the market.

natural monopoly See *Monopoly.*

nonprofit firm A firm "owned" by a charitable group which has a special social purpose. Examples include most hospitals, the Red Cross, and city orchestras.

normal good See *Income Elasticity of Demand.*

normal return Corresponds to an economic profit of zero. It represents the rate of return equal to the return the firm could make in the most profitable alternative use of resources.

normative economics Normative economics concerns value judgments, or what ought to be. A normative statement usually expresses ethical standards and values.

oligopoly A market structure dominated by a group of leading firms. There is often a fringe of smaller competitors. A distinctive characteristic of oligopoly is the recognition of interdependence by the firms in the industry.

Tight oligopoly refers to markets in which the four largest firms account for 60 percent of market sales. Loose oligopoly refers to cases in which the four largest firms account for 20 to 40 percent of market sales.

open shop See *Labor Union.*

opportunity cost The cost of taking one action in terms of foregone alternatives.

perfect competition See *Competition.*

physical capital See *Capital.*

positive economics Positive economics concerns facts: What is happening or has happened.

price ceiling See *Price Controls.*

price controls Legal maximum or minimum prices. Price ceilings set the maximum price allowed by law, while price floors set the minimum price allowed by law.

price discrimination Setting different price-cost ratios for different customers, rather than one price/cost ratio for all.

price effect The increasing cost of leisure resulting from higher wages.

price elasticity of demand (elastic demand, inelastic demand, unitary demand) Price elasticity of demand $\frac{\%\Delta Q}{\%\Delta P}$ measures the relative responsiveness of quantity demanded to changes in price. Because of the inverse relation between changes in price and quantity, price elasticity will always be negative. The tradition is to ignore the negative sign. If the absolute value of the price elasticity is greater than 1, demand is elastic, or relatively responsive to changes in price. If the absolute value of price elasticity is less than 1, demand is inelastic, or relatively unresponsive to changes in price. When price elasticity equals 1, demand is called unitary elastic. In most cases, elasticity will differ from one point on the demand curve to another.

price floor See *Price Controls.*

private enterprise A firm owned by individuals or by other firms and operated with the primary aim of making profits for its owners.

production efficiency Average cost is as low as possible for a given level of output.

production function Shows the relation between inputs and output. It is often stated as a mathematical equation.

production-possibility boundary A downward-sloping boundary showing the maximum amount of goods which an economy can produce if all of its resources are used efficiently.

productivity The amount of output resulting from the use of inputs. Productivity can be stated as output per unit of input (Average Product) or the increased output resulting from an additional unit of input (Marginal Product).

profit (accounting and economic) Accounting profit refers to a firm's total revenues minus dollars paid out. It is equal to revenue minus direct costs. Economic profit refers to a firm's total revenue minus economic cost. Economic cost is the sum of direct costs (dollars paid out) plus imputed or implicit costs.

progressive tax See *Tax.*

public enterprise A firm, such as the U.S. Postal Service or the Tennessee Valley Authority, which is owned by the citizens through their government.

public good (social good) Consumption of the good by one person does not reduce the supply available to others. Examples of such goods include parks, roads, and fire protection.

quantity control A legal restriction on the quantity of a good or service that a producer may supply.

quantity demanded A particular point on the demand curve, representing a specific price-quantity combination.

quantity supplied A particular point on the supply curve representing a specific price-quantity combination.

regressive tax See *Tax.*

revenue Total revenue is the price of each unit of output times the quantity of output sold.

sales tax A common form of governmental levy, imposed in most states of the U.S. It is a tax levied on goods when they are sold. An example of a sales tax would be a per gallon tax on each gallon of gasoline sold, or a tax per package of cigarettes. The consumers' burden of a sales tax is the increase in price per unit of the good which results from the tax. The producers' burden of a sales tax is the reduction in revenue per unit of the good which results from the tax.

short run A period of time during which at least one input is fixed.

slope The degree of slant or tilt of a line.

social benefits and costs See *External Effects*.

social good See *Public Good*.

specialization Performing a task repeatedly so that one can become fast, skilled, and efficient at it.

stock A value at a point in time, such as wealth held by an individual.

substitution effect The change in quantity demanded of a good that occurs as consumers substitute one good for another in response to a price change.

supply The entire relationship between price and quantity supplied; the entire supply schedule.

tax The taking of money from a person or organization by a government. There are personal taxes such as income taxes and *in rem* taxes (taxes on things) such as sales taxes and property taxes.

A progressive tax is any type of tax which takes a higher percentage of income as income rises, falling more heavily on the rich. A regressive tax takes a decreased percentage of income as income rises, falling more heavily on the poor. A propor-

tional tax takes the same percentage of income at every level of income.

tax friction The loss of production that occurs when people alter their economic decisions in order to lighten their tax burdens.

tax incidence Analysis of who bears the burden of a tax.

technology The state of the art with respect to production. It encompasses all of the known methods of production.

time series A graph that shows how an economic variable has moved or behaved over time.

total cost / average total cost / marginal cost Total cost refers to the total cost of production; the sum of fixed and variable costs. Average total cost is total cost per unit of output. Marginal cost is the change in total cost resulting from a one-unit change in output.

total product / average product / marginal product Total product refers to total output. Average product refers to output per unit of input. Marginal product refers to the change in output that results from a one-unit change in input.

total utility See *Utility*.

transfer earnings A payment to an input which is equal to the amount necessary to elicit supply.

transfer payments Government spending which is not made in exchange for a good or service. Transfer payments involve a transfer of income from the government to an individual or firm. Examples of such payments include unemployment compensation, welfare payments, and subsidies.

union See *Labor Union*.

union shop See *Labor Union*.

utility The satisfaction derived from the consumption of a good.

value of marginal product See *Marginal Revenue Product*.

variable costs Costs that vary with the level of output, such as payments for inputs. Average variable cost refers to variable cost per unit of output.

vertical merger See *Merger.*

windfall gains Increases in economic rent which occur with no added effort or contribution by the owners of the inputs.

x-inefficiency Internal slack may result in the firm's costs for given levels of output rising above the lowest possible levels.

Index

Accounting:
  choices of regulated utilities, 281
  simple, of enterprises, 138–41
Accounting cost, defined, 138, 150
  (see also Direct costs)
Accounts receivable, 140
Addyston Pipe and Steel Company case,
  254, 265 *tab.*, 267
Advertising:
  annual expenditures, 58
  as entry barrier, 223
After-tax profit, 139
Age, and income, 404
Aggregate concentration, 241–42
Agricultural economics, 457–62
Agricultural products:
  inelasticity of demand and
    supply, 87–89
  price supports, 96–97
  selected, estimated elasticities of
    supply, 101 *tab.*
Agricultural sector:
  basic conditions, 457
  energy scarcity, 458–59
  farm policies, 459–62
  productivity growth, 350 *tab.*,
    351, 457–58
  topsoil erosion and water
    shortage, 459
Aid to Dependent Children (ADC),
  404, 415
Airlines industry:
  deregulation, 283
  private enterprises, 284 *fig.*
  response to fuel price increase,
    173
Alcoa case, 255, 262 *tab.*
Allocative efficiency, 195–96 (see
  also Efficient allocation)
Allocative inefficiency, 209–11,
  212

Altruism, utility analysis, 121
Aluminum Company of America,
  227
American Broadcasting Company
  (ABC), 255–56
American Can Company, 255
American Economic Review, 12 *fn.*
American Electric Power Company,
  268
American Stock Exchange, 344
American Telephone and
    Telegraph Company
    (AT&T), 6, 126, 147
  antitrust case, 252, 256, 262 *tab.*
American Tobacco Company, 227,
  254, 262 *tab.*
Amtrak, 286
*Antitrust and Trade Regulations
  Reporter,* 261 *fn.,* 267
Antitrust policies, 249–70
  agencies and laws, 253–54
  economic criteria, 256–58
  economic effects, 258–59
  exempt organizations, 259 *tab.*
  toward existing concentrations,
    257–58, 259–64
  history, 254–56
  toward mergers, 135, 257 *tab.*,
    258, 264–67
  and minimum optimal scale, 171
  origins, 250–52
  toward price discrimination, 258,
    268–69
  toward price fixing, 257 *tab.*, 258,
    267–68
  standards, 252
Aquinas, Thomas, 8
Aristotle, 7
Army Corps of Engineers, 383
Arrow, Kenneth J., 42
Artificial scarcity, of labor, 319, 324

"As if" proposition, 22, 107
Assets:
  on balance sheet, 139–40
  claims against, 140 (see also
    Liabilities)
  of firms, 53, 128–29 *tab.*
  household preferences, 19–20, 51
  of major sectors, 52 *tab.*
  and regulated price levels, 274,
    277, 281
  "writing off," 142
Asset values, 343–49
Austria, 11, 284 *fig.*
Autolite, 258
Automobile industry:
  autonomous innovation, 353
  emission standards, 432–33
  market share concentration ratio,
    229
  market type, 200
  partial competition, 223 *tab.*
  public enterprises, 284 *fig.*
  ripple effects, 365
Autonomous inventions, 353
Average cost, and efficient
    production, 194
Average fixed cost (AFC), 159 *tab.*,
  160
Average product (AP), 154–58, 159
  tab.
  and average variable cost, 160–62
Average total cost (ATC):
  calculation, 159 *tab.*, 160, 162
  economies and diseconomies of
    scale, 167–71
  and long-run equilibrium,
    192–93
  long vs. short run, 164–67
  and marginal cost, 162–63
  and profit maximization, 180,
    188

Average variable cost (AVC):
  and average product, 160–62
  calculation, 159 *tab.*, 160
  and marginal cost, 162–63
  and price, 186–87
  and profit maximization, 180
  and short-run equilibrium, 191
  and short-run supply curve, 184,
    187–88

Babylonia, 7
Balance sheet, 138, 139–41
Barron's, 132
Belgium, 284 *fig.*
Benefit-cost analysis (*see* Cost-
  benefit analysis)
Bentham, Jeremy, 106
Berle, A. A., 127
Bias:
  in econometric diagrams, 50–51
  in present value analysis of
    natural resource use, 457
Bilateral monopoly, 325–26
Birth rate, and future resources,
  465
Black markets, 96
Blacks:
  housing discrimination, 408–9
  job discrimination, 406
  poverty among, 404
  unemployment rate, 6
Bloomsbury Group, 10
Blue-collar jobs, pay rates, 315–16
Bonds:
  asset values, 344–46, 347
  and cost of capital, 337
  interest rates, 342
  published price listings, 131, 132
    tab.
  ratings, 341
  tax-exempt, 397
Bribes, response to price ceilings,
  96
Britain (*see* Great Britain)
British East India Company, 244
Brown Shoe—Kinney Shoe merger,
  265 *tab.*
Bubble concept, 434, 435
Burger, Warren E., 256, 257
Business cycle, 11, 35, 36
Business firms (*see* Firms)
Business sector (*see* Industrial
  sector; Manufacturing sector)
Business Week, 132, 256

California, 273 *tab.*, 425, 459
Campbell Soup Company, 224
Canada, 4, 393 *tab.*
Capital (Marx), 8, 9, 12
Capital, 331–54
  asset valuation, 343–49
  characteristics, 332
  costs of, 139, 335–36
  human, 316–18
  as input to production, 20–21,
    137, 153
  investment decisions, 142,
    333–37
  management of, 136, 137
  market demand, 337
  market supply, 337–38

  price of, and least-cost
    production, 171–72
  and productive capacity, 5
  productivity of, 332
  real or physical vs. money or
    portfolio types, 331–32
  return on, 141, 332, 338–43
  and technological change, 349–53
Capital goods, 331–33
Capital intensity, 77–78, 148 *fn.*
Capitalism:
  in classical economics, 8
  defined, 21
  Marxist view, 13
Capital stock, 30
Carlson, Chester, 405
Carnegie, Andrew, 405
Carnegie-Mellon University, 405
Cartels:
  defined, 234
  in nuclear fuels, 463–64
  in petroleum (*see* Organization of
    Petroleum-Exporting
    Countries [OPEC])
Cash, on balance sheet, 140
Central America, 444
Charity:
  provision of public goods, 385
  utility analysis of contributions,
    121
Charts (*see* Diagrams)
Chicago School, 13
China, 7, 10
Choices (*see* Economic choices)
Chrysler Corporation, 147, 229, 258
Circular flow, 18–19, 23–24, 33–34
Civil Aeronautics Board (CAB), 273
  tab., 274, 283
Civil War, 250
Clark, Colin, 393
Classical economics, 8, 12
Classical liberals, 13
Clayton Act (1914), 254 *tab.*, 255,
  257 *tab.*, 264
Clinical analysis, 14
Clorox Chemical Company, 266
Closed shop, 320, 321
Coal industry, public enterprises,
  284 *tab.*
Collective bargaining (*see* Labor
  unions)
College, public financing issues,
  422–23, 425–28
Collusion:
  antitrust cases, 267–68
  antitrust policy, 254 *tab.*
  vs. competition, 232–33
  conditions favorable toward,
    233–34
  types, 234–35
Colorado, 273 *tab.*
Commercial banks, five largest, 129
  tab.
Commodities:
  heavily taxed, 94
  market prices, 56 *tab.*
  published price listings, 131, 133
    tab.
Common-property resources, 369,
  456

Communications industry,
  productivity growth, 350 *tab.*,
  351
Communist Manifesto (Marx and
  Engels), 9
Companies (*see* Enterprises; Firms)
Comparative advantage, and job
  selection, 307
Comparative static analysis, 57
Competition:
  defined, 180
  degrees of, 221–47 (*see also*
    Partial competition)
  and efficient allocation, 194–96,
    358–64
  entry barriers (*see* Entry barriers)
  ideal model (*see* Pure
    competition)
  from imports, 244
  limits on efficiency of, 196,
    364–70
  and maximization of consumer
    surplus, 210
  vs. monopoly, 200
  natural, 170
  nature of, 180–81
  of oligopoly firms, 232
  perfect (*see* Perfect competition)
  policies that reduce, 259 *tab.*
  policies to increase (*see* Antitrust
    policies)
  public school voucher proposal,
    424–25
  recent market share trends,
    243–44
  for regulated utilities, 282–83
  and rivalry, 181
  Schumpeter's theory, 231, 260
  unfair, 204
  U.S. faith in, 249
Complementary goods:
  cross-elasticity of demand, 70–71
  defined, 58
  and derived demand, 120
Computer industry, 261–63, 269
Concentration:
  aggregate, 241–42
  and antitrust policy, 259–67
  and economies of scale, 239–40
  in monopolistic competition, 240
  and oligopolistic collusion, 232, 234
  and oligopoly characteristics,
    229–30, 231
  recent trends, 242–44
Conglomerate firms:
  characteristics, 126–27
  effect on competition, 244–46
Conglomerate mergers:
  antitrust policy, 256, 257 *tab.*,
    258, 265 *tab.*, 266–67
  recent trends, 130–35, 245
Conservation, 448–57
Conservative economists, 13, 36
Construction industry, productivity
  growth, 350 *tab.*, 351
Consumer demand:
  basis for, 20
  and derived demand, 297
  (*see also* Demand; Individual
    demand)

Consumer durable goods, 333
Consumer goods, markets for, 23
Consumer Product Safety
    Commission (CPSC), 435
    tab., 436–37
Consumers:
    rational choices, 105–7, 120–21
    share of sales taxes, 92–94
    (*see also* Household sector)
Consumer surplus:
    and marginal utility, 117–18
    and market demand, 120
    Marshall's contribution, 106
    reduction in, due to monopoly,
        210
Consumption:
    and disposable income, graphing,
        41–43, 46–48
    household patterns, 19–20,
        104–5
    of social vs. private goods,
        375–76
Contracts:
    exclusive and tying, antitrust
        policy, 254 *tab.*
    government, 204
Cooperatives, 135
Corporate income tax, 396
Corporate profits:
    of largest firms, 128–29 *tab.*
    long-term trends, 342–43
    (*see also* Profits)
Corporate securities, ownership,
    402 (*see also* Bonds; Stock)
Corporations, 125–27 (*see also*
    Firms)
Cost-benefit analysis:
    antitrust standard, 252
    of capital goods, 332–37
    and choices of enterprises,
        136–37
    and economic approach, 14
    of environmental protection,
        430–32, 434, 435 *fig.*
    of finding and harvesting natural
        resources, 453–54
    for government choices, 32
    of marginal input, 290
    and marginal utility, 116, 117
    and opportunity cost, 25 (*see also*
        Opportunity cost)
    of public expenditures, 378–83
    of worker and consumer safety
        programs, 436–37
    (*see also* Efficient allocation;
        Present value analysis)
Cost-plus pricing, 439–40
Costs, 147–74
    accounting, 150
    accounting vs. economic, 138
    average, 194
    average fixed, 159 *tab.*, 160
    average total, 159 *tab.*, 160,
        162–63, 164–71, 180, 188,
        192–93
    average variable, 159 *tab.*,
        160–63, 180, 184, 186–88,
        191
    of capital, 139, 335–38
    defined, 149

direct, 150, 151–53, 297–98,
    453–54
discounted (*see* Present value
    analysis)
and economic profit, 151–53
effects of regulation on, 281–82
explicit, 150
external vs. social, 364–66
fixed vs. variable, 159
of foregone alternatives, 149–50
    (*see also* Opportunity cost)
implicit, 150
imputed, 150
and productivity, 153–73
sunk, 150, 151
and technology, 148–49
and transfer earnings, 299–300
Council on Environmental Quality,
    429
Craft unions, 322, 323–24
Cream skimming, 282
Creative destruction, theory of, 231
Cross-elasticity of demand, 70–71
Cultural values, and efficient
    allocation, 368
Culture, effect of monopoly on,
    213
Current assets, 140

Dark Ages, 8
Das Kapital (*see* Capital)
Debt financing, cost of, 337, 338
Decision making:
    in households, 18, 19–20
    individual, 117
    and innovation, 352–53
    and investment, 333–34
    (*see also* Cost-benefit analysis;
        Economic choices)
Defense spending (*see* Military
    spending)
Demand, 58–71
    for capital, 337
    cross-elasticity of, 70–71
    derived, 120, 297, 311
    diminishing marginal effect, 27
    elastic, 86–87
    elasticity and total revenue,
        66–67
    and income, 34–35
    income elasticity, 67–70
    individual vs. total, 104, 118–20
    inelastic, 87–90
    influences on, 58–59
    for inputs, of firm, 290–97
    interaction with supply, 78–80
    for labor, 311–13, 324
    for money, 215–20
    price elasticity, 63–67
    vs. quantity demanded, 61–63
    for social goods, 376–77
    (*see also* Demand and supply;
        Demand curve; Individual
        demand; Market demand)
Demand and supply, 55–83,
    85–102
    for agricultural products, 460
    for college education, 425–27
    effects of elasticities on market
        outcomes, 86–91

household-enterprise interaction,
    18–19
interaction of, 78–80
interferences with market
    processes, 91–98
for investment funds, 34–35
and market prices, 23, 55–57
measuring, 98–101
for soldiers, 443–44
tendency toward equilibrium, 32
(*see also* Demand; Supply)
Demand curve, 59–61
    of dominant firm, 222–23
    for free vs. scarce goods, 112–13
    graphing convention, 41–43
    of individuals, 104, 107, 110–11,
        116–17
    intersection with supply curve,
        78–80
    kinked, of oligopoly, 236–39
    in monopolistic competition,
        240–41
    in monopoly, 200–202
    in perfect competition, 181–82
    in pure competition, 180
    (*see also* Elasticity of demand)
Democracy, effect of monopoly on,
    213
Dependent variable, 41, 46–47
Depreciation, 139, 140
Depressions, in Keynesian theory,
    11 (*see also* Great Depression)
Deregulation, 282–83
Derived demand:
    defined, 120
    for labor, 311
    method of computing, 297
Diagrams, 40–50
    of distributions, 41, 49–50
    economic models, 44–48
    functions, 40–41
    of linear equations, 41–44
    problems of bias and deception,
        50–51
    three main types, 41
    of time series, 48–49
Diminishing marginal effect, 26–27
    of market disequilibrium, 32
    and production-possibility
        boundary, 29, 30 *fig.*
    and public choice, 32–33
Diminishing marginal returns (*see*
    Law of diminishing marginal
    returns)
Diminishing marginal utility (*see*
    Marginal utility)
Direct costs:
    defined, 150
    and economic profit, 151–53
    and input market supply curve,
        297–98
    of natural resources, 453–54
    vs. opportunity costs, 149–50,
        151
Discounted future values (*see*
    Present value analysis)
Discrimination:
    in employment, 406–8
    in housing, 408–9
    programs to combat, 413–16

Diseconomies of scale, 167–71
Disposable income:
  and consumption, econometric
    diagrams, 41–43, 46–48
  taxation effects, 410–11
Distribution, economic choices, 2–3
    (*see also* Income distribution)
Distributions, econometric
    diagrams, 41, 49–50
Distribution sector, productivity
    growth, 350 *tab.*
Disutility, 108, 306
Diversification:
  of large corporations, 126–27
  and risk reduction, 341
Dividends:
  and asset values, 347–48
  and cost of capital, 337
  and income statement, 139
  long-term trends, 342
  vs. retained earnings, 140–41
Dividend yield, 348
Dominant firms, 222–29
  antitrust policy, 258, 259–64
  causes, 224–29
  characteristics, 222–23
  instances and effects, 223–24,
    225 *tab.*, 228 *tab.*
  and market type, 201 *tab.*
  predatory pricing, 269
  price discrimination, 216
  recent market share trends,
    243–44
Dow Jones Industrial Average, 343,
    345 *fig.*
Duke, James B., 405
Duke University, 405
Duopoly, 236
DuPont Corporation, 245, 262 *tab.*,
    265 *tab.*, 266
DuPont family, 403, 405

Eastman Kodak Company, 171,
    229, 263
Econometrics, 39–54
  distributions, 49–50
  fitting techniques, 47
  linear equations, 41–44
  model building, 44–48
  Nobel Prize winners, 42–43
  problem of bias and deception,
    50–51
  stocks and flows, 51–53
  time series, 48–49
  use of diagrams, 40–41
Economic analysis, 7–14
  in ancient times, 7–8
  classical, 8
  of demand and supply, 85–102
    (*see also* Demand and supply)
  economic approach, 13–14
  economic choices, 2
  focus on markets, 23
  literature, 12–13
  methods and measurements (*see*
    Econometrics)
  neoclassical, 8–12
  positive and normative, 4
  of utility and demand, 104–20
    (*see also* Economics; Economists)

Economic choices:
  in classical economics, 8
  and efficient allocation, 359
  of enterprises, 20, 136–37, 138
  as focus of economics, 1–2
  and general equilibrium, 356–58
  of households, 18, 19–20
  individual decision making, 117
  intergenerational, 454–55
  of investors, and equalization of
    returns, 348
  in job selection, 307
  marginal conditions, 25–26
  maximizing behavior, 22
  of monopolist, 204–9
  opportunity costs, 25, 149–50,
    151
  and production-possibility
    boundary, 27–31
  production questions, 2–3, 24–25
  of production technologies,
    148–49
  public, 32–33
  vs. public school monopoly,
    423–25
  rational, 105–7, 120–21
  restrictions due to monopoly,
    212–13
  in the short and long run,
    166–67
  taxation effects, 387–89
Economic cost, 149, 150 (*see also*
    Opportunity cost)
Economic goals, 3–4
Economic growth:
  and investment levels, 30
  and population growth, 465–66
Economic models, 41, 44–49
Economic obsolescence, 352–53
Economic profit, 151–53, 338
Economic rent:
  and elasticity of supply, 299–301
  Marshall's contribution, 106
  and natural resources, 448
  and price of farmland, 460–61
  taxing of, 301–2
Economics:
  agricultural, 457–62
  applied fields, 222
  defined, 1–2
  as the "dismal science," 448
  of energy, 462–65
  evolution of, 12
  Nobel Prize, 42
  political process, 373
  principles, 17–37
    (*see also* Economic analysis;
    Economists;
    Macroeconomics;
    Microeconomics)
Economic sectors, 4–5
  stocks and flows, 51–53
Economic systems, 2–7
  circular flow of goods and
    services, 18–19, 23–24,
    33–34
  distribution of income and
    wealth, 6–7
  in economic analysis, 13–14
  and economic goals, 3–4

  influence of scarcity and choice,
    2–3
  major sectors, 4–5
  productivity factors, 5–6
  stocks and flows, 52 *tab.*, 53
  tendency toward equilibrium, 32
Economies of scale, 167–71
  antitrust criteria, 261
  as cause of dominance, 224–27,
    229
  as entry barrier, 223
  and monopoly power, 203, 218,
    368
  of oligopoly, 239–40
  and regulation of utilities, 272,
    273, 275
Economists:
  debate over government
    stabilization policy, 36
  desirable attributes, 14, 40
  generalists vs. specialists, 11–12
  major figures, 8–11
  Nobel Prize winners, 42–43, 357
  publications, 12–13
  schools and groups, 13
Edison, Thomas, 217
Education, 420–28
  expenditures on, 422–23
  private benefits, 316–19, 420–21
  public benefits, 421
  public colleges, 425–28
  public school monopoly, 423–25
Efficiency:
  in antitrust standards, 252
  conditions for, 194–96
  economies and diseconomies of
    scale, 167–71 (*see also*
    Economies of scale)
  and financing of public colleges,
    425–28
  of income distribution, 405
  and monopoly power, 203
  and production-possibility
    boundary, 27–31
  in public action, 32
  of public enterprises, 286–87
  purpose of public sector, 374
  and regulated price levels,
    276–77, 281
  X-level, 165 (*see also* X-efficiency)
Efficient allocation:
  and college financing, 427
  conditions of, 195–96, 358–61
  effect of farm price supports, 460
  and general equilibrium, 355
  limits, 196, 364–70
  of natural resources, 448–49
    (*see also* Efficiency)
Effluent fees, 434
Effort, and income distribution,
    405
Egypt, 7
Eisenhower, Dwight D., 438
Elastic demand, defined, 65
Elasticity:
  defined, 63
  main types and ranges, 82 *tab.*
  and market outcomes, 86–91
Elasticity of demand:
  cross-elasticity, 70–71

effect on future world resources, 466
and incidence of taxation, 387
for an input, 294–95
with kinked demand curve, 236–39
for labor, 314, 320–21
and monopoly conditions, 208, 211
price discrimination based on, 213–16
and regulation, 273
relative to income, 67–70, 82 *tab.*
relative to price, 63–67, 82 *tab.*
and sales tax burden, 92–93
(*see also* Demand curve)
Elasticity of supply, 75–78
and economic rent, 299–301
and incidence of taxation, 387
of individual laborers, 308
of labor market, 314–15
and sales tax burden, 93–94
(*see also* Supply curve)
Elastic supply, defined, 75
Elderly, poverty among, 404
Electrical Equipment Conspiracy, 265 *tab.*, 267–68
Electric power companies:
as monopolies, 217–18
productivity growth, 350 *tab.*, 351
public enterprises, 284 *fig.*
regulated price levels, 272, 277, 278–81
(*see also* Utilities)
Elements of Pure Economics (Walras), 357
Employment:
discrimination, 406–8
effects of labor unions on, 322–23
equal opportunity programs, 413–16
and minimum wage law, 416–17
(*see also* Unemployment; Work)
Energy:
economics of, 462–65
effect of scarcity on farming, 458–59
England (*see* Great Britain)
Enterprises, 123–45
accounting concepts, 138–41
choices and outcomes, 136–37
defined, 135–36
diversity in size, 6
functions in economic system, 18–19, 20
income requirements, 20
input categories, 20–21
inputs, outputs, and production, 137–38
maximizing behavior, 21–22
new, a case history, 142–45
patterns, 124–35
public, 20, 135, 283–87
success indicators, 141–42
(*see also* Firms; Private enterprises)
Entrepreneurship, 342, 352
Entry barriers:
absence of, as condition of competition, 181, 240, 241

in craft unions and professional groups, 324
due to monopoly, 202, 212–13
of oligopoly, 232
types and causes, 223
Environmental protection, 428–35
automobile emission case, 432–33
cost-benefit analysis, 430–32
issues and programs, 428–30
steel industry case, 433
use of incentives, 433–35
Environmental Protection Agency (EPA), 429, 432, 433, 434
Equal Employment Opportunity Commission (EEOC), 413–16
Equalization of returns, 348
Equal Opportunity Act (1964), 413
Equilibrium:
of marginal utilities and prices, 113–17
microeconomic principle, 31–32
of prices and quantity, 78–80
short- and long-run, under perfect competition, 190–93
(*see also* General equilibrium)
Equity (*see* Fairness)
Equity capital:
on balance sheet, 140
cost, 337, 338
rate of return on, 141
Essay on the Principle of Population (Malthus), 8
Estate taxes, 396
Ethics, and natural resource use, 454–55 (*see also* Values)
Europe, 8, 11 (*see also* Western Europe)
Excess profits:
of dominant firms, 224
of monopoly, 211
of oligopoly firms, 232–33
regulation to prevent, 272
Excise taxes, 413 (*see also* Sales taxes)
Expectations:
and asset values, 343, 346–47
effect on demand, 58
effect on prices, 455, 462
Explicit costs, defined, 150
External effects:
as limits to efficient allocation, 364–69
and public policy, 32–33, 375 *tab.*, 377–78
and rate of use of natural resources, 369, 457
External funds, 337
Exxon Corporation, 126, 141, 203, 217

Factors of production, 20–21 (*see also* Inputs)
Fairness:
and efficient allocation, 367–68
equity in public sector, 374
and financing of public colleges, 425–28
Family size, and income, 404–5
Farmers, poverty among, 404

Farming (*see* Agricultural sector)
Farmland:
effect of price supports on value, 460, 462
erosion of topsoil, 459
land bank program, 461
Farm policy, 459–62
Fascism, 213
Fast-food restaurants, case study of partial competition, 223 *tab.*
Federal Communications Commission (FCC), 273 *tab.*, 274
Federal Energy Regulatory Commission, 273 *tab.*, 274
Federal Farm Loan program, 396
Federal Trade Commission (FTC), 253, 255, 256, 257 *tab.*
Du Pont case, 262 *tab.*
Procter and Gamble case, 265 *tab.*, 266
Xerox case, 262 *tab.*, 263–64
Federal Trade Commission Act, 254 *tab.*
Fibers and textiles:
market prices, 56 *tab.*
published price listings, 133 *tab.*
Figures (*see* Diagrams)
Final demand, vs. derived demand, 120
Financial industry:
productivity growth, 350 *tab.*, 351
public enterprises, 283
Financial markets, 23, 34 (*see also* Stock market)
Fines, 383
Finished goods, 137
Firms:
conditions of efficient allocation, 358 *tab.*
corporations, 125–27
derived demand, 120
dominant (*see* Dominant firms)
economic choices, 2
influences on supply, 72
investment demand, 34–35
news stories, 131
public (*see* Public enterprises)
scope of term, 123
stocks and flows, 51–53
supply of capital to, 338
(*see also* Enterprises; Industrial sector)
Fixed assets, 140
Fixed costs:
average, 160
defined, 159
effect on short-run supply curve, 190
total, 160
Fixed inputs, 153
Flows, vs. stocks, 51–53 (*see also* Circular flow)
Food and Drug Administration (FDA), 435, 436–37
Foods:
commodity price listings, 133 *tab.*
market prices, 56 *tab.*
(*see also* Agricultural products)
Forbes, 132, 256

Ford Motor Company, 51–53, 229, 258
Forecasting, and use of natural resources, 456–57
Foregone alternatives, 149–50 (*see also* Opportunity cost)
Foreign aid, and farm policy, 461
Foreign currencies, 131, 134 *tab.*
Foreign trade, 18
Fortune, 132, 256
Forward pricing, 455
France, 284 *fig.*, 393 *tab.*
Franchises:
    monopolistic, 203–4
    of regulated utilities, 272, 274
Franklin, Benjamin, 443
Free goods:
    and consumer surplus, 118
    and marginal utility, 112–13
Free-market economists, 13
French Physiocrats, 8, 302 *tab.*
French Socialists, 8, 302 *tab.*
Friedman, Milton, 42, 424
Frisch, Ragnar, 42
Fuels:
    conservation by airlines, 173
    economies of use, 462–65
    effect of scarcity on farming, 458–59
    elasticity of demand, 466
    price controls, 95
    (*see also entries under* Oil)
Future (*see* Expectations)
Future values, discounted (*see* Present value analysis)

Galbraith, John Kenneth, 260
Gasoline industry, public enterprises, 284 *fig.* (*see also* Oil industry)
Gasoline taxes, 387, 395
General Electric Company, 227, 245, 265 *tab.*, 268, 269
General equilibrium, 355–70
    adjusting toward, 356–58
    conditions, 358–61
    Invisible Hand concept, 361, 364, 367, 370, 456
    limits on competitive efficiency, 364–70
    ripple effects, 356, 361–64, 365
General Foods Company, 245
General Motors Corporation, 2, 6, 22, 135, 171, 200, 203, 224, 229, 245, 259, 266, 265 *tab.*
General Theory of Employment, Interest and Money (Keynes), 10, 11, 12
Geography:
    and income levels, 404
    and market definition, 57, 261
    and ripple effect, 364
George, Henry, 301
Georgia, 273 *tab.*
Gillette Company, 227
Gold:
    commodity price listings, 133 *tab.*
    market value, 56 *tab.*, 57
Goods:
    in circular flow, 23, 24 *fig.*, 33–34
    complementary, 58, 70–71, 120

costs of producing, and supply, 71–72
    with inelastic supply, 87
    intermediate, 137
    market definition, 57, 261
    necessities, 67
    normal vs. inferior, 69–70
    as output of enterprises, 138
    related, 72
    scarce vs. free, 111–13
    selected, price elasticities of demand, 100 *tab.*
    social vs. private, 375–76
    substitutable, 57, 58, 60, 67, 70–71
Government (*see also* Local government; State government; *and entries under* Federal; U.S.)
Government contracts, 204
Government intervention, views of various schools, 11, 13
Government policy:
    conglomerate pressures on, 245–46
    effect on competition, 244
    farm policy, 459–62
    toward monopoly power, 203–4, 249–70 (*see also* Antitrust policies)
    (*see also* Public policy)
Government regulation (*see* Regulation)
Government sector:
    criteria for economic choices, 32–33
    influence on economic system, 18
    interference with market process, 94–98
    public goods provided by, 113
    purchases, 385–86, 392, 393 *fig.*, 394
    stocks and flows, 52 *tab.*, 53
    in U.S. economy, 4
Grains and feeds, prices, 56 *tab.*, 133 *tab.*
Gramlich, Edward M., 417 *fn.*
Graphs (*see* Diagrams)
Great Britain, 8, 11, 284 *fig.*, 368
Great Depression, 10, 11, 255
Great Plains region, 6, 459
Great Society, 392, 394
Greece, 7
Growth (*see* Economic growth; Population growth)

Harvard University, 231, 357
Hayek, Friedrick A. von, 43
Health maintenance organizations, 385
Heavy industries (*see* Capital intensity)
Henry George Society, 301
Hicks, John R., 42
Hispanics, 406
Hoarding, vs. conservation, 449
Holiday Inns, 344, 354 *fig.*
Holland (*see* Netherlands)
Horizontal mergers, 130, 135
    antitrust policy, 257 *tab.*, 258, 264–66
    as cause of firm dominance, 227

Households, defined, 19
Household sector:
    conditions of efficient allocation, 358 *tab.*
    consumption patterns, 104–5
    functions in economic system, 18–19
    income sources, 19, 34
    maximizing behavior, 21–22
    saving and investment decisions, 19–20, 34–35
    stocks and flows, 51, 52 *tab.*
    (*see also entries under* Consumer)
Housing:
    discrimination, 408–9
    income effect on demand, 60
    supply elasticity, 78
Human capital, 316–18 (*see also* Labor)
Hume, David, 9

Imitation, phase of technological change, 352
Implicit costs, 25, 150
Imports, competition from, 244
Imputed costs, 150, 152
Incentives:
    for environmental protection, 433–35
    and income support, 415–16
    taxation effects, 387–89
Income:
    allocation of, and marginal utility, 113–16
    and education, 316–19
    effect of labor unions on, 326–27
    of farmers, 460–62
    household sources, 19, 34
    as influence on demand, 58, 60
    and investment demand, 34–35
    by job type, 316 *tab.*
    and output, 34
    and preferences, 110–11
    and price elasticity of demand, 67
    requirement of enterprises, 20
    and tax incidence, 411–13
Income distribution, 401–18
    and allocative efficiency, 196
    economic forces shaping, 405
    as influence on demand, 58
    and marginal productivity, 401
    monopoly effects, 211–12
    and public enterprise, 283
    public finance effects, 389–92
    and public policy, 409–17
    unfair or inequitable, 367–68, 375 *tab.*, 402–9, 457
    in U.S., 6, 50
Income effect, 61, 308–9
Income elasticity of demand, 67–70
Income stabilization, and price supports, 460–61
Income statement, 138–39
Income support, and work incentives, 415–16
Income taxes (*see* Personal income tax)
Independent variable, 41–43, 46–47, 48
India, 393 *tab.*

Individual demand, 103–22
  and consumer surplus, 117–18
  debate over microeconomic
    theory, 120–21
  and derived demand, 120
  marginal utility concepts, 107–9,
    113–17
  and market demand, 118–20
  preferences and income effects,
    110–11
  rational choices, 105–7, 120–21
  for scarce vs. free goods, 111–13
  (see also Demand)
Induced inventions, 353
Industrial mix, 226–27
Industrial Revolution, 250
Industrial sector:
  aggregate concentration trends,
    242
  and antitrust policy, 259
  largest firms, 128 fig.
  supply of capital to, 338
  in U.S. economy, 4–5
  (see also Industries)
Industrial structure:
  patterns and trends, 241–46
  and public policy, field of, 222
Industrial unions, 322–23 (see also
    Labor unions)
Industries:
  capital intensity effects, 77–78
  diversification of firms among,
    126–27
  with elastic demand and supply,
    87
  life cycles, 275 tab.
  minimum optimum scale, 171 tab.
  news stories, 131
  primary, 4, 5 fig.
  publicly owned, 283, 284 fig.
  size influences, 77
  supply curve shifts, 189–90
Inefficiency:
  allocative, 209–11, 212
  in military weapons production,
    438–40
  X-level (see X-inefficiency)
Inelastic demand, 65–66, 67
Inelastic supply, 75
Inequality:
  and discrimination, 406–9
  and income distribution, 367–78,
    375 tab., 401–5, 457
  in public school system, 423–25
Inferior goods, 69–70
Inflation, 11, 36
Innovation:
  to create and maintain monopoly
    power, 203
  decision-making issues, 352–53
  effects of monopoly on, 212
  induced vs. autonomous, 353
  phase of technological change,
    352
  process vs. product type, 352
  return on, 342
  Schumpeter's theory, 231
  (see also Technological change)
Input markets, 23, 289–304
  economic rent concept, 299–302
  equilibrium in, 298–99

supply and demand factors,
    18–19, 290–98
  and value of production, 302–3
Input-output analysis, 357, 362
Inputs:
  accounting vs. opportunity costs,
    149–50, 151
  categories, 20–21, 137
  cost calculation, 153
  efficient allocation of, 361
  key, and monopoly power, 204
  least-cost combination, 171–73
  price of, and supply, 71, 72
  relative value, 367
  scarce, and elasticity of supply, 77
  in the short vs. long run, 153
  (see also Input markets)
In rem taxes, 386
Institutional investors, 130
Insurance industry:
  largest companies, 129 tab.
  public enterprises, 283
Insurance pooling, 385
Intercept, in graphs, 44, 45 figs.
Interdependence:
  absence of, in monopolistic
    competition, 240
  macroeconomic concept, 33, 34,
    36
  in oligopoly, 230–31
Interest payments, 139, 140
  foregone, 335–36, 337
Interest rates:
  and asset values, 346–48
  and internal rate of return, 334
  published listings, 131, 134 tab.
  and return to capital, 338,
    341–42
  usury laws, 95
Intergenerational choices, 454–55
Interlocking directorates, 254 tab.
Intermediate goods, 137
Internal funds, 337
Internal rate of return, 334–35
International Business Machines
    Corporation (IBM), 126,
    171, 203, 224, 229
  antitrust issues, 256, 257–58,
    261–63, 269
International Telephone &
    Telegraph Company (ITT),
    126, 244, 265 tab., 266
Interstate Commerce Commission
    (ICC), 251, 273 tab., 274
Invention:
  effects of monopoly, 212
  induced vs. autonomous, 353
  patent system, 203, 227, 353
  phase of technological change,
    352
  (see also Innovation)
Inventories, 140
Investment:
  cost of capital, 335–36
  demand for, and savings, 34–35
  and economic growth, 30
  internal rate of return criterion,
    334
  in job training and education,
    316–19
  marginal return curve, 334–35

present-value criterion, 333–34
  (see also Present value
    analysis)
  profit-maximizing, 336–37
  profits as a signal for, 142
  and rate base of regulated
    utilities, 276, 277, 281–82
  risk-return relationship, 338–41
  as source of capital, 332–33
Investors, 127–30
Invisible Hand, 361, 364, 367, 370,
    456
Iowa, 21, 457
Italy, 284 fig.

Japan, 4, 30, 125, 393 tab., 432–33
Jevons, William Stanley, 8, 106
Jobs:
  discriminatory policies, 406–8
  pay rates, 315–16
  selection of, 306
  varieties of, 315
  (see also Employment)
Job training:
  entry barriers, 324
  return on investment, 316–19
Johnson, Lyndon B., 11
Journal of Economic History, 12 fn.
Journal of Economic Theory, 12 fn.
Journal of Political Economy, 12 fn.

Kantrovich, Leonid V., 42
Kellogg Company, 227
Key inputs, 204
Keynes, John Maynard, 10, 11, 12
Keynesian economics, 11, 12, 13
Kinked demand curve, 236–39
Klein, Lawrence R., 43
Koopmans, Tjalling C., 42
Korean War, 95
Kuznets, Simon, 42

Labor:
  costs of, on income statement, 139
  price of, and least-cost
    production, 171–72
  as production factor, 20, 137,
    302
  productivity trends, 349–51
  as variable input, 153
  (see also Labor market)
Labor force participation rate,
    309–11
Labor-intensity, 148
Labor market, 305–29
  artificial scarcity of supply, 324
  demand factors, 311–13, 324
  equilibrium of supply and
    demand, 313–15
  individual supply schedules,
    308–9
  job selection factors, 307
  marginal utility of work, 306–7
  market supply curve, 309–11
  with monopsonist demand,
    325–26
  scarcity of talent, 319–20
  training effects, 316–19
  union effects, 320–28 (see also
    Labor unions)
  variations in pay rates, 315–16

Labor unions, 320–28
  choice of goals and methods, 322–23
  control over supply, 320–21
  for craft and professional groups, 323–24
  effect on demand, 324
  effect on workers' incomes, 326–27
  leverage, 321–22
  monopoly power, 204
  and monopsonists, 325–26
Land, Edwin, 405
Land:
  economic rent, 299, 301–2
  as production factor, 20, 21, 137
  taxation of, 301–2
  (see also Farmland)
Land bank program, 461
Law of diminishing marginal returns, 27
  vs. concept of economies and diseconomies of scale, 167
  and educational investment, 318
  and marginal revenue product, 291
  and short-run productivity, 157–59
Law of diminishing marginal utility, 27, 107, 306–7 (see also Marginal utility)
Law of large numbers, 341
Leontief, Wassily, 42, 357
Lewis, Arthur W., 43
Liabilities:
  on balance sheet, 140
  of firms, 53
  of households, 51
  of major sectors, 52 tab.
Liberal economists, 13, 36, 302 tab.
Life cycles:
  human and income distribution, 405
  of industries, 257 tab.
Liggett and Meyers Company, 255
Light industries, 78
Linear equations, 41–44, 45 figs., 46–47
Liquidity, defined, 140
Loan guarantee program, 395–96
Loans, 337, 342
Local government:
  spending trends, 394, 395
  tax incidence, 411–13
  tax revenues, 396 tab.
Location, 138, 148–49 (see also Geography)
Logarithmic scales, 48–49
Logic, 13, 47
Long run:
  defined, 153
  equilibrium, 190–92, 197
  productivity and costs, 163–73
  supply, 193–94, 197
Loose oligopoly, 201 tab.
  concentration ratio, 230
  and tacit collusion, 235
Lorenze curve, 410
Los Angeles, 378, 428
Losses, minimizing, 186–87

Loss leaders, 216
Luck, 405

MacAvoy, Paul W., 464
Macroeconomics:
  central concept, 33, 34
  defined, 11
  principles, 33–37
Malthus, Thomas, 8, 448, 466 fn.
Management, and scale economies, 168, 169
Managerial revolution, 127
Manchester School, 8, 302 tab., 367
Manufacturing sector:
  industrial structure, 242–43
  large corporations, 126
  productivity growth, 350 tab., 351
  (see also Industrial sector)
Marginal analysis, 14, 57, 106
Marginal benefits, 27 tab., 136, 379–80
Marginal choices, and efficient allocation, 359
Marginal concepts, 27 tab., 32–33
Marginal conditions, 25–26, 171–73, 359
Marginal cost:
  and allocative efficiency, 195–96
  calculation of, 159 tab., 162–63
  in competitive markets, 360–61
  defined, 27 tab., 182–83
  and elasticity of demand, 294
  equal to marginal revenue, 293, 297
  equal to price, 185–86
  of external funds, 337
  of input vs. output, 290
  and monopoly conditions, 206–9
  and predatory pricing, 269
  and profit maximization, 178–79
  and regulated price levels, 272, 276, 277, 278–81
  and supply curves, 183–90, 193–94
Marginal effect (see Diminishing marginal effect)
Marginal product (MP):
  calculation of, 154–58, 159 tab.
  defined, 27 tab.
  and least-cost combination of inputs, 171–73
  and marginal cost, 162
  and marginal revenue product, 290–92, 295
  value of, 291, 296, 298
Marginal productivity:
  and income distribution, 367–68, 401
  and minimum wage law, 417
Marginal profit, 178–80
Marginal propensity, 27 tab.
Marginal returns on investment (MRI), 334–35, 336–38 (see also Law of diminishing marginal returns)
Marginal revenue:
  defined, 27 tab.
  of dominant firm, 223
  equal to marginal cost, 293, 297
  with kinked demand curve, 238

and marginal revenue product, 290–92
  under monopoly conditions, 205–7, 209
  with perfect competition, 181–82, 183 fig., 295–96
  and profit maximization, 178–80
  and supply, 183–88
Marginal revenue product (MRP), 290–97
  derivation, 290–92
  and firm's demand schedule, 293–95, 311
  in perfect vs. partial competition, 295–97
  and profit-maximizing level of input use, 292–93
  shifts in curve, 295
  and value of individual inputs to production, 303
Marginal tax rates, 390
Marginal utility:
  defined, 27 tab., 108–9
  diminishing, law of, 27, 107
  of free vs. scarce goods, 111–13
  origin of concept, 106
  preference and income effects, 110–11
  and prices, equilibrium levels, 113–17
  and total utility, 107–8
  validity of concept, 121
  and variety of goods, 110–11
  of work, 306–7
Marijuana, government controls, 97–98
Marketable permits, 434, 435
Market demand:
  and individual demand, 118–20
  with perfect competition, 181–82
  with pure monopoly, 204–6, 207–9
  (see also Demand)
Market equilibrium, 78–80
  government intervention, 94–98
  in input markets, 298–99, 300
  in labor market, 313–15
  in oil market, 90–91
Market exchange, defined, 22–23
Market power, defined, 200 (see also Monopoly power)
Market price:
  concerns of microeconomics, 55–57
  and consumer surplus, 117–18
  defined, 22, 23
  and demand curve, 58, 59–67
  effect of expectations, 58
  equilibrium point, 78–80
  and individual demand, 110
  and marginal utilities, 113–17
  of selected commodities and retail items, 56 tab.
  of stocks and bonds, published listings, 131, 132–33, tab.
  and supply, 71, 72–74, 75–78
  (see also Prices)
Markets:
  antitrust criteria, 256–57, 260–61
  basic functions, 57

causes of failure, 364–70, 374–75
conditions of efficient allocation,
    358–61
defined, 22, 57
disequilibrium effects, 32
effect of conglomerates, 244–46
elasticity effects, 86–91
as focus of economic analysis, 23
input vs. output, 18–19 (see also
    Input markets)
interferences with, 91–98
interrelatedness, and ripple
    effect, 356, 361–64
microeconomic analysis, 10–11
minimum optimum scale, 170–71
naturally competitive, 226
pull toward equilibrium, 356–58
recent trends in concentration,
    241–44
relevant, 260–61
types, 23, 200, 201 tab.
in Walrasian theory, 10, 357
(see also Demand and supply)
Market share:
    antitrust criteria, 257–58, 259–60
    concentration ratio, 229–30 (see
        also Concentration)
    of dominant firm, 222–23, 224
        fig.
    and innovation, 203
    mergers to increase, 203
    and minimum optimum scale,
        170–71
    in monopolistic competition, 240
    and monopoly power, 202
    of oligopoly, 229–30, 239–40
Market value:
    defined, 23
    determinants, 106
    and market prices, 55–57
Marshall, Alfred, 8–10, 25–26, 43,
    106, 355
Marx, Karl, 8, 9–10, 12, 302 tab.
Marxist theory, 13
Maximizing behavior, 21–22, 25
Meade, James E., 43
Means, Gardiner C., 127
Measurement:
    of demand and supply, 98–101
    diagrams, 40–50
    interpretation of numbers, 50–53
    (see also Econometrics)
Medicaid, 404, 413, 415
Medicare, 286, 404
Medicine, entry barriers, 319, 324
Mellon, Andrew, 405
Mellon family, 403, 405
Menger, Carl, 10, 106
Mercantilists, 8, 302 tab.
Mergers:
    antitrust policy, 254, 255 fig.,
        256, 257 tab., 258, 264–67
    conglomerate, 245
    and firm dominance, 227
    kinds, 130–35
    and monopoly power, 203
Microeconomics:
    competitive assumption, 180
    debate over utility theory of
        demand, 120–21

defined, 10–11, 24
distinguished from
    macroeconomics, 33
focus on market prices, 55–57
new problems, 11
principles, 24–33
"secret password," 150
unifying concept, 355, 357
Middle Ages, 94, 387
Middle East, 444, 462, 463
Military draft, 442–44
Military spending, 437–45
    avoiding production waste,
        438–40
    efficient levels and arms race
        dynamics, 440–42
    government contracts and
        monopoly power, 204
    pricing problems, 281, 439–40
    ripple effect, 365
    volunteer army, economic basis,
        442–45
Minimum optimum scale (MOS),
    170–71
Minimum wage laws, 99, 416–17
Mining industry, 350 tab.
Minorities:
    discrimination against, 406–9
    equal opportunity programs,
        413–16
Misallocation burden, 211
Mobil Oil Corporation, 217
Monetarism, 11
Money, flow of, 23, 24 fig., 34,
    51–53
Money capital, 332
Monopolistic competition, 201 tab.,
    240–41
    concentration ratio, 230
    distinctive concept, 222
    instances, 225 tab.
Monopoly, 199–218:
    advantages of, for common
        property resources, 457
    and allocative efficiency, 196
    antitrust policy, 254 tab.
    bilateral, 325–26
    cases of, 216–18
    characteristics, 200–203, 204 tab.
    creation and maintenance of,
        203–4
    effects of, 204–16, 218
    and income distribution, 211–12,
        405
    labor unions as, 320, 325–26
    laws against, 251
    natural (see Natural monopoly)
    and natural resource use, 455
    and patent system, 353
    public school system as, 423–25
    pure (see Pure monopoly)
    varieties of, 200
    (see also Monopoly power)
Monopoly franchises, 203–4
Monopoly power, 218
    antitrust policies, 249–70 (see also
        Antitrust policies)
    creation and maintenance, 203–4
    effect on demand for inputs,
        295–97

effect on profits, 211, 343
gradations of, 200
indications of, 202–3
as limit on efficient allocation,
    368–69
and market failure, 375 tab.
regulation and public enterprises,
    271–87 (see also Regulation)
(see also Dominant Firms;
    Monopolistic Competition;
    Monopoly; Oligopoly)
Monopsony, 320, 325–26
Moody's Industrial Manuals, 138
Moody's Investor's Service, 132,
    341
Morgan, J. P., 250
Multinational firms, response to
    strikes, 321
Myrdal, Gunnar, 42

National Broadcasting Company
    (NBC), 255
National Can Company, 255
National Highway Traffic Safety
    Administration (NHSA), 435
    tab., 436
Native Americans, 406
Natural competition, 170, 274–75
Natural gas, price controls, 95
Natural monopoly, 170
    basic sources, 282
    limits to efficient allocation, 368
    regulation of, 271, 272–73, 275,
        282
    (see also Regulation)
    (see also Monopoly)
Natural resources, 447–67
    agricultural economics, 457–62
    basic concepts, 448–57
    depletion of, 447–48
    energy, 462–65
    environmental protection,
        428–35
    future of, 465–66
    as input to production process,
        137
    limits to efficient allocation,
        369–70
    main types, 21, 448 tab.
    and productive capacity, 5
    scarcity of, 1–2
    supply curve, 298
Natural scarcity, 319
Necessities, 67, 272–73
Negative income tax, 416
Negative slope, 44, 45 figs.
Neoclassical economics:
    development, 8–12
    and efficient allocation, 355
    focus on marginal choices, 25
    incompleteness, 12
    and liberal school, 13
    and limits of competition, 196
    marginal utility analysis, 106
    and value of production factors,
        302 tab.
Netherlands, 284 fig., 393 tab., 425
Net income, 137 (see also Profits)
Net plant and equipment, 140
Net worth, of households, 51

Newspapers:
    dominance and scale economies, 228–29
    relevant market, 260–61
Newton, Isaac, 48
New York City, 95, 378, 384, 403, 404
New York State, 273 *tab.*, 425
New York Stock Exchange (NYSE), 343, 344, 345 *fig.*
New York Times, 68–69
Nixon, Richard, 374
Nobel Prize, 42–43, 357
Nonprofit enterprises, 20, 135, 385
Normal curve, 49, 50 *fig.*
Normal goods, 69–70
Normative economic analysis, 4
Nuclear fuels, cartel, 463
Nuclear power plants, 369–70

Obsolescence, technological vs. economic, 352–53
Occupational Safety and Health Administration (OSHA), 435 *tab.*, 436–37
Ohlin, Bertil, 43
Oil industry:
    and alternative fuel sources, 454, 462–64
    economics of exploration, 464–65
    largest firms, 128 *tab.*
    price fixing, 464
    Standard Oil monopoly (*see* Standard Oil Company)
Oil prices:
    government controls, 95
    market equilibrium, 90–91
    1973 increases, 11
    OPEC effects, 90, 234, 464
    recent levels, 56 *tab.*
    ripple effects, 363–64
Oligopoly, 229–40, 246
    arms race as, 441
    central tendency, 235–36
    collusion, 232–35
    competition within, 232
    concentration and leading firms, 229–30
    demand curves, 236–39
    distinctive concept, 222
    economies of scale, 239
    instances, 225 *tab.*
    interdependence of firms, 230–31
    types, 201 *tab.*, 231–32
Open shop, 320, 321
Opportunity cost, 25, 26
    basic concept, 149–50, 151
    and economic profit, 151–53
    of internal funds, 337
    of loan guarantee program, 396
    and marginal cost, 182
    of military draft, 442–44
    and production-possibility boundary, 29
    and production questions, 178
    of public expenditures, 379, 383
    and supply curve, 297
Optimum rate of use, of natural resources, 449–57
Optimum scale, 194
    minimum, 170–71

Organization of Petroleum-Exporting Countries (OPEC), 90, 234, 464
Output:
    changes in, 35
    of enterprises, 138
    and income, 34
    level of, and variability of costs, 159
    long-term growth rate, 349–51
    markets, 18–19
    as monopolist's choice, 207
    potential, 35–36
    and pricing, under pefect competition, 177–97
    and productivity, 153
    profit-maximizing level, 178–80

Parallel pricing, 234
Paramount Pictures case, 256
Partial competition, 201 *tab.*, 221–47
    dominant firm, 222–29 (*see also* Dominant firms)
    marginal revenue schedule, 291, 295–96
    monopolistic competition, 222, 230, 240–41
    oligopoly, 229–40 (*see also* Oligopoly)
    recent trends, 241–46
Patent system:
    economic questions, 353
    and firm dominance, 227
    and monopoly power, 203
Pavarotti, Luciano, 319
Peak-load pricing, 278–81
Penn-Central Railroad, 245
Perfect competition, 177–97
    economic assumptions, 181
    firm and market demand, 181–82
    marginal revenue product schedule, 291, 295–97
    short- and long-run equilibrium, 190–93
    short-run supply curve, 183–88
Personal income tax, 386
    and income distribution, 410, 411
    "negative," 416
    trends, 396
    and work incentives, 387–89
Personal taxes, 386
Petroleum (*see* Fuels; *and entries under* Oil)
Photocopier market, 263–64
Physical capital, 331–33
Physical laws, and economies and diseconomies of scale, 168, 169
Physiocrats, 8, 302 *tab.*
Pittsburgh, 378, 428
Planning-programming-budgeting (PPB) analysis, 380 (*see also* Cost-benefit analysis)
Plato, 7
Pleasure (*see* Utility, marginal analysis)
P. Lorillard Company, 255

Polaroid Corporation, 203, 227–29, 344, 345 *fig.*
Political influence, and natural resource use, 457
Pollution:
    rules and fines, 384–85, 432
    social cost, 378
    social regulation, 428–35
    (*see also* Environmental protection)
Population:
    and income distribution, 6
    as influence on demand, 58
Population growth:
    and future world resources, 465–66
    Malthus's view, 8, 448, 466 *fn.*
    and production-possibility boundary, 29
Portfolio capital, 332
Positive economic analysis, 4
Positive slope, 44, 45 *figs.*
Post offices, public enterprises, 284 *fig.* (*see also* U.S. Postal Service)
Potential output, 35–36
Poverty:
    benchmark level, 6–7
    incidence in U.S., 402–4
Precious metals:
    market prices, 56 *tab.*
    mercantilist view, 8
    published price listings, 131
Predatory pricing:
    antitrust policy, 262, 269
    by regulated utilities, 282
Preferences:
    vs. actual market outcomes, 61
    changes in, and marginal utility, 116
    in household decision making, 19–20
    and income, 110–11
    as influence on demand, 58, 61, 104
    of seller, during price ceilings, 96
    for social goods, 377
    variety of, 109–10
Prepaid goods, 113
Present value analysis:
    and expected rate of return, 346, 347
    of future uses of natural resources, 449–55, 456
    of social goods, 382–83
    use in investment decisions, 333–34
Preservation, vs. conservation, 449
Price ceilings, 95–96
Price controls, 94–97
Price cutting:
    by oligopoly firms, 232–33, 234, 237–38
    by regulated utilities, 282
Price discrimination:
    antitrust policies, 258, 268–69
    by dominant firms, 224, 229
    by electric companies, 218
    due to monopoly, 213–16, 218
    by regulated utilities, 272, 277, 279, 282

by Standard Oil, 217
by Xerox, 263
Price effect, on labor supply curve,
    308–9
Price elasticity of demand, 63–67
    and consumer surplus, 118, 119
        fig., 120
    determinants, 67
    estimating, precautions, 68–69
    for selected goods and services,
        100 *tab.*
Price fixing:
    antitrust policies, 251, 254, 258,
        267–68
    of fuels, 463–64
    by oligopoly, 232–33, 234–35
Price floors, 96–97, 99
Price leadership, 234
Prices:
    and allocative efficiency, 195–96
    and average variable cost, 186–87
    and demand, in perfect
        competition, 181–82
    and determination of costs, 153
    and economic choices of
      . enterprises, 138
    effects on, of dominant firms,
        224
    and least-cost production, 171–73
    and marginal cost, 185–86,
        360–61
    micro vs. macroeconomic
        questions, 33
    under monopoly, 207–8, 209
    regulation of, 272–83
    rigid, of oligopoly, 236–39
    and scarcity of natural resources,
        452, 455–56
    and social values, 195, 196, 207
    and supply, 71, 72
    (*see also* Market price; Pricing)
Price signaling, 234
Price structure, regulatory issues,
    272, 277
Price supports, 96–97, 460–61
Price takers, 180, 290
Pricing:
    of military weapons, 439–40
    under perfect competition,
        177–97
    predatory, 262, 269, 282
    by public enterprises, 287
Primary industries, 4, 5 *fig.*
Principles of Economics (Marshall),
    10, 26
Principles of Political Economy
    (Marshall), 106
Private enterprises:
    aim, 20
    corporations, 125–28
    defined, 124
    diversification, 126–27
    mergers, 130–35
    ownership and control, 127
    small business, 124–25
    stock ownership, 127–30
    (*see also* Enterprises; Firms)
Private good, 375–76
Private market system:
    external effects, 33

and natural resource use, 455–57
    (*see also entries under* Market)
Process innovations, 352
Procter and Gamble Company, 140,
    266
Producers, share of sales taxes,
    92–94
Product (*see* Marginal product;
    Total product)
Product differentiation:
    as entry barrier, 223
    in monopolistic competition, 240
    of oligopoly, 232
Product innovation, 352
Production:
    basic input factors, 20–21
    basic units, 20
    capacity and growth, 5–6
    diversity of techniques, 138
    and economic choices, 2, 136–37
    efficient, 194–96
    of households, 20
    and income distribution, 6
    least-cost production, 27, 171–73
    supply and demand factors,
        18–19, 71–72, 297–98
    three basic questions, 2, 19,
        24–25
    valuing individual inputs to,
        302–3
Production function, 154–55
Production-possibility boundary,
    27–31, 35–36
Production process:
    choice of technology, 148–49
    innovations, 352
    inputs, 137–38
Productivity:
    of agricultural sector, 457–58
    of capital, 332
    defined, 153
    economies and diseconomies of
        scale, 167–71
    in the long run, 163–73
    in the short run, 153–63
    and technological change, 349–51
Product type, antitrust market
    criteria, 260–61
Professional groups, 322, 323–24
Profitability:
    correct measure of, 141
    and monopoly power, 202–3
    (*see also* Profits)
Profit maximization:
    capital investment criteria,
        334–37
    as condition for equilibrium, 191
    as goal of private enterprise, 20,
        22, 124, 127, 137
    and input use, 290, 292–93
    and least-cost technology, 148
    by minimizing short-term losses,
        186–88
    under monopoly, 205, 207, 209
    rules for, 178–80, 183, 184,
        190–91
    and short-run supply curve,
        183–84
    unnecessary in public enterprises,
        283, 287

Profits:
    accounting vs. economic, 138
    after-tax, 139
    and average variable costs,
        186–88
    calculation of, 137
    components, 342–43
    distribution of, 34
    economic, 151–53
    excess, 211, 224, 232–33, 272
    joint, of colluding oligopoly,
        232–33
    and regulated price levels, 274,
        277, 281
    reinvestment of, 337
    as signal for investment, 142
    (*see also* Corporate profits; Profit
        maximization; Return to
        capital)
Progressive taxes, 389–93, 410–13
Property (*see* Assets)
Property taxes, 301–2, 410, 413
Proportional taxes, 410–13
Public benefits, of education, 421
Public choice, principle of, 32–33
Public enterprises, 20, 135, 283–87
Public expenditures:
    alternatives to, 383–85
    categories, 385–86
    composition by level of
        government, 393–94, 395 *fig.*
    cost-benefit analysis, 378–83
    on education, 422–28
    and income distribution, 413, 414
        fig.
    program types, 395–96
    sources of funds, 383
    tax loophole effect, 396–98
    trends, 392–93
Public finance, 373–98
    economic concepts, 374–86
    major patterns, 392–98
    taxation issues, 386–92
    (*see also* Public expenditures)
Public goods:
    and consumer surplus, 118
    costs, 366–67
    marginal utility, 32, 113
Public policy:
    economic concepts, 374–86
    environmental, 428–35
    and income distribution, 409–17
    and military spending, 437–45
    worker and consumer safety,
        435–37
    (*see also* Government policy)
Public schools, cost-benefit issues,
    422–28
Public sector, 374
Public utilities, regulation of, 249,
    251 (*see also* Utilities)
Pure competition:
    concentration ratio, 229
    demand curve, 201
    economic assumptions, 181
    and input pricing, 290
    vs. monopolistic competition, 241
    vs. monopoly, 200, 201, 218
    nature of, 180
    vs. perfect competition, 181

Pure monopoly, 200, 201 *tab.*, 218
  dominant firm likened to, 223
  and market demand curve,
    204–6
  recent market share trends,
    243–44
Pure public good, 286

Quantity controls, 97–98
Quantity demanded:
  vs. demand, 61–63
  equilibrium with quantity
    supplied, 78–80
  by individuals, 117
  and market price, 59–61
  and price elasticity of demand,
    63–67
Quantity supplied:
  equilibrium with quantity
    demanded, 78–80
  and market price, 72–73
  vs. supply, 73–74
Quarterly Journal of Economics, 12 *fn.*
Queuing, 96

Radical economists, 13
Radio Corporation of America
    (RCA), 244, 269
Railroad industry:
  life-cycle stage, 275 *tab.*
  monopolies, 250–51
  public enterprises, 284 *fig.*
Rate base, for regulated prices,
    276, 277, 281–82
Rationing, 96
Raw materials, as variable inputs,
    153
Reagan administration:
  antitrust policy, 256, 261, 263,
    264
  economic program, 387, 392,
    393, 416
  safety regulation policy, 437
Reaganomics, 11
Real assets, 346
Real capital, 331–32
Real estate taxes, 387, 389, 391
Recessions, 6
Regressive taxes, 389, 390–91,
    410–13
Regulation, 272–83
  applications, 272–73
  background and evolution,
    274–75
  commissions, 273–74
  cream skimming and
    competition, 282
  decisions on price levels and
    structures, 275–77
  and deregulation, 282–83
  economic objective, 272
  effects on cost, 281–82
  marginal cost pricing, 276, 277,
    278–81
  problems and criticism, 272
  process, 275
  social, 428–37
Related goods, 72
Relevant market, antitrust criteria,
    259–61
Rent, economic (*see* Economic rent)

Rent controls, 95
Replacement-level birth rate, 465
Research and development (R&D):
  by colleges and universities, 423
  military, 438
  and technological change, 351–53
Resource allocation:
  and competition, 180
  efficient, 355
  monopoly effects, 209–11
  (*see also* Efficient allocation;
    Natural resources)
Retail firms, largest, 129 *tab.*
Retail items, market prices, 56 *tab.*
Retained earnings:
  effects, 342
  on income statement, 139
  and stockholder's equity, 140–41
Return to capital, 338–43
  and asset values, 346–47
  equalization of, 348
  expected rates, 346–48
  and interest rate, 341–42
  and productivity, 332
  profit components, 342–43
  risk-return factors, 338–41
  as success indicator, 141
  (*see also* Profits)
Revenue sharing, 394
Review of Economics and Statistics, 12
    fn.
Ricardo, David, 8, 9, 23, 448
Ripple effects, 356, 361–64, 365
Risk:
  and cost of capital, 337
  defined, 338–40
  diversification to reduce, 341
Riskless rate of return, 340, 342
Risk premium, 338, 340–41, 342
Rivalry, 181, 196, 202
Robber barons, 405
Robinson-Patman Act (1936), 254
    tab.
Rockefeller, John D., 217, 229, 405
Rockefeller family, 403, 405
Rockefeller University, 405
Rome, 7, 8
Roosevelt, Theodore, 254
Rules:
  to limit pollution, 432
  and public policy, 383–85
Russia (*see* Soviet Union)

Safety, social regulation, 435–37
Sales revenues:
  in income statement, 138–39
  of largest firms, 128–29 *tab.*
Sales taxes:
  incidence, 387
  and income distribution, 410, 413
  as in rem tax, 386
  interference with market process,
    91–94
  as regressive tax, 390–91
Salvage operations, 284–86
Samuelson, Paul, 42
Satisfaction (*see* Utility)
Savings, and investment demand,
    34–35
Scale economies (*see* Economies of
    scale)

Scarce goods, 111–12
Scarcity:
  and elasticity of supply, 77
  of energy, effect on farming,
    458–59
  as focus of economics, 1–2
  of fuel, 462–65
  of labor talent, 319–20
  and least-cost production, 172–73
  of natural resources, 448, 452,
    455–56
  and opportunity costs, 149, 150
  and production-possibility
    boundary, 27–31
  and production questions, 2–3
Schools, public financing issues,
    422–28
Schultz, Theodore W., 43
Schumpeter, Joseph A., 231, 260
Sears, 344, 345 *fig.*
Self-interest, 21–22
Seller's preferences, 96
Semifinished goods, 137
Services:
  in circular flow, 23, 24 *fig.*
  input to production process, 137
  output of enterprises, 138
  selected, price elasticities of
    demand, 100 *tab.*
Service sector, 4–5, 350 *tab.*
Shakespeare, William, 14
Shepherd, William G., 242 *fn.*
Sherman Antitrust Act (1890), 234,
    251, 254, 255, 257 *tab.*
Shipbuilding industry, 284 *fig.*
Shopping Bag chain, 264
Short run:
  costs, 158–63
  defined, 153
  equilibrium, 190–91, 197
  vs. long-run efficiency, 166–67
  productivity, 153–58
  supply curve, 183–89, 197
Simon, Herbert A., 43
Simon, Julian, 466 *fn.*
Single-parent families, 404
Size (*see* Economies of scale)
Skills:
  differences in, 315–20
  inadequate, due to
    discrimination, 406–8
  and productive capacity, 5
  as public benefit of education,
    421
Slope:
  of demand curve, 60, 64, 104,
    110
  of linear relationship, 44
  of supply curve, 72–73, 75–77
Small business, 124–25
Smith, Adam, 8, 9, 12, 23, 168, 302
    tab., 361, 448
Social benefits, of public schools,
    423
Social costs:
  vs. external costs, 364–66
  of public schools, 423
Social goods:
  allocating spending among,
    378–80
  demand curve, 376–77

funding, 383, 385
  vs. private goods, 375–76
  and public policy, 374–76
Socialists, 8, 302 *tab.*
Social preference, and public
  enterprises, 284
Social regulation, 428–37
  vs. economic regulation, 428 *fn.*
  of environment, 428–35
  worker and consumer safety,
    435–37
  (*see also* Regulation)
Social Security system, 394, 396
Social services, 283
Social values, 195, 196
South, 6, 404
Southwest, 403, 404
Soviet bloc, 10
Soviet Union, 357, 441–42
Spain, 284 *fig.*
Specialization, and scale economies,
  168–69
Spillovers, 32 (*see also* External
  effects)
Springsteen, Bruce, 319
Stabilization, 36, 374
Standard Oil Company, 200, 217,
  229, 254, 258, 262 *tab.*, 269
Standard and Poor's, 132, 341
Stanford, Leland, 405
Stanford University, 405
State government:
  spending trends, 394
  tax incidence, 411–13
  tax revenues, 396 *tab.*
Static analysis, 57, 149
Statistical methods, use in data
  fitting, 57 (*see also*
  Econometrics)
Steel industry:
  pollution standards, 433
  public enterprises, 284 *fig.*
Stock:
  accounting vs. market value, 140
  asset value, 347–48
  ownership, 127–30, 140–41
  price as performance indicator,
    141–42, 348–49
  published listings, 131, 132 *tab.*
Stock market:
  and asset values, 343–44, 345
    figs.
  as a control system, 348–49
  crash of 1929, 255
  main parts, 344
Stocks, vs. flows, 51–53
Strachey, Lytton, 10
Strikes, 321–22, 327–28
Subsidies:
  for public enterprises, 286–87
  for school system, 422–28
Substitutable goods, 58, 60
  cross-elasticity of demand, 70–71
  and derived demand, 120
  and marginal utility, 116
  and market definition, 57
  and price elasticity of demand,
    67
Substitution effect, 60, 116,
  294–95, 312
Sumeria, 7

Sunk costs, 150, 151
Supply, 71–80
  of capital, 337–38
  diminishing marginal effect, 27
  elastic, 86–87
  elasticity of, 75–78
  firms as basis for, 20, 123–45
  inelastic, 87–90
  influences on, 71–72
  in input markets, 297–303
  interaction with demand, 78–80
  long-run, 193–94
  and the nature of costs, 147–74
  vs. quantity supplied, 73–74
  (*see also* Demand and supply;
    Supply curve)
Supply curve, 72–73
  elasticity vs. slope, 75–77
  graphing convention, 41–43
  of individual laborers, 308–9
  intersection with demand curve,
    78–80
  of labor market, 309–11
  long-run, 193–94
  under monopoly conditions, 206,
    208–9
  under perfect competition,
    183–89
  under pure competition, 180
  shifts in, 189–90
  upward slope, 72–73
  (*see also* Elasticity of supply)
Supply side economics, 11
Sweden, 284 *fig.*, 393 *tab.*
Switzerland, 284 *fig.*, 393 *tab.*
Systems (*see* Economic systems)

Tacit collusion, 234–35, 257 *tab.*,
  268
Taft, William H., 255, 267
Taft-Hartley Act (1947), 320
Talent:
  and income distribution, 405
  scarcity of, 319–20
  and training, 318
  (*see also* Skills)
Taxes:
  categories, 386
  on economic rent, 301–2
  effect of education on tax base,
    421
  on emitting pollution, 434–35
  incentive effects, 387–89
  (*see also* Tax incidence; Tax
    revenues)
Tax expenditures, 396–98
  on colleges, 423, 426
Tax friction, 389
Tax incidence, 386–87
  and income distribution, 411–13
  progressive vs. regressive, 389–93
  and public expenditures on
    benefits, 413, 414 *fig.*,
    415–16
Tax loopholes (*see* Tax
  expenditures)
Tax policy, 410–13
Tax revenues:
  alternative sources of funds,
    383–85
  as percent of GNP, 393

  for social goods, 383
  trends, 396
Technological change:
  and capital investment, 349–53
  decision-making issues, 352–53
  future, and natural resource use,
    454
  patent system, 353
  phases, 352
  and production-possibility
    boundary, 29
  and productivity, 5–6, 349–51
  and pure competition, 196
  sources, 353
  (*see also* Technology)
Technological obsolescence, 352
Technology:
  agricultural, 458–59
  and cost of production, 71–72,
    148–49
  and economic choices, 138
  and economies of scale, 227
  least-cost, identifying, 164–67
  and supply curve, 189
Telecommunications, public
  enterprises, 284 *fig.*
Telephone system:
  and economies of scale, 227
  regulated price levels, 277, 279,
    280 *fig.*
Tennessee Valley Authority, 284
Theory of Political Economy (Jevons),
  106
Third-party effects, 32
Thurow, Lester, 260
Tight oligopoly, 201 *tab.*
  antitrust policy, 258
  concentration ratio, 230
  price-fixing cases, 267–68
  recent market share trends,
    243–44
  strategy requirement, 230–31
  tacit collusion, 235
Time discounting (*see* Present value
  analysis)
Time Inc., 344, 345 *fig.*
Time series, 41, 48–49
Tinbergen, Jan, 42
Tobin, James, 43
Total cost (TC):
  calculating lowest in long run,
    164
  defined, 159–60
  of inputs to enterprises, 136–37
Total factor productivity (TFP),
  349–51
Total fixed cost (TFC), 159 *tab.*,
  160
Total product (TP), 154–58, 159
  tab.
Total revenue, 63, 66, 136–37
Total utility, 107–8
Total variable costs (TVC), 159 *tab.*,
  160
Toyota, 229
Trademarks, 203, 223, 227
Transfer earnings, 299–300
Transfer payments:
  to farmers, proposal for, 461–62
  government expenditures, 386
  trends, 394–95

Transportation industry, 227, 350 *tab.*
Trusts, 250, 251 (*see also* Antitrust policies)

Unemployment:
 macroeconomic concern, 36
 micro- vs. macroeconomic questions, 33
 and minimum wage, 99
 positive and normative statements, 4
 post-1973 rise, 11
 during recessions, 6
 time series diagram, 49
Unfair competition, 204, 254 *tab.*
Unfair distribution, 367–68, 375 *tab.*, 457
Union shop, 320
United Fruit, 229
United Kingdom, 393 *tab.* (*see also* Great Britain)
United Shoe Machinery, 227
United States:
 antitrust policies, 250–69
 consumption patterns, 104–5
 distinctiveness of regulatory system, 272
 distribution of wealth and income, 6–7, 50, 402–4
 Gilded Age, 368
 input-output analysis, 362–63
 largest firms, 128–29 *tab.*
 merger boom, 130
 number of private firms, 124
 number of stock owners, 127
 oil production, 462
 productivity growth, 349–51
 public enterprises, 283–86
 role of corporations in, 124, 125–27
 school enrollment, 422 *tab.*
 tax incidence study, 411–13
 topsoil losses, 459
 trends in competition, 241–44
 trends in public expenditures, 393–94
 (*see also entries under* Federal; Government; U.S.)
United Technologies, 126
U.S. Army, 442–45
U.S. Census Bureau, 126, 229 *fn.*, 242
U.S. Congress:
 antitrust policy, 253–54, 259
 budgetary actions, 374
 environmental protection policy, 429, 432
 regulatory policy, 274
 transfer payments, 394
U.S. Department of Agriculture, 460, 461
U.S. Department of Defense (Pentagon), 254, 420, 438, 440–41
U.S. Department of Justice, Antitrust Division, 253, 257 *tab.*, 261–62, 266, 268
U.S. Postal Service, 135, 204, 252, 271, 286
U.S. Steel Company, 227

U.S. Supreme Court:
 antitrust rulings, 217, 254, 256, 257, 265, 266
 and regulatory commissions, 274
 safety ruling, 437
Usury laws, 95
U.S. v. Addyston Pipe and Steel, 254, 265 *tab.*, 267
U.S. v. Alcoa, 255, 262 *tab.*
U.S. v. American Telephone and Telegraph, 252, 256, 262 *tab.*
U.S. v. American Tobacco, 254, 262 *tab.*
U.S. v. Dupont, 262 *tab.*, 265 *tab.*, 266
U.S. v. General Electric and Westinghouse, 265 *tab.*, 268
U.S. v. International Business Machines, 256, 257–58, 261–63, 269
U.S. v. Socony-Vacuum, 265 *tab.*
U.S. v. Standard Oil, 254, 262 *tab.*
U.S. v. Von's Grocery Company, 264–66
Utilitarians, 106
Utilities:
 largest firms, 129 *tab.*
 life-cycle stages, 275 *tab.*
 as monopolies, 203
 price discrimination, 216, 218
 public enterprises, 283
 regulation of, 272–83
 in U.S. economy, 4, 5
Utility, 104–20
 marginal analysis, 106
 maximization of, 105–7, 114
 total vs. marginal, 107–9
 of work, 306

Value:
 of assets, 343–49
 consumer surplus, 117–18
 of foregone alternatives, 149, 150
 (*see also* Opportunity cost)
 of inputs to production, 302–3
 of marginal product, 291, 296, 298
 (*see also* Market value)
Values:
 cultural, 368
 private vs. social, 364–66
Vanderbilt, Cornelius, 405
Vanderbilt University, 405
Variable cost:
 average, 160
 defined, 159
 and marginal cost, 162
 total, 160
Variable inputs, 153
Variables, 41, 43, 46–47, 48
Vertical mergers, 130, 135
 antitrust policy, 257 *tab.*, 258, 265 *tab.*, 266
Vietnam War, 11, 392
Von's Grocery chain, 264–66

Wages:
 discriminatory, 406–8
 effect of labor unions on, 322–23, 326–27
 as household income, 34

micro- vs. macroeconomic questions, 33
 military, proposal for reform, 445
 minimum wage laws, 416–17
Wagner Act (1935), 204
Wall Street Journal, 131–34, 256, 344
Walras, Leon, 10, 106, 355, 356, 357
Warren, Earl, 256, 257
Washington Star, 229
Water shortage, 459
Wealth:
 distribution in U.S., 6–7, 50
 (*see also* Income distribution)
 mercantilist vs. Physiocrat views, 8
 unfair distribution, 211–12, 367–68, 375 *tab.*, 402–4
Wealth of Nations (Smith), 8, 9, 12, 168
Welfare payments, 415–16
Welfare triangle, 210–11
West Coast, 6, 404
Western Europe, 4, 125, 283, 284 *fig.*
West Germany, 284 *fig.*, 393 *tab.*
Westinghouse, 265 *tab.*, 268
White-collar jobs, 315–16
Wilson, Woodrow, 255
Windfall gains, 301
Wisconsin, 273 *tab.*, 274
Wisconsin Electric Power Company, 279–81
Women:
 effect of minimum wage laws on, 417
 equal opportunity programs, 416
 job discrimination, 406, 407–8
Woolf, Virginia, 10
Work:
 household preferences, 19
 job selection, 307
 marginal utility, 306–7
 and scarcity of resources, 361
 (*see also* Employment)
Workers:
 attitudes of, and scale economies, 227
 safety regulations, 435–37
 (*see also* Labor)
Work incentives:
 taxation effects, 387
 and welfare payments, 415–16
World War I, 10, 393
World War II, 11, 95, 392

X-efficiency, 165
 and competition, 194
 and monopoly power, 203
 and regulated price levels, 277
Xerox Corporation, 200, 203, 227
 antitrust case, 256, 258, 262 *tab.*, 263–64
X-inefficiency, 165
 in electric companies, 218
 due to monopoly, 212
 due to regulated price levels, 281

Yugoslavia, 284 *fig.*